Bruce Dawes

technology of MACHINE TOOLS

second edition

S. F. KRAR

J. W. OSWALD

J. E. ST. AMAND

McGRAW-HILL RYERSON LIMITED

Toronto Montreal New York London Sydney
Johannesburg Mexico Panama Düsseldorf
Singapore Rio De Janeiro Kuala Lumpur New Delhi

TECHNOLOGY OF MACHINE TOOLS, SECOND EDITION

ISBN 0-07-082437-1

2 3 4 5 6 7 8 9 BP 5 4 3 2 1 0 9

Printed and Bound in Canada

PREFACE

New machining methods and techniques are constantly being developed because of the rapidly changing technology. These developments have broadened the range of knowledge required by the trainee in today's machine shop. To make this second edition as comprehensive as possible, the authors have included the basic and advanced machine operations and theory as well as the recent technological developments. The wide scope of this text makes it suitable for use in vocational and secondary schools, community colleges, apprenticeship training, and adult retraining programs.

This book is based on the authors' many years of practical experience as skilled tradesmen and as specialists in teaching. To keep abreast of rapid technological change, the authors have researched the latest technical information available, and have attended specialized courses offered by industries which are leaders in their field. Many sections of this book were reviewed by key personnel in various manufacturing firms, so that the most accurate and up-to-date information is presented. The authors appreciated the opportunity to incorporate into the text the suggestions and recommendations made by these people.

To make this text easily understood, each chapter contains many new illustrations and photographs. Colour has been used throughout to emphasize important points and to make the illustrations more meaningful. Each operation is explained in a step-by-step procedure which students can readily follow. Each advanced operation is introduced by problems, followed by a step-by-step solution and then the machining procedure.

In recent years there has been increasing pressure, in both Canada and the United States, to change from the Imperial (inch) system to SI (Système International), or the Metric system. The need for this changeover in North America has been brought about by the desire to standardize the measuring system throughout the world so that trade with other countries can be carried on with less confusion.

Although both Canada and the United States are now committed to conversion to the metric system as rapidly as possible, it is likely to be several years before all machine tools and measuring devices are redesigned or converted. The change to metric in the machine shop trade will be gradual because of the long life-expectancy of the costly machine tools and measuring equipment involved. It is probable, therefore, that those involved in the machine shop trade will have to be familiar with both the metric and inch systems during the long changeover period.

Wherever possible, metric tools and information are included. In some cases, due to lack of information at the time of publication, only inch information is given, while in other cases dual dimensioning has been used.

The purpose of this text is to assist instructors to give their students a basic training in the operation of machine tools, and to help them understand the latest machining processes and developments. The material is organized so that instructors may readily select the topics most suitable for class projects, or to suit the individual differences of students. The questions at the end of each chapter can be used for review, or for homework assignments to prepare the student for subsequent operations.

A technician in the machine shop trade should be neat, develop sound work habits, and have a good knowledge of mathematics and blueprint reading. To keep up to date on technological change, he must continue to expand his knowledge by reading specialized texts, trade literature, and magazine articles in this field.

S.F.K., J.W.O., J.E.St.A.

ABOUT THE AUTHORS

Steve F. Krar majored in Machine Shop Practice and spent fifteen years in the trade, first as a machinist and finally as a tool and diemaker. After this period he entered Teachers' College and graduated from the University of Toronto with a Specialist's Certificate in Machine Shop Practice. During his nineteen years of teaching, Mr. Krar was active in Vocational and Technical education and served on the executive of many educational organizations. For ten years he was on the summer staff of the University of Toronto, involved in teacher training programs. Active in machine tool associations, Steve Krar has been a senior member of the Society of Manufacturing Engineers for over 20 years. He is also co-author of the following McGraw-Hill Ryerson Ltd. publications: *Machine Shop Training, Machine Shop Operations*, and the overhead transparency kits: *Machine Tools, Measurement and Layout, Threads and Testing Equipment*, and *Cutting Tools*.

Joseph E. St. Amand served his apprenticeship in general machine shop work, jigs and fixtures, and tool and die work. After twelve years in industry he entered Teachers' College and graduated with a Specialist's Certificate in Machine Shop Practice from the University of Toronto. During his thirty-three years of teaching, Joe St. Amand served on several educational committees which were involved with technical research, courses, and standardized examinations. For more than twenty-five years he has been active in chapter work for the Society of Manufacturing Engineers. He is co-author of the texts: *Machine Shop Training, Machine Shop Operations*, and Machine Shop Transparency Kits: *Machine Tools, Measurement and Layout, Threads and Testing Equipment*, and *Cutting Tools*.

J. William Oswald served an apprenticeship in machine shop, and after sixteen years in the trade attended Teachers' College at the University of Toronto. After graduation, he received a Specialist's Certificate in Machine Shop Practice and taught machine shop work for twenty-five years. During this time he attended several up-grading courses in the operation of the latest machine shop and testing equipment. For several years Mr. Oswald served on the teacher-training staffs at the University of Toronto and the University of Western Ontario. He had also worked with various technical educational committees and organizations. Mr. Oswald is a co-author of *Machine Shop Operations*, and the overhead transparency kits: *Machine Tools, Measurement and Layout, Threads and Testing Equipment* and *Cutting Tools*.

ACKNOWLEDGEMENTS

The authors wish to express their sincere thanks and appreciation to Alice H. Krar for her untiring devotion in reading, typing, and checking the manuscript for this text. Without her supreme efforts, this text could not have been produced.

Special thanks are due to Mr. Oliver Coley, formerly Technical Director, Garson-Falconbridge Secondary School; Mr. Nelson Durst, formerly of the Arthur Voaden Vocational School, St. Thomas; Mr. J. Demaline of the Hagersville Secondary School; and to all the teachers who offered suggestions which we were happy to include.

Our deep thanks go to the following firms which reviewed sections of the manuscript and offered suggestions which were incorporated to make this text as accurate and up to date as possible: American Superior Electric Co., Bendix Corporation, Carborundum Co., FAG Bearing Co. Ltd., Federal Products Corporation and Moore Special Tool Co. Cincinnati Milacron Inc. was most helpful in offering advice and in reviewing several sections on milling and special processes.

We are grateful to the following firms who have assisted in the preparation of this text by supplying illustrations and technical information.

Allen, Chas. G. & Co.
American Chain and Cable Co. Inc., Wilson Instrument Division
"American Machinist"
American Superior Electric Co. Ltd.
Ametek Testing Equipment
Armstrong Bros. Tool Co.
Ash Precision Equipment Inc.
Atlas Press Co., Clausing Division
Avco-Bay State Abrasive Company
Bendix Corporation, Automation Group
Bethlehem Steel Corporation
Boston Gear Works
Brown & Sharpe Manufacturing Co.
Buffalo Forge Co.
Butterfield Division, Union Twist Drill Co.

Canadian Blower and Forge Co. Ltd.
Canadian Tap and Die Co. Ltd.
Carborundum Company
Cincinnati Lathe and Tool Co.
Cincinnati Milacron Inc.
Cincinnati Shaper Co.
Cleveland Tapping Machine Co.
Cleveland Twist Drill (Canada) Ltd.
Colchester Lathe & Tool Co.
Coleman Engineering Co. Inc.
Covel Manufacturing Co.
Delmar Publishers Inc.
Delta File Works
DeVlieg Machine Co.
Dillon, W. C. and Co. Inc.
DoALL Company

Elliott Machine Tools
Enco Manufacturing Co.
Ex-Cell-O Corp.
Explosive Fabricators Division, Tyco Corp.
FAG Bearing Co. Ltd.
Federal Products Corp.
Firth-Brown Tools (Canada) Ltd.
General Electric Co. Ltd.
General Motors of Canada
Greenfield Tap and Die Co.
Hones, Charles H. Inc.
Inland Steel Co.
Jacobs Manufacturing Co.
Jones and Lamson Division of Waterbury Farrel
Kaiser Steel Corp.
Kostel Enterprises Ltd.
LeBlond, R. K. Machine Tool Co.
Lionite Abrasives Ltd.
Mahr Gage Co. Inc.
Mobil Oil Corporation
Moore Special Tool Co.
Morse Twist Drill and Machine Co.
National Broach & Machine Division, Lear Siegler Inc.
Neill, James & Co. (Sheffield) Ltd.
Nicholson File Co. of Canada Ltd.
Norton Company of Canada Ltd.

Pedersen Machine Co.
Powder Metallurgy Parts Manufacturers' Association
Pratt & Whitney Co. Inc., Machine Tool Division
Precision Diamond Tool Co.
Retor Developments Ltd.
Rockford Machine Tool Co.
Shore Instrument & Mfg. Co. Inc.
Slocomb, J. T. Co.
South Bend Lathe Inc.
Standard-Modern Tool Co. Ltd.
Stanley Tools Division, Stanley Works
Starrett, L. S. Co.
Sun Oil Co.
Taft-Peirce Manufacturing Co.
Taper Micrometer Corp.
Union Carbide Corp., Linde Division
United States Steel Corporation
Watts Bros. Tool Works
Weldon Tool Co.
Whitman & Barnes
Wickman, A. C. Ltd.
Wilkie Brothers Foundation
Williams, A. R., Machinery Co. Ltd.
Williams, J. H. & Co.
Woodworth, W. J., and J. D. Woodworth

CONTENTS

1 MACHINE TOOLS

Almost all the products used by man, whether in farming, mining, manufacturing, construction, transportation, communication, or the professions, are dependent on the use of machine tools. Constant improvements to and efficient use of machine tools affect the standard of living of any nation. Only through the use of machine tools has man been able to enjoy such pleasures as the automobile, airplane, television, home furnishings, appliances, and many other items on which we rely in our daily life.

Through constant improvement, modern machine tools have become more accurate and efficient. Improved production and accuracy have been made possible through the application of hydraulics and electronic devices such as numerical control to basic machine tools.

To operate today's machines, skilled technicians are indispensable. Such men are not just machine operators. They must be trained to approach and solve new problems as they arise. They must be capable of carrying out ideas and plans that call for the production of extremely intricate parts, and, in addition to skill, must possess many other characteristics to be successful. Care of self, orderliness, accuracy, judgment, confidence, and safe work habits are some of the essentials required to become a skilled craftsman.

Machinists must have had enough experience, acquired enough information, and developed enough judgment to be able

Courtesy DoALL Company

to set up and operate any standard machine tool and perform any bench operation. In addition, they should be capable of making, hardening, tempering, and grinding machine shop cutting tools.

A *toolmaker* qualifies substantially as a first-class general machinist. Generally speaking, toolmaking involves more precision workmanship, more mathematical calculations, and more advanced use of machine tools and their attachments. An expert toolmaker must possess all the qualities of a machinist, plus expertness in planning, in making precise measurements, and in advanced machine production.

Webster says, "Work is a physical or intellectual effort directed to some end." Machine shop work is a lively occupation. Gears revolving at terrific speeds, cams snapping back and forth, levers and arms guiding precise automatic instruments faster than the eye can see, and cutters

1

chewing off quantities of cuttings per minute that can only be seen by the use of a television camera—all these things offer excitement for the machinist.

With study and application, a machinist can advance to become a toolmaker, a designer, an engineer, a teacher, or a successful manufacturing businessman.

COMMON MACHINE TOOLS

Machine tools are generally power-driven metal-cutting or forming machines used to shape metals by:
1. the removal of chips
2. pressing, drawing, or shearing
3. controlled electrical machining processes

Any machine tool generally has the capability of:
1. Holding and supporting the workpiece.
2. Holding and supporting a cutting tool.
3. Imparting a suitable movement (rotational or longitudinal) to the cutting tool or the work.
4. Feeding the cutting tool or the work so that the desired cutting action and accuracy will be achieved.

The machine tool industry is divided into several different categories such as the general machine shop, the toolroom, and the production shop. The machine tools found in the metal trade fall into three broad categories:
1. **Chip producing machines** which form metal to size and shape by cutting away the unwanted sections. These machine tools generally alter the shape of steel products produced by casting, forging, or rolling in a steel mill.
2. **Non-chip producing machines** which form metal to size and shape by pressing, drawing, or shearing. These machine tools generally alter the shape of sheet steel products and granular or powdered materials.
3. **New generation machines** which were developed to perform operations which would be very difficult, if not impossible, to perform on chip or non-chip

producing machines. Electro-discharge and electro-chemical machines, for example, use either electrical or chemical energy to form metal to size and shape.

A general machine shop contains a number of standard machine tools that are basic to the production of a variety of metal components. Operations such as turning, boring, threading, drilling, reaming, sawing, milling, filing, and grinding are most commonly performed in a machine shop. Machines such as the drill press, engine lathe, power saw, shaper, milling machine, and grinder are usually considered the basic machine tools in a machine shop.

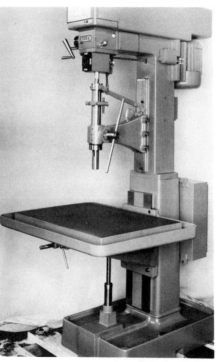

Courtesy Chas. G. Allen Co.

Fig. 1-1 A standard upright drill press

DRILL PRESS

The drill press or drilling machine (Fig. 1-1), probably the first mechanical device developed by prehistoric man, is used primarily to produce round holes. Drill presses range from the simple hobby type

to the more complex automatic and numerically controlled machines used for production purposes. The function of a drill press is to grip and revolve the cutting tool (generally a twist drill) so that a hole may be produced in a piece of metal or other material. Operations such as drilling, reaming, spot facing, countersinking, counterboring, and tapping are commonly performed on a drill press.

Courtesy Cincinnati Milacron Inc.

Fig. 1-2 An engine lathe is used to produce round work

ENGINE LATHE

The engine lathe (Fig. 1-2) is used to produce round work. The workpiece, held by a work-holding device mounted on the lathe spindle, is revolved against a cutting tool which produces a cylindrical form. Straight turning, tapering, facing, drilling, boring, reaming, and thread cutting are some of the common operations performed on a lathe.

METAL SAW

The metal-cutting saws are used to cut metal to the proper length and shape. There are two main types of metal-cutting saws: the bandsaw (horizontal and vertical) and the reciprocating cut-off saw. On the vertical bandsaw (Fig. 1-3) the workpiece is held on the table and brought into contact with the continuous-cutting saw blade. It can be used to cut work to length and shape. The horizontal bandsaw and the reciprocating saw are used to cut work to length only. The material is held in a vise and the saw blade is brought into contact with the work.

Courtesy DoALL Company

Fig. 1-3 A contour cutting bandsaw

SHAPER

The shaper (not illustrated) is generally used for producing flat, curved, or angular surfaces on metal workpieces. The cutting tool moves back and forth in a horizontal plane across the face of the work, which may be held in a vise or fastened to the table. The work is moved across for successive cuts either by hand or automatic feed. Shapers are manufactured with either the crank type or the hydraulic driving mechanism.

Courtesy Cincinnati Milacron Inc.

Fig. 1-4 A horizontal milling machine

MILLING MACHINE

The horizontal milling machine (Fig. 1-4) and the vertical milling machine are two of the most useful and versatile machine tools. Both machines use one or more rotating milling cutters having single or multiple cutting edges. The workpiece, which may be held in a vise, fixture, accessory, or fastened to the table, is fed into the revolving cutter. Equipped with proper accessories, milling machines are capable of performing a wide variety of operations such as drilling, reaming, boring, counterboring, and spot facing, and of producing flat and contour surfaces, grooves, gear teeth, and helical forms.

Courtesy DoALL Company

Fig. 1-5 A surface grinder is used to grind flat surfaces

GRINDER

Grinders use an abrasive cutting tool to bring a workpiece to an accurate size and produce a high surface finish. In the grinding process, the surface of the work is brought into contact with the revolving grinding wheel. The most common types of grinders are the surface, cylindrical, cutter and tool, and the bench or pedestal grinder.

Surface grinders (Fig. 1-5) are used to produce flat, angular, or contoured surfaces on a workpiece.

Cylindrical grinders are used to produce internal and external diameters which may be straight, tapered, or contoured.

Cutter and tool grinders are generally used to sharpen milling machine cutters.

Bench and pedestal grinders are used for offhand grinding and the sharpening of cutting tools such as chisels, punches, drills, and lathe and shaper tools.

SPECIAL MACHINE TOOLS

Special machine tools are designed to perform all the operations necessary to produce a single component. Some special-purpose machine tools include gear-generating machines; centreless, cam, and thread grinders; turret lathes; and automatic screw machines. The introduction of electro-discharge machining, electro-chemical machining, and electrolytic grinding has made it possible to machine materials and produce shapes which were difficult or often impossible to produce by other methods. Numerical and computer control of machine tools has greatly increased production and improved the quality of the finished product.

With the introduction of the numerous special machines and special cutting tools, production has increased tremendously over standard machine methods. Many products are produced automatically by a continuous flow of finished parts from these special machines. With product control and high production rates, everyone can enjoy the pleasures and conveniences of the automobile, power lawn mowers, automatic washers, stoves, and scores of other products produced today. Without the basic machine tools to produce the first pieces required to develop these ideas of production and automation, the costs of many luxuries that we now enjoy would be prohibitive.

CHAPTER 1 - REVIEW QUESTIONS

1. Why are machine tools so important to our society?
2. How have improved production and accuracy been achieved with basic machine tools?
3. List five qualifications of a good machinist.
4. What are the requirements to become a good toolmaker?
5. Name three categories of machine tools used in the metalworking trade.
6. List five operations which can be performed on each of the following:
   a) drill press
   b) lathe
   c) milling machine
7. Name four types of grinders found in a machine shop.
8. What is the importance of the electro-machining processes?
9. What effect has numerical and computer control had on manufacturing?

2 SAFETY

All hand and machine tools can be dangerous if used improperly or carelessly. Working safely is one of the first things a student or apprentice should learn because the safe way is usually the most correct and efficient way. A person learning to operate machine tools *must first* learn the safety regulations and precautions for each tool or machine. Far too many accidents are caused by carelessness in work habits, or by horseplay. It is easier and much more sensible to develop safe work habits than to suffer the consequences of an accident. *SAFETY IS EVERYONE'S BUSINESS AND RESPONSIBILITY.*

The safety programs initiated by accident prevention associations, safety councils, governmental agencies, and industrial firms are constantly attempting to reduce the number of accidents. *Nevertheless,* each year accidents which could have been avoided result not only in millions of dollars' worth of lost time and production, but also in a great deal of pain and many lasting physical handicaps. Modern machine tools are equipped with safety features, but it is still the operator's responsibility to use these machines wisely and safely.

CAUSES OF ACCIDENTS

Accidents don't just happen; they are caused. The cause of an accident can usually be traced to carelessness on someone's part. Accidents can be avoided, and a person learning the machine shop trade must

first develop safe work habits. A safe worker should:
a) be neat and tidy at all times,
b) develop a responsibility to himself,
c) learn to consider the welfare of fellow workers,
d) derive satisfaction from performing work accurately and safely.

Safety in a machine shop may be divided into four general categories: *personal grooming, housekeeping, securing the workpiece,* and *machining the workpiece.* Although it would be impossible to list every safety rule or unsafe practice that a person may encounter in each of these areas, some general rules are offered.

PERSONAL GROOMING

1. Never wear loose clothing around any machine. Remove or tuck in a tie and roll up the sleeves to the elbow to prevent them from getting caught in the machine (Fig. 2-1).

Courtesy Clausing Corp.

Fig. 2-1 Loose clothing can easily be caught in moving parts of machinery

5

2. Remove any watches, rings, or bracelets; these can get caught in the machine (Fig. 2-2).

Courtesy Clausing Corp.

Fig. 2-2   Wearing rings and watches can be the cause of serious injuries

3. Long hair must be protected by a hair net or an approved protective shop cap. Remember, one of the most common accidents on a drill press is long, unprotected hair becoming caught in the revolving drill.
4. Always wear approved safety glasses when operating a drill press. Be sure the glasses are clean and in good repair.

HOUSEKEEPING

The operator should remember that good housekeeping will never interfere with safety or efficiency; therefore, the following points should be observed.

1. *ALWAYS STOP THE MACHINE BEFORE YOU ATTEMPT TO CLEAN IT.*
2. Always keep the machine clean. Oily surfaces can be dangerous. Metal chips left on the table surface may interfere with the safe clamping of a workpiece. Always use a brush and proper T-slot tool to remove any chips. Oily surfaces should be cleaned with a cloth.
3. Do not place tools and materials on the drill table—use a bench near the drill press.

4. Keep the floor free from oil and grease (Fig. 2-3).
5. Sweep up the metal chips on the floor frequently. They become embedded in the soles of shoes and can cause dangerous slippage if a person walks on a terrazzo or concrete floor. A scraper should be used to remove these chips.
6. Never place tools or materials on the floor close to the machine where they will interfere with the operator's ability to move safely around the machine.

Courtesy Clausing Corp.

Fig. 2-3   Grease and oil on floors can cause dangerous falls

SECURING THE WORKPIECE

1. Before you handle any workpiece, remove all burrs and sharp edges with a file.
2. Do not attempt to lift heavy or odd-shaped objects which are difficult to handle on your own.
3. For heavy objects, follow safe lifting practices. Use your leg muscles for lifting and not your back.
4. Be sure the work is clamped securely in the vise or to a machine table.
5. Whenever work is clamped, be sure the bolts are placed closer to the workpiece than to the clamping blocks.
6. Never start a machine until you are sure that the cutting tool and machine parts will clear the workpiece (Fig. 2-4).
7. Use the proper wrench for the job, and replace nuts with worn corners.

Courtesy Kostel Enterprises Ltd.

Fig. 2-4   Make sure the cutting tool and parts of a machine will clear the work

8. It is safer to pull on a wrench than to push on it.

MACHINING THE WORKPIECE

1. *Do not operate any machine before understanding its mechanism and knowing how to stop it quickly.* Knowing how to stop a machine quickly can prevent a serious injury.
2. *Keep hands away from moving parts.* It is dangerous practice to "feel" the surface of the revolving work or to stop a machine by hand.
3. *Always stop a machine before measuring, cleaning, or making any adjustments.* It is dangerous to do any type of work around moving parts of a machine (Fig. 2-5).

Courtesy Kostel Enterprises Ltd.

Fig. 2-5   The machine must be stopped before the work is measured

4. *Never operate a machine unless all safety guards are in place.* Safety guards

are used to protect an operator from being drawn into moving machine parts.

5. *Never use a rag near the moving parts of a machine.* The rag may be drawn into the machine, along with the hand that is holding it.

6. *Never have more than one person operate a machine at the same time.* Not knowing what the other person would or would not do has caused many accidents.

7. *Get first aid immediately for any injury, no matter how small.* Report the injury and be sure that the smallest cut is treated to prevent the chance of a serious infection.

WORK AND THINK SAFELY AT ALL TIMES.

CHAPTER 2 - REVIEW QUESTIONS

1. What is one of the first things that a person entering the machine shop trade must learn?
2. List four qualities of a safe worker.
3. Why is loose clothing dangerous around machines?
4. How should long hair be protected to avoid an accident?
5. List two advantages of keeping a machine clean and tidy.
6. Explain how metal chips on the floor can cause an accident.
7. How should heavy objects be lifted?
8. What precautions should be taken before starting a machine?
9. Why is it unwise to operate any machine before understanding its mechanism?
10. List three other safety precautions which should be observed when machining the workpiece.

3 MEASUREMENT SYSTEMS, PRECISION MEASUREMENT, AND INSPECTION

Courtesy DoALL Company

Man's progress has depended on some form of measurement system since the beginning of civilization. The Egyptians, for example, used a unit of length called the cubit, a unit equal to the length of the forearm from the middle finger to the elbow. James Watt, on the other hand, improved his steam engine by maintaining its tolerances to the thickness of a thin shilling, an English coin. The days of such crude measurements, however, have gone. Today we live in a demanding world where products must be built to very precise tolerances. These same products may start out as components built by several sub-industries and find their way to other industries which use them in the manufacture of final consumer products. From start to finish the product may cover several industries located in widely separate places, often nations away, and then be sold at still another location. *Interchangeable manufacture*, world trade, and the need for high precision have all contributed towards the need for a *highly accurate international* measurement system. Consequently, in 1960 the SI (Système International) metric system was developed to satisfy this need.

MEASUREMENT SYSTEMS

Currently, two major systems of measurement are used in the world: the metric (decimal) systems, and the inch-pound (Imperial Canadian, U.S. Customary) systems. Over 90% of the world's population uses some form of the metric system; the inch-pound system is the one that has been traditionally used in Canada and the U.S.

METRIC (DECIMAL) SYSTEMS

On January 16, 1970, the Canadian Government adopted SI for implementation throughout Canada by 1980. On December 8, 1975, the United States Senate passed Metric Bill S100 to make the metric system the predominant system in the United States.

Although both Canada and the United States are now committed to conversion to the metric system as rapidly as possible, it is likely to be some years before all machine tools and measuring devices are redesigned or converted. The change to the metric system in the machine shop trade will be gradual because of the long life expectancy of the costly machine tools and measuring equipment involved. It is probable, therefore, that people involved in the machine shop trade will have to be familiar with both the metric and the inch-pound systems during the long changeover period.

THE CHANGEOVER PERIOD

The problems that faced the authors of this book at the time of publication were:

a) students had to expect to work in a dual measurement system world for some years yet,

b) many measuring tools were not available in metric sizes, and information was not obtainable as to when and in what sizes some items would become available.

To accommodate these two problems, the following policy has been adopted throughout this book. This policy should enable you to work effectively in both systems now, while permitting an easy transition to full metric as the new materials and tools become available.

a) Where general measurements or references to quantity are not related specifically to inch-pound standards, tools, or products, only metric units are given.

b) Where the student may be exposed to equipment designed to both metric and inch-pound standards, separate information is given on both types of equipment in *exact* dimensions.

c) Where only inch-pound standards, tools, or products exist at the present time, inch measurements are given with a soft conversion to metric provided in parentheses, marked with a ■.

SYMBOLS FOR USE WITH SI (SYSTEME INTERNATIONAL)

Table 3-1A provides a list of some common SI quantities, names, and symbols which you are likely to encounter in your work in the machine shop.

Quantity	Name	Symbol
length*	metre	m
volume*	litre	l and l
mass*	gram	g
time	minute	min
	second	s
force	newton	N
pressure, stress*	pascal	Pa
temperature	degrees Celsius	°C
area*	square metre	m²
velocity (speed)	metres per minute and	m/min and m/s
	metres per second	
angles	degrees	°
	minutes	′
	seconds	″
electric potential	volt	V
electric current	ampere	A
frequency	hertz	Hz
electric capacitance	farad	F

Table 3-1B provides a list of prefixes often used with the quantities indicated by * in Table 3-1A

prefix	meaning	multiplier	symbol
micro	one millionth of a	.000 001	μ
milli	one thousandth of a	.001	m
centi	one hundredth of a	.01	c
deci	one tenth of a	.1	d
deca	ten	10	da
hecto	one hundred	100	h
kilo	one thousand	1 000	k
mega	one million	1 000 000	M

STYLE DIFFERENCES BETWEEN SI AND INCH-POUND

Because SI is an international language, all countries adopting it must follow the approved style. The approved SI style is followed throughout this text wherever standards, tools, products, or processes are described in metric terms. The approved SI style is also followed as much as possible where the *inch-pound* system is used. The student should, however, be aware of one particular difference between SI and inch-pound styles. In SI, a zero is placed in front of the decimal marker when no other figure is there (e.g. 0.25). The zero is not required in the inch-pound system and is not used in this text where inch-pound terms are shown.

BASIC MEASUREMENT

METRIC MEASUREMENTS

Linear metric dimensions are expressed in multiples and sub-multiples of the metre. In the machine shop trade the millimetre is used for the expression of most metric dimensions. Fractions of the millimetre are expressed in decimals.

INCH-POUND MEASUREMENTS

The unit of length in this system is the inch, which may be divided into fractional or decimal divisions.

FRACTIONAL MEASUREMENT

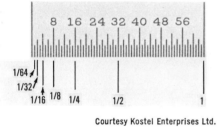

Courtesy Kostel Enterprises Ltd.

Fig. 3-1   Fractional divisions of an inch

Fractional dimensions, often called *scale dimensions*, can be measured with such instruments as rules or calipers. The steel rules used in machine shop work are graduated either in divisions of centimetres, millimetres, and half millimetres or in divisions of 1, 1/2, 1/4, 1/8, 1/16, 1/32, and 1/64 of an inch (Fig. 3-1). Divisions of 0.5 mm or 1/64 of an inch are about as fine as can be seen on a rule without the use of a magnifying glass. Precision measuring instruments such as micrometers, verniers, etc., are required when metric-drawn blueprints show any dimensions of less than 0.5 mm or when inch-drawn blueprints show any dimensions in decimals.

STEEL RULES

Metric Steel Rules

Metric steel rules (Fig. 3-2), usually graduated in millimetre and half millimetre, are

used for making linear metric measurements which do not require great accuracy. A wide variety of metric rules are available in lengths from 15 cm to 1 m.

Courtesy The L. S. Starrett Company

Fig. 3-2   Metric rules are graduated to measure in millimetres and half-millimetres

Fractional Steel Rules

The common fractions found on inch steel rules are 1/64, 1/32, 1/16, and 1/8 of an inch. Several varieties of inch steel rules may be used in machine shop work, such as *spring tempered, flexible, narrow,* and *hook.* Lengths range from 1 to 72 inches. Again, these rules are used for measurements which do not require great accuracy. Spring tempered (quick-reading) 6 in. rules (Fig. 3-3A) with No. 4 graduations are the most frequently used inch rules in machine shop work. These rules have four separate scales, two on each side. The front is graduated in eighths and sixteenths and the back is graduated in thirty-seconds and sixty-fourths of an inch. Every fourth line is numbered to make reading in thirty-seconds and sixty-fourths easier and quicker.

Courtesy The L. S. Starrett Company

Fig. 3-3A   A spring tempered (quick-reading) 6 in. rule

Hook rules (Fig. 3-3B) are used to make accurate measurements from a shoulder, step, or edge of a workpiece. They may also be used to measure flanges, circular pieces, and for setting inside calipers to a dimension.

Courtesy The L. S. Starrett Company

Fig. 3-3B   A hook rule is used to make accurate measurements from an edge or shoulder

Short length rules (Fig. 3-3C) are useful in measuring small openings and hard-to-reach locations where an ordinary rule cannot be used. Five small rules come to a set; they range between 1/4 in. and 1 in. in length and can be interchanged in the holder.

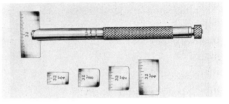

Courtesy The L. S. Starrett Company

Fig. 3-3C   Short length rules are used for measuring small openings

Decimal rules (Fig. 3-4) are most often used when it is necessary to make linear measurements smaller than 1/64 in. Since linear dimensions are sometimes specified on blueprints in decimals, these rules are very useful to the machinist. The most common graduations found on decimal rules are .100 (1/10 of an inch), .050 (1/20 of an inch), .020 (1/50 of an inch), and .010 (1/100 of an inch).

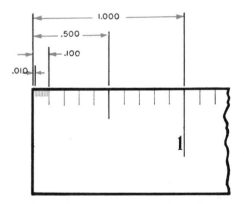

Fig. 3-4   Decimal readings on a rule provide an accurate and simple form of measurement

MEASURING LENGTHS

With a reasonable amount of care, fairly accurate measurements can be made using steel rules. Whenever possible, it is advisable to butt the end of a rule against a shoulder or step (Fig. 3-5) to assure an accurate measurement.

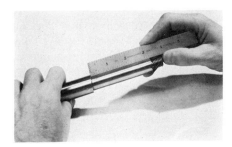

Fig. 3-5 Butting a rule against a shoulder

Through constant use, the end of a steel rule becomes worn. Measurements taken from the end are, therefore, often inaccurate. Accurate measurements of flat work can be made by placing the 1 cm or 1 in. graduation line on the edge of the work, taking the measurement, and subtracting 1 cm or 1 in. from the reading (Fig. 3-6A and B). When you measure the diameter of round stock, it is also advisable to start from the 1 cm or 1 in. graduation line.

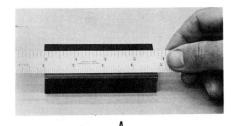

A

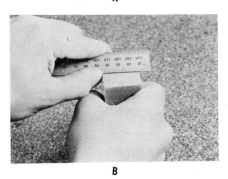

B

Courtesy Kostel Enterprises Ltd.

Fig. 3-6A & B Measuring with a rule starting at the 1 in. or 1 cm line

The Rule as a Straightedge

The edges of a steel rule are ground flat. The rule may therefore be used as a straightedge to test the flatness of workpieces. The edge of a rule should be placed on the work surface which is then held up to the light. Inaccuracies as small as 0.05 mm or a few thousandths of an inch can easily be seen by this method.

OUTSIDE CALIPERS

Outside calipers are tools used to measure the outside surface of either round or flat work. They are made in several styles such as *spring joint* and *firm joint calipers*. The spring joint caliper, Figure 3-7A, consists of two curved legs, a spring, and an adjusting nut. The outside spring joint caliper is most commonly used because it can easily be adjusted to size. The caliper itself cannot be read directly and therefore must be set to a steel rule or a standard size gauge.

Setting an Outside Caliper

Outside calipers are usually set to size using a steel rule. The rule should be held in the left hand with the forefinger extending slightly beyond the end of the rule (Fig. 3-7A). The caliper is held in the right hand and one leg of the caliper, supported by the forefinger of the left hand, is held against the end of the rule. The caliper is then adjusted to size using the thumb and first finger of the right hand. Always make sure that the leg of the caliper *splits* the desired graduation line on the rule in half.

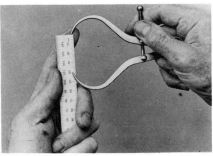

Courtesy Kostel Enterprises Ltd.

Fig. 3-7A Setting an outside caliper to a size with a rule

Measuring with Outside Calipers

Never attempt to measure work while the work is moving or revolving. Not only is it a dangerous practice which could result in an accident, but any measurements taken will not be accurate. Calipers should be held lightly between the thumb and forefinger in order to get the most accurate measurement. The caliper must be held at right angles (Fig. 3-7B) and never forced over the work, otherwise the measurement will not be accurate. When the caliper just slides over the work, the work is the same diameter as the caliper setting. Through practice, a *feel* or sense of touch can be developed which will enable a machinist to achieve a reasonable degree of accuracy using calipers. *NOTE*: When work must be accurate within hundredths of a millimetre or thousandths of an inch, a micrometer should be used.

Courtesy Kostel Enterprises Ltd.

Fig. 3-7B Checking a diameter with an outside caliper

INSIDE CALIPERS

Inside calipers are used to measure the diameter of holes or the width of keyways and slots. They are made in several styles, such as the *spring joint* and the *firm joint calipers*.

Measuring an Inside Diameter

Fairly accurate measurements of holes and slots may be made using an inside caliper and a rule.

1. Place one leg of the caliper near the bottom edge of the hole, Figure 3-8A.

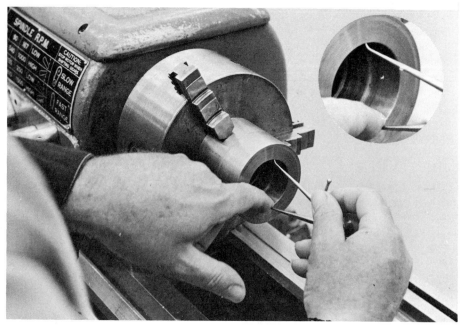

Courtesy Kostel Enterprises Ltd.

Fig. 3-8A Adjusting an inside caliper to the size of a hole

2. Hold the caliper leg in this position with a finger.
3. Keep the caliper legs vertical or parallel to the hole.
4. Move the top leg in the direction of the arrows and turn the adjusting nut until a slight drag is felt on the caliper leg.
5. Find the size of the setting by placing the end of a rule and one leg of the caliper against a flat surface.
6. Hold the legs of the caliper parallel to the edge of the rule and note the reading on the rule.

Courtesy Kostel Enterprises Ltd.

Fig. 3-8B An inside caliper setting being transferred to a micrometer

Transferring Measurements

When an accurate measurement is required, the caliper setting should be checked with an outside micrometer.

1. Hold the micrometer in the right hand so that it can be easily adjusted with the thumb and forefinger, Figure 3-8B.
2. Place one leg of the caliper on the micrometer anvil and hold it in position with a finger.
3. Rock the top leg of the caliper in the direction of the arrows.
4. Adjust the micrometer thimble until *only a slight drag* is felt as the caliper leg passes over the measuring face.

PRECISION SQUARES

Precision squares are used chiefly for inspection and setup purposes. They are hardened and accurately ground and must be handled carefully to preserve their accuracy. A great variety of squares is manufactured for specific purposes. The squares are all variations of the *solid square* or the *adjustable square*, however.

BEVELLED-EDGE SQUARES

The better quality standard squares used in inspection have a bevelled-edge blade which is hardened and ground. The bevelled edge allows the blade to make a line contact with the work, thereby permitting a more accurate check. Two methods of using a bevelled-edge square for checking purposes are illustrated in Figures 3-9A and B. In Figure 3-9A, if the work is

Fig. 3-9A Using paper between the blade of the square and the work to check for squareness

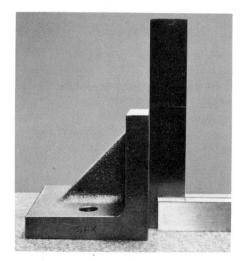

Fig. 3-9B Light shines through where the blade of the square does not make line contact with the surface

square (90°), both pieces of paper will be tight between the square and the work. In Figure 3-9B, the light is shut out only where the blade makes line contact with the surface of the work. Light shows through where the blade of the square does not make line contact with the surface being checked.

TOOLMAKER'S SURFACE PLATE SQUARE

The *toolmaker's surface plate square* (Fig. 3-10) provides a convenient method of checking work for squareness on a surface plate. Since it is of one-piece construction, there is little chance of any inaccuracy developing, as is the case with a blade and beam square.

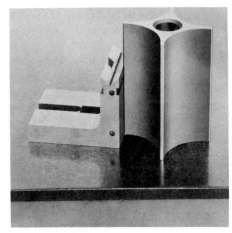

Courtesy Brown & Sharpe Mfg. Co.

Fig. 3-10   A toolmaker's surface plate square

CYLINDRICAL SQUARES

Cylindrical squares are commonly used as master squares against which other squares may be checked. The square consists of a thick-walled alloy steel cylinder which has been hardened, ground, and lapped. The outside diameter is a nearly true cylinder, and the ends are ground and lapped square with the axis. The ends are recessed and notched to decrease the inaccuracy from dust and to reduce friction. When a cylindrical square is used, it must be set carefully on a clean surface plate and rotated

slightly to force particles of dust and dirt into the end notches; the square can then make the proper contact with surface plate. Cylindrical squares provide a perfect line contact with the part being checked.

Another type of cylindrical square is the *direct reading cylindrical square* (Fig. 3-11) which indicates directly the amount that the part is out of square. One end of the cylinder is lapped square with the axis, while the other end is ground and lapped slightly out of square. The circumference is etched with several series of dots which form elliptical curved lines. Each curve is numbered at the top to indicate the amount the workpiece is out of square over the length of the square. Absolute squareness, or *zero deviation*, is indicated by an etched, vertical, dotted line on the square.

When used, the square is carefully placed in contact with the work and turned until no light is seen between it and the

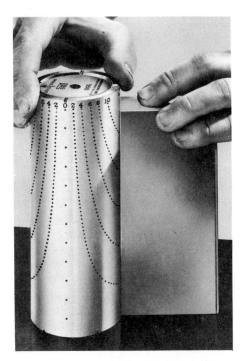

Courtesy Brown & Sharpe Mfg. Co.

Fig. 3-11   Checking a part for squareness using a direct reading cylindrical square

part being inspected. The uppermost curved line in contact with the work is noted and followed to the top where the number shows the amount the work is out of square. This square may also be used as a conventional cylindrical square if the opposite end which is ground and lapped square with the axis is used.

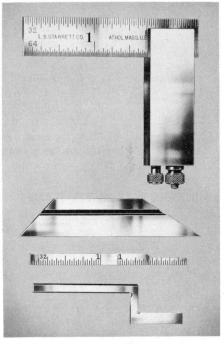

Courtesy The L. S. Starrett Company

Fig. 3-12   A diemaker's square is useful for checking the clearance on dies

ADJUSTABLE SQUARES

The *adjustable square*, while not providing the accuracy of a good solid square, is used by the toolmaker where it would be impossible to use a fixed square.

A *diemaker's square* (Fig. 3-12) is used to check the clearance angle on dies. The blade is adjusted to the angle of the workpiece by means of a blade adjusting screw. This angular setting must then be checked with a protractor. Another form of diemaker's square is the *direct reading* type which indicates the angle at which the blade is set.

Courtesy Ash Precision Equipment Inc.

Fig. 3-13 The amount a part is out of square can be read on an adjustable micrometer square

ADJUSTABLE MICROMETER SQUARE

The *adjustable micrometer square* (Fig. 3-13) may be used to check a part for squareness accurately. When a piece of work is being checked and light shows between the blade and the work, turn the micrometer head until the full length of the blade, which may be tilted, touches the work. The amount the part is out of square may be read from the micrometer head. When the micrometer head is set at zero, the blade is perfectly square with the beam.

STRAIGHTEDGES

A *straightedge* is used to check surfaces for flatness and to act as a guide when scribing long, straight lines in layout work. Straightedges are generally rectangular bars of hardened and accurately ground steel, having both edges flat and parallel. They are supplied with either plain or bevelled edges. Long straightedges are generally made of cast iron with ribbed construction.

SURFACE PLATES

A *surface plate* is a rigid block of granite or cast iron, the flat surface of which is used as a reference plane for layout, setup, and inspection work. Surface plates generally have a three-point suspension to prevent rocking when mounted on an uneven surface.

Cast-iron plates are well ribbed and supported to resist deflection under heavy loads. They are made of close-grained cast iron, which has high strength and good wear-resistance qualities. After a cast-iron surface plate has been machined, its surface must be scraped by hand to a flat plane. This operation is long and tedious; therefore, the cost of these plates is high.

Granite surface plates (Fig. 3-14) have many advantages over the cast-iron types and are replacing them in many shops. They may be manufactured from grey, pink, or black granite and are obtainable in several degrees of accuracy. Extremely flat finishes are produced by lapping.

The advantages of granite plates are:
a) They are not appreciably affected by temperature change. Granite will not burr as does cast iron; therefore the accuracy is not impaired.
b) These plates are nonmagnetic.
c) They are rustproof.

d) Abrasives will not embed themselves as easily in the surface; thus they may be used near grinding machines.

Courtesy The L. S. Starrett Company

Fig. 3-14 Granite surface plates are not affected by temperature change

Care of Surface Plates

1. Keep surface plates clean at all times, and wipe them with a dry cloth before using.
2. Clean them occasionally with solvent or surface plate cleaner to remove any film.
3. Protect them with a wooden cover when not in use.
4. Use parallels whenever possible to prevent damage to plates by rough parts or castings.
5. Remove burrs from the workpiece before placing it on the plate.
6. Slide heavy parts onto the plate rather than place them directly on the plate, since a part might fall and damage the plate.
7. Remove all burrs from cast-iron plates by honing.
8. When they are not in regular use, cover cast-iron plates with a thin film of oil to prevent rusting.

PRECISION MEASURING TOOLS

Although fixed gauges are convenient for checking hole sizes, they do not measure the actual size of the part. The machinist must use some form of precision measuring instrument to give him this desired size. Precision measuring tools may be divided into five categories, namely, **tools** used for outside measurement, inside measurement, depth measurement, thread measurement, and height measurement.

OUTSIDE MEASURING INSTRUMENTS

MICROMETERS

The *micrometer caliper*, usually called the *micrometer,* is the most commonly used measuring instrument when accuracy is required. The *standard inch micrometer,* shown in a cut-away view in Fig. 3-15, measures accurately to one-thousandth of an inch. Since many phases of modern manufacturing require greater accuracy, the *vernier micrometer,* capable of even finer measurements, is being used to an increasingly greater extent.

The only difference in construction and reading between the standard inch and the vernier micrometer is the addition of the vernier scale on the sleeve above the index or centre line.

PRINCIPLE OF THE INCH MICROMETER

There are 40 threads per inch on the spindle of the inch micrometer. Therefore, one complete revolution of the spindle will either increase or decrease the distance between the measuring faces by 1/40 (.025) in. The 1 in. distance marked on the micrometer sleeve is divided into 40 equal divisions, each of which equals 1/40 (.025) in.

If the micrometer is closed until the measuring faces just touch, the zero line on the thimble should line up with the index line on the sleeve (barrel). If the thimble is revolved counterclockwise one complete revolution, it will be noted that one line has appeared on the sleeve. Each line on the sleeve indicates .025 in. Thus, if three lines were showing on the sleeve (or barrel), the micrometer would have opened 3 × .025, or .075 in.

Every *fourth* line on the sleeve is longer than the others and is numbered to permit easy reading. Each numbered line indicates a distance of .100 in. For example, #4 showing on the sleeve indicates a distance between the measuring faces of 4 × .100, or .400 in.

The thimble has 25 equal divisions about its circumference, each of these divisions representing .001 in.

To read a standard inch micrometer, note the last number showing on the sleeve, multiply this by .100, multiply the number of small lines visible past that number by .025, and add the number of divisions on the thimble from zero to the line that coincides with the centre or index line on the sleeve.

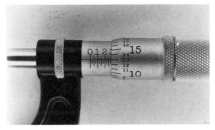

Fig. 3-16   Micrometer reading of .288

In Fig. 3-16

#2 is shown on the sleeve	2 × .100 = .200 in.
3 lines are visible past the number	3 × .025 = .075 in.
#13 line on thimble coincides with the index line	13 × .001 = .013 in.
Total reading	.288 in.

VERNIER MICROMETER

The *vernier inch micrometer* (Fig. 3-17) has, in addition to the graduations found on a standard micrometer, a *vernier scale* on the sleeve. This vernier scale consists of 10 divisions which run *parallel to and above* the index line. It will be noted that these ten divisions on the sleeve occupy the same distance as nine divisions (.009) on the thimble. One division on the vernier scale, therefore, represents 1/10 × .009, or .0009 in. Since one graduation on the thimble represents .001 or .0010 in., the difference between one thimble division and one vernier scale division represents .0010 − .0009, or .0001. Therefore, each division on the vernier scale has a value of .0001 in.

To Read a Vernier Micrometer

1. Read the micrometer as you would a standard micrometer.
2. Note the line on the vernier scale that coincides with a line on the thimble. This line will indicate the number of ten-thousandths that must be added to the above reading.

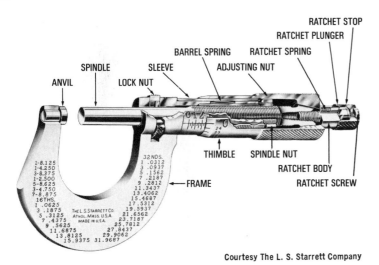

Fig. 3-15   Cut-away view of a standard micrometer with ratchet stop

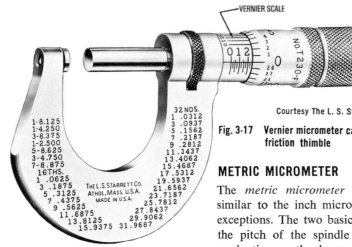

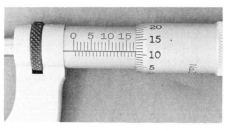

Fig. 3-17   Vernier micrometer caliper with friction thimble

METRIC MICROMETER

The *metric micrometer* (Fig. 3-19) is similar to the inch micrometer with two exceptions. The two basic differences are the pitch of the spindle screw and the graduations on the sleeve and thimble.

The pitch of the screw is 0.5 mm; therefore, a complete revolution of the thimble increases or decreases the distance between the measuring faces 0.5 mm. Above the index line on the sleeve, the graduations are in millimetres (from zero to 25) with every fifth line being numbered. Below the index line, each millimetre is subdivided into two parts of 0.5 mm, which corresponds to the pitch of the thread. It is apparent, therefore, that two turns of the thimble will be required to move the spindle 1 mm.

The circumference of the thimble is divided into 50 equal divisions, with every fifth line being numbered. Since one revolution of the thimble advances the spindle 0.5 mm, each graduation on the thimble equals $1/50 \times 0.5$ mm = 0.01 mm.

To Read a Metric Micrometer

1. Note the number of the last main division showing *above the line* to the left of the thimble. Multiply this by 1 mm.
2. If there is a half-millimetre line showing *below the index line*, between the whole millimetre and the thimble, then add 0.5 mm.
3. Add the number of the line on the thimble that coincides with the index line.

In Fig. 3-20A there are:

17 lines above the index line	17×1	= 17.00 mm
1 line below the index line	1×0.5	= 0.50 mm
11 lines on the thimble	11×0.01	= 0.11 mm
Total reading		17.61 mm

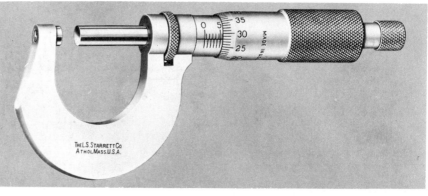

Fig. 3-20A   Metric micrometer reading of 17.61 mm

Referring to Fig. 3-18A, the reading of the vernier micrometer is as follows.

#2 is shown on the sleeve	$2 \times .100$	= .200 in.
1 line is visible past the number	$1 \times .025$	= .025 in.
#11 line on the thimble is just past the index line	$11 \times .001$	= .011 in.
#3 line on the vernier scale coincides with a line on the thimble	$3 \times .0001$	= .0003 in.
Total reading		= .2363 in.

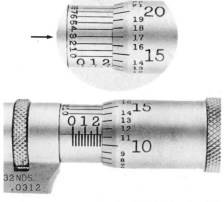

Fig. 3-18   Vernier micrometer reading of .2363

Fig. 3-19   Metric micrometer

METRIC VERNIER MICROMETER

The *metric vernier micrometer* in addition to the graduations found on the standard micrometer has 5 vernier divisions on the barrel each representing 0.002 mm. In the vernier micrometer reading illustrated in Fig. 3-20B, each major division (below the index line) has a value of 1 mm. Each minor division (above the index line) has a value of 0.50 mm. There are 50 divisions around the thimble, each having a value of 0.01 mm.

To Read a Metric Vernier Micrometer

1. Read the micrometer as you would for a standard metric micrometer.
2. Note the line on the vernier scale that coincides with a line on the thimble. This line will indicate the number of two thousandths of a millimetre that must be added to the above reading.

Referring to Fig. 3-20B, the reading of the metric vernier micrometer would be:

Major divisions
(below the index line)
(10×1.00) = 10.00 mm
Minor divisions
(above the index line)
(1×0.05) = 0.50 mm
Thimble divisions
(16×0.01) = 0.16 mm
The 2nd vernier division
coincides with a thimble
line (2×0.002) = 0.004 mm
Reading = 10.664 mm

MICROMETER ADJUSTMENTS

Proper care and use of a micrometer is necessary if its accuracy is to be preserved and adjustments kept to a minimum. Minor adjustments to micrometers can easily be made; however, it is extremely important that all parts of the micrometer be kept free from dust and foreign matter during any adjustment.

To Remove Play in the Micrometer Threads

To remove play (looseness) in the spindle threads due to wear:

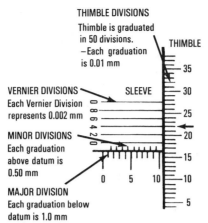

THIMBLE DIVISIONS
Thimble is graduated in 50 divisions.
—Each graduation is 0.01 mm

THIMBLE

VERNIER DIVISIONS
Each Vernier Division represents 0.002 mm

SLEEVE

MINOR DIVISIONS
Each graduation above datum is 0.50 mm

MAJOR DIVISION
Each graduation below datum is 1.0 mm

Fig. 3-20B A metric vernier micrometer reading of 10.664 mm

1. Back off the thimble as shown in Fig. 3-21A.
2. Insert the C-spanner into the slot or hole of the adjusting nut.

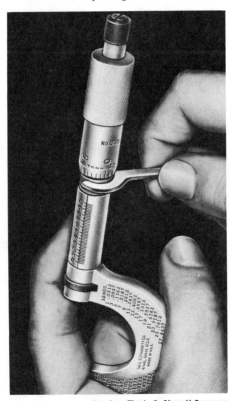

Fig. 3-21A Removing the play in the spindle screw threads

3. Turn the adjusting nut clockwise until play between the threads has been eliminated.

NOTE: After the micrometer has been adjusted, it should advance the spindle freely while turning the ratchet stop or friction thimble.

To Adjust the Accuracy of a Micrometer

Should the accuracy of a micrometer require adjustment:

1. Clean the measuring faces, and inspect them for damage.
2. Close the measuring faces carefully by turning the ratchet stop or friction thimble.
3. Insert the C-spanner into the hole or slot provided in the sleeve (Fig. 3-21B).
4. Carefully turn the *sleeve* until the index line on the sleeve coincides with the zero line on the thimble.
5. Recheck the accuracy of the micrometer by opening the micrometer and then closing the measuring faces by turning the ratchet stop or friction thimble.

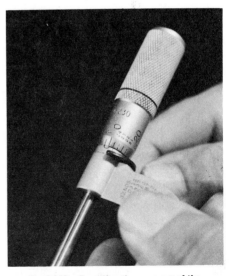

Fig. 3-21B Resetting the accuracy of the micrometer

MICROMETER ACCESSORIES

Although the design of most micrometers is fairly standard, certain desired refinements may be added to the basic design. Items such as the lock ring, ratchet, friction thimble, and carbide measuring faces increase the accuracy of these instruments. Figs. 3-22A, B, and C illustrate several models of outside micrometers.

INDICATING MICROMETER

Fig. 3-23 shows an *indicating micrometer*, employing an indicating dial and a movable anvil, which permits accurate measurements to ten-thousandths of an inch. This type of micrometer may also be used as a comparator by setting it to the desired size with gauge blocks or a standard and locking the spindle. The tolerance arms are then set to the required limits. As each piece of work is inserted, the relieving button is depressed. After the button is released, a comparative or a limit reading will be indicated on the dial.

VERNIER CALIPERS

Vernier calipers (Fig. 3-24) are precision tools used to make accurate measurements to within 0.02 mm or .001 in., depending on whether they are metric or inch. They consist of an L-shaped bar and movable jaw which are graduated on both sides, one side for taking outside measurements and the other for inside measurements. The bar contains the main graduations and the vernier graduations are on the movable jaw. Two types of vernier calipers are available: one has 25 divisions on the vernier scale of the movable jaw, and the other has 50 divisions.

The bar of the vernier caliper with the 25-division vernier scale on the movable jaw is graduated exactly the same as a micrometer. Each inch is divided into 40 equal divisions, each having a value of .025 in. Every fourth line, representing 1/10 or .100, is numbered. The vernier

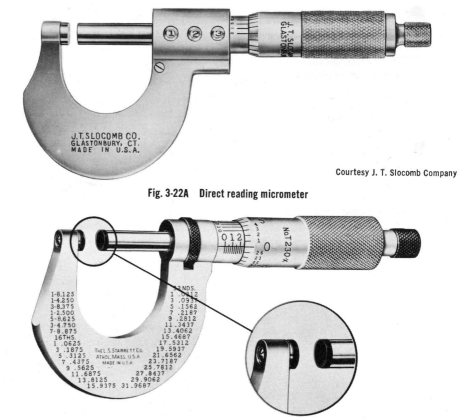

Courtesy J. T. Slocomb Company

Fig. 3-22A   Direct reading micrometer

Courtesy The L. S. Starrett Company

Fig. 3-22B   Micrometer with carbide measuring faces

Courtesy The L. S. Starrett Company

Fig. 3-22C   Tubular frames are used in larger size micrometers to reduce weight

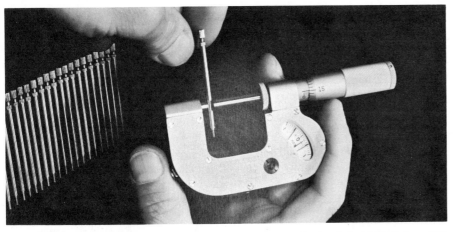

Courtesy Federal Products Corporation

Fig. 3-23   An indicating micrometer used for inspection work

scale on the movable jaw has 25 equal divisions, each representing .001. The 25 divisions on the vernier scale, which are .600 in length, are equal to 24 divisions on the bar. The difference between *one* division on the bar and one vernier division equals .025 − .024, or .001 in. Therefore, only one line of the vernier scale will line up exactly with a line on the bar at any one setting.

Some vernier calipers are provided with two small indentations, or points, on the bar and movable jaw (Fig. 3-24) which may be used to set dividers accurately to a specific dimension or radius.

To Read a 25-Division Vernier Inch Caliper

1. The last large number above the main scale on the bar and to the left of the vernier scale represents the number of whole inches.

2. Note the last small number on the bar to the left of the zero on the vernier scale. Multiply this number by .100.

3. Note how many graduations are showing on the bar between the last number and the zero on the vernier scale. Multiply this number by .025.

4. Observe which line on the vernier scale coincides with a line on the bar. Multiply this number by .001.

In Fig. 3-25:

The large #1 on the bar		= 1.000 in.
The small #4 past the #1	4 × .100 =	.400 in.
One line is visible past the #4	1 × .025 =	.025 in.
The 11th line on the vernier scale coincides with a line on the bar	11 × .001 =	.011 in.
Total reading		= 1.436 in.

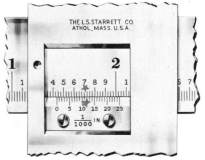

Courtesy The L. S. Starrett Company

Fig. 3-25   A 25-division vernier caliper reading of 1.436

The 50-Division Vernier Inch Caliper

Because 25-division vernier calipers are often difficult to read, many vernier calipers are now manufactured with 50 divisions (equal to 49 on the main scale) on the vernier scale of the movable jaw. Each of these scales on the bar and movable jaw is equal to 2.450 in. in length. Each division on the bar then equals 2.450 divided by 49 divisions, or .050 in. in length. Each division on the vernier scale would equal 2.450 divided by 50 divisions, or .049 in. in length. The *difference in length* between one main scale division and one vernier division equals .050 − .049, or .001 in.

Each line on the main scale of a 50-division vernier caliper has a value of .050 in. Each line on the vernier scale has a value of .001 in.

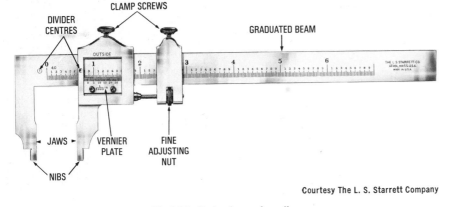

Courtesy The L. S. Starrett Company

Fig. 3-24   Parts of a vernier caliper

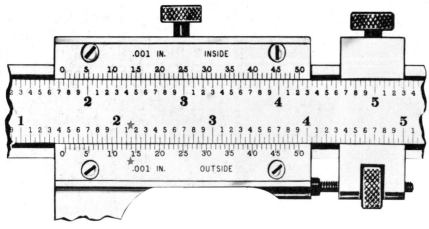

Courtesy The L. S. Starrett Company

Fig. 3-26 A 50-division vernier caliper reading of 1.464

In Fig. 3-26:

The large #1 on the bar		= 1.000 in.
The small #4 past the #1	4 × .100 =	.400 in.
1 line is visible past #4	1 × .050 =	.050 in.
The 14th line on the vernier scale coincides with a line on the bar	14 × .001 =	.014 in.
Total reading		= 1.464 in.

THE METRIC VERNIER CALIPER

Vernier calipers are also made with metric readings and many of these vernier calipers have both metric and inch graduations on the same instrument (Fig. 3-27). The parts of metric vernier calipers are the same as those of the inch vernier.

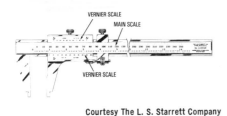

Courtesy The L. S. Starrett Company

Fig. 3-27 Vernier caliper with metric and inch readings

The *main scale* is graduated in millimetres and every main division is numbered. Each numbered division has a value of 10 mm, for example, #1 represents 10 mm, #2 represents 20 mm, etc. There are 50 graduations on the sliding or *vernier scale* with every fifth one being numbered. These 50 graduations occupy the same space as 49 graduations on the main scale (49 mm).

$$\text{Therefore 1 vernier division} = \frac{49}{50}\text{ mm}$$
$$= 0.98\text{ mm}$$

The difference between 1 main scale division and 1 vernier scale division
$$= 1 - 0.98$$
$$= 0.02\text{ mm}$$

To Read a Metric Vernier Caliper

1. The last numbered division on the bar to the left of the vernier scale represents the number of millimetres multiplied by 10.
2. Note how many full graduations are showing between this numbered division and the zero on the vernier scale. Multiply this number by 1 mm.
3. Find the line on the vernier scale which coincides with a line on the bar. Multiply this number by 0.02 mm.

In Fig. 3-28:

The large #4 graduation on the bar (4 × 10 mm)	= 40 mm
Three full lines past the #4 graduation (3 × 1 mm)	= 3 mm
The 9th line on the vernier scale coincides with a line on the bar (9 × 0.02)	= 0.18 mm
Total reading	= 43.18 mm

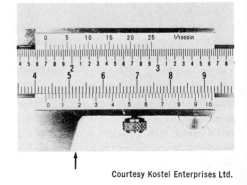

Courtesy Kostel Enterprises Ltd.

Fig. 3-28 A metric vernier caliper reading of 43.18 mm

DIRECT READING DIAL CALIPER

An instrument which resembles the vernier caliper is the *direct reading dial caliper*, capable of reading to .001 in. A dial indicator, the hand of which is attached to a

Fig. 3-29 A direct reading dial caliper

pinion, is mounted on the sliding jaw. For the inch dial caliper, one revolution of the hand represents .200 in. of travel. The dial is divided into 200 divisions, each representing .001 in. The pinion meshes with a rack attached to the bar which is graduated in inches (1.000) and tenths of an inch (.100). Dial calipers are quickly set and more easily read than vernier calipers.

GEAR TOOTH VERNIER CALIPER

The *gear tooth vernier caliper* (Fig. 3-30) consists basically of a vernier caliper and a vernier depth gauge mounted at right angles to each other. This caliper is used to measure the thickness of gear teeth at the pitch-circle line. It may be used also to measure the width of Acme threads at the pitch line. Inch instruments are manufactured in two ranges: 20 diametral pitch to two diametral pitch, and 10 diametral pitch to one diametral pitch, measuring in thousandths of an inch.

Metric gear tooth vernier calipers are graduated in steps of 0.02 mm and come in the 1.25 to 12.00 mm range and the 2.5 to 25.00 mm range.

Corrected Addendum. When measuring gear teeth, it is necessary to set the gear-tooth vernier caliper to the *corrected addendum*, which is a point slightly lower than the *true addendum* of the gear. If the vernier depth slide is set to the true addendum, the caliper will measure the sides of the tooth at a point above the pitch circle and not give a true measurement (Fig. 3-31A and B). Most handbooks contain tables giving the corrected addendum of gear teeth. If tables are not available, the following formula may be used to calculate the corrected addendum.

$$CA = A + \left[1/2\,PD \left(1 - \cos\frac{90°}{N} \right) \right]$$

CA = corrected addendum
A = addendum
PD = pitch diameter
N = number of teeth in the gear

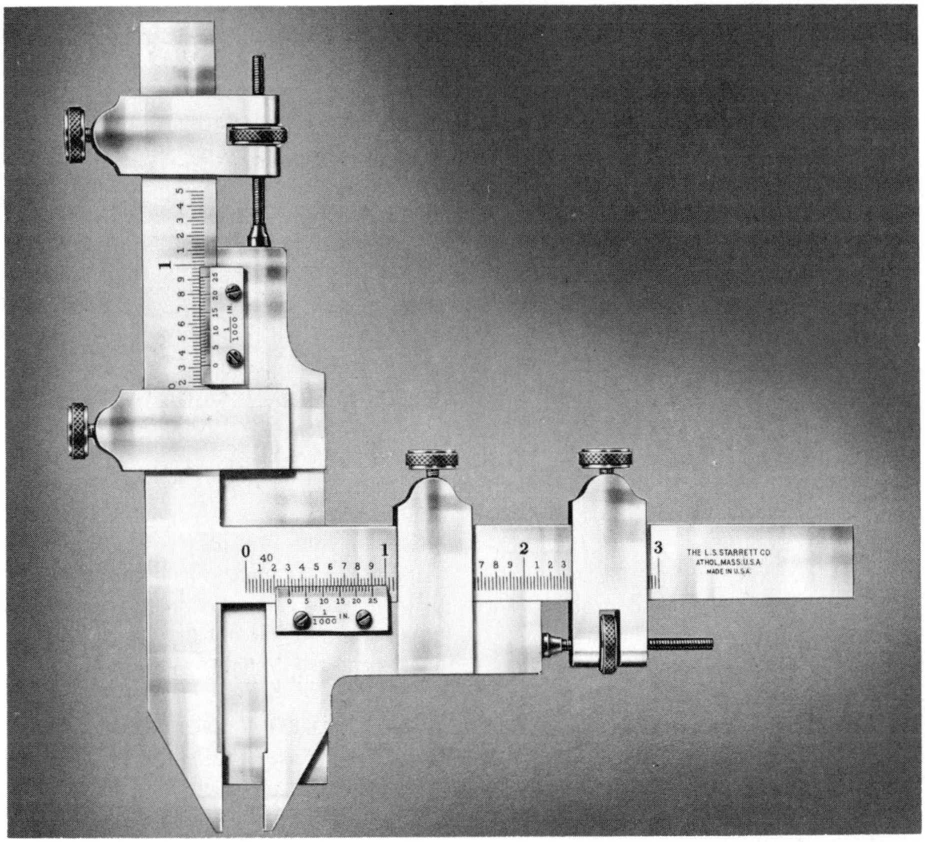

Fig. 3-30   A gear tooth vernier caliper

Courtesy The L. S. Starrett Company

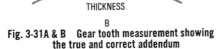

TRUE ADDENDUM   CORRECTED ADDENDUM

PITCH CIRCLE
DIFFERENCE
A

CHORDAL THICKNESS
B

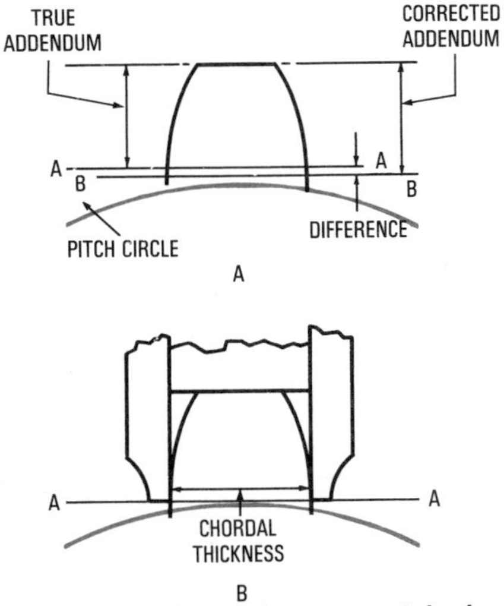

Fig. 3-31A & B   Gear tooth measurement showing the true and correct addendum

To Check Gear-Tooth Dimensions

1. Set the vertical slide to the *corrected addendum* of the gear.
2. Place the slide on top of the gear tooth to be measured.
3. Using the adjusting nut, set the horizontal slide to the thickness of the tooth.
4. Note the reading on the horizontal scale and check it with the required thickness.

INSIDE MEASURING INSTRUMENTS

INSIDE MICROMETER CALIPERS

The inside micrometer caliper (Fig. 3-32) is designed for measuring holes, slots,

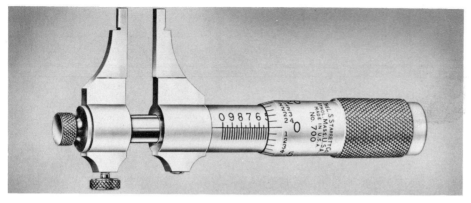

Fig. 3-32 An inside micrometer caliper

grooves, etc., from 40 to 1000 mm, or from .200 to 1.200 in. for the inch-designed instruments. The nibs or ends of the jaws are hardened and ground to a small radius to permit the accurate measurement of holes. A locking nut provided with this micrometer can be used to lock the micrometer at any desired size.

The inside micrometer caliper employs the same principle as a standard micrometer; however, the barrel readings on some calipers are reversed (as shown in Fig. 3-32). Extreme care must be taken in reading this type of instrument. Other in-side micrometer calipers have the reading on the spindle and are read in the same manner as a standard outside micrometer. Inside micrometer calipers are special purpose tools and are not used in mass production measurement.

To Use an Inside Micrometer Caliper

1. Adjust the jaws to slightly less than the diameter to be measured.
2. Hold the fixed jaw against one side of the hole, and adjust the movable jaw until the proper "feel" is obtained. *NOTE:* Move the movable jaw back

and forth to ensure that the measurement taken is across the diameter.

3. Set the lock nut, remove the instrument, and check the reading.

INSIDE MICROMETERS

For internal measurements larger than 40 mm (1-1/2 in. for inch-designed instruments), inside micrometers (Fig. 3-33) are used. The inside micrometer set consists of a micrometer head, having a range of 25 mm (1/2 in. or 1 in. for inch tools), several extension rods of different lengths which may be inserted into the head, and a 1/2 in. spacing collar. These sets cover a range from 40 to 1000 mm, or from 1-1/2 in. to over 100 in. for inch tools. Sets that are used for the larger ranges generally have hollow tubes, rather than rods, for greater rigidity.

The inside micrometer is read in the same manner as the standard micrometer. Since there is no locking nut on the inside micrometer, the thimble nut is adjusted to a tighter fit on the spindle thread to prevent a change in the setting while it is being removed from the hole.

To Measure with an Inside Micrometer

1. Measure the size of the hole with a rule.
2. Insert the correct micrometer extension rod after having carefully cleaned the shoulders of the rod and the micrometer head.

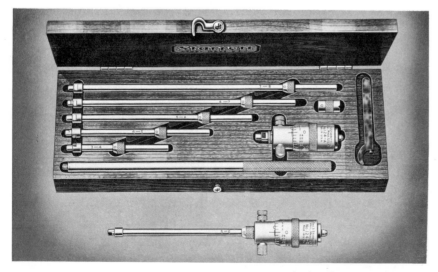

Fig. 3-33 An inside micrometer set

Fig. 3-34 Using an inside micrometer

3. Align the zero marks on the rod and micrometer head, and lock the rod firmly in place with the knurled set screw.

4. Adjust the micrometer to slightly less than the diameter to be measured.

5. Hold the head in a fixed position and adjust the micrometer to the hole size while moving the rod end in the direction of the arrows (Fig. 3-34).

6. When a micrometer is properly adjusted to size, there should be a slight drag or feel when the rod end is moved past the centre line of the hole.

7. Carefully remove the micrometer and note the reading.

8. To this reading, add the length of the extension rod and collar.

SMALL HOLE GAUGES

Small hole gauges are available in sets of *four*, covering a range from 1/8 in. to 1/2 in. (3.1 to 12.7 mm■). They are manufactured in *two* types (Fig. 3-35A and B).

The small hole gauges shown in Fig. 3-35A have a small, round end, or ball, and are used for measuring holes, slots,

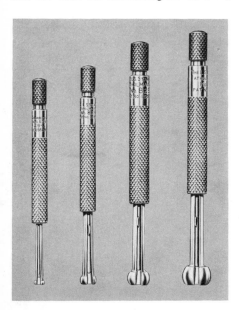

Courtesy The L. S. Starrett Company

Fig. 3-35A   Small hole gauges with hardened ball

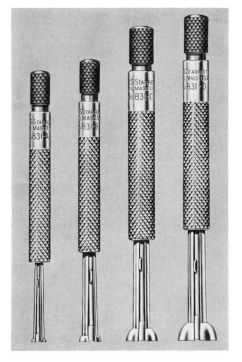

Courtesy The L. S. Starrett Company

Fig. 3-35B   Small hole gauges with flat bottom

grooves, and recesses which are too small for inside calipers or telescope gauges. Those shown in Fig. 3-35B have a flat bottom and are used for similar purposes. The flat bottom permits the measurement of shallow slots, recesses, and holes impossible to gauge with the rounded type.

Both types are of similar construction and are adjusted to size by turning the knurled knob on the top. This draws up a tapered plunger, causing the two halves of the ball to open up and contact the hole.

To Use a Small Hole Gauge

Small hole gauges require extreme care in setting since it is easy to get an incorrect setting when checking the diameter of a hole.

1. Measure the hole to be checked with a rule.
2. Select the proper small hole gauge.
3. Clean the hole and the gauge.
4. Adjust the gauge until it is slightly

smaller than the hole and insert into the hole.

5. Adjust the gauge until it can be felt just touching the sides of the hole or slot.

6. Swing the handle back and forth, and adjust the knurled end until the proper "feel" is obtained across the widest dimension of the ball.

7. Remove the gauge and check the size with an outside micrometer.

NOTE: It is important that when transferring the measurement, the same "feel" is obtained as when adjusting the gauge to the hole.

TELESCOPE GAUGES

Telescope gauges (Fig. 3-36) are used for obaining the size of holes, slots, and recesses from 5/16 to 6 in. (8 to 152 mm■). They are T-shaped instruments, each consisting of a pair of telescoping tubes or plungers connected to a handle. The plungers are spring-loaded to force them apart. The knurled knob on the end of the handle locks the plungers into position when turned in a clockwise direction.

NOTE: In some sets, only one plunger moves.

To Measure Using a Telescope Gauge

1. Measure the hole size and select the proper gauge.
2. Clean the gauge and the hole.
3. Depress the plungers until slightly smaller than the hole diameter and clamp them in this position.
4. Insert it into the hole and, with the handle tilted upwards slightly, then release the plungers.
5. *Lightly* snug up the knurled knob.
6. Hold the bottom leg of the telescope gauge in position with one hand.
7. Move the handle downwards through the centre while slightly moving the top leg from side to side.
8. Tighten the plungers in position.
9. Recheck the "feel" on the gauge by testing it in the hole again.

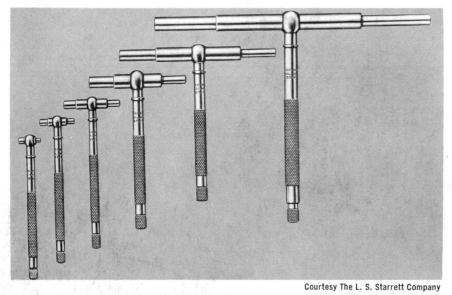

Fig. 3-36   Set of telescope gauges

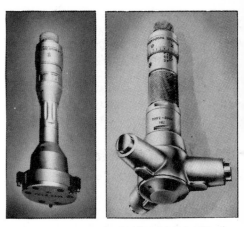

Fig. 3-38   Intramiks — Style A   Style B

10. Check the gauge size with outside micrometers, maintaining the same "feel" as in the hole.

DIAL BORE GAUGES

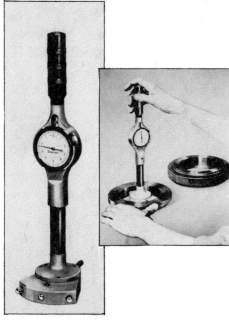

Fig. 3-37   Dial bore gauge

A quick and accurate method of checking hole diameters and bores for size, out-of-round, taper, bell-mouth, hour-glass, or barrel shapes, is by means of the *dial bore gauge* (Fig. 3-37).

Gauging is accomplished by three spring-loaded centralizing plungers in the head, one of which actuates the dial indicator, graduated in ten-thousandths of an inch, or in 0.01 mm graduations for metric tools.

These instruments are available in six sizes to cover a range from 75 to 300 mm, or from 3 to 12 in. Each instrument is supplied with extensions to increase its range. The dial bore gauge must be set to a size with a master gauge, and then the hole size is compared to the gauge setting. Should the hole size vary, it is not necessary to adjust the gauge, as long as the size remains within the range of the gauge.

INTRIMIK

A difficulty encountered in measuring hole sizes with instruments employing only two measuring faces is that of properly measuring the diameter and not a chord of the circle. An instrument which eliminates this problem is the *Intrimik* (Fig. 3-38).

The Intrimik consists of a head with three contact points spaced 120° apart; this head is attached to a micrometer-type body. The contact points are forced out to contact the inside of the hole by means of a tapered or conical plug attached to the micrometer spindle (Fig. 3-39). The construction of a head with three contact points permits the Intrimik to be self-centring and self-aligning. It is more accurate because it provides a direct reading, eliminating the necessity of transferring measurements to determine hole size as with telescope or small hole gauges.

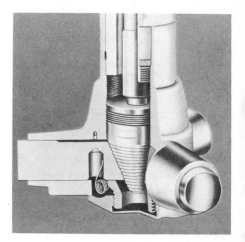

Fig. 3-39   Construction of the Intramik head

The range of these instruments is from .275 to 12.000 in., and the accuracy varies between .0001 and .0005 in., depending on the head used. Metric Intrimiks have a range from 6 mm to 300 mm, with graduations in 0.001 mm. The accuracy of the Intrimik should be checked periodically with a setting ring or master ring gauge.

DEPTH MEASUREMENT

MICROMETER DEPTH GAUGE

Micrometer depth gauges are used for measuring depth of blind holes, slots, recesses, and projections. Each gauge consists of a flat base attached to a micrometer sleeve. An extension rod of the required length fits through the sleeve and protrudes through the base (Fig. 3-40). This rod is held in position by a threaded cap on the top of the thimble.

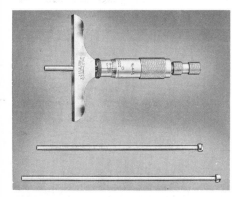

Courtesy The L. S. Starrett Company

Fig. 3-40   Micrometer depth gauge and extension rods

Micrometer extension rods are available in various lengths, providing a range up to 75 mm or, for inch tools, up to 9 in. The micrometer screw has a range of 0.25 mm for metric tools, and for inch tools of 1/2 in. or 1 in. Depth micrometers are available with both round or flat rods which are *not interchangeable* with other depth micrometers. The accuracy of these micrometers is controlled by a nut on the end of each extension rod which can be adjusted if necessary.

Courtesy The L. S. Starrett Company

Fig. 3-41   Measuring the depth of a shoulder

To Measure with a Micrometer Depth Gauge

1. Remove burrs from the edge of the hole and the face of the workpiece.
2. Hold the micrometer base firmly against the surface of the work (Fig. 3-41).
3. Rotate the thimble lightly with the tip of one finger, in a clockwise direction,

Courtesy The L. S. Starrett Company

Fig. 3-42   Graduations on a depth micrometer are reversed from those on an outside micrometer

until the bottom of the extension rod touches the bottom of the hole or recess.
4. Recheck the micrometer setting a few times to make sure that not too much pressure was applied in the setting.
5. Carefully note the reading.

NOTE: The numbers on the thimble and the sleeve are the reverse of those on a standard micrometer (Fig. 3-42).

VERNIER DEPTH GAUGES

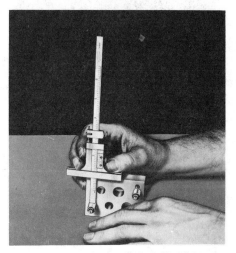

Courtesy The L. S. Starrett Company

Fig. 3-43   Checking toolmaker's buttons using a vernier depth gauge

The depth of holes, slots, and recesses may also be measured by a vernier depth gauge. This instrument is read in the same manner as a standard vernier caliper. Fig. 3-43 illustrates how the toolmaker's button may be set up with this instrument.

Depth measurements may also be made with certain types of vernier calipers which are provided with a thin sliding blade or depth gauge attached to the movable jaw. The blade protrudes from the end of the bar opposite the sliding jaw. The caliper is placed vertically over the depth to be measured, and the end of the bar is held against the shoulder while the blade is inserted into the hole to be measured. Depth readings are identical to standard vernier readings.

THREAD MEASUREMENT

SCREW THREAD MICROMETERS

Sharp-V, American National, Unified, and ISO threads may be measured with reasonable accuracy with a screw thread micrometer (Fig. 3-44). These micrometers have a pointed spindle and a double-V swivel anvil which are shaped to contact the pitch diameter of the thread being measured (Fig. 3-44). The micrometer reading indicates the pitch diameter of the thread which is equal to the outside diameter less the depth of one thread.

Each thread micrometer is limited to measuring a certain range of threads; this range is stamped on the micrometer frame. One-inch thread micrometers are manufactured in four ranges to cover the following range of threads per inch (tpi).

a) 8 to 13 tpi

b) 14 to 20 tpi

c) 22 to 30 tpi

d) 32 to 40 tpi

Metric thread micrometers are available in sizes from 0 to 25 mm, 25 to 50 mm, 50 to 75 mm, and 75 to 100 mm. A set of twelve anvil and spindle inserts are available for thread pitches from 0.4 to 6 mm.

To check the accuracy of a thread micrometer, carefully bring the measuring faces into light contact; the micrometer reading for this setting should be zero.

When measuring threads, the micrometer gives a slightly distorted reading because of the helix angle of the thread. In order to overcome this inaccuracy, set the thread micrometer to a thread plug gauge or to a thread which must be duplicated.

To Measure with a Thread Micrometer

1. Thoroughly clean the measuring surfaces.
2. Check the micrometer for accuracy by bringing the measuring faces together; the reading should be zero.
3. Clean the thread to be measured.
4. Set the micrometer to the required thread plug gauge and note the reading.
5. Fit the swivel anvil onto the threaded workpiece.
6. Adjust the spindle until the point just bears against the opposite side of the thread.
7. Carefully roll the micrometer over the thread to get the proper feel.
8. Note the readings and compare them to the micrometer reading of the thread plug gauge.

Threads may also be checked by the *screw-thread-comparator micrometer* (Fig. 3-45) which has two conical measuring surfaces. Since it does not measure the pitch diameter, it is important to set this instrument to a thread plug gauge before measuring a threaded workpiece. The screw micrometer is used for quick comparison of threads, as well as for checking small grooves and recesses where regular micrometers cannot be used.

When thread micrometers or comparators are not available, threads may be accurately checked by the *3-wire method* which is fully discussed in Chapter 9.

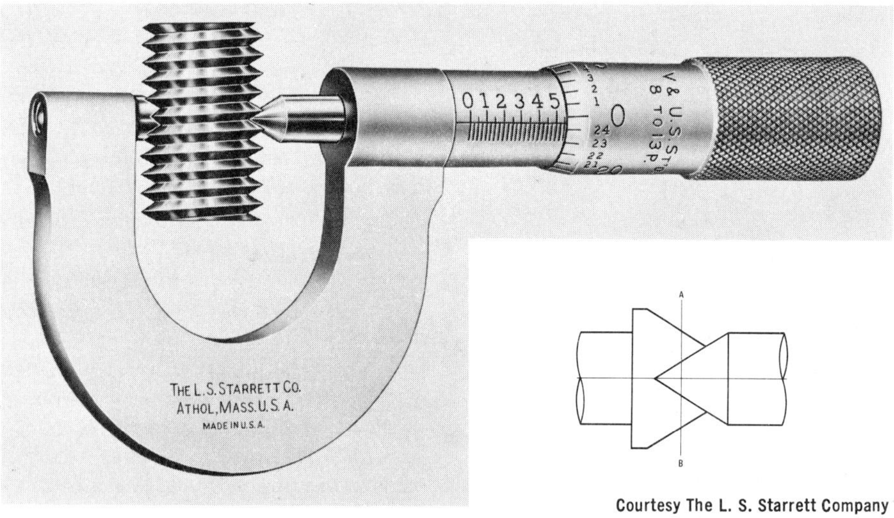

HEIGHT MEASUREMENT

VERNIER HEIGHT GAUGE

The vernier height gauge is a precision instrument used in toolrooms and inspection departments on layout and jig and fixture work to measure and mark off distances accurately. These instruments are available in a variety of sizes from 300 to 1000 mm sizes, or from 12 in. to 72 in. for inch-designed tools, and can be accurately set at any height to within 0.02 mm or .001 in., respectively. Basically, a vernier height gauge is a vernier caliper with a hardened, ground, and lapped base in lieu of a fixed jaw and is always used with a surface plate or an accurate flat surface. The sliding jaw assembly can be raised or lowered to any position along the beam. Fine adjustments are made by means of an adjusting nut. The vernier height gauge is read in the same manner as a vernier caliper.

The vernier height gauge is particularly suited to accurate layout work and may be used for this purpose if a scriber is mounted on the movable jaw (Fig. 3-46). The scriber height may be set either by means of the vernier scale or by setting the scriber to the top of a gauge block buildup.

Courtesy The L. S. Starrett Company

Fig. 3-44 Screw thread micrometer and insert showing the measuring faces

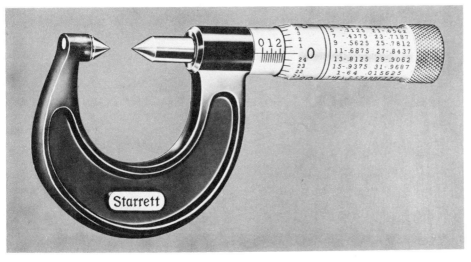

Fig. 3-45 Screw-thread-comparator micrometer

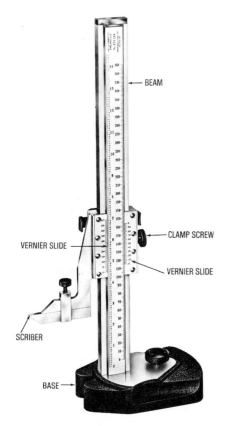

Fig. 3-46 Vernier height gauge

The *offset scriber* (Fig. 3-47) is a vernier height gauge attachment which permits the setting of heights from the face of the surface plate. When using this attachment, it is not necessary to consider the height of the base or the width of the scriber and clamp.

A *depth gauge attachment* may be fastened to the movable jaw, permitting the measurement of height differences which may be difficult to measure by other methods.

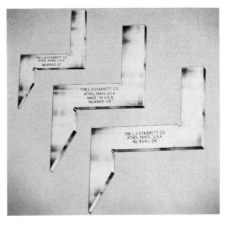

Fig. 3-47 Offset scribers are used with a vernier height gauge for accurate layout work

Another important use for the vernier height gauge is in inspection work. A dial indicator may be fastened to the movable jaw of the height gauge (Fig. 3-48), and distances between holes or surfaces can be checked to within an accuracy of .001 in. on the vernier scale. If greater accuracy (.0001 in. or less) is required, the indicator may be used in conjunction with gauge blocks.

In Fig. 3-48, the height gauge is being used to check the location of reamed holes in relation to the edges of the plate and to each other.

Fig. 3-48 Using a height gauge and dial indicator to check a height

To Measure with a Vernier Height Gauge and Dial Indicator

1. Thoroughly clean the surface plate, height gauge base, and work surface.
2. Place the work on the surface plate and clamp it against an angle plate if required.
3. Insert a snug-fitting plug in the hole to be checked with about 12 mm projecting beyond the work.
4. Mount the dial indicator on the movable jaw of the height gauge.
5. Adjust the movable jaw until the indicator almost touches the surface plate.
6. Lock the upper slide, and use the adjusting nut to move the indicator until the needle registers about one-quarter turn.
7. Set the indicator dial to zero.
8. Record the reading of the vernier height gauge.

9. Adjust the vernier height gauge until the indicator registers zero on the top of the plug. Record this vernier height gauge reading.

10. From this reading, subtract the initial reading plus half the diameter of the plug. This will indicate the distance from the surface plate to the centre of the hole.

11. Check other hole heights using the same procedure.

To Measure Heights Using Gauge Blocks

When hole locations must be accurate to 0.010 mm (.0005 in.) or less, a gauge block buildup is made for the proper dimension from the surface plate to the top of a plug fitted in the hole.

1. Prepare the required gauge block buildup (the centre of the hole height plus one-half the hole diameter).

2. Mount a suitable reading dial indicator on a surface or vernier height gauge.

3. Set the dial indicator to register zero on the top of the gauge blocks.

4. Move the indicator over the top of the plug. The difference between the gauge block buildup and the top of the plug will be registered on the dial indicator.

PRECISION HEIGHT GAUGE

The precision height gauge (Fig. 3-49) provides a quick and accurate means of setting any height within the range of the instrument, eliminating the need for calculating and assembling specified gauge blocks for comparative measurements. A surface plate is used as the reference surface.

The precision height gauge is made from a hardened and ground round steel bar, with ground and lapped measuring steps or discs spaced exactly at 1 in. (25.4 mm) intervals. The measuring bar or column is raised or lowered by turning the large micrometer thimble which is graduated by steps of 0.002 mm, or .001 in. if the instrument is inch-designed. The column may be raised or lowered 25 mm or a full inch, permitting any reading from

Fig. 3-49 Checking hole locations with a precision height gauge and a height transfer gauge

zero to the range of the instrument in increments of 0.002 mm or .001 in., respectively. Some models have a vernier scale below the micrometer thimble; readings in increments of 0.000 25 mm, or in .000 010 in. increments are then possible. It is important that the accuracy of precision height gauges be checked periodically with a master set of gauge blocks.

Height gauges are available in 6 in., 12 in., 24 in., and 36 in. models, and their range may be increased by the use of riser blocks under the base. Metric gauges range from 300 to 450 mm.

To Use a Precision Height Gauge

1. Clean the surface plate and the feet of the height gauge.

2. Clean the bottom of the work to be checked and place it on the surface plate, using parallels and an angle plate if required.

3. Insert plugs into the holes to be checked.

4. Mount a dial indicator on the movable jaw of a vernier height gauge.

5. Adjust the height gauge until the dial indicator registers approximately .015 in. (0.40 mm■) across the top of the plug.

6. Turn the dial of the indicator to zero.

7. Move the dial indicator over the nearest disc of the precision height gauge, and raise the column by turning the micrometer until the dial indicator reads zero.

8. Check the micrometer reading. This reading will indicate the distance from the surface plate to the top of the plug.

9. Subtract half the diameter of the plug from this reading.
   NOTE: If the work is set on parallels, this height must be subtracted from the precision height gauge reading.

GAUGE BLOCKS

Man has continually striven to improve the system of measurement. Various standards of measurement were applied until light waves were finally used to designate a unit of measurement. Today the metre and inch are defined as equal to certain quantities of wave lengths of helium light. Gauge blocks are more than just blocks of special steel; they are the *physical representation* of wave lengths of helium light. Gauge blocks, an acceptable standard of accuracy, have provided industry with a means of maintaining sizes to specific standards or tolerances, a feature which has resulted in a high rate of production and has made interchangeable manufacture possible.

GAUGE BLOCK MANUFACTURE

Gauge blocks are rectangular blocks of hardened and ground alloy steel which have been stabilized through alternate subjections of extreme heat and cold until the crystalline structure of the metal is without strain. The two measuring surfaces are lapped and polished to an optically flat surface and to a specific size accurate to within 0.000 05 mm. The size of each block is stamped on one of its surfaces. Chrome-plated gauge blocks are also available and when long wear is desirable, carbide blocks are used. Great care is exercised in their manufacture; the final calibration is made under ideal conditions where the temperature is maintained at 20°C. Therefore, a centimetre or inch is accurate to size *only* when measured at the standard temperature of 20°C.

Uses

Industry has found gauge blocks to be invaluable tools. Because of their extreme accuracy, they are used for the following purposes.

a) to check the dimensional accuracy of fixed gauges to determine the extent of wear, growth, or shrinkage

b) to calibrate adjustable gauges, such as micrometers and vernier calipers, imparting accuracy to these instruments

c) to set comparators, dial indicators, and height gauges to exact dimensions

d) to set sine bars and sine plates when extreme accuracy is required in angular setups

e) with the use of attachments, for precision layout work

f) in machine tool setups

g) to measure and inspect the accuracy of finished parts in inspection rooms

GAUGE BLOCK SETS
INCH STANDARD GAUGE BLOCKS

Gauge blocks are manufactured in a variety of sets that vary from a few blocks

Courtesy DoALL Company

Fig. 3-50 An 83-piece set of gauge blocks

to as many as 115 in a set. The most commonly used is the 83-piece set (Fig. 3-50) from which it is possible to make over 120 000 different measurements ranging from one hundred-thousandth of an inch to over 25 inches. The blocks which comprise an 83-piece set are listed in Table 3-2A.

Two *wear* blocks are furnished with an 83-piece set. Some manufacturers supply .050 in. wear blocks, while others have .100 in. wear blocks. They should be used at each end of a combination, especially if the blocks will be in contact with hard surfaces or abrasives. In this way, the wear which occurs during use will be on the two wear blocks only, rather than on many blocks, and the useful life and accuracy of the set will be prolonged. During use, it is considered good practice always to expose the same face of the wear block to the work surface. A good habit to formulate is always to have the words "Wear Block" appear on the outside of the combination. This way, all the wear will be on one surface and the wringing quality of the other surface will be preserved.

METRIC GAUGE BLOCKS

Metric gauge blocks are supplied by most manufacturers in sets of 47, 88 and 113 piece blocks. The most common set is the 88-piece set (Table 3-2B). Each of the above sets contains a pair of 2 mm wear blocks. These blocks are used at each end of the buildup to prolong the accuracy of the other blocks in the set.

ACCURACY

Gauge blocks in the inch-pound and metric standards are manufactured in three common degrees of accuracy, depending on the purpose for which they are used.

a) The *Class AA* set, commonly called a *laboratory* or *master* set, is accurate to ±.000 002 in. in the inch standard. The metric gauge block set is accurate to ±0.000 05 mm. These gauge blocks are used in temperature-controlled laboratories as references to compare or

check the accuracy of working gauges.

b) The *Class A* set is used for inspection purposes and is accurate to ±.000 004 in. in the inch standard. The metric gauge block set is accurate to +0.000 15 mm and −0.000 05 mm.

c) The *Class B* set, commonly called the *working* set, is accurate to ±000 008 in. in the inch standard. The metric gauge block set is accurate to +0.000 25 mm and −0.000 15 mm. These blocks are used in the shop for machine tool setups, layout work, and measurement.

THE EFFECT OF TEMPERATURE

While the effect of temperature on ordinary measuring instruments is negligible, changes in temperature are important when precision gauge blocks are handled. Gauge blocks have been calibrated at 20°C, while the human body temperature is around 37°C. A 0.5°C rise in temperature will cause a 100 mm stack of gauge blocks to expand approximately 0.0006 mm; therefore it is important that these blocks be handled as little as possible. The following suggestions are offered to eliminate as much error as possible due to temperature change.

1. Handle gauge blocks only when they must be moved.

2. Hold them for as little time as possible.

3. Hold them between the tips of the fingers so that the area of contact is small.

4. Have the work and gauge blocks at the same temperature. If a temperature-controlled room is not available, both the work and gauge blocks may be placed in kerosene until both are at the same temperature.

5. Where extreme accuracy is necessary, use insulating gloves and tweezers to prevent temperature change during handling.

TABLE 3-2A
SIZES IN AN 83-PIECE SET OF INCH-POUND STANDARD GAUGE BLOCKS

FIRST: .0001 in. Series – 9 Blocks								
.1001	.1002	.1003	.1004	.1005	.1006	.1007	.1008	.1009

SECOND: .001 in. Series – 49 Blocks								
.101	.102	.103	.104	.105	.106	.107	.108	.109
.110	.111	.112	.113	.114	.115	.116	.117	.118
.119	.120	.121	.122	.123	.124	.125	.126	.127
.128	.129	.130	.131	.132	.133	.134	.135	.136
.137	.138	.139	.140	.141	.142	.143	.144	.145
.146	.147	.148	.149					

THIRD: .050 in. Series – 19 Blocks									
.050	.100	.150	.200	.250	.300	.350	.400	.450	.500
.550	.600	.650	.700	.750	.800	.850	.900	.950	

FOURTH: 1.000 in. Series – 4 Blocks			
1.000	2.000	3.000	4.000
TWO .050 in. WEAR BLOCKS			

TABLE 3-2B SIZES IN AN 88-PIECE SET OF METRIC GAUGE BLOCKS								
0.001 mm Series – 9 Blocks								
1.001	1.002	1.003	1.004	1.005	1.006	1.007	1.008	1.009
0.01 mm Series – 49 Blocks								
1.01	1.02	1.03	1.04	1.05	1.06	1.07	1.08	1.09
1.10	1.11	1.12	1.13	1.14	1.15	1.16	1.17	1.18
1.19	1.20	1.21	1.22	1.23	1.24	1.25	1.26	1.27
1.28	1.29	1.30	1.31	1.32	1.33	1.34	1.35	1.36
1.37	1.38	1.39	1.40	1.41	1.42	1.43	1.44	1.45
1.46	1.47	1.48	1.49					
0.5 mm Series – 1 Block								
0.5								
0.5 mm Series – 18 Blocks								
1	1.5	2	2.5	3	3.5	4	4.5	5
5.5	6	6.5	7	7.5	8	8.5	9	9.5
10 mm Series – 9 Blocks								
10	20	30	40	50	60	70	80	90
TWO 2 mm WEAR BLOCKS								

GAUGE BLOCK BUILDUPS

Gauge blocks are manufactured to great accuracy; they adhere to each other so well when wrung together properly that they can withstand a 1000 N pull. Many theories have been advanced to explain this adhesion. Scientists have felt that it may be atmospheric pressure, molecular attraction, the flat surfaces of the blocks, or a minute film of oil which give the blocks this quality. Possibly a combination of any of these could be responsible.

When the blocks required to make up a dimension are being calculated, the following procedure should be followed to save time, reduce the chance of error, and use as few blocks as possible. For example, if a measurement of 1.6428 in. is required:

Step 1 – Write the dimension required on paper   1.6428 in.

Step 2 – Deduct the size of two wear blocks (2 × .050 in.)   .100 in.
Remainder   1.5428 in.

Step 3 – Use a block which will eliminate the right-hand digit   .1008 in.
Remainder   1.4420 in.

Step 4 – Use a block which will eliminate the right-hand digit and at the same time bring the digit to the left of it to a zero (0) or a five (5)   .142 in.
Remainder   1.300 in.

Step 5 – Continue to eliminate the digits from right to left until the dimension required is attained   .300 in.
Remainder   1.000 in.

Step 6 – Use a 1.000 in. block   1.000 in.
Remainder   .000 in.

To eliminate the possibility of error in subtraction while making a buildup, it is good practice to use two columns for this calculation. As the following example illustrates, the left-hand column is where the gauge blocks are subtracted from the original dimension, and the right-hand column is used as a check column. For example, to build up a dimension of 3.8716 in.:

	Procedure Column	Check Column
	3.8716 in.	
a) Two wear blocks (2 × .050 in.)	.100 in.	.100 in.
	3.7716 in.	
b) Use .1006 in.	.1006 in.	.1006 in.
	3.6710 in.	
c) Use .121 in.	.121 in.	.121 in.
	3.550 in.	
d) Use .550 in.	.550 in.	.550 in.
	3.000 in.	
e) Use 3.000 in.	3.000 in.	3.000 in.
	.000 in.	3.8716 in.

When using metric blocks for a buildup of 57.150 mm, proceed as follows:

Step 1 – Write the dimension required on paper   57.150 mm

Step 2 – Deduct the size of 2 wear blocks (2 × 2 mm)   4.000 mm
Remainder   53.150 mm

Step 3 – Use a block which will eliminate the right-hand digit

	1.050 mm
Remainder	52.100 mm

Step 4 – Use a block to eliminate the right-hand digit

	1.100 mm
Remainder	51.000 mm

Step 5 – Use a 1 mm block

	1.000 mm
Remainder	50.000 mm

Step 6 – Use a 50 mm block

	50.000 mm
Remainder	0.000 mm

For a metric buildup of 27.781 mm, proceed as follows:

	Procedure Column	Check Column
	27.781 mm	
a) Two wear blocks (2 × 2 mm)	4.000 mm	4.000 mm
	23.781 mm	
b) Use 1.001mm	1.001 mm	1.001 mm
	22.780 mm	
c) Use 1.080 mm	1.080 mm	1.080 mm
	21.700 mm	
d) Use 1.700 mm	1.700 mm	1.700 mm
	20.000 mm	
e) Use 20.000 mm	20.000 mm	20.000 mm
	0.000 mm	27.781 mm

To Wring Blocks Together

It is important when wringing blocks together to take care not to damage them. The sequence of movement to wring blocks together correctly is illustrated in Fig. 3-51.

1. Clean the blocks with a clean, soft cloth.
2. Wipe each of the contacting surfaces on the clean palm of the hand or wrist.

This procedure removes any dust particles left by the cloth and also applies a light film of oil.
3. Place the end of one block over the end of another block as shown in Fig. 3-51.
4. While applying pressure on the two blocks, slide one block over the other.
5. If the blocks do not adhere to each other, it is generally because the blocks have not been thoroughly cleaned.

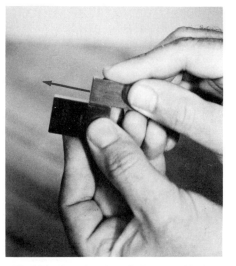

Fig. 3-51 Procedure for wringing gauge blocks

Care of Gauge Blocks

1. Gauge blocks should always be protected from dust and dirt by being kept in a closed case when not in use.
2. Gauges should not be handled unnecessarily since they absorb the heat of the hand. Should this occur, the gauge blocks must be permitted to settle down to room temperature before use.
3. Fingering of lapped surfaces should be avoided to prevent tarnishing and rusting.
4. Care should be taken that gauge blocks are not dropped or their lapped surfaces scratched.
5. Immediately after use, each block should be cleaned, oiled, and replaced in its case.

6. Before gauge blocks are wrung together, their faces must be free of oil and dust.
7. Gauge blocks should never be left wrung together for any length of time. The slight moisture between the blocks can cause rusting which will permanently damage the block.

ANGULAR MEASUREMENT

Precise angular measurement and setups constitute an important phase of machine shop work. The most commonly used tools for accurately laying out and measuring angles are the universal bevel protractor, sine bar, and sine plate.

THE UNIVERSAL BEVEL PROTRACTOR

The *universal bevel protractor* is a precision instrument capable of measuring angles to within 5′ (0.083°). It consists of a *base* to which a *vernier scale* is attached. A *protractor dial*, graduated in degrees with every tenth degree being numbered, is mounted onto the circular section of the base. A *sliding blade* is fitted into this dial; it may be extended in either direction and

Courtesy The L. S. Starrett Company

Fig. 3-52 Measuring an obtuse angle using a universal bevel protractor

set at any angle to the base. The blade and the dial are rotated as a unit. Fine adjustments are obtained with a small knurled-headed pinion which when turned engages with a gear attached to the blade mount. The protractor dial may be locked in any desired position by means of the *dial clamp nut*.

The vernier protractor (Fig. 3-52) is being used to measure an obtuse angle, or an angle greater than 90° but less than 180°. An *acute angle attachment* is fastened to the vernier protractor to measure angles less than 90° (Fig. 3-53).

Courtesy The L. S. Starrett Company

Fig. 3-54   Vernier protractor reading of 50°20′ (50.33°)

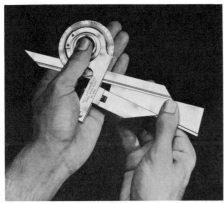

Courtesy The L. S. Starrett Company

Fig. 3-53   Measuring an acute angle

The vernier protractor employs the following principle. The protractor dial, or main scale, is divided into two arcs of 180°. Each arc is divided into two quadrants of 90° and has graduations from zero to 90° to the left and right of the "0" line.

The vernier scale is divided into 12 spaces on each side of the "0" line which occupy the same space as 23° on the protractor dial. By simple calculation, it is easy to prove that one vernier space is 5′, or 0.083°, less than two graduations on the main scale. If the zero on the vernier scale coincides with a line on the main scale, the reading will be in degrees only. However, if any other line on the vernier scale coincides with a line on the main scale, the number of vernier graduations beyond the zero should be multiplied by

five and added to the number of full degrees indicated on the protractor dial.

To Read a Vernier Protractor

1. Note the number of whole degrees between the zero on the main scale and the zero on the vernier scale.
2. Proceeding in the *same direction* beyond the zero on the vernier scale, note which vernier line coincides with a main scale line.
3. Multiply this number by five and add it to the number of degrees on the protractor dial.

In Fig. 3-54, the angular reading is determined as follows. The number of degrees indicated on the main scale is 50 plus. The fourth line on the vernier scale *to the left* of the zero coincides with a line on the main scale. Therefore, the reading is:

Number of full degrees	$= 50°$
Value of vernier scale 4 × 5′	$= \underline{\quad 20′\ (0.33°)}$
Reading	$= 50°20′\ (50.33°)$

NOTE: A double check of the reading would locate the vernier scale line on the other side of zero which coincides with a protractor scale line. This line should always equal the complement of 60′. In Fig. 3-54, the 40′ line to the right of the zero

coincides with a line on the protractor scale. This reading, when added to the 20′ on the left of the scale, is equal to 60′, or 1°.

THE SINE BAR

A *sine bar* (Fig. 3-55) is used when the accuracy of an angle must be checked to less than 5′ (0.083°) or work must be located to a given angle within close limits. The sine bar consists of a steel bar with two cylinders of equal diameter secured near the ends. The centres of these cylinders are on a line exactly parallel with the edge of the bar. The distance between the

Fig. 3-55   A 5 in. sine bar with gauge block buildup is used to set up work to an angle

centres of these lapped cylinders is usually 5 in. or 10 in. Sizes for metric sine bars were not available at the time of publication. These bars are generally made of stabilized tool steel, hardened, ground, and lapped to extreme accuracy. They are used on surface plates, and any desired angle can be set by raising one end of the bar to a predetermined height with gauge blocks.

Sine bars are generally made 5 in. or multiples of 5 in. in length. That is, the lapped cylinders are 5 in. ±.0002 or 10 in. ±.00025 between centres. The face of the sine bar is accurate to within .00005 in. in 5 in. In theory, the sine bar merely becomes the hypotenuse of a right-angle triangle. The gauge block buildup forms the side opposite, while the face of the surface plate forms the side adjacent in the triangle.

Using trigonometry, it is possible to calculate the side opposite or gauge block buildup for any angle between zero and 90° as follows.

$$\text{Sine of a given angle} = \frac{\text{side opposite}}{\text{hypotenuse}}$$
$$= \frac{\text{gauge block buildup}}{\text{length of sine bar}}$$

When using a 5 in. sine bar, this would become:

$$\text{Sine of the angle} = \frac{\text{buildup}}{5}$$

Therefore, by transposition, the gauge block buildup for any required angle with a 5 in. bar is as follows.
Buildup = 5 × sine of the required angle

EXAMPLE:

Calculate the gauge block buildup required to set a 5 in. sine bar to an angle of 30°.

$$\begin{aligned} \text{Buildup} &= 5 \sin 30 \\ &= 5 \times .5000 \text{ in.} \\ &= 2.5000 \text{ in.} \end{aligned}$$

A   Set the sine bar to the complement of the angle

Fig. 3-56   Setting up for an angle greater than 60°

NOTE: This formula is applied only to angles up to 60°.

When an angle greater than 60° is to be checked, it is better to set up the work using the complement of the angle (Fig. 3-56A). The angle plate is then turned 90° to produce the correct angle (Fig. 3-56B). The reason is that when the sine bar is in a near-horizontal position, a small change in the height of the buildup will produce a smaller change in the angle than when the sine bar is in the near-vertical position. This change in gauge block height may be shown by calculating the buildups required for 75° and also for the complementary angle of 15°.

Buildup required for:

$$\begin{aligned} 75°1' (75.017°) &= 5 \sin 75°1' (.9660) \\ &= 4.8300 \text{ in.} \\ 75° &= 5 \sin 75° (.96592) \\ &= 4.82960 \text{ in.} \end{aligned}$$
Difference in buildup for 1' (0.017°)
$$= .00040 \text{ in.}$$

Buildup required for:
$$\begin{aligned} 15°1' (15.017°) &= 5 \sin 15°1' (.25910 \\ &\quad \text{in.)} \\ &= 1.29550 \text{ in.} \\ 15° &= 5 \sin 15° (.25882) \\ &= 1.29410 \text{ in.} \end{aligned}$$
Difference in buildup for 1' (0.017°)
$$= .00140 \text{ in.}$$

B   Turn the angle plate 90° on its side

This example shows that exactly 3.5 times the buildup is required to produce a change of 1' (0.017°) at 15°, than is required for 1' (0.017°) at 75°. Therefore, a small inaccuracy in setup would result in a smaller error at a smaller angle than it would at a larger one. If the complementary angles of 80° and 10° are used, this ratio increases to over 5:1.

When small angles are to be checked, it is sometimes impossible to get a buildup small enough to place under one end of the sine bar. In such situations, it will be necessary to place gauge blocks under both rolls of the sine bar, having a net difference in measurement equal to the required buildup. For example, the buildup required for 2° is .1745 in. Since it is impossible to make this buildup, it is necessary to place the buildup for 1.1745 under one roll and a 1.000 block under the other roll, giving a net difference of .1745.

Before the sine bar is used to check a taper, it is necessary to calculate the angle of the taper so that the proper gauge block buildup may be made. Figures 3-57A and B illustrate how this is done.
In the right-angled triangle *ABD*:

$$\begin{aligned} \text{Tan } \frac{a}{2} &= \frac{1/2}{12} \\ &= .04166 \\ &= 2°23'10'' (2.411°) \\ \therefore a &= 4°46'20'' (4.822°) \end{aligned}$$

From this solution, the following formula for solving the included angle when the taper per foot is known is derived.

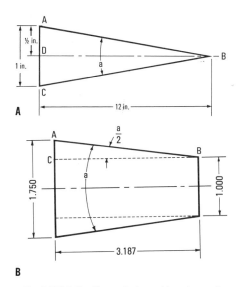

A

B

Fig. 3-57A & B   The angle formed by a taper of 1 in. per foot

$$\text{Tan} \frac{a}{2} = \frac{\text{TPF}}{24}$$

NOTE: When calculating the angle of a taper *do not* use the formula $\text{Tan } a = \dfrac{\text{TPF}}{12}$ since the triangle *ABC* is not a right-angled triangle.

By transposition, if the included angle is given, the taper per foot may be calculated as follows. $\text{TPF} = \tan \dfrac{1}{2} a \times 24$.

If the taper per foot is not known, the angle may be calculated as shown in Fig. 3-57B.

SOLUTION:

$$AC = \frac{1.750 - 1.000}{2}$$

$$= \frac{.750}{2}$$

$$= .375$$

$$\text{Tan} \frac{a}{2} = \frac{.375}{3.187}$$

$$= .11766$$

$$= 6°42'22'' \ (6.761°)$$

$$\therefore a = 13°24'44'' \ (13.522°)$$

To check the accuracy of this taper using a 5 in. sine bar, it is necessary to calculate the buildup as follows.

$$\text{Buildup} = 5 \sin 13°24'44'' \ (13.522°)$$
$$= 5 \times .23196$$
$$= 1.1598$$

Metric tapers are expressed as a ratio of 1 mm per unit of length; for example, a taper having a ratio of 1:20 would taper 1 mm in diameter in 20 mm of length. (See Chapter 9.)

Tapers can be checked conveniently and accurately with a *taper micrometer*. This measuring instrument measures work to sine bar accuracy while the work is still in the machine. See "Checking a Taper" in Chapter 9.

SINE PLATE

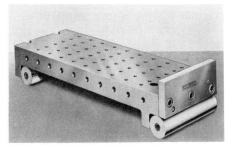

Courtesy The Taft-Peirce Manufacturing Company

Fig. 3-58   Work may be clamped to a sine plate

The *sine plate* (Fig. 3-58) uses the same principle as the sine bar and is similar in construction except that it is wider. Sine bars are up to 1 in. in width, while sine plates are generally more than 2 in. wide. (Sizes for metric sine plates were not available at the time of publication.) They have several tapped holes in the surface which permit the work to be clamped to the surface of the sine plate. An end stop on a sine plate prevents the workpiece from moving during machining.

Sine plates may be hinged to a base (Fig. 3-59) and are often called *sine tables*. Both types are supplied in 5 in. and 10 in. lengths and have a step or groove of .100 in. or .200 in. deep ground in the

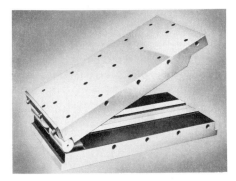

Courtesy Brown & Sharpe Mfg. Co.

Fig. 3-59   A hinged sine plate may be clamped to the machine table

base to permit the buildup for small angles to be placed under the free roll.

THE COMPOUND SINE PLATE OR TABLE

The *compound sine plate* (Fig. 3-60) consists of one sine plate superimposed on another sine plate. The lower plate is hinged to a base and may be tilted to any angle from zero to 60° by placing gauge blocks under the free roll or cylinder. The upper base is hinged to the lower base so that its cylinder and hinge are at right angles to those of the lower plate. The upper plate may also be tilted to any angle up to 60°. This feature permits the setting of compound angles (angles in two directions).

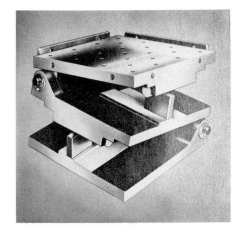

Courtesy The Taft-Peirce Manufacturing Company

Fig. 3-60   A compound sine plate permits the setting of angles in two directions

Compound sine plates have a side and end plate on the top table to facilitate setting up work square with the table edge and to prevent movement of the work during machining. A step or groove of .100 in. or .200 in. deep ground in the base and in the lower table permits the setup for small angles, as the gauge block buildup may be placed in the groove. Sizes and dimensions of metric compound sine plates were not available at the time of publication.

Since most angles are machined in fixtures, sine plates are not used until the finishing operation which is generally grinding. To facilitate the holding of parts, both simple and compound sine plates are available with built-in magnetic chucks.

GAUGES AND GAUGING

Although modern production processes have reached a high degree of precision, because of their high cost it would be impossible to produce all parts to an exact dimension. Industrial production processes therefore permit certain variations from the exact dimension. Both the machinist and the inspector must be familiar with certain basic terms since they apply to all forms of measurement and inspection. (See Table 3-3.)

Basic dimension is the exact size of a part from which all limiting variations are made.

Limits are the maximum and minimum dimensions of a part (the high and low dimensions).

Tolerance is the permissible variation of a part. This is often shown on the drawing by the basic dimension plus or minus the amount of variation allowed. If a part on a drawing was dimensioned to 3.00 mm ±0.02, the tolerance would be 0.04 mm.

If the tolerance is in one direction only, that is plus *or* minus, it is said to be *unilateral tolerance*. However, if the tolerance is both plus *and* minus, it is referred to as *bilateral tolerance*.

TABLE 3-3		
An example of limits and tolerances		
Nominal size	3 mm	
Basic Dimension	3.00	Decimal equivalent of nominal size
Basic Dimension and amount of Bilateral tolerance permitted	3.00 ±0.02	1/2 tolerance
Limits	3.02	Largest size permitted
	2.98	Smallest size permitted
Tolerance	0.04	Difference between minimum and maximum limits

Allowance is the intentional difference in the dimensions of mating parts, for example, the difference between the maximum diameter of the shaft and the minimum diameter of the mating bore.

FIXED GAUGES

Fixed gauges are used in inspection procedures because they provide a quick means of checking a specific dimension. These gauges must be easy to use and accurately finished to the required tolerance. They are generally finished to one-tenth the tolerance they are designed to control. For example, if the tolerance of a piece being checked is to be maintained at 0.001 mm, then the gauge must be finished to within 0.0001 mm of the required size.

CYLINDRICAL PLUG GAUGES

Plain *cylindrical plug gauges* (Fig. 3-61) are used for checking the inside diameter of a straight hole and are generally of the "go" and "no-go" variety. This type consists of a handle and a plug on each end ground and/or lapped to a specific size. The smaller diameter plug, or the "go" gauge, checks the lower limit of the hole.

Courtesy The Taft-Peirce Manufacturing Company

Fig. 3-61 A cylindrical plug gauge is used to check hole sizes

The larger diameter plug, or the "no-go" gauge, checks the upper limit of the hole (Fig. 3-62). For instance, if a hole size is to be maintained at 1.00 ±0.05 the "go" end of the gauge would be designed to fit into a hole 0.995 in diameter. The larger end ("no-go") would not fit into any hole smaller than 1.005 in diameter.

The dimensions of these gauges are usually stamped on the handle at each end adjacent to the plug gauge. "Go" gauges are made longer than the "no-go" end for easy identification. Sometimes a groove is cut on the handle near the "no-go" gauge to distinguish it from the "go" end.

Due to the wear caused by the constant use of plug gauges, many of them are equipped with carbide tips which greatly increase their life.

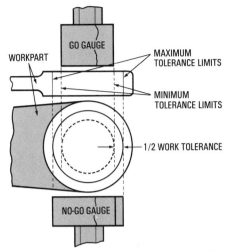

Courtesy Bendix Corporation

Fig. 3-62 The "go" end of the gauge checks the minimum tolerance limit, while the "no go" checks the maximum tolerance

To Use a Cylindrical Plug Gauge

1. Select a plug gauge of the correct size and tolerance for the hole being checked.
2. Clean both ends of the gauge and the hole in the workpiece with a clean, dry cloth.
3. Check the gauge (both ends) and the workpiece for nicks and burrs.
4. Wipe both ends of the gauge with an oily cloth to deposit a thin film of oil on the surfaces.
5. Start the "go" gauge *squarely* into the hole (Fig. 3-63). If the hole is within the limits, the gauge will enter easily.

Fig. 3-63 Checking a hole size with a plug gauge

DO NOT FORCE OR TURN IT. The plug should enter the hole for the full length, and there should be no excessive play between the plug and the part. *NOTE*: If the gauge enters only part way, there is a taper in the hole. Excessive play or looseness in one direction indicates that the hole is elliptical (out of round).

6. After the hole has been checked with the "go" gauge, it should be checked with the "no-go" end. This gauge should not begin to enter the hole. An entry of more than 1.6 mm indicates an oversize, bell-mouth, or tapered hole.

PLAIN RING GAUGES

Plain ring gauges, used to check the outside diameter of pieces, are ground and lapped internally to the desired size. The size is stamped on the side of the gauge. The outside diameter is knurled, and the "no-go" gauge is identified by an annular groove on the knurled surface (Fig. 3-64). The precautions and procedure regarding the use of a ring gauge are similar to those outlined for a plug gauge and should be followed carefully.

TAPER PLUG GAUGES

Taper plug gauges (Fig. 3-65), made with standard or special tapers, are used to check the size of the hole and the accuracy of the taper. Some of these gauges used for inspection purposes have "go" and "no-go" rings scribed on them. If the gauge fits into the hole between these two rings, the hole is then within the required tolerances. Other taper plug gauges have steps ground on the large end to indicate the limits. The rings or steps measure hole size limits only. An incorrect taper is evidenced by a wobble between the plug gauge and the hole.

To Check an Internal Taper Using a Taper Plug Gauge

1. Select the proper taper gauge for the hole being checked.

A — "go" gauge

Courtesy The Taft-Peirce Manufacturing Company

B — "no go" gauge

Fig. 3-64 Plain ring gauges are used to check the diameter of round work

Fig. 3-65 Taper ring and plug gauges

2. Wipe the gauge and the hole with a clean, dry cloth.
3. Check both the gauge and hole for nicks and burrs.

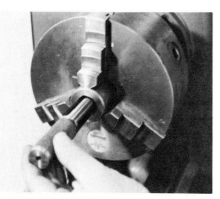

Fig. 3-66 Checking a tapered hole with a tapered plug gauge

4. Apply a *thin* coating of Prussian blue to the surface of the plug gauge.
5. Insert the plug gauge into the hole as far as it will go (Fig. 3-66).
6. Maintaining light end-pressure on the plug gauge, rotate it in a *counter-clockwise* direction for approximately one-quarter turn.
7. Check the diameter of the hole. A proper size is indicated when the edge of the workpiece lies between the limit steps or lines on the gauge.
8. Check the taper of the hole by attempting to move the gauge radially in the hole. Any discrepancy in the taper will be indicated by play at either end between the hole and the gauge. Movement or play at the large end indicates excessive taper; movement at the small end indicates insufficient taper.
9. Remove the gauge from the hole to see if the bluing has rubbed off evenly along the length of the gauge, a result which would indicate a proper fit. A poor fit is evident if the bluing has been rubbed off more at one end than the other.

TAPER RING GAUGES

Taper ring gauges (Fig. 3-65) are used to check both the accuracy and the outside diameter of the taper. Ring gauges often have scribed lines or a step ground on the small end to indicate the "go" and "no-go" dimensions.

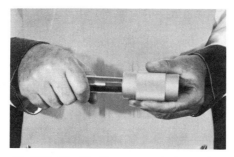

Fig. 3-67 Checking the accuracy of a taper using chalk lines

For a taper ring gauge, the precautions and procedures are similar to those outlined for a taper plug gauge. However, when work which has not been ground or polished is being checked, three equally spaced chalk lines around the circumference and extending for the full length of the tapered section may be used to indicate the accuracy of the taper (Fig. 3-67). If the work has been ground or polished, it is advisable to use three thin lines of Prussian blue.

Care of Plug and Ring Gauges

Gauge life is dependent on the following factors.
a) materials from which the gauge is made
b) material of the part being checked
c) class of fit required
d) proper care of the gauge

In order to preserve the accuracy and life of gauges, observe the following points.

1. Store gauges in divided wooden trays to protect them from being nicked or burred.
2. Check them frequently for size and accuracy.
3. Correctly align gauges with the workpiece to prevent binding.
4. Do not force or twist a plain plug or ring gauge. Forcing or twisting will cause excessive wear.
5. Clean the gauge and workpiece thoroughly before checking the part.
6. Use a light film of oil on the gauge to help prevent binding.

7. Make provision for air to escape when gauging blind holes with a plug gauge.
8. Have gauges and work at room temperature to ensure accuracy and prevent damage to the gauge.
9. Never use an inspection gauge as a working gauge.

THREAD PLUG GAUGES

Courtesy The Taft-Peirce Manufacturing Company

Fig. 3-68 Thread plug gauges are used to check the size and accuracy of an internal thread

Internal threads are checked with *thread plug gauges* (Fig. 3-68) of the "go" and "no-go" variety and employ the same principle as cylindrical plug gauges.

When a thread plug gauge is used, the "go" end, which is the longer end, should be turned in flush to the bottom of the hole. The "no-go" end should just start into the hole and become quite snug before the third thread enters.

Since thread plug gauges are quite expensive, certain precautions should be observed in their use.

1. Thread plug gauges have a chip groove cut along the thread to clear loose chips. Do not depend on this for removing burrs or loose chips. To prolong the life of the gauge, it is advisable to remove burrs and loose chips (wherever possible) by means of an old tap.
2. Before using the thread plug gauge, apply a little oil to its surface.
3. Never force the gauge.

THREAD RING GAUGES

The most popular gauge of this type is the *adjustable thread ring gauge*. These gauges, used to check the accuracy of an external thread, have a threaded hole in the centre with three radial slots and a set screw to permit small adjustment. The outside diameter is knurled, and the "no-go" gauge is identified by an annular groove cut on the knurled surface. Both the "go" and "no-go" gauges are generally assembled in one holder for checking the part easily (Fig. 3-69).

Courtesy Bendix Corporation

Fig. 3-69 "Go" and "no go" thread ring gauges in a holder

When these gauges are used, the thread being checked should fully enter the "go" gauge, but should not enter the "no-go" gauge by more than 1-1/2 turns. Before checking a thread, remove any dirt, grit, or burrs. A little oil will help to prolong the life of the gauge.

SNAP GAUGES

Snap gauges, one of the most common types of comparative measuring instruments, are faster to use than micrometers, but are limited in their use. They are used to check diameters within certain limits by comparing the part size to the pre-set dimension of the snap gauge. Snap gauges generally have a C-shaped frame with adjustable gauging anvils which are set to the "go" and "no-go" limits of the part. These gauges are supplied in several styles, some of which are shown in Fig. 3-70.

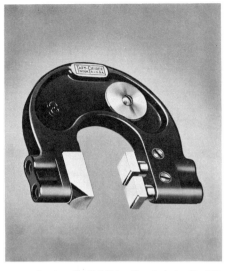

Courtesy The Taft-Peirce Manufacturing Company

A — Adjustable snap gauge

Courtesy The Taft-Peirce Manufacturing Company

B — Adjustable roll snap gauge
Fig. 3-70   Various types of snap gauges

To Use a Snap Gauge to Check a Dimension

Proper use of a snap gauge is required to prevent springing the gauge and marring the work surface.

1. Thoroughly clean the anvils of the gauge.
2. Set the "go" and "no-go" anvils to the required limits using gauge blocks or a standard.

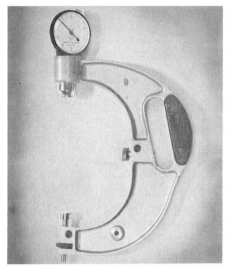

Courtesy Bendix Corporation

C — Dial indicator adjustable snap gauge

3. Lock the anvils in position and recheck the accuracy of the settings.
   NOTE: If a dial indicator gauge is used, set the bezel (outer ring) of the indicator to read zero and lock it into position.
4. Clean the surface of the work.
5. Hold the gauge in the right hand, keeping it square with the work.
6. With the left hand, hold the lower anvil in position on the workpiece.
7. Push the gauge over the work surface with a rolling motion. Only light hand pressure should be used to pass the "go" pins.
   NOTE: Do not force the gauge; if the work is the correct size, the gauge will pass easily over the work.
8. Advance the gauge until the "no-go" anvils or rolls contact the work. If the gauge stops at this point, the work is within the limits.

COMPARISON MEASUREMENT

Manufacturing processes have now become so precise that component parts are often made in several areas, then shipped to a central location for final assembly. In order for this process of *interchangeable manufacture* to be economical, there must be some assurance that these parts will fit on assembly. The components are therefore made to within certain limits, and further inspection or *quality control* insures that only properly sized parts will be used.

Much of this inspection is done rapidly, accurately, and economically by a process called *comparison measurement*. This consists of comparing the measurement of the part to a known standard or master of the exact dimension required. Basically, *comparators* are gauges that incorporate some means of amplification to compare the part size to a set standard, usually gauge blocks.

Mechanical, optical, mechanical-optical comparators, and air, electrical, and electronic gauges all employ the same principle of comparison measurement.

DIAL INDICATORS

Dial indicators are used to compare sizes and measurements to a known standard and to check the alignment of machine tools, fixture, and workpieces prior to machining.

Many types of dial indicators operate on a gear and rack principle (Fig. 3-72). A *rack* cut on the *plunger or spindle* is in mesh with a *pinion* which in turn is connected with a *gear train*. Any movement of the spindle is then amplified and transmitted to a *hand or pointer* over a *graduated dial*. Inch-designed dials may be graduated in thousandths of an inch or less. The dial, attached to a *bezel*, may be adjusted to and locked in any position.

During use, the contact point on the end of the spindle bears against the work and is held in constant engagement with the work surface by the rack spring. A hair spring is attached to the gear that meshes with the centre pinion. This flat spiral spring takes up the backlash from the gear train and prevents any lost motion from affecting the accuracy of the
e.

Fig. 3-71   A long range continuous reading dial indicator is often used on machine tools

Dial indicators are generally available in two types: the continuous reading dial indicator and the dial test indicator.

The *continuous reading dial indicator* (Fig. 3-71), numbered clockwise for 360°, is available in two types: the regular range and the long range indicator. The regular range dial indicator has only about 2-1/2 revolutions of travel. It is generally used for comparison measurement and setup purposes. The long range dial indicator (Fig. 3-71) is often used to indicate table travel or cutting tool movement on machine tools. It has a second smaller hand that indicates the number of revolutions that the large hand has travelled.

Dial test indicators (Fig. 3-72) may have a balanced type dial, that is, one which reads both to the right and left from zero and indicates a plus or minus value. Indicators of this type have a total spindle travel of only 2-1/2 revolutions. These instruments may be equipped with tolerance pointers to indicate the permissible variation of the part being measured.

Perpendicular dial test indicators or back plunger indicators have the spindle at right angles (90°) to the dial. They are used extensively in setting up lathe work and for machine table alignment.

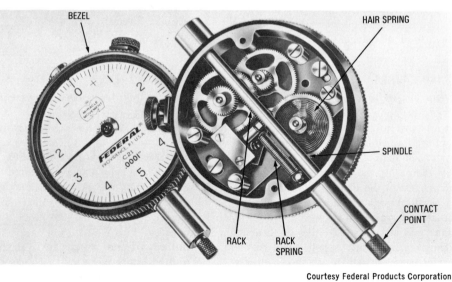

Fig. 3-72   A balanced type dial test indicator showing the internal mechanism

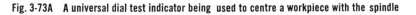

Courtesy Federal Products Corporation

Fig. 3-73A   A universal dial test indicator being used to centre a workpiece with the spindle

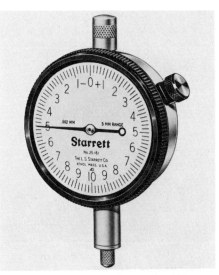

Courtesy The L. S. Starrett Company

Fig. 3.74   A metric indicator with a balanced dial

Courtesy Federal Products Corporation

Fig. 3-73B   Checking measurements with a dial test indicator and a height gauge

The *Universal* dial test indicator (Fig. 3-73) has a contact point that may be set at several positions through a 180° arc. This type of indicator may be conveniently used to check internal and external surfaces. Figs. 3-73A and B illustrate typical applications of this type of indicator.

Metric dial indicators (Fig. 3-74) are available in both the balanced and continuous reading types. The type used for inspection purposes is usually graduated in 0.002 mm and has a range of 0.5 mm. The regular indicators are usually graduated in 0.01 mm and have a range up to 25 mm.

To Measure with a Dial Test Indicator and Height Gauge

1. Clean the face of the surface plate and the vernier height gauge.
2. Mount the dial test indicator on the movable jaw of the height gauge (Fig. 3-73B).
3. Lower the movable jaw until the indicator point just touches the top of a gauge block resting on the surface plate.
4. Tighten the upper locking screw on the vernier and loosen the lower locking screw.
5. Carefully turn the adjusting nut until the indicator needle registers approximately one-quarter turn.
6. Turn the bezel to set the indicator to zero.

7. Note the reading on the vernier and record it on a piece of paper.
8. Raise the indicator to the height of the first hole to be measured.
9. Adjust the vernier until the indicator reads zero.
10. Note the vernier reading again and record it.
11. Subtract the first reading from the second and add the height of the gauge block.
12. Proceed in this manner to record the location of all other holes.

COMPARATORS

A comparator may be classified as any instrument which is used to compare the size of a workpiece to a known standard. The simplest form of comparator is a dial indicator mounted on a surface gauge. All comparators are provided with some means of amplification by which variations from the basic dimensions are noted easily.

MECHANICAL COMPARATORS

The *mechanical comparator* (Fig. 3-75) consists of a base, a column, and a gauging head. Mechanical comparators operate

Courtesy Mahr Gage Co. Inc.

Fig. 3-75   A mechanical comparator showing tolerance pointers to indicate upper and lower limits

on several principles. Some employ the gear and rack principle used in some dial indicators while others use a system of levers similar to the universal dial indicator (Fig. 3-73B). The mechanical comparator uses two twisted steel ribbons which are tensioned when the comparator is set to a standard. Any variance from the standard size changes the tension of the ribbons and the position of the pointer. All types are used in inspection to check the size of a part against a master gauge. The variation between the part and the master is shown in a scale as a plus or minus quantity.

To Measure with a Mechanical Comparator

1. Clean the anvil and master gauge of the required size.
2. Place the master on the anvil.
3. Carefully lower the gauging head until the stylus touches the master and indicates a movement of the needle.
4. Lock the gauging head to the column.
5. Adjust the needle to zero using the fine adjustment knob, and set the limit pointers on the face.
6. Recheck the setting by removing the master and replacing it.
7. Substitute the work being gauged for the master and note the reading. If the

reading is to the right of zero, the work is too large; if to the left, it is too small.

OPTICAL COMPARATORS

An *optical comparator* or *shadowgraph* (Fig. 3-76) projects an enlarged shadow onto a screen where it may be compared to lines, or to a master form which indicates the limits of the dimensions or the contour of the part being checked. The optical comparator is a fast, accurate means of measuring or comparing the workpiece with a master. It is often used when the workpiece is difficult to check by other methods. Optical comparators are particularly suited to the checking of extremely small or odd-shaped parts which would be difficult to inspect without the use of expensive gauges.

Optical comparators are available in bench and floor models, identical in principle and operation (Fig. 3-77). Light from a *lamp* passes through a *condenser lens* and is projected against the workpiece. The shadow caused by the workpiece is transmitted through a *projecting lens* system which magnifies the image and casts it onto a *mirror*. The

Courtesy Jones & Lamson Division of Waterbury Farrel

Fig. 3-76   Intricate parts can be easily checked with an optical comparator

image is then reflected to the *viewing screen* and is further magnified in this process.

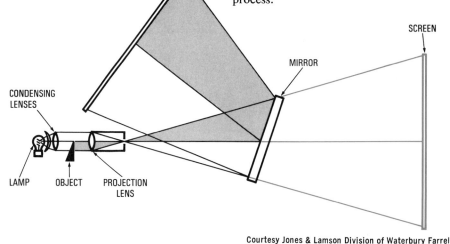

Courtesy Jones & Lamson Division of Waterbury Farrel

Fig. 3-77   The principle of the optical comparator

The extent of the image magnification depends on the lens used. Interchangeable lenses for optical comparators are available in the following magnifications: 5X, 10X, 31.25X, 50X, 62.5X, 90X, 100X, and 125X.

A comparator chart or master form mounted on the viewing screen is used to compare the accuracy of the enlarged image of the workpiece being inspected. Charts are usually made of translucent material, such as cellulose acetate or frosted glass. There are many different charts available for special jobs, but the most commonly used are linear-measuring, radius, and angular charts. A vernier protractor screen is also available for checking angles. *Since charts are available in several magnifications, care must be taken to use a chart of the same magnification as the lens mounted on the comparator.*

Many accessories are available for the comparator, increasing the versatility of the machine. Some of the most common are: *tilting work centres* which permit the workpiece to be tilted to the required helix angle when checking threads; a *micrometer work stage* which permits quick and accurate measuring of dimensions in both directions; and *gauge blocks*, *measuring rods*, and *dial indicators* used on comparators for checking measurement. The surface of the workpiece may be checked by a *surface illuminator* which lights up the face of the workpiece adjacent to the projecting lens system and permits this image to be projected onto the screen.

To Check the Angle of a 60° Thread Using an Optical Comparator

1. Mount the correct lens into the comparator.
2. Mount the tilting centres on the micrometer cross-slide stage.
3. Set the tilting centres to helix angle of the thread.
4. Set the workpiece between centres.

5. Mount the vernier protractor chart and align it horizontally on the screen.
6. Turn on the light switch.
7. Focus the lens so that a clear image appears on the screen.
8. Move the micrometer cross-slide stage until the thread image is centralized on the screen.
9. Revolve the vernier-protractor chart to show a reading of 30°.
10. Adjust the cross-slides until the image coincides with the protractor line.
11. Check the other side of the thread in the same manner.
    NOTE: If the thread angle is not correct or square with the centre line, adjust the vernier-protractor chart to measure the angle of the thread image.

Other dimensions of the thread, such as depth, diameters, and width of flats, may be measured with the micrometer measuring stages or devices such as rods, gauge blocks, and indicators.

MECHANICAL-OPTICAL COMPARATORS

Fig. 3-78   A reed type comparator employs both the mechanical and optical principles of measurement

The *mechanical-optical comparator* (Fig. 3-78), or the *reed* type comparator, combines a reed mechanism with a light beam to cast a shadow on a magnified scale to indicate the dimensional variation of the part. It consists of a base, and a column, as well as a gauging head which contains the reed mechanisms and light source.

THE REED MECHANISM

Fig. 3-79 illustrates the principle of the reed mechanism. A fixed steel block A and a movable block B have two pieces of spring steel, or reeds, attached to them (Fig. 3-79B). The upper ends of the reeds are joined and connected to a pointer. Since block A is fixed, any movement of the spindle attached to block B will move this block up or down, causing the pointer to move a much greater distance to the right or left (Fig. 3-79C).

A light beam passing through an aperture illuminates the scale (Fig. 3-80). The pointer, with a *target* attached, is located below the aperture so that a movement of block B will cause the target to interrupt the light beam, casting a highly amplified shadow on the scale. The movement of the pointer and target is obviously greater than the movement of the spindle. Also, the shadow cast on the scale will be larger than the movement of the target. Therefore, the measurement on the scale will be much greater than the movement of the spindle.

To illustrate the total magnification of this instrument, suppose that the ratio of target movement to the stylus is 25:1; the ratio to the light beam lever is 20:1. By combining these two movements, the shadow cast would then be 25 × 20 or 500 times as large as the movement of the stylus. This large amplification would permit extremely accurate gauging to be performed on this type of instrument. Reed type comparators are manufactured with magnifications from 500:1 to 20 000:1.

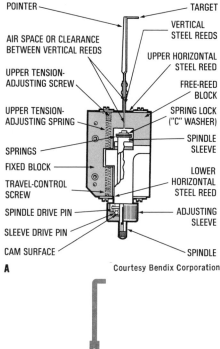

POINTER
TARGET
VERTICAL STEEL REEDS
AIR SPACE OR CLEARANCE BETWEEN VERTICAL REEDS
UPPER HORIZONTAL STEEL REED
UPPER TENSION-ADJUSTING SCREW
FREE-REED BLOCK
UPPER TENSION-ADJUSTING SPRING
SPRING LOCK ("C" WASHER)
SPINDLE SLEEVE
SPRINGS
FIXED BLOCK
LOWER HORIZONTAL STEEL REED
TRAVEL-CONTROL SCREW
SPINDLE DRIVE PIN
ADJUSTING SLEEVE
SLEEVE DRIVE PIN
CAM SURFACE
SPINDLE

A   Courtesy Bendix Corporation

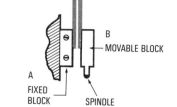

B
MOVABLE BLOCK
A
FIXED BLOCK
SPINDLE

B   Courtesy "Fundamentals of Dimensional Metrology," Delmar Publishers Inc., Albany, N.Y.

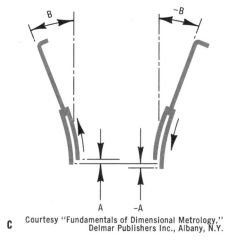

B   ~B
A   –A

C   Courtesy "Fundamentals of Dimensional Metrology," Delmar Publishers Inc., Albany, N.Y.

Fig. 3-79A,B,C   Construction and principle of the reed mechanism (mechanical lever)

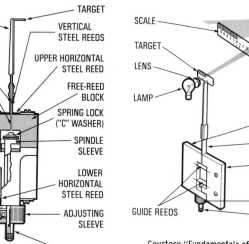

SCALE
MIRROR
TARGET
LENS
LAMP
MOVABLE BLOCK
MAIN REED
FIXED BLOCK
GUIDE REEDS
FINE ADJUSTMENT
SPINDLE

Courtesy "Fundamentals of Dimensional Metrology," Delmar Publishers Inc., Albany, N.Y.

Fig. 3-80   The light beam or optical lever amplifies the target movement

The scales for these instruments are graduated in plus and minus with zero being in the centre of the scale. The value for each graduation is marked on the scale of every machine.

To Measure with a Reed Comparator

1. Raise the gauging head above the required height, and clean the anvil and master thoroughly.
2. Place the master gauge or gauge block buildup on the anvil.
3. Carefully lower the gauging head until the end of the spindle *just touches the master.*
   NOTE: A shadow will begin to appear on the left side of the scale.
4. Clamp the gauging head to the column.
5. Turn the adjusting sleeve until the shadow coincides with the zero on the scale.

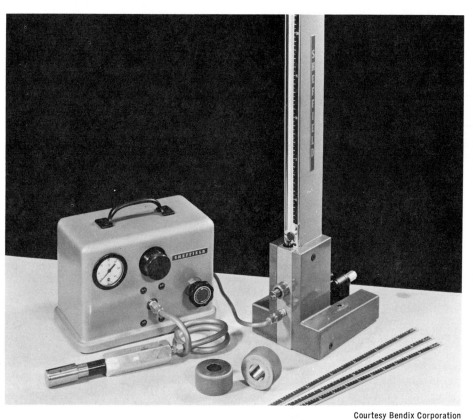

Courtesy Bendix Corporation

Fig. 3-81   A flow or column type air gauge

6. Remove the gauge blocks and carefully slide the workpiece between the anvil and the spindle.

7. Note the reading. If the shadow is to the right of the zero, the part is oversize; if to the left, it is undersize.

AIR GAUGES OR PNEUMATIC COMPARATORS

Air gauging, a form of comparison measurement, is used to compare workpiece dimensions with those of a master gauge by means of air pressure or flow.

Air gauges are of two types: the *flow or column type* (Fig. 3-81) which indicates air velocity, and the *pressure type* (Fig. 3-83) which indicates air pressure in the system.

COLUMN TYPE AIR GAUGE

After air has been passed through a filter and a regulator, it is supplied to the gauge at about 70 kPa (Fig. 3-82). The air flows through a transparent tapered tube in which a float is suspended as a result of this air flow. The top of this tube is connected to the gauging head by a plastic tube.

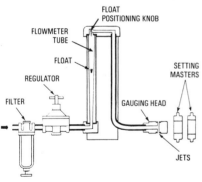

Courtesy Bendix Corporation

Fig. 3-82 Principle of the column type air gauge

The air flowing through the gauge exhausts through the passages in the gauging head into the clearance between the head and the workpiece. The rate of flow is proportional to the clearance indicated by the position of the float in the column. The gauge is set to a master and the float is then positioned by means of an adjusting knob. The upper and lower limits for the workpiece are then set. If the hole in the workpiece is larger than the hole size of the master, more air will flow through the gauging head, and the float will rise higher in the tube. Conversely, if the hole is smaller than the master, the float will fall in the tube. Amplification from 1000:1 to 40 000:1 may be obtained with this type of gauge. Snap, ring, and plug type gauging heads may be fitted to this type of gauging device.

PRESSURE TYPE AIR GAUGE

In the pressure type air gauge, air passes through a filter and regulator and is then divided into two channels (Fig. 3-84). The air in the *reference channel* escapes to atmosphere through a zero setting valve. The air in the *measuring channel* escapes to atmosphere through the gauge head jets. The two channels are connected by an extremely accurate differential pressure meter.

The master is placed over the gauging spindle and the zero setting valve is adjusted until the gauge needle indicates zero. Any deviation in the workpiece size from the master size changes the reading. If the workpiece is too large, more air will escape through the gauging plug; therefore, pressure in the measuring channel will be less and the dial gauge hand will move counterclockwise, indicating how much the piece is oversize. A diameter smaller than the master gauge indicates a reading on the right side of the

Courtesy Federal Products Corporation

Fig. 3-83 Gauging a hole using a pressure-type air gauge

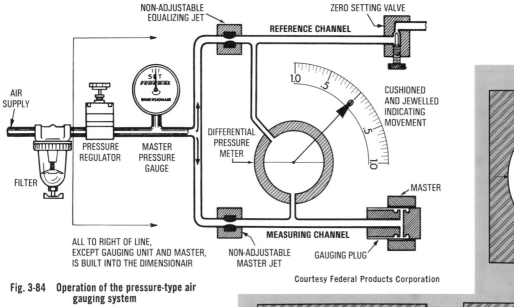

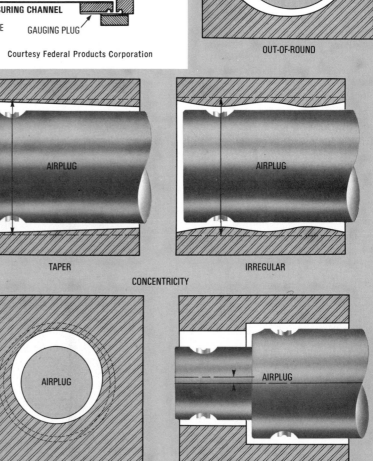

Fig. 3-84 Operation of the pressure-type air gauging system

Courtesy Federal Products Corporation

dial. Amplification from 2500:1 to 20 000:1 may be obtained with this type of gauge. Pressure type air gauges may also use plug, ring, or snap gauging heads for a wide variety of measuring jobs.

Air gauges are widely used since they have several advantages over other types of comparators.

a) Holes may be checked for taper, out-of-roundness, concentricity, and irregularity more easily than with mechanical gauges (Fig. 3-85).

b) The gauge does not touch the workpiece; therefore there is little chance to mar the finish.

c) Gauging heads last longer than fixed gauges since wear is reduced between the head and the workpiece.

d) Less skill is required to use this type of gauging equipment than other types.

e) Gauges may be used at a machine or bench.

f) More than one diameter may be checked at the same time.

Courtesy Federal Products Corporation

Fig. 3-85 Irregular-shaped holes may be easily checked with an air gauge

ELECTRONIC COMPARATORS

The *electronic comparator* (Fig. 3-86), a highly accurate form of comparator, uses the Wheatstone bridge circuit to transform minute changes in spindle movement into a relatively large needle movement on the gauge. This degree of magnification is controlled by a selector on the front of the *amplifier*. The widely spaced graduations represent values from 0.002 mm to 0.0002 mm (or .0001 in. to .000 01 in. depending on the scale selected).

When it is not necessary to know the exact dimension of a part, but rather if it falls within the required limits, a signal light attachment may be installed on the gauge. When a workpiece is tested, an amber light indicates that it is within the prescribed limits. A red light indicates

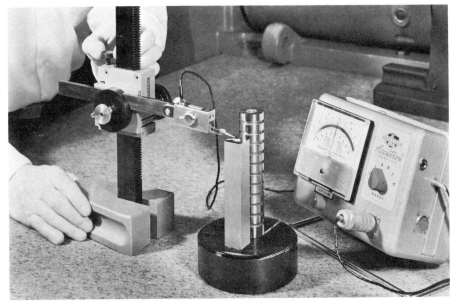

Fig. 3-87   The electronic gauge with a rectangular head is used to accurately check heights

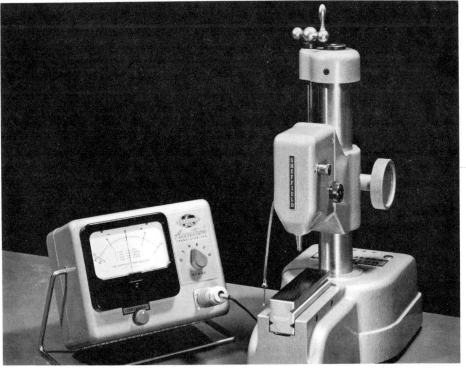

Fig. 3-86   The value of the scale divisions on an electronic comparator can be readily changed to suit the accuracy required

that the workpiece is too small, and a blue light indicates that it is too large.

Electronic units may also be used as height gauges by mounting a rectangular gauging head on a height gauge stand (Fig. 3-87). This method is particularly suited to the checking of soft, highly polished surfaces because of the light gauging pressure required.

OPTICAL FLATS

One of the most accurate and reliable means of measurement is the use of light waves. *Optical flats* (Fig. 3-88), used with a monochromatic light, employ this principle to check work for flatness, parallelism, and size (Fig. 3-89A, B, and C).

Optical flats are discs of clear fused quartz, lapped to within 0.05 μm of flatness. They are generally used with a helium light source which produces a greenish-yellow light, having a wave length of 0.587 56 μm.

The optical flat, a perfectly flat, transparent disc, is placed on the surface of the work to be checked. The functioning surface of the optical flat is the surface

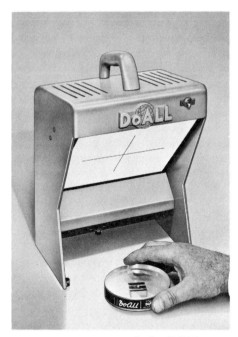

Courtesy DoALL Company

Fig. 3-88   Checking a gauge block using an optical flat and a helium light source

Courtesy DoALL Company

Fig. 3-89A   Checking flatness

Courtesy DoALL Company

Fig. 3-89B   Checking parallelism

Courtesy DoALL Company

Fig. 3-89C   Checking size

adjacent to the workpiece. It is transparent and capable of reflecting light; therefore all light waves that strike this surface are split into two parts (Fig. 3-90). One part is reflected back by the lower surface of the flat. The other part passes through this surface and is reflected by the upper surface of the work. Whenever the reflected split portions of two light waves cross each other, or *interfere*, they become visible and produce dark interference bands or fringe lines. This happens whenever the distance between the lower surface of the flat and the upper surface of the workpiece is *only one half of a wave length* or multiples thereof (Fig. 3-90).

Since the wave length of helium light is 0.587 56 μm, each half wave length will represent 0.293 78 μm. Each dark band then represents a progression of 0.293 78 μm above the point of contact between the workpiece and the optical flat. Therefore, when a height is checked, the number of bands between two points on a surface multiplied by 0.293 78 μm will indicate the height difference between two surfaces.

For comparison measurements, the difference in height between a master block and the workpiece can be determined as shown in Fig. 3-91. This illustrates the method used for checking accurately the height of an unknown surface by comparing it with a gauge block of a known height. It is necessary first to know which block is larger before the unknown block can be measured. To determine the larger block, apply finger pressure to points X and Y. If this pressure at X makes no change in the band pattern and the pressure at Y causes the bands to separate, the master block (M) is larger. If the opposite is true, the unknown block (U) is larger. In Fig. 3-91, two bands appear on the low block; therefore the unknown block is two bands, or 2 $\times$ 0.29 378 = 0.587 56 μm below the master.

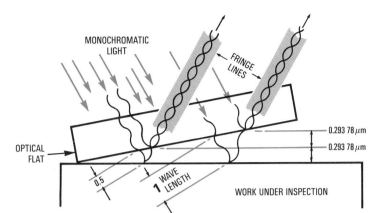

MONOCHROMATIC LIGHT

FRINGE LINES

OPTICAL FLAT

0.293 78 μm
0.293 78 μm

0.5

1 WAVE LENGTH

WORK UNDER INSPECTION

Fig. 3-90 The principle of the optical flat

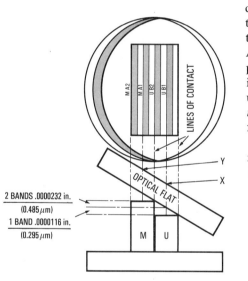

MA2 MA1 UB2 UB1

LINES OF CONTACT

OPTICAL FLAT

Y

X

2 BANDS .0000232 in.
(0.485 μm)
1 BAND .0000116 in.
(0.295 μm)

M U

Fig. 3-91 Checking the height of a block with a master block

SURFACE FINISH MEASUREMENT

Modern technology has demanded improved surface finishes to assure proper functioning and long life of machine parts. Pistons, bearings, and gears depend to a great extent on a good surface finish for proper functioning and therefore require little or no break-in period. Finer finishes often require additional operations, such as lapping or honing, and are more costly to produce. To indicate the desired finish on a print and to convey this information to the machinist, a system of symbols has been devised by the American Standards Association. This provides a standard system of determining and indicating surface finish. The inch unit of surface finish measurement is the *microinch*. The metric unit for surface finish is the *micrometre* (μm).

The most common instrument used to measure finish is the *surface indicator* (Fig. 3-92).

This device consists of a *tracer head* and an *amplifier*. The tracer head houses a diamond stylus, having a point radius of 0.013 mm, which bears against the surface of the work. It may be moved along the work surface by hand or it may be motor-driven. Any movement of the stylus caused by surface irregularities is converted into electrical fluctuations by the tracer head. These signals are magnified by the amplifier and registered on the meter by a hand or needle. The reading shown on the meter indicates the *average* height of surface roughness or the departure of this surface from the reference (centre) line.

Readings may be in either *Arithmetical Average* (*AA*) or *Root Mean Square* (*rms*). A highly magnified cross-section of a workpiece would appear as in Fig. 3-93 with "hills and valleys" above and below the centre line. To calculate the surface finish without a surface indicator, the height of these deviations must be measured and recorded as shown. The arithmetical average or the root mean square could then be calculated as in Fig. 3-93. The rms is considered the better

Fig. 3-92 Using a surface indicator to check the surface finish of a part

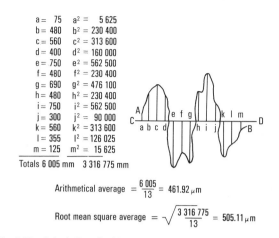

$$
\begin{array}{ll}
a = 75 & a^2 = 5\,625 \\
b = 480 & b^2 = 230\,400 \\
c = 560 & c^2 = 313\,600 \\
d = 400 & d^2 = 160\,000 \\
e = 750 & e^2 = 562\,500 \\
f = 480 & f^2 = 230\,400 \\
g = 690 & g^2 = 476\,100 \\
h = 480 & h^2 = 230\,400 \\
i = 750 & i^2 = 562\,500 \\
j = 300 & j^2 = 90\,000 \\
k = 560 & k^2 = 313\,600 \\
l = 355 & l^2 = 126\,025 \\
m = 125 & m^2 = 15\,625 \\
\end{array}
$$

Totals 6 005 mm   3 316 775 mm

$$\text{Arithmetical average} = \frac{6\,005}{13} = 461.92\,\mu m$$

$$\text{Root mean square average} = \sqrt{\frac{3\,316\,775}{13}} = 505.11\,\mu m$$

Fig. 3-93   Calculation of arithmetical average and root mean square

method of determining surface roughness since it emphasizes extreme deviations.

For accurate determination of the surface finish, the indicator must first be calibrated by setting it to a precision reference surface on a test block calibrated to ASA standards.

The symbols used to identify surface finishes and characteristics are shown in Fig. 3-94.

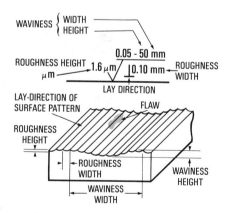

Fig. 3-94   Surface characteristics and symbols

SURFACE FINISH DEFINITIONS

Surface deviations — any departures from the nominal surface in the form of waviness, roughness, flaws, lay, and profile.

Waviness — surface irregularities which deviate from the mean surface in the form of waves; they may be caused by vibrations in the machine or work. These are generally widely spaced.

Roughness — relatively finely spaced irregularities superimposed on the waviness pattern and caused by the cutting tool or the abrasive grain action and the machine feed. These irregularities are much narrower than the waviness pattern.

Flaws — irregularities such as scratches, holes, cracks, ridges, or hollows that do not follow a regular pattern as in the case of waviness and roughness.

Lay — the direction of the predominant surface pattern caused by the machining process.

Profile — the contour of a specified section through a surface.

Microinch or Micrometre — the unit of measurement used to measure the surface finish. The microinch is equal to .000 001 in.; the micrometre to 0.000 001 m.

The following symbols indicate the direction of the lay.

‖ parallel to the boundary line of the surface indicated by the symbol

⊥ perpendicular to the boundary line of the surface indicated by the symbol

X angular in both directions on the surface indicated by the symbol

M multidirectional

C approximately circular to the centre of the surface indicated by the symbol

R approximately radial in relation to the centre of the surface indicated by the symbol

AVERAGE SURFACE ROUGHNESS PRODUCED BY STANDARD MACHINING PROCESSES

	Microinches	Micrometres
turning	100 – 250	2.5 – 6.3 μm
drilling	100 – 200	2.5 – 5.1 μm
reaming	50 – 150	1.3 – 3.8 μm
grinding	20 – 100	0.5 – 2.5 μm
honing	5 – 20	0.13 – 0.51 μm
lapping	1 – 10	0.025 – 0.254 μm

To Measure Surface Finish with a Surface Indicator

1. Turn the switch on and allow the intrument to warm up for approximately three minutes.

2. Check the machine calibration by moving the stylus over the 125 microinch (3.2 μm) test block at approximately 1/8 in. per second (3 mm/s).

3. If necessary, adjust the calibration control so that the instrument registers the same as the test block.

4. Unless otherwise specified, use the .030 in. (0.76 mm) cutoff range for surface roughness of 30 microinches (0.76 μm) or more. For surfaces less than 30 microinches (0.76 μm) use the .010 in. (0.25 mm) cutoff range. *NOTE*: When measuring a surface where the roughness is unknown, it is good practice to set the range switch at a high setting to avoid damage to the instrument. After an initial test, the range switch may be turned to a finer setting for an accurate surface reading.

5. Thoroughly clean the surface to be measured, to ensure accurate readings and reduce wear on the rider cap protecting the stylus.

6. With a smooth, steady movement of the stylus, trace the work surface at

TABLE 3-4: SURFACE FINISHES OBTAINED BY VARIOUS MACHINING OPERATIONS*

	Operation	Material	Speed	Feed	Tool	Analyzer Setting Cut-off	Analyzer Setting Range	Surface Finish (RMS)
CUT-OFF SAW	sawing	2½ in. diameter aluminum	320 f/min (97.5 m/min)	—	10 pitch saw	.030 in. (0.76 mm)	1000	300–400
SHAPER	shaping a flat surface	machine steel	100 f/min (30.5 m/min)	.005 in. (0.13 mm)	3/64 in. radius HSS	.030 in. (0.76 mm)	300	225–250
VERTICAL MILLING MACHINE	fly cutting (flat surface)	machine steel	820 r/min	.015 in. (0.38 mm)	1/16 in. radius Stellite	.030 in. (0.76 mm)	300	125–150
HORIZONTAL MILLING MACHINE	slab milling	cast aluminum	225 r/min	2½ in./min (63.5 mm/min)	slab cutter, 4 in. diameter HSS	.030 in. (0.76 mm)	100	40–50
LATHE	turning	2½ in. diameter aluminum	500 r/min	.010 in. (0.25 mm)	3/64 in. radius HSS	.030 in. (0.76 mm)	300	100–200
	turning	2½ in. diameter aluminum	500 r/min	.007 in. (0.18 mm)	5/64 in. radius HSS	.030 in. (0.76 mm)	100	50–60
	facing	2 in. diameter aluminum	600 r/min	.010 in. (0.25 mm)	1/32 in. radius HSS	0.30 in. (0.76 mm)	300	200–225
	facing	2 in. diameter aluminum	800 r/min	.005 in. (0.13 mm)	1/32 in. radius HSS	.030 in. (0.76 mm)	100	30–40
	filing	¾ in. diameter machine steel	1200 r/min	—	10 in. lathe file	.010 in. (0.25 mm)	100	50–60
	polishing	¾ in. diameter machine steel	1200 r/min	—	#120 abrasive cloth	.010 in. (0.25 mm)	30	13–15
	machine reaming	aluminum	500 r/min	—	machine reamer HSS, ¾ in. diameter	.030 in. (0.76 mm)	100	25–32
SURFACE GRINDER	grinding a flat surface	machine steel	—	.030 in. (0.76 mm)	60 grit grinding wheel	.003 in. (0.076 mm)	10	7–9
TOOL AND CUTTER GRINDER	cylindrical grinding	1 in. machine steel	—	hand (slow)	46 grit grinding wheel	.010 in. (0.25 mm)	30	12–15
LAPPING	flat lapping	⅞ in. × 5½ in. tool steel (hardened)	—	hand	600 grit abrasive	.010 in. (0.25 mm)	10	1–2
	cylindrical lapping	½ in. diameter tool steel (hardened)	—	hand	600 grit abrasive	.010 in. (0.25 mm)	10	1–2

* Metric figures given represent soft conversions. New metric standards for many of the product sizes and operating procedures were not established at the time of publication.

approximately 1/8 in. per second (3 mm/s).

7. Note the reading from the meter scale.

A more elaborate device for measuring surface finish is the *surface analyzer*. This incorporates a recording device which produces a graph ink line record of the surface irregularities on a graduated chart.

Although the surface indicator is the most common, other methods may be used to measure surface finish with reasonable accuracy during machining processes.

1. *Comparison blocks* are used for comparing the finish on the workpiece with the calibrated finish on a test block using the fingernail test.

2. *Commercial sets of standard finished specimens*. Standard sets having up to 25 different surface finish samples are available for checking surface finish. They consist of blocks or plates having surfaces varying from the smoothest to the roughest likely to be required.

Table 3-4 shows the results obtained on pieces of round and flat metal by various machining operations. A model B-1 110 brush surface analyzer was used to obtain the readings. The speeds, feeds, and tool radii used are those recommended for a high-speed steel toolbit.

LIGHT WAVE PRECISION MEASUREMENT

The coordinate measuring system uses a pattern of dark and light bands as a means of achieving accurate measurements. It is one of the latest developments in the machine tool industry. This system employs the *moire fringe pattern* and has been applied extensively to machine tools such as lathes, milling machines, and jig borers (Fig. 3-95A and B). Coordinate measuring machines (Fig. 3-95C) are used widely in the fields of measurement and inspection.

Various units may be mounted on a machine tool to give readings for the X

A   Courtesy Bendix Corporation

B   Courtesy Bendix Corporation

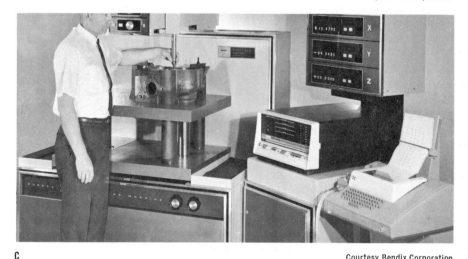

C   Courtesy Bendix Corporation

Fig. 3-95A,B,C   Applications of coordinate measuring systems

(length), *Y* (width), and *Z* (depth) axis. A unit providing direct readout in degrees, minutes, and seconds, is available for angular positioning and measurement.

The measuring unit has three basic components: *a machined spar with a calibrated grating,* Fig. 3-96(A), a *reading head,* Fig. 3-96(B), and a *counter with a digital readout display,* Fig. 3-96(C).

above the main grating. Mounted in the reading head are a small light, a collimating lens, and four photoelectric cells (Fig. 3-97).

NOTE: This electro-optical system "counts" the moire fringes, and produces the high resolution measurement accuracy of the Sheffield Cordax Measuring System.

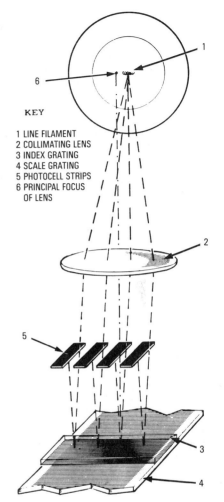

KEY

1 LINE FILAMENT
2 COLLIMATING LENS
3 INDEX GRATING
4 SCALE GRATING
5 PHOTOCELL STRIPS
6 PRINCIPAL FOCUS
   OF LENS

Courtesy Bendix Corporation

Fig. 3-97   Principle of the coordinate measuring system

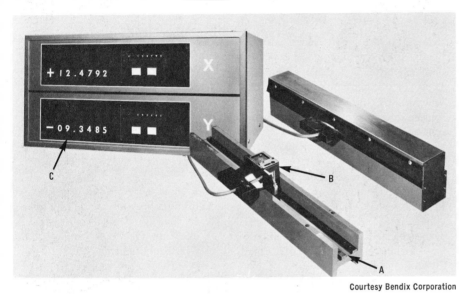

Courtesy Bendix Corporation

Fig. 3-96   Components of a coordinate measuring system

The main element in this system is an accurately ruled grating (Fig. 3-96A) of the desired length of travel. The face of this grating for systems having .0001 in. (0.002 mm) resolution, is etched for its entire length with lines spaced .001 in. (0.02 mm) apart. For machines capable of greater accuracy, the grating spar is etched with 2500 lines per inch, so that the digital readout resolution is .000 050 in. Metric readings are obtained by pushing a button on the side of the machine.

A *transparent index grating,* having the same graduations as the grating spar, is mounted in the reading head. The index grating is positioned so that its lines are at a slight angle to the lines on the spar. The reading head is mounted so that the index grating is positioned just 0.05 mm

PRINCIPLE OF THE MOIRE FRINGE

To illustrate the Moire fringe pattern, draw a series of equally spaced lines on two pieces of plastic sheeting (Fig. 3-98).

One sheet should then be placed over the other at an angle as in Fig. 3-98. Where these lines cross, dark bands appear. If the top sheet is moved to the right, the position of these bands will shift down and the pattern appear as a series of dark and light bands moving vertically on the sheet. Thus, any longitudinal movement will produce a vertical movement of the light bands. This principle can also be illustrated by placing one comb upon another at a small angle and moving one across the face of the other.

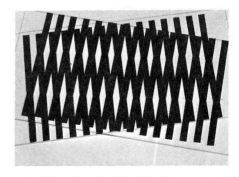

Fig. 3-98   Principle of the Moire fringe pattern

OPERATION OF THE MEASURING UNIT

Since the etched lines on the reading-head grating are at an angle to the lines on the main spar, a series of bands would appear when viewed from directly above. Let us consider one band only, to explain the operation of the system.

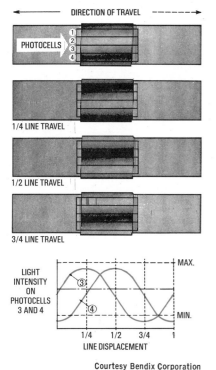

Fig. 3-99   Lateral movement of the fringe pattern

Light from the lamp (Fig. 3-97) passes through the collimating lens and is converted into a parallel beam of light. This beam strikes the fringe pattern and is reflected back up to one of four photo-electric cells which convert the fringe pattern into an electrical signal. As the reading head is moved longitudinally, the band moves vertically on the face of the spar and will be picked up by the next photo-electric cell creating another signal. These signals from the photo-electric cells (output signals) are transmitted to the digital readout display box where they indicate accurately the head travel at any point. A signal from the next photo-electric cell will increase or decrease the reading on the digital readout box by .0001 in. (0.002 mm), depending on the direction of the movement.

NOTE: The fringe pattern shifts laterally and continuously across the grating path.

Advantages of the Coordinate Measuring Systems

1. Readout boxes provide clear visible numbers which eliminate the possibility of misreading a dial gauge.
2. It provides a constant readout of the tool (or table) position.
3. The reading indicates the exact position of the tool (or table) and is not affected by machine or lead screw wear.
4. This system eliminates the need for gauge blocks and measuring rods on jig borers and vertical milling machines.
5. The need for operator calculations and the inherent possibility of errors are eliminated.
6. Machine setup time is greatly reduced.
7. Production is increased since the workpiece need only be checked for one size. For example, when a workpiece having several diameters is to be machined in a lathe, it is necessary to measure the first diameter only. Once the machine has been set to this size, all other diameters will be accurate.
8. The need for operator skill is reduced.
9. Scrap and rework are virtually eliminated.
10. Most machine tools can be fitted with this system.

CHAPTER 3 - REVIEW QUESTIONS

SI

1. What is the common unit of length in SI?

STEEL RULES

2. How are metric rules usually graduated?
3. Name four types of steel rules used in machine shop work.
4. Describe a rule with No. 4 graduations.
5. State the purpose of:
   a) hook rules
   b) decimal rules

OUTSIDE CALIPERS

6. Name and describe two types of outside calipers.
7. What is the procedure for setting an outside caliper to a size?
8. Explain how you would know when the work is the same size as the caliper setting.

INSIDE CALIPERS

9. Explain the procedure for setting an inside caliper to the size of a hole.
10. In point form, list the procedure for checking an inside caliper setting with a micrometer.

PRECISION SQUARES

11. Name two types of solid squares and state the advantage of each.
12. Why are bevelled-edge squares used in inspection work?
13. What procedure should be followed when using a cylindrical square?
14. State the purpose of a diemaker's square.
15. How can the angle of the workpiece be determined using each type of diemaker's square?

SURFACE PLATES

16. What is the purpose of a surface plate?
17. Name three types of granite used in making surface plates.
18. State five advantages of granite over cast-iron surface plates.
19. List eight points necessary for the care of surface plates.

MICROMETERS

20. How many threads per inch are there on a standard inch micrometer?
21. What is the value of:
    a) each line on the sleeve?
    b) each numbered line on the sleeve?
    c) each line on the thimble?
22. Read the following standard micrometer settings.

A

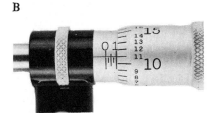

B

C

D

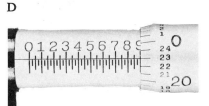

23. Describe briefly the principle of the vernier micrometer.
24. Describe the procedure for reading a vernier micrometer.
25. Read the following vernier micrometer settings.

A

B

C

D

26. Explain how to adjust a micrometer
    a) to remove play in the spindle threads
    b) for accuracy

METRIC MICROMETERS

27. What are the basic differences between a metric and an inch micrometer?
28. What is the value of one division on:
    a) the sleeve above the index line?
    b) the sleeve below the index line?
    c) the thimble?
29. Read the following metric micrometer settings.

A

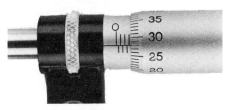

B

C

D

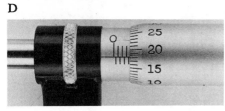

INDICATING MICROMETER

30. State two uses for an indicating micrometer.
31. What is the purpose of the relieving button on the indicating micrometer?

VERNIER CALIPER

32. Describe the principle of
    a) the 25-division vernier
    b) the 50-division vernier
33. Describe the procedure for reading a vernier caliper.
34. What are the following vernier caliper readings?

A

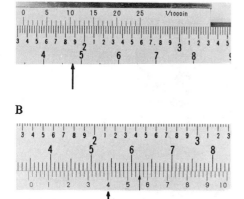

B

C

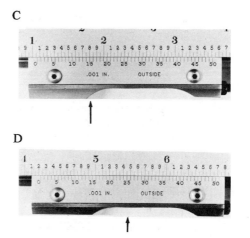

D

METRIC VERNIER CALIPER

35. Describe the principle of the metric vernier caliper.
36. Read the following metric caliper settings.

A

B

GEAR-TOOTH VERNIER CALIPER

37. A 16-diametral pitch gear has 54 teeth.
    a) Calculate the corrected addendum.
    b) Explain how to measure the gear tooth.

INSIDE MICROMETER CALIPERS

38. a) On what type of inside micrometer calipers are the readings reversed to an outside micrometer?
    b) What type are read the same as an outside micrometer?

39. What precautions must be observed in taking a measurement with an inside micrometer caliper?

INSIDE MICROMETERS

40. What construction feature compensates for a lock nut on inside micrometers?
41. What precautions must be taken when:
    a) assembling the inside micrometer and extension rod?
    b) using the inside micrometer?
42. What is the correct "feel" with an inside micrometer?

SMALL HOLE GAUGES

43. Name two types of small hole gauges and state the purpose of each.
44. What precaution must be observed when using a small hole gauge to obtain a dimension?

TELESCOPE GAUGES

45. List the steps required to measure a hole with a telescope gauge.

DIAL BORE GAUGES

46. What hole defects may be conveniently measured with a dial bore gauge?

INTRIMIK

47. Why is an Intrimik particularly suited to measure hole sizes?
48. Why is an Intrimik more accurate than a telescope gauge for measuring a hole size?

MICROMETER DEPTH GAUGE

49. How is the accuracy of a micrometer depth gauge adjusted?
50. How must the workpiece be prepared prior to measuring the depth of a hole or slot with a micrometer depth gauge?
51. Explain the procedure for measuring a depth with a depth micrometer.

52. How does the reading of a depth micrometer differ from that of a standard outside micrometer?

SCREW THREAD MICROMETERS

53. Describe the construction of the contact points of a screw thread micrometer.
54. What dimension of the thread is indicated on a screw thread micrometer reading?
55. List the four ranges covered by screw thread micrometers.
56. How may threads be measured *accurately* with a screw thread micrometer?

VERNIER HEIGHT GAUGE

57. State the two main applications for the vernier height gauge.
58. What accessories are required for a vernier height gauge to check *accurately* the height of a workpiece?

PRECISION HEIGHT GAUGE

59. What are the advantages of using a precision height gauge in lieu of a gauge block buildup?
60. What dimension(s) must be subtracted from the reading so that the correct reading for the height of a hole being checked will be obtained?

GAUGE BLOCKS

61. How are gauge blocks stabilized, and why is this necessary?
62. State five general uses for gauge blocks.
63. For what purpose are wear blocks used?
64. How should wear blocks always be assembled into a buildup?
65. State the difference between a master set and a working set of gauge blocks.

66. What precautions are necessary when handling gauge blocks in order that the effect of heat on the blocks is minimal?
67. List five precautions necessary for the proper care of gauge blocks.
68. Calculate the gauge blocks required for the following buildups.
    a) 2.1743 in.   d) 32.079 mm
    b) 6.2937 in.   e) 74.213 mm
    c) 7.8923 in.   f) 89.694 mm

UNIVERSAL BEVEL PROTRACTOR

69. Name the parts of a universal bevel protractor, and state the purpose of each.
70. Describe the principle of the vernier protractor.
71. Sketch a vernier protractor reading of:
    a) 34°20′ (34.33°)
    b) 17°45′ (17.75°)

SINE BAR

72. Describe the construction and principle of a sine bar.
73. What are the accuracies of the 5 in. and the 10 in. sine bars?
74. Calculate the gauge block buildup for the following angles using a 5 in. sine bar:
    a) 7°40′ (7.67°)
    b) 25°50′ (25.83°)
    c) 40°10′ (40.17°)
75. What procedure should be followed to check an angle of 72° using a sine bar and gauge blocks? Why is this procedure recommended?
76. In calculating the angle of a taper, why is the formula

$$\mathrm{Tan}\ \frac{1}{2}\,a = \frac{\mathrm{TPF}}{24}\ \text{used, rather than}$$

$$\mathrm{Tan}\ a = \frac{\mathrm{TPF}}{12}\ ?$$

Illustrate by means of a suitable sketch.

SINE PLATE

77. Describe a sine plate and state its purpose.
78. What is the advantage of a hinged sine plate?
79. What is the purpose of a compound sine plate?

PRECISION MEASUREMENT AND INSPECTION QUESTIONS

80. For each of the following dimensions indicate the basic diameter, upper limit, lower limit, and tolerance:
    a) 12.50 ± 0.02 mm
    b) 1.750 + .002 in.
            − .000 in.
    c) .625 + .0015 in.
            − .0000 in.
    d) 20.500 + 0.000 mm
              − 0.015 mm
    e) 0.500 ± 0.005 mm
81. State whether the tolerances for each size in question 80 are unilateral or bilateral.

FIXED GAUGES

82. What purpose do fixed gauges serve in industry?
83. To what tolerance are fixed gauges finished?
84. If a hole size is to be maintained at 1.75 ± 0.02 mm, what would be the sizes of the "go" and "no-go" gauges?

CYLINDRICAL PLUG GAUGES

85. How are the "go" and "no-go" ends of a cylindrical plug gauge identified?
86. What precautions must be observed when a cylindrical plug gauge is used?

PLAIN RING GAUGES

87. How is a "no-go" ring gauge distinguished from a "go" ring gauge?

TAPER PLUG AND RING GAUGES

88. How may the limits of a taper plug gauge be indicated on the gauge?
89. List the precautions to observe when checking with a taper plug or ring gauge.
90. When may chalk be used to check an external taper, and when should bluing be used?
91. Why should a taper plug or ring gauge be rotated no more than one-quarter of a turn when checking a taper?

THREAD PLUG AND RING GAUGES

92. What parts of a thread are checked with a "go" gauge? A "no-go" gauge?
93. List three precautions to observe when using a thread plug gauge.
94. How should an external thread of the proper size fit into the thread ring gauge?

SNAP GAUGES

95. Describe a snap gauge.
96. What advantage has the dial indicator snap gauge over an adjustable snap gauge?
97. List the precautions necessary when a workpiece is checked with a snap gauge.

COMPARISON MEASUREMENT

98. Describe
   a) quality control
   b) comparison measurement

DIAL INDICATORS

99. What is the difference between a regular range dial indicator and a long range indicator?

100. Compare a perpendicular dial indicator with a dial test indicator.
101. How are metric dial indicators usually graduated?

COMPARATORS

102. Define a comparator.
103. List three principles used in mechanical comparators.
104. Why is high amplification necessary in any comparison measurement process?
105. Describe the procedure for measuring a workpiece with a reed-type comparator.

OPTICAL COMPARATORS

106. List the advantages of an optical comparator.
107. Describe the principle of an optical comparator. Illustrate by means of a suitable sketch.
108. What precautions are necessary when charts are used on an optical comparator?

AIR GAUGES

109. Describe the principle of the column type air gauge. Illustrate by means of a suitable sketch.
110. Describe and neatly illustrate the principle of the pressure type air gauge.
111. List six advantages of air gauges.

ELECTRONIC COMPARATORS

112. What circuit is employed in electronic comparators?
113. Describe the operation of the signal light attachment for electrical or electronic gauges.

OPTICAL FLATS

114. Describe an optical flat.
115. What light source is used with optical flats and what is its wave length?
116. Describe, and illustrate in detail, the principle of an optical flat.
117. When measuring the height of a block using a gauge block and an optical flat, how is it possible to determine the higher block?

SURFACE FINISH MEASUREMENT

118. Explain why present-day standards for surface finish are very important to industry.
119. Define the following surface finish terms: microinch, lay, flaw, roughness, waviness, root mean square (rms), arithmetical average (AA).
120. Explain each symbol and number (inches) as it applies to surface finish:

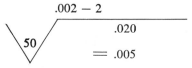

121. Explain what the following lay symbols represent: $=$, $\perp$, X, M, C, R .

122. Describe briefly the principle and operation of a surface indicator and a surface analyzer in measuring surface finish.

4 LAYOUT TOOLS

Laying out a workpiece may involve the scribing of lines, radii, circles, and the location of holes to specifications on the drawing or blueprint. This is done to assist the machinist in setting up and machining a workpiece.

The importance of proper layout cannot be overemphasized. The blueprint does not show how much material must be removed from each surface of the casting or workpiece; it merely shows which surfaces are to be finished.

The layout for holes, whether in cored or solid material, is as important as the layout for other dimensions of the workpiece.

The degree of accuracy required on the layout will determine the tools to be used. If the part does not have to be precise, time should not be spent in making a precision layout. It is advisable, therefore, to keep the layout as simple as the workpiece requirements permit.

LAYOUT TABLES

Layout work is generally done on a special table with a heavy cast-iron or granite top which provides a reference or starting surface for the laying out operation (Fig. 4-1). The granite layout table is better than the cast-iron type because it does not become burred and is not affected by temperature change. The cast-iron table top should be kept clean and free of burrs and nicks since these can

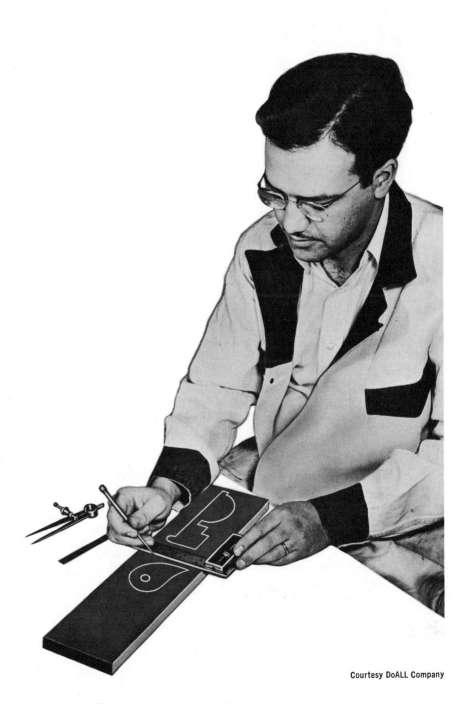

Courtesy DoALL Company

59

Fig. 4-1   A layout table provides an accurate reference surface for layout work

seriously affect the accuracy of precision layout. The layout table should be treated with the same care as a machine table to preserve its accuracy.

SURFACE PREPARATION OF THE METAL FOR LAYOUT

The surface of the metal is usually coated with a layout solution to make layout lines visible. There are several types of layout solutions available. Regardless of the type used, the surface should be clean and free of grease.

The most commonly used layout solution is *layout dye*, or *bluing*. This quick-drying solution, when coated lightly on the surface of any metal, will produce a background for sharp, clear-cut lines. Layout dye may be applied with a cloth, a brush, a dauber, or sprayed on the work surface.

A copper-coloured surface can be produced if the clean surface of a steel workpiece is coated with a copper sulphate ($CuSO_4$) solution to which a few drops of sulphuric acid have been added. When this solution is used, the surface of the workpiece must be absolutely clean and free from grease and finger marks. *NOTE*: Copper sulphate should be used on ferrous metal only.

Steel may be blued by heating the surface of the workpiece with a torch until it turns blue, and then quenching the workpiece to prevent further colour change. Care must be taken to avoid distortion when heating the workpiece.

A mixture of vermilion powder and shellac is often used for aluminum since some layout compounds corrode the aluminum. Alcohol should be used to thin this solution or to remove it from the workpiece.

The surfaces of castings and hot-rolled steel are often prepared for layout by merely chalking the surface. A mixture of lime and alcohol which readily clings to the rough surface of the castings is often used for this purpose.

METHODS OF SCRIBING LINES PARALLEL TO A SURFACE OR EDGE

The *scriber* (Fig. 4-2) has a hardened steel point, or points, and may be used in conjunction with a combination square,

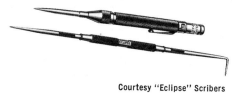

Courtesy "Eclipse" Scribers

Fig. 4-2   A pocket and double-end scriber

Fig. 4-3   Sharpening a scriber on an oilstone

a rule, or a straightedge to draw straight lines. Any layout, to be accurate, requires fine lines; therefore, the scriber point must always be sharp. The points of scribers, hermaphrodite calipers, dividers, and trammels should be honed frequently on a fine oilstone (Fig. 4-3) for sharp points to be maintained. When extremely fine lines are required, knife-edge scribers should be used.

One of the most useful tools used for layout and checking is the *combination set* (Fig. 4-4).

The *combination square* and scriber may be used to draw lines parallel to an edge (Fig. 4-5) or at 45° and 90° to an edge (Fig. 4-6).

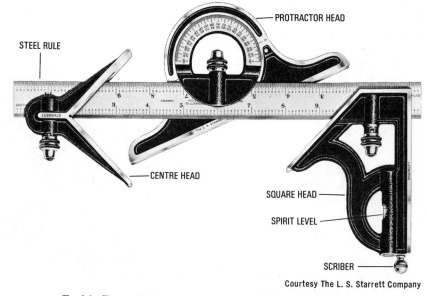

STEEL RULE

PROTRACTOR HEAD

CENTRE HEAD

SQUARE HEAD

SPIRIT LEVEL

SCRIBER

Courtesy The L. S. Starrett Company

Fig. 4-4   The combination set is used for laying out and checking work

Courtesy Kostel Enterprises Ltd.

Fig. 4-5   Scribing a line parallel to an edge

When scribing lines by this method, take care to keep the scriber point against the edge of the rule and always at the same angle relative to the rule and workpiece.

A more accurate method of scribing lines parallel to a surface is with a *surface gauge* (Fig. 4-7). This method eliminates errors caused by the variable angle of the hand-held scriber.

The scriber can be swung to any position on the spindle and can be set to a rule with reasonable accuracy by the adjusting screw. Lines may be drawn parallel to an edge, by depressing two pins in the base and placing the gauge base on the workpiece so that these two pins bear against, and over, the edge of the work. The pins must remain in contact with the edge during the scribing process if the scribed line is to be parallel to the edge of the workpiece.

Courtesy Kostel Enterprises Ltd.

Fig. 4-7   Scribing a line parallel to an edge using a surface gauge

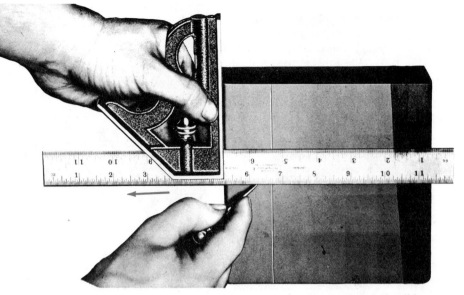

Courtesy The L. S. Starrett Company

Fig. 4-6   Scribing a line at 90° to an edge

The base of the surface gauge has a V-shaped groove machined in the bottom to permit it to be used on round surfaces.

When the layout lines must be accurate to within 0.02 mm or .001 in., a *vernier height gauge* (Fig. 4-8) may be used.

Courtesy The L. S. Starrett Company

Fig. 4-8   A vernier height gauge is used when an accurate layout is required

When lines are being laid out parallel to a surface, the highest degree of accuracy is obtained by setting the scriber of a height gauge to a *gauge block build-up* (Fig. 4-9). When this method is used, care must be taken that the scriber is set with the pointed side down, as shown.

Fig. 4-9   Setting a vernier height gauge scriber to a gauge block buildup

The following points should be observed when a surface or a height gauge is used for laying out lines.

1. Thoroughly clean the surface plate and the base of the surface or height gauge.
2. Hold the gauge so that the scriber point is approximately 45° to the surface being laid out (Figs. 4-7 and 8).
3. Press down firmly on the surface or height gauge base.
4. Always pull the gauge to maintain an accurate layout line. Pushing tends to make the scriber point dig in and tip the gauge, producing inaccurate layout lines.

ANGULAR LAYOUT

Angles may be laid out on a workpiece to an accuracy of about 0.5° by means of a *bevel protractor head and rule* (Fig. 4-10). A *Universal bevel protractor* may be used if an accuracy of 0.0833° (5′) is required.

If extreme accuracy is required for angular layout, it is advisable to use a *sine bar* or *sine plate*, *gauge blocks*, and a *vernier height gauge* as shown in Fig. 4-11.

Fig. 4-10   Laying out an angle with a protractor head and rule

Fig. 4-11   Making a precise angular layout using a sine bar and gauge blocks

CIRCULAR LAYOUT

Dividers are used for scribing arcs and circles on a layout and for transferring measurements. The divider should be set by placing one point in the 1 cm or 1 in. graduation line on a steel rule. Adjust the other point until it fits into the graduation line on the rule which indicates the desired measurement (Fig. 4-12). Care must be taken to keep the points of the divider parallel to the edge of the rule when making a setting.

Fig. 4-12   Setting a divider to 3-3/4 in. by placing the points in the 1 in. and 4-3/4 in. graduations

Trammels (Fig. 4-13) are used for transferring measurements and scribing circles and radii beyond the range of the divider. When a circle is laid out from a hole, a ball attachment may be substituted for one of the scriber points. This ball attachment fits into the hole and serves as the centre point when arcs are scribed.

The *Centre head*, the last component of the combination set, may be used to find the centre of round, square, or octagonal stock (Fig. 4-14).

PERMANENT LAYOUT

After the layout lines have been scribed on the workpiece, they should be permanently marked by means of prick-punch marks along the layout. This step will ensure that the layout line location will still be visible should the line be rubbed off through handling. The intersection of the centre lines of a circle should be carefully prick punched and then enlarged with a centre punch.

NOTE: Extreme care should be taken when the intersections of layout lines are being prick punched. Regardless of how accurate the layout is, it is impossible to mark locations with a prick punch to closer than 0.075 to 0.100 mm.

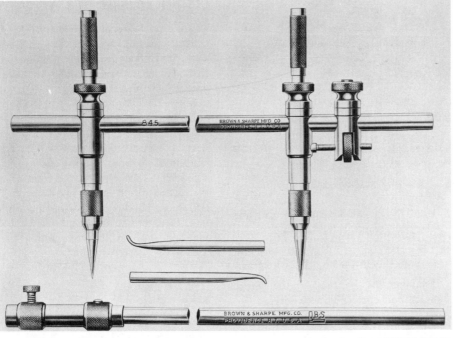

Courtesy Brown & Sharpe Mfg. Co.

Fig. 4-13   Trammels are used for work beyond the range of a divider

The *prick punch* and the *centre punch* (Fig. 4-15) differ only in the angle of the point. The *prick punch* is ground to an angle of 30 to 60° and is used to mark permanently the location of layout lines. The narrower angle of this punch makes a smaller and neater indentation in the metal surface.

The *centre punch* is ground to an angle of 90° and is used to mark the location of the centres of holes. The wider indentation permits easier and more accurate starting of a drill point.

Uniform layout punch marks may be obtained with an automatic centre punch (Fig. 4-16). This punch contains a striking block which is released by downward pressure; the block then strikes the punch proper, causing it to indent the metal. The impression size can be changed by adjusting the tension on the screw cap on the upper end of the tool. This type of punch produces marks uniform in size, which improve the appearance of the workpiece. Automatic centre punches may also have a spacing attachment which provides uniformity in the spacing of the layout punch marks.

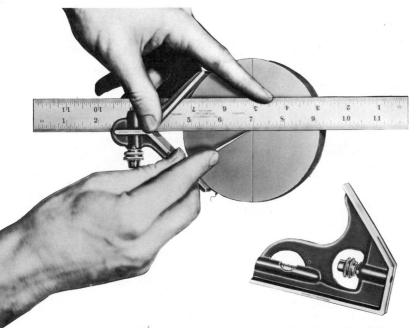

Courtesy The L. S. Starrett Company

Fig. 4-14   Using a centre head to locate the centre of a round piece of stock

Courtesy Kostel Enterprises Ltd.

Fig. 4-15   A prick punch and a centre punch are used in layout work

persian angle plate

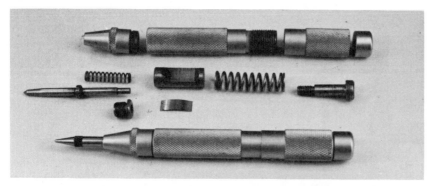

Fig. 4-16 An automatic centre punch produces uniform indentations on a layout

On straight lines or large curves, prick-punch marks should be spaced approximately every 12 mm. For hole layouts up to 12 mm in diameter, four marks around the circumference should be sufficient.

The following points should be observed when using a centre or a prick punch.

1. Always make sure that the point of the punch is sharp.

2. Hold the punch at a 45° angle, and place the point on the layout line.

3. Bring the punch to a vertical position, and tap it gently with a light hammer.

4. Examine the position of the punch mark and correct if necessary.

5. Using a centre punch, enlarge all the centre marks of the holes to be drilled so that the drill point can centre itself in the indentation.

LAYOUT ACCESSORIES

In addition to regular layout tools, certain accessories are helpful in layout work. When lines are required on the face of a plate, it is customary to clamp the work to an *angle plate* (Fig. 4-17) with a *toolmaker's clamp*. This will hold the work in a vertical plane so that the layout lines will be accurately positioned. Since an accurate angle plate will have all adjacent surfaces at 90° to each other, it is possible to accurately scribe lines which intersect at 90°. This is achieved by scribing all the horizontal lines on the workpiece then turning the angle plate on its side and scribing the intersecting lines (Fig. 4-18 A and B).

Fig. 4-18A Horizontal lines should be scribed first

Fig. 4-18B The angle plate is turned on its end and intersecting lines are scribed

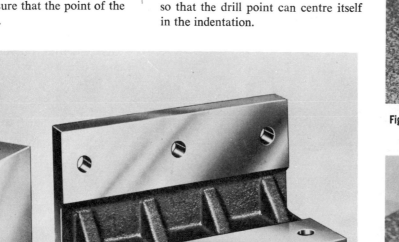

Courtesy The Taft-Peirce Manufacturing Company

Fig. 4-17 Angle plates have sides at 90° to each other

Courtesy The Taft-Peirce Manufacturing Company

Fig. 4-19   Parallels keep the bottom surface of the work parallel with the surface plate

Parallels (Fig. 4-19) may be used when it is necessary to raise the workpiece to a desired height and to maintain the work surface parallel to the top of the surface plate.

V-blocks are used to hold round work for layout and for inspection. They may be used singly or in pairs. Some blocks are so constructed that they may be rotated 90° on their sides without the work having to be removed. This feature permits the laying out of lines at 90° on a shaft without a change in the position of the work in the V-block (Fig. 4-20).

Keyseat rules are used to lay out keyseats on shafts or to draw lines parallel to the axis of the shaft. A solid keyseat rule resembles two straightedges machined at 90° to each other (Fig. 4-21A). *Keyseat clamps* when attached to a rule or straightedge will convert it to a keyseat rule (Fig. 4-21B).

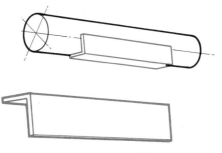

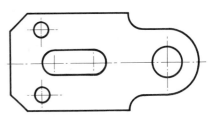

A — Solid keyseat rule

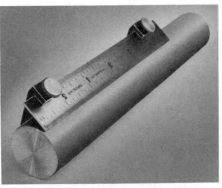

B — Keyseat rule and clamp

Fig. 4-21   Keyseat rules are used to scribe lines parallel to the axis of a cylinder

LAYOUT OPERATIONS

Although the layout required will naturally not be the same for each workpiece, there are certain procedures which should be followed in any layout. The following list of jobs is intended to acquaint the reader with layout methods and procedures.

To Lay Out Hole Locations, Slots, and Radii

1. Study Fig. 4-22 and select the proper stock.

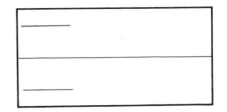

Fig. 4-22   A layout exercise

2. Cut off the stock, allowing enough material to square the ends if required.
3. Remove all burrs.
4. Clean the surface thoroughly, and apply layout dye.
5. Place a suitable angle plate on a surface plate.
   NOTE: Clean both plates.
6. Clamp the work to the angle plate with a finished edge of the part against the surface plate or on a parallel. Leave one end of the angle plate protruding beyond the workpiece.

Fig. 4-23A   Centre lines are scribed parallel to the base

7. With the surface gauge set to the proper height, scribe a centre line for the full length of the workpiece (Fig. 4-23A).
8. Using the centre line as a reference, set the surface gauge as required and scribe the centre lines for all hole and radii locations (Fig. 4-23A).

Fig. 4-20   Lines may be conveniently marked at 90° with a special V-block

9. Turn the angle plate 90°, scribe the base line at the bottom of the workpiece (Fig. 4-23B).

10. Using the base line as a reference line, locate and scribe the other centre lines for each hole or arc (Fig. 4-23B).

NOTE: All measurements for any location must be taken from the base line or finished edge.

Fig. 4-23B   Centre lines are scribed at 90°

11. Locate the starting points for the angular layout (Fig. 4-23B).

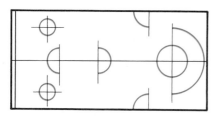

Fig. 4-23C   Arcs and circles are scribed

12. Remove the workpiece from the angle plate.

13. Carefully prick punch the centre of all hole or radii locations.

14. Using a divider set as required, scribe all circles and arcs (Fig. 4-23C).

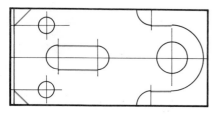

Fig. 4-23D   Arcs and circles are connected

15. Scribe any lines required to connect the arcs or circles (Fig. 4-23D).

16. Draw in the angular lines (Fig. 4-23D).

PRECISION LAYOUT

If a very accurate layout is required for hole positions and angles as shown in Fig. 4-24, this may be done by using a sine bar, gauge blocks, and toolmaker's buttons to accurately position the hole locations.

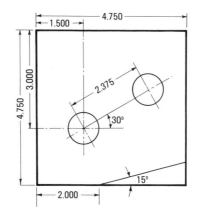

Fig. 4-24   An accurate layout for precision work (dimensions in inches)

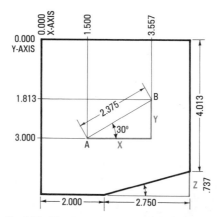

Fig. 4-25   The position of hole B is calculated by trigonometry (dimensions in inches)

Procedure

NOTE: This example is given in inch dimensions as the calculation involved is dependent upon an inch tool.

1. Check the blueprint for the required dimensions.

2. Machine and grind a plate square to size 4.750 in. × 4.750 in.

3. Clean the surface of the workpiece, and coat it with layout dye.

4. Set the work on edge on a surface plate, and clamp it to an angle plate.

5. Using a vernier height gauge, scribe the centre lines for hole *A* (Fig. 4-25).

6. Calculate the position of hole *B* as follows:

Length of side x

$$\frac{x}{2.375} = \cos 30°$$
$$x = 2.375 \cos 30°$$
$$= 2.375 \times .86603$$
$$= 2.0568 \text{ in.}$$

Length of side y

$$\frac{y}{2.375} = \sin 30°$$
$$y = 2.375 \sin 30°$$
$$= 2.375 \times .5000$$
$$= 1.1875 \text{ in.}$$

The position of the centre of hole *B* is then 2.0568 in. to the right of the centre line for hole *A* and 1.1875 in. above the centre line for hole *A*. It is now possible to position the hole using the coordinate method. (See Chapter 12 for an explanation of coordinates.)

The vertical centre line for hole *B* would then be located 1.500 + 2.0568 = 3.5568 in. along the *x* axis.

The horizontal centre line for hole *B* would be located 3.000 − 1.1875 = 1.8125 in. along the *y* axis.

7. Using a vernier height gauge, mark off the centre line for hole *B*.

8. Carefully prick punch and then centre punch the intersection of the centre lines of these holes.

9. Drill with a #38 drill, and tap using a 5 − 40 NC tap.

10. Lightly fasten the toolmaker's buttons (.400 diameter) to the plate.

Fig. 4-26A   Using gauge blocks to quickly set toolmaker's buttons to within .001 in. of location

11. Place the angle plate on its side (Fig. 4-26A); place side *y* of the work down against the surface plate and side *x* tightly against the corner of the angle plate.

12. Clamp the workpiece securely in this position.

13. Toolmaker's buttons can be set quickly to within at least .001 of location by the following steps:

   i) Calculate the distance for hole *A* from the bottom of the button to edges *x* and *y*.

   $$x = 3.000 - .200$$
   $$= 2.800 \text{ in.}$$
   $$y = 1.500 - .200 \text{ (1/2 the}$$
   diameter of the button)
   $$= 1.300 \text{ in.}$$

   ii) Make gauge block buildups for 1.300 and 2.800, and place them in the proper position under or along the side of the toolmaker's button (Fig. 4-26A).

   iii) Press the toolmaker's button firmly against both gauge block buildups, and tighten the screw snugly.

   iv) Repeat this same procedure for locating the button at hole *B*. *NOTE*: If desired, a depth micrometer could be used to measure from side *x* and *y* and

approximately locate the buttons.

14. To check the position of the buttons accurately, follow the steps listed below.

   i) Mount a dial indicator on a surface or height gauge.

   ii) Calculate the distance from side *x* to holes *A* and *B*, and add one-half the diameter of the toolmaker's button.

   iii) Make a gauge block buildup for both these dimensions.

   iv) Set the indicator to zero over one gauge block buildup for hole *A* and check the button to see how it compares with the indicator setting (Fig. 4-26B).

   v) If the button reading varies from the gauge block reading, lightly tap the toolmaker's button to the proper location using a brass or aluminum rod.

   vi) Locate the button for hole *B* in the same manner.

   vii) Recheck the location of both buttons.

   viii) Turn the angle plate 90°, and repeat procedures (i) to (vii) to locate the buttons from side *y*.

15. After the toolmaker's buttons are accurately located, tighten the screw securely.

Fig. 4-26B   Checking the position of the toolmaker's buttons

16. Double check the position of the buttons by measuring over the buttons with a micrometer. This measurement should be the distance between centres plus the diameter of one button. This equals 2.375 + .400, or 2.775 in.
   NOTE: If this dimension is not correct, recheck the position of both buttons and readjust as required.

17. Set the workpiece up on a vertical milling machine or on the faceplate of a lathe.
   NOTE: If the work is to be machined on a vertical milling machine, a dial indicator is mounted (on a grasshopper leg) in the machine spindle. The work is adjusted until the needle of the indicator shows no movement, as the indicator is rotated by hand around the toolmaker's button.

   If the holes on the workpiece are to be bored out on a lathe, the work should be mounted in a 4-jaw chuck or on a faceplate (see *lathe*, Chapter 9), and a dial indicator mounted in the toolpost. With the contact point bearing against the button, the work is rotated by hand and adjusted until there is no movement of the indicator needle.

18. After both holes have been machined, remove the work.

19. To lay out the 15° angle at the corner of the plate, calculate the buildup for 15° using a 5 in. sine bar.

   $$\text{Buildup} = 5 \sin 15°$$
   $$= 5 \times .25882$$
   $$= 1.2941 \text{ in.}$$

20. Place the buildup under one end of a sine bar (on a surface plate).

21. Place the workpiece, angled edge up, on a sine bar and clamp to an angle plate.

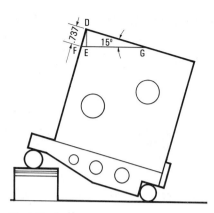

Fig. 4-27   To accurately locate the line EG, the distance DE must be known (dimensions in inches)

22. Calculate the length of DF (Fig. 4-27) as follows:

$$\frac{DF}{2.750} = \tan 15°$$

$$\frac{DF}{2.750} = .26795$$

$$DF = .26795 \times 2.750$$

$$DF = .7368 \text{ in.}$$

23. Calculate the length of the line DE (Fig. 4-27).

    In order to accurately scribe the line at 15° as required in Fig. 4-24, it is necessary first to calculate the length of the line DE (Fig. 4-27) since this is the vertical distance below D that the line must be scribed. By previous calculations it was determined that the line DF was .737 in.

    In the triangle DEF the angle FDE is 15°.

$$\therefore \frac{DE}{DF} = \cos 15°$$

$$DE = \cos 15° \times DF$$

$$= .96592 \times .737$$

$$= .7118$$

$$= .712 \text{ in.}$$

24. Set the scriber on the vernier height gauge to the uppermost corner of the plate (point D).

25. Lower the scriber .712 and scribe the line GF. This will locate the point G at a position 2.000 in. from the side of the plate as required in Fig. 4-24.

26. Remove the workpiece from the angle plate.

27. Lightly prick punch the layout line.

28. Machine the excess stock off to about .010 in. above the layout line.

29. Remount the plate on the sine bar (buildup 1.294 in.), and clamp to the angle plate.

30. Place the angle plate and workpiece on the surface grinder, and grind to the layout line.

31. Check the accuracy of the ground surface with a vernier height gauge and indicator.

LAYING OUT A CASTING HAVING A CORED HOLE

When a casting which requires a hole in it is molded in a foundry, a core is used to produce the rough hole which may have to be machined later. Often the core shifts out of place and the hole is cast off-centre as shown in Fig. 4-28. If the hole must be machined concentric with the outside of the casting, it may be necessary to lay out the location of the hole.

Procedure

1. Grind the scale off the surface to be laid out.

2. Tap a tightly fitting wooden block into the cast hole (Fig. 4-28).

3. Coat the surface to be laid out and the wooden plug with a solution of slaked lime and alcohol or layout dye.

4. With the hermaphrodite calipers scribe four arcs as shown, using the outside diameter of the shoulder as the reference surface.

5. Using the intersection of these arcs as a centre, scribe a circle of the required diameter on the casting. The hole should be concentric with the outside of the casting (Fig. 4-28).

6. Prick punch the layout line at about eight equidistant points around the layout circle.

To Lay Out a Keyseat in a Shaft

1. Apply layout dye to the end of the shaft and to the area where the keyseat is to be laid out.

2. Mount the workpiece in a V-block.

3. Set the surface gauge scriber to the centre of the shaft.

4. Scribe a line across the end and continue it along the shaft to the keyseat location (Fig. 4-29).

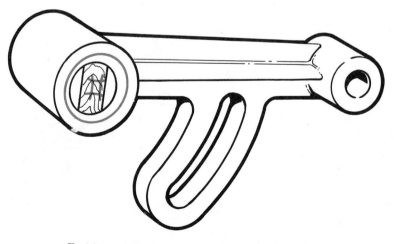

Fig. 4-28   Method of centring a hole layout with the casting

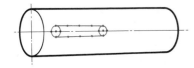

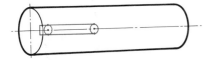

Fig. 4-29 Keyseat layouts

5. Rotate the work in the V-block, and mark the length and the position of the keyseat on the shaft.
6. Set the dividers to half the width of the keyseat, and scribe a circle at each end of the layout (Fig. 4-29).
7. Using a keyseat rule and scriber, connect the circles with a line on either side of the centre line and tangent to the circles.
8. Prick punch the layout of the keyseat, and centre punch the centres of the circles.
9. If it is necessary to drill holes at the end of the keyseat, it is advisable to set up the shaft by aligning the end layout line in a vertical position with a square.

CHAPTER 4 - REVIEW QUESTIONS

1. State two reasons why a layout is necessary.
2. Why should the layout be as simple as possible?

LAYOUT TABLES

3. Why is a granite layout table considered better than a cast-iron type?

SURFACE PREPARATION OF THE METAL FOR LAYOUT

4. What is the purpose of a layout solution?
5. Name four layout solutions, and state one application of each.
6. State two methods of preparing the surface of a casting prior to laying out the workpiece.

METHODS OF SCRIBING LINES PARALLEL TO A SURFACE OR EDGE

7. List two precautions that must be observed when using a scriber.
8. Describe the construction of a surface gauge.
9. What is the purpose of the two pins in the base of a surface gauge?
10. What precautions should be taken when a vernier height gauge is used to scribe a layout line?

ANGULAR LAYOUT

11. List three methods of making angular layouts, and state the accuracy of each.

CIRCULAR LAYOUT

12. State two precautions to observe when setting dividers or trammels to size.

PERMANENT LAYOUT

13. Why should a prick punch rather than a centre punch be used to permanently mark layout lines?
14. Describe the operation of an automatic centre punch.
15. List the points which should be observed when using a centre or prick punch.

LAYOUT ACCESSORIES

16. How may lines which intersect at 90° be accurately scribed on a workpiece?
17. State two purposes of parallels.
18. What are keyseat clamps, and how are they used?

LAYOUT OPERATIONS

19. Outline the main steps that should be followed in making a layout comprised of straight lines, slots, and radii.
20. Name four tools which may be used for precision layout.
21. Describe how the toolmaker's buttons can be set up quickly and accurately to a desired location.
22. The cored hole in a casting must be bored out but is not concentric with the outside shoulder. Describe how to lay out the hole concentric with the ontside shoulder of the casting.
23. Outline the main steps for laying out a keyseat in a shaft.

5 HAND TOOLS AND BENCH WORK

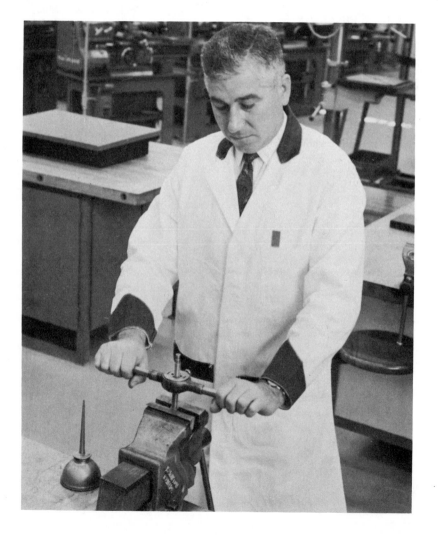

The machine trade may be divided into two categories: hand tool and machine tool operations.

Although this era is looked upon as the machine age, the importance of hand tool operations or bench work should not be overlooked. Bench work may refer to the operations of laying out, fitting, and assembling. These operations may involve sawing, chipping, filing, polishing, scraping, reaming, and threading. A good machinist should be capable of using all hand tools skilfully. Effective selection and use of these tools is possible only with continued practice.

THE BENCH VISE

The machinist's, or bench, vise (Fig. 5-1) is used to hold small work securely for sawing, chipping, filing, polishing, drilling, reaming, and tapping operations.

Vises are mounted close to the edge of the bench; they permit long work to be held in a vertical position. Vises may be made of cast iron or cast steel. The vise size is determined by the width of the jaws.

A machinist's vise may be of the solid base or swivel base type. The swivel base vise (Fig. 5-1) differs from the solid base type by having a swivel plate added to the bottom of the vise. This allows the vise to be swung in any circular position.

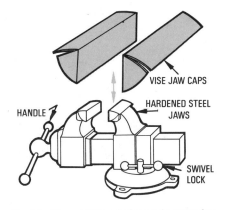

Fig. 5-1   The swivel bench vise can be rotated to any position

When gripping finished work or soft materials, use jaw caps made of brass, aluminum, or copper to protect the work surface from being marred or damaged.

HAMMERS

There are many types of hammers used by the machinist, the most common being the *ball peen hammer* (Fig. 5-2A). The larger striking surface is called the *face*, and the smaller, rounded end is the *peen*. Ball peen hammers are made in a variety of sizes, with head masses ranging from approximately 55 to 1400 g. The smaller sizes are used for layout work, and the larger ones are for general work. The peen is generally used in riveting or peening operations.

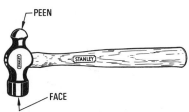

Courtesy Stanley Tools Division of the Stanley Works

Fig. 5-2A   A ball peen hammer

Soft-faced hammers (Fig. 5-2B) have heads made of plastic, rawhide, copper, or lead. These heads are fastened to a steel body and can be replaced when

worn. Soft-faced hammers are used in assembling or dismantling parts so the finished surface of the work will not be marred. Lead hammers are often used to seat the workpiece properly on parallels when setting up work in a vise for milling or shaping operations.

Courtesy Stanley Tools Division of the Stanley Works

Fig. 5-2B   A soft faced hammer

SCREWDRIVERS

Screwdrivers (Fig. 5-3) are manufactured in a variety of shapes, types, and sizes. Some of the more common types are the standard, stubby, and offset screwdrivers. Blades for smaller screwdrivers are generally made of round stock, and blades for larger screwdrivers are often square so that a wrench may be applied for leverage.

Courtesy Stanley Tools Division of the Stanley Works

Fig. 5-3A   A standard screwdriver

Courtesy Stanley Tools Division of the Stanley Works

Fig. 5-3B   An offset screwdriver is often used in confined spaces

Care of a Screwdriver

1. Choose the correct size of screwdriver for the job. If too small a screwdriver is used, both the screw slot and the tip of the driver may become damaged.
2. Do not use the screwdriver as a pry, chisel, or wedge.
3. When the point becomes worn or

broken, it should be redressed to shape (Fig. 5-4).

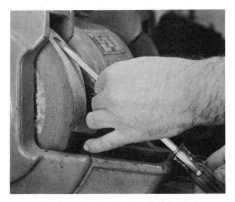

Fig. 5-4   Regrinding a screwdriver blade

REGRINDING A SCREWDRIVER BLADE

When regrinding the tip, make the sides of the blade slightly concave (Fig. 5-4) by holding the side of the blade tangential to the periphery of the grinding wheel (Fig. 5-4). Grind an equal amount off each side of the blade. This shape will enable the blade to maintain a better grip in the slot. Care should be taken that the original taper, width, and thickness of the tip are retained and that the end is ground square with the centre line of the blade.

NOTE: When grinding, remove a minimum amount of metal so as not to grind past the hardened zone in the tip. Quench frequently in cold water so as not to draw the temper from the blade.

THE HAND HACKSAW

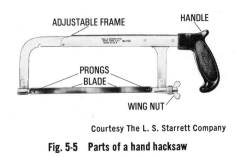

Courtesy The L. S. Starrett Company

Fig. 5-5   Parts of a hand hacksaw

The *pistol grip hand hacksaw* (Fig. 5-5) is composed of three main parts: the *frame*, the *handle*, and the *blade*. The frame can be of either the solid or adjustable type. The solid frame is more rigid and will accommodate blades of only one specific length. The adjustable frame is more commonly used and will take blades which range from 200 to 300 mm long. A wing nut at the back of the frame provides adjustment for blade tensioning.

Hacksaw blades are made of high-speed molybdenum or tungsten-alloy steel that has been hardened and tempered. There are two types: the solid, or all-hard, blade and the flexible blade. Solid blades are hardened throughout and are very brittle. They break easily if not used properly. Only the teeth of the flexible blade are hardened, while the back of the blade is soft and flexible. Although this type of blade will stand more abuse than the all-hard blade, it will not stand up as long for general use.

Solid blades are usually used on brass, tool steel, cast iron, and larger sections of mild steel since they do not run out of line when pressure is applied. Flexible blades may be used on channel iron, tubing, copper, and aluminum since they do not break as easily on material with thin cross sections.

Blades are manufactured in various pitches* (number of teeth per inch) such as: 14, 18, 24 and 32. The pitch is the most important factor to consider when selecting the proper blade for a job. An 18-tooth blade (18 teeth per inch) is recommended for general use. When selecting a blade, choose as coarse a blade as possible in order to provide plenty of chip clearance and cut through the work as quickly as possible. The blade selected should have at least two teeth in contact with the work at all times. This will prevent the work from jamming between the teeth and stripping the teeth from the blade. Fig. 5-6 will provide a guide for proper blade selection.

*Metric pitches for saw blades were not established at the time of publication.

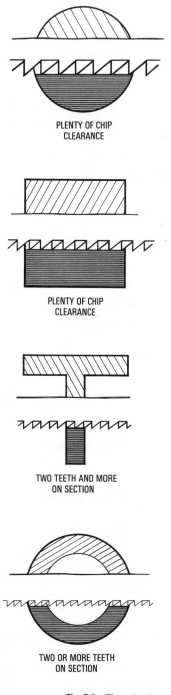

CORRECT PITCH

PLENTY OF CHIP CLEARANCE

PLENTY OF CHIP CLEARANCE

TWO TEETH AND MORE ON SECTION

TWO OR MORE TEETH ON SECTION

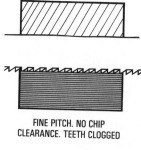
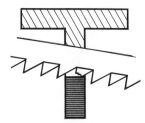

INCORRECT PITCH

FINE PITCH. NO CHIP CLEARANCE. TEETH CLOGGED

FINE PITCH. NO CHIP CLEARANCE. TEETH CLOGGED

COARSE PITCH STRADDLES WORK STRIPPING TEETH

COARSE PITCH STRADDLES WORK

Fig. 5-6   The selection of the proper blade for the job is very important

To Use the Hand Hacksaw

1. Check that the blade is of the proper pitch for the job and that the teeth point away from the handle.
2. Adjust the blade tension so that the blade cannot flex or bend.
3. Mount the stock in the vise so that the cut will be about 5 mm from the vise jaws.
4. Grasp the hacksaw as shown in Fig. 5-7. Assume a comfortable stance, standing erect with the left foot slightly ahead of the right foot.

Courtesy Kostel Enterprises Ltd.

Fig. 5-7   Correct method of holding a hacksaw

5. Start the saw cut just outside and parallel to a previously scribed line. *NOTE*: If the saw does not start in the desired spot, file a V-shaped nick at the starting point.
6. After the cut has started, apply pressure only on the forward stroke. Use about 50 strokes per minute.
7. When cutting thin material, hold the saw at an angle to have at least two teeth in contact with the work at all times. Thin work is often clamped between two pieces of wood, and the cut is made through all three pieces (Fig. 5-7).
8. When nearing the end of the cut, slow down to control the saw as it breaks through the material.

NOTE: If a saw blade breaks or becomes dull in a partly finished cut, start the new blade in another place. A new blade will bind in an old cut and the "set" of the new teeth will be ruined quickly.

FILES

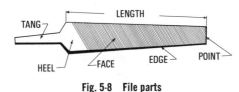

Fig. 5-8   File parts

A *file* is a hand cutting tool made of high-carbon steel, having a series of teeth cut on the body by parallel chisel cuts. Files are used to remove surplus metal and to produce finished surfaces. Files are manufactured in a variety of types and shapes, each for a specific purpose. They may be divided into two classes: single cut and double cut (Fig. 5-9).

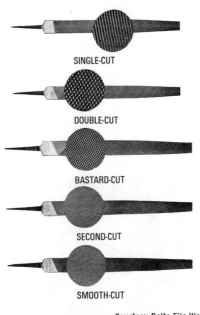

Courtesy Delta File Works

Fig. 5-9   File classification

Single cut files have a single row of parallel teeth running diagonally across the face. They include *mill*, *long-angle lathe*, and *saw files*. Single cut files are used when a smooth finish is desired or when hard materials are to be finished.

Double cut files have two intersecting rows of teeth. The first row is usually coarser and is called the "overcut." The other row is called the "upcut." These intersecting rows produce hundreds of cutting teeth which provide for fast removal of metal and easy clearing of chips.

DEGREES OF COARSENESS

Both single and double cut files are manufactured in various degrees of coarseness, such as *rough*, *coarse*, *bastard*, *second cut*, *smooth*, and *dead smooth*. Those most commonly used by the machinist are the bastard, second cut, and smooth (Fig. 5-9).

MACHINISTS' FILES

The types of files most commonly used are the *flat*, *hand*, *round*, *half-round*, *square*, *pillar*, *three-quarter* (triangular), *warding*, and *knife* (Fig. 5-10).

Care of Files

Because files are relatively inexpensive hand tools, they are often abused. Proper care, selection, and use are most important if good results are to be obtained with files. The following points should be observed in the care of files:

1. Do not store files where they will rub together. Hang or store them separately.
2. Never use a file as a pry or a hammer. Since the file is hard, it snaps easily, often causing small pieces to fly, which may result in a serious eye injury.
3. Do not knock a file on a vise or other metallic object to clean it. Always use a file card or brush for this purpose.
4. Apply pressure only on the forward stroke when filing. Pressure on the return stroke will dull the file.
5. Do not press too hard on a new file. Too much pressure tends to break off the cutting edges and shorten the life of the file.

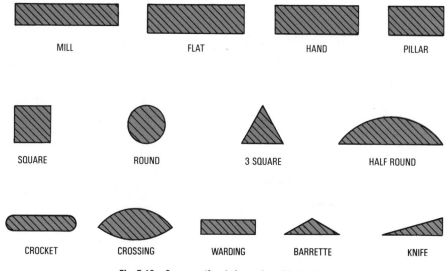

Fig. 5-10   Cross-sectional views of machinist files

6. Too much pressure also results in "pinning" (small particles being wedged between the teeth) which causes scratches on the surface of the work. Keep the file clean. A piece of soft steel, brass, copper, or wood pushed through the teeth will remove the "pins." Applying chalk to the face of the file will lessen the tendency for the file to become "pinned."

FILING PRACTICE

Filing is an important hand operation, and one that can be mastered only through patience and practice. The following points should be observed when cross filing:

1. Never use a file without a handle. Ignoring this rule is a dangerous practice. Serious hand injury may result should the file slip.
2. Fasten the work to be filed, at about elbow height, in a vise.
3. To produce a flat surface, the right hand, right forearm, and left hand should be held in a horizontal plane (Fig. 5-11). Push the file across the work face in a straight line and do not rock the file.

4. Apply pressure only on the forward stroke.
5. Never rub the fingers or hand across a surface being filed. Grease or oil from the hand causes the file to slide over instead of cutting the work. Oil will also clog the file.
6. Keep the file clean by using a file card frequently.

For rough filing, use a double cut file and cross the stroke at regular intervals to help keep the surface flat and straight

Courtesy Nicholson File Co. of Canada Ltd.

Fig. 5-11   The file must be kept level when filing

(Fig. 5-12). When finishing, use a single cut file and take shorter strokes to keep the file flat.

Test the work for flatness occasionally by laying the edge of a steel rule across its surface. A steel square should be used to test the squareness of one surface to another.

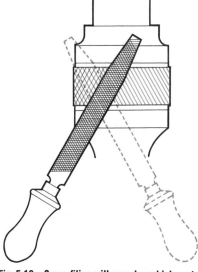

Fig. 5-12   Cross filing will reveal any high spots on the surface

DRAW FILING

Draw filing is used to produce a smooth, flat surface on the workpiece. This method of filing removes file marks and scratches left by cross filing.

NOTE: When draw filing, hold the file as in Fig. 5-13 and move the file back and forth along the length of the work.

Fig. 5-13   Draw filing is used to produce a flat smooth surface

POLISHING

After a surface has been filed, it may be finished with abrasive cloth to remove small scratches left by the file. This may be done with a piece of abrasive cloth held under the file which is moved back and forth along the work.

SPECIAL FILES

Long-angle lathe files are used for filing on a lathe as they provide a better shearing action than mill files. The long angle of the teeth tends to clean the file, helps eliminate chatter, and reduces the possibility of tearing the metal.

Aluminum files are designed for soft, ductile metals, such as aluminum and white metal, because regular files tend to clog quickly when used on this type of material.

The modified tooth construction on aluminum files tends to reduce clogging. The upcut tooth is deep, and the overcut is fine. This produces small scallops on the upcut which breaks up the chips and permits them to clear more easily.

Brass files have a small upcut angle and a fine, long-angle overcut which produces small, easily-cleared chips. The almost straight upcut prevents grooving the surface of the work.

Shear tooth files combine a long angle and a single cut coarse tooth for filing materials such as brass, aluminum, copper, plastics, and hard rubber.

PRECISION FILES

Precision files comprise swiss pattern, needle, and riffler files. *Swiss pattern* and *needle files* (Fig. 5-14) are small files having very fine tooth cuts and round integral handles. They are made in several shapes and are generally used in tool and die shops for finishing delicate and intricate pieces. *Die sinker rifflers* are curved up at the ends to permit filing the bottom surface of a die cavity.

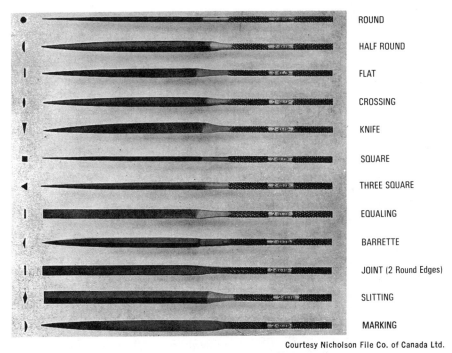

ROUND
HALF ROUND
FLAT
CROSSING
KNIFE
SQUARE
THREE SQUARE
EQUALING
BARRETTE
JOINT (2 Round Edges)
SLITTING
MARKING

Courtesy Nicholson File Co. of Canada Ltd.

Fig. 5-14   Needle files are used for intricate work

ROTARY FILES AND BURRS

The increased use of portable electric and pneumatic power tools has developed the widespread application of rotary files and burrs. The wide range of shapes and sizes available makes these tools particularly suitable for metal pattern making and die sinking.

Rotary files. The teeth of rotary files (Fig. 5-15) are hand cut and form broken lines in contrast to the unbroken flutes of the ground burr (Fig. 5-16). The teeth of the rotary file tend to dissipate the heat of friction, a feature which makes this tool particularly useful for work on tough die steels, forgings, and scaly surfaces.

Ground burrs (Fig. 5-16) may be made of high-speed steel or carbide. The flutes of a burr are generally machine ground to a master burr to ensure uniformity of tooth shape and size. Ground high-speed burrs are used more efficiently on nonferrous metals, such as aluminum, brass, bronze, and magnesium, since they have better chip clearance than rotary files.

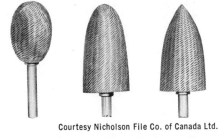

Courtesy Nicholson File Co. of Canada Ltd.

Fig. 5-15   The broken line teeth of rotary files tend to dissipate heat quickly

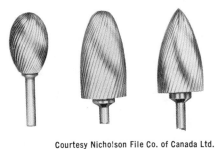

Courtesy Nicholson File Co. of Canada Ltd.

Fig. 5-16   Ground burrs are used on non-ferrous metals

Carbide burrs may be used on hard or soft materials with good results and will last up to 100 times longer than a high-speed steel burr.

Using High-Speed Steel Rotary Files and Burrs

For best results, the following points should be observed when using rotary files or burrs.

1. Move the file or burr at an even rate to produce a smooth surface. An uneven rate of pressure produces work with ridges and hollows.
2. Use the proper speed for the burr diameter or file as recommended by the manufacturer.
3. Use only sharp burrs or files.
4. For more accurate control of the burr or file, grip the grinder as close as possible to the end.
5. Medium cut burrs and files generally provide satisfactory metal removal and finish for most jobs. If greater stock removal is required, use a coarse burr or file. For an extra-smooth finish, use a fine burr or file.

SCRAPERS

When a truer surface is required than can be produced by machining, the surface may be finished by scraping. However, this is a long and tedious process. Most bearing surfaces (flat and curved) are now finished by grinding, honing, or broaching.

Scraping is a process of removing small amounts of metal from specific areas to produce an accurate bearing surface. It is used to produce flat surfaces on cast-iron surface plates or in fitting brass and babbitt bearings to shafts.

Scrapers are made in various shapes, depending on the surface to be scraped (Fig. 5-17). They are generally made of high grade tool steel, hardened and tempered. Carbide-tipped scrapers are very popular because they maintain the cutting edge longer than other types.

HAND TAPS

Taps are cutting tools used to cut internal threads. They are made from high quality tool steel, hardened and ground. Two, three, or four flutes are cut lengthwise across the threads to form cutting edges, provide room for the chips, and admit cutting fluid to lubricate the tap. The end of the shank is square so that a tap wrench (Fig. 5-19) can be used to turn the tap into a hole. For inch-built taps, the major diameter, number of threads per inch, and type of thread are usually found stamped on the shank of a tap. For example, 1/2 in. — 13 UNC represents:

a) 1/2 in. = major diameter of the tap
b)   13 = number of threads per inch
c)   UNC = Unified National Coarse (a type of thread)

Hand taps are usually made in sets of three, called *taper*, *plug*, and *bottoming* (Fig. 5-18).

A *taper tap* is tapered from the end approximately six threads and is used to start a thread easily. It can be used for tapping a hole which goes *through* the work, as well as for starting a *blind* hole (one that does not go through the work).

A *plug tap* is tapered for approximately three threads. Sometimes the plug tap is the only tap used to thread a hole going through a piece of work.

A *bottoming tap* is not tapered but chamfered at the end for one thread. It is used for threading to the bottom of a blind hole. When tapping a blind hole, first use the taper tap, then the plug tap, and complete the hole with a bottoming tap.

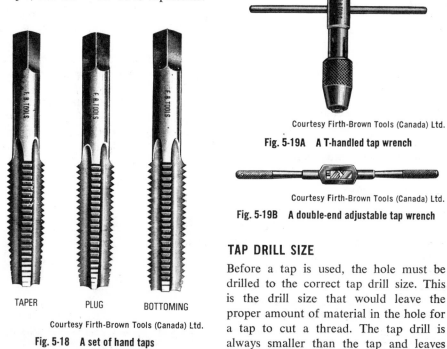

Courtesy Firth-Brown Tools (Canada) Ltd.

Fig. 5-19A   A T-handled tap wrench

Courtesy Firth-Brown Tools (Canada) Ltd.

Fig. 5-19B   A double-end adjustable tap wrench

TAP DRILL SIZE

Before a tap is used, the hole must be drilled to the correct tap drill size. This is the drill size that would leave the proper amount of material in the hole for a tap to cut a thread. The tap drill is always smaller than the tap and leaves

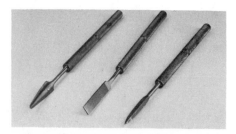

Fig. 5-17   A set of hand scrapers

TAPER   PLUG   BOTTOMING

Courtesy Firth-Brown Tools (Canada) Ltd.

Fig. 5-18   A set of hand taps

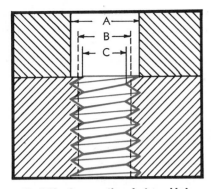

Fig. 5-20 Cross-section of a tapped hole
A — body size
B — tap drill size
C — minor diameter

enough material in the hole for the tap to produce 75% of a full thread.

When a chart is not available, the tap-drill size for any American National or Unified thread can be found easily by applying this simple formula:

$$TDS = D - \frac{1}{N}$$

TDS = tap drill size
D = major diameter of tap
N = number of threads per inch

EXAMPLE:
Find the tap drill size for a 7/8 in. — 9 NC tap.

$$TDS = 7/8 - \frac{1}{9}$$
$$= .875 - .111$$
$$= .764 \text{ in.}$$

The nearest drill size to .764 in. is .765 in. (49/64). Therefore, 49/64 in. is the tap drill size for a 7/8 in. — 9 NC tap.

METRIC TAPS

Although there are several thread forms and standards in the Metric thread system, the International Standards Organization (ISO) have adopted a standard Metric thread which will be used throughout Canada, the United States, and many other countries throughout the world. This new series will have only 25 thread

sizes ranging from 1.6 mm to 100 mm diameter. See Table provided in the appendix for the size and pitch of the threads in this series. Also see Chapter 9 for the thread form and dimensions of the ISO metric thread.

Like inch taps, metric taps are available in sets of three: the *taper, plug,* and *bottoming* tap. They are identified with the letter M followed by the nominal diameter of the thread in millimetres times the pitch in millimetres.

A tap with the markings M 4 × 0.7 would indicate

M – a metric thread
4 – the nominal diameter of the thread in millimetres
0.7 – the pitch of the thread in millimetres

TAP DRILL SIZES FOR METRIC TAPS

The tap drill size for metric taps is calculated in the same manner as for U.S. Standard threads.

$$TDS = \text{major diameter (mm)} - \text{pitch (mm)}$$

EXAMPLE
Find the tap drill size for a 22 — 2.5 mm thread.

$$TDS = 22 - 2.5$$
$$= 19.5 \text{ mm}$$

TAPPING A HOLE

Tapping is the operation of cutting an internal thread using a tap and tap wrench. Because taps are hard and brittle, they

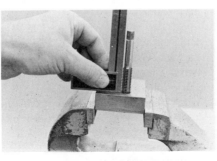

Courtesy Kostel Enterprises Ltd.

Fig. 5-21 Checking a tap for squareness while work is held in the vise

are easily broken. *Extreme* care must be used when tapping a hole to prevent breakage. A broken tap in a hole is difficult to remove and often results in scrapping the work.

To Tap a Hole by Hand

1. Select the correct taps and tap wrench for the job.
2. Apply a suitable cutting fluid to the tap.
   NOTE: No cutting fluid is required when tapping brass or cast iron.
3. Place the tap in the hole as vertically as possible, press downward on the wrench applying equal pressure on both handles, and turn clockwise (for right-hand thread) for about two turns.
4. Remove the tap wrench and check the tap for squareness.
   NOTE: Check at two positions at 90° to each other (Fig. 5-21).
5. If the tap has not entered squarely, remove it from the hole and restart it by applying pressure in the direction from which the tap leans. *Be careful* not to exert too much pressure in the straightening process.
6. When a tap has been properly started, feed it into the hole by turning the tap wrench.
7. Turn the tap clockwise one-quarter turn, and then turn it backward about one-half turn to break the chip. This must be done with a steady motion to prevent the tap from breaking.
   NOTE: When tapping blind holes, use all three taps in order: taper, plug, and then the bottoming tap. Before using the bottoming tap, remove all the chips from the hole and be careful not to hit the bottom of the hole with the tap.

REMOVING BROKEN TAPS

If extreme care is not used when cutting a thread, particularly in a blind hole, the tap may break in the hole and considerable work will be required to remove it. In some cases, it may not be possible and another piece of work must be started.

Several methods may be used to remove a broken tap; some may be successful, others will not.

TAP EXTRACTOR

This tool (Fig. 5-22) has four fingers that slip into the flutes of a broken tap. It is adjustable in order to support the fingers close to the broken tap, even when the broken end is below the surface of the work. A wrench is fitted to the extractor and turned counterclockwise to remove a right-hand tap. Tap extractors are made to fit all sizes of taps.

Fig. 5-22   A tap extractor being used to remove a broken tap

To Remove a Broken Tap Using a Tap Extractor

1. Select the proper extractor for the tap to be removed.
2. Slide *collar A*, to which the fingers are attached, down *body B* so that the fingers project well below the end of the body.
3. Slide the fingers into the flutes of the broken tap, making sure they go down into the hole as far as possible.
4. Slide the body down until it rests on top of the broken tap. This will give the maximum support to the fingers.
5. Slide the *collar C* down until it rests on top of the work. This also provides support for the fingers.

6. Apply a wrench to the square section on the top of the body.
7. Turn the wrench *gently* in a counter-clockwise direction.
   NOTE: Do not force the extractor as this will damage the fingers. It may be necessary to turn the wrench back and forth carefully to free the tap sufficiently to back it out.

DRILLING

If the broken tap is made of carbon steel, it may be possible to drill it out.

Procedure

1. Heat the broken tap to a bright red colour, and allow it to cool *slowly*.
2. Centre punch the tap as close to the centre as possible.
3. Using a drill considerably smaller than the distance between opposite flutes, proceed *carefully* to drill a hole through the broken tap.
4. Enlarge this hole to remove as much of the metal between the flutes as possible.
5. Collapse the remaining part with a punch and remove the pieces.

ACID METHOD

If the broken tap is made of high-speed steel and cannot be removed with a tap extractor, it is sometimes possible to remove it by the acid method.

Procedure

1. Dilute one part nitric acid with five parts water.
2. Inject this mixture into the hole. The acid will act upon the steel and cause the tap to become loose.
3. Remove the tap with an extractor or a pair of pliers.
4. Wash the remaining acid from the thread with water so that it will not continue to act on the threads.

TAP DISINTEGRATORS

Taps may sometimes be successfully removed by a tap disintegrator which may

be held in the spindle of a drill press. The disintegrator employs the Electrical Discharge Principle to cut its way through the tap, using a hollow brass tube as an electrode. Taps may also be removed using the same method on any Electrical Discharge machine (see Chapter 19).

THREADING DIES

Threading dies are used to cut external threads on round work. The most common threading dies are the solid, adjustable split, and the adjustable and removable screw plate die.

**Fig. 5-23   A — A solid die nut
B — An adjustable round split die**

The *solid die* (Fig. 5-23A) is used for chasing or recutting damaged threads and may be driven by a suitable wrench. It is not adjustable.

The *adjustable split die* (Fig. 5-23B) has an adjusting screw which permits an adjustment over or under the standard depth of thread. This type of die fits into a die stock (Fig. 5-24).

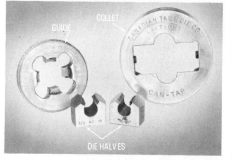

Courtesy Canadian Tap & Die Co. Limited

Fig. 5-23C   An adjustable screw plate die

The *adjustable screw plate die* (Fig. 5-23C) is probably a more efficient die since it provides for greater adjustment

Courtesy Cleveland Twist Drill (Canada) Ltd.

Fig. 5-24   A die stock is used to turn the die onto the workpiece

than the split die. Two die halves are held securely in a collet by means of a threaded plate which also acts as a guide when threading. The plate, when tightened into the collet, forces the die halves with tapered sides into the tapered slot of the collet. Adjustment is provided by means of two adjusting screws which bear against each die half. The threaded section at the bottom of each die half is tapered to provide for easy starting of the die. Note that the upper side of each die half is stamped with the manufacturer's name, while the lower side of each is stamped with the same serial number. Care should be taken in assembling the die that both serial numbers are facing down. *Never* use two die halves with different serial numbers.

HAND REAMERS

A hand reamer is a tool used to finish drilled holes accurately and provide a good finish. Reaming is generally performed by machine, but there are times when a hand reamer must be used to finish a hole. Hand reamers, when used properly, will produce holes accurate to size, shape, and finish.

Courtesy Cleveland Twist Drill (Canada) Ltd.

Fig. 5-25   A solid hand reamer

TYPES OF HAND REAMERS

The *solid hand reamer* (Fig. 5-25) may be made of carbon steel or high-speed steel. These straight reamers are available in metric sizes from 1 mm to 26 mm in diameter, and in inch sizes of from 1/8 in. to 1-1/2 in. in diameter. For easy starting, the cutting end of the reamer is ground to a slight taper for a distance equal to the diameter of the reamer. Solid reamers are not adjustable and may have straight or helical flutes. Straight fluted reamers should not be used on work with a keyway or any other interruption. Since hand reamers are designed to remove only small amounts of metal, no more than 0.10 to 0.25 mm should be left for reaming, depending on the diameter of the hole. A square on the end of the shank provides the means of driving the reamer with a tap wrench.

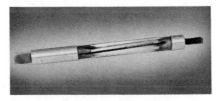

Fig. 5-26   An expansion hand reamer

The *expansion hand reamer* (Fig. 5-26) is designed to permit an adjustment of approximately 0.05 mm above the nominal diameter. The reamer is made hollow and has slots cut along the length of the cutting section. A tapered threaded plug, fitted into the end of the reamer, provides for limited expansion. If the reamer is expanded too much, it will be easily broken. *Metric expansion hand reamers* are available in sizes from 4 mm to 25 mm. The maximum amount of expansion on these reamers is 1% over the nominal size. For example, a 10 mm diameter reamer can be expanded to 10.1 mm (10 + 1%). On *inch expansion hand reamers*, the limit of adjustment is up to .006 in. over the nominal size on reamers

up to 1/2 in. and about .015 in. on reamers over 1/2 in. The cutting end of the reamer is ground to a slight taper for easy starting.

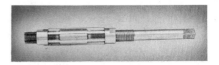

Fig. 5-27   An adjustable hand reamer

The *adjustable hand reamer* (Fig. 5-27) has tapered slots cut in the body for the entire length. The inner edge of the cutting blades have a corresponding taper so that the blades remain parallel for any setting. The blades are adjusted to size by upper and lower adjusting nuts. *Metric adjustable hand reamers* are available in sizes from #000 (adjustable from 6.4 to 7.2 mm) to #16 (adjustable from 80 to 95 mm). The blades on inch adjustable hand reamers have an adjustment range of 1/32 in. on the smaller reamers to almost 5/16 in. on the larger ones. They are manufactured in sizes 1/4 to 3 in. in diameter.

Courtesy Whitman & Barnes

Fig. 5-28   A roughing taper reamer

Taper reamers are made to standard tapers and are used to finish tapered holes accurately and smoothly. They may be made with either spiral or straight teeth. Because of its shearing action and its tendency to reduce chatter, the spiral-fluted reamer is superior to the straight one. A *roughing reamer* (Fig. 5-28), with nicks ground at intervals along the teeth, is used for more rapid removal of surplus metal. These nicks or grooves break up the chips into smaller sections; they prevent the tooth from cutting and overloading along its entire length. When a roughing reamer is not available, an old taper reamer is often used prior to finishing the hole with a finishing reamer.

The *finishing taper reamer* (Fig. 5-29) is used to finish the hole smoothly and to size after the roughing reamer. This reamer, which has either straight or left-hand spiral flutes, is designed to remove only a small amount of metal (about 0.25 mm) from the hole. Since taper reamers do not clear themselves readily, they should be removed frequently from the hole and the chips cleared from the flutes.

Courtesy Whitman & Barnes

Fig. 5-29   A finishing taper reamer

To Ream a Hole with a Straight Reamer

1. Check the size of the drilled hole. It should be between 0.10 mm and 0.25 mm smaller than the finished hole size.
2. Place the end of the reamer into the hole and place the tap wrench on the square end of the reamer.
3. Rotate the reamer in a clockwise direction to allow it to align itself with the hole.
4. Check the reamer for squareness with the work by testing it with a square at several points around the circumference.
5. Brush cutting fluid over the end of the reamer if required.
6. Rotate the reamer slowly in a clockwise direction and apply downward pressure. Feed should be fairly rapid and steady to prevent the reamer from chattering.
   NOTE: The rate of feed should be about one quarter the diameter of the reamer for each turn.

Precautions when Reaming

1. Never turn a reamer backwards (counterclockwise) as it will dull the cutting teeth.
2. Use a cutting lubricant where required.

3. Always use a helical fluted reamer in a hole that has a keyway or oil groove cut in it.
4. Never attempt to remove too much material with a hand reamer; about 0.10 mm should be the maximum.
5. Frequently clear a taper reamer (and the hole) of chips.

BROACHING

Broaching is a process in which a special tapered multi-toothed cutter is forced through an opening or along the outside of a piece of work to enlarge or change the shape of the hole or to form the outside to a desired shape.

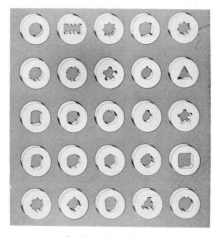

Courtesy National Broach & Machine Co.

Fig. 5-30   Examples of internal broaching

Broaching was first used for producing internal shapes, such as keyways, splines, and other odd internal shapes (Fig. 5-30). Its application has been extended to exterior surfaces, such as the flat face on automotive engine blocks and cylinder heads. Most broaching is now performed on special machines which either pull or push the broach through or along the material. Hand broaches are used in the machine shop for such operations as keyway cutting.

The cutting action of a broach is performed by a series of successive teeth,

each protruding about 0.07 mm further than the preceding tooth (Fig. 5-31). The last three teeth are generally of the same depth and provide the finish cut.

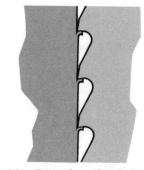

Fig. 5-31   The cutting action of a broach

Broaching has many advantages and an extremely wide range of applications.

a) It is possible to machine almost any irregular shape, providing it is parallel to the broach axis.
b) It is rapid; the entire machining process is usually completed in one pass.
c) Roughing and finishing cuts are generally combined in the same operation.
d) A variety of forms, either internal or external, may be cut simultaneously and the entire width of a surface may be machined in one pass.

Fig. 5-32   Using an arbor press to cut a keyway with a broach

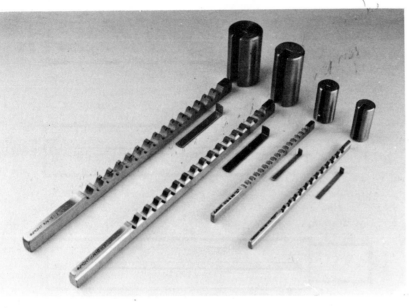

Fig. 5-33   A broach set for cutting internal keyways

CUTTING A KEYWAY WITH A BROACH

Keyways may be cut by hand in the machine shop quickly and accurately by means of a broach set and an arbor press (Fig. 5-32).

A broach set (Fig. 5-33) covers a wide range of keyways and is a particularly useful piece of equipment when many keyways must be cut. The equipment necessary to cut a keyway is a bushing to suit the hole size in the workpiece, a broach the size of the keyway to be cut, and shims to increase the depth of the cut of the broach.

Procedure

1. Determine the keyway size required for the size of the workpiece.
2. Select the proper broach, bushing, and shims.
3. Place the workpiece on the arbor press. Use an opening on the base smaller than the opening in the workpiece so that the bushing will be properly supported.

4. Insert the bushing and the broach into the opening. Apply cutting fluid if the workpiece is made of steel.

Fig. 5-34   Two shims are used when making the final pass with the broach

5. Press the broach through the workpiece (Fig. 5-34), maintaining constant pressure on the arbor-press handle.
6. Remove the broach, insert one shim, and press the broach through the hole.
7. Insert the second shim, if required, and press the broach through again. This will cut the keyway to the proper depth.
8. Remove the bushing, broach, and shims.

LAPPING

Lapping is an abrading process used to remove minute amounts of metal from a surface which must be flat, accurate to size, and smooth. Lapping may be performed for any of the following reasons.
a) to increase the wear life of a part
b) to improve accuracy and surface finish
c) to improve surface flatness, sometimes to provide better seals and eliminate the need for gaskets

Lapping may be performed by hand or machine, depending on the nature of the job. Lapping is intended only to take off small amounts of material, usually about 0.010 mm. Lapping by hand is a long, tedious process and should be avoided unless absolutely necessary because of the time required to remove a small amount of material.

LAPPING ABRASIVES

Both natural and artificial abrasives are used for lapping. Flour of emery and fine powders made of silicon carbide or aluminum oxide are used extensively. Abrasives used for rough lapping should be no coarser than 150 grit; fine powders used for finishing run up to about 600 grit.* For fine work, diamond dust, generally in paste form, is used.

*Metric grit classifications had not been determined at the time of publication.

TYPES OF LAPS

Laps may be used to finish flat surfaces, holes, or the outside of cylinders. In each case, the lap material must be *softer* than the workpiece.

FLAT LAPS

Laps for producing flat surfaces are made from close-grained cast iron. For the roughing operation or "blocking down," the lapping plate should be scored with narrow grooves about 12 mm apart, both lengthwise and crosswise or diagonally to form a square or diamond pattern (Fig. 5-35A). Finish lapping is done on a smooth cast-iron plate (Fig. 5-35B).

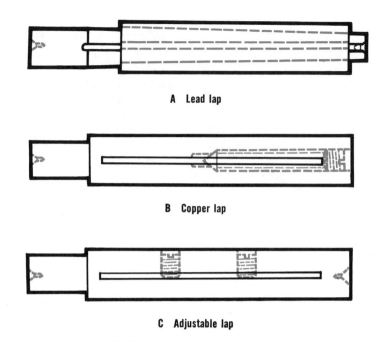

A   Lead lap

B   Copper lap

C   Adjustable lap

Fig. 5-36   Various types of internal laps

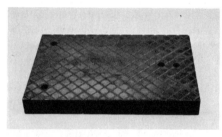

Fig. 5-35A   A roughing lapping plate

Fig. 5-35B   A finishing lapping plate

CHARGING THE FLAT LAPPING PLATE

Spread a thin coating of abrasive powder over the surface of the plate and press the particles into the surface of the lap with a hardened steel block or roll. Rub as little as possible. When the entire surface appears to be charged, clean the surface with varsol and examine it for bright spots. If any spots appear, recharge the lap until the entire surface assumes a gray appearance after it has been cleaned.

LAPPING A FLAT SURFACE

If work is to be roughed down, oil should be used on the roughing plate as a lubricant. As the work is rubbed over the lap, the abrasive powder will be washed from the grooves and act between the surface of the work and the lap. If the work has been surface ground, rough lapping or "blocking down" is not required.

Procedure

1. Place a little varsol on a finish lapping plate which has been properly charged.
2. Place the work on top of the plate, and gently push it back and forth over the full surface of the lap using an irregular movement. *Do not dwell in one spot.*
3. Continue this movement with a light pressure until the desired surface finish is obtained.

Precautions to be Observed for Flat Lapping

1. Do not dwell in one area; cover the full surface of the lap.
2. Never add a fresh supply of loose abrasive. If this is required, recharge the lap.
3. Never press too hard on the work because the lap will become "stripped" in places.
4. Always keep the lap moist.

INTERNAL LAPS

Holes may be accurately finished to size and smoothness by lapping. Internal laps may be made of brass, copper, or lead and may be of three types.

The *lead lap* (Fig. 5-36A) is made by pouring lead around a tapered mandrel which has a groove cut along its length. The lap is turned to a running fit into the hole, and it is then sometimes slit on the outside to trap the loose abrasive during the lapping operation. Adjust this type by lightly tapping the large end of the mandrel on a soft block. This will cause the lead sleeve to move along the mandrel and expand.

The *internal lap* (Fig. 5-36B) may be made of copper, brass, or cast iron. A threaded-taper plug fits into the end of the lap which is slit for almost its entire length. The lap diameter may be adjusted by the threaded-taper plug.

The *adjustable lap* (Fig. 5-36C) may be made from copper or brass. The lap is split for almost its full length, but both ends remain solid. Slight adjustment is provided by means of two set screws in the centre section of the lap.

Charging and Using an Internal Lap

Before charging, the lap should be a running fit in the hole.

1. Sprinkle some lapping powder evenly on a flat plate.
2. Roll the lap over the powder, applying sufficient pressure to embed the abrasive into the surface of the lap.
3. Remove any excess powder.
4. Mount a lathe dog on the end of the lap.
5. Fit the workpiece over the end of the lap.
   NOTE: The lap should now be a wringing fit in the hole of the work and about 2.5 times the length of the workpiece.
6. Place some oil or varsol on the lap.
7. Mount the lap and the work between lathe centres.
8. Set the machine to run at a slow speed, 150 to 200 r/min for a 25 mm diameter.
9. Grasp the work and start the machine.
10. Run the work back and forth along the entire length of the lap.
11. Remove the work and rinse in varsol to remove the abrasive and to bring it to room temperature.
12. Gauge the hole for size.

NOTE: Always keep the lap moist and never add loose abrasive to the lap. This will cause the work to become bell-mouthed at the ends. If more abrasive is necessary, recharge the lap and adjust as required.

EXTERNAL LAPS

External laps are used to finish the outside of cylindrical workpieces. They may be of several forms (Fig. 5-37); however, the basic design is the same. External laps may be made of cast iron or may have a split brass bushing mounted inside by means of a set screw. There must be some provision for adjusting the lap.

Charging and Using an External Lap

1. Mount the workpiece in a 3-jaw chuck on the lathe or drill press.
2. Adjust the lap until it is a running fit on the workpiece.
3. Grip the end of the lap in a vise.
4. Sprinkle abrasive powder in the hole.
5. With a hardened steel pin, roll the abrasive evenly around the inside surface of the lap.
6. Remove any excess lapping powder.
7. Place the lap on the workpiece. It should now be a wringing fit.
8. Set the machine to run at a slow speed (150 to 200 r/min for a 25 mm diameter piece of work).
9. Add some varsol to the workpiece and the lap.
10. Grasp the lap and start the machine.
11. Move the lap back and forth along the work.
    NOTE: Always keep the lap moist.
12. In order to gauge the work, remove the lap and clean the workpiece with varsol.

BEARINGS

Bearings contribute to the smooth operation of rotating parts of machinery and motors. They are used to support and position a shaft and to reduce the friction created by the rotating part, particularly when under load. They must also be capable of absorbing and transmitting loads for the required speeds and temperatures. Bearings may be divided into two general classifications: *plain* and *rolling*.

PLAIN TYPE BEARINGS

Plain type bearings operate on the oil film principle, that is, when rotating, the shaft is actually supported on a thin film of oil.

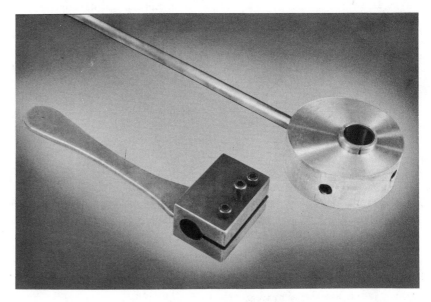

Fig. 5-37 External laps

Plain bearings are generally used in machines or components running at slower speeds. The bearing material is usually of a different material from the shaft, although great success has been claimed with hardened steel shafts rotating in hardened steel bearings at relatively high speeds. Plain bearings may be of the *solid*, *split*, or *thrust* type.

Solid bearings (Fig. 5-38) are of the sleeve type and often found in electric motors. They may be made of bronze, sintered bronze, or even cast iron in slowly rotating equipment. Straight sleeve bearings have no provision for adjustment and often present problems when not kept properly lubricated. Sleeve bearings on some machines have a slight taper on the outside to provide for wear adjustment. Bearings of sintered bronze are made by the powdered metallurgy process and often contain graphite between the bronze particles, which aids in the lubrication of the bearing. The porosity created by the powdered metallurgy process also provides a reservoir for oil. This tends to create a much longer lasting bearing than the plain bronze bushing. Sleeve bearings are usually made to standard sizes and are easily replaceable.

Fig. 5-38   A plain type sleeve bearing has no adjustment

Split bearings are often used on larger machines which operate at slower speeds. They may be made of bronze, bronze with babbitt, or have a babbitt metal lining. Adjustment is usually provided for by means of laminated shims between the upper and lower bearing halves. Oil grooves chipped or machined in the bearing provide a channel for lubrication.

Thrust bearings are used to take the longitudinal thrust of a shaft. They may be flat, kidney-shaped, babbitt-faced pieces, or shoes. They bear against a collar or collars on a shaft which rotates in oil. The bearings operate on the oil wedge principle whereby the oil is drawn up by the rotating shaft and forms a wedge between the bearing and the collar of the shaft. These bearings may be used on large equipment where there is considerable end thrust. They prevent damage to the equipment and maintain the position of the rotating part.

ROLLING TYPE BEARINGS

Rolling bearings are used in preference to plain bearings for several reasons.
a) They have a lower coefficient of friction, especially at start-up.
b) They are compact in design.
c) They have high running and dimensional accuracy.
d) The wear is not as great as on plain type bearings.
e) They are easily replaced because of standardized sizes.

The following rolling bearing types are commonly available.

A. RADIAL BEARINGS
1. *Ball Bearings*
   a) single row deep groove ball bearing
   b) double row deep groove ball bearing
   c) single row angular contact ball bearing
   d) double row angular contact ball bearing
   e) self-aligning ball bearing

2. *Roller Bearings*
   a) cylindrical roller bearing
   b) double row spherical roller bearing
   c) single row spherical roller bearing
   d) tapered roller bearing
   e) needle bearing

B. THRUST BEARINGS
   a) ball thrust bearing
   b) cylindrical roller thrust bearing
   c) spherical roller thrust bearing
   d) taper roller thrust bearing

TYPES OF RADIAL BEARINGS

Ball bearings (Fig. 5-39) are widely used because of their low coefficient of friction and their suitability for high speeds. They are capable of absorbing medium to high radial and thrust loads. Ball bearings may be of single row design for light to medium loads and of double row design for heavy loads. There is no means of adjustment in this type of bearing.

Courtesy FAG Bearing Company Limited

Fig. 5-39   Single and double row ball bearings

Single row angular contact ball bearings (Fig. 5-40A) are designed for high radial and high thrust loads in one direction. *Double row angular contact ball bearings* (Fig. 5-40B) are designed for high radial and high thrust loads in both directions. Both types are suitable for high speeds.

Courtesy FAG Bearing Company Limited

Fig. 5-40 Angular contact bearings provide for high radial and axial thrust

When mounting single row angular contact ball bearings, take care to have the thrust applied to the proper side of the bearing.

TYPES OF ROLLER BEARINGS

When it is necessary to support heavy loads under medium to high speeds, roller bearings are used since their basic dynamic load rating is higher than that of ball bearings of the same dimensions. The higher basic dynamic load rating is achieved by the greater area of contact between the rolling elements and the bearing raceways.

Cylindrical roller bearings (Fig. 5-41A) may be single or double row and are designed for heavy radial loads at medium to high speeds.

Double row self-aligning roller bearings (Fig. 5-41B) consist of two rows of rollers, either spherical or barrel-shaped, revolving in a spherical outer race. They are capable of absorbing very high radial loads and moderate thrust loads in both directions. The self-aligning feature of these bearings permits shaft deflection up to 0.5° without impairing the basic dynamic load rating.

Tapered roller bearings (Fig. 5-41C) are manufactured as single row, double row, or four row and are capable of absorbing high radial and high thrust loads at moderate speeds. Provision for adjustment makes these bearings versatile. They are used extensively in machine tool manufacture.

Needle bearings employ long cylindrical rollers of small diameter. They are used where a longer bearing surface is required and where limited installation space is available. Needle bearings are designed for radial loads and moderate speeds.

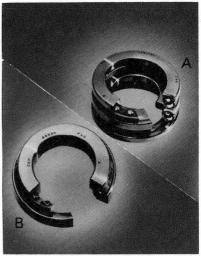

Courtesy FAG Bearing Company Limited

Fig. 5-42 Ball and roller thrust bearings

TYPES OF THRUST BEARINGS

Thrust bearings consist of a set of balls or rollers held in a retainer ring between two races or washers. They are designed for heavy thrust loads and, in some instances, for combined high thrust and medium radial load.

Ball thrust bearings (Fig. 5-42A) are designed for medium to high thrust loads at moderate speeds. No radial load may be applied.

Roller thrust bearings may be of two types: cylindrical roller and spherical roller.

a) *Cylindrical roller thrust bearings* (Fig. 5-42B) are designed for high thrust load and low speed. No radial load can be applied.

b) *Spherical roller thrust bearings* are capable of aborbing very high thrust loads and moderate radial loads at low speeds. The track in the housing washer is spherical, which permits a shaft misalignment of 3°.

Bearing Installation

When a bearing must be replaced, it is advisable to select a duplicate bearing for replacement. If another make of bearing is chosen, the maker's catalogue should be

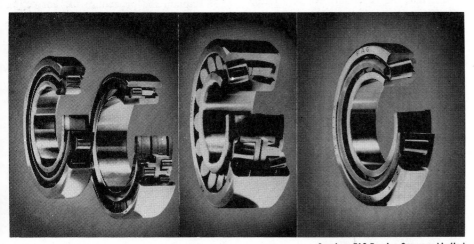

Courtesy FAG Bearing Company Limited

A — Single and double row cylindrical   B — Double row self aligning   C — Taper
Fig. 5-41 Types of roller bearings

consulted so that a bearing of the same specifications is used. Once the replacement bearing has been secured, the following precautions should be observed in the installation of rolling bearings.

1. Check the shaft and housing tolerances.
2. Make sure tolerances are within the range recommended by the bearing supplier.
3. Clean the installation area and mating parts.
4. Do not unwrap the bearings until they are required for installation.
5. Do not expose a bearing to dust or dirt.
6. Do not wash a new bearing as this will remove the protective film.
7. Under no condition mount the bearing by exerting force over or through the rolling elements.

NOTE: The outer ring is generally a hand push fit into the housing while the inner ring has a light to heavy interference fit on the shaft (depending on the application).

LUBRICATION OF BALL AND ROLLER BEARINGS

Bearings operating under moderate speed and temperature conditions are generally lubricated with grease, since grease can easily be retained in the bearings and housings. It also tends to create a seal to keep out dirt and foreign matter. Oil lubrication is generally used on bearings operating at high speeds and temperatures and also in such mechanisms as closed gear trains.

Double-sealed or shielded bearings are lubricated by the manufacturer and, unless special provisions have been made, may not be relubricated.

PRECAUTIONS IN HANDLING BEARING LUBRICANTS

Because of the danger of any small particles of dirt or grit entering the bearings, grease or oil should be stored in covered containers. Grease fittings and oil caps should be wiped clean before lubricant is added. Over-lubrication of ball and roller bearings must be avoided since this may result in high operating temperatures, rapid deterioration of the lubricant, and premature bearing failure.

HAND TOOLS AND BENCH WORK QUESTIONS

THE BENCH VISE

1. What is the advantage of the swivel base vise over the solid base vise?
2. How may finished work be held in a vise without the surface being marred or damaged?

HAMMERS

3. Describe the most common hammer used by a machinist.
4. For what purpose are soft-faced hammers used?

SCREWDRIVERS

5. List three important points which should be observed in the care of a screwdriver.
6. Explain the procedure for regrinding the tip of a screwdriver blade.

THE HAND HACKSAW

7. Compare the flexible blade and the solid, or all-hard, hacksaw blade.
8. What pitch hacksaw blade should be selected to cut:
   a) tool steel?
   b) thin wall tubing?
   c) angle iron and copper?
9. What procedure is recommended if a saw blade breaks or becomes dull in a partially finished cut?

FILES

10. Describe and state the purpose of:
    a) single cut files
    b) double cut files

11. Name the most commonly used degrees of coarseness in which files are manufactured.
12. List four important points which should be observed in the care of files.
13. How can "pinning" of a file be kept to a minimum?
14. Describe and state the purpose of:
    a) long-angle lathe files
    b) aluminum files
    c) shear tooth files
15. Describe and state the purpose of:
    a) swiss pattern files
    b) die sinker rifflers
16. Compare rotary files and ground burrs.
17. List three important points which should be observed when rotary files or ground burrs are used.

HAND TAPS

18. Name, describe, and state the purpose of the three taps in a set.
19. Define tap drill size.
20. Use the formula and calculate the tap drill size for:
    a) 1/2 — 13 NC tap
    b) M 42 — 4.5 mm tap
21. Why should care be used when a hole is being tapped?
22. Explain the procedure for correcting a tap which has not started squarely.
23. Briefly explain the method of removing a broken tap using a tap extractor.

HAND REAMERS

24. What is the purpose of a hand reamer?
25. Describe and state the purpose of:
    a) the solid hand reamer
    b) the adjustable hand reamer
    c) the taper finishing reamer
26. How much metal should be removed with a hand reamer?
27. List four important precautions which should be observed while reaming.

BROACHING

28. Define the term "broaching".

29. Describe the cutting action of a broach.
30. State three advantages of broaching.
31. Briefly describe the procedure for broaching a keyway on an arbor press.

LAPPING

32. State three reasons for lapping.
33. What abrasives are generally used for lapping?

34. Why must the lap be softer than the workpiece?
35. Explain the procedure for charging a flat lapping plate.
36. Briefly describe the process of lapping a flat surface.
37. How are internal laps charged?

BEARINGS

38. Explain the difference between a plain type and an anti-friction type bearing.

39. Why are anti-friction bearings preferred over plain type bearings?

40. Name three types of ball bearings and state the purpose of each.

41. Describe and state the purpose of any three types of roller bearings.

42. List three important precautions which should be observed when bearings are being installed.

6 PHYSICS OF METAL CUTTING

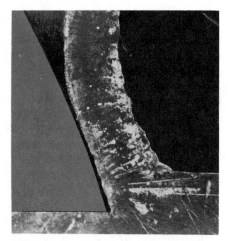

Courtesy Cincinnati Milacron Inc.

Fig. 6-1 The simile of an axe splitting wood was often used incorrectly to illustrate the action of a cutting tool

Throughout civilization man has continually used new developments without fully understanding the theory behind them. The cave man used fire to cook his food but he had no knowledge of pyrology; in early battles, man used the boughs of trees to hurl large stones although he did not have a knowledge of physics or trajectory. Many hundreds of years ago, iron was mined, smelted, and forged into swords by the craftsmen of Damascus although metallurgy was then unknown. Without knowledge of basic fundamentals, man progresses at a slow rate, but progress accelerates tremendously as these fundamentals are understood.

Man has been using tools to cut metal for hundreds of years without really understanding how the metal was cut or

Courtesy Cincinnati Milacron Inc.

Fig. 6-2 A false conception of metal cutting

what was occurring where the cutting tool met the metal. For many years, it was felt that the metal ahead of the cutting tool split in a manner similar to the way that wood splits in front of an axe (Fig. 6-1). This, according to the original theory, accounted for the wear which occurred on the cutting tool face some distance away from the cutting edge. An early cutting fluid advertisement illustrated this same theory by showing the metal splitting in front of a cutting tool during a lathe-turning operation (Fig. 6-2).

NEED FOR METAL CUTTING RESEARCH

The manufacture of dimensionally accurate, closely fitting parts is essential to interchangeable manufacture. The accuracy and wearability of mating surfaces is directly proportional to the surface finish produced on the part. Every year in the United States alone, over 1.3 billion tonnes of metal are cut into chips at a cost of well over 10 billion dollars. In order to reduce the cost of machining, prolong the life of cutting tools, and maintain high surface finishes, it was essential for research to be carried out in the area of metal cutting. Since the Second World War, a great deal of research has been conducted in areas such as the theory of metal cutting, measurement of cutting forces and temperatures, machinability of metals, machining economics, and the theory of cutting fluid action. This research has found that metal of the workpiece, instead of rupturing or breaking a little before the cutting tool, is compressed and then flows up the face of the cutting tool. New cutting tools, speeds and feeds, cutting tool angles and clearances, and cutting fluids have been developed as a result of this research. All of these new developments have greatly assisted in the economical machining of metals; however, much work remains to be done before all the factors affecting surface finish, tool life, and machine output are controlled.

METAL CUTTING TERMINOLOGY

A number of terms resulted from the research conducted on metal cutting, and it may be wise to clearly define these terms.

Courtesy Cincinnati Milacron Inc.

Fig. 6-3A   Chip-tool interface

A built-up edge is a layer of compressed metal from the material being cut which adheres to and piles up on the cutting tool edge during a machining operation (Fig. 6-3A).

The chip-tool interface is that portion of the face of the cutting tool upon which the chip slides as it is cut from the metal (Fig. 6-3A).

Crystal elongation is the distortion of the crystal structure of the work material which occurs during a machining operation (Fig. 6-3B).

Courtesy Cincinnati Milacron Inc.

Fig. 6-3B   A photomicrograph of a chip showing the crystal elongation and plastic deformation

The deformed zone is the area in which the work material is deformed during a cutting action.

Plastic deformation is the deformation of the work material occurring in the shear zone during a cutting action (Fig. 6-3B).

Plastic flow is the flow of metal occurring on the shear plane which extends from the cutting tool edge A to the corner between the chip and the unmachined work surface B in Fig. 6-3B.

A rupture is the tear that occurs when brittle materials, such as cast iron, are cut and the chip breaks away from the work surface. This generally occurs when discontinuous or segmented chips are produced.

The shear angle or plane is the angle of the area of material where plastic deformation is occurring (Fig. 6-3A).

The shear zone is the area where plastic deformation of the metal occurs. It is along a plane from the cutting edge of the tool to the original work surface.

PLASTIC FLOW OF METAL

In order to understand more fully what occurred to the metal while it was being deformed in the shear zone, researchers made many tests on various types of materials. Flat punches were used on ductile material to study the stress pattern, direc-

tion of material flow, and the distortion created in the metal. To observe easily what occurs when pressure is applied to one spot, blocks of photoelastic materials, such as celluloid and bakelite, were used in tests. Stress lines created when pressure was exerted on the punch were observed by polarized light, through a suitable analyzer, as a series of coloured bands known as *isochromatics*.

Three different types of punches (flat, narrow-faced, and knife-edge) were used on the photoelastic material to observe the various stresses created.

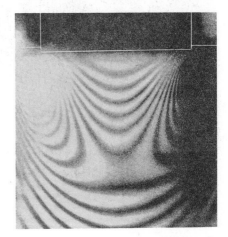

Courtesy Cincinnati Milacron Inc.

Fig. 6-4   The stress distribution created by a flat punch in photoelastic material

FLAT PUNCH

When a flat punch is forced into a block of photoelastic material, the lines of constant maximum shearing stress appear, indicating the distribution of stress. In Fig. 6-4, the shape of these stress lines, or isochromatics, appears as a family of curves almost passing through the corners of the flat punch. The greatest concentration of stress lines occurs at each corner of the punch, and larger circular stress lines appear further away from the punch. The spacing of the isochromatics is relatively wide.

NARROW-FACED PUNCH

When a narrow-faced punch is forced into a block of photoelastic material, the stress lines are still concentrated at the punch corners and where the punch meets the top surface of the work. As can be noted in Fig. 6-5, the isochromatics are spaced closer than with the flat punch.

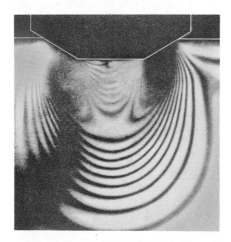

Courtesy Cincinnati Milacron Inc.

Fig. 6-5 The stress distribution created by a narrow-faced punch

KNIFE-EDGE PUNCH

When a knife-edge punch is forced into the block of photoelastic material (Fig. 6-6), the isochromatics become a series of circles tangent to the two faces of the punch. In this case, the flow of material occurs upward from the point towards the free area along the faces of the punch.

When a cutting tool engages a workpiece, this flow of material takes place, and the compressed material escapes up the tool face. As the tool advances, opposition to the upward flow of material creates stresses in the material ahead of the tool, due to the friction of the chip flow up the tool face. These stresses are somewhat relieved by the plastic flow or rupture of the material along a plane leading from the cutting edge of the tool to the surface of the unmachined metal. From Figs. 6-4, 6-5, and 6-6 it can be concluded

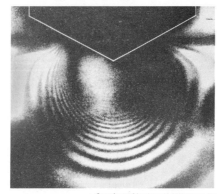

Courtesy Cincinnati Milacron Inc.

Fig. 6-6 The stress lines created by a knife-edge punch

that internal stresses are created during metal-cutting operations.

a) Because of the forces exerted by the cutting tool, a compression of metal occurs in the material.

b) As the cutting tool or work moves forward during a cut, the stress lines concentrate at the cutting tool edge and radiate from here to the material (Fig. 6-6).

c) This concentration of stresses causes the chip to shear from the material and flow along the chip-tool interface.

d) By either plastic flow or rupture, the metal tries to flow along the chip-tool interface. Since most metals are ductile to some degree, a plastic flow generally occurs.

Whether plastic flow or rupture occurs as the metal flows along the chip-tool interface will determine the type of chip which will be produced. When brittle materials, such as cast iron, are being cut, the metal has a tendency to rupture and produce discontinuous or segmented chips. When relatively ductile metals are being cut, a plastic flow occurs, and continuous or flow-type chips are produced.

CHIP FORMATION

Machining operations performed on lathes, shapers, milling machines, or similar machine tools, produce chips which fall into three basic types: discontinuous chip (Fig. 6-7A), continuous chip (Fig. 6-7B), and continuous chip with a built-up edge (Fig. 6-7C).

TYPE 1 - DISCONTINUOUS (SEGMENTED) CHIP

Discontinuous or segmented chips (Fig. 6-7A) are produced when brittle metals, such as cast iron and hard bronze, or some ductile metals are cut under poor

Courtesy Cincinnati Milacron Inc.

Fig. 6-7A Discontinuous chip

Courtesy Cincinnati Milacron Inc.

Fig. 6-7B Continuous chip

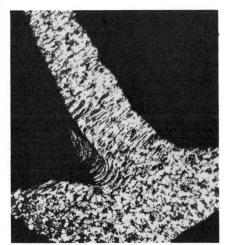

Courtesy Cincinnati Milacron Inc.

Fig. 6-7C   Continuous chip with a built-up edge

cutting conditions. As the point of the cutting tool contacts the metal, some compression occurs, as can be noted in Fig. 6-8B and C, and the chip begins flowing along the chip-tool interface. As more stress is applied to brittle metal by the cutting action, the metal compresses until it reaches a point where rupture occurs (Fig. 6-8D) and the chip separates from the unmachined portion. This cycle is repeated indefinitely during the cutting operation with the rupture of each segment occurring on the shear angle or plane. Generally, as a result of these successive ruptures, a poor surface is produced on the workpiece.

Excessive machine chatter sometimes causes discontinuous chips to be produced when ductile metal is cut.

The following conditions would be favourable to the production of a type 1 discontinuous chip:

a) brittle work material

b) small rake angle on the cutting tool

c) large chip thickness (coarse feed)

d) low cutting speed

TYPE 2 - CONTINUOUS CHIP

The type 2 chip is a continuous ribbon produced when the flow of metal next to

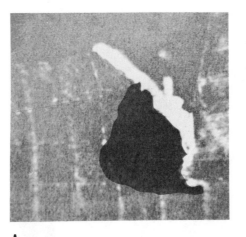

A

B

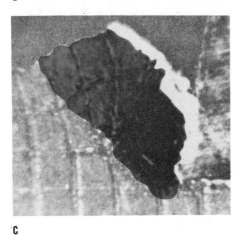

C

the tool face is not greatly retarded by a built-up edge or friction at the chip-tool

D

E

Courtesy Cincinnati Milacron Inc.

Fig. 6-8A,B,C,D,E   Formation of a discontinuous chip

interface. The continuous ribbon chip is considered ideal for efficient cutting action because it results in better surface finishes.

When ductile materials are cut, plastic flow in the metal takes place by the deformed metal sliding on a great number of crystallographic slip planes. As is the case with the type 1 chip, fractures or ruptures do not occur because of the ductile nature of the metal.

In Fig. 6-3B it can be seen that the crystal structure of the ductile metal is elongated when it is compressed by the action of the cutting tool and as the chip separates from the metal. The process of chip formation occurs in a single plane

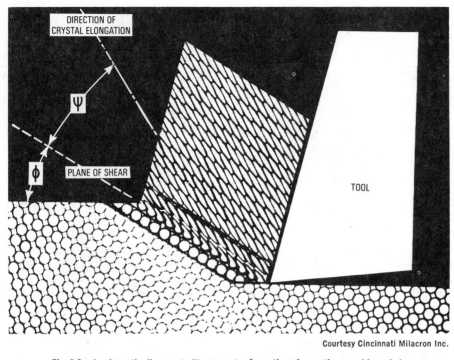

Courtesy Cincinnati Milacron Inc.

Fig. 6-9   A schematic diagram to illustrate the formation of a continuous chip and show the deformation of the crystal structure

extending from the cutting tool to the unmachined work surface. The area where plastic deformation of the crystal structure and shear occurs is called the *shear zone*. The angle on which the chip separates from the metal is called the *shear plane* or *shear angle*.

The mechanics of chip formation can best be understood with the aid of the schematic diagram in Fig. 6-9. As the cutting tool or work progresses, the metal immediately ahead of the cutting tool is compressed with resultant deformation or elongation of the crystal structure. This elongation does not take place in the direction of shear. As this process of compression and elongation continues, the material above the cutting edge is forced along the chip-tool interface and away from the work.

Machine steel generally forms a continuous (unbroken) chip with little or no built-up edge when machined with a cemented-carbide cutting tool. In order to reduce the amount of resistance occurring as the compressed chip slides along the chip-tool interface, a suitable rake angle is ground on the tool, and cutting fluid is used during the cutting operation. This allows the compressed chip to flow relatively freely along the chip-tool interface. A shiny layer on the back of a continuous-type chip indicates ideal cutting conditions with little resistance to chip flow.

The conditions favourable to producing a type 2 continuous chip are:
a) ductile work material
b) small chip thickness (relatively fine feeds)
c) sharp cutting tool edge
d) a large rake angle on the cutting tool
e) high cutting speeds
f) the cutting tool and work kept cool by use of cutting fluids
g) a minimum of resistance to chip flow by:
   i) a high polish on the cutting tool face

ii) use of cutting fluids to prevent the formation of a built-up edge
iii) use of cutting-tool materials, such as cemented carbides, which have a low coefficient of friction.

TYPE 3 - CONTINUOUS CHIP WITH A BUILT-UP EDGE

Low-carbon machine steel, when cut with a high-speed steel cutting tool without the use of cutting fluids, generally produces a continuous type chip with a built-up edge.

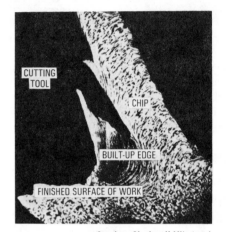

Courtesy Cincinnati Milacron Inc.

Fig. 6-10   A type 3 continuous chip with a built-up edge being formed

The metal ahead of the cutting tool is compressed and forms a chip which begins to flow along the chip-tool interface (Fig. 6-10). As a result of the high temperature, the high pressure, and the high frictional resistance against the flow of the chip along the chip-tool interface, small particles of metal begin adhering to the edge of the cutting tool while the chip shears away. As the cutting process continues, more particles adhere to the cutting tool; a larger buildup results, which affects the cutting action. The built-up edge increases in size and becomes more unstable; eventually a point is reached where fragments are torn off. Portions of these fragments which break off stick to both the chip and the workpiece. The buildup and break-down of the built-up edge occur rapidly during a cutting action and cover the machined surface with a multitude of built-up fragments. These fragments adhere to and score the machined surface; the result is a poor surface finish.

The continuous chip with the built-up edge, as well as creating a poor surface finish on the workpiece, also shortens the cutting tool life. Two factors have an effect on the cutting tool life with this type of chip.

a) The fragments of the built-up edge cause an abrasion of the tool flank as they escape with the workpiece and chip.

b) A cratering effect is caused a short distance back from the cutting edge where the chip contacts the tool face. As this cratering continues, it eventually extends closer to the cutting edge until fracture or breakdown occurs.

MACHINABILITY OF METALS

Machinability describes the ease or difficulty with which a metal can be machined. Such factors as cutting tool life, surface finish produced, and power required must be considered. Machinability has been measured by the length of the cutting tool life in minutes or by the rate of stock removal in relation to the cutting speed employed, that is, depth of cut. For finish cuts, machinability refers to the life of the cutting tool and the ease with which a good surface finish is produced.

GRAIN STRUCTURE

The machinability of a metal is affected by its microstructure and will vary if the metal has been annealed. The ductility and shear strength of a metal can be modified greatly by operations such as annealing and normalizing. Certain chemical and physical modifications of steel will improve their machinability. Free-machining steels have generally been modified in the following manner by:

a) the addition of sulphur
b) the addition of lead
c) the addition of sodium sulphite
d) cold working which modifies the ductility

By making these (free-machining) modifications to the steel, three main machining characteristics become evident:

a) Tool life is increased.
b) A better surface finish is produced.
c) Lower power consumption is required for machining.

LOW-CARBON (MACHINE) STEEL

The microstructure of low-carbon steel may have large areas of ferrite (iron) interspersed with small areas of pearlite (Fig. 6-11A and B). Ferrite is soft with high ductility and low strength, while pearlite, a combination of ferrite and iron carbide, has low ductility and high strength. When the amount of ferrite in steel is greater than pearlite or the ferrite is arranged in alternate layers with pearlite (Fig. 6-11C and D), the amount of power required to remove material increases and the surface finish produced is poor. Fig. 6-12 illustrates a more desirable microstructure in steel because the pearlite is well distributed and is therefore better for machining purposes.

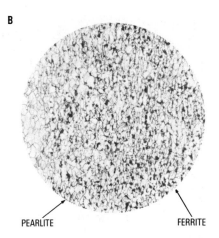

PEARLITE   FERRITE

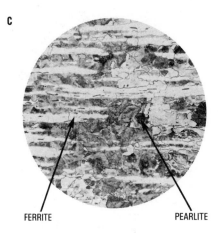

FERRITE   PEARLITE

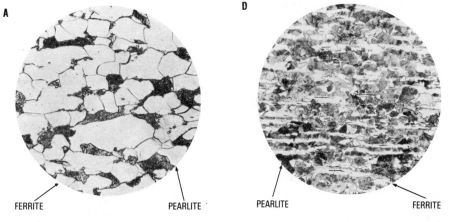

A
FERRITE   PEARLITE

D
PEARLITE   FERRITE

Courtesy Cincinnati Milacron Inc.

Fig. 6-11A,B,C,D Photomicrographs indicating undesirable steel microstructures

A

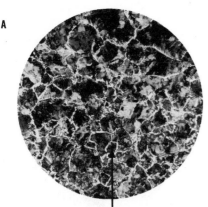

QUENCHED AND TEMPERED
STRUCTURE

B

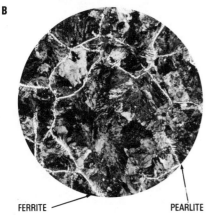

FERRITE   PEARLITE

Courtesy Cincinnati Milacron Inc.

Fig. 6-12A & B   Photomicrographs showing a desirable microstructure in steel

HIGH-CARBON (TOOL) STEEL

A greater amount of pearlite is present in high-carbon (tool) steel because of the higher carbon content. The greater the amount of pearlite (low ductility and high strength) present in the steel, the more difficult it becomes to machine the steel efficiently. It is, therefore, desirable to anneal these steels to alter their microstructure and, as a result, improve their machining qualities.

ALLOY STEEL

Alloy steels, which are a combination of two or more metals, are generally a little more difficult to machine than low- or high-carbon steels. In order to improve their machining qualities, combinations of sulphur and lead or sulphur and manganese in proper proportions are sometimes added to alloy steels. A combination of normalizing and annealing is also used with some types of alloy steels to create desirable machining characteristics. The machining of *stainless steel*, generally difficult because of its work-hardening qualities, can be greatly eased by the addition of selenium.

CAST IRON

Cast irons, consisting generally of ferrite, iron carbide, and free carbon, form an important group of materials used by industry. The microstructure of cast iron can be controlled by the addition of alloys, the method of casting, the rate of cooling, and by heat treating. *White cast iron* (Fig. 6-13A), cooled rapidly after casting, is usually hard and brittle because of the formation of hard iron carbide. *Grey cast iron* (Fig. 6-13B) is cooled gradually; its structure is composed of compound pearlite, a mixture of fine ferrite and iron carbide, and flakes of graphite. Because of the gradual cooling, it is softer and therefore easier to machine.

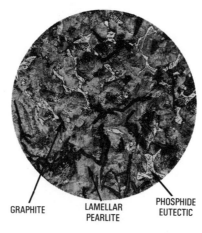

GRAPHITE   LAMELLAR   PHOSPHIDE
               PEARLITE   EUTECTIC

Courtesy Cincinnati Milacron Inc.

Fig. 6-13A   The microstructure of white cast iron

MOTTLED GRAY AND
WHITE IRON

Courtesy Cincinnati Milacron Inc.

Fig. 6-13B   The microstructure of grey cast iron

Iron carbide and the presence of sand on the outer surface of the casting generally make cast iron a little difficult to machine. Through annealing, the microstructure is altered. The iron carbide is broken down into graphitic carbon and ferrite; the cast iron is thus made easier to machine. The addition of silicon, sulphur, and manganese gives cast iron different qualities and improves its machinability.

CUTTING TOOL SHAPE

The shape of the cutting tool is very important to the efficient removal of metal. Every time a machine must be stopped to recondition or replace a worn cutting tool, production rates decrease. The life of a cutting tool is generally reported as:

a) the number of minutes that the tool has been cutting

b) the length which was cut

c) the number of cubic centimetres (cm³) or cubic inches that has been removed

d) in the case of drills, the number of millimetres or inches of hole depth that has been drilled

To prolong cutting tool life, reduce the friction between the chip and the tool as much as possible. This can be accomplished by providing the cutting tool with a suitable rake angle and by highly polishing the cutting-tool face with a honing stone. The polished cutting face reduces the friction on the chip-tool interface, reduces the size of the built-up edge, and generally results in better surface finish. The rake angle on cutting tools allows chips to flow away freely and reduces friction and the amount of power required for the machining operation.

Fig. 6-14A   Large rake angle ground on a cutting tool

The rake angle of the cutting tool also affects the shear angle or plane of the metal which in turn determines the area of plastic deformation. If a *large rake angle* is ground on the cutting tool, a large shear angle is created in the metal during the cutting action (Fig. 6-14A). The results of a large shear angle are:

a) A thin chip is produced.
b) The shear zone is relatively short.
c) Less heat is created in the shear zone.
d) Good surface finish is produced.
e) Less power is required for the machining operation.

A *small or negative rake angle* on the cutting tool (Fig. 6-14B) creates a small shear angle in the metal during the cutting process with the following results:

a) A thick chip is produced.

b) The shear zone is long.
c) More heat is produced.
d) The surface finish is not quite as good as with large rake angle cutting tools.
e) More power is required for the machining operation.

Two types of rake angles are found on cutting tools: *positive rake* (Fig. 6-14A) where the point of the cutting tool and the cutting edge contact the metal first and *negative rake* (Fig. 6-14B) where the face of the cutting tool contacts the metal first. Each type of rake angle serves a specific purpose. The type used depends upon the machining operation being performed and the characteristics of the work material. Rake angles can be ground on cutting tools or, in the case of cutting tool inserts, they can be held in suitable holders which provide the rake angle desired.

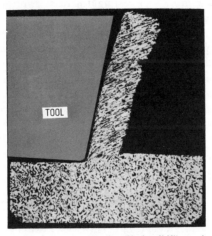

Fig. 6-14B   Small or negative rake angle ground on a cutting tool

POSITIVE RAKE ANGLE

A positive rake angle (Fig. 6-14A) is considered best for the efficient removal of metal. It creates a large shear angle at the shear zone, reduces friction and heat, and allows the chip to flow freely along the chip-tool interface. Positive rake angle cutting tools are generally used for continuous cuts on ductile materials which are not too hard or abrasive in character. Even

though positive rake angle tools remove metal efficiently, they are not recommended for all work materials or cutting applications. The following factors must be considered when the type and the amount of rake angle for a cutting tool are being determined.

a) the hardness of the metal to be cut
b) the type of cutting operation (continuous or interrupted)
c) the material and shape of the cutting tool
d) the strength of the cutting edge

NEGATIVE RAKE ANGLE

A negative rake angle (Fig. 6-14B) is used for interrupted cuts and when the metal is tough or abrasive in quality. A negative rake angle on the tool creates a small shear angle at the rear zone; therefore more friction and heat are created. Although the increase in heat may seem to be a disadvantage, it is desirable when tough metals are machined with carbide cutting tools. Face milling cutters with carbide tool inserts are a good example of the use of negative rake for interrupted and high speed cutting.

The advantages of negative rake on cutting tools are:

a) The shock of the work meeting the cutting tool is on the face and not the point or edge, which prolongs the life of the tool.
b) The hard outer scale on the metal does not contact the cutting edge.
c) Surfaces with interrupted cuts can be readily machined.
d) Higher cutting speeds can be employed.

The shape of a chip can be altered in a number of ways to improve the cutting action and reduce the power required. A continuous *straight* ribbon chip on a lathe can be changed to a continuous curled ribbon by a chip breaker being ground behind the cutting edge of the tool. A helix angle on a milling cutter affects the cutting performance by providing a shearing action when the chip is removed.

TOOL LIFE

The wear or abrasion of the cutting tool will determine its life. Three types of wear are generally associated with cutting tools: *flank wear*, *nose wear*, and *crater wear* (Fig. 6-15).

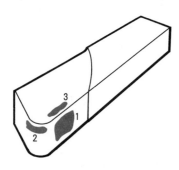

Fig. 6-15   The tool wear of a cutting tool
1 flank wear 2 nose wear 3 crater wear

Flank wear is the wear occurring on the side of the cutting edge as a result of friction between the side of the cutting-tool edge and the metal being machined. Too much flank wear increases friction and makes more power necessary for machining. When the flank wear is 0.40 to 0.80 mm long, the tool requires regrinding.

Nose wear is the wear occurring on the nose or point of the cutting tool as a result of friction between the nose and the metal being machined. Wear on the nose of the cutting tool affects the quality of the surface finish on the workpiece.

Crater wear is the wear occurring a slight distance away from the cutting edge as a result of the chips sliding along the chip-tool interface due to a built-up edge on the cutting tool. Too much crater wear eventually breaks down the cutting edge.

The following factors affect the life of a cutting tool:
a) the type of material being cut
b) the microstructure of the material
c) the hardness of the material
d) the type of surface on the metal (smooth or scaly)
e) the material of the cutting tool
f) the profile of the cutting tool
g) the type of machining operation being performed
h) speed, feed, and depth of cut

THE EFFECTS OF TEMPERATURE AND FRICTION

In the process of cutting metals, heat is created by:
a) the plastic deformation occurring in the metal during the process of forming a chip
b) the friction created by the chips sliding along the cutting-tool face

The cutting temperature varies with each type of metal and increases with the cutting speed employed and the rate of metal removal. The *greatest heat* is generated when cutting ductile material of high tensile strength, such as steel. The *lowest heat* is generated when cutting soft material of low tensile strength, such as aluminum. The maximum temperature attained during the cutting action will affect the cutting tool life, quality of the surface finish, rate of production, and accuracy of the workpiece.

At times, the temperature of metal immediately ahead of the cutting tool comes close to the melting temperature of the metal being cut. This great heat affects the life of the cutting tool. High-speed steel cutting tools cannot withstand the same high temperatures that cemented-carbide tools can without the cutting edges breaking down.

High-speed steel cutting tools can withstand temperatures of about 540°C; however, above this the heat tends to soften them, and the cutting edge breaks down.

Cemented-carbide cutting tools can be used efficiently at temperatures up to 870°C. The carbide tools are harder than high-speed steel tools, but also have a greater wear-resistance. Therefore, much higher cutting speeds can be used with carbide tools than with high-speed steel tools.

FRICTION

For efficient cutting action, it is important that the friction between the chip and tool face be kept as low as possible. As the coefficient of friction increases, the more possibility there is of a built-up edge forming on the cutting edge. The larger the built-up edge, the more friction is created, which results in the breakdown of the cutting edge and poor surface finish. Every time the machine must be stopped to regrind or replace a cutting tool, production rates decrease.

The temperature created by the friction also affects the accuracy of the machined part. Even though the workpiece does not reach the same temperature as the cutting-tool point, it is still high enough to cause the metal to expand. If a part that has been heated by the cutting action is machined to size, the part will be smaller than required when it cools to room temperature. A good supply of cutting fluid will help reduce friction at the chip-tool interface and also help maintain efficient cutting temperatures.

SURFACE FINISH

Many factors affect the surface finish produced by a machining operation, the most common being the feed rate, the nose radius of the tool, the cutting speed, and the temperature generated during the machining process.

If a high temperature is created during the cutting action, there is a marked tendency for a rough surface finish to result. The reason for this is that at high temperatures metal particles tend to adhere to the cutting tool and form a built-up edge. A direct relationship between the temperature of the workpiece and the quality of the surface finish is illustrated in Fig. 6-16.

Courtesy Cincinnati Milacron Inc.

Fig. 6-16A   Machining aluminum at 95°C

Fig. 6-16A shows the results of machining a piece of aluminum without cutting fluid at 95°C. The rough surface finish indicates the presence of a built-up edge on the cutting tool. The same piece of aluminum was machined under the same conditions, but at a room temperature of 24°C (Fig. 6-16B). A considerable improvement can be noted between

Courtesy Cincinnati Milacron Inc.

Fig. 6-16B   Machining aluminum at 24°C

Courtesy Cincinnati Milacron Inc.

Fig. 6-16C   Machining aluminum cooled to −50°C

the surface finishes of the samples in Figs. 6-16A and B. When the piece of aluminum was cooled to −50°C and machined, a further improvement in the surface finish was evident. By cooling the work material to −50°C the temperature of the cutting tool edge was considerably reduced and resulted in a much better surface finish than that which was produced at 95°C.

EFFECTS OF CUTTING FLUIDS

Cutting fluids are important to most machining operations in that they make it possible to cut metals at higher rates of speed. They perform two important functions.
a) They reduce the temperature of the cutting action.
b) They reduce the friction of the chips sliding along the tool face.
Some cutting fluids form a nonmetallic film on the metal surface which prevents the chip from sticking to the cutting edge. This prevents a built-up edge from forming and as a result a better surface finish is produced. The surface finish of most metals can be improved considerably by the use of the proper types of cutting fluids.

Cutting fluids are generally used when machining steel, alloy steel, brass, and bronze with high-speed steel cutting tools. As a rule, cutting fluids are not generally used with cemented carbide tools, unless a great quantity of cutting fluid can be applied to ensure uniform temperatures, which will prevent the carbide inserts from cracking. Cast iron, aluminum, and magnesium alloys are generally machined dry; however, cutting fluids have been used with good results in some cases.

PHYSICS OF METAL CUTTING QUESTIONS

1. Explain the original theory of what occurred during a metal cutting operation.

2. Why was extensive research carried out in the area of metal cutting?
3. Explain the new theory of what occurs when a cutting tool removes a chip from a piece of metal.

METAL CUTTING TERMINOLOGY
4. Define the following metal cutting terms:
   a) built-up edge
   b) chip-tool interface
   c) plastic deformation
   d) shear angle or plane

PLASTIC FLOW OF METAL
5. Why was research conducted to determine the plastic flow in metal?
6. Briefly describe what occurs when the following are forced into a block of photoelastic material:
   a) a flat punch
   b) a narrow-faced punch
   c) a knife-edge punch
7. Describe the two fundamental processes which are involved in metal cutting.

CHIP FORMATION
8. Describe briefly how each of the chip types are produced:
   a) discontinuous
   b) continuous
   c) continuous with a built-up edge
9. Which is the most desirable chip? Give reasons for your answer.
10. What conditions must be present in order to produce the type 2 chip?
11. Explain how a built-up edge is formed, and state its effect on the cutting tool life.

MACHINABILITY OF METALS
12. Define *machinability*.
13. What factors affect the machinability of a metal?
14. Compare the microstructure of low-carbon and high-carbon steels with respect to their machinability.

15. How can the machining qualities of alloy steels be improved?

16. What factors in cast iron make it a little difficult to machine? How can these factors be altered?

CUTTING TOOL SHAPE

17. Name two methods which can be used to improve the life of a cutting tool.

18. What results can be expected from grinding a large rake angle on the cutting tool?

19. How does negative rake on a tool affect the cutting process?

20. Compare the advantages and disadvantages of positive and negative rake angles.

TOOL LIFE

21. Define *flank wear*, *nose wear*, and *crater wear*.

22. List six important factors that affect the life of a cutting tool.

EFFECTS OF TEMPERATURE AND FRICTION

23. Name two methods by which heat is created during machining.

24. How does high temperature affect a machining operation?

25. Why is it important that friction between the chip and tool be kept to a minimum?

SURFACE FINISH

26. What common factors determine surface finish?

27. Why does high temperature affect the surface finish produced?

EFFECTS OF CUTTING FLUIDS

28. List four ways in which cutting fluids assist the machining of metals.

29. What precaution should be taken when cutting fluids are used with carbide tools?

7 CONTOUR BANDSAW

Courtesy DoALL Company

The vertical bandsaw is the latest basic machine tool to be developed. Since its development in the early 1930s, it has been widely accepted by industry as a fast and economical method of cutting metal and other materials.

Band cut-off saws differ from power hacksaws in that they have a continuous cutting action on the workpiece, while the latter cuts only on the forward stroke and on a limited section of the blade.

The contour-cutting bandsaw (vertical bandsaw) offers several features not found on other metal cutting machines. These advantages are illustrated in Fig. 7-1.

BASIC BANDSAW APPLICATIONS

Many operations may be performed on the contour bandsaw much faster than on other types of machines. These basic applications are as follows.

Notching. Sections of metal can be removed in one piece rather than in chips.

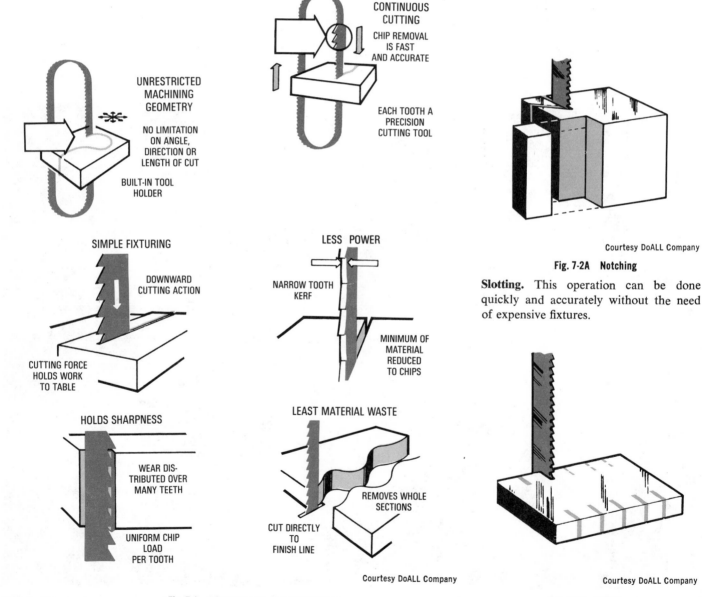

UNRESTRICTED MACHINING GEOMETRY

NO LIMITATION ON ANGLE, DIRECTION OR LENGTH OF CUT

BUILT-IN TOOL HOLDER

CONTINUOUS CUTTING

CHIP REMOVAL IS FAST AND ACCURATE

EACH TOOTH A PRECISION CUTTING TOOL

SIMPLE FIXTURING

DOWNWARD CUTTING ACTION

CUTTING FORCE HOLDS WORK TO TABLE

LESS POWER

NARROW TOOTH KERF

MINIMUM OF MATERIAL REDUCED TO CHIPS

HOLDS SHARPNESS

WEAR DISTRIBUTED OVER MANY TEETH

UNIFORM CHIP LOAD PER TOOTH

LEAST MATERIAL WASTE

REMOVES WHOLE SECTIONS

CUT DIRECTLY TO FINISH LINE

Courtesy DoALL Company

Courtesy DoALL Company

Fig. 7-2A Notching

Slotting. This operation can be done quickly and accurately without the need of expensive fixtures.

Courtesy DoALL Company

Fig. 7-1 Advantages of a contour bandsaw

Fig. 7-2B Slotting

Three-dimensional shaping. Complicated shapes may be cut; simply follow the layout lines.

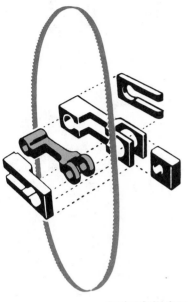

Courtesy DoALL Company

Fig. 7-2C   Three dimensional shaping

Radius cutting. Internal or external contours may be cut easily. Internal sections are generally removed in one piece as shown.

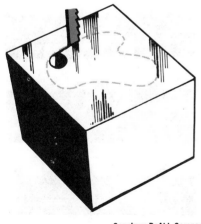

Courtesy DoALL Company

Fig. 7-2D   Radius cutting

Splitting. This can be accomplished quickly with a minimum waste of material.

Courtesy DoALL Company

Fig. 7-2E   Splitting

Angular cutting. The work may be clamped at any angle and fed through the saw. The table may be tilted for compound angles.

Courtesy DoALL Company

Fig. 7-2F   Angular cutting

CONTOUR BANDSAW CONSTRUCTION

The construction of contour band machines differs from most other machines in that the band machine is generally fabricated from steel rather than being of cast construction. There are three basic parts to the contour bandsaw (Fig. 7-3).

BASE

The *base* supports the *column* and houses the *variable-speed drive assembly* which drives the *lower band carrier wheel*, which in turn drives the *saw band* or blade. It also houses the *air pump* which provides air to blow the chips away from the cutter-work interface. The worktable is attached to the base by means of a *trunnion* (Figs. 7-4, 7-11), which permits the table to be tilted 45° to the right or 10° to the left for making angular cuts. The *lower saw guide* is attached to the base of the trunnion. Mounted in the worktable is the removable *filler plate slide* and the *centre plate*. Hydraulic feed models have a *hydraulic reservoir* and *pump* for operating the power-feed table, as well as a *coolant system* incorporated in the base.

COLUMN

The *column* supports the *head*, the left-hand *blade guard*, and the *welding unit and grinder* which is used to weld, anneal, and grind the saw blades. It houses the control to the variable-speed drive unit and provides mounting positions for the *start/stop buttons*, the *band tension indicator*, and the *speed indicator*.

HEAD

The *head* houses the *upper saw band carrier* and its *tension* and *tracking controls*. It supports the *adjustable saw guide post* which in turn supports the *upper saw guide*, the *saw band guard*, and the *air nozzle*. The saw guide may be adjusted vertically and locked in place by means of handles at the back of the head casing.

Band machines may be of two types. The machine used in many toolrooms has two band carrier wheels, while the larger capacity saws have three carrier wheels

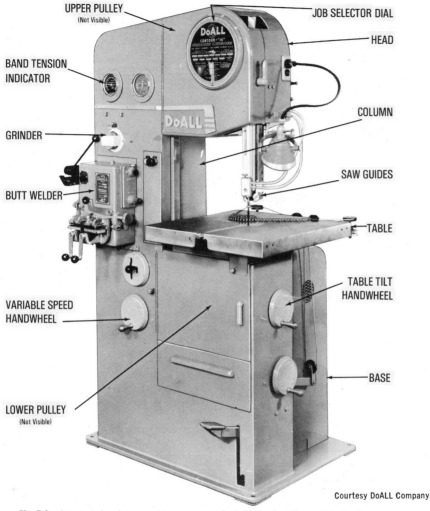

UPPER PULLEY (Not Visible)

JOB SELECTOR DIAL

BAND TENSION INDICATOR

HEAD

GRINDER

COLUMN

BUTT WELDER

SAW GUIDES

TABLE

TABLE TILT HANDWHEEL

VARIABLE SPEED HANDWHEEL

BASE

LOWER PULLEY (Not Visible)

Courtesy DoALL Company

Fig. 7-3   A contour bandsaw provides an economical means of cutting metals to shape

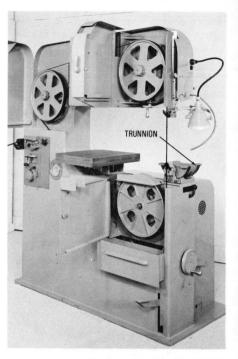

TRUNNION

Courtesy "Fundamentals of Band Machining," Delmar Publishers, Inc.

Fig. 7-4   A three carrier wheel contour bandsaw with the table removed

(Fig. 7-4). On the larger capacity saws, both upper wheels may be tilted so that the band will track properly. When the blade in this type of machine becomes too short, it need not be discarded. It may be shortened to fit over the upper and lower band carrier wheels (Fig. 7-4); the capacity of the machine is reduced, but this adjustment permits the economical use of the saw blade.

BANDSAW BLADE TYPES AND APPLICATIONS

There are three kinds of blades commonly used in bandsawing: carbon-alloy, high-speed steel, and tungsten carbide tipped blades. In order to obtain the best results from any bandsaw, it is necessary to select the proper blade for the job. Consideration must be given to the kind of saw-blade material, tooth form, pitch set, width, and gauge for the material being cut.

TOOTH FORMS

Carbon and high-speed steel blades are available in three types of tooth forms (Fig. 7-5).

Precision or regular tooth. This is the most generally used type of tooth. It has a zero rake angle and about 30° back clearance angle. It is used when a fine finish and an accurate cut are required.

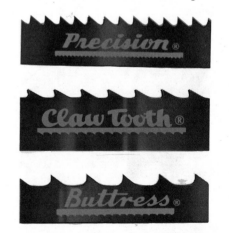

Courtesy DoALL Company

Fig. 7-5   Bandsaw blade tooth forms

Claw or hook tooth. This tooth form has a positive rake on the cutting face and slightly less back clearance than the precision or buttress blade. It has the same general application as the buttress-tooth form. It is faster cutting and longer lasting than the buttress tooth, but will not produce as smooth a finish.

Buttress or skip tooth. This tooth form is similar to the precision tooth; however, the teeth are spaced further apart to provide more chip clearance. The tooth angles are the same as on the precision type. Buttress, or skip-tooth, blades are used to advantage on thick work sections and on deep cuts in soft material.

PITCH

Each of the tooth forms is available in various pitches, or numbers of teeth per standard reference length. Metric saw blade pitch is determined by the number of teeth per 25 mm; inch blade pitch by the number of teeth per inch.

The thickness of the material to be cut determines the pitch of the blade to be used. When cutting thick materials, use a coarse-pitch blade; thin materials require a fine-pitch blade. It is well to remember when the proper pitch is being selected that there must be at least two teeth in contact with the material being cut.

SET

The set of a blade is the amount that the teeth are offset on either side of the centre to produce clearance for the back of the band or blade. There are three common set patterns (Fig. 7-6).

Raker set has one tooth offset to the right, one to the left, while the third tooth is straight. This is the most common pattern and is used for most sawing applications.

Wave set has a group of teeth offset to the right and the next group to the left, a pattern which produces a wave-like appearance. Wave set blades are generally

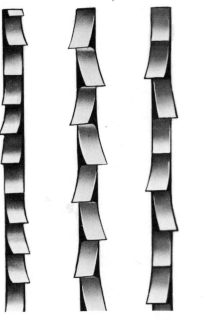

Courtesy DoALL Company

Fig. 7-6   Common set patterns
(A) Wave   (B) Straight   (C) Raker

used when the cross section of the workpiece changes, such as on structural-steel sections or on pipe.

Straight set has one tooth offset to the right and the next to the left. It is used for cutting light nonferrous castings, thin sheet metal, tubing, and Bakelite.

WIDTH

When making straight, accurate cuts, it is advisable to select a wide blade. Narrow blades are used to cut small radii. Radius charts, advising the proper width blade to use for contour sawing, are generally found on all bandsaws. When selecting a blade for contour cutting, it is advisable to select the widest blade which can cut the smallest radius on the workpiece.

GAUGE

The gauge is the thickness of the saw blade. This has been standardized according to the width of the blade. Blades up

TO INCREASE	Faster Tool Velocity (more teeth per min)	Slower Tool Velocity (less teeth per min)	Finer Pitch Band Tool (more teeth & smaller gullets)	Coarser Pitch Band Tool (less teeth & larger gullets)	Slower Feeding Rate (decreases chip load)	Faster Feeding Rate (increases chip load)	Medium Feeding Rate	Claw Tooth (positive rake angle)	Precision & Buttress (0° rake angle)
CUTTING RATE	✔			✔		✔		✔	
TOOL LIFE		✔	✔				✔	✔	
FINISH	✔		✔		✔				✔
ACCURACY	✔				✔				

TRY ONE OR MORE OF THE FOLLOWING (column header spanning)

JOB REQUIREMENT CHART

TABLE 7-1

to 1/2 in. (12.7 mm■) wide are .025 in. (0.64 mm■) thick, 5/8 in. (15.88 mm■) and 3/4 in. (19.05 mm■) blades are .032 in. (0.81 mm■) thick, while 1 in. (25.4 mm■) wide blades are .035 in. (.89 mm■) thick. Since thick blades are stronger than thin blades, the thickest blade possible should be used for sawing tough material.

At the time of publication, gauges were not available in metric sizes. The soft conversions to metric are provided for information only.

JOB REQUIREMENTS

The bandsaw operator should be familiar with the various types of blades and be able to select the one which will do the job to the specified requirements of finish and accuracy at the lowest cost. Table 7-1 will serve as a guide to more efficient cutting.

THE SAW BAND WELDING ATTACHMENT

The butt welder (Fig. 7-7) adds greatly to the versatility of the bandsaw. It permits the blade to be conveniently welded for the removal of internal sections. Blades can be cut from coil stock and welded into a continuous band, while broken blades may be welded and used again. Welders on vertical bandsaws are resistance-type welders which fuse the ends of the blade together when the correct current is applied and the blade is held properly.

In addition to knowing how to select the proper blade for the job, the operator must also be able to weld the blade. Improper welds will cause the blade to break, and it will require rewelding which is costly and time-consuming. Unless the weld is as strong as the band itself, it is not a good weld. In making a weld, the butted ends of the blade must not overlap in width, set, or pitch of the teeth.

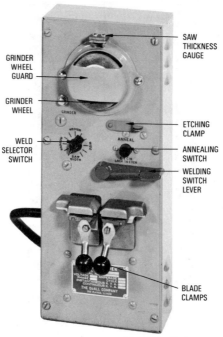

Courtesy DoALL Company

Fig. 7-7   Parts of a butt welder

To Weld a Bandsaw Blade

1. Select the proper blade for the job by checking the chart on the machine.
2. Determine the length of blade required. The blade length for a two-wheel machine is determined by adding twice the centre-to-centre distance of the wheels plus the circumference of one wheel. If the upper

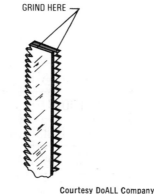

GRIND HERE

Courtesy DoALL Company

Fig. 7-8   Method of grinding blade ends prior to welding

wheel is extended the full distance, deduct 25 mm to allow for the stretch of the blade.

3. Place the blade in the cut-off shear, and cut it to the required length. Make sure that the blade is held straight and up against the blade-squaring bar on the shear.
4. If the ends of the blade are not square, hold them firmly with the teeth reversed, as in Fig. 7-8, and grind both ends in one operation.
   If the ends are not square after grinding, it will not matter since when the blade ends are placed together for welding, the ends will match perfectly.
5. In order to get the proper tooth spacing after the blade has been welded, it is necessary to grind off some teeth at the ends of the blade to the depth of the gullet prior to welding. This is necessary since the welding operations on a DoALL welder consume about 5 mm of the blade length. Other types of welders may vary in the blade length consumed by welding. The number of teeth that are ground off will depend on the pitch of the blade. Fig. 7-9 illustrates the amount to grind off each type of blade from 4 to 10 pitch.
6. Clean the welder jaws and position the inserts for the blade size and pitch.
7. Adjust the jaw pressure by turning the selector handle for the width of the blade being welded.

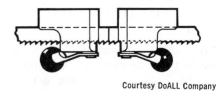

Courtesy DoALL Company

Fig. 7-10   Blade clamped properly for welding

8. Clamp the blade as shown in Fig. 7-10. Make sure that the blade is against the aligning surface on the

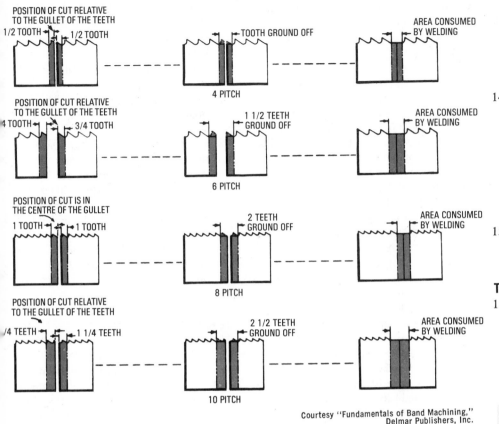

POSITION OF CUT RELATIVE
TO THE GULLET OF THE TEETH
1/2 TOOTH — 1/2 TOOTH

TOOTH GROUND OFF

AREA CONSUMED
BY WELDING

4 PITCH

POSITION OF CUT RELATIVE
TO THE GULLET OF THE TEETH
4 TOOTH — 3/4 TOOTH

1 1/2 TEETH
GROUND OFF

AREA CONSUMED
BY WELDING

6 PITCH

POSITION OF CUT IS IN
THE CENTRE OF THE GULLET
1 TOOTH — 1 TOOTH

2 TEETH
GROUND OFF

AREA CONSUMED
BY WELDING

8 PITCH

POSITION OF CUT RELATIVE
TO THE GULLET OF THE TEETH
/4 TEETH — 1 1/4 TEETH

2 1/2 TEETH
GROUND OFF

AREA CONSUMED
BY WELDING

10 PITCH

Courtesy "Fundamentals of Band Machining,"
Delmar Publishers, Inc.

Fig. 7-9 Amounts to grind off various blades to achieve proper tooth spacing

back of the jaws and centred between the two jaws. If the ends of the blades do not butt against each other for the full width, they should be removed and reground.

9. Depress the welding switch or lever and hold it until the weld has cooled. *NOTE*: Stand to one side and wear safety glasses to avoid injury from the welding flash.

10. Release the movable jaw clamp and then release the welding lever.

11. Remove the blade and check the weld for the following points.
    i) The flash material should be uniform on both sides
    ii) The spacing of the teeth should be uniform.
    iii) The weld should be in the centre of the gullet.
    iv) The back of the blade should be straight.

    If the blade does not meet all of these requirements, it should be broken, prepared again, and rewelded.

12. Move the reset lever to the anneal position and clamp the blade, with the weld in the centre of the jaws and the teeth to the rear.

13. Set the selector switch at the proper setting for the blade to be annealed. Push in the anneal switch button and jog it intermittently until the band reaches a dull red colour.

CAUTION: Do not permit the blade to become too hot at this time as it will air harden on cooling. As the weld starts to cool, jog the anneal switch occasionally to permit the blade to cool slowly.

14. Remove the blade and grind off the welding flash. Grind the weld to the same thickness as the blade, being careful not to grind the teeth. Continually check the thickness of the blade in the thickness gauge located on the welder. When properly ground, it should just slide through the thickness gauge.

15. After the blade has been ground to the proper thickness, it is advisable to anneal the blade to a blue colour.

To Mount a Saw Band

1. Select and mount the proper saw inserts in the upper and lower saw guides using the proper gauge for the thickness of the blade being used. Allow 0.03–0.05 mm clearance to ensure that the blade will not bind.

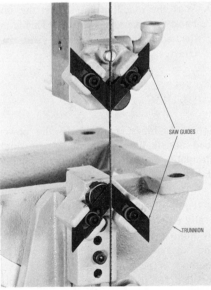

Courtesy DoALL Company

Fig. 7-11 Upper and lower saw guides of bandsaw with table removed. Note table support or trunnion

2. Lower the upper saw band carrier wheel to ensure that the blade will slide over the wheels when installed.

3. Mount the blade over the upper and lower wheels with the teeth pointing downward.

4. Adjust the upper wheel until some tension is registered on the blade-tension gauge.

5. Set the gearshift lever in the neutral position and turn the upper saw band wheel by hand to see that the saw band rides on the centre of the crown. If the saw is not tracking properly, the upper wheel must be tilted until the saw band rides on the centre of the crown. When the blade is tracking properly, it should be very close to, but not touching, the back-up bearing when the saw is not cutting.

6. Re-engage the gearshift lever and close the doors on the upper and lower carrier housing.

7. Replace the filler plate in the table.

8. Lower the upper saw guide as close as possible to the work in order to ensure a straight and accurate cut.

9. Start the machine and adjust the saw band to the proper tension. This is indicated on the band-tension gauge and chart.

COOLANTS

Some machines, particularly the power feed models, have a cooling system which circulates and discharges coolant against the faces of the blade and work.

In fixed table machines where coolant is required, a mist coolant system is generally employed. The mist system uses air to atomize the coolant and direct it onto the faces of the blade and the work. This method is very efficient and is recommended for the high-speed machining of nonferrous metals, such as aluminum and magnesium alloys. Tough, hard-to-machine alloys can also be cut successfully using the mist coolant system.

Grease type lubricants and coolants may be applied directly to the blade to assist in cutting on machines having no coolant system.

POWER FEED

Some of the heavier band cutting machines are equipped with power-feed tables. The work and the table are fed towards the blade by means of a hydraulic feed system.

On fixed table machines, power feeding is accomplished by means of a device which uses the force of gravity to provide a steady mechanical feeding pressure. This allows the operator to use both hands to guide the work into the saw. The workpiece is held against a work jaw and is forced into the blade by means of cables and pulleys.

The force applied to the blade can be varied up to about 360 N. However, for regular sawing, the feeding force of about 130–180 N should be used.

Greater feed force may be used for sawing straight lines than for cutting contours. In order to determine the feed to use for any particular job or operation, consult the job selector dial on the band-saw.

BANDSAW OPERATIONS

To Cut an External Section

1. Study the print and check the layout for accuracy.

2. Check the job selector and determine the proper blade to use for the job. Consideration must be given to the material, thickness, type of cut (straight or curved), and the finish desired.
   NOTE: When making curved cuts, it is advisable to use as wide a blade as possible.

3. Mount the proper saw blade and guides on the machine.

4. Place the work on the table and lower the upper saw guide until it

just clears the work by 5 mm. Clamp the guide in place.

5. Start the machine and see that the band is tracking properly.

6. Consult the job selector dial and set the proper speed.

7. Place the material against the work-holding jaw or against a block of wood.

8. Carefully bring the workpiece up to the blade and start the cut.
   NOTE: When the workpiece is to be finished by some other machining operation, the cut should be made about 0.8 mm outside the layout line.

9. Carefully feed the workpiece into the saw. *Do not use too much force. Keep fingers clear of the moving blade.*

10. Saw to the layout lines.

To Remove an Internal Section

The bandsaw is particularly suited to the removal of internal sections. It is possible to use this internal cutting technique to make short-run trimming and blanking dies. By this process, the internal section, or slug, becomes the punch, while the external material forms the die (Fig. 7-12). When doing work of this type, it is necessary to tilt the table to provide the proper clearance for the die.

Procedure

1. Drill a small starting hole at the correct angle shown on the print for the angular clearance on the die. This hole should just touch the layout line on the inside of the layout (Fig. 7-13).

2. Tilt the table to an angle slightly *less* than the angle of the starting hole.

3. Select a narrow, precision saw blade and cut it to the required length.

4. Thread the end of the blade through the drilled hole, with the teeth pointing in the direction of the blade travel.

5. Weld the ends of the blade.

6. Grind and anneal the weld.

Courtesy "Fundamentals of Band Machining,"
Delmar Publishers, Inc.

Fig. 7-12   The internal section can be used to make the die punch

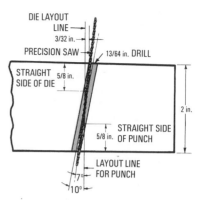

Courtesy "Fundamentals of Band Machining,"
Delmar Publishers, Inc.

Fig. 7-13   Section showing the starting hole and the sawcut angle

7. Mount the blade on the upper and lower band wheels and apply the proper tension.

8. Insert table filler plate.

9. Set the proper band speed.

10. Carefully cut out the internal section just inside the line.

11. Remove the blade from the machine.

12. Cut the blade at the weld on the cut-off shear.

13. Remove the workpiece and the blade.

NOTE: When this method is used to make a die, there is sufficient material left on the die so that it can be further machined or filed to the layout line. Once the die is finished, the excess material on the punch may be removed to fit the hole in the die.

	TABLE 7-2 SAWING PROBLEMS AND POSSIBLE CAUSES											
	Possible Cause											
Problem	Too heavy feed	Too light feed	Improper blade tracking	Improper blade tension	Saw guides too far apart	Incorrect saw speed	Pitch too coarse	Pitch too fine	Wrong type of blade	Blade dull on one side	Blade dull on both sides	Machine too light
Blade wanders	X		X	X	X					X		
Blade not cutting		X		X	X	X			X	X		X
Blade dulls quickly	X					X			X			
Poor finish	X			X	X	X	X		X	X	X	X
Severe diagonal waviness	X		X	X	X	X						X
Saw teeth chipping	X						X		X			
Saw teeth clogging						X		X	X			

ACCURACY AND FINISH

As with any other machine, the accuracy and finish produced on a bandsaw depend upon the operator's ability to properly set up and operate the machine. Table 7-2 indicates some of the problems which may be encountered and the suggested remedies.

FRICTION SAWING

Friction sawing (Fig. 7-14) is the fastest means of sawing ferrous metals up to 25 mm in thickness. In this process, the metal is fed into a bandsaw which is travelling at a high velocity (up to 4575 m/min). The tremendous heat generated by friction heats the metal immediately ahead of the saw teeth to a plastic state, and the teeth easily remove the softened metal. Since the thermal conductivity of steel is very low, the depth to which the metal is softened is only about 0.05 mm.

The temperature of the saw blade remains quite low, since each tooth is only momentarily in contact with the metal and has time to cool as it travels around the carrier wheels before contacting the metal again. This method of sawing leaves a small burr which is easily removed from the workpiece.

Friction sawing is used on hardened ferrous alloys, armour plate, and parts having a thin wall or section which would be damaged by other sawing methods. Friction sawing is particularly suited to the cutting of stainless steel alloys since this metal is difficult to cut because it work hardens so quickly. It is not suitable for sawing most cast irons because grains break off before the metal softens. Aluminum and brass cannot be cut by friction sawing because the high thermal conductivity of the metal does not let the heat concentrate just ahead of the blade. These metals also melt almost immediately after softening and will weld to the blade and clog the teeth. Most thermoplastics react in the same manner as the nonferrous metals.

Courtesy "Fundamentals of Band Machining,"
Delmar Publishers, Inc.

Fig. 7-14   Friction sawing uses a high saw band speed

Friction sawing machines resemble the standard vertical band machines, but are of heavier construction in the frame, bearings, spindles, and guides, to withstand the vibrations created by the high speeds required. The saw band is almost completely covered to protect the operator from the shower of sparks produced by friction sawing.

Friction sawing bands are made of standard carbon-alloy steel but are thicker than standard blades to provide greater strength. They may be obtained in 1/2 in., 3/4 in., and 1 in. (12.7, 19.05, and 25.4 mm▪) widths and in 10 and 14 pitch with raker set only.

The teeth on a standard saw blade travelling at the high velocity required for friction sawing would dull very quickly; therefore, the teeth on friction saws are not sharpened. Since dull teeth create more friction than sharp teeth, they are more efficient for friction sawing.

The procedure for setting up a machine for friction sawing is basically the same as for conventional sawing.

HIGH SPEED SAWING

High speed band sawing is performed at speeds ranging from 600 to 1800 m/min. It is merely a standard sawing procedure performed at higher than standard speeds on non ferrous metals, such as aluminum, brass, bronze, magnesium, zinc, and other materials such as wood, plastic and rubber.

The same machine setups and procedures apply as for conventional sawing. In high speed sawing, the chips must be removed rapidly; consequently, buttress, or claw-tooth blades are the most efficient for this operation.

BAND FILING

When a better finish than that produced by conventional sawing is required on the edge of the workpiece, it may be produced by means of a *band file*.

The band file consists of a steel band onto which are riveted a number of short, interlocking file segments (Fig. 7-15). The ends of the band are locked together to form a continuous loop. Band files may be obtained in flat, oval, and half-round cross-sections, in bastard and medium cuts, and in widths of 1/4 in., 3/8 in., and 1/2 in. (6.35, 9.53, and 12.7 mm■). Special file guides and a file-adaptor table-filler plate are used for band filing.

Fig. 7-15 Segments of a band file

To Set Up for Band Filing

1. Select the proper band file for the job by consulting the job-selector dial. Consideration must be given to material being filed, the shape, size, and cut of the file.
2. Set the gearshift lever into neutral position.
3. Remove the saw guides and filler plate.
4. Mount the proper file guide and back-up support.
5. Lock the ends of the file blade together.
6. Mount the file band, with the teeth pointing in the proper direction, on the bandsaw carrier wheels.
   NOTE: On some makes of machines, or when filing internal sections, it may be necessary to mount the file band then join the ends.
7. Lightly tension the band.
8. Check the alignment and tracking of the file band.
9. Lower the upper guide post to the proper work thickness. The distance should not exceed 2 in. (51.4 mm■) for a 1/4 in. (6.35 mm■) file band, and 4 in. (101.6 mm■) for a 3/8 in. or 1/2 in. (9.5 or 12.7 mm■) band.
10. Mount the proper table filler plate.
11. Set the gearshift lever into low gear and start the machine.
12. Adjust the band file to the proper tension.
13. Adjust the machine to the proper speed for the material being filed.

ADDITIONAL BAND TOOLS

Although the saw blade and band file are the most commonly used, several other band tools make this machine particularly versatile.

Knife-edge blades (Fig. 7-16) are available with knife, wavy, and scalloped edges, and are used for cutting soft, fibrous materials such as cloth, cardboard, cork, and rubber. Scalloped-edge

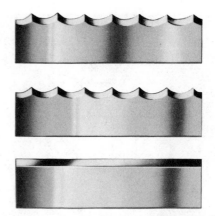

Fig. 7-16 Knife edge blades

blades are particularly suited for cutting thin corrugated aluminum. Special guides must be used with knife-edge blades.

Spiral-edge blades (Fig. 7-17) are round and have a continuous helical cutting edge around the circumference. This provides a cutting edge of 360° and permits the machining of intricate contours and patterns (Fig. 7-18) without the workpiece having to be turned.

.020 in. DIA.

.050 in. DIA.

Fig. 7-17 Spiral edge blades

Spiral-edge blades are made in two types: the spring-tempered blade which is used for plastics and wood, and the all-hard blade which is used for light metals. These blades are manufactured in diameters of .020, .040, .050, and .074 ins. (0.51, 1.02, 1.27, and 1.88 mm■). Special

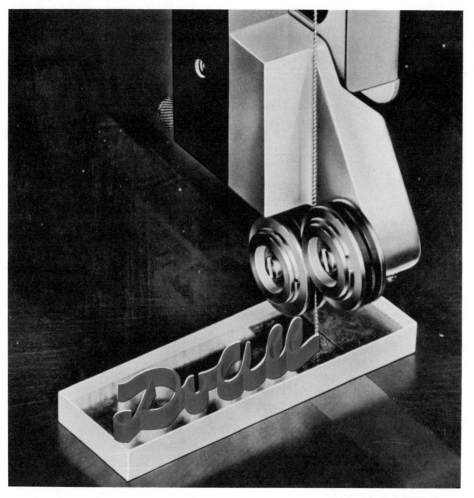

Fig. 7-18   Intricate forms may be cut with spiral edge blades

guides (Fig. 7-18) are used on the machine with this blade. When spiral blades are welded, sheet copper is used to protect the cutting edges from the welder jaws.

Line grinding bands (Fig. 7-19) have an abrasive (either aluminum oxide or silicon carbide) bonded to the thin edge of the steel band. These bands are used to cut hardened steel alloys, and other materials such as brick, marble, and glass, which could not be cut by band sawing.

This type of machining requires a high speed - 900-1500 m/min - and the use of coolant because of the heat generated. A diamond dressing stick is used to dress line grinding bands.

Diamond-edge blades (Fig. 7-20) are used to cut super-hard space-age materials, as well as ceramics, glass, silicon, and granite. This type of blade has diamond particles fused to the edges of the saw teeth. These blades operate at about 900

m/min and generally require coolant for most efficient operation.

Although diamond-edge bands are very expensive, they will outlast 200 steel blades when cutting asbestos-cement pipe.

Polishing bands are used to remove burrs and provide a good finish to surfaces which have been sawed or filed. They may also be used for sharpening carbide toolbits. A polishing band is a continuous loop of 25 mm wide abrasive cloth manufactured to a specific length to fit the machine. They are available in several grain sizes in both aluminum oxide and silicon carbide abrasive.

The polishing band is mounted in the same manner as a saw band. The special polishing guide uses the same back-up support as the file bands. A special polishing-band centre plate is used during band polishing. Most polishing bands are marked with an arrow on the back to indicate the direction of travel.

Electro-band machining (Fig. 7-21). This latest development in band machining is used to machine such materials as thin-wall tubing, stainless steel, aluminum, and titanium honeycombing.

By this process, a low voltage, high amperage current is fed into the saw blade. The workpiece is connected to the opposite pole of the circuit. When the work comes close to the fast-moving band 1800 m/min, a continuous electric spark passes from the knife edge of the saw to the work. This arc acts on the material and disintegrates it. The blade does not touch the work. Coolant is flooded onto the cutting area to prevent damage to the material by the heat created. Power feed must be used in this type of machining operations.

BANDSAW ATTACHMENTS

Several standard attachments can be obtained which will increase the scope of the band machine. Some of the most common follow.

The work-holding jaw (Fig. 7-22) is a device used by the operator to hold and guide the work into the saw. Since it is usually connected to the weight-type power feed, the operator merely steers the work with the work-holding jaw and does not have to apply any feed force.

The disc-cutting attachment (Fig. 7-23) permits the cutting of accurate circles from approximately 67-760 mm in diameter.

The cut-off and mitring attachment is used to support the work when square or angular cuts are being made.

The ripping fence provides a means for cutting long sections of flat bar stock or plate into narrow parallel sections.

When special work-holding devices are required, they are generally made in the shop to suit the specific job. These devices are usually attached to the machine table and are called *fixtures*.

Courtesy "Fundamentals of Band Machining,"
Delmar Publishers, Inc.

Fig. 7-19 Line grinding bands are used to cut hardened metals

Courtesy "Fundamentals of Band Machining,"
Delmar Publishers, Inc.

Fig. 7-20 Diamond edge blades are used to cut super hard materials

Courtesy "Fundamentals of Band Machining,"
Delmar Publishers, Inc.

Fig. 7-22   A work-holding jaw is used to guide the
work into the saw blade

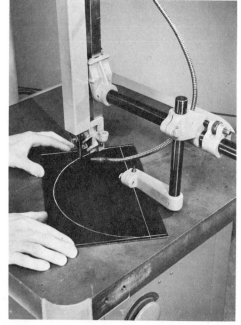

Courtesy "Fundamentals of Band Machining,"
Delmar Publishers, Inc.

Fig. 7-21   Cutting a heat exchanger by electro-
band machining

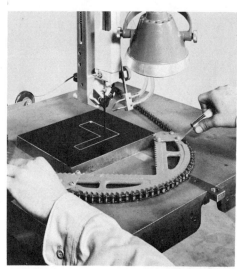

Courtesy "Fundamentals of Band Machining,"
Delmar Publishers, Inc.

Fig. 7-23   The disc cutting attachment is used to
cut circular shapes

CONTOUR BANDSAW QUESTIONS

1. Describe the cutting action of a contour bandsaw.
2. List six advantages of the contour bandsaw.

BASIC BANDSAW OPERATIONS

3. Make neat sketches of four basic operations that may be performed on the contour bandsaw.

CONTOUR BANDSAW CONSTRUCTION

4. List the parts which are contained in the
   a) base
   b) column
   c) head
5. State two advantages of a three carrier wheel contour bandsaw.

BANDSAW BLADE TYPES AND APPLICATIONS

6. Name three types of blades used in the contour bandsaw, and state their purpose.

TOOTH FORMS, PITCH, SET

7. Name three tooth forms and state the purpose of each.
8. a) What rule should be applied when selecting the proper pitch band for a job?
   b) How is the pitch on metric blades measured?
9. Name and describe three common set patterns.

WIDTH, GAUGE

10. What width blade should be selected for:
    a) a straight cut?
    b) a contour cut?
11. What is the thickness of a 1/2 in. blade? a 1 in. blade?

JOB REQUIREMENTS

12. Name four factors that can improve
    a) the cutting rate
    b) the finish

THE SAW BAND WELDING ATTACHMENT

13. List the main steps required to weld a bandsaw blade.
14. How is the length of a blade calculated when the upper carrier wheel is extended the full distance?
15. Make a sketch to show how the ends of the bandsaw are positioned for grinding prior to welding.
16. In order to obtain the correct tooth spacing, how many teeth should be ground off each end of a 10-pitch blade? A 14-pitch blade?
17. What are the characteristics of a good weld on a bandsaw blade?
18. What precautions must be observed when the flash is being ground from a blade weld?

TO MOUNT A BANDSAW BLADE

19. Describe how to make the blade track properly.
20. Why must the upper saw guide be close to the top of the work?

COOLANTS

21. Describe the principle of a mist-coolant system.
22. On what material should mist coolant be used?

POWER FEED

23. How is power feed accomplished on
    a) heavier band cutting machines?
    b) fixed table machines?

TO CUT AN EXTERNAL SECTION

24. What factors should one consider when selecting a blade for a contour cut?
25. List two precautions that will help prevent the blade from wandering.

TO REMOVE AN INTERNAL SECTION

26. List the main steps required to remove an internal section from a piece of work.
27. When a die is made, how can the internal section be used as a punch?

ACCURACY AND FINISH

28. How can the following bandsawing problems be corrected?
    a) blade wander
    b) poor finish

FRICTION SAWING

29. Describe the principle of friction sawing.
30. Why is friction sawing particularly suited to cutting stanless steel?
31. Explain why friction sawing is not suitable for sawing aluminum, brass, and thermoplastics.
32. Why are the teeth on a friction saw band dull?

HIGH-SPEED SAWING

33. How does high-speed sawing differ from friction sawing?

34. What type of blades should be used for high-speed sawing? Explain why.

BAND FILING

35. Describe a band-file blade. State what shapes, cuts, and sizes are available.
36. List the main steps required to set up the machine for band filing.
37. List the precautions to be taken when setting the upper saw-guide post.

ADDITIONAL BAND TOOLS

38. Sketch and name three types of knife bands.
39. Name five materials that can be cut satisfactorily with knife-edge bands.
40. Describe a spiral-edge band.
41. Name two types of spiral-edge bands and state two uses for each.
42. Describe a line-grinding band and state its purpose.
43. Name five materials which may be cut with a diamond-edge band.
44. At what speed should a diamond band operate?
45. In what type and grain sizes are abrasive belts manufactured?

ELECTRO-BAND MACHINING

46. Describe the principle of electro-band machining.
47. On what materials is electro-band machining used?
48. Describe and state the purpose of:
    a) a work-holding jaw
    b) a disc-cutting attachment
    c) a mitring attachment

8 DRILLING MACHINES

Courtesy Cincinnati Milacron Inc.

Probably one of the first mechanical devices developed by prehistoric man was a drill to bore holes in various materials. A bow string was wrapped around an arrow and then rapidly sawed back and forth. This process not only produced fire, but it also wore a hole in the wood. The principle of a rotating tool making a hole in various materials is the one on which all drill presses operate.

The *drilling machine* or *drill press* is an essential in any metal-working shop. Fundamentally, a drilling machine consists of a spindle which turns the drill and which can be advanced into the work, either automatically or by hand, and a work table which holds the workpiece rigidly in position as the hole is drilled. A drilling machine is used primarily to produce holes in metal; however, operations such as tapping, reaming, counterboring, countersinking, boring, and spot-facing can also be performed. A wide variety of drill presses are available, ranging from the simple sensitive drill to the highly complex automatic and numerically controlled machines.

SIZES OF DRILL PRESSES

Drilling machines vary in sizes from 12 to 30 ins. (300 to 760 mm■) in the bench, upright, and multiple-spindle machines. The size is determined by the distance from the edge of the column to the centre of the spindle; that is, a 15 in. (380 mm■) drill press will measure 15 in. (380 mm■) from the column to the centre of the spindle.

PRINCIPAL TYPES OF DRILLING MACHINES

The simplest type of precision drilling machine is the so-called *"sensitive" drill press*. It is a light, high-speed machine used primarily for drilling small parts; however, other drill press operations may also be performed on this machine.

SENSITIVE DRILL PRESS PARTS

Although drill presses are manufactured in a wide variety of types and sizes, all drilling machines contain certain basic parts. The main parts on the bench and floor type models are *base, column, table,* and the *drilling head* (Fig. 8-1). The floor type model is larger and has a longer column than the bench type.

Base – The base, usually made of cast iron, provides stability for the machine and also rigid mounting for the column. The base is usually provided with holes so that it may be bolted to a table or bench. The slots or ribs in the base allow the workholding device or the workpiece to be fastened to the base.

Column – The column is an accurate cylindrical post which fits into the base. The table, which is fitted to the column, may be adjusted to any point between the base and head. The head of the drill press is mounted near the top of the column.

Table – The table, either round or rectangular in shape, is used to support the workpiece to be machined. The table, whose surface is at 90° to the column, may be raised, lowered, and swivelled around the column. On some models it is possible to tilt the table in either direction for drilling holes on an angle. Slots are provided in

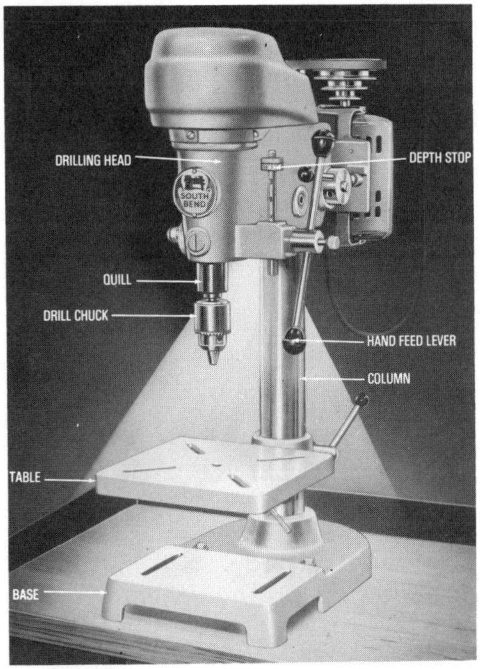

Fig. 8-1 photo labels: DRILLING HEAD, DEPTH STOP, QUILL, DRILL CHUCK, HAND FEED LEVER, COLUMN, TABLE, BASE

Courtesy South Bend Lathe Inc.

Fig. 8-1 A bench-type sensitive drill press

most tables to allow jigs, fixtures, or large workpieces to be clamped directly to the table.

Drilling Head – The head, mounted close to the top of the column, contains the mechanism which is used to revolve the cutting tool and advance it into the workpiece. The *spindle*, which is a round shaft that holds and drives the cutting tool, is housed in the *spindle sleeve* or *quill*. The spindle sleeve does not revolve but slides up and down inside the head to provide a downfeed for the cutting tool. The end of the spindle may have a tapered hole to hold taper shank tools, or may be threaded or tapered for attaching a *drill chuck* (Fig. 8-1).

The *hand feed lever* is used to control the vertical movement of the spindle sleeve and the cutting tool. A *depth stop*, attached to the spindle sleeve, can be set to control the depth that a cutting tool enters the workpiece.

UPRIGHT DRILLING MACHINE

The standard *upright drilling machine* (Fig. 8-2) is similar to the sensitive type drill, except that it is larger and heavier. The basic differences are:
a) It is equipped with a gear box to provide a greater variety of speeds.
b) The spindle may be advanced by three methods.
  i) manually with a hand lever
  ii) manually with a handwheel
  iii) automatically by the feed mechanism
c) The table may be raised or lowered by means of a table-raising mechanism.
d) Some models are equipped with a reservoir in the base for the storage of coolant.

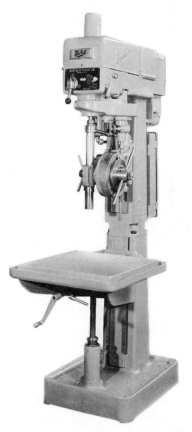

Courtesy The Canadian Blower & Forge Co. Ltd.

Fig. 8-2 A standard upright drilling machine with a square, or production-type, table

GANG DRILLS

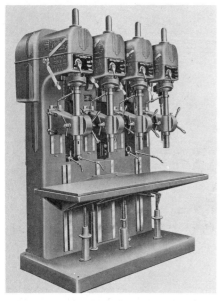

Courtesy Buffalo Forge Co.

Fig. 8-3   A gang drilling machine

Gang drills (Fig. 8-3) are drilling machines equipped with more than one work or drilling head mounted on a single table.

Courtesy The Cleveland Tapping Machine Co.

Fig. 8-4   A multi-spindle drilling head

They are used when several operations must be performed on a single job; for example, a drill, reamer, and tap may be mounted on successive spindles so that the work may be advanced quickly from one operation to the next.

For high-speed production work, a number of spindles may be mounted on a single head. This *multi-spindle head* (Fig. 8-4) may incorporate as many as 20 or more spindles on a single head driven by a drilling machine spindle. Several heads equipped with multi-spindle attachments may be combined and controlled automatically to drill as many as 100 holes in a single operation. This type of automated drilling is used, for example, by the automotive industry for the drilling of engine blocks.

RADIAL DRILLING MACHINE

The *radial drilling machine* (Fig. 8-5), sometimes called a radial-arm drill, has been developed primarily for the handling of larger workpieces than is possible on upright machines. The advantages of this machine over the upright drill are:

a) Larger and heavier work may be machined.

b) The drilling head may be easily raised or lowered to accommodate various heights of work.

c) The drilling head may be moved rapidly to any desired location, while the workpiece remains clamped in one position; this feature permits greater production.

d) The machine has more power; thus, larger cutting tools can be used.

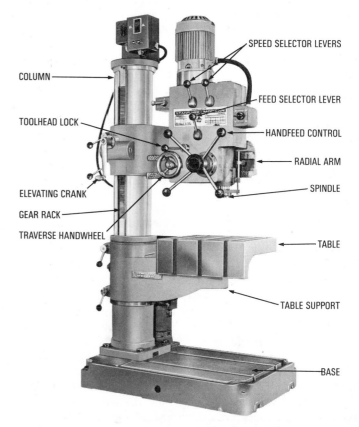

Courtesy The A. R. Williams Machinery Company Limited

Fig. 8-5   A radial drilling machine permits large parts to be drilled

e) On universal models, the head may be swivelled so that holes can be drilled on an angle.

RADIAL DRILLING MACHINE PARTS

Base. The base is made of heavy, box-type ribbed cast iron or of welded steel. The base, or pedestal, is used to bolt the machine to a floor or bench and also to provide a coolant reservoir. Large work may be clamped directly to the base for drilling purposes. For convenience in drilling smaller work, a *table* may be bolted to the base.

Column. The column is an upright cylindrical member fitted to the base which supports the radial arm at right angles.

Radial arm. The arm is attached to the column and may be raised and lowered by means of a *power-driven elevating screw*. The arm may also be swung about the column and may be clamped in any desired position. It also supports the drive motor and drilling head.

Drilling head. The drilling head is mounted on the arm and may be moved along the length of the arm by means of a *traverse handwheel*. The head may be clamped at any position along the arm. The head houses the change gears and controls for the spindle speeds and feeds. The drill spindle may be raised or lowered manually by means of the spindle-feed handles. When the spindle-feed handles are brought together, automatic feed is provided to the drill spindle.

STANDARD OPERATIONS

Drilling machines may be used for performing a variety of operations besides drilling a round hole. A few of the more standard operations, cutting tools, and work setups will be briefly discussed.

Drilling may be defined as the operation of producing a hole by removing metal from a solid mass using a cutting tool called a *twist drill*.

Fig. 8-6A   Drilling

Spot-facing is the operation of smoothing and squaring the surface around a hole to provide a seat for the head of a cap screw or a nut. A boring bar, with a pilot section on the end to fit into the existing hole, is generally fitted with a double-edged cutting tool. The pilot on the bar provides rigidity for the cutting tool and keeps it concentric with the hole. For the spot-facing operation, the work being machined should be securely clamped and the machine set to approximately 25% of the drilling speed.

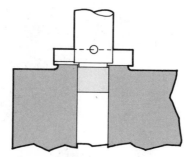

Fig. 8-6B   Spot Facing

Countersinking is the operation of producing a tapered or cone-shaped enlargement to the end of a hole.

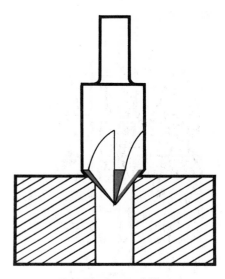

Fig. 8-6C   Countersinking

Tapping is the operation of cutting internal threads in a hole with a cutting tool called a tap. Special machine taps or gun taps are used with a tapping attachment when this operation is performed by power in a machine.

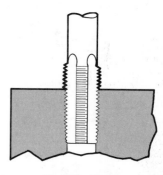

Fig. 8-6D   Tapping

Reaming is the operation of sizing and producing a smooth round hole from a previously drilled or bored hole with the use of a cutting tool having several cutting edges.

Boring is the operation of truing and enlarging a hole by means of a single point cutting tool which is usually held in a boring bar.

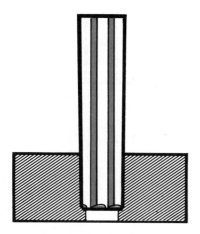

Fig. 8-6E Reaming

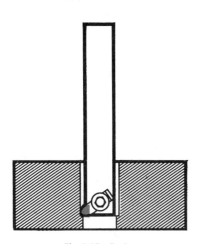

Fig. 8-6F Boring

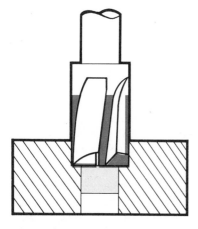

Fig. 8-6G Counterboring

Counterboring is the operation of producing a straight hole having a square shoulder on the end of an existing hole to provide a recess for the head of a cap screw or nut.

DRILL-HOLDING DEVICES

Drill-holding devices are used to hold and provide the drive to the drill. Straight drills are held in a *drill chuck* (Fig. 8-7) which may be either tightened by hand (on some models) or by a key. On larger drill presses, the chuck is held in the drill press spindle by means of a self-holding taper.

Taper shank drills may be held directly in the drill press spindle by means of a *drill sleeve* (Fig. 8-8A) or by means of a *drill socket* (Fig. 8-8B). The drill sleeve is used when the tapered shank of the drill is smaller than the taper in the drill press spindle. Drill sockets are generally used when the drill shank is larger than the taper in spindle.

Courtesy Kostel Enterprises Ltd.

Fig. 8-7 A key-type drill chuck is used for holding straight shank drills

Courtesy Kostel Enterprises Ltd.

Fig. 8-8A A drill sleeve
Fig. 8-8B A drill socket

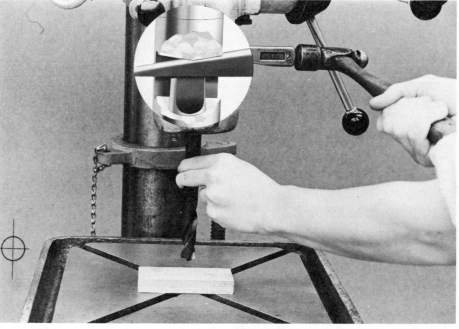

Courtesy Kostel Enterprises Ltd. and The Cleveland Twist Drill Co.

Fig. 8-9 Removing a taper-shank drill with a drill drift. Notice the board to prevent damage to the table if the drill drops.

A flat wedge-shaped tool called a *drill drift* is used to remove tapered shank drills or accessories from the drill press spindle. When using a drill drift (Fig. 8-9) always place the rounded edge up so that this edge will bear against the round slot in the spindle. A hammer is used to tap the drill drift and loosen the tapered drill shank in the spindle. A board or a piece of masonite should be used to protect the table in case the drill drops when it being removed.

WORK-HOLDING DEVICES

All workpieces must be fastened securely before cutting operations are performed on a drilling machine. If the work moves or springs during drilling, the drill usually breaks. Serious accidents can be caused by work becoming loose and spinning around during a drilling operation. Some of the commonly used work-holding devices used on drill presses are listed.

A drill vise (Fig. 8-10) may be used to hold round, rectangular, square, and odd-shaped pieces for any operation that can

Fig. 8-11   An angle drill vise permits holes to be drilled at an angle in workpieces

be performed on a drill press. It is a good practice to clamp or bolt the vise to the drill table or to provide a table stop to prevent the vise from moving during the drilling operation.

An angle vise (Fig. 8-11) has an angular adjustment on its base to allow the operator to drill holes at an angle without tilting the drill press table.

V-blocks (Fig. 8-12A), made out of cast iron or steel, are generally used in pairs to support round work for drilling. A U-shaped strap may be used to fasten the work in a V-block (Fig. 8-12A), or work may be held with a T-bolt and a strap clamp (Fig. 8-12B).

Step blocks (Fig. 8-13) are used to provide support for strap clamps when work is being fastened for drilling machine operations. They are made in various sizes and steps.

The angle plate (Fig. 8-14) is an L-shaped piece of cast iron or steel machined to

an accurate 90° angle. It is made in a variety of sizes and has slots or holes (clearance and tapped) which provide a means for fastening work for drilling. The angle plate may be bolted or clamped to the table.

Fig. 8-10   A drill vise should be clamped to the table when larger holes are being drilled

Courtesy Brown & Sharpe Mfg. Co.

Fig. 8-12A   V-blocks are used to hold round work for drilling

Fig. 8-12B   Work clamped in a V-block

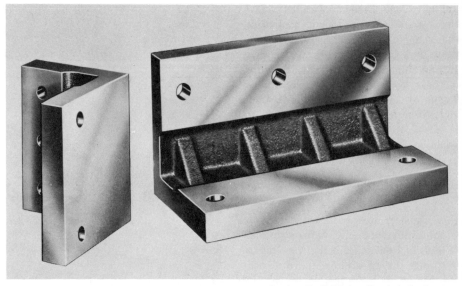

Fig. 8-14   Angle plates

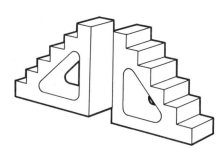

Fig. 8-13   Step blocks support the end of the clamp

Drill jigs (Fig. 8-15) are use in production for drilling holes in a large number of identical parts. They eliminate the need of laying out a hole location, avoid incorrectly located holes, and allow holes to be drilled quickly and accurately.

Clamps or straps (Fig. 8-16), used to fasten work to the drill table or an angle plate for drilling, are made in various sizes. They are usually supported at the

Fig. 8-15   A drill jig permits identical parts to be drilled quickly and accurately

end by a step block and bolted to the table by a T-bolt that fits into the table T-slot. It is good practice to place the T-bolt in the clamp or strap as close to the work as possible, so that pressure will be exerted on the workpiece. Modifications of the above clamps are the *double-finger* and *gooseneck* clamps.

Courtesy J. H. Williams & Co.

Fig. 8-16A   Finger clamp

Courtesy J. H. Williams & Co.

Fig. 8-16B   U-clamp

Courtesy J. H. Williams & Co.

Fig. 8-16C   Straight clamp

CLAMPING STRESSES

Whenever work is clamped for any machining operation, stresses are created. It is important that these clamping stresses should not be great enough to cause springing or distortion of the workpiece.

When work is to be held for drilling, reaming, or any machining operation, it is important that the workpiece be held securely. The clamps, bolts, and step blocks should be properly located and the work clamped firmly enough to prevent

movement, yet not enough to cause the workpiece to spring or distort. It is important that the clamping pressures be applied to the work, not to the packing or step block.

Fig. 8-17A illustrates the correct clamping procedure, the main pressure being applied to the workpiece.

NOTE: The step block is slightly higher than the workpiece and the bolt is close to the work.

Fig. 8-17B shows a piece of work incorrectly clamped. The bolt is located close to the step block, which is slightly lower than the workpiece. The main clamping pressure with this type of setup is applied to the step block, not the workpiece.

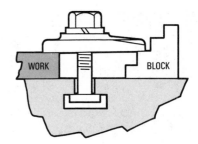

Fig. 8-17A   Work is correctly clamped when bolt is close to work

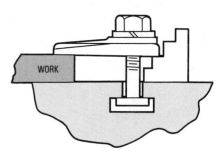

Fig. 8-17B   Work is incorrectly clamped; the clamping pressure is on the step block

Clamping Hints

The following suggestions should be observed when work is being clamped so that good clamping pressure will be obtained and work distortion avoided.

1. Always place the bolt as close as possible to the workpiece.
2. Have the packing or step block slightly higher than the work surface being clamped.
3. Insert a piece of paper between the machine table and workpiece to prevent the work from shifting during the machining process.
4. Place a metal shim between the clamp and workpiece to spread the clamping force over a wider area.
5. It is wise to use a sub-base or liner under a rough casting to prevent damage to the machine table.
6. Parts which do not lie flat on a machine table should be shimmed to prevent the work from rocking. This will prevent distortion when the work is clamped.

TWIST DRILLS

Twist drills are end-cutting tools used to produce holes in most types of material. Two helical grooves, or flutes, are cut lengthwise around the body of the drill. They provide cutting edges and space for the cuttings to escape in the drilling process. Since this is one of the most efficient cutting tools, it is necessary to know the main parts, how to sharpen the cutting edges, and the correct speeds and feeds for drilling various metals.

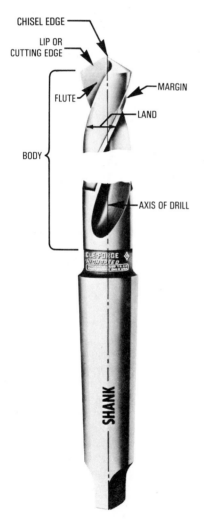

Courtesy The Cleveland Twist Drill Co.

Fig. 8-18   Parts of a twist drill

Twist drills can be made from both carbon and high-speed steels. Carbon steel drills are cheaper but are not recommended for machine shop work as the cutting edge tends to break down quickly. In most cases, high-speed steel drills have replaced carbon-steel drills since they can be operated at double the cutting speed and the cutting edge lasts longer. Since the introduction of *carbide-tipped* drills, speeds for production drilling have increased up to 300% over high-speed steel drills. Carbide drills have made it possible to drill certain materials that would not be possible with high-speed steels.

PARTS

A drill (Fig. 8-18) may be divided into three main parts: *shank, body,* and *point.*

SHANK

Generally drills up to 12 mm or ½ in. in diameter have straight shanks, while those over this diameter usually have tapered shanks (Fig. 8-18). *Straight shank* drills are held in a drill chuck; *tapered shank* drills fit into the internal taper of the drill press spindle. A tang is provided on the end of tapered shank drills to prevent the drill from slipping while it is cutting and to allow the drill to be removed from the spindle or socket without the shank being damaged.

BODY

The *body* is the portion of the drill between the shank and the point. It consists of a number of parts important to the efficiency of the cutting action.
a) The *flutes* are two or more helical grooves, cut around the body of the drill. They form the cutting edges, admit cutting fluid, and allow the chips to escape from the hole.
b) The *margin* is the narrow, raised section on the body of the drill. It is immediately next to the flutes and extends along the entire length of the flutes. Its purpose is to provide a full size to the drill body and cutting edges.
c) The *body* clearance is the undercut portion of the body between the margin and the flutes. It is made smaller to reduce friction between the drill and the hole during the drilling.
d) The *web* (Fig. 8-19) is the thin partition in the centre of the drill which extends the full length of the flutes. This part forms the chisel edge at the cutting end of the drill. The web gradually increases in thickness towards the shank to give the drill strength.

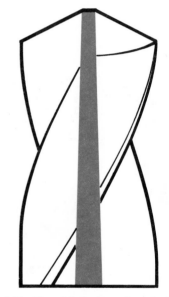

Fig. 8-19   The web is the tapered metal column which separates the flutes

POINT

The *point* of a twist drill (Fig. 8-20) consists of the chisel edge, lips, lip clearance, and heel. The chisel edge is the chisel-shaped portion of the drill point. The *lips* (cutting edges) are formed by the intersection of the flutes. The lips must be of equal length and have the same angle so that the drill will run true and will not cut a hole larger than the size of the drill.

The *lip clearance* is the relief which is ground on the point of the drill extending

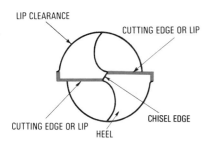

LIP CLEARANCE
CUTTING EDGE OR LIP
CUTTING EDGE OR LIP
HEEL
CHISEL EDGE

Fig. 8-20   The point of a twist drill

from the cutting lips back to the heel (Fig. 8-21). The average lip clearance is from 8 to 12° depending upon the hardness or softness of the material to be drilled.

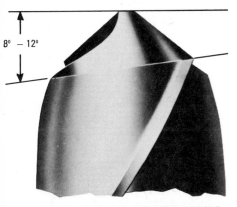

8° – 12°

Courtesy The Cleveland Twist Drill Co.

Fig. 8-21   The lip clearance angle or the relief back angle of the cutting edge should be 8-12°

SYSTEMS OF DRILL SIZES

Drill sizes are designated under four systems: Millimetre (metric), fractional, number, and letter sizes.

Millimetre (Metric) Drills are produced in a wide variety of sizes. Miniature metric drills range from 0.04 to 0.09 in steps of 0.01 mm. Straight shank standard metric drills are available in sizes from 0.5 to 20 mm. Taper shank metric drills are manufactured in sizes from 8 mm up to 80 mm.

The *fractional* size drills range from 1/64 to 3-1/4 in. varying in steps of 1/64 in. from one size to the next.

Fig. 8-22A   Checking a drill for size using a drill gauge

The *number* size drills range from #1, measuring .228 in. to #97 which measures 0.0059 in.

The *letter* size drills range from A to Z. Letter-A drill is the smallest in the set (0.234 in.) and Z is the largest (0.413 in.).

Drill sizes may be checked by using a drill gauge (Fig. 8-22A). These gauges are available in millimetre, fractional, letter, and number sizes. The size of a drill may also be checked by measuring the drill, *over the margins*, with a micrometer.

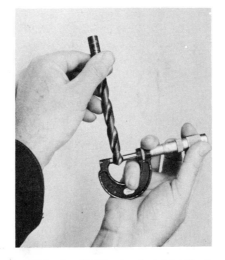

Fig. 8-22B   Checking the size of a twist drill using a micrometer

Fig. 8-23A   Core drill

SPECIAL DRILLS

The most commonly used drill is the two-fluted twist drill; however, for high production and special purposes, various types of drills are used. A few of the more common types of special drills and their uses are listed.

A core drill (Fig. 8-23A), designed with three or four flutes, is used primarily to enlarge cored, drilled, or punched holes. This drill has advantages over the two fluted drills in productivity and finish. In some cases, a core drill may be used in place of a reamer for finishing a hole. Core drills are produced in sizes from 1/4 to 3 in. in diameter.

A saw type hole cutter (Fig. 8-23B) is a cylindrical diameter cutter with a twist drill in the centre to provide a guide for cutting teeth on the hole cutter. This type of cutter is made in various diameters and is generally used for drilling holes in thin materials. It is especially valuable for drilling holes in pipe and sheet metal as little burr is produced and the cutter does not have a tendency to jam as it is breaking through.

Courtesy The L. S. Starrett Company

Fig. 8-23B   Saw-type hole cutter

Oil hole drills (Fig. 8-23C) have one or two oil holes running from the shank to the cutting point through which compressed air, oil, or cutting fluid can be forced when deep holes are being drilled. That the cutting edge is cooled and the chips flushed out are the main advantages of oil holes. These drills are generally used on turret lathes or screw machines.

Courtesy Greenfield Tap & Die Company

Fig. 8-23C   Oil hole drill

Straight fluted drills (Fig. 8-23D) are recommended for drilling operations on soft materials such as brass, bronze, copper, and various types of plastic. The straight flute prevents the drill from drawing itself into the material (digging in) while cutting.

If a straight fluted drill is not available, a conventional drill can be modified by grinding a small flat (approximately 1.6 mm wide) on the face of both cutting edges of the drill.

NOTE: The flat must be ground parallel to the axis of the drill.

Courtesy The Cleveland Twist Drill Co.

Fig. 8-23D   Straight fluted drill

High helix drills (Fig. 8-23E) are designed for drilling deep holes in aluminum, copper, die-cast material, and other metals where the chips have a tendency to jam in a hole. The high helix angle (35 to 40°) and the wider flutes of these drills assist in clearing chips from the hole.

Courtesy Greenfield Tap & Die Company

Fig. 8-23E   High helix drill

Deep hole or gun drills (Fig. 8-23F) are used for producing holes from approximately 9.5 to 75 mm in diameter and as deep as 6.1 m. The most common gun drill consists of a round, tubular stem, on the end of which is fastened a flat, two-fluted drilling insert. Cutting fluid is forced through the centre of the stem to flush the chips from the hole. When the drilling insert becomes dull, it can be replaced quickly by loosening one screw which holds it to the tubular stem.

Courtesy Greenfield Tap & Die Company

Fig. 8-23F   Gun drills

DRILLING SPEEDS AND FEEDS

SPEED

The speed at which a drill is operated is probably the most important factor which determines the life of the drill. Too fast a

TABLE 8-1: SPEEDS FOR HIGH SPEED STEEL DRILLS											
		STEEL CASTING		TOOL STEEL		CAST IRON		MACHINE STEEL		BRASS AND ALUMINUM	
DRILL SIZE		CUTTING SPEEDS IN METRES PER MINUTE OR FEET PER MINUTE									
		12 m/min	40 ft./min	18 m/min	60 ft./min	24 m/min	80 ft./min	30 m/min	100 ft./min	60 m/min	200 ft./min
mm	in.										
2	1/16	1910	2445	2865	3665	3820	4890	4775	6110	9550	12225
3	1/8	1275	1220	1910	1835	2545	2445	3185	3055	6365	6110
4	3/16	955	815	1430	1220	1910	1630	2385	2035	4775	4075
5	1/4	765	610	1145	915	1530	1220	1910	1530	3820	3055
6	5/16	635	490	955	735	1275	980	1590	1220	3180	2445
7	3/8	545	405	820	610	1090	815	1365	1020	2730	2035
8	7/16	475	350	715	525	955	700	1195	875	2390	1745
9	1/2	425	305	635	460	850	610	1060	765	2120	1530
10	5/8	350	245	520	365	695	490	870	610	1735	1220
15	3/4	255	205	380	305	510	405	635	510	1275	1020
20	7/8	190	175	285	260	380	350	475	435	955	875
25	1″	150	155	230	230	305	305	380	380	765	765

NOTE: There is no direct relationship between the metric and inch drill sizes.

cutting speed results in the cutting edges of the drill dulling rapidly and requiring frequent regrinding. Too slow a cutting speed generally results in a broken drill. The recommended cutting speeds for drilling various types of materials may be found in Table 8-1.

The speed of a twist drill is generally referred to as *cutting speed, surface speed,* or *peripheral speed*: it is the distance that a point on the circumference of a drill will travel in one minute.

A wide range of drills and drill sizes is used to cut various metals; an equally wide range of speeds is required for the drill to cut efficiently. For every job, there is the problem of choosing the drill speed which will result in the best production rates and the least amount of down-time for regrinding the drill. The most economical drilling speed depends upon many variables such as:

a) the type and hardness of the material
b) the diameter and material of the drill
c) the depth of the hole
d) the type and condition of the drill press
e) the efficiency of the cutting fluid employed
f) the accuracy and quality of the hole required
g) the rigidity of the work setup

Although all these factors are important in the selection of economical drilling speeds, the type of work material and the diameter of the drill are the most important.

When reference is made to the speed at which a drill should revolve, the cutting speed of the material in *metres per minute* (m/min) or *surface feet per minute* is implied unless otherwise stated. The number of revolutions of the drill necessary to attain the proper cutting speed for the metal being machined is called the *revolutions per minute* (r/min). A small drill operating at the same r/min as a larger drill will travel fewer metres per minute; it naturally would cut more efficiently at a higher number of r/min.

REVOLUTIONS PER MINUTE

To determine the correct number of revolutions per minute of a drill press spindle for a given size drill, the following should be known.

a) the type of material to be drilled
b) the recommended cutting speed of the material
c) the type of material from which the drill is made

Formula (S.I. or Metric System)

$$r/min = \frac{CS \text{ (metres per minute)}}{\pi D \text{ (drill circumference in metres)}}$$

EXAMPLE:

Calculate the r/min required to drill a 15 mm hole in tool steel (CS 18) using a high speed steel drill.

$$r/min = \frac{CS}{\pi D}$$

$$= \frac{18}{3.1416 \times 15 \text{ mm}}$$

$$= \frac{18}{3.1416 \times 0.015 \text{ m}}$$

$$= 382$$

Formula (Inch system)

$$r/min = \frac{CS \text{ (feet per minute} \times 12)}{\pi D \text{ (drill circumference in inches)}}$$

CS = the recommended cutting speed in *feet per minute* for the material being drilled.

NOTE: This would vary, depending on the material from which the drill is made.

D = the diameter of the drill being used.

Since only a few machines can be set to the exact calculated speed, π (3.1416) is divided into 12 to arrive at a simplified formula which is accurate enough for most drilling operations.

$$r/min = \frac{CS \times 4}{D}$$

EXAMPLE:

Calculate the r/min required to drill a 1/2 in. hole in cast iron (CS 80) with a high-speed steel drill.

$$r/min = \frac{CS \times 4}{D}$$

$$= \frac{80 \times 4}{1/2}$$

$$= 640$$

FEED

Feed is the distance that a drill advances into the work for each revolution. Drill feeds may be expressed in millimetres, decimals, or fractions of an inch. Since the feed rate is a determining factor in the rate of production and the life of the drill, it should be carefully chosen for each job. The rate of feed is generally governed by:

a) the diameter of the drill
b) the material of the workpiece
c) the condition of the drilling machine

A general rule of thumb is that the feed rate increases as the drill size increases. For example, a 6 mm drill should have a feed of only 0.05 to 0.10, while a 25 mm drill will have a feed of 0.25 mm to 0.63 mm per revolution. Too coarse a feed may chip the cutting edges or break the drill. Too light a feed causes a chattering or scraping noise which quickly dulls the cutting edges of the drill.

The drill feeds listed in Table 8-2 are recommended for general-purpose work. When drilling alloy or hard steels, use a somewhat slower feed. Softer metals such as aluminum, brass, or cast iron, can usually be drilled with a faster feed. Whenever chips coming from a hole turn blue, it is wise to stop the machine and examine the drill. Blue chips indicate too much heat at the cutting edge. This heat is caused by either a dull cutting edge or too high a speed.

CUTTING FLUIDS

Drilling work at the recommended cutting speeds and feeds causes considerable heat to be generated at the drill point. This

TABLE 8-2: DRILL FEEDS			
DRILL SIZE		**FEED PER REVOLUTION**	
MILLIMETRES	INCHES	MILLIMETRES	INCHES
3 and smaller	⅛ and smaller	0.02 to 0.05	.001 to .002
3 to 6	⅛ to ¼	0.05 to 0.10	.002 to .004
6 to 13	¼ to ½	0.10 to 0.18	.004 to .007
13 to 25	½ to 1	0.18 to 0.38	.007 to .015
25 to 38	1 to 1½	0.38 to 0.63	.015 to .025

heat must be dissipated as quickly as possible; otherwise, it will cause a drill to dull rapidly.

The purpose of a *cutting fluid* is to provide both cooling and lubrication. For a liquid to be most effective in dissipating heat, it must be able to absorb heat readily, have a good resistance to evaporation, and have a high thermal conductivity. Unfortunately, oil has poor cooling qualities. Water is the best coolant; however, it is rarely used by itself because it promotes rust and has no lubrication value. Basically, a good cutting fluid should:

a) Cool the workpiece and tool.
b) Reduce friction.
c) Improve the cutting action.
d) Protect the work against rusting.
e) Provide anti-weld properties.
f) Wash away the chips.

See Chapter 16, Table 16-1, for the recommended cutting fluids for drilling various metals.

DRILL POINT CHARACTERISTICS

Efficient drilling of the wide variety of materials used by industry requires a great variety of drill points. The most important factors which determine the size of the drilled hole are the characteristics of the drill point.

A drill is generally considered a roughing tool capable of removing metal quickly. It is not expected to finish a hole to the accuracy possible with a reamer.

However, a drill can often be made to cut more accurately and efficiently by proper drill point grinding. The use of various point angles and lip clearances, in conjunction with the thinning of the drill web, will:

a) Control the size, quality, and straightness of the drilled hole.
b) Control the size, shape, and formation of the chip.
c) Control the chip flow up the flutes.
d) Increase the strength of the drill's cutting edges.
e) Reduce the rate of wear at the cutting edges.
f) Reduce the amount of drilling pressure required.
g) Control the amount of burr produced during drilling.
h) Reduce the amount of heat generated.
i) Permit the use of various speeds and feeds for more efficient drilling.

DRILL POINT ANGLES AND CLEARANCES

Drill point angles and clearances are varied to suit the wide variety of material which must be drilled. Three general drill points are commonly used to drill various materials; however, there may be variations of these to suit various drilling conditions.

Conventional point (118°) (Fig. 8-24A). This is the most commonly used drill point and gives satisfactory results for most

Fig. 8-24A A drill point angle of 118° is suitable for most general work

general purpose drilling. The point angle should be ground with 8 to 12° lip clearance for best results.

Too much lip clearance weakens the cutting edge and causes the drill to chip and break easily. Too little lip clearance results in the use of heavy drilling pressure; this pressure causes the cutting edges to wear quickly because of the excessive heat generated and also places undue strain on the drill and equipment.

Fig. 8-24B A drill point angle of 60-90° is used for soft materials

Long angle point (60 to 90°) (Fig. 8-24B). The long angle drill point is commonly used on low helix drills for the drilling of nonferrous metals, soft cast irons, plastics, fibres, wood, etc. The lip clearance on long angle point drills is generally from 12 to 15°. On standard drills, a flat may be ground on the face of the lips to prevent the drill from drawing itself into the soft material.

Fig. 8-24C A drill point angle of 135-150° is best for hard materials

Flat angle point (135 to 150°) (Fig. 8-24C). The flat angle drill point is generally used to drill hard and tough materials. The lip clearance on flat angle point drills is generally only 6 to 8° to provide as much support as possible for the cutting edges. The shorter cutting edge tends to reduce the friction and heat generated during drilling.

WEB THINNING

Most drills are manufactured with webs that gradually increase in thickness towards the shank to give the drill strength. As the drill becomes shorter, the web becomes thicker (Fig. 8-25) and more pressure is required in order to cut. This increase in pressure results in more heat, which shortens the drill life. To reduce the amount of drilling pressure and resultant heat, the web of a drill is generally thinned. Webs can be thinned on a special web-thinning grinder, on a tool and cutter grinder, or freehand on a conventional grinder. It is important when thinning a web to grind equal amounts off each edge; otherwise the drill point will be off-centre (Fig. 8-26B).

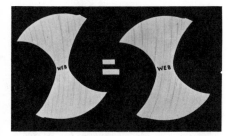

Courtesy The Cleveland Twist Drill Co.

Fig. 8-25   Notice the difference in web thickness between the drill cross-section near the shank (right) and the point (left)

DRILLING FACTS AND PROBLEMS

The most common drill problems encountered are illustrated in Fig. 8-26A and Fig. 8-26B. It is wise to study these various

EXCESSIVE SPEED WILL CAUSE WEAR AT OUTER CORNERS OF DRILL. THIS PERMITS FEWER REGRINDS OF DRILL DUE TO AMOUNT OF STOCK TO BE REMOVED IN RECONDITIONING. DISCOLORATION IS WARNING SIGN OF EXCESSIVE SPEED.

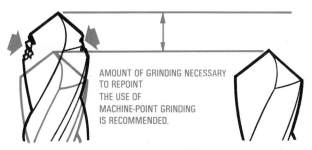

AMOUNT OF GRINDING NECESSARY TO REPOINT THE USE OF MACHINE-POINT GRINDING IS RECOMMENDED.

EXCESSIVE FEED SETS UP ABNORMAL END THRUST WHICH CAUSES BREAKDOWN OF CHISEL POINT AND CUTTING LIPS. FAILURE INDUCED BY THIS CAUSE WILL BE BROKEN OR SPLIT DRILL.

EXCESSIVE CLEARANCE RESULTS IN LACK OF SUPPORT BEHIND CUTTING EDGE WITH QUICK DULLING AND POOR TOOL LIFE DESPITE INITIAL FREE CUTTING ACTION. CLEARANCE ANGLE BEHIND CUTTING LIP FOR GENERAL PURPOSES IS 8° — 12°

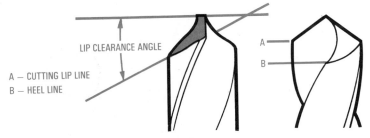

LIP CLEARANCE ANGLE

A — CUTTING LIP LINE
B — HEEL LINE

INSUFFICIENT CLEARANCE CAUSES THE DRILL TO RUB BEHIND THE CUTTING EDGE. IT WILL MAKE THE DRILL WORK HARD, GENERATE HEAT AND INCREASE END THRUST. RESULTS IN POOR HOLES AND DRILL BREAKAGE.

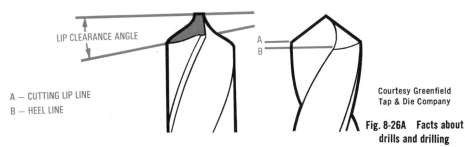

LIP CLEARANCE ANGLE

A — CUTTING LIP LINE
B — HEEL LINE

Courtesy Greenfield Tap & Die Company

Fig. 8-26A   Facts about drills and drilling

IMPROPER WEB THINNING IS THE RESULT OF TAKING MORE STOCK FROM ONE CUTTING EDGE THAN FROM THE OTHER, THEREBY DESTROYING THE CONCENTRICITY OF THE WEB AND OUTSIDE DIAMETER.

THE WEB IS THE TAPERED CENTRAL PORTION OF THE BODY THAT JOINS THE LANDS.

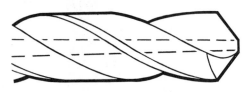

WRONG   RIGHT

CUTTING LIPS WITH UNEQUAL ANGLES WILL CAUSE ONE CUTTING EDGE TO WORK HARDER THAN THE OTHER. THIS CAUSES TORSION STRAIN, BELLMOUTH HOLES, RAPID DULLING, POOR TOOL LIFE.

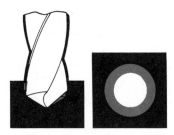

64°
54°

CUTTING LIPS UNEQUAL IN LENGTH CAUSE CHISEL POINT TO BE OFF CENTRE WITH AXIS AND WILL DRILL HOLES OVERSIZE BY APPROXIMATELY TWICE THE AMOUNT OF ECCENTRICITY.

FAST SPIRAL DRILL

REGULAR DRILL

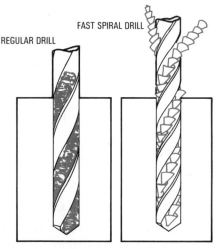

LOADING AND GALLING IS CAUSED BY POOR CHIP REMOVAL WITH INSUFFICIENT DISSIPATION OF HEAT SO THAT MATERIAL ANNEALS ITSELF TO THE CUTTING EDGE AND FLUTE. THIS CONDITION FREQUENTLY RESULTS FROM USING WRONG DRILLS FOR THE JOB OR INADEQUATE CUTTING FLUID APPLICATION.

Courtesy Greenfield Tap & Die Company

Fig. 8-26B Facts about drills and drilling

problems to ensure that the amount of drill breakage, regrinding, and down-time is kept to a minimum.

DRILL GRINDING

Before a drill is used, it is wise first to examine its condition. To cut properly and efficiently, a drill should have the following characteristics.

a) The cutting edges should be free from nicks or wear.

b) Both cutting edges should have the same angle.

c) Both cutting edges should be the same length.

d) The margin should be free of wear.

e) There should be a proper amount of lip clearance.

If the drill does not meet all of these requirements, it will be necessary to recondition the point by grinding.

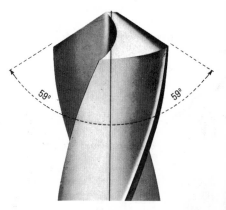

59°   59°

Courtesy The Cleveland Twist Drill Co.

Fig. 8-27A The point angle for a general purpose drill is 118°

To Grind a Drill

A general purpose drill has an included point angle of 118° and a lip clearance of from 8° to 12° (Fig. 8-27A and B).

1. Examine the drill point and the margins for wear. If there is any wear on the margins, it will be necessary to grind the point of the drill back until all margin wear has been removed.

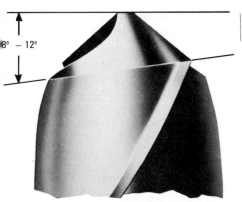

Courtesy The Cleveland Twist Drill Co.

Fig. 8-27B   The lip clearance for a general purpose drill is 8-12°

2. Hold the drill near the point with one hand, and with the other hand hold the shank of the drill slightly lower than the point (Fig. 8-28).

3. Move the drill so that it is approximately 59° to the face of the grinding wheel (Fig. 8-29).
   NOTE: A line scribed on the toolrest at 59° to the wheelface will assist in holding the drill at the proper angle.

4. Hold the lip or cutting edge of the drill parallel to the grinder tool rest.

5. Bring the lip of the drill against the grinding wheel and slowly lower the drill shank. **DO NOT TWIST THE DRILL.**

6. Remove the drill from the wheel without moving the position of the body or

Courtesy Kostel Enterprises Ltd.

Fig. 8-28   To provide lip clearance, lower the shank of the drill when grinding

Courtesy Kostel Enterprises Ltd.

Fig. 8-29   The drill is held at 59° to the face of the grinding wheel

hands, rotate the drill one-half turn, and grind the other cutting edge.

7. Check the angle of the drill point and length of the lips with a drill point gauge (Fig. 8-30).

8. Repeat operations 4 to 6 until the cutting edges are sharp and the lands are free from wear.

REAMERS

It is impossible to produce a hole which is round, smooth, and accurate to size by drilling. Whenever a hole must meet these specifications, it can be finished with a reamer.

A reamer is a rotary cutting tool with several straight or helical cutting edges along its body. It is used to accurately size

Courtesy Kostel Enterprises Ltd.

Fig. 8-30   Checking the drill point angle with a drill point gauge

and smooth a hole which has been previously drilled or bored. Some reamers are operated by hand (hand reamers), while others may be used under power in any type of machine tool (machine reamers).

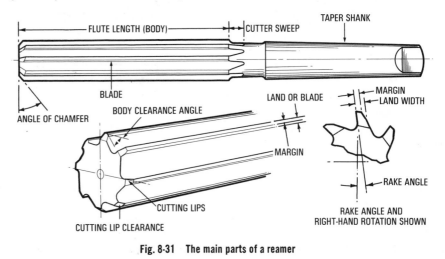

Fig. 8-31   The main parts of a reamer

REAMER PARTS

Reamers generally consist of three main parts: shank, body, and angle of chamfer (Fig. 8-31).

The shank, straight or tapered, is used to drive the reamer. The shank of machine reamers may be round or tapered, while hand reamers have a square on the end to accommodate a tap wrench.

The body of a reamer contains several straight or helical grooves, or flutes, and lands (the portion between the flutes). A margin (the top of each tooth) runs from the *angle of chamfer* to the end of the flute. The *body clearance angle* is a relief or clearance behind the margin which reduces friction while the reamer is cutting. The *rake angle* is the angle formed by the face of the tooth when a line is drawn from a point on the front marginal edge through the centre of the reamer (Fig. 8-31). If there is no angle on the face of the tooth, the reamer is said to have *radial land*.

The angle of chamfer is the part of the reamer which actually does the cutting. It is ground on the end of each tooth and there is clearance behind each chamfered cutting edge. On rose reamers, the angle of chamfer is ground on the end only and the cutting action occurs at this point. On fluted reamers, each tooth is relieved and most of the cutting is done by the reamer teeth.

TYPES OF REAMERS

Reamers are available in a variety of designs and sizes; however, they all fall into two general classifications: *hand* and *machine* reamers.

HAND REAMERS

Hand reamers (Fig. 8-32) are finishing tools used when a hole must be finished to a high degree of accuracy and finish. Holes to be hand reamed should be bored to

within 0.08 to 0.12 mm of the finish size. NEVER attempt to ream more than 0.12 mm with a hand reamer.

Courtesy Greenfield Tap & Die Company

Fig. 8-32   Straight and helical fluted hand reamers

A square on the shank end allows a wrench to be used in turning the reamer into the hole. The teeth on the end of the reamer are tapered slightly for a distance equal to the reamer diameter so that it can enter the hole which is to be reamed.

A hand reamer should never be used under mechanical power. When using a hand reamer, it is important to keep it true and straight with the hole. The dead centre in a lathe or a stub centre in a drill press will help keep the reamer aligned during the hand reaming operation.

Courtesy Whitman & Barnes

Fig. 8-33A   Roughing taper reamer

Courtesy Whitman & Barnes

Fig. 8-33B   Finishing taper reamer

Taper hand reamers (Fig. 8-33) both roughing and finishing, are available for all standard size tapers. Because chips do not fall out readily, a taper reamer should be removed from the hole and the flutes cleaned frequently.

MACHINE REAMERS

Machine reamers may be used in any machine tool for both roughing and finishing a hole. They are also called chucking reamers because of the method used to hold them for the reaming operation. Machine reamers are available in a wide variety of types and styles. Only some of the more common types will be discussed.

Courtesy The Cleveland Twist Drill Co.

Fig. 8-34A   A rose reamer cuts on the end angle only

Rose reamers (Fig. 8-34A) can be purchased with straight or tapered shanks and with straight or helical flutes. The teeth on the end have a 45° chamfer which is backed off to produce the cutting edge. The lands (teeth) are nearly as wide as the flutes and are not backed off. Rose reamers cut on the end only and can be used to remove material quickly and bring the hole fairly close to the size required. Rose reamers are usually made .003 to .005 in. (0.08 to 0.13 mm■) under the nominal size.

Courtesy The Cleveland Twist Drill Co.

Fig. 8-34B   The fluted reamer has more teeth than a rose reamer and cuts on the sides and end

Fluted reamers (Fig. 8-34B) have more teeth than those reamers for a comparable diameter. The lands are relieved for the entire length, and fluted reamers therefore cut along the side as well as at the chamfer on the end. These reamers are considered as finishing tools and are used to bring a hole to size.

Courtesy The Cleveland Twist Drill Co.

Fig. 8-35   A carbide-tipped reamer

Carbide-tipped reamers (Fig. 8-35) were developed to meet the ever-increasing demand for higher production rates. They are similar to rose or fluted reamers, except that carbide tips have been brazed to their cutting edges. Because of the hardness of the carbide tips, these reamers resist abrasion and maintain sharp cutting edges even at high temperatures. Carbide-tipped reamers outlast high-speed steel reamers, especially on castings where hard scale or sand is a problem. Because carbide-tipped reamers can be run at higher speeds and still maintain their size, they are used extensively for long production runs.

Courtesy The Cleveland Twist Drill Co.

Fig. 8-36 Shell reamers are economical for reaming large holes

Shell reamers (Fig. 8-36) are reamer heads mounted on a driving arbor. The shank of the driving arbor may be straight or tapered, depending on the size and type of shell reamer used. Two slots in the end of this reamer fit into lugs on the driving arbor. Sometimes a locking screw in the end of the arbor holds the shell reamer in place.

The advantages of shell reamers are:
a) They are economical for larger holes.
b) Various head sizes can be easily interchanged on one arbor.
c) When a reamer becomes worn, it may be thrown away without the driving arbor.

Adjustable reamers (Fig. 8-37) have inserted blades which can be adjusted approximately at .015 in. (0.38 mm■) over or under the nominal reamer size. The threaded body has a series of tapered grooves cut lengthwise into which blades are fitted. Adjusting nuts on either end can be used to increase or decrease the size of the reamer.

Hand or machine adjustable reamers can be readily sharpened and are available with either high-speed steel or carbide inserts.

Courtesy The Cleveland Twist Drill Co.

Fig. 8-37 An adjustable reamer with inserted blades

Expansion reamers (Fig. 8-38) are similar in purpose to adjustable reamers; however, the amount they can be expanded is very limited. The body of this reamer is slotted, and a tapered, threaded plug is fitted into the end. Turning this plug will allow a 1 in. (25.4 mm■) reamer to expand up to .005 in. (0.13 mm■). Expansion reamers are meant not to be oversize reamers, but to give longer life to finishing reamers.

Courtesy The Cleveland Twist Drill Co.

Fig. 8-38 An expansion-type reamer can be expanded slightly

Emergency reamers, drills whose corners (at the lip and land) have been slightly rounded and honed, may be used with fairly good results if a reamer of a particular size is not available. First drill the hole as close as possible to the required size. Then run the reaming drill at a fairly high speed, and feed it into the hole slowly.

REAMING ALLOWANCES

The amount of material left in a hole for the reaming operation depends on a number of factors. If a hole has been punched, rough drilled, or bored, it requires more metal for reaming than a hole which has already been reamed with a roughing reamer. The type of machining operation prior to reaming must be considered as well as the material being reamed.

General rules for the amount of material which should be left in a hole for machine reaming are as follows.
1. For holes up to 1/2 in. diameter, allow 1/64 in. for reaming.
2. For holes over 1/2 in. diameter, allow 1/32 in. for reaming.
NOTE: Never leave more than .003 to .005 in a hole for hand reamers up to 1/2 in. diameter. On larger holes, a proportional allowance should be left to make a good finish possible.

For metric size reamers allow 0.10 mm for holes up to 12 mm in diameter. For holes over 12 mm, allow 0.20 mm for reaming.

REAMING SPEEDS AND FEEDS

Speeds. The selection of the most efficient speed for machine reaming is dependent upon the following factors.
a) the type of material being reamed
b) the rigidity of the setup
c) the tolerance and finish required in the hole

Generally, reaming speeds should be from 1/2 to 2/3 the speed used for drilling the same material.

Higher reaming speeds can be used when the setup is rigid; slower speeds should be used when the setup is less rigid. A hole requiring close tolerances and a fine finish should be reamed at slower speeds. The use of coolants improves the surface finish and allows higher speeds to be used.

Reamers do not work well when they chatter; the speed selected should always be low enough to eliminate chatter.

Table 8.3 gives the recommended reaming speeds for high-speed steel reamers. Carbide reamers may be operated at higher speeds.

TABLE 8-3: RECOMMENDED REAMING SPEEDS FOR HIGH SPEED STEEL REAMERS		
MATERIAL	SPEED	
	m/min	ft./min
Aluminum	39–60	130–200
Brass	39–55	130–180
Bronze	15–30	50–100
Cast iron	15–24	50–80
Machine steel	15–21	50–70
Steel alloys	9–12	30–40
Stainless steel	12–15	40–50
Magnesium	52–82	170–270

Feeds. The feed used for reaming is usually two to three times greater than that used for drilling. The feed rate will vary with the material being reamed; however, it should be approximately 0.02 to 0.10 mm per flute per revolution. Feeds which are too low generally result in glazing, excessive reamer wear, and sometimes chatter. Too high a feed tends to reduce the hole accuracy and sometimes results in poor surface finish. Generally, feeds should be the highest possible which will still produce the hole accuracy and finish required.

An exception to these feed rates occurs when tapered holes are being reamed. As tapered reamers cut along their entire length, a light feed is necessary. The reamer should be removed occasionally and the flutes cleaned.

REAMER CARE

The accuracy and surface finish of a hole, as well as the life of a reamer, depend greatly on the care a reamer receives. It is wise to remember that a reamer is a finishing tool and should be handled carefully.

1. Never turn a reamer backward; this will ruin the cutting edges.

2. Always store reamers in separate containers to prevent the cutting edges from being nicked or burred. Plastic or cardboard tubes make excellent reamer containers.
3. Never roll or drop reamers on metal surfaces, such as bench tops, machines, plates, etc.
4. When not in use, a reamer should be oiled, especially on the cutting edges, to prevent rusting.
5. A fine, free-cutting grinding wheel should be used for resharpening reamers. Burring of the cutting edges destroys the life of the reamer, while a rough cutting edge produces a rough hole and the reamer dulls quickly.

REAMING HINTS

1. Examine a reamer and remove all burrs from the cutting edges with a hone so that good surface finishes will be produced.
2. Cutting fluid should be used in the reaming operation to improve the hole finish and prolong the life of the reamer.
3. Helical fluted reamers should always be used when long holes and those with keyways or oil grooves are reamed.
4. Straight fluted reamers are generally used when extreme accuracy is required.
5. To obtain hole accuracy and good surface finish, use a roughing reamer first and then a finishing reamer. An old reamer which is slightly undersize may be used as a roughing reamer.
6. Never, *under any circumstances*, turn a reamer backwards.
7. Never attempt to start a reamer on an uneven surface; the reamer will go towards the point of least resistance and will not produce a straight, round hole.
8. If chatter occurs, stop the machine, reduce the speed, and increase the feed. To overcome the chatter marks,

it may be necessary to restart the reamer slowly by pulling the drill press belt by hand.
9. To avoid chatter, select a reamer with an incremental cut (unequally spaced teeth).
10. When hand reaming in a drill press, always use a stub centre in the drill press spindle to keep the reamer aligned.

DRILL PRESS OPERATIONS

A wide variety of operations can be performed on a drill press by the use of various types of cutting tools. No attempt has been made to explain every operation; only those most commonly performed are discussed.

DRILL PRESS SAFETY

Before proceeding with any drill press operation, it may be wise to carefully study the following safety precautions.

1. Never attempt to hold the work by hand; a table stop or clamp should be used to prevent the work from spinning.
2. Never set speeds or adjust the work unless the machine is stopped.
3. Keep your head well back from revolving parts of a drill press to prevent your hair from being caught.
4. As the drill begins to break through the work, ease up on the drilling pressure and allow the drill to break through gradually.
5. Always remove burrs from a drilled hole with a file or scraper.
6. Never leave a chuck key in the drill chuck *at any time*.
7. Never attempt to grab work which may have caught in the drill. *Stop the machine.*

LATHE CENTRE HOLES

Work to be turned between the centres on a lathe must have a hole drilled in each end for the lathe centres to enter. A

A — regular type

B — Bell type

Courtesy The Cleveland Twist Drill Co.

Fig. 8-39   Two types of centre drills

combination drill and countersink (Fig. 8-39), more commonly called a *centre drill*, is used for this operation.

To ensure an adequate bearing surface for the work on the lathe centre, it is important that centre holes be drilled to the correct size and depth (Fig. 8-40A).

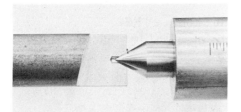

Courtesy Kostel Enterprises Ltd.

Fig. 8-40A   A centre hole drilled to the proper depth

A centre hole which is too shallow is illustrated in Fig. 8-40B. This results in poor support for the work and possible damage to both the lathe centre and the work.

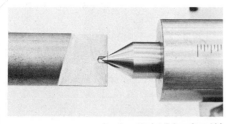

Courtesy Kostel Enterprises Ltd.

Fig. 8-40B   A centre hole drilled too shallow

Fig. 8-40C shows a centre hole which has been drilled too deep. The taper on the lathe centre cannot contact the taper of the centre hole; the result is poor support for the work.

Courtesy Kostel Enterprises Ltd.

Fig. 8-40C   A centre hole drilled too deep

To Drill a Lathe Centre Hole

1. Select the proper size centre drill to suit the diameter of the work.
2. Fasten the centre drill in the drill chuck, having it extend beyond the chuck only about 12 mm.
3. Place the work to be centre drilled in the drill vise as shown in Fig. 8-41.

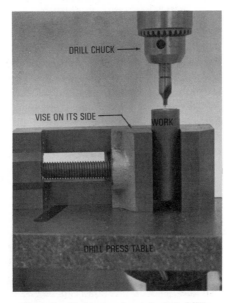

Courtesy Kostel Enterprises Ltd.

Fig. 8-41   Work set up for centre hole drilling

4. Set the drill press at the proper speed and start the machine.
5. Locate the centre punch mark in the work directly below the centre drill point.
6. Carefully feed the centre drill into the centre punch mark in the work for about 1.6 mm.
7. Raise the centre drill, apply a few drops of cutting fluid, and continue drilling.
8. Frequently remove the drill from the hole to apply cutting fluid, remove the chips, and measure the diameter of the top of the centre hole.
9. Continue drilling until the hole is the proper size.

To Drill to an Accurate Layout

Before the work can be drilled to the exact location, the position of the holes must be accurately laid out.

1. Coat the surface of the work with a layout dye.
2. Scribe lines at right angles as in Fig. 8-42A and centre punch where the lines intersect.
3. With a divider, scribe a circle the size of the hole required (Fig. 8-42B).
4. Scribe a test circle 1.6 mm smaller than the hole size (Fig. 8-42C).
5. Place four light punch marks on both circles if they are 19 mm or less in diameter and eight punch marks if they are larger, as in Fig. 8-42C.
6. Spot the hole to a depth equal to one-half or two-thirds of the *drill point size*, as shown in Fig. 8-43A.
7. Stop the drill press spindle and examine the spotting caused by the drill point.
8. If the spotting is off-centre, cut shallow V-grooves with a round nose or diamond point chisel on the side toward which the drill must be moved (Fig. 8-43B).
9. Start the drill in the spotted and grooved hole. The drill will be drawn toward the circle and witness marks.

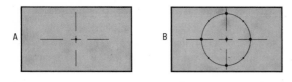

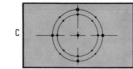

Fig. 8-42A,B,C   Layout for a hole to be drilled

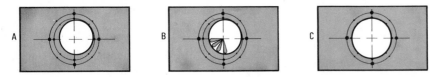

Fig. 8-43A,B,C   Drawing the drill point to the layout

Fig. 8-45A   A set of counterbores

10. Continue cutting grooves into the spotted hole until the drill point is drawn to the centre of the scribed circles, as shown in Fig. 8-43C.
NOTE: The drill point must be drawn to the centre of the scribed circle before the drill has cut to its full diameter.

11. Continue to drill the hole to the desired depth.

DRILLING LARGE HOLES

As drills increase in size, the thickness of the web also increases to give the drill added strength. The thicker the web, the thicker will be the point or chisel edge of the drill. As the chisel edge becomes larger, poorer cutting action results and more pressure must be applied for the drilling operation. A thick web will not follow the centre-punch mark accurately and the hole may not be drilled in the proper location. Two methods are generally employed to overcome the poor cutting action of a thick web on large drills.

a) The web is thinned, as stated previously in this chaper.
b) A smaller lead, or pilot, hole is drilled.

The usual procedure for drilling large holes is that first a pilot, or lead, hole (Fig. 8-44), the diameter of which is slightly larger than the thickness of the web, is drilled. *Care must be taken that the pilot hole is drilled on-centre.* The pilot hole is

Courtesy Kostel Enterprises Ltd.

Fig. 8-44   Drilling a pilot or lead hole helps the larger drill cut easily and accurately

then followed with a larger drill. This method may also be used to drill average-size holes when the drill press is small and does not have sufficient power to drive the drill through the solid metal.

NEVER drill a pilot hole any bigger than necessary; otherwise, the larger drill may:
a) cause chattering
b) drill the hole out-of-round
c) spoil the top (mouth) of the hole

COUNTERBORING

Counterboring is the operation of enlarging the end of a hole which has been drilled previously. A hole is generally counterbored to a depth slightly greater than the head of the bolt, cap screw, or pin which it is to accommodate.

Counterbores (Fig. 8-45A) are supplied in a variety of styles, each having a pilot in the end to keep the tool in line with the hole being counterbored. Some counterbores are available with interchangeable pilots to suit a variety of hole sizes.

To Counterbore a Hole

1. Set up and fasten the work securely.

Fig. 8-45B   A counterbore is used to enlarge the end of a hole

2. Drill the proper size hole in the work-piece to suit the body of the pin or screw.

3. Mount the correct size counterbore in the drill press (Fig. 8-45B).

4. Set the drill press speed to approximately one-quarter of that used for drilling.

5. Bring the counterbore close to the work and see that the pilot turns freely in the drilled hole.

6. Start the machine, apply cutting fluid, and counterbore to the required depth.

COUNTERSINKING

Countersinking is the process of enlarging the top end of a hole to the shape of a cone to accommodate the head of a flat- or oval-head machine screw. The cutting tool used is called a countersink (Fig. 8-46A). An 82° countersink is used to enlarge the top of a hole so that it will accommodate a flat-head machine screw (Fig. 8-46B). The hole is countersunk until the head of the machine screw is flush with or slightly below the top of the work surface (Fig. 8-46B). All holes that are to be threaded should be countersunk slightly larger than the tap diameter to protect the start of the thread.

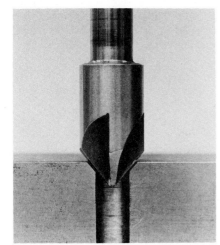

Courtesy Kostel Enterprises Ltd.

Fig. 8-46A Countersinking produces a tapered hole to fit a flat head machine screw

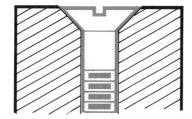

Fig. 8-46B Countersunk until the hole is slightly larger than the diameter of the screw head

The speed recommended for countersinking is approximately one quarter of the drilling speed.

TRANSFERRING HOLE LOCATIONS

During the construction of dies, jigs, fixtures, and machine parts, it is often necessary to transfer the location of holes accurately from one part to another. Three common methods of transferring hole locations are:

a) spotting with a twist drill
b) using transfer punches
c) using transfer screws

Regardless of which method is used, the holes in the existing part are used as a master or guide to transfer the hole locations.

To Spot with a Twist Drill

1. Remove the burrs from the mating surfaces on both parts.

2. Align both parts accurately and clamp them together.

3. Mount a drill of the same diameter as the hole to be transferred in the drill press spindle.

4. Start the drill into the hole of the guide part and spot drill the second part (Fig. 8-47A).
   NOTE: Never spot drill deeper than the diameter of the drill.

5. Spot drill all the holes that are to be transferred.

6. Remove the original part.

7. Drill the spotted holes to the required diameter.

Fig. 8-47A Transferring hole locations by spotting with a drill

To Use Transfer Punches

1. Remove the burrs from the mating surfaces on both parts.

2. Align both parts accurately and clamp them together.

3. Secure a transfer punch (Fig. 8-47B) of the same diameter as the hole to be transferred.

Fig. 8-47B Transferring hole locations using a transfer punch

4. Place the punch in the hole and *lightly* strike it with a hammer to mark the hole location.

5. Use the correct size of transfer punch on all the holes that are to be transferred.

6. Remove the original part.

7. Use a divider to lay out proof circles for the holes to be drilled.

8. With a centre punch, deepen the existing transfer punch marks.

9. Use the method outlined in "Drilling to a Layout" to drill the holes to location accurately.

To Use Transfer Screws

Many times it is necessary to transfer the location of threaded holes. This may be easily accomplished by the use of transfer screws (Fig. 8-47C) which have been hardened and sharpened to a point. Two flats are ground on the point to allow the screws to be threaded into a hole with a small wrench or a pair of needle nose pliers.

Fig. 8-47C   Transfer screws are used to transfer threaded hole locations

1. Remove all burrs from the mating surfaces.

2. Thread transfer screws into the holes to be transferred, allowing the points to extend beyond the work surface approximately 0.8 mm.

3. Align both parts accurately and then sharply strike one part with a hammer.

4. Remove the original part, and deepen the marks left by the transfer screws with a centre punch.

5. Drill all holes to the required size.

DRILL JIGS

A drill jig is used whenever it is necessary to drill holes to an exact location in a large number of identical parts. Drill jigs are used to save layout time, to avoid incorrectly located holes, and to produce holes accurately and economically. The advantages of using a drill jig are:

a) Since it is not necessary to lay out the hole locations, layout time is eliminated.

b) Each part is quickly and accurately aligned.

c) The part is held in position by a clamping mechanism.

d) The drill jig bushings provide a guide for the drill.

e) The hole locations in each part will be exactly the same; therefore the parts produced are interchangeable.

f) Unskilled labour can be used.

Courtesy The Canadian Blower & Forge Co. Ltd.

Fig. 8-48   Using a drill jig to locate and hold the workpiece. Notice the jig bushing used to guide the drill

A drill jig (Fig. 8-48) is designed so that the part to be drilled may be fastened into it and drilled immediately. Hardened drill jig bushings, used to guide and keep the drill in location, are located in the drill jig wherever holes must be drilled. When two or more different size holes are to be drilled in the same part, it is preferable to have a gang or multi-spindle drill press set up. A different size drill is mounted in each spindle, and the drill jig is passed from one spindle to the next for each hole.

DRILLING HINTS

The following hints should help to prevent many problems which could affect the accuracy of the hole and the efficiency of the drilling operation.

1. Always examine the condition of the drill point before use, and if necessary, resharpen it.

2. Set the correct r/min for the size of drill being used. Too high speed quickly dulls a drill, and too low speed causes a small drill to break.

3. Arrange the work setup so that the drill will not cut into the table, parallels, or drill vise as it breaks through the workpiece.

4. The work should always be clamped securely for the drilling operation. For small diameter holes, a clamp or stop fastened to the left-hand side of the table will prevent the work from spinning.

5. The end of the workpiece farthest from the hole should be placed on the left-hand side of the table so that if the work catches, it will not swing towards the operator.

6. Always clean a tapered drill shank, sleeve, and the machine spindle before inserting a drill.

7. It is a good practice to start each hole with a centre drill. The small point of the centre drill will pick up a centre-punch mark accurately; the centre-drilled hole will provide a guide for the following drill.

8. Thin workpieces, such as sheet metal, should be clamped to a hardwood block for drilling. This prevents the work from catching and also steadies the drill point as it breaks through the workpiece.

9. A drill squeak usually indicates a dull drill. Stop the machine and examine the condition of the drill point.

10. When increased pressure must be applied during a drilling operation, the reason is generally a dull drill, or a chip caught in the hole between the drill and the work.

BORING

Boring is the operation of enlarging a drilled or cored hole by means of a single- or double-edged cutting tool held in a boring bar. Although boring is generally not done on a drill press, sometimes, because of the nature of the workpiece, it may be necessary to use this machine for a boring operation.

Many large drill presses have a hole in the centre of the table into which a bushing can be inserted. A pilot on the end of the boring bar fits into the table bushing and keeps the boring bar rigid and aligned during the machining operation.

To Bore in a Drill Press

1. Mount as large a boring bar as possible into the drill press spindle.
2. Swing the drill press table to allow the boring bar pilot to enter the table bushing hole.
3. Lock the drill press table in position.
4. Mount the work on parallels to allow the chips to clear the hole and also to prevent cutting into the drill press table.
5. Centralize the hole to be machined to the boring bar, and clamp it securely in position.
6. Set the drill press to the correct r/min and feed for the material being cut. Roughing feeds may be as high as 0.40 mm, while finishing feeds are approximately 0.02 to 0.12 mm.
7. Set the toolbit and take a light trial cut approximately 5 mm deep.
8. Stop the machine and measure the size of the hole with inside calipers or telescoping gauges.

9. Reset the cutting tool for the depth of cut desired.
10. Continue to bore the hole to the required size by setting the cutting tool for each cut.

NOTE: In order to produce an accurate hole with a good surface finish, keep the drill press spindle adjusted snugly, use a sharp cutting tool, and apply cutting fluid.

TAPPING

Tapping in a drill press may be performed either by hand or with the use of a tapping attachment. The advantage of using a drill press for tapping a hole is that the tap can be started squarely and maintained that way through the entire length of the hole.

To Tap a Hole by Hand in a Drill Press

1. Mount the work on parallels with the centre punch in line with the spindle, and clamp the work securely to the drill-press table.
2. Adjust the drill press table so that the drill may be removed after the hole has been drilled without moving the table or work.

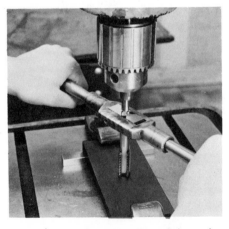

Fig. 8-49A   Guiding a tap into the workpiece, using a stub centre held in a drill chuck

3. Drill the hole to the correct *tap drill size* for the tap to be used.
NOTE: The work or table *must not* be moved after the drilling.

4. Mount a stub centre in the drill chuck (Fig. 8-49A).

OR

Remove the drill chuck and mount a special centre in the drill press spindle.

5. Place the tap in the drilled hole, and lower the drill press spindle until the centre fits into the centre hole in the tap shank.
6. Turn the tap wrench to start the tap into the hole, and at the same time keep the centre in light contact with the tap.
7. Continue to tap the hole in the usual manner; keep the tap aligned by applying light pressure on the drill press downfeed lever.

A *tapping attachment* (Fig. 8-49B) may be mounted in a drill press spindle to rotate the tap by power. It has a built-in

Fig. 8-49B   A tapping attachment mounted in a drill press

friction clutch which drives the tap clockwise when the drill press spindle is fed downwards. If there is excessive pressure against the tap because it is stuck or jammed in a hole, the clutch slips before the tap will break. The tapping attachment has a reversing mechanism, engaged by the drill press spindle being raised, to back a tap out of the hole.

Two- or three-fluted machine or gun taps are used for tapping under power because of their ability to clear the chips. Tapping speed for most materials ranges from 60 to 100 r/min.

RADIAL DRILL PRESS

The main advantage of a radial drill press over other types of drilling machines is that it is capable of performing a variety of operations in large workpieces without the work having to be shifted continually from one location to another.

To Drill a Hole on a Radial Drill Press

1. Mount the work on parallels when through holes are to be drilled, and clamp it securely to the table.
2. Loosen the column clamp and swing the radial arm over the workpiece.
3. Bring the radial arm to the required height by means of the elevating crank.
4. Drill all hole locations with a centre drill and pilot drill, if required.
5. Mount the correct size of drill in the spindle or drill chuck.
6. Set the speeds and feeds for the size of the drill and the work material.
7. Start the machine, bring the revolving drill down into the centre-drilled hole, then lock the radial arm in position.
8. Engage the spindle feed, apply cutting fluid, and proceed to drill all the holes.

DRILLING SPECIAL-SHAPED HOLES

Square, hexagon, octagon, and special-shaped holes can be quickly and accurately cut in a drill press. A special floating chuck, angular drill, guide plate, and slip bushing are required for this operation (Fig. 8-50A, B, C, D).

The principle of drilling holes with angular sides is the same as that used for drilling round holes. It is an accepted fact that a circle is composed of a series of minute chords (degrees) of which there are 360 to a full circle.

Courtesy Watts Bros. Tool Works

Fig. 8-50A   Floating chuck

Courtesy Watts Bros. Tool Works

Fig. 8-50B   Angular drill

Courtesy Watts Bros. Tool Works

Fig. 8-50C   Guide plate

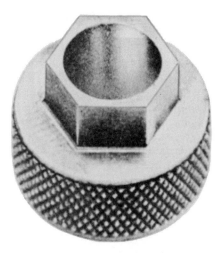

Courtesy Watts Bros. Tool Works

Fig. 8-50D   Slip bushing

Fig. 8-51 illustrates the various positions of the cutting lips of a square drill as it rotates in the guide plate. The centre of the drill does not follow a circle, but a series of minute alternate cycloid-like curves whose chords are parallel to the sides of the hole being drilled. The full-floated chuck takes up the driving and floating action and allows the drill to operate as freely as an ordinary drill. Special-shaped holes can be drilled on a drill press, lathe, or any spindle-driven machine if the tools illustrated in Fig. 8-50 are used.

Courtesy Watts Bros. Tool Works

Fig. 8-51 Drilling a square hole in a plate

To Drill Special-Shaped Holes

1. Align and clamp the work to be drilled under the centre of the drill press spindle.
2. Locate and fasten the guide plate to the workpiece in the required position.
3. Insert the slip bushing into the guide plate, and drill the lead hole. The lead hole allows the chips to clear and gives the drill freedom to turn the corners. Lead holes should be approximately 25% smaller than the distance across the flats of the hole to be drilled.
4. Insert a drill of the correct size into the full-floating chuck. The setscrew in the chuck should be tightened securely on the flat of the drill shank.
5. Mount the chuck into the drill press spindle.
6. With the drill press spindle in its uppermost position, raise the table until the workpiece is close to the drill.
7. Snug up the drill press spindle sleeve bearing to prevent chatter.
8. Lower the drill into the guide plate and turn the machine spindle by hand to see that the drill turns freely.
9. Set the drill press to approximately one-quarter the speed and feed used for regular drilling.
10. Start the machine, lubricate the drill, and apply steady cutting pressure to avoid chatter while drilling to depth.

DRILL PRESS QUESTIONS

1. Name six operations which can be performed on a drill press.
2. Explain how the size of a drill press is determined.

TYPES OF DRILLING MACHINES

3. Compare a sensitive drill press with an upright drilling machine.
4. Describe a gang drill and state the purpose for which it is used.
5. What are the advantages of a radial drilling machine?
6. Describe and state the purpose of the following parts of a sensitive drill press.
   a) base
   b) column
   c) drilling head
   d) table
   e) depth stop

RADIAL DRILL PRESS

7. Compare the construction of the radial drill press to that of a standard upright drill press.

STANDARD OPERATIONS

8. Define: drilling, boring, reaming.
9. How does counterboring differ from countersinking?

DRILL HOLDING DEVICES

10. What is the purpose of the following?
    a) drill chuck
    b) drill sleeve
    c) drill socket
11. What precautions should be observed when removing a drill from the spindle with a drill drift?

WORK-HOLDING DEVICES

12. Why is it necessary to fasten work securely for drilling?
13. List four work-holding devices and state the purpose of each.

CLAMPING STRESSES

14. Why is it important that work be clamped properly for any machining operation?
15. Explain the procedure for clamping a workpiece properly.
16. List four important clamping hints.

TWIST DRILLS

17. Name three materials used to manufacture drills and state the advantage of each.
18. Describe the body, web, and point of a twist drill.
19. List four systems of drill sizes and give the range of each.

SPECIAL DRILLS

20. Describe and state the purpose of:
    a) a core drill
    b) a straight-fluted drill
    c) a high-helix drill

DRILLING SPEEDS

21. Why is it important that a drill be operated at the correct speed?
22. Explain the difference between cutting speed and revolutions per minute.
23. What factors determine the most economical drilling speed?
24. Calculate the r/min which would be required to drill:
    a) a 3/8 in. diameter hole in tool steel
    b) a 1 in. diameter hole in aluminum
    c) a 9 mm hole in a steel casting
    d) a 20 mm hole in cast iron

DRILLING FEEDS

25. Define feed and state the factors which govern the rate of feed.
26. Discuss the effects of feed which is:
    a) too coarse
    b) too fine

DRILL POINT CHARACTERISTICS

27. Why are various drill points and clearances used for drilling operations?

28. Describe and state the purpose of the following drill points:
    a) conventional
    b) long angle
    c) flat angle
29. Why is it necessary to thin the web of a drill?

DRILLING FACTS AND PROBLEMS

30. What problems generally result from the use of excessive speed and excessive feed?
31. Discuss excessive lip clearance and insufficient lip clearance.
32. What is the effect of:
    a) drills with unequal angles on the cutting lips?
    b) drills with cutting lips of unequal length?

DRILL GRINDING

33. What are the characteristics of a properly ground drill?
34. List the main steps in grinding a general-purpose drill.

REAMERS

35. What is the purpose of a reamer?
36. Define the following reamer parts:
    a) body
    b) angle of chamfer
    c) body clearance angle
    d) radial land
37. How may a hand reamer be recognized, and for what purpose is it used?
38. Compare a rose reamer and a fluted reamer.
39. State the advantages of carbide-tipped reamers.
40. Describe briefly the following types of reamers and state their purpose.
    a) shell
    b) adjustable
41. How much material should be left in a hole for:
    a) machine reamers?
    b) hand reamers?

42. What is the recommended speed and feed for reaming?
43. Discuss the effects of too high or too low reaming speeds and feeds.
44. List three important points which should be observed in the care of reamers.
45. List seven of the most important reaming hints.

DRILL PRESS OPERATIONS

46. Select three of the most important safety suggestions, and explain why they should be observed.
47. State three reasons why a centre drill should be removed from the work frequently.
48. How may work be held in a drill vise so that it will be square when centre holes are drilled?
49. Briefly explain the results of centre holes which are drilled:
    a) too shallow
    b) too deep
50. Explain how a drill may be drawn over to a layout.
51. What are pilot holes and why are they necessary?
52. Why should pilot holes not be drilled any larger than necessary?
53. List the procedure for counterboring a hole.
54. Why should holes that are to be tapped be countersunk?

TRANSFERRING HOLE LOCATIONS

55. Name three methods of transferring the location of holes from one part to another.
56. Explain the procedure for spotting with a twist drill.
57. What are transfer punches and how are they used?
58. Describe transfer screws and explain how they are used.

DRILL JIGS

59. State the advantages of using a drill jig for drilling holes in a large number of identical parts.
60. Briefly describe a drill jig.

DRILLING HINTS

61. Why is it important that the correct r/min be set for the size of drill being used?
62. List three precautions to observe before starting to drill a hole.
63. How can a centre punch mark location be picked up accurately?
64. Explain how thin workpieces should be drilled.

BORING

65. Explain how a drill press may be set up for boring a hole.
66. What requirements are necessary for an accurate hole with a good surface finish to be produced?

TAPPING

67. What is the advantage of tapping a hole by hand in a drill press?
68. Describe the procedure for tapping a hole by hand in a drill press.
69. Explain how a tapping attachment operates.

RADIAL DRILL PRESS

70. What advantages has a radial drill press over other types of drilling machines?
71. List the steps for drilling a hole on a radial drill press.

DRILLING SPECIAL-SHAPED HOLES

72. What tools are required for drilling special-shaped holes?
73. Explain the procedure for drilling special-shaped holes on a standard drill press.

9 THE ENGINE LATHE

Courtesy Cincinnati Milacron Inc.

Historically, the engine lathe is the father of all machine tools. The first application of the lathe principle was probably the potter's wheel used by prehistoric man. This machine rotated a mass of clay which enabled the clay to be formed into a cylindrical shape.

Basically the modern lathe operates on the same principle. The work is held and rotated on its axis while the cutting tool is advanced along the lines of a desired cut (Fig. 9-1). The lathe is one of the most versatile machine tools used in industry. With suitable attachments, the lathe may be used for turning, tapering, form turning, screw cutting, facing, drilling, boring, spinning, grinding, and polishing operations. Cutting operations are performed with a cutting tool fed either parallel or at right angles to the axis of the work. The cutting tool may also be fed at an angle, relative to the axis of the work, for machining tapers and angles.

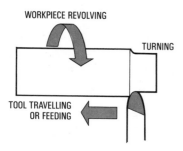

Fig. 9-1   Lathe cutting action

Three common engine lathes are the tool room, heavy-duty, and gap-bed lathes. Modern production has led to the development of many special types of lathes, such as multiple-spindle, profiling, tracing, spinning, and numerically controlled machines. The engine lathe, which is basic to all lathes, will be discussed in detail.

LATHE SIZE AND CAPACITY

Lathe size is designated by the *largest work diameter* which can be swung over the lathe ways and generally the *maximum*

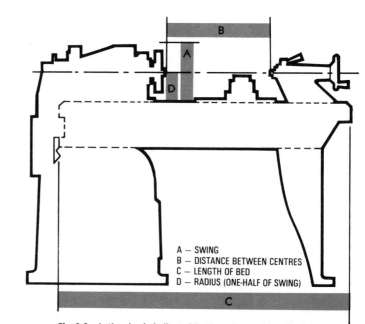

A — SWING
B — DISTANCE BETWEEN CENTRES
C — LENGTH OF BED
D — RADIUS (ONE-HALF OF SWING)

Fig. 9-2   Lathe size is indicated by the swing and length of the bed

distance between centres (Fig. 9-2). Some manufacturers designate the lathe size by the largest work diameter which can be swung over the ways and the overall bed length.

Lathes are manufactured in a wide range of sizes, the most common being from 9 to 30 in. swing, with a capacity of 16 in. to 12 ft. between centres. A typical lathe may have a 13 in. swing, a 6 ft. long bed, and a capacity to turn work 36 in. long between centres (Fig. 9-2).

The average metric lathe used in school shops may have a 230 to 330 mm swing and have a bed length of from 500 to 3000 mm in length.

PARTS OF THE ENGINE LATHE

HEADSTOCK

The *headstock* (Fig. 9-3A and B) is clamped on the left-hand side of the bed. The *headstock spindle*, a hollow cylindrical shaft supported by bearings, provides a drive from the motor to work-holding devices. A live centre, a faceplate or a chuck can be fitted to the spindle nose to hold and drive the work. The live centre has a 60° point which provides a bearing for the work to turn between centres.

Headstock spindles can be driven either by a cone pulley and a belt, or by transmission of gears in the headstock. The lathe with a cone pulley drive is generally called a belt-driven lathe; the gear-driven lathe is referred to as a geared-head lathe.

The *feed reverse lever*, mounted on the headstock, reverses the rotation of the feed rod and lead screw.

QUICK-CHANGE GEARBOX

The *quick-change gearbox* (Fig. 9-3A and B) containing a number of different sized gears, provides the *feed rod* and *lead screw* with various speeds for turning and thread-cutting operations. The feed rod advances the carriage for turning operations when the *automatic feed lever* is engaged. The lead screw advances the carriage for thread-cutting operations when the *split-nut lever* is engaged.

CARRIAGE

The *carriage* (Fig. 9-3A and B) consisting of three main parts, the *saddle*, *cross-slide*,

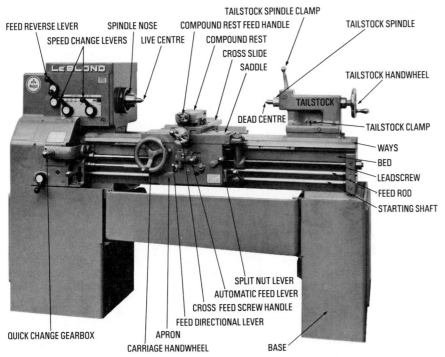

Fig. 9-3A Parts of an engine lathe

FEED REVERSE LEVER
SPEED CHANGE LEVERS
SPINDLE NOSE
LIVE CENTRE
TAILSTOCK SPINDLE CLAMP
COMPOUND REST FEED HANDLE
COMPOUND REST
CROSS SLIDE
SADDLE
TAILSTOCK SPINDLE
TAILSTOCK HANDWHEEL
TAILSTOCK
DEAD CENTRE
TAILSTOCK CLAMP
WAYS
BED
LEADSCREW
FEED ROD
STARTING SHAFT
SPLIT NUT LEVER
AUTOMATIC FEED LEVER
CROSS FEED SCREW HANDLE
FEED DIRECTIONAL LEVER
APRON
CARRIAGE HANDWHEEL
BASE
QUICK CHANGE GEARBOX

Courtesy The R. K. LeBlond Machine Tool Co.

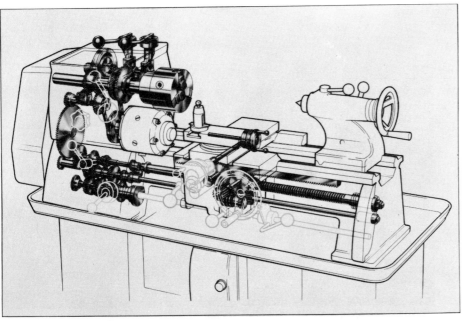

Courtesy Colchester Lathe & Tool Co.

Fig. 9-3B Phantom view of an engine lathe showing the gear drives

and *apron*, is used to move the cutting tool along the lathe bed.

The *saddle,* an H-shaped casting mounted on the top of the lathe ways, provides a means of mounting the cross-slide and the apron.

The *cross-slide,* mounted on top of the saddle, provides a manual or automatic cross-movement for the cutting tool. The *compound rest,* fitted on top of the cross-slide, is used to support the cutting tool. It can be swivelled to any angle for taper-turning operations, and is moved manually. The cross-slide and compound rest both have graduated collars which insure accurate cutting tool settings in hundredths of a millimetre or thousandths of an inch.

The *apron* is fastened to the saddle and contains the carriage and cross-slide controls. The *apron handwheel* can be turned manually to move the carriage along the lathe bed. This handwheel is connected to a gear which meshes in a rack fastened to the lathe bed.

The *automatic feed lever* engages a clutch which provides automatic feed to the carriage. The *feed change lever* can be set for longitudinal feed or for cross-feed. When in the neutral position, the feed change lever permits the split-nut lever to be engaged for thread cutting. For thread cutting operations, the carriage is moved automatically when the split-nut lever is engaged. This causes the threads of the split-nut to engage into the threads of the revolving lead screw and move the carriage at a predetermined rate.

TAILSTOCK

The *tailstock* (Fig. 9-4), consisting of the upper and lower tailstock castings, can be adjusted for taper or parallel turning by two screws set in the base. The tailstock can be locked in any position along the bed of the lathe by the *tailstock clamp.* The *tailstock spindle* has an internal taper to receive the *dead centre,* which provides support for the right-hand end of the work. Other standard tapered shank tools, such as reamers and drills, can be held in the

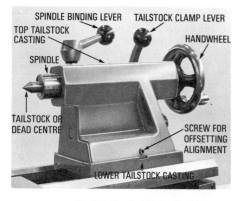

Fig. 9-4   The tailstock assembly

tailstock spindle. A *spindle binding lever* or lock handle is used to hold the tailstock spindle in a fixed position. The *tailstock handwheel* moves the tailstock spindle in or out of the tailstock casting. It can also be used to provide a hand feed for drilling and reaming operations.

SETTING SPEEDS ON A LATHE

Engine lathes are designed to operate at various spindle speeds for machining of different materials. These speeds are measured in revolutions per minute (r/min) and are changed by the cone pulleys or gear levers.

On a *belt-driven lathe*, various speeds are obtained by changing the flat belt and the back gear drive.

On the *geared-head lathe* (Fig. 9-5) speeds are changed by moving the speed levers into proper positions according to the r/min chart fastened to the headstock. While shifting the lever positions, place one hand on the faceplate or chuck, and turn the face plate slowly by hand. This will enable the levers to engage the gear teeth without clashing.

NOTE: Never change speeds when the lathe is running. On lathes equipped with *variable speed drives*, the speed is changed by turning a dial or handle while the machine is running.

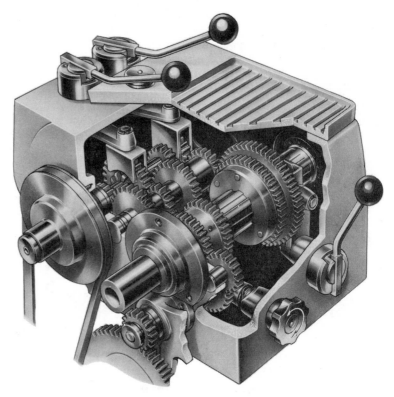

Fig. 9-5   A geared headstock

Fig. 9-6A   The quick-change gearbox

MASTER 6½ in.	LEVERS	ENGLISH—THREADS PER INCH		METRIC-PITCH IN mm	
		SLIDING FEEDS IN THOUSANDTHS	SURFACING ¼	SLIDING	
	D B	60 56 52 48 44 40 38 36 32			
		0.5 mm .005 .005 .006 .006 0.75 mm .007 .008 .009			
MADE BY	C B	30 28 26 24 22 20 19 18 16			
THE COLCHESTER LATHE CO. LTD.		1 mm .010 .011 1.25 mm .013 1.5 mm .015 .016 .017			
COLCHESTER	D A	15 14 13 12 11 10 9½ 9 8			
ENGLAND		2 mm .020 .021 2.5 mm .025 3 mm .029 .031 .034			
	C A	7½ 7 6½ 6 5½ 5 4¾ 4½ 4			
		4 mm .039 .042 5 mm .050 6 mm .058 .061 .068			

FILL WITH SHELL TELLUS OIL 33 TO MARK ON SIGHT GLASS
OIL OBTAINABLE FROM SHELL OIL COMPANIES THROUGHOUT THE WORLD

Feeds & threads available from Master gearbox

Courtesy Colchester Lathe & Tool Co.

Fig. 9-6B A quick-change gearbox chart. Note the settings for metric threads

SETTING FEEDS

The feed of an engine lathe, or the distance the carriage will travel in one revolution of the spindle, depends on the speed of the feed rod or lead screw. This is controlled by the change gears in the quick-change gearbox (Fig. 9-6A). This quick-change gearbox obtains its drive from the headstock spindle through the end gear train (Fig. 9-3B). A chart mounted on the front of the quick-change gearbox indicates the various feeds and metric pitches or threads per inch which may be obtained by setting levers to the positions indicated (Fig. 9-6B).

To Set the Feed for the Apron (Carriage Drive)

1. Select the desired feed on the chart.
2. Move tumbler lever #4 (Fig. 9-6A) into the hole directly below the selected feed.
3. Follow the row in which the selected feed is found to the left, and set the *feed change levers* (#1 and #2) to the letters indicated.
4. Set lever #3 to disengage the lead screw.
   NOTE: Before turning on the lathe, be sure all levers are fully engaged by turning the headstock spindle by hand, and see that the feed rod turns.

SHEAR PINS AND SLIP CLUTCHES

To prevent damage to the feed mechanism due to overload or sudden torque, some lathes are equipped with either *shear pins* or *slip clutches*. Shear pins, usually made of brass, may be found on the feed rod, leadscrew, and the end gear train. Spring-loaded slip clutches are found only on feed rods. When the feed mechanism is overloaded, either the shear pin will break or the slip clutch will slip, causing the automatic feed to stop. This prevents damage to the gears or shafts of the feed mechanism.

LATHE ACCESSORIES

Many lathe accessories are available to increase the variety of work which can be machined. Work-holding and work-supporting devices are used to hold or support the workpiece for a machining operation. Lathe centres, chucks, faceplates, mandrels, and steady rests are some of the more common lathe accessories.

LATHE CENTRES

Most turning operations can be performed between centres on a lathe. Work to be turned between centres must have a centre hole drilled in each end (usually 60°) to provide a bearing surface which allows the work to turn on the centres. The centres merely support the work while the cutting operations are performed. A lathe dog, fitted into a driving plate, provides a drive for the work (Fig. 9-7A).

A variety of lathe centres are used to suit various operations or workpieces. The revolving *dead centre* (Fig. 9-7B), sometimes called a live dead centre, is commonly used to support long work held in a chuck. This centre usually contains anti-friction bearings which allow the centre to revolve with the work. No lubrication is required between the centre and the workpiece, and the centre tension is not affected by workpiece expansion during the cutting action.

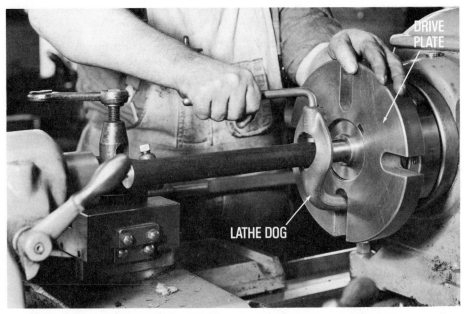

DRIVE PLATE

LATHE DOG

Courtesy J. H. Williams & Co.

Fig. 9-7A Work mounted between centres is usually driven by a lathe dog

- REMOVABLE POINT
- ROTATING COVER
- ROLLER AND CAGE ASSEMBLY
- SPRING RING
- BODY
- SPINDLE
- LOCKING SCREW
- NEEDLE ROLLER BEARING
- SCREWED RETAINER
- O-RING
- END CAP

Courtesy Enco Manufacturing Company

Fig. 9-7B   A revolving dead centre

Courtesy Enco Manufacturing Company

Fig. 9-7C   A micro-set adjustable dead centre

A *micro-set adjustable centre* (Fig. 9-7C) fits into the tailstock spindle and provides a means of aligning lathe centres or producing slight tapers on work being machined between centres. An eccentric, or sometimes a dovetail slide, allows this type of centre to be adjusted a limited amount to each side of centre. Lathe centres are quickly and easily aligned with an offset centre.

Courtesy Cincinnati Milacron Inc.

Fig. 9-7D   A self-driving live centre

The *self-driving centre* (Fig. 9-7D), mounted in the headstock spindle, is used when machining the entire length of a workpiece in one operation, and a chuck or lathe dog could not be used to drive the work. Grooves ground around the circumference of the lathe centre point provide the drive for the workpiece. The work (usually a soft material) is forced onto the driving centre; a revolving dead centre is used to support the work and keep it against the grooves of the driving centre.

CHUCKS

Some workpieces, because of their size

and shape, cannot be held and machined between lathe centres. Lathe chucks are used extensively for holding work for machining operations. The most commonly used lathe chucks are: the three-jaw universal, four-jaw independent, and the collet chuck.

The three-jaw universal chuck (Fig. 9-8A) is used to hold round and hexagonal work. It grasps the work quickly and within a few hundredths of a millimetre or thousandths of an inch of accuracy, because the three jaws move simultaneously when adjusted by the chuck wrench. This simultaneous motion is caused by a scroll plate into which all three jaws fit. Three-jaw chucks are made in various sizes from 4 to 16 in. (100-400 mm■) in diameter. They are usually provided with two sets of jaws, one for outside chucking and the other for inside chucking.

The four-jaw independent chuck (Fig. 9-8B) has four jaws, each of which can be adjusted independently by a chuck

wrench. They are used to hold round, square, hexagonal, and irregular-shaped workpieces. The jaws can be reversed to hold work by the inside diameter.

Universal and independent chucks can be fitted to the three types of headstock spindles. Fig. 9-9A shows a threaded spindle nose, Fig. 9-9B a tapered spindle nose, Fig. 9-9C a cam-lock spindle nose. The threaded type turns in a clockwise direction; the tapered type is held by a lock nut that tightens on the chuck. The cam lock is held by tightening the cam locks using a T-wrench. On the taper and cam lock types, the chuck is aligned by the taper on the spindle nose.

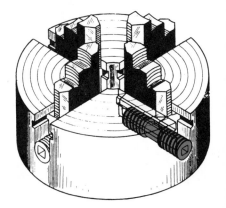

Fig. 9-8B   A four-jaw independent chuck

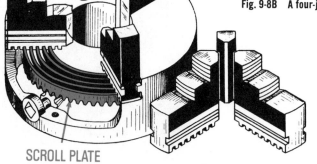

SCROLL PLATE

Fig. 9-8A   A three-jaw universal geared scroll chuck

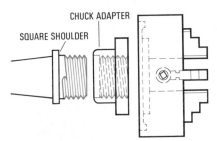

Fig. 9-9A   A threaded spindle nose

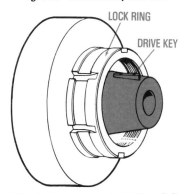

Fig. 9-9B   An American standard lathe spindle nose

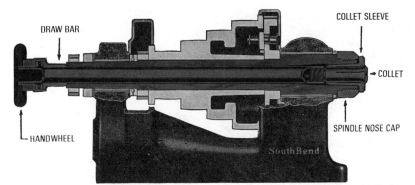

Courtesy South Bend Lathe Inc.

Fig. 9-10   Cross-section view of a belt drive headstock showing the construction of a draw-in collet chuck attachment

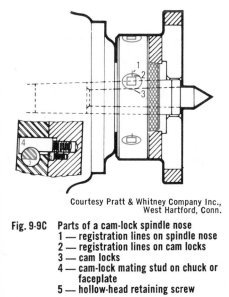

Courtesy Pratt & Whitney Company Inc.,
West Hartford, Conn.

Fig. 9-9C   Parts of a cam-lock spindle nose
1 — registration lines on spindle nose
2 — registration lines on cam locks
3 — cam locks
4 — cam-lock mating stud on chuck or faceplate
5 — hollow-head retaining screw

The collet chuck (Fig. 9-10) is the most accurate chuck and is used for high-precision work and small tools. Spring collets are available to hold round, square, or hexagon-shaped workpieces. Each collet has a range of only a few hundredths of a

millimetre or thousandths of an inch over or under the size stamped on the collet.

A special adaptor is fitted into the taper of the headstock spindle, and a hollow draw bar having an internal thread is inserted in the opposite end of the headstock spindle. As the handwheel (and draw bar) is revolved, it draws the collet into the tapered adaptor, causing the collet to tighten on the workpiece. This type of chuck is also referred to as a *spring collet chuck*. Another form of spring collet chuck uses a chuck wrench to tighten the collet on the workpiece. This type is mounted on the spindle nose in the same manner as standard chucks and can hold larger size work than the draw-in type.

Courtesy The Jacobs Manufacturing Company

Fig. 9-11   The Jacobs collet chuck has a wider range than other types of collet chucks

Courtesy James Neill & Company (Sheffield) Ltd.

Fig. 9-12   Work may be held on a magnetic chuck for turning operations

Faceplates are used to hold work that is too large or of such a shape that it cannot be held in a chuck or between centres. Faceplates are equipped with several slots to permit the use of bolts to secure the work or angle plate (Fig. 9-13), so that the axis of the workpiece may be aligned with the lathe centres. When work is mounted off-centre, a counterbalance (Fig. 9-13) should be fastened to the faceplate to prevent imbalance and the resultant vibrations when the lathe is in operation.

A steady rest (Fig. 9-14) is used to support long work held in a chuck or between lathe centres. It is located on, and aligned by,

Courtesy Standard-Modern Tool Co.

Fig. 9-14   A steady rest is often used to support long or slender work during a machining operation

The Jacobs collet chuck (Fig. 9-11) has a wider range than the spring collet chuck. Instead of a draw bar, it incorporates an impact-tightening handwheel to close the collets on the workpiece. A set of 11 rubber-flex collets, each capable of a range of almost 3.2 mm, makes it possible to hold a wide range of work diameters. When the handwheel is turned clockwise, the rubber-flex collet is forced into a taper, causing it to tighten on the workpiece. When the handwheel is turned counterclockwise, the collet opens and releases the workpiece.

Magnetic chucks (Fig. 9-12) are used to hold iron or steel parts that are too thin, or that may be damaged if held in a conventional chuck. These chucks are fitted to an adaptor mounted on the headstock spindle. Work is held lightly for aligning purposes by turning the chuck wrench approximately 1/4 turn. After the work has been trued, the chuck is turned to the

full-on position to hold the work securely. This type of chuck is used only for light cuts and for special grinding applications.

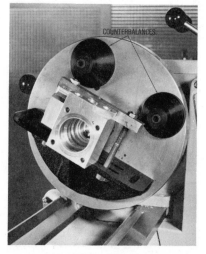

COUNTERBALANCES

Courtesy Colchester Lathe & Tool Co.

Fig. 9-13   An angle plate fastened to a faceplate is used to hold the work for machining

the ways of the lathe, and may be positioned at any point along the lathe bed provided it clears the carriage travel. The three jaws, tipped with plastic, bronze, or rollers, may be adjusted to support any work diameter within the steady rest capacity. During machining operations performed on or near the end of a workpiece, a steady rest supports the end of work held in a chuck, when the work cannot be supported by the tailstock centre. A steady rest also supports the centre of long work to prevent springing when the work is machined between centres.

A follower rest (Fig. 9-15), mounted on the saddle, travels with the carriage to prevent work from springing up and away from the cutting tool. The cutting tool is generally positioned just ahead of the follower rest to provide a smooth bearing surface for the two jaws of the follower rest.

Fig. 9-16 A plain mandrel

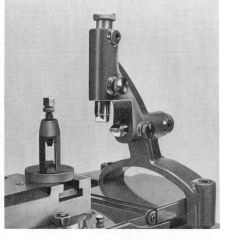

Fig. 9-15 A follower rest mounted on the saddle may be used to support long, slender work when machining

A mandrel holds an internally machined workpiece between centres so that further machining operations are concentric with the bore. There are several types of mandrels, the most common being the *plain mandrel* (Fig. 9-16), the *expanding mandrel*, and the *gang mandrel*.

CUTTING SPEEDS AND FEEDS

Lathe work *cutting speed* may be defined as the rate at which a point on the work circumference travels past the cutting tool. Cutting speed is always expressed in metres per minute (m/min) or in feet per minute (ft./min). Industry demands that machining operations be performed as

TABLE 9-1: LATHE CUTTING SPEEDS IN METRES PER MINUTE AND FEET PER MINUTE USING A HIGH SPEED TOOLBIT						
	TURNING AND BORING				**THREADING**	
	ROUGH CUT		**FINISH CUT**			
MATERIAL	m/min	ft./min	m/min	ft./min	m/min	ft./min
MACHINE STEEL	27	90	30	100	11	35
TOOL STEEL	21	70	27	90	9	30
CAST IRON	18	60	24	80	8	25
BRONZE	27	90	30	100	8	25
ALUMINUM	61	200	93	300	18	60

quickly as possible; therefore correct cutting speeds must be used for the type of material being cut. If a cutting speed is too high, the cutting tool edge breaks down rapidly, resulting in time lost to recondition the tool. With too slow a cutting speed, time will be lost for the machining operation, resulting in low production rates. Based on research and testing by steel and cutting tool manufacturers, the cutting speeds for high-speed steel tools listed in Table 9-1 are recom-

mended for efficient metal removal rates. These speeds may be varied slightly to suit factors such as the condition of the machine, the type of work material, and sand or hard spots in the metal. The cutting speeds for cemented carbide and ceramic cutting tools may be found in Chapter 15, Tables 15-4 and 15-7.

The r/min (revolutions per minute) at which the lathe should be set for cutting metals is as follows:

METRIC MEASUREMENTS

Formula: $r/min = \dfrac{CS \text{ (in metres)}}{\pi D \text{ (in metres)}}$

Where   CS = cutting speed
D = diameter of work to be turned

EXAMPLE: Calculate the r/min required to turn a 45 mm diameter piece of machine steel.

(CS of machine steel = 30 m/min)

Since the diameter of the workpiece is given in millimetres, this must first be changed to metres.

$45 \div 1000 = 0.045$

$$r/min = \frac{CS}{\pi D}$$

$$= \frac{30}{3.1416 \times 0.045}$$

$$= \frac{30}{0.141}$$

$$= 212.8$$

INCH MEASUREMENTS

Formula: $r/min = \dfrac{CS \times 12}{\pi D}$

However, because most lathes provide only a limited number of speed settings, a simpler formula is usually used:

$$r/min = \frac{CS \times 4}{D}$$

Thus, to calculate the r/min required to rough-turn a 2 in. diameter piece of machine steel (CS 90)

$$r/min = \frac{CS \times 4}{D}$$

$$= \frac{90 \times 4}{2}$$

$$= 180$$

LATHE FEED

The feed of a lathe is defined as the distance the cutting tool advances along the length of the work for every revolution of the spindle. For example, if the lathe is set for a 0.40 mm feed, the cutting tool will travel along the length of the work 0.40 mm for every complete turn that the

work makes. The feed of an engine lathe is dependent upon the speed of the lead screw or feed rod. The speed is controlled by the change gears in the *quick-change gearbox* (Fig. 9-6A).

Whenever possible, only two cuts should be taken to bring a diameter to size: a roughing cut and a finishing cut. Since the purpose of a roughing cut is to remove excess material quickly and surface finish is not too important, a coarse feed should be used. The finishing cut is used to bring the diameter to size and produce a good surface finish and therefore a fine feed should be used. For general purpose machining, a 0.25 mm to 0.40 mm or a .010 in. to .015 in. feed for roughing and a 0.07 mm to 0.12 mm or a .003 in. to .005 in. feed for finishing is recommended. Table 9-2 lists the recommended feeds for cutting various materials when using a high-speed steel cutting tool.

LATHE TOOLHOLDERS

Most toolbits used in lathe cutting operations are square and are generally held in a standard type toolholder (Fig. 9-17). These toolholders are made in various styles and sizes to suit different machining operations. Toolholders for turning operations are available in three styles: left-hand offset, right-hand offset, and straight.

Each of these toolholders has a square hole to accommodate the square toolbit which is held in place by a set screw. The hole in the toolholder is at an angle of approximately 15 to 20° to the base of the toolholder (Fig. 9-17C). When the cutting tool is set on centre, this angle provides the proper amount of back rake in relation to the workpiece.

Courtesy J. H. Williams & Co.

Fig. 9-17A   A left-hand offset toolholder

TABLE 9-2: FEEDS FOR VARIOUS MATERIALS (USING A HIGH SPEED CUTTING TOOL)

MATERIAL	ROUGH CUTS		FINISH CUTS	
	Millimetres	Inches	Millimetres	Inches
MACHINE STEEL	0.25–0.50	.010–.020	0.075–0.25	.003–.010
TOOL STEEL	0.25–0.50	.010–.020	0.075–0.25	.003–.010
CAST IRON	0.40–0.65	.015–.025	0.13 –0.30	.005–.012
BRONZE	0.40–0.65	.015–.025	0.075–0.25	.003–.010
ALUMINUM	0.40–0.75	.015–.030	0.13 –0.25	.005–.010

The *left-hand offset* toolholder (Fig. 9-17A) is designed for machining work close to the chuck or faceplate and for cutting from right to left. This type of toolholder is designated by the letter L to indicate the direction of cut.

Courtesy J. H. Williams & Co.

Fig. 9-17B A right-hand offset toolholder

The *right-hand offset* toolholder (Fig. 9-17B) is designed for machining work close to the tailstock, for cutting from left to right, and for facing operations. This type of toolholder is designated by the letter R.

Courtesy J. H. Williams & Co.

Fig. 9-17C A straight toolholder

The *straight* toolholder (Fig. 9-17C) is a general purpose type. It can be used for

taking cuts in either direction and for general machining operations. This type of toolholder is designated by the letter S.

Courtesy J. H. Williams & Co.

Fig. 9-17D A carbide toolholder (straight)

The *carbide* toolholder (Fig. 9-17D) has a square hole, parallel to the base of the toolholder, to accommodate carbide-tipped toolbits. When using carbide tipped toolbits, it is important that the toolbit be held so that there is little or no back rake (Fig. 9-17D). Toolholders of this type are designated by the letter C. The correct methods of using this and other types of carbide toolholders are fully explained in Chapter 15.

The *turret-type* toolholder (Fig. 9-18) provides a convenient means of holding toolbits when several operations, such as turning, threading, grooving, and parting, must be performed. This type of toolholder is suitable for carbide tipped tools, since no provision is made for back rake. Four different types of toolbits may be mounted in this toolholder and each may

be brought into position by loosening the locking handle and rotating the turret head until the desired toolbit is in the cutting position. The handle is then turned to lock the head in place.

CUTTING TOOL MATERIALS

Lathe toolbits are generally made of four materials: high-speed steel, cast alloys such as stellite, cemented carbides, and ceramics.

The properties that each of these materials possesses are different and the application of each depends on the material being machined, and the condition of the machine.

Lathe toolbits should possess the following properties.

a) They should be hard.
b) They should be wear-resistant.
c) They should be capable of standing up to high temperatures developed during the cutting operation.
d) They should be able to withstand shock during the cutting operation.

HIGH-SPEED STEEL TOOLBITS

Probably the toolbit most commonly used in schools for lathe operations is the high-speed steel toolbit. High-speed steels may contain combinations of tungsten, chromium, vanadium, molybdenum, and cobalt. They are capable of taking heavy cuts, withstanding shock, and maintaining a sharp cutting edge under red heat.

High-speed steel toolbits are generally of two types: molybdenum-base (Group M) and tungsten-base (Group T). The most widely used tungsten-base toolbit is known as T_1, which is sometimes called 18-4-1 since it contains about 18% tungsten, 4% chromium, and 1% vanadium.

A general purpose molybdenum-base high-speed steel toolbit is known as M_1 or 8-2-1. This alloy contains about 8% molybdenum, 2% tungsten, 1% vanadium, and 4% chromium.

These two types are general purpose tools; if more red hardness is desired, one

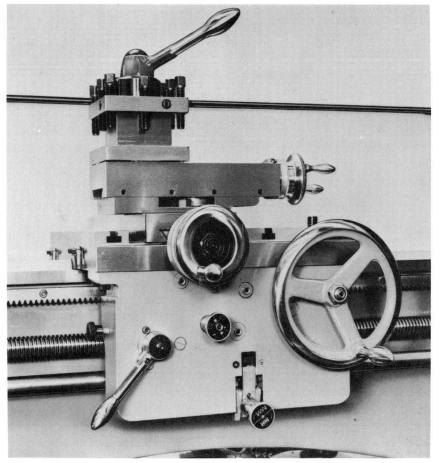

Courtesy Colchester Lathe & Tool Co.

Fig. 9-18   A turret-type toolholder may hold up to four cutting tools for different machining operations

steel shank and the throwaway type of insert (see Chapter 15). Carbide toolbits have low toughness, but high hardness and excellent red-hardness qualities. Carbides are available in different grades to suit the material being machined. Tungsten carbide toolbits are generally used for cutting cast iron and nonferrous metals, whereas titanium and tantalum carbides are used for machining various types of steel. Cemented carbide toolbits are capable of speeds three to four times greater than high-speed steel toolbits.

CERAMIC AND DIAMOND CUTTING TOOLS

The most recent development in lathe cutting tools is the application of ceramic and diamond cutting tools. These tools are capable of much higher cutting speeds than those of any other cutting tools. They are discussed in detail in Chapter 15.

CUTTING TOOL NOMENCLATURE

Cutting tools used on a lathe are generally single-pointed cutting tools, and although the shape of the tool is changed for various applications, the same nomenclature applies to all cutting tools (Fig. 9-19A).

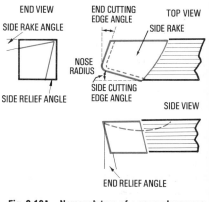

Fig. 9-19A   Nomenclature of a general purpose lathe toolbit

containing more cobalt should be selected. Since there are many different grades of high-speed steel toolbits, it is advisable to refer to the manufacturer's recommendations for a toolbit for a specific job. Table 17-1 indicates the properties imparted to a high-speed steel toolbit by the various alloying elements.

CAST ALLOY TOOLBITS

Cast alloy (stellite) toolbits usually contain 25% to 35% chromium, 4% to 25% tungsten, 1% to 3% carbon; the remainder is cobalt. These toolbits have high hardness, high resistance to wear, and

excellent red-hardness qualities. Since they are cast, they are weaker and more brittle than high-speed steel toolbits. Stellite toolbits are capable of high speeds and feeds on deep uninterrupted cuts. They may be operated at about two to two-and-a-half times the speed of a high-speed steel toolbit.

NOTE: When grinding stellite toolbits, light pressure only should be used and the toolbit should not be quenched in water.

CEMENTED CARBIDES

Cemented carbide toolbits for lathe work may be of two types; those brazed to a

The base is the bottom surface of the tool shank.

The **cutting edge** is the leading edge of the toolbit that does the cutting.

The **face** is the surface against which the chip bears as it is separated from the work.

The **flank** is the surface of the tool which is adjacent to and below the cutting edge.

The **nose** is the tip of the cutting tool formed by the junction of the cutting edge and the front face.

The **nose radius** is the radius to which the nose is ground. The size of the radius will affect the finish. For rough turning, a small nose radius (about 0.40 mm) is used. A larger radius (about 1.6 to 3.2 mm) is used for finish cuts.

The **point** is the end of the tool that has been ground for cutting purposes.

The **shank** is the body of the toolbit or the part held in the toolholder.

LATHE TOOLBIT ANGLES AND CLEARANCES

Proper performance of a toolbit depends on the clearance and rake angles which must be ground on the toolbit. Although these angles vary for different materials, the nomenclature is the same for all toolbits.

Side Cutting Edge Angle – the angle which the cutting edge forms with the side of the tool shank (Fig. 9-19A). Side cutting angles for a general purpose lathe cutting tool may be from 10 to 20°, depending on the material being cut. If this angle is too large (over 30°), the tool will tend to chatter.

End Cutting Edge Angle – the angle formed by the end cutting edge and a line at right angles to the centre line of the toolbit (Fig. 9-19A). This angle may vary from 5 to 30° depending on the type of cut and finish desired. An angle of 5 to 15° is satisfactory for roughing cuts; angles between 15 and 30° are used for general

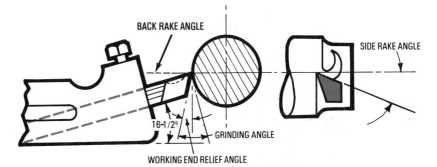

Fig. 9-19B   Lathe cutting tool angles and clearances

purpose turning tools. The larger angle permits the cutting tool to be swivelled to the left when taking light cuts close to the dog or chuck, or when turning to a shoulder.

Side Relief (Clearance) Angle – the angle ground on the flank of the tool below the cutting edge (Fig. 9-19A). This angle is generally 6 to 10°. The side clearance on a toolbit permits the cutting tool to advance lengthwise into the rotating work and prevents the flank from rubbing against the workpiece.

End Relief (Clearance) Angle – the angle ground below the nose of the toolbit which permits the cutting tool to be fed into the work. It is generally 10 to 15° for general purpose tools (Fig. 9-19A). This angle must be measured when the toolbit is held in the toolholder. The end

relief angle varies with the hardness and type of material and the type of cut being taken. The end relief angle is smaller for harder materials, to provide support under the cutting edge.

Side Rake Angle – the angle at which the face is ground away from the cutting edge. For general purpose toolbits, the side rake is generally 14° (Fig. 9-19A). Side rake creates a keener cutting edge and allows the chips to flow away quickly. For softer materials, the side rake angle is generally increased.

Back (Top) Rake – the backward slope of the tool face away from the nose. The back rake angle is generally about 20° and is provided for in the toolholder (Fig. 9-19B). Back rake permits the chips to flow away from the point of the cutting tool.

TABLE 9-3: RAKE AND RELIEF ANGLES IN DEGREES FOR HIGH-SPEED STEEL LATHE TOOLS				
Material	**Side Relief**	**Front Relief**	**Side Rake**	**Back Rake**
Aluminum	12	8	15	35
Brass	10	8	5 to −4	0
Bronze	10	8	5 to −4	0
Cast iron	10	8	12	5
Copper	12	10	20	16
Machine steel	10 to 12	8	12 to 18	8 to 15
Tool steel	10	8	12	8
Stainless steel	10	8	15 to 20	8

GRINDING LATHE CUTTING TOOLS

Because of the number of turning operations which can be performed on a lathe, a wide variety of cutting tools are used. In order for these cutting tools to perform effectively, they must possess certain angles and clearances for the material being cut. All lathe tools cut if they have front and side clearance. The addition of side and top rake enables the chips to escape quickly from the cutting edge, making the tool cut better. All lathe cutting tools must have certain angles and clearances regardless of shape; therefore, only the grinding of a general purpose cutting tool (Fig. 9-20) will be explained in detail.

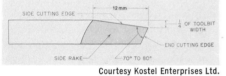

Courtesy Kostel Enterprises Ltd.

Fig. 9-20   The shape and dimensions of a general purpose toolbit

To Grind a General Purpose Toolbit

1. Grip the toolbit firmly while supporting the hands on the grinder toolrest (Fig. 9-21).
2. Hold the toolbit at the proper angle to grind the cutting edge angle. At the same time, tilt the bottom of the toolbit in towards the wheel and grind the 10° side relief or clearance angle on the cutting edge.
   NOTE: The cutting edge should be approximately 12 mm long and should be over about one quarter the width of the toolbit (Fig. 9-21).
3. While grinding, move the toolbit back and forth across the face of the wheel. This accelerates grinding and prevents grooving the wheel.
4. The toolbit must be cooled frequently during the grinding operation. NEVER OVERHEAT A TOOLBIT.
   NOTE: Stellite or cemented carbide tools should never be quenched.

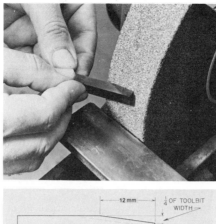

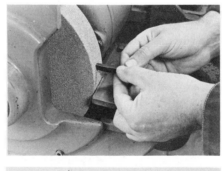

Courtesy Kostel Enterprises Ltd.

Fig. 9-21   Grinding the side cutting edge and side relief angles on a toolbit

5. Grind the end cutting edge so that it forms an angle a little less than 90° with the side cutting edge (Fig. 9-22). Hold the tool so that the end cutting edge angle and end relief angle of 15° are ground at the same time.

Courtesy Kostel Enterprises Ltd.

Fig. 9-22   Grinding the end relief angle on a lathe toolbit

6. Check the amount of end relief when the toolbit is in the toolholder (Fig. 9-23).

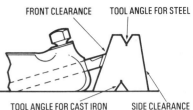

Courtesy South Bend Lathe Inc.

Fig. 9-23   Checking the end relief angle of a toolbit while it is in a toolholder

7. Hold the top of the toolbit at approximately 45° to the axis of the wheel and grind the side rake to approximately 14° (Fig. 9-24).
   NOTE: When grinding the side rake, *be sure that the top of the cutting edge is not ground below the top of the toolbit*. If a step is ground in the top of the toolbit, a chip trap is formed which reduces the efficiency of the cutting tool.

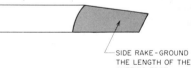

Courtesy Kostel Enterprises Ltd.

Fig. 9-24   Grinding the side rake on a lathe toolbit

8. Grind a slight radius on the point of the cutting tool, *being sure to maintain the same front and side clearance angle*.
9. With an oilstone, hone the cutting edge of the toolbit slightly. This will lengthen the life of the toolbit and enable it to produce a better surface finish.

LATHE SAFETY

The lathe, like most other machine tools, can be hazardous if not operated properly. A good lathe operator is a safe operator who realizes the importance of keeping the machine and the surrounding area clean and tidy. Accidents on any machine do not just happen; they are usually caused by carelessness and could generally be avoided. To minimize the chance of accidents when you are operating a lathe, the following precautions should be observed.

Courtesy The Clausing Corporation

Fig. 9-25A   Wearing rings and watches around machines is a dangerous practice

1. Always wear approved safety glasses.
2. Roll up sleeves, remove ties, and tuck in loose clothing.
3. Never wear a ring or watch (Fig. 9-25A).
4. Do not operate a lathe until you fully understand its controls.
5. Never operate a machine if any safety guards are removed.
6. Stop the lathe before you measure the work, and before you clean, oil or adjust the machine.
7. Do not use a rag to clean the work or the machine when the lathe is in operation; it may be drawn into the machine.
8. Never attempt to stop a lathe chuck or faceplate with your hand.
9. Be sure the chuck or faceplate is mounted securely before you start the lathe.

Courtesy The Clausing Corporation

Fig. 9-25B   Always remove the chuck wrench before starting a lathe

10. Always remove the chuck wrench before you start the machine (Fig. 9-25B).
11. Always revolve the lathe spindle one turn by hand before you start the lathe to ensure that all parts will clear without jamming.
12. Keep the floor around the machine free from grease, oil, metal cuttings, tools, and workpieces (Fig. 9-25C).

Courtesy The Clausing Corporation

Fig. 9-25C   Oil and grease on floors can be dangerous

MOUNTING AND REMOVING LATHE CENTRES

Any work machined between lathe centres is generally turned for some portion of its length, then reversed, and the other end finished. It is important, when machining work between centres, that the live centre run absolutely true. If the live centre does not run true, when the work is reversed to machine the opposite end, the two turned diameters will not be concentric with each other and the part may have to be scrapped.

To Mount Lathe Centres

1. Thoroughly clean the tapers on the lathe centres and in the headstock and tailstock spindles.
   NOTE: Never attempt to clean the taper in the headstock spindle while the lathe is running.
2. If there are any burrs on the centre or in the lathe spindle, remove them.
3. Partially insert the cleaned centre in the lathe spindle.
4. With a quick snap, force the centre into the spindle. When mounting a tailstock centre, observe the same procedure.

After a centre has been mounted in the headstock spindle, it should be checked for trueness. Start the lathe and observe if the centre runs true. Whenever accuracy is required, it is wise to check the trueness of the centre with a dial indicator. If the centre is not running true, and has been mounted properly, it should be either turned or ground.

To Remove Lathe Centres

The *live centre* may be removed by using a *knockout bar* that is pushed through the headstock spindle (Fig. 9-26). A slight tap is required to remove the centre. When removing the live centre with a knockout bar, place a cloth over the centre and hold it with one hand to prevent an accident or damage to the centre.

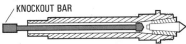

KNOCKOUT BAR

Fig. 9-26   Removing the live centre with a knockout bar

The dead centre can be removed by turning the tailstock handwheel to draw the spindle back into the tailstock. The end of the screw contacts the end of the dead centre, forcing it out of the spindle.

ALIGNMENT OF LATHE CENTRES

To produce a parallel diameter when machining work between centres, it is important that the lathe centres be aligned; that is, the two lathe centres must be in line with each other and true with the centre line of the lathe. If the centres are not aligned, the work being machined will be tapered.

Three common methods are used to align lathe centres.

a) By aligning the centre lines on the back of the tailstock with each other (Fig. 9-27). This is only a visual check and therefore not too accurate.

b) The trial cut method (Fig. 9-28) where a small cut is taken from each end of the work and the diameters are measured with a micrometer.

c) By using a parallel test bar and dial indicator (Fig. 9-29). This is the fastest and most accurate method of aligning lathe centres.

To Align Centres by Adjusting the Tailstock

1. Loosen the tailstock clamp nut or lever.
2. Loosen one of the adjusting screws G or F (Fig. 9-27), depending upon the direction the tailstock must be moved. Tighten the other adjusting screw until the line on the top half of the tailstock aligns exactly with the line on the bottom half.

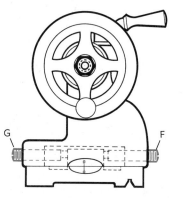

Courtesy South Bend Lathe Inc.

Fig. 9-27   The lines on the tailstock must be in line to produce a parallel diameter

3. Tighten the loosened adjusting screw to lock both halves of the tailstock in place.
4. Lock the tailstock clamp nut or lever.

To Align Centres by the Trial Cut Method

1. Take a light cut (approximately 0.10 mm) to a true diameter, from Section A at the tailstock end for 6 mm long.
2. Stop the feed and note the reading on the graduated collar of the crossfeed handle.
3. Move the cutting tool away from the work with the crossfeed handle.
4. Bring the cutting tool close to the headstock end.
5. Return the cutting tool to the same collar setting as at Section A.
6. Cut a 12 mm length at Section B and then stop the lathe.
7. Measure both diameters with a micrometer (Fig. 9-28).
8. If both diameters are not the same size, adjust the tailstock either toward or away from the cutting tool one-half the difference between the two readings.

Courtesy Kostel Enterprises Ltd.

Fig. 9-28   A trial cut at each end of the work is used to check centre alignment

9. Take another light cut at A and B. Measure these diameters and adjust the tailstock, if required.

To Align Centres Using a Dial Indicator

1. Clean the lathe and work centres and mount the test bar.
2. Adjust the test bar snugly between centres and tighten the tailstock spindle clamp.

3. Mount a dial indicator on the toolpost or lathe carriage. Be sure that the indicator plunger is parallel to the lathe bed and that the contact point is set on centre.
4. Adjust the cross-slide so that the indicator registers approximately 0.65 mm or .025 in. at the tailstock end.
5. Move the carriage by hand so that the indicator registers on the diameter at the headstock end (Fig. 9-29) and note the indicator reading.
6. If both indicator readings are not the same, adjust the tailstock by the adjusting screws until the indicator registers the same reading at both ends.

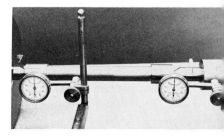

Courtesy Kostel Enterprises Ltd.

Fig. 9-29   Tailstock alignment may be accurately checked using a parallel test bar and dial indicator

MOUNTING WORK BETWEEN CENTRES

Work mounted between centres can be machined, removed, or set up for additional machining, and still maintain the same degree of accuracy. Turning on a lathe is one of the most important machining operations in a machine shop. It is very important that the cutting tool and work be properly set up, or damage to the machine, work, and lathe centres will result.

To Set Up a Cutting Tool for Machining

1. Move the toolpost to the left-hand side of the T-slot in the compound rest.
2. Mount a toolholder in the toolpost so that the set screw in the toolholder is approximately 25 mm beyond the toolpost (Fig. 9-30).

Fig. 9-30 The toolholder and toolbit being set up for a machining operation

When taking heavy cuts, it is advisable to set the toolholder at right angles to the work (Fig. 9-31A). If the toolholder should move under pressure of the cut, the cutting tool would swing away from the work and make the diameter larger.

If the toolholder were set as in Fig. 9-31B and it moved under pressure of the cut, the toolbit would swing into the work, causing the diameter to be cut undersize. A toolholder can be set as in Fig. 9-31B for light finishing cuts.

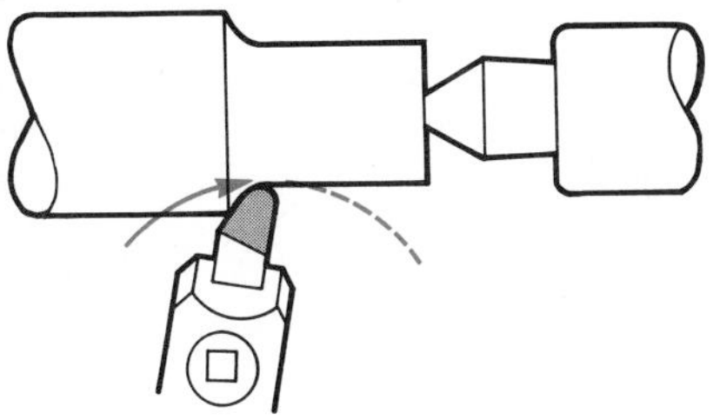

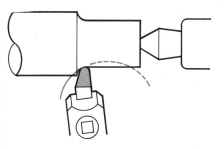

Fig. 9-31A The toolholder set to prevent the tool from digging into the work

Fig. 9-31B The toolholder improperly set for taking a heavy cut

3. Insert the proper cutting tool into the toolholder, having the tool extend only 12 mm beyond the toolholder.
4. Set the cutting tool point to centre height. Check it against the lathe centre point (Fig. 9-30).
5. Tighten the toolpost securely to prevent it from moving during a cut.

To Mount Work Between Lathe Centres

1. Check that the live centre is running true. If it is not running true, remove the centre, clean all surfaces, and replace the centre. Check again for trueness.
2. Clean the lathe centre points and the centre holes in the workpiece.
3. Adjust the tailstock spindle until it projects about 65 to 75 mm beyond the tailstock.
4. Loosen the tailstock clamp nut or lever.
5. Place a lathe dog on the left-hand end of the work (Fig. 9-32) and leave it loose.
6. Apply a suitable centre lubricant to the right-hand end of the work.

7. Place the end of the work with the lathe dog on the live centre, and slide the tailstock up until it supports the other end of the work.
8. Tighten the tailstock clamp nut or lever.
9. Adjust the tail of the dog in the drive plate slot, making sure it does not bind, and tighten the lathe dog screw.
10. Turn the drive plate by hand until the tail of the lathe dog is parallel to the bed of the lathe.
11. Hold the tail of the dog *up* in the slot and with the other hand lightly tighten the tailstock handwheel.
12. Carefully turn the tailstock handwheel backwards until the tail of the dog drops in the drive plate slot.
13. Hold the tailstock handwheel in this position, and, with the other hand, tighten the tailstock spindle clamp.
14. Check the centre tension. The tail of the dog should drop by gravity into the slot, and there should be no end play between the centres.

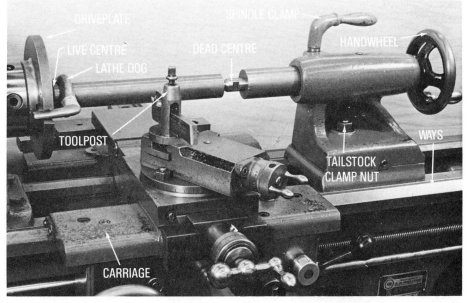

Courtesy Kostel Enterprises Ltd.

Fig. 9-32 Work mounted for machining between centres

15. Move the carriage to the furthest position of the cut and revolve the lathe by hand to make sure that the lathe dog clears the compound rest.

FACING BETWEEN CENTRES

Workpieces to be machined are generally cut a little longer than required, and then end faced to the proper length. Facing is an operation of machining the ends of a workpiece square with its axis. To produce a flat, square surface when facing between centres, the lathe centres must be in line.

The purposes of facing are:

a) to provide a true, flat surface, square with the axis of the work
b) to provide an accurate surface from which to take measurements
c) to cut the work to the required length

To Face Work Between Centres

1. Move the toolpost to the left-hand side of the compound rest, and set the right-hand facing toolbit to the height of the lathe centre point (Fig. 9-33A).
2. Clean the lathe and work centres, and mount the work between centres.
   NOTE: Use a half centre in the tailstock if it is available.
3. Set the facing toolbit pointing left, as shown in Fig. 9-33A.
   NOTE: The point of the toolbit must be closest to the work and a space must be left along the side.
4. Set the lathe to the correct speed for the diameter and type of material being cut.
5. Start the lathe and bring the toolbit as close to the lathe centre as possible (Fig. 9-33B).
6. Move the carriage to the left, using the apron handwheel, until a small cut is started.
7. Feed the cutting tool out by turning the crossfeed handle and cut from the centre outwards. If the automatic crossfeed is used for feeding the cutting tool, the carriage should be locked in position.

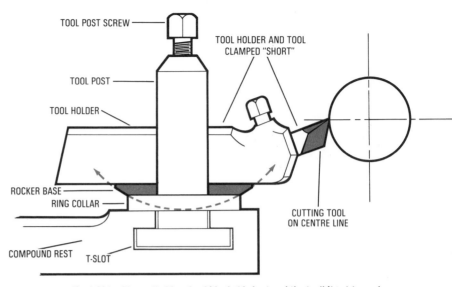

Fig. 9-33A The toolholder should be held short and the toolbit set to centre

8. Repeat operations 5, 6, and 7 until the work is cut to the correct length. (It is advisable, before facing, to mark the correct length with centre punch marks and then face until the punch marks are cut in half.)

NOTE: When facing, finishing cuts should begin at the centre of the workpiece and be fed toward the outside.

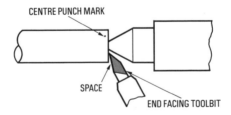

Fig. 9-33B Point of toolbit set for facing a surface

GRADUATED MICROMETER COLLARS

Graduated micrometer collars are sleeves or bushings that are mounted on the compound rest and crossfeed screws (Fig. 9-34). They assist the lathe operator to set

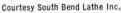

Courtesy South Bend Lathe Inc.

Fig. 9-34 Micrometer collars on the compound rest and crossfeed handles permit machining the work to an accurate size. The thumbscrew "A" is used to lock the collar in place

the cutting tool accurately to remove the required amount of material from the workpiece. The micrometer collars on lathes using the metric system of measurement are usually graduated in steps of two hundredths of a millimetre (0.02 mm). The collars on lathes using the inch system of measurement, are usually graduated in thousandths of an inch (.001).

METRIC LATHES

The circumference of the crossfeed and compound rest screw collars on lathes using the metric system of measurement is usually divided into 200 or 250 equal divisions, each having a value of 0.02 mm. Therefore if the crossfeed screw is turned *clockwise* 30 graduations, the cutting tool will be moved 30 × 0.02 mm or 0.6 mm towards the work. Because the work in a lathe revolves, a 0.6 mm depth of cut will remove 1.2 mm from the diameter of a workpiece.

INCH LATHES

The circumference of the crossfeed and compound rest screw collars on lathes using inch systems of measurement are usually divided into 100 or 125 equal divisions, each having a value of .001 in. Therefore, if the crossfeed screw is turned *clockwise* 10 graduations, the cutting tool will be moved .010 in. towards the work. Because the work in a lathe revolves, a .010 in. depth of cut will be taken from the entire work circumference, thereby reducing the diameter .020 in. (2 × .010 in.) (Fig. 9-35A).

Machine tools equipped with graduated collars generally fall into two classes.

a) *Machines where the work revolves.* These include lathes, vertical boring mills, cylindrical grinders, etc.

When you machine the *circumference of work* on machines where the work revolves, it is wise to remember that since material is removed from the entire circumference, the cutting tool should be set

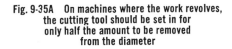

TOOL FEED → .010
MATERIAL REMOVED .020

Fig. 9-35A On machines where the work revolves, the cutting tool should be set in for only half the amount to be removed from the diameter

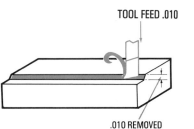

TOOL FEED .010

.010 REMOVED

Fig. 9-35B On machines where the work does not revolve, the cutting tool should be set in for the amount of material to be removed

in only half the amount of material to be removed.

b) *Machines where the work does not revolve.* These include shapers, milling machines, surface grinders, etc.

On machines where the work does not revolve, the material removed from a workpiece is equal to the amount set on the graduated collar, because the machining is taking place only on one surface. Therefore, if a 0.50 mm depth of cut is set, 0.50 mm will be removed from the work (Fig. 9-35B).

Hints on Graduated Collar Use

1. If the graduated collar has a locking screw, make sure the collar is secure before setting a depth of cut (Fig. 9-34).

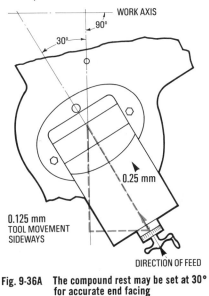

WORK AXIS
90°
30°
0.25 mm
0.125 mm
TOOL MOVEMENT
SIDEWAYS
DIRECTION OF FEED

Fig. 9-36A The compound rest may be set at 30° for accurate end facing

2. All depths of cut must be made by feeding the cutting tool *towards the workpiece.*
3. If the graduated collar is turned past the desired setting, it must be turned backwards a half-turn and then fed into the proper setting to remove the backlash.
4. Never hold a graduated collar when setting a depth of cut. Graduated collars with friction devices can be moved easily if held when setting a depth of cut.
5. The graduated collar on the compound rest can be used for accurately setting the depth of cut for the following operations.

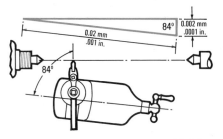

84°
0.02 mm
.001 in.
0.002 mm
.0001 in.
84°

Fig. 9-36B The compound rest set at 84°16′ (84.27°) for making fine settings

a) *Facing.* When facing, the compound rest may be set to 30° (to the cross-slide). The side movement of the cutting tool is always half the amount of the compound rest feed. For example, if the compound rest is fed in 0.25 mm, the side movement of the tool, or the amount of material removed from the end of the workpiece will be 0.125 mm (Fig. 9-36A).

b) *Shoulder turning.* When a series of shoulders must be spaced accurately along a piece of work, the compound rest should be set at 90° to the cross-slide. With the carriage locked in position, the graduated collar of the compound rest can be used for the spacing of shoulders to within 0.02 mm (or .001 in. on inch collars) accuracy.

c) *Machining accurate diameters.* When accurate diameters must be machined or ground in a lathe, the compound rest should be set to 84°16′ (84.27°) to the cross-slide. A 0.02 mm movement of the compound rest results in a 0.002 mm infeed movement of the cutting tool. On similar inch calibrated compound rests, a .001 in. movement would result in a .0001 in. infeed movement of the tool (Fig. 9-36B).

PARALLEL TURNING

Work is generally machined on a lathe for two reasons: to cut it to size and to produce a true diameter. Work that must be cut to size and have the same diameter along the entire length of the workpiece involves the operation of parallel turning. Many factors determine the amount of material which can be removed on a lathe at one time. However, whenever possible, a diameter should be cut to size in two cuts: a roughing cut and a finishing cut (Fig. 9-37).

NOTE: To remove metal from a cylindrical piece of work and have the same diameter at each end, *the lathe centres must be in line.*

Before either the rough or finish cut is taken, the cutting tool must be set accurately for the depth of cut desired.

To Set an Accurate Depth of Cut

1. Move the toolpost to the left-hand side of the compound rest and set the toolbit height to centre.
2. Start the lathe and take a light cut (approximately 0.10 mm or until a true diameter is produced) 5 mm long at the right-hand end of the work.
3. Stop the lathe, but *DO NOT* move the crossfeed screw handle.
4. Move the cutting tool to the end of the work by turning the carriage handwheel.

5. Measure the work and calculate the amount of material which must be removed.
6. Advance the graduated collar half the amount of material to be removed. (For example, if 1.00 mm must be removed, the graduated collar should be turned in 0.50 mm, since the cut is taken off the circumference of the work.)

ROUGH TURNING

The operation of rough turning is used to remove as much metal as possible in the shortest length of time. Accuracy and surface finish are not important in this operation; therefore a 0.50 mm to 0.75 mm (or a .020 in. to .030 in.) feed is recommended. Work is generally rough turned to within 0.80 mm (or 1/32 in.) of the finished size in as few cuts as possible (preferably one cut).

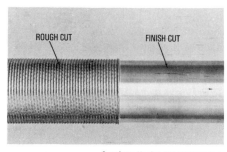

ROUGH CUT   FINISH CUT

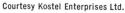

Courtesy Kostel Enterprises Ltd.

Fig. 9-37   Rough and finish turning

To Rough Turn Work

1. Set the lathe to the correct speed for the type and size of material being cut (Table 9-1).
2. Adjust the quick-change gearbox for a 0.25 mm to 0.76 mm (or a .010 in. to .030 in.) feed, depending on the depth of cut and condition of the machine.
3. Move the toolholder to the left-hand side of the compound rest and set the toolbit height to centre.
4. Tighten the toolpost *securely* to prevent the toolholder from moving during the machining operation.

5. Take a light trial cut at the right-hand end of the work for 5 mm length.
6. Measure the work and adjust the toolbit for the proper depth of cut.
7. Cut along for 5 mm, stop the lathe, and check the diameter for size. (The diameter should be approximately 0.80 mm (or 1/32 in.) over the finish size.)
8. Readjust the depth of cut, if necessary.

FINISH TURNING

Finish turning, which follows rough turning, produces a smooth surface finish, and cuts the work to an accurate size. Factors such as the condition of the cutting tool, the rigidity of the machine and work, and the lathe speeds and feeds, affect the type of surface finish produced.

To Finish Turn Work

1. See that the cutting edge of the toolbit is free from nicks, burrs, etc. It is good practice to hone the cutting edge before you take a finish cut.
2. Set the toolbit on centre; check it against the lathe centre point.
3. Set the lathe to the recommended speed and feed. The feed used depends upon the surface finish required.
4. Take a light trial cut (5 mm long) at the right-hand end of the work to
   a) produce a true diameter
   b) set the cutting tool to the diameter
   c) set the graduated collar to the diameter
5. Stop the lathe and measure the diameter.
6. Set the depth of cut for half the amount of material to be removed.
7. Cut along for 5 mm, stop the lathe and check the diameter.
8. Readjust the depth of cut, if necessary, and finish turn the diameter.

NOTE: In order to produce the truest diameter possible, finish turn work to the required size. Should it be necessary to finish a diameter by filing or polishing, *never* leave more than 0.05 mm to 0.08 mm (or .002 in. to .003 in.) for this operation.

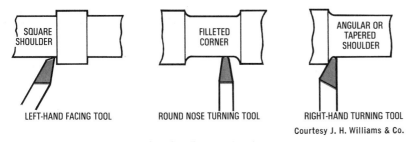

LEFT-HAND FACING TOOL   ROUND NOSE TURNING TOOL   RIGHT-HAND TURNING TOOL

Courtesy J. H. Williams & Co.

Fig. 9-38 Types of shoulders

TURNING TO A SHOULDER

When turning more than one diameter on a piece of work, the change in diameters, or step, is known as a shoulder. Three common types of shoulders are illustrated in Fig. 9-38.

To Turn a Square Shoulder

1. With the work mounted in a lathe, lay out the shoulder position from the finished end of the work. In case of filleted shoulders, allow sufficient length to permit the proper radius to be formed on the finished shoulder.
2. Place the point of the toolbit at this mark and cut a *small* groove around the circumference to mark off the length.
3. With a turning tool, rough and finish turn the work to within 1.5 mm of the required length.
4. Set up an end facing tool, chalk the small diameter of the work, and bring the cutting tool up until it just removes the chalk mark.
5. Note the reading on the graduated collar of the crossfeed handle.
6. Face (square) the shoulder, cutting to the line *using hand feed.*
7. For successive cuts, return the crossfeed handle to the same graduated collar setting.

If a filleted corner is required, a toolbit having the same radius is used for finishing the shoulder. Angular or chamfered edges may be obtained by setting the cutting edge of the tool to the desired angle of chamfer and feeding it against the shoulder, or by setting the compound rest to the desired angle.

FILING IN A LATHE

Work should be filed in a lathe only to remove a small amount of stock, to remove burrs, or round off sharp corners. Work should always be turned to within 0.05 mm to 0.08 mm (or .002 in. to .003 in.) of size, if the surface is to be filed. When larger amounts must be removed,

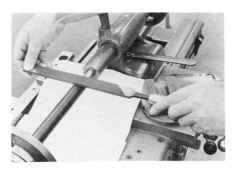

Courtesy Kostel Enterprises Ltd.

Fig. 9-39 Hold the file handle in the left hand to avoid injury when filing on a lathe

the work should be machined, since excessive filing will produce work which is out-of-round and not parallel. The National Safety Council recommends filing with the left hand, so that the arms and hands can be kept clear of the revolving chuck or drive plate (Fig. 9-39).

NOTE: Before attempting to file or polish in a lathe, it is good practice to cover the lathe bed with a piece of paper, to prevent filings from getting into the slides and causing excessive wear and damage to the lathe. Cloth is not suitable for this purpose because it tends to get caught in the revolving work or the lathe.

To File in a Lathe

1. Set the spindle speed to approximately twice that used for turning.
2. Mount the work between centres, lubricate, and carefully adjust the dead centre in the workpiece. Use a revolving dead centre if one is available.
3. Move the carriage as far to the right as possible and remove the toolpost.
4. Disengage the lead screw and feed rod.
5. Select a 10- or 12-inch (250 mm or 300 mm■) *mill file* or a *long-angle lathe file*.
   NOTE: Be sure that the file handle is properly secured on the tang of the file.
6. Start the lathe.
7. Grasp the file handle in the left hand and support the file point with the right hand fingers.
8. Apply light pressure and push the file forward to its full length. Release pressure on the return stroke.
9. Move the file about half the width of the file for each stroke and continue filing, using 30 to 40 strokes per minute until the surface is finished.
10. When filing in a lathe, the following points should be observed.
    a) Roll up sleeves.
    b) Remove watches and rings.
    c) Never use a file without a properly fitted handle.
    d) Never apply too much pressure to the file. Excessive pressure produces out-of-roundness and causes the file teeth to clog and damage the work surface.
    e) Clean the file frequently with a file brush. Rub a little chalk into the file teeth to prevent clogging and facilitate cleaning.

POLISHING IN A LATHE

After the work surface has been filed, the finish may be improved by polishing with abrasive cloth.

Courtesy Kostel Enterprises Ltd.

Fig. 9-40   A high surface finish can be produced with abrasive cloth

To Polish in a Lathe

1. Select the correct type and grade of abrasive cloth for the finish desired; use a piece about 150 to 200 mm long and 25 mm wide. For ferrous metals, use aluminum oxide abrasive cloth. Silicon carbide abrasive cloth should be used for nonferrous metals.
2. Set the lathe to run at high speed.
3. Disengage the feed rod and lead screw.
4. Lubricate and adjust the dead centre.
5. Roll up sleeves and tuck in any loose clothing.
6. Start the lathe.
7. Hold the abrasive cloth on the work as shown in Fig. 9-40.
8. With the right hand, press the cloth firmly on the work while *tightly* holding the other end of the abrasive cloth with the left hand.
9. Move the cloth slowly back and forth along the work.

    NOTE: For normal finishes, 80 to 100 grit abrasive cloth should be used. For better finishes, use a finer grit abrasive cloth.

KNURLING

Knurling is a process of impressing a diamond-shaped or straight line pattern into the surface of the workpiece to improve its appearance, or to provide a better gripping surface. Straight knurling is often used to increase the workpiece diameter when a press fit is required.

The knurling tool (Fig. 9-41A) is a toolpost type toolholder on which a pair of hardened steel rolls are mounted. These rolls may be obtained in diamond and straight line patterns, and in coarse, medium, and fine pitches. Some knurling tools are made with the three various pitched rollers on one holder (Fig. 9-41B).

To Knurl in a Lathe

1. Mount the work between centres and mark the required length to be knurled.

Courtesy J. H. Williams & Co.

Fig. 9-41A   A knurling tool with one set of rolls in a self-centring head

NOTE: If the work is held in a chuck for knurling, the right end of the work should be supported with the tailstock centre.

2. Set the lathe to run at one-quarter the speed required for turning.
3. Set the carriage feed to 0.40 mm to 0.76 mm (or .015 in. to .030 in. for inch calibrated feeds).
4. Set the centre of the floating head of the knurling tool even with the dead centre point.
5. Set the knurling tool at right angles to the workpiece and tighten in this position.
6. Start the machine and lightly touch the rolls against the work to see that they are tracking properly (Fig. 9-42). Adjust if necessary.
7. Move the knurling tool to the end of the work so that only half the roll

Courtesy J. H. Williams & Co.

Fig. 9-41B   A knurling tool with three sets of rolls in a revolving head

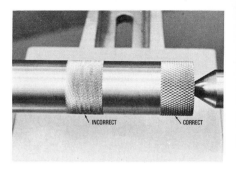

Courtesy Kostel Enterprises Ltd.

Fig. 9-42   Correct and incorrect knurling patterns

face bears against the work. If the knurl does not extend to the end of the workpiece, the knurling tool is set at the correct limit of the section to be knurled.

8. Force the knurling tool into the work approximately 0.5 mm and start the lathe.
9. Apply oil along the section to be knurled.
10. Engage the automatic feed and knurl for the required length.
11. If necessary, reverse the automatic feed and take another pass over the work until the knurl comes to a diamond point.

    NOTE: Never disengage the automatic feed until the full length has been knurled, since rings will be formed on the knurled pattern (Fig. 9-43).

Courtesy Kostel Enterprises Ltd.

Fig. 9-43   Disengaging the automatic feed will damage the knurling pattern

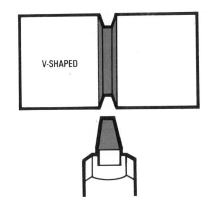

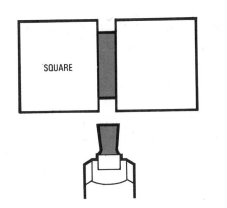

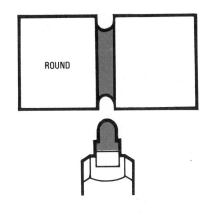

Fig. 9-44   Types of grooves

GROOVING

Grooving, commonly called *recessing*, *undercutting*, or *necking*, is often done at the end of a thread to permit full travel of the nut up to a shoulder, or at the edge of a shoulder to ensure a proper fit of mating parts. Grooves are generally square, round, or V shaped (Fig. 9-44).

Rounded grooves are usually used where there is a strain on the part, and where a square corner would lead to fracturing of the metal at this point.

To Cut a Groove

1. Grind a toolbit to the desired size and shape of the groove required.
2. Lay out the location of the groove.
3. Set the lathe to half the speed for turning.
4. Mount the workpiece in the lathe.
5. Set the toolbit to centre height.
6. Feed the toolbit into the work *slowly* using the crossfeed handle.
7. Apply cutting fluid to the point of the cutting tool. To ensure that the cutting tool will not bind in the groove, move the carriage slightly to the left and to the right while grooving. Should chatter develop, the spindle speed of the lathe should be reduced.
8. Stop the lathe and check the depth of groove with outside calipers or knife-edge verniers.
NOTE: Safety goggles should always be worn when grooving on a lathe.

TAPERS

A *taper* may be defined as a uniform change in the diameter of a workpiece measured along its axis. Metric tapers are expressed as a ratio of 1 mm per unit of length; for example 1:20 taper would have a 1 mm change in diameter in 20 mm of length. Tapers in the inch system are expressed in taper per foot or taper per inch. A taper provides a rapid and accurate method of aligning machine parts and an easy method of holding tools such as twist drills, lathe centres, and reamers.

Machine tapers (those used on machines and tools) are now classified by the American Standards Association as *self-holding tapers* and *steep or self-releasing tapers*.

SELF-HOLDING TAPERS

Self-holding tapers, when seated properly, remain in position due to the wedging action of the small taper angle. The most common forms of self-holding tapers are the Morse, the Brown and Sharpe, and the 3/4 in. per foot Machine taper. See Table 9-4.

The smaller sizes of self-holding tapered shanks are provided with a tang to help drive the cutting tool. Larger sizes employ a tang drive with the shank held in by a key, or a key drive with the shank held in with a draw bolt.

STEEP TAPERS

Steep tapers (self-releasing) have a 3-1/2 in. taper per foot. This was formerly called the standard milling machine taper. It is used mainly for alignment of milling machine arbors and accessories. A steep taper has a key drive and uses a draw-in bolt to hold it securely in the milling machine spindle.

NON-STANDARD TAPERS

Although many of the tapers referred to in Table 9-4 are taken from the Morse and Brown and Sharpe taper series, those not listed in this table are classified as non-standard machine tapers.

The *Morse taper* which has approximately 5/8 in. taper per foot is used for most drills, reamers, and lathe centre shanks. Morse tapers are available in eight sizes ranging from #0 to #7.

The *Brown and Sharpe taper*, available in sizes from #4 to #12, has approximately .502 in. taper per foot, except #10 which has a taper of .516 in. per foot. This self-holding taper is used on Brown and Sharpe machines and drive shanks.

The *Jarno taper*, .600 in. taper per foot, was used on some lathe and drill spindles in sizes from #2 to #20. The taper number indicates the large diameter in eighths of an inch and the small diameter in tenths of an inch. The taper length is indicated by the taper number divided by two.

TABLE 9-4: BASIC DIMENSIONS OF SELF-HOLDING TAPERS

Number of Taper	Taper per Foot	Diameter at Gauge Line (A)	Diameter at Small End (D)	Length (P)	Series Origin
.239	.502	.2392	.200	15/16	Brown and Sharpe Taper Series
.299	.502	.2997	.250	1-3/16	
.375	.502	.3752	.3125	1-1/2	
*0	.624	.3561	.252	2	Morse Taper Series
1	.5986	.475	.369	2-1/8	
2	.5994	.700	.572	2-9/16	
3	.6023	.938	.778	3-3/16	
4	.6233	1.231	1.020	4-1/16	
4-1/2	.624	1.500	1.266	4-1/2	
5	.6315	1.748	1.475	5-3/16	
6	.6256	2.494	2.116	7-1/4	
7	.624	3.270	2.750	10	
200	.750	2.000	1.703	4-3/4	3/4 in. Taper per Foot Series
250	.750	2.500	2.156	5-1/2	
300	.750	3.000	2.609	6-1/4	
350	.750	3.500	3.063	7	
400	.750	4.000	3.516	7-3/4	
450	.750	4.500	3.969	8-1/2	
500	.750	5.000	4.422	9-1/4	
600	.750	6.000	5.328	10-3/4	
800	.750	8.000	7.141	13-3/4	
1000	.750	10.000	8.953	16-3/4	
1200	.750	12.000	10.766	19-3/4	

* Taper #0 is not a part of the self-holding taper series. It has been added to complete the Morse taper series.

The *standard taper pins* used for positioning and holding parts together have 1/4 in. taper per foot. Standard sizes in these pins range from #6/0 to #10.

LATHE SPINDLE NOSE TAPERS

There are two types of tapers used on lathe spindle noses.

The *Type D-1* has a very short tapered section (3 in. taper per foot) and is used on cam lock spindles (Fig. 9-45A).

Fig. 9-45A Tapered lathe spindle nose Type D-1

Fig. 9-45B Tapered lathe spindle nose Type L

The *Type L* lathe spindle nose has a taper of 3-1/2 in. per foot and has a considerably longer taper than the Type D-1. The chuck or drive plate is held on by a threaded lock ring fitted on the spindle behind the taper nose. A key drive is employed in this type of taper (Fig. 9-45B).

TAPER CALCULATIONS

To machine a taper, particularly by the tailstock offset method, it is often necessary to make calculations to ensure accurate results. Since tapers are often expressed in *taper per foot* or *taper per inch*, it may be necessary to calculate either of these dimensions.

To Calculate the Taper per Foot

To calculate the taper per foot (tpf) it is necessary to know the large diameter, the small diameter and the length of taper. The taper per foot can be calculated by applying the following formula.

$$tpf = \frac{(D - d)}{\text{length of taper}} \times 12$$

To calculate the tpf for the workpiece in Fig. 9-46.

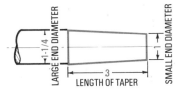

Fig. 9-46   The main parts of an inch taper

$$tpf = \frac{(1\text{-}1/4 - 1)}{3} \times 12$$

$$= \frac{1}{4} \times \frac{1}{3} \times 12$$

$$= 1$$

To Calculate the Tailstock Offset

When calculating the tailstock offset, the taper per foot and the total length of the work must be known (Fig. 9-47).

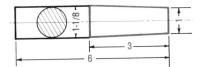

Fig. 9-47   Dimensions of a workpiece having a taper

$$\text{Tailstock offset} = \frac{tpf \times \text{total length of work}}{24}$$

1. $$tpf = \frac{(1\text{-}1/8 - 1)}{3} \times 12$$

$$= \frac{1}{8} \times \frac{1}{3} \times 12$$

$$= 1/2 \text{ in.}$$

2. Tailstock offset $$= \frac{1/2 \times 6}{24}$$

$$= \frac{1}{2} \times \frac{1}{24} \times 6$$

$$= 1/8 \text{ in.}$$

In cases where it is not necessary to find the taper per foot, the following simplified formula can be used to calculate the amount of tailstock offset.

$$\text{Tailstock ofset} = \frac{OL}{TL} \times \frac{(D - d)}{2}$$

OL = overall length of work
TL = length of the tapered
     section
D = diameter at the large end
d = diameter at the small end
    of the taper

For example, to find the tailstock offset required to cut the taper for the work in Fig. 9-47:

$$\text{Tailstock offset} = \frac{6}{3} \times \frac{1}{8} \times \frac{1}{2}$$

$$= 1/8 \text{ in.}$$

METRIC TAPERS

Metric tapers are expressed as a ratio of one millimetre per unit of length. In Fig. 9-48 the work would taper 1 mm in a distance of 20 mm. This taper would then be expressed as a ratio of 1:20 and would be indicated on a drawing as Taper = 1:20.

Since the work tapers 1 mm in 20 mm of length, the diameter at a point 20 mm from the small diameter (d) will be 1 mm larger ($d + 1$).

Some common metric tapers are:

Milling machine
   spindle   – 1:3.429
Morse taper shank – approximately 1:20
Tapered pins and
   pipe threads   – 1:50

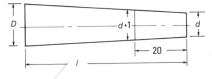

Fig. 9-48   The characteristics of a metric taper

METRIC TAPER CALCULATIONS

If the small diameter (d), the unit length of taper (k) and the total length of taper (l) are known, the large diameter (D) may be calculated.

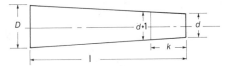

Fig. 9-49   Dimensions of a metric taper

In Fig. 9-49, the large diameter (D) will be equal to the small diameter plus the amount of taper. The amount of taper for the unit length (k) is $(d + l) - (d)$ or 1 mm. Therefore the amount of taper per mm of

unit length $= \dfrac{1}{k}$

The *total amount of taper* will be the

taper per millimetre $\left(\dfrac{1}{k}\right)$ multiplied by the

total length of taper (l).

$$\text{Total taper} = \frac{1}{k} \times l \text{ or } \frac{l}{k}$$

$$D = d + \text{total amount of taper}$$

$$D = d + \frac{l}{k}$$

EXAMPLE:

Calculate the large diameter D for a 1:30 taper having a small diameter of 10 mm and a length of 60 mm.

SOLUTION:

Since taper is 1:30 $k = 30$

$$D = d + \frac{l}{k}$$

$$= 10 + \frac{60}{30}$$

$$= 10 + 2$$

$$= 12 \text{ mm}$$

METRIC TAILSTOCK OFFSET CALCULATIONS

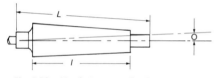

Fig. 9-50   Metric taper turning by the tailstock offset method

If the taper is to be turned by offsetting the tailstock, the amount of offset is calculated as follows. See Fig. 9-50.

$$\text{Offset (o)} = \frac{D - d}{2 \times l} \times L$$

D = large diameter
d = small diameter
l = length of taper
L = total length of work

EXAMPLE:

Calculate the tailstock offset required to turn a 1:30 taper × 60 mm long on a workpiece 300 mm long. The small diameter of the tapered section is 20 mm.

SOLUTION:

$$\text{Large diameter of taper } (D) = d + \frac{l}{k}$$

$$= 20 + \frac{60}{30}$$

$$= 20 + 2$$

$$= 22 \text{ mm}$$

$$\text{Tailstock offset} = \frac{D - d}{2 \times l} \times L$$

$$= \frac{22 - 20}{2 \times 60} \times 300$$

$$= \frac{2}{120} \times 300$$

$$= 5 \text{ mm}$$

METRIC TAPER ATTACHMENT OFFSET CALCULATIONS

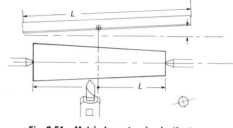

Fig. 9-51   Metric taper turning by the taper attachment method

When the taper attachment is used to turn a taper, the amount the guide bar is set over may be determined as follows:

a) If the angle of taper is given on the blueprint, set the guide bar to one-half the angle (Fig. 9-51).

b) If the angle of taper is not given on the blueprint, use the following formula to find the amount of guide bar setover.

$$\text{Guide bar setover} = \frac{D - d}{2} \times \frac{L}{l}$$

D = large diameter of taper
d = small diameter of taper
l = length of taper
L = length of taper attachment guide bar

EXAMPLE:

Calculate the amount of setover for a 500 mm long guide bar to turn a 1:50 × 250 mm long taper on a workpiece. The small diameter of the taper is 25 mm.

$$\text{Large diameter of taper} = d + \frac{l}{k}$$

$$= 25 + \frac{250}{50}$$

$$= 30 \text{ mm}$$

$$\text{Guide bar setover} = \frac{D - d}{2} \times \frac{L}{l}$$

$$= \frac{30 - 25}{2} \times \frac{500}{250}$$

$$= \frac{5}{2} \times 2$$

$$= 5 \text{ mm}$$

TAPER TURNING

Taper turning in a lathe can be performed on work held between centres or in a lathe chuck. There are three methods of producing a taper.

a) By offsetting the tailstock.

b) By means of the taper attachment which has been set to the proper taper per foot or the proper taper angle of the workpiece. On metric tapers, by calculating the guide bar offset; or on inch tapers, by means of the taper attachment which has been set to the taper per foot or angle of the workpiece.

c) By adjusting the compound rest to the angle of the taper.

The method used to machine any taper depends on the work length, taper length, taper angle and number of pieces to be machined.

THE TAILSTOCK OFFSET METHOD

The tailstock offset method is generally used to cut a taper when no taper attachment is available. This involves moving the tailstock centre out of line with the headstock centre. However, the amount that the tailstock may be offset is limited. This method will not permit steep tapers to be turned, or standard tapers to be turned on the end of a long piece of work.

METHODS OF OFFSETTING THE TAILSTOCK

The tailstock may be offset by three methods.

a) By using the graduations on the end of the tailstock (visual method).

b) By means of the graduated collar and feeler gauge.

c) By means of a dial indicator.

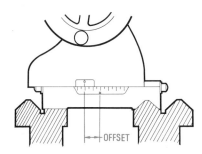

Fig. 9-52   Offsetting the tailstock using the graduated scale

To Offset the Tailstock by the Visual Method

1. Loosen the tailstock clamp nut.

2. Offset the upper part of the tailstock by loosening one set screw and tightening the other until the required amount is indicated on the graduated scale at the end of the tailstock (Fig. 9-52).

Fig. 9-53   Offsetting the tailstock using a dial indicator

NOTE: Before machining the work be sure that both set screws are snugged up to prevent any lateral movement of the tailstock.

To Offset the Tailstock Accurately

The tailstock may be accurately offset by using a dial indicator (Fig. 9-53).

1. Adjust the tailstock spindle to the distance it will be used in the machining setup and lock the tailstock spindle clamp.

2. Mount a dial indicator in the toolpost with the plunger in a horizontal position and on centre.

3. Using the crossfeed handle, move the indicator so that it registers approximately 0.50 mm (or .020 in.) on the work, and set the indicator and crossfeed graduated collars to zero. If the amount of offset required is less than the indicator range, adjust the tailstock until the required offset is shown on the indicator.

4. Move the cross-slide out until the required offset is shown on the graduated collar. *Be sure to remove the backlash.*

5. Adjust the tailstock until the dial indicator reads zero after both offset screws have been snugged up.

The tailstock may also be offset fairly accurately by using a feeler gauge between the toolpost and the tailstock spindle in conjunction with the crossfeed graduated collar (Fig. 9-54).

Fig. 9-54   Offsetting the tailstock using the crossfeed graduated collar and a feeler

To Turn a Taper by the Tailstock Offset Method

1. Loosen the tailstock clamp nut.

2. Offset the tailstock the required amount.

3. Set up the cutting tool as for parallel turning.
   NOTE: The cutting tool *must* be on centre.

4. Starting at the small diameter, take successive cuts until the taper is 1.25 mm to 1.50 mm (or .050 in. to 0.60 in.) oversize.

5. Check the taper for accuracy using a taper ring gauge, if required. (See Taper Ring Gauges, Chapter 3.)

6. Finish turn the taper to the size and fit required.

TAPER TURNING USING THE TAPER ATTACHMENT

The use of a taper attachment provides many advantages when taper turning.

a) The lathe centres remain in alignment, preventing the distortion of centres on the workpiece.

b) The setup is simple and permits changing from taper to parallel turning with no time lost to align the centres.

c) The length of the workpiece does not matter, since duplicate tapers may be turned on any length of work.

d) Tapers may be produced on work held between centres, in a chuck, or in a collet.

e) Internal tapers can be produced by this method.

f) Metric taper attachments are graduated in millimetres and degrees, while inch attachments are graduated in both degrees and inches of taper per foot. This eliminates the need of lengthy calculations and set up.

g) A wider range of tapers may be produced.

There are two types of taper attachments.

a) *the plain taper attachment* (Fig. 9-55)

b) *the telescopic taper attachment* (Fig. 9-56)

Courtesy Kostel Enterprises Ltd.

Fig. 9-55   The parts of a plain taper attachment

When using the plain taper attachment, remove the binding screw which holds the cross-slide to the crossfeed screw nut. The binding screw is then used to connect the sliding block to the slide of the taper attachment. With the plain taper attachment, the depth of cut is made by using the compound rest feed handle.

When a telescopic taper attachment is used, the crossfeed screw is not disengaged and the depth of cut can be set by the crossfeed handle.

To Cut a Taper Using a Telescopic Taper Attachment

1. Clean and oil the guide bar B (Fig. 9-56).

2. Loosen the lock screws D^1 and D^2 and offset the end of the guide bar the required amount or, for inch attachments, set the bar to the required taper in degrees or taper per foot.

3. Tighten the lock screws.

4. Set up the cutting tool on centre.

5. Set the workpiece in the lathe and mark the length of taper.

6. Tighten the connecting screw G on the sliding block E.
   NOTE: If a plain taper attachment is being used, remove the binding screw in the cross-slide and use it to connect the sliding block and the connecting slide. The compound rest must also be set at right angles to the lathe bed.

7. Move the carriage until the centre of the attachment is opposite the length to be tapered.

8. Lock the anchor bracket A to the lathe bed.

9. Take a cut 1.5 mm long, stop the lathe, and check the end of the taper for size.

10. Set the depth of the roughing cut to 1.25 mm to 1.50 mm (or to .050 in. to .060 in.) oversize, and machine the taper.
    NOTE: Start the feed about 12 mm before the start of the cut to remove any play in the taper attachment.

11. Readjust the taper attachment if necessary, take a light cut, and recheck the taper fit.

12. Finish turn and fit the taper to a gauge.

When standard tapers must be produced on a piece of work, a taper plug gauge may be mounted between centres and the taper attachment adjusted to this

Courtesy R. K. LeBlond Tool Co. Ltd.

Fig. 9-56   The telescopic taper attachment

angle by using a dial indicator mounted on centre in the toolpost.

When an *internal taper* is cut, the same procedure is followed, except that the guide bar is set to the side of the centre line opposite to that used when turning an external taper.

When mating external and internal tapers must be cut, it is advisable first to machine the internal taper to a plug gauge. The external taper is then fitted to the internal taper.

TAPER TURNING USING THE COMPOUND REST

To produce short or steep tapers stated in degrees, the compound rest method is used. The tool must be fed in by hand, using the compound rest feed handle.

To Cut a Taper with the Compound Rest

1. Refer to the drawing for the amount of taper required in degrees.
2. Loosen the compound rest lock screws.
3. Swivel the compound rest to half the included angle desired (Fig. 9-57).
4. Tighten the compound rest lock screws.
5. Set the toolbit on centre and feed the cutting tool, using the compound rest feed screw.
6. Check the taper for size and fit.

CHECKING A TAPER

Inch tapers can be checked by scribing two lines exactly 1 in. apart on the taper and carefully measuring the taper at these points with a micrometer. The difference in readings will indicate the taper per inch of the workpiece. Tapers may be more accurately checked by using a sine bar (see Chapter 3).

To obtain a more accurate taper, a taper ring gauge is used to check external tapers. A taper plug gauge is used to check internal tapers (see Chapter 1).

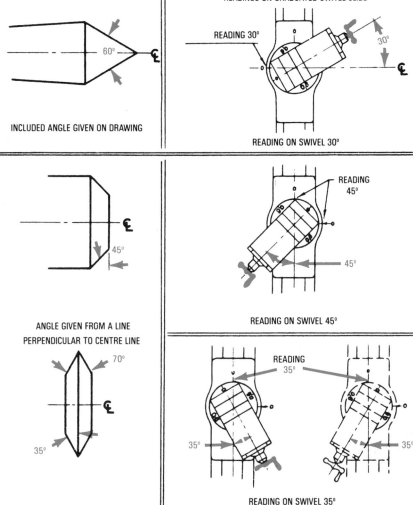

Fig. 9-57 Direction to swing the compound rest for cutting various angles

Courtesy Taper Micrometer Corporation

Fig. 9-58A Using a taper micrometer for checking an external taper

The *taper micrometer* (Fig. 9-58A), recently developed, quickly and accurately measures tapers while the workpiece is still in the machine. This instrument incorporates an adjustable anvil and a 1 in. sine bar, attached to the frame, which is adjustable by the micrometer thimble. The micrometer reading indicates the taper per inch, which can be readily converted to taper per foot or angles. The anvil can be adjusted to accommodate a wide range of work sizes.

Taper micrometers are available in various models for measuring internal tapers and dovetails (Fig. 9-58B), and in bench models incorporating two indicators for quickly checking the accuracy of tapered parts.

The advantages of taper micrometers are:

a) The taper accuracy can be checked while the workpiece is still in the machine.
b) They provide a quick and accurate means of checking tapers.
c) They are simple to operate.
d) The need for costly gauging equipment is eliminated.
e) They can be used for measuring external tapers, internal tapers, and dovetails.

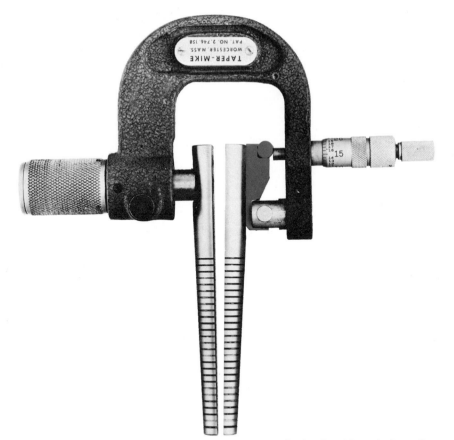

Courtesy Taper Micrometer Corporation

Fig. 9-58B   Taper micrometer for measuring internal tapers

To Fit an External Taper

1. Make three equally spaced lines with chalk or mechanics blue along the taper (see Chapter 3, Taper Ring Gauges).
2. Insert the taper into the ring gauge and turn *counterclockwise* for one-half turn.
3. Remove the workpiece and examine the chalk marks. If the chalk has spread along the whole length of the taper, the taper is correct. If the chalk lines are rubbed from only one end, the taper setup must be adjusted.
4. Make a slight adjustment to the taper attachment and taking trial cuts, machine the taper until the fit is correct.

To Check a Metric Taper

1. Check the drawing for the taper required.
2. Clean the tapered section of the work and apply layout dye.
3. Lay out two lines on the taper which are the same distance apart as the second number in the taper ratio.

Example: If the taper was 1:20, the lines would be 20 mm apart.

NOTE: If the work is long enough, lay out the lines at double or triple the length of the tapered section and increase the difference in diameters by the appropriate amount. For instance, on a 1:20 taper the lines may be laid out 60 mm apart or three times the unit length of the taper. Therefore the difference in diameters would then be 3 × 1 or 3 mm. This will give a more accurate check of the taper.

4. Measure the diameters carefully with a metric micrometer at the two lines. The difference between these two diameters should be 1 mm for each unit of length.
5. If necessary, adjust the taper attachment setting to correct the taper.

MOUNTING AND REMOVING CHUCKS

To Mount a Chuck

1. Remove the drive plate and live centre.
2. Clean all surfaces of the spindle nose and the mating parts of the chuck.

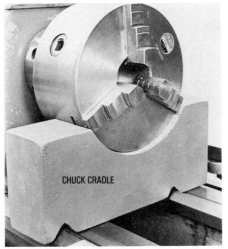

Courtesy Kostel Enterprises Ltd.

Fig. 9-59 A properly fitted cradle block makes mounting and removal of chucks easy and safe

3. Place a cradle block on the lathe bed in front of the spindle and place the chuck on the cradle (Fig. 9-59).
4. Slide the cradle close to the lathe spindle nose and mount the chuck.
   a) *Threaded Spindle Nose Chucks*
      i) Revolve the lathe spindle *by hand* in a counterclockwise direction and bring the chuck up to the spindle. *NEVER START THE MACHINE.*
      ii) If the chuck and spindle are correctly aligned, the chuck should easily thread onto the lathe spindle.
      iii) Never bring the chuck up against the shoulder with a quick snap; otherwise, removing it may be very difficult.
   b) *Taper Spindle Nose Chucks*
      i) Revolve the lathe spindle by hand until the key on the spindle nose aligns with the keyway in the tapered hole of the chuck.
      ii) Slide the chuck onto the lathe spindle, and, at the same time, turn the lock ring in a counterclockwise direction.

iii) Tighten the lock ring securely with a spanner wrench.
   c) *Cam Lock Spindle Nose Chucks*
      i) Align the registration line of each cam lock with the registration line on the lathe spindle nose.
      ii) Revolve the lathe spindle by hand until the holes in the spindle align with the cam lock studs of the chuck (Fig. 9-60A).
      iii) Slide the chuck onto the spindle and tighten each cam lock in a clockwise direction.

Courtesy Kostel Enterprises Ltd.

Fig. 9-60A The cam lock studs and the clearance holes must be aligned when a cam lock chuck is being mounted

To Remove a Chuck

1. Set the lathe in the slowest speed. *STOP THE MOTOR.*
2. Place a cradle block under the chuck (Fig. 9-59).
3. Remove the chuck by the following methods.
   a) *Threaded Spindle Nose Chucks*
      i) Turn the chuck until a wrench hole is in the top position, insert the chuck wrench into the hole and pull it *sharply* towards the front of the lathe.

      OR

      ii) Place a block or short stick under the chuck jaw and revolve the lathe by hand in a clockwise direction.
   b) *Taper Spindle Nose Chucks*
      i) Secure the proper C-spanner wrench and place it around the

lock ring of the spindle with the handle in an upright position.
      ii) Place one hand on the curve of the spanner wrench to prevent it from slipping off the lock ring (Fig. 9-60B).
      iii) With the palm of the other hand, *sharply* strike the handle of the wrench in a clockwise direction.

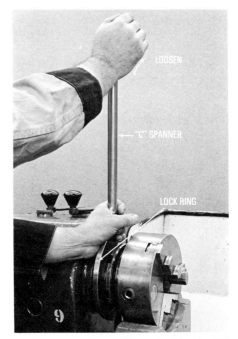

Courtesy Kostel Enterprises Ltd.

Fig. 9-60B A C-spanner wrench is used to loosen the locking ring which holds the chuck on a taper nose spindle

      iv) Hold the chuck with one hand, and with the other hand remove the lock ring from the chuck.
      NOTE: The lock ring may turn a few turns and then become tight. It may be necessary to use the spanner wrench again to loosen the taper contact between the chuck and the spindle nose.
   c) *Cam Lock Spindle Nose Chucks*
      i) With the chuck wrench, turn

each cam lock in a counter-clockwise direction until its registration line coincides with the registration line on the lathe spindle nose.

ii) Place one hand on the chuck face, and with the palm of the other hand *sharply* strike the top of the chuck. This is necessary to break the taper contact between the chuck and the lathe spindle.

NOTE: Sometimes it may be necessary to use a soft-faced hammer for this operation.

4. Slide the chuck clear of the spindle and place it carefully in a storage compartment.

To True Work in a 4-Jaw Chuck

1. Measure the diameter of the work to be chucked.
2. With a chuck wrench adjust the jaws to the approximate size according to the ring marks on the face of the chuck (Fig. 9-61).

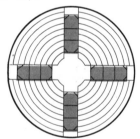

Fig. 9-61   All jaws line up with the same ring on the face of the chuck

3. Set the work in the chuck and set the jaws snugly against the work surface.
4. Start the lathe, and with a piece of chalk held in the hand, lightly mark the high spot on the diameter (Fig. 9-62A).

OR

Place a *surface gauge* on the lathe bed and adjust the point of the scriber so that it is close to the work surface (Fig. 9-62B).

NOTE: When using a surface gauge, do not run the lathe by power.

Courtesy Kostel Enterprises Ltd.

Fig. 9-62A   Using chalk to indicate the high spot on the work

5. Stop the lathe and check the chalk mark. If it is an even, lightly marked line around the work, the work is true.
6. If there is only one mark, loosen the jaw opposite the chalk mark and tighten the jaw next to the chalk mark.
7. Continue this operation until the chalk marks lightly around the work or leaves two marks opposite each other.

Courtesy Kostel Enterprises Ltd.

Fig. 9-62B   Using a surface gauge to true work in a four-jaw chuck

To True Work in a 4-Jaw Chuck Using a Dial Indicator

A dial indicator should be used whenever a machined diameter must be aligned to within a few hundredths of a millimetre (or thousandths of an inch).

1. Mount the work and true it approximately, using either the chalk or surface gauge method.
2. Mount an indicator, preferably with a range of at least 2.5 mm (or .100 in.) in the toolpost of the lathe (Fig. 9-63).
3. Set the indicator spindle in a *horizontal position* with the contact point set to centre height.
4. Bring the indicator point against the work diameter so that it registers approximately 0.50 mm (or .020 in.) and revolve the lathe *by hand*.
5. Note the highest and the lowest reading on the dial indicator.
6. Slightly loosen the chuck jaw at the lowest reading, and tighten the jaw at the high reading until the work is moved half the difference between the two indicator readings.
7. Continue to adjust *only these two opposite jaws* until the indicator registers the same at both jaws.

NOTE: Disregard the indicator readings on the work between these two jaws.

8. Adjust the other set of opposite jaws in the same manner until the indicator registers the same at any point on the work circumference.
9. Tighten all jaws evenly to secure the workpiece firmly.
10. Rotate the lathe spindle by hand and recheck the indicator reading.

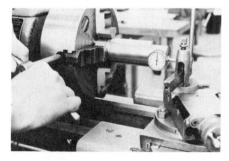

Fig. 9-63   Truing a workpiece in a chuck using a dial indicator

To Face Work Held in a Chuck

The purpose of facing work in a chuck is the same as that of facing between centres: to obtain a true, flat surface and to cut the work to length.

1. True up the work in a chuck using the chalk or dial indicator method. (This is not necessary if a 3-jaw universal chuck is used.)
2. Have at least an amount equal to the diameter of the work projecting from the chuck jaws.
3. Swivel the compound rest at 90° (right angles) to the cross-slide.
4. Set up the facing toolbit to the height of the dead centre and pointing slightly to the left.
5. Lock the carriage in position.
6. Set the depth of cut by using the graduated collar on the compound rest screw, and face to the required length.

To Spot and Drill Work in a Chuck

Spotting ensures that a drill will start in the centre of the work. A spotting tool is used to make a shallow, V-shaped hole in the centre of the work, which provides a guide for the drill to follow. In most cases, a hole can be spotted quickly and fairly accurately by using a centre drill (Fig. 9-64). Where extreme accuracy in spotting is necessary, a spotting toolbit should be used.

1. Mount work true in a chuck.
2. Set the lathe to the proper speed for the type of material to be drilled.

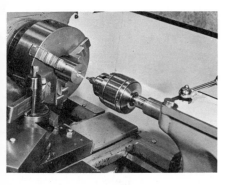

Fig. 9-64 Using a centre drill to spot a hole

3. Check the tailstock centre and make sure it is in line.
4. Spot the hole with a centre drill or spotting tool.
5. Mount the twist drill in the tailstock spindle, in a drill chuck or in a drill holder (Fig. 9-65, A,B,C).

Courtesy Kostel Enterprises Ltd.

Fig. 9-65A A tapered shank drill mounted in the spindle is prevented from turning by a lathe dog

NOTE:

i) When a tapered shank drill is mounted directly in the tailstock spindle, a dog should be used to stop the drill from turning and scoring the tailstock spindle taper (Fig. 9-65A).

Courtesy Kostel Enterprises Ltd.

Fig. 9-65B Supporting the end of a drill will prevent it from wobbling when starting a hole

ii) The end of the drill may be supported with the end of a toolholder so that the drill will start on centre (Fig. 9-65B).
iii) Tapered shank drills are often mounted in a drill holder. The point of the drill is positioned in the hole, while the end of the hold-

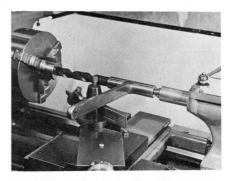

Fig. 9-65C Drilling a hole with a drill mounted in a drill holder and supported on the dead centre

er is supported by the dead centre. The handle of the holder rests on the toolholder and against the toolpost to prevent the drill from turning and from pulling into the work (Fig. 9-65C).

6. Start the lathe and drill to the desired depth, applying cutting fluid frequently.
7. To gauge the depth of the hole, use the graduations on the tailstock spindle, or measure the depth with a steel rule (Fig. 9-66).
8. Withdraw the drill frequently to remove the chips and measure the depth of the hole.

CAUTION: Always ease the force on the feed as the drill breaks through the work.

Courtesy Kostel Enterprises Ltd.

Fig. 9-66 Drilling a depth

BORING

Boring is the operation of enlarging and truing a drilled or cored hole with a single-point cutting tool. Special diameter holes, for which no drills are available, can be produced by boring.

Holes may be drilled in a lathe; however, such holes are generally not considered accurate although the drill may have started straight. During the drilling process, the drill may become dull or hit a hard spot or blowhole in the metal, which will cause the drill to wander or run off centre. If such a hole is reamed, the reamer will follow the drilled hole, and, as a result, the hole will not be straight. Therefore, if it is important that a reamed hole be straight and true, the hole should first be drilled, then bored and reamed.

Courtesy R. K. LeBlond Tool Co. Ltd.

Fig. 9-67   Boring may be used to true an inside diameter

To Bore Work in a Chuck

1. Mount the work in a chuck, face, spot, and drill the hole approximately 1.5 mm undersize.
2. Select a boring bar as large as possible and have it extend beyond the holder only enough to clear the depth of the hole to be bored.
3. Mount the boring bar holder in the toolpost on the left-hand side of the compound rest.
4. Set the boring toolbit to centre (Fig. 9-67).
5. Set the lathe to the proper speed and select a medium feed.

6. Start the lathe and bring the boring tool into contact with the inside diameter of the hole.
7. Take a light trial cut (approximately 0.10 mm or until a true diameter is produced) 5 mm long at the right-hand end of the work.
8. Stop the lathe and measure the hole diameter with a telescopic gauge or inside micrometer.
9. Determine the amount of material to be removed from the hole.
   NOTE: Leave approximately 0.25 mm to 0.50 mm for a finish cut.
10. Set the depth of cut for half the amount of metal to be removed.
11. Start the lathe and take the roughing cut.
    NOTE: If chatter or vibration occurs during machining, slow the lathe speed and increase the feed until it is eliminated.
12. Stop the lathe and bring the boring tool out of the hole without moving the crossfeed handle.
13. Set the depth of the finish cut and bore the hole to size. For a good surface finish, a fine feed is recommended.

REAMING

Courtesy South Bend Lathe Inc.

Fig. 9-68   Setup for reaming in a lathe

Reaming may be performed in a lathe to quickly obtain an accurately sized hole and to produce a good surface finish. Reaming may be performed after a hole has been drilled or bored. If a true, accurate hole is required, it should be bored before the reaming operation.

To Ream Work in a Lathe

1. Mount the work in a chuck; face, spot and drill the hole to size. Holes under 12 mm (or 1/2 in.) in diameter, drill 0.40 mm (or 1/64 in.) undersize; holes over 12 mm (or 1-1/2 in.) in diameter drill 0.80 mm (or 1/32 in.) undersize. If the holes must be true, they should be bored 0.25 mm (or .010 in.) undersize.
2. Mount the reamer in a drill chuck or drill holder (Fig. 9-68). When reaming holes 16 mm (or 5/8 in.) diameter and larger, fasten a lathe dog near the reamer shank and support the tail on the compound rest to prevent the reamer from turning.
3. Set the lathe to approximately half the drilling speed.
4. Bring the reamer close to the hole and lock the tailstock in position.
5. Start the lathe, apply cutting fluid to the reamer, and slowly feed it into the drilled or bored hole with the tailstock handwheel.
6. Occasionally remove the reamer from the hole to clear chips from the flutes and apply cutting fluid.
7. Once the hole has been reamed, stop the lathe and remove the reamer from the hole.
   CAUTION: Never turn the lathe spindle or reamer backwards for any reason. This will damage a reamer.
8. Clean the reamer and store it carefully to prevent it from being nicked or damaged.

TAPPING

Tapping is one method of producing an internal thread on a lathe. The tap is

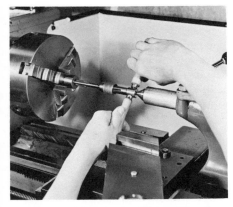

Fig. 9-69 Using a tap to cut internal threads

aligned by placing the point of the lathe dead centre in the shank end of the tap to guide it while the tap is turned by a tap wrench. A standard tap may be used for this operation; however, a gun tap is preferred because the chips are cleared ahead of the tap. When tapping a hole in a lathe, the spindle is locked and the tap is turned by hand (Fig. 9-69).

To Tap a Hole in a Lathe

1. Mount the work in the chuck, face, and centre-drill.
2. Select the proper tap drill for the tap to be used.
3. Set the lathe to the proper speed and drill with the tap drill to the required depth. Use cutting fluid if required.
4. Chamfer the edge of the hole slightly larger than the tap diameter.
5. Stop the lathe and lock the spindle, or put the lathe in its lowest speed.
6. Place a taper tap in the hole and support the shank with the dead centre.
7. With a suitable wrench, turn the tap, keeping the dead centre snug into the shank of the tap by turning the tailstock handwheel.
8. Apply cutting fluid while tapping the hole (Fig. 9-69).
9. Back off the tap frequently to break the chip.
10. Remove the taper tap and complete tapping the hole with a plug or bottoming tap.

CUTTING OFF WORK IN A CHUCK

Cut-off tools, often called parting tools, are used for cutting off work projecting from a chuck, for grooving, and for undercutting. The inserted blade-type parting tool is most commonly used, and it is provided in three holders (Fig. 9-70).

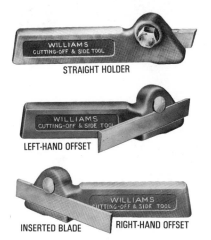

Courtesy J. H. Williams & Co.

Fig. 9-70 Inserted blade cut-off or parting tool

To Cut Off Work in a Chuck

1. Mount the work in the chuck with the part to be cut off as close to the jaws as possible.
2. Mount the cut-off tool on the left-hand side of the compound rest with the cutting edge set on centre.
3. Place the holder as close to the toolpost as possible to prevent vibration and chatter (Fig. 9-71).
4. Extend the cutting blade beyond the holder half the diameter of the work to be cut, plus 3 mm (or 1/8 in.) for clearance.
5. Set the lathe to approximately one-half the turning speed.
6. Move the cutting tool into position (Fig. 9-71).
7. Start the lathe and feed the cut-off tool into the work by hand, keeping a steady feed during the operation. Cut brass and cast iron dry, but use cutting fluid for steel.

8. When grooving or cutting off deeper than 6 mm (or 1/4 in.), it is good practice to move the parting tool sideways slightly. This may be accomplished by moving the carriage handwheel back and forth a few hundredths of a millimetre during the cutting operation. This side motion cuts a little wider groove and prevents the tool from jamming.
9. Before the cut is completed, remove the burrs from each side of the groove with a file.
   NOTE: To avoid chatter, keep the tool cutting and apply cutting fluid constantly during the operation. Feed slowly when the part is almost cut off.

Courtesy South Bend Lathe Inc.

Fig. 9-71 Cutting off with the workpiece held in a chuck

FOLLOWER AND STEADY RESTS
FOLLOWER REST

A follower rest, mounted on the saddle, moves along with the carriage to prevent work from springing up and away from the cutting tool. The follower rest, positioned immediately behind the cutting tool, can be used to support long work for successive operations such as thread cutting (Fig. 9-72).

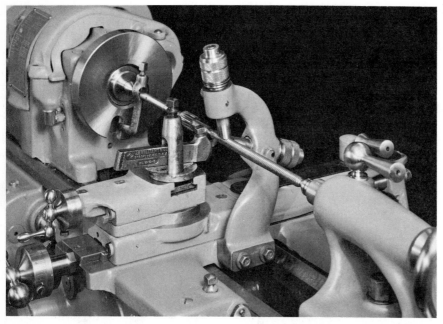

Courtesy South Bend Lathe Inc.

Fig. 9-72   Follower rest used to support long, slender work between centres while thread cutting

To Set Up a Follower Rest

1. Mount the work between centres.
2. Fasten the follower rest to the saddle of the lathe.
3. Position the cutting tool in the toolpost so that it is just to the left of the follower rest jaws.
4. Turn the work diameter, for approximately 40 mm long, to the desired size.
5. Adjust both jaws of the follower rest until they lightly contact the turned diameter.
6. Tighten the lock screw on each jaw.
7. Lubricate the work and the follower rest jaws to prevent marring the finished diameter.
8. If successive cuts are required, readjust the follower rest jaws as in step 4.

STEADY REST

A steady rest (Fig. 9-73) is used to support long, slender work and prevent it from springing while being machined between centres. A steady rest may also be used when it is necessary to perform a machining operation on the end of a workpiece which is held in a chuck. The steady rest is fastened to the lathe bed and its three jaws are adjusted to the surface of the work to provide a supporting bearing. The jaws on a steady rest are generally made of soft material, such as fibre or brass, to prevent damaging the work surface. Other follower rests have rollers attached to the jaws to provide good support for the work.

To Set Up a Steady Rest

1. Mount the work between centres.
   OR
   Set up and true the work in a chuck.
2. a) If the work diameter is not round, turn a true spot on the diameter (slightly wider than the steady rest jaws) at the point where the steady rest will be supporting the work. Long work in a chuck should be first supported by the tailstock centre. If the diameter is rough, turn a section for the steady rest and one near the chuck to the same diameter.

   b) If it is impossible to turn a true diameter (due to the shape of the workpiece), mount and adjust a *cathead* (Fig. 9-74) on the work.

Courtesy South Bend Lathe Inc.

Fig. 9-73   Using a steady rest to support the end of long work held in a chuck

Fig. 9-74 The cathead can be adjusted to provide a true surface for the steady rest even if square work is being turned

3. Move the carriage to the tailstock end of the lathe.
4. Place the steady rest on the lathe bed at the desired position. If work diameter is turned and held in a chuck, slide the steady rest up close to the chuck.
5. Adjust the lower two jaws to the work diameter, using a paper feeler to provide clearance between the jaws and the work.
6. Slide the steady rest to the desired position and fasten it in place.
7. Close the top section of the steady rest and adjust the top jaw, using a paper feeler.
8. Apply white or red lead to the diameter at the steady rest jaws.
9. Start the lathe and carefully adjust each jaw until it just touches the diameter.
   NOTE: The white or red lead will smear when the jaw contacts the work.
10. Tighten the lock screw on each jaw and then apply a suitable lubricant.
11. Before machining, it is wise to indicate the top and front of the turned diameter at the chuck and at the steady rest, to check for alignment. If the indicator reading varies, adjust the steady rest until it is correct.

To True a Damaged Centre Hole

1. Mount and true the work in a chuck and steady rest, if necessary.

2. Grind a 60° spotting tool (Fig. 9-75) and mount it on centre in the toolholder.
3. Start the lathe and gradually bring the spotting tool into the damaged centre hole.
4. Recut the centre hole until the damaged section is removed.
5. Remove the workpiece, mount it between centres, and turn the diameter as required.

Fig. 9-75 A 60° spotting tool set up to recut a damaged centre

THREADS

Metric information on threads has been included wherever possible. However, due to the lack of uniform standards and scarcity of information at the time of printing, most of the information in the threading section is given in the inch-pound system. While the operations involved in cutting the various threads are explained with inch examples, the actual procedure for thread cutting is, of course, the same in both the inch and metric systems.

A thread may be defined as a helical ridge of uniform section formed on the inside or outside of a cylinder or cone. Threads are used for several purposes.
a) For fastening devices such as screws, bolts, studs, and nuts.
b) To provide accurate measurement as in a micrometer.
c) To transmit motion. The threaded lead screw on the lathe causes the carriage to move along when threading.

d) To increase torque. Heavy work can be raised with a screw jack.

THREAD TERMINOLOGY

To understand and calculate thread parts and sizes, the following definitions relating to screw threads should be known. (Fig. 9-76)

A screw thread is a helical ridge of uniform section formed on the inside or outside of a cylinder or cone.

An external thread is cut on an external surface or cone such as on a cap screw or a wood screw.

An internal thread is produced on the inside of a cylinder or cone, such as the thread on the inside of a nut.

The major diameter is the largest diameter of an external or internal thread.

The minor diameter is the smallest diameter of an external or internal thread. This was formerly known as the root diameter.

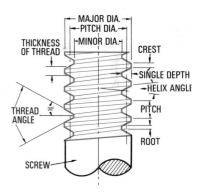

Fig. 9-76 Parts of a screw thread

The pitch diameter is the diameter of an imaginary cylinder which passes through the thread at a point where the groove and thread widths are equal.

The pitch diameter is equal to the major diameter minus a single depth of thread. The tolerance and allowances on threads are given at the pitch diameter line. The pitch diameter is also used to determine the outside diameter for rolled threads. The diameter of the blank is always equal to the pitch diameter of the thread to be rolled. Thread rolling is a displacement operation and the amount of metal displaced is forced up to form the thread above the pitch line.

NOTE: Pitch diameter is not used as a basis for determining ISO metric thread dimensions.

The number of threads is the number of crests or roots per inch of threaded section. This term does not, of course, apply to metric threads.

Pitch is the distance from a point on one thread to a corresponding point on the next thread, measured parallel to the axis. Pitch is expressed in millimetres for metric threads.

Lead is the distance a screw thread advances axially in one revolution. On a single start thread, the lead and the pitch are equal.

Root is the bottom surface joining the sides of two adjacent threads. The root of an external thread is on its minor diameter. The root of an internal thread is on its major diameter.

Crest is the top surface joining two sides of a thread. The crest of an external thread is on the major diameter while the crest of an internal thread is on the minor diameter.

A flank (side) is a thread surface which connects the crest with the root.

Depth of thread is the distance between the crest and root measured perpendicular to the axis.

Angle of thread is the included angle between the sides of a thread measured in an axial plane.

The helix angle (lead angle) is the angle which the thread makes with a plane perpendicular to the thread axis.

A right-hand thread is a helical ridge of uniform cross-section onto which a nut is threaded in a clockwise direction.

When the thread is held in a horizontal position with its axis pointing from right to left, a right-hand thread will slope *down* and to the right. When a right-hand thread is cut on a lathe, the toolbit advances from right to left.

A left-hand thread is a helical ridge of uniform cross-section onto which a nut is threaded in a counterclockwise direction.

When the thread is held in a horizontal position with its axis pointing from right to left, the thread will slope *down* and to the left. When a left-hand thread is cut on a lathe the toolbit advances from left to right.

THREAD FORMS

THE ISO METRIC THREAD

Over the past several decades, one of the world's major industrial problems has been the lack of an international thread standard whereby the thread standard used in any country could be interchanged with that of another country. In April 1975, the International Organization for Standardization (ISO) drew up an agreement covering a standard metric thread profile, the sizes and pitches for the various threads in the new ISO Metric Thread Standard. The new series has only 25 thread sizes ranging in diameter from 1.6 mm to 100 mm. Countries throughout the world have been encouraged to adopt the ISO series (See Table 9-5).

These metric threads are identified by the letter M, the nominal diameter and the pitch. For example, a metric thread with an outside diameter of 5 mm and a pitch of 0.8 mm would be identified as follows: M 5 × 0.8.

The new ISO series will not only simplify thread design but will generally

TABLE 9-5: ISO METRIC PITCH AND DIAMETER COMBINATIONS			
NOMINAL DIA. (mm)	THREAD PITCH (mm)	NOMINAL DIA. (mm)	THREAD PITCH (mm)
1.6	0.35	20	2.5
2.0	0.40	24	3.0
2.5	0.45	30	3.5
3.0	0.50	36	4.0
3.5	0.60	42	4.5
4.0	0.70	48	5.0
5.0	0.80	56	5.5
6.3	1.00	64	6.0
8.0	1.25	72	6.0
10	1.50	80	6.0
12	1.75	90	6.0
14	2.00	100	6.0
16	2.00		

produce stronger threads for a given diameter and pitch and will reduce the large inventory of fasteners now required by industry.

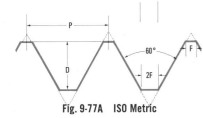

Fig. 9-77A ISO Metric

The new ISO metric thread has a 60° included angle and a crest equal to 0.125 times the pitch, similar to the National Form thread. The main difference, however, is the depth of thread, which is 0.54127 times the pitch. Because of these dimensions, the root of the thread is larger than that of the National Form thread. The root of the new ISO metric thread is 1/4 of the pitch (0.250P).

The most commonly used thread forms in North America at the present time are:

The American National Standard thread (Fig. 9-77B) is divided into four main series, all having the same shape and proportions. National Coarse (NC), National Fine (NF), National Special (NS), and National Pipe (NPT). This thread has a 60° angle with a root and crest truncated to one-eighth the pitch. This thread is used in fabrication, machine construction and assembly, and for components where easy assembly is desired.

$$D = .6495 \times P \text{ or } \frac{.6495}{N}$$

$$F = .125 \ \times P \text{ or } \frac{.125}{N}$$

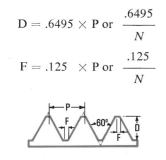

Fig. 9-77B   American National

The British Standard Whitworth thread (BSW) (Fig. 9-77C) has a 55°-V form with rounded crests and roots. This thread application is the same as for the American National form thread.

$$D = .6403 \times P \text{ or } \frac{.6403}{N}$$

$$R = .1373 \times P \text{ or } \frac{.1373}{N}$$

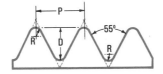

Fig. 9-77C   Whitworth

The Unified thread (Fig. 9-77D) was developed by the United States, Britain, and Canada, so that equipment produced by these countries would have a standardized thread system. Until this thread was developed, many problems were created by

$$D - \text{(external thread)} = .6134 \times P \text{ or } \frac{.6134}{N}$$

$$- \text{(internal thread)} = .5413 \times P \text{ or } \frac{.5413}{N}$$

$$F - \text{(external thread)} = .125 \ \times P \text{ or } \frac{.125}{N}$$

$$- \text{(internal)} \text{ thread)} = .250 \ \times P \text{ or } \frac{.250}{N}$$

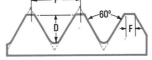

Fig. 9-77D   Unified

the non-interchangeability of threaded parts being used in these countries. The Unified thread is a combination of the British Standard Whitworth and the American National form thread. This thread has a 60° angle with a rounded root, and the crest may be rounded or flat.

$$D = \text{minimum } .500P$$
$$= \text{maximum } .500 \ P + .010$$
$$F = .3707 \ P$$
$$C = .3707 \ P - .0052$$
$$\text{(for maximum depth)}$$

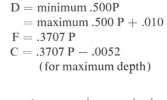

Fig. 9-77E   Acme

The American National Acme thread (Fig. 9-77E) is replacing the square thread in many cases. It has a 29° angle and is used for feed screws, jacks, and vises.

The Brown and Sharpe Worm thread (Fig. 9-77F) has a 29° included angle as the Acme thread; however, the depth is

$$D = .6866 \ P$$
$$F = .335 \ P$$
$$C = .310 \ P$$

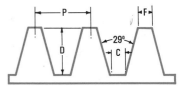

Fig. 9-77F   Brown and Sharpe Worm

greater, and the widths of the crest and root are different. This thread is used to mesh with worm gears and transmit motion between two shafts at right angles to each other but not in the same plane. The self-locking feature makes it adaptable to winches and steering mechanisms.

$$D = .500\,P$$
$$F = .500\,P$$
$$C = .500\,P + .002$$

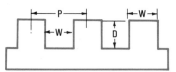

Fig. 9-77G   Square

The Square thread (Fig. 9-77G) is frequently being replaced by the Acme thread due to the difficulty of cutting it, particularly with taps and dies. Square threads were often found on vises and jack screws.

$$D = .7035\,P \text{ (maximum)}$$
$$.6855\,P \text{ (minimum)}$$
$$F = .125\,P$$
$$R = .0633\,P \text{ (maximum)}$$
$$.054\,P \text{ (minimum)}$$

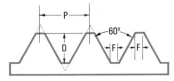

Fig. 9-77H   International Metric

The International Metric thread (Fig. 9-77H) is a standardized thread used in Europe. This thread has a 60° included angle with a crest and root truncated to one-eighth the depth. Although this thread is used extensively throughout Europe, its use in North America has been confined mainly to plugs and the manufacture of instruments.

THREAD FITS AND CLASSIFICATIONS

Certain terminology is used when referring to thread classifications and fits. To properly understand any thread system, the terminology relating to thread fits should be understood.

Fit is the range of tightness between two mating parts. This is determined by the clearance or interference of parts when they are assembled.

Allowance is the intentional difference in size of the mating parts or the minimum clearance between mating parts. With threads, the allowance is the permissible difference between the largest external thread and the smallest internal thread. This produces the tightest fit acceptable for any given classification.

The allowance for a 1 in. – 8 UNC Class 2A and 2B fit is:
Minimum pitch diameter
of the internal thread (2B) = .9188 in.
Maximum pitch diameter
of the external thread (2A) = .9168 in.
Allowance or intentional ——
difference   = .002 in.

Tolerance is the variation permitted in part size. The tolerance may be expressed as plus, minus, or both. The total tolerance is the sum of the plus and minus tolerances. For example, if a size is 1.000

±.002, the total tolerance is .004. In the Unified and National systems, the tolerance is plus on external threads and minus on internal threads. Thus, when a thread varies from the basic or nominal size, it will ensure a freer rather than a tighter fit.

The tolerance for a 1 in. – 8 UNC Class 2A thread is:
Maximum pitch diameter
of the external thread (2A) = .9168 in.
Minimum pitch diameter
of the external thread   = .9100 in.
Tolerance or permitted   ——
variation   = .0068 in.

Limits are the maximum and minimum dimensions of a part.

The limits for a 1 in. – 8 UNC Class 2A thread are:
Maximum pitch diameter
of the external thread (2A) = .9168 in.
Minimum pitch diameter
of the external thread (2A) = .9100 in.
The pitch diameter of this thread must be between .9168 in. (upper limit) and .9100 in. (lower limit).

Nominal size is the designation used to identify the size of the part. For example, in the designation 1 in. – 8 UNC, the figure 1 indicates a 1 in. diameter thread.

Actual size is the measured size of a thread or part. Although the basic major diameter of a 1 in. – 8 UNC Class 2A thread is 1.000 in., the actual size may vary from .998 in. to .983 in.

CLASSIFICATION OF THREAD FITS

With wide use of threads, it became necessary to establish certain limits and tolerances to properly identify classes of fit.

ISO Metric Tolerances and Allowances

The ISO metric screw thread tolerance system provides for allowances and tolerances defined by tolerance grades, tolerance positions, and tolerance classes.

Tolerance Grades

A medium tolerance, used on a general-purpose thread, is indicated by the number

6. Any number below 6 indicates a finer tolerance and any number above 6 indicates a greater tolerance. The tolerance for the thread at the pitch line and for the major diameter may be shown on the drawing (see example).

Allowance

Symbols are used to indicate the allowance for external threads:

Small "e" indicates a large allowance
Small "g" indicates a small allowance
Small "h" indicates no allowance

For internal threads:

Large "G" indicates a small allowance
Large "H" indicates no allowance

EXAMPLE: An external metric thread may be designated as follows:

		Pitch	Outside
	Nominal	Diam.	Diam.
Metric	Size	Pitch Tolerance	Tolerance
↓	↓	↓ ↓	↓
M	6	× 0.75 – 5g	6g

The thread fit between mating parts is indicated by the internal thread designation followed by the external thread tolerance:

$$M20 \times 2 - 6H/5g\,6g$$

Unified thread fits have been divided into three categories and the applications of each have been defined by the Screw Thread Committee. External threads are classified as 1A, 2A and 3A, and internal threads as 1B, 2B and 3B.

Classes 1A and 1B include those threads for work which must be readily assembled. They have the loosest fit, with no possibility of interference between the mating external and internal threads when the threads are dirty or bruised.

Classes 2A and 2B are used for the majority of commercial fasteners. These threads provide a medium or free fit and permit power wrenching with minimum galling and seizure.

Classes 3A and 3B are used where a more accurate fit and lead are required.

No allowance is provided and the tolerances are 75% of those used for 2A and 2B fits.

By classifying the tolerances of threads, the cost of threaded parts is reduced, since the manufacturer may use any combination of mating threads that suits his needs. With the former system of identifying classes of tolerances (Classes 1, 2, 3, 4), it was felt that a Class 3 internal thread should be used with a Class 3 external thread.

With reference to the Unified system it should be noted that "Class" refers to tolerance or tolerance and allowance, and does not refer to fit. The fit between the mating parts is determined by the selected combination used for a specific application. For example, if a closer-than-normal fit is required, a Class 3B nut may be used on a Class 2A bolt. The basic dimensions, tolerances and allowances for these threads may be found in any machine handbook.

THREAD CALCULATIONS

To cut a correct thread on a lathe, it is necessary first to make calculations so that the thread will have proper dimensions. The following diagrams and formulas will be helpful when calculating thread dimensions. The symbols used in these diagrams and formulas are:

D – single depth of thread
P – pitch

EXAMPLE 1: What is the pitch, depth, minor diameter, width of crest, and width of root for a M6.3 × 1.0 thread?

$$\text{Pitch} = 1 \text{ mm}$$

$$\begin{aligned} \text{Depth} &= 0.54127 \times 1 \\ &= 0.54 \text{ mm} \end{aligned}$$

$$\begin{aligned} \text{Minor Diameter} &= \text{Major Diameter} - \\ & \quad (D + D) \\ &= 6.3 - (0.54 + 0.54) \\ &= 5.22 \text{ mm} \end{aligned}$$

$$\begin{aligned} \text{Width of Crest} &= 0.125 \times \text{pitch} \\ &= 0.125 \times 1 \\ &= 0.125 \text{ mm} \end{aligned}$$

$$\begin{aligned} \text{Width of Root} &= 0.250 \times \text{pitch} \\ &= 0.250 \times 1 \\ &= 0.250 \text{ mm} \end{aligned}$$

EXAMPLE 2: Calculate the pitch, depth, minor diameter, and width of flat for a 3/4 – 10 NC thread.

$$\begin{aligned} P &= \frac{1}{\text{Number of threads per inch}} \\ &= \frac{1}{10} \\ &= .100 \text{ in.} \end{aligned}$$

$$\begin{aligned} \text{Depth} &= .6495 \times \text{Pitch} \\ &= .6495 \times \frac{1}{10} \\ &= .065 \text{ in.} \end{aligned}$$

$$\begin{aligned} \text{Minor Diameter} &= \text{Major Diameter} - \\ & \quad (D + D) \\ &= .750 - (.065 + .065) \\ &= .620 \text{ in.} \end{aligned}$$

$$\begin{aligned} \text{Width of Flat} &= \frac{P}{8} \\ &= \frac{1}{8} \times \frac{1}{10} \\ &= .0125 \text{ in.} \end{aligned}$$

To Set the Quick-Change Gearbox for Threading

The quick-change gearbox provides a means of quickly setting the lathe for the desired pitch of the thread in millimetres on metric lathes or number of threads per inch on inch-pound system lathes. This unit contains a number of different size gears which vary the ratio between headstock spindle revolutions and the rate of carriage travel when thread cutting.

1. Check the blueprint for the pitch in millimetres or number of threads per inch required.

SLIDING GEAR

TOP LEVER

GEAR BOX

TUMBLER LEVER

STANDARD-MODERN

INCH SERIES 2000

Fig. 9-78   Quick change gear mechanism used on a 2000 series Standard-Modern lathe

2. From the chart on the quick-change gearbox, find the *whole number* which represents the pitch in millimetres or number of threads per inch.

3. With the lathe stopped, engage the *tumbler lever* into the hole which is in line with the pitch in millimetres or number of threads per inch (Fig. 9-78).

4. Set the *top lever* into the proper position as indicated on the chart.

5. Engage the *sliding gear* in or out as required.
   NOTE: Some lathes have two levers on the gearbox which take the place of the top lever and sliding gear, and these should be set as indicated on the chart.

6. Turn the lathe spindle by hand to ensure that the leadscrew revolves.

7. Recheck the lever settings to avoid errors.

THREAD CHASING DIAL

To cut a thread on a lathe, the lathe spindle and the leadscrew must be in the same relative position for each successive cut. Most lathes have a thread chasing dial either built into, or attached to, the carriage for this purpose. The chasing dial indicates when the split-nut should be engaged with the leadscrew to follow the previously cut groove.

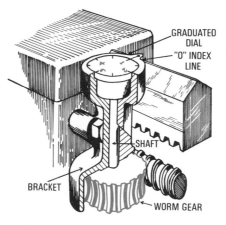

GRADUATED DIAL

"0" INDEX LINE

SHAFT

BRACKET

WORM GEAR

Fig. 9-79   Thread chasing dial mechanism

The thread chasing dial is connected to a worm gear which meshes with the threads of the leadscrew (Fig. 9-79). The dial is graduated into eight divisions, four numbered and four unnumbered, and it revolves as the leadscrew turns. Fig. 9-80 indicates when the split-nut lever should be engaged for cutting various numbers of threads per inch. Insufficient information was available on metric lathes to include here at the time of publication.

THREAD CUTTING

Thread cutting on a lathe is a process that produces a helical ridge of uniform section on a workpiece. This is performed by taking successive cuts with a threading toolbit the same shape as the thread form required. Work to be threaded may be held between centres or in a chuck. If work is held in a chuck, it should be turned to size and threaded before the work is removed.

To Set Up a Lathe for Threading (60° Thread)

1. Set the lathe speed to about 1/4 the speed used for turning.

2. Set the quick-change gearbox for the required pitch in millimetres or required thread per inch.

3. Engage the leadscrew.

4. Secure a 60° threading toolbit and check the angle using a thread centre gauge (Fig. 9-81).

5. Set the compound rest at 29° to the right (Fig. 9-81); to the left for a left-hand thread.

6. Set the cutting tool to the height of the lathe centre point.

7. Mount the work between centres. Make sure the lathe dog is tight on the work. If the work is mounted in a chuck, it must be held tightly.

8. Set the toolbit at right angles to the work, using a thread centre gauge (Fig. 9-81).
   NOTE: Never jam a toolbit into a thread centre gauge. This can be avoided by aligning only the cutting edge (leading side) of the toolbit with the gauge. A piece of paper on the cross-slide under the gauge and toolbit makes it easier to check tool alignment.

9. Arrange the apron controls to allow the split-nut lever to be engaged.

EVEN NUMBER OF THREADS	ENGAGE AT ANY GRADUATION ON THE DIAL	1 1-1/2 2 2-1/2 3 3-1/2 4 4-1/2	
ODD NUMBER OF THREADS	ENGAGE AT ANY MAIN DIVISION	1 2 3 4	
FRACTIONAL NUMBER OF THREADS	½ THREADS, E.G. 11½, ENGAGE AT EVERY OTHER MAIN DIVISION— 1 & 3, OR 2 & 4. OTHER FRACTIONAL THREADS ENGAGE AT SAME DIVISION EVERY TIME		
THREADS WHICH ARE A MULTIPLE OF THE NUMBER OF THREADS PER INCH IN THE LEAD SCREW	ENGAGE AT ANY TIME THAT SPLIT NUT MESHES		USE OF DIAL UNNECESSARY

Fig. 9-80   Split-nut engagement rules for thread cutting

Courtesy Kostel Enterprises Ltd.

Fig. 9-81   Setting a threading tool square with the work

THREAD CUTTING OPERATION

Thread cutting is one of the more interesting operations which can be performed on a lathe. It involves manipulation of the lathe parts, correlation of the hands, and strict attention to the operation. Before proceeding to cut a thread for the first time on any lathe, it is wise to take several trial passes, without cutting, in order to get the feel of the machine.

To Cut a 60° Thread

1. Check the major diameter of the work for size. It is good practice to have the diameter 0.05 mm (or .002 in.) undersize.

2. Start the lathe and chamfer the end of the workpiece with the side of the threading tool to just below the minor diameter of the thread.

3. Move the toolbit until it just scratches the diameter to be threaded.

4. Set both the crossfeed and compound rest graduated collars to zero.

5. Move the carriage until the toolbit clears the end of the work.

6. Move the compound rest in 0.08 mm (or .003 in.), engage the split-nut lever at the correct line of the thread chasing dial and take a trial cut. At the end of the cut, back out the toolbit with the crossfeed handle and with the other hand disengage the split-nut lever.

7. Stop the lathe and check the pitch in millimetres or number of threads per inch, with a thread pitch gauge, rule, or the side of a thread centre gauge (Fig. 9-82).

8. Return the carriage to the start of the thread and turn the crossfeed handle back to zero.

9. Set the depth of cut with the compound rest handle.
   a) The first two cuts should be 0.40 mm to 0.50 mm (or .015 in. to 0.20 in.) deep.
   b) Other cuts should be governed by the depth of the thread, generally 0.12 mm to 0.25 mm (or .005 in. to .010 in.) deep.

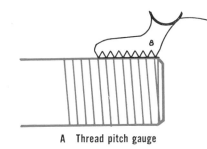

A   Thread pitch gauge

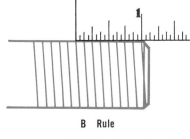

B   Rule

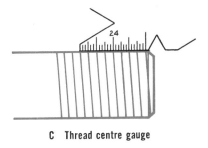

C   Thread centre gauge

Fig. 9-82   Three methods of checking the number of threads per inch

c) The last few cuts should be 0.02 mm to 0.05 mm (or .001 in. to .002 in.) deep.

NOTE: The depth of each cut is set by the compound rest handle. In this way, most of the metal is removed by the leading edge of the threading tool (Fig. 9-83).

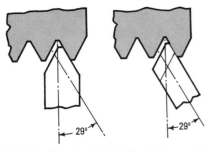

Fig. 9-83 When the tool is fed in at 29°, most of the cutting is done by the leading edge of the toolbit

10. Apply cutting fluid and continue to take successive cuts until the thread fits a gauge nut freely with no end play.
11. Whenever the work is removed from between centres, mark the slot into which the tail of the dog fits so that the thread will not be ruined if successive cuts are necessary.

Table 9-6 lists the amount the compound rest should be fed in when cutting various threads.

To Reset a Threading Tool

A threading tool must be reset: whenever it is necessary to remove partly threaded work and finish it at a later time; if the threading tool is removed for regrinding; or if the work slips under the lathe dog.

1. Set up the lathe and work for thread cutting.
2. Start the lathe, and with the toolbit clear of the work, engage the split-nut lever on the correct line.
3. Allow the carriage to travel until the toolbit is opposite any portion of the unfinished thread (Fig. 9-84).
4. Stop the lathe, *leaving the split-nut lever engaged.*

	Compound Rest Setting		
tpi	0°	30°	29°
24	.027	.031	.0308
20	.0325	.0375	.037
18	.036	.0417	.041
16	.0405	.0468	.046
14	.0465	.0537	.0525
13	.050	.0577	.057
11	.059	.068	.0674
10	.065	.075	.074
9	.072	.083	.082
8	.081	.0935	.092
7	.093	.1074	.106
6	.108	.1247	.1235
4	.1625	.1876	.1858

TABLE 9-6
DEPTH SETTINGS WHEN CUTTING 60° NATIONAL FORM THREADS

NOTE: When using this table for cutting National form threads, the correct width of flat (.125P) must be ground on the toolbit, otherwise the thread will not be the correct width.

Courtesy Kostel Enterprises Ltd.

Fig. 9-84 Resetting the threading tool in a partially cut groove using the crossfeed and compound rest feed handles

5. Feed the toolbit into the thread groove using ONLY the compound rest and crossfeed handles until the right-hand edge of the toolbit touches the rear side of the thread.

NOTE: Do not have the cutting edge of the toolbit contacting the thread at this time.

6. Set the crossfeed graduated collar to zero.
7. Back out the threading tool using the crossfeed handle, disengage the split-nut lever and move the carriage until the toolbit clears the start of the thread.
8. Set the crossfeed handle back to zero and take a trial cut without setting the compound rest.
9. Set the depth of cut using the compound rest handle and finish the thread to the required depth.

To Convert an Inch-Designed Lathe to Metric Threading

Metric threads may be cut on a standard quick-change gear lathe by using a pair of change gears having 50 and 127 teeth respectively. Since the lead screw has inch dimensions and is designed to cut threads per inch, it is necessary to convert the pitch in millimetres to centimetres and then into threads per inch. To do this, it is first necessary to understand the relationship between inches and centimetres.

1 inch = 2.54 centimetres

Therefore the ratio of inches to centi-

metres is 1:254 or $\dfrac{1}{2.54}$

To cut a metric thread on an inch lathe, it is necessary to incorporate certain gears in the gear train which will produce a ratio of 1/2.54. These gears are:

$$\frac{1}{2.54} \times \frac{50}{50} = \frac{50}{127} \quad \text{teeth}$$

In order to cut metric threads, two gears having 50 and 127 teeth must be placed in the gear train of the lathe. The 50 tooth gear is used as the spindle or drive gear and the 127 tooth gear is placed on the leadscrew.

To Cut a 2 mm Metric Thread on a Standard Quick-Change Gear Lathe

1. Mount the 127 tooth gear on the leadscrew.
2. Mount the 50 tooth gear on the spindle.
3. Convert the 2 mm pitch to threads per centimetre.

   $$10 \text{ mm} = 1 \text{ cm}$$

   $$\text{Pitch} = \frac{10}{2} = 5 \text{ threads/cm}$$

4. Set the quick-change gearbox to 5 threads/inch. By means of the 50 and 127 tooth gears, the lathe will now cut 5 threads/cm or 2 mm pitch.
5. Set up the lathe for thread cutting. See *To Set Up a Lathe For Threading (60° thread)*.
6. Take a light trial cut. At the end of the cut back out the cutting tool and stop the machine but *do not disengage the split nut*.
7. Reverse the spindle rotation until the cutting tool has just cleared the end of the threaded section.
8. Check the thread with a metric screw pitch gauge.
9. Cut the thread to the required depth (Table 9-7).
   NOTE: Never disengage the split nut until the thread has been cut to depth.

To Cut a Left-hand Thread (60°)

A left-hand thread is used to replace a right-hand thread on certain applications

TABLE 9-7: DEPTH SETTINGS WHEN CUTTING 60° ISO METRIC THREADS			
	COMPOUND RESET SETTING (in mm)		
PITCH (mm)	0°	30°	29°
0.35	0.19	0.21	0.21
0.4	0.21	0.25	0.24
0.45	0.24	0.28	0.27
0.5	0.27	0.31	0.31
0.6	0.32	0.37	0.37
0.7	0.37	0.43	0.43
0.8	0.43	0.50	0.49
1.0	0.54	0.62	0.62
1.25	0.67	0.78	0.77
1.5	0.81	0.93	0.93
1.75	0.94	1.09	1.08
2.0	1.08	1.25	1.24
2.5	1.35	1.56	1.55
3.0	1.62	1.87	1.85
3.5	1.89	2.19	2.16
4.0	2.16	2.50	2.47
4.5	2.44	2.81	2.78
5.0	2.71	3.13	3.09
5.5	2.98	3.44	3.40
6.0	3.25	3.75	3.71

Courtesy Kostel Enterprises Ltd.

Fig. 9-85 The compound rest is set 29° to the left when left-hand threads are cut

where the nut may loosen due to the rotation of a spindle.

The procedure for cutting left-hand threads is basically the same as for right-hand threads with a few exceptions.

1. Set the lathe speed and the quick-change gear box for the pitch of the thread to be cut.
2. Engage the feed direction lever so that the leadscrew will revolve in the *opposite* direction to that for a right-hand thread.
3. Set the compound rest to 29° to the *LEFT* (Fig. 9-85).
4. Set up the left-hand threading tool and square it with the work.
5. Cut a groove at the left end of the section to be threaded. This gives the cutting tool a starting point.
6. Proceed to cut the thread to the same dimensions as for a right-hand one.

Cutting a Thread on a Tapered Section

When a tapered thread, such as a pipe thread, is required on the end of a workpiece, either the taper attachment or the offset tailstock may be used for cutting the taper. The same setup is then used as for regular thread cutting. When setting up the threading tool, it is most important that it be set at 90° to the axis of the work and not square with the tapered surface.

THREAD MEASUREMENT

Interchangeable manufacture demands that all parts be made to certain standards in order that, on assembly, they will fit the intended component properly. This is especially important for threaded components, and therefore the measurement and inspection of threads is important.

Threads may be measured by a variety of methods; the most common are:

a) a thread ring gauge
b) a thread plug gauge
c) a thread snap gauge
d) a screw thread micrometer
e) a thread comparator micrometer
f) an optional comparator
g) the three-wire method

The description and use of the ring gauge, plug gauge, snap gauge, screw-thread micrometer, thread comparator micrometer, and optical comparator for checking threads are fully described in Chapter 3.

THREE-WIRE METHOD OF MEASURING THREADS

The three-wire method of measuring threads is recommended by the Bureau of Standards and the National Screw Thread Commission. It is recognized as one of the best methods of checking the pitch diameter because the results are least affected by an error which may be present in the included thread angle. For threads which require an accuracy of 0.02 mm or .001 in., a micrometer can be used to measure the distance over the wires. An electronic comparator should be used to measure the distance over the wires for threads requiring greater accuracy.

Three wires, of equal diameter, are placed in the thread; two on one side and one on the other side (Fig. 9-86). The wires used should be hardened and lapped

to three times the accuracy of the thread to be inspected. A standard micrometer may then be used to measure the distance over the wires (M). Different sizes and pitches of threads require different size wires. For the greatest accuracy, the *best wire size* should be used. This is one that will contact the thread at the pitch diameter (middle of the sloping sides). If the best size wire is used, the pitch diameter of the thread can be calculated by subtracting the wire constant (found in any handbook) from the measurement over the wires.

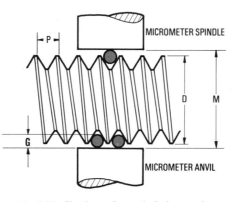

Fig. 9-86   The three-wire method of measuring 60° threads

To Calculate the Measurement Over the Wires

The measurement over the wires for American National Threads (60°) can be calculated by applying the following formula.

$$M = D + 3G - \frac{1.5155}{N}$$

where M = measurement over the wires
D = major diameter of the thread
G = diameter of the wire used
N = number of threads per inch

Any of the following formulas can be used to calculate the wire size (G).

a) largest size wire $= \dfrac{1.010}{N}$ or $1.010P$

b) best size wire $= \dfrac{.57735}{N}$ or $.57735P$

c) smallest size wire $= \dfrac{.505}{N}$ or $.505P$

For the most accurate thread measurement, the best size wire (.57735P) should be used, since this wire contacts the thread at the pitch diameter.

EXAMPLE:
To find M (measurement over the wires) for a 3/4 − 10 NC thread.
1. Calculate G (wire size).

$$G = \frac{.57735}{10}$$
$$= .0577$$

2. Calculate M (measurement over the wires).

$$M = D + 3G - \frac{1.5155}{N}$$
$$= .750 + (3 \times .0577) - \frac{1.5155}{10}$$
$$= .750 + .1731 - .1516$$
$$= .9231 - .1516$$
$$= .7715$$

MULTIPLE THREADS

Multiple threads are used when it is necessary to obtain an increase in lead and a deep, coarse thread cannot be cut. Multiple threads may be double, triple, or quadruple, depending on the number of starts around the periphery of the workpiece (Fig. 9-87).

The *pitch* of a thread is always the distance from a point on one thread to the corresponding point on the next thread. The *lead* is the distance a nut advances lengthwise in one complete revolution. On a single-start thread, the pitch and lead are equal. On a double-start thread, the lead will be twice the pitch. On triple-start threads the lead will be three times the pitch.

Multiple-start threads are not as deep as single-start threads and therefore have a more pleasing appearance. For example, a double-start thread having the same lead

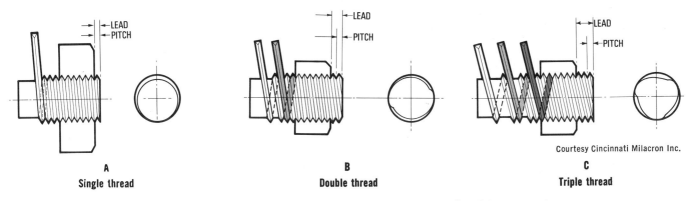

A
Single thread

B
Double thread

C
Triple thread

Courtesy Cincinnati Milacron Inc.

Fig. 9-87 The relationship between the pitch and lead for a single-start and multiple-start threads

as a single-start thread would be cut only half as deep.

Multiple threads may be cut on a lathe by:

a) Using an accurately slotted drive plate or faceplate.
b) Disengaging the intermediate gear of the end gear train and rotating the spindle the desired amount.
c) Using the thread chasing dial (only for double-start threads with an odd number lead).

To Cut an 8-Thread per Inch Double Thread

1. Set up the lathe and cutting tool as for cutting a single-start thread.
2. Set the quick change gearbox to 4 threads per inch. (The lead of this thread is 1/4 in.).
3. Cut the first thread to half the depth required for 4 threads per inch.
4. Leave the crossfeed handle set to the depth of the thread and *note the reading on the compound rest graduated collar.*
5. Withdraw the threading tool from the work using the *compound rest handle.*
6. Revolve the work exactly one-half turn by either of the following methods.
   a) i) Remove the work from the lathe with the lathe dog attached.
      ii) Replace the work in the lathe with the tail of the dog in the slot exactly opposite the one used for the first thread.

Fig. 9-88 Marking the spindle and intermediate gear before indexing the work exactly one-half turn for cutting a double thread

NOTE: An accurately slotted drive plate or faceplate must be used for this method of indexing. A special indexing plate may also be used for this purpose.

OR

   b) i) Turn the lathe by hand until a tooth of the spindle gear is exactly between two teeth of the intermediate gear.

   ii) With chalk, mark both the spindle tooth and the space in the intermediate gear (Fig. 9-88).
   iii) Disengage the intermediate gear from the spindle gear.
   iv) Starting with the tooth *next* to the marked tooth on the spindle gear, count the number required for a half revolution of the spindle. For example, if the spindle gear has 24 teeth, count 12 teeth and mark this one with chalk.
   v) Revolve the lathe spindle by hand one-half turn to bring the marked tooth in line with the chalk mark on the intermediate gear.
   vi) Re-engage the intermediate gear.

7. Reset the crossfeed handle to the same position as when cutting the first thread.
8. Cut the second thread, feeding the compound rest handle until the graduated collar is at the same setting as for the first thread.

THE THREAD CHASING DIAL METHOD OF CUTTING MULTIPLE THREADS

Double-start threads with an odd numbered lead (example 1/5, 1/7, etc.) may be cut using the thread chasing dial.

1. Take one cut on the thread by engaging the split-nut at a numbered line on the chasing dial.
2. Without changing the depth of cut, take another cut at an unnumbered line on the chasing dial. The second thread will be exactly in the middle of the first thread.
3. Continue cutting the thread to depth, taking two passes (one on a numbered line, the other on an unnumbered line) for every depth of cut setting.

SQUARE THREADS

Square threads were often found in vise screws, jacks, and other devices where maximum power transmission was required. Because of the difficulty of cutting this thread with taps and dies, it is being replaced by Acme thread. With care, square threads can be readily cut on a lathe.

THE SHAPE OF A SQUARE THREADING TOOL

The square threading tool looks like a short cutting-off tool. It differs from it in that both sides of the square threading tool must be ground at an angle to conform to the helix angle of the thread (Fig. 9-89).

The helix angle of a thread, and therefore the angle of the square threading tool, depends upon two factors.
a) The helix angle changes for each *different lead* on a given diameter. The greater the lead of the thread, the greater will be the helix angle.
b) The helix angle changes for each *different diameter* of thread for a given lead. The larger the diameter, the smaller will be the helix angle.

The helix angle of either the leading or following side of a square thread can be represented by a right-angle triangle (Fig. 9-89). The side opposite equals the *lead* of the thread, while the side adjacent equals the circumference of either the major or minor diameter of the thread. The angle between the hypotenuse and the side adjacent represents the helix angle of the thread.

To Calculate the Helix Angles of the Leading and Following Sides of a Square Thread

Tan leading angle

$$= \frac{\text{lead of thread}}{\text{circumference of minor diameter}}$$

Tan following angle

$$= \frac{\text{lead of thread}}{\text{circumference of major diameter}}$$

CLEARANCE

If a square toolbit is ground to the same helix angles as the leading and following sides of the thread, it has no clearance and the sides would rub. To prevent the tool from rubbing, it must be provided with approximately 1° clearance on each side, making it thinner at the bottom (Fig. 9-90). For the leading side of the tool, *add 1°* to the calculated helix angle. On the following side, subtract *1°* from the calculated angle.

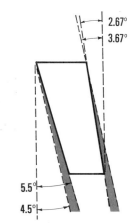

Fig. 9-90   Helix angles of the thread and the clearance angles necessary for a square threading tool

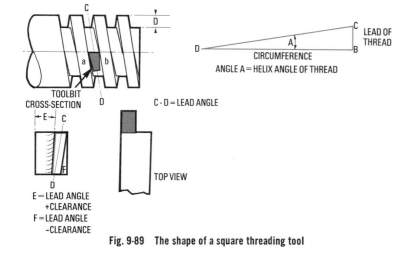

Fig. 9-89   The shape of a square threading tool

EXAMPLE:
To find the leading and following angles of a threading tool to cut a 1-1/4 in. — 4 square thread.

SOLUTION:

$$\text{Lead} = .250 \text{ in.}$$
$$\text{Single depth} = \frac{.500 \text{ in.}}{4}$$
$$= .125 \text{ in.}$$
$$\text{Double depth} = 2 \times .125$$
$$= .250 \text{ in.}$$
$$\text{Minor diameter} = 1.250 - .250$$
$$= 1.000 \text{ in.}$$

$$\text{Tan leading angle} = \frac{\text{lead}}{\text{circumference of}}$$
$$\text{minor diameter}$$

$$= \frac{.250}{1.000 \times \pi}$$

$$= \frac{.250}{3.1416}$$

$$= .0795 \text{ in.}$$

$\therefore$ The angle of the thread
$$= 4°33'$$

The toolbit angle $= 4°33'$ plus $1°$
clearance
$$= 5°33'$$

$$\text{Tan following angle} = \frac{\text{lead}}{\text{circumference of}}$$
$$\text{major diameter}$$

$$= \frac{.250}{1.250\pi}$$

$$= \frac{.250}{3.927}$$

$$= .0636 \text{ in.}$$

$\therefore$ The angle of the thread
$$= 3°38'$$

The toolbit angle $= 3°38'$ minus $1°$
clearance
$$= 2°38'$$

To Cut a Square Thread

1. Grind a threading tool to the proper leading and following angles. The width of the tool should be approximately .002 in. (0.05 mm) wider than the thread groove. This will allow the completed screw to fit the nut readily. Depending on the size of the thread, it may be wise to grind two tools; a roughing tool .015 in. (0.40 mm) undersize, and a finishing tool .002 in. (0.05 mm) oversize.
2. Align the lathe centres and mount the work.
3. Set the quick-change gearbox for the required pitch in millimetres or number of threads per inch.
4. Set the compound rest at 30° to the

right. This will provide side movement if it becomes necessary to reset the cutting tool.
5. Set the threading tool square with the work and on centre.
6. Cut the right-hand end of the work to the minor diameter for approximately 1/16 in. (1.5 mm) long. This will indicate when the thread is cut to the full depth.
7. If the work permits, cut a recess at the end of the thread to the minor diameter. This will provide room for the cutting tool to "run out" at the end of the thread.
8. Calculate the single depth of the thread
$$\left(\frac{.500}{N} \right)$$
9. Start the lathe and just touch the tool to the work diameter.
10. Set the *crossfeed graduated collar* to zero.
11. Set a .003 in. (0.08 mm) depth of cut with the *crossfeed screw* and take a trial cut.
12. Check the thread with a thread pitch gauge.
13. Apply cutting fluid and cut the thread to depth, moving the *crossfeed* in from .002 in. to .010 in. (0.05 mm to 0.25 mm) for each cut. The depth of the cut will depend on the thread size and the nature of the workpiece.

NOTE: Since the thread sides are square, *all cuts* must be set using the *crossfeed screw*.

ACME THREAD

The *Acme thread* is gradually replacing the square thread because it is stronger and easier to cut with taps and dies. It is used extensively for leadscrews because the 29° angle formed by its sides allows the split nut to be engaged readily during thread cutting.

The Acme thread is provided with .010 in. clearance for both the crest and root on

all sizes of threads. The hole for an internal Acme thread is cut .020 in. larger than the minor diameter of the screw, and **the major diameter of a tap or internal thread is .020 in. larger than the major diameter of the screw. This provides .010 in. clear**ance between the screw and nut on both the top and bottom.

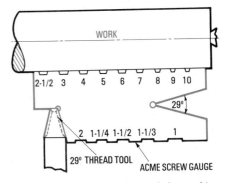

Fig. 9-91 An Acme thread gauge being used to set up and align the cutting tool with the workpiece

To Cut an Acme Thread

1. Grind a toolbit to fit the end of the Acme thread gauge (Fig. 9-91). Be sure to provide sufficient side clearance so that the tool will not rub while cutting the thread.
2. Grind the point of the tool flat until it fits into the slot of the gauge indicating the number of threads per inch to be cut.

   NOTE: If a gauge is not available, the width of the toolbit point may be calculated:

$$\text{Width of point} = \frac{.3707}{N} - .0052 \text{ in.}$$

3. Set the quick-change gearbox to the required number of threads per inch.
4. Set the compound rest 14-1/2° to the right (half the included thread angle).
5. Set the Acme threading tool on centre and square it with the work using the gauge shown in Fig. 9-91.
6. At the right-hand end of the work, cut a section 1/16 in. long to the minor diameter. This will indicate when the thread is to the full depth.

7. Cut the thread to the proper depth by feeding the cutting tool, using the *compound rest*.

MEASURING ACME THREADS

For most purposes, the *one-wire method* of measuring Acme threads is accurate enough. A single wire or pin of the correct diameter is placed in the thread groove (Fig. 9-92), and measured with a micrometer. The thread is the correct size when the micrometer reading over the wire is the same as the major diameter of the thread and the *wire is tight in the thread*. NOTE: It is important that the burrs be removed from the diameter before using the one-wire method.

The diameter of the wire to be used can be calculated as follows:

$$\text{Wire diameter} = .4872 \times \text{pitch}$$

For example, if 6 threads per inch are being cut, the wire diameter should be:

$$\text{Wire size} = .4872 \times \frac{1}{6}$$
$$= .081 \text{ in.}$$

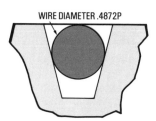

WIRE DIAMETER .4872P

Fig. 9-92   Using one wire to measure the accuracy of an Acme thread

INTERNAL THREADS

Most internal threads are cut with taps; however, there are times when a tap of a specific size is not available and the thread must be cut on a lathe. Internal threading, or cutting threads in a hole, is an operation performed on work held in a chuck, collet, or mounted on a faceplate. The threading tool is similar to a boring toolbit, except

the shape is ground to the form of the thread to be cut.

To Cut a 1-3/8 in. - 6 NC Internal Thread

1. Calculate the tap drill size of the thread.

$$\text{Tap drill size} = \text{major diameter} - \frac{1}{N}$$
$$= 1.375 - \frac{1}{6}$$
$$= 1.375 - .166$$
$$= 1.209 \text{ in.}$$

2. Mount the work to be threaded in a chuck, collet, or on a faceplate.
3. Drill a hole, approximately 1/16 in. smaller than the tap drill size in the workpiece. For this thread it would be 1.209 − .062 = 1.147 or a 1-5/32 in. hole.
4. Mount a boring tool in the lathe and bore the hole to the tap drill size (1.209). The boring bar should be as large as possible and held short. The boring operation cuts the hole to size and makes it true.
5. Recess the start of the hole to the major diameter of the thread (1.375) 1/16 in. (1.5 mm) for length. During the thread cutting operation, this will indicate when the thread is cut to depth.
6. If the thread does not go through the workpiece, a recess should be cut at the end of the thread to the major diameter (Fig. 9-93). This recess

should be wide enough to allow the threading tool to "run out" and permit time to disengage the split-nut lever.
7. Set the compound rest at 29° to the left (Fig. 9-93); to the right for left-hand threads.
8. Mount a threading toolbit into the boring bar and set it to centre.
9. Square the threading tool with a thread centre gauge (Fig. 9-94).

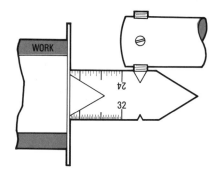

Fig. 9-94   Using a thread centre gauge to square the threading tool with the work

10. Place a mark on the boring bar, measuring from the threading tool, to indicate the length of hole to be threaded. This will show when the split-nut lever should be disengaged.
11. Start the lathe and turn the crossfeed handle *out* until the threading tool just scratches the internal diameter.
12. Set the crossfeed graduated collar to zero.

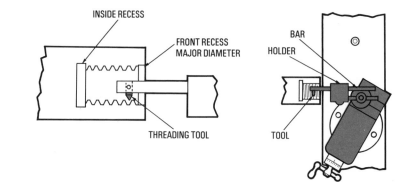

INSIDE RECESS

FRONT RECESS
MAJOR DIAMETER

THREADING TOOL

BAR

HOLDER

TOOL

Fig. 9-93   The compound rest is set at 29° to the left for cutting right-hand internal threads

13. Set a 0.08 mm (or .003 in.) depth of cut by feeding the compound rest *out* and take a trial cut.

14. At the end of *each* cut on an internal thread, disengage the split-nut lever and feed the crossfeed handle *in* to clear the thread.

15. Clear the threading tool from the hole and check the pitch of the thread.

16. Return the crossfeed handle to zero and set the depth of cut by turning the compound rest *out* the desired amount.

17. Cut the thread to depth; check the fit with a screw or threaded plug gauge.
NOTE: The last few cuts should not be deeper than 0.02 mm (or .001 in.) each to eliminate the spring of the boring bar.

MANDRELS

A *mandrel* (Fig. 9-95) is a precision tool which, when pressed into the hole of a workpiece, provides centres for a machining operation. They are especially valuable for thin work such as flanges, pulleys, gears, etc., where the outside diameter must run true with the inside diameter and it would be difficult to hold the work in a chuck.

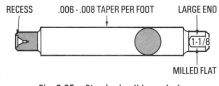

Fig. 9-95   Standard solid mandrel

CHARACTERISTICS OF A STANDARD MANDREL

a) Mandrels are usually hardened and ground, and tapered .006 in. to .008 in. per foot (0.50 to 0.66 mm/m▪).

b) The nominal size is near the middle and the small end is usually .001 in. (0.02 mm▪) under; the large end is .004 in. (0.10 mm▪) over the nominal size.

c) Both ends are turned smaller than the body and provided with a flat so that the lathe dog does not damage the accuracy of the mandrel.

d) The size of the mandrel is stamped on the large end.

e) The centre holes, which are recessed slightly, are large enough to provide a good bearing surface and to withstand the strain caused by machining a workpiece.

TYPES OF MANDRELS

Many types of mandrels are used to suit various types of workpieces or machining operations. Descriptions and purposes of some of the more common types follow.

The solid mandrel (Fig. 9-95) is available for most of the standard hole sizes. It is a general purpose mandrel which may be used for a variety of workpieces.

The expansion mandrel (Fig. 9-96A) consists of a sleeve, with four or more grooves cut lengthwise, fitted over a solid mandrel. A taper pin fits into the sleeve to expand it to hold work that does not have a standard size hole. Another form of expansion mandrel has a slotted bushing fitting over a tapered mandrel. Various size bushings can be used with this mandrel, increasing its range.

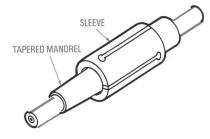

Fig. 9-96A   Expansion mandrel

The gang mandrel (Fig. 9-96B) is used to hold a number of identical parts for a machining operation. The body of the mandrel is parallel (no taper) and has a shoulder or flange on one end. The other end is threaded for a locking nut.

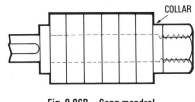

Fig. 9-96B   Gang mandrel

The threaded mandrel (Fig. 9-96C) is used for holding workpieces having a threaded hole. An undercut at the shoulder ensures that the workpiece will seat squarely and is not canted on the threads.

Fig. 9-96C   Threaded mandrel

The taper-shank mandrel (Fig. 9-96D) may be fitted to the tapered hole in the headstock spindle. The projecting portion may be machined to any desired form to suit the workpiece. This type of mandrel is often used for small workpieces or those which have blind holes.

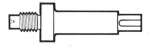

Fig. 9-96D   Taper-shank mandrel

To Mount Work on a Plain Mandrel

1. Secure a mandrel to fit the hole in the workpiece.

2. Thoroughly clean the mandrel and apply a thin film of oil on the diameter.

3. Clean and remove any burrs from the hole in the workpiece.

4. Start the small end of the mandrel into the hole (the large end has the size stamped on it) by hand.

5. Place the work on an arbor press with a machined surface down so that the hole is at right angles (Fig. 9-97).

6. Press the mandrel firmly into the workpiece.

Fig. 9-97   Using an arbor press to press a mandrel into a workpiece

To Turn Work on a Mandrel

Work pressed on a mandrel is held in position by friction; therefore cutting operations should be toward the large end of the mandrel. This will tend to keep the work tight on the mandrel.

1. Fasten the lathe dog on the *large end* of the mandrel (where the size is stamped).
2. Clean the lathe and mandrel centres and then mount the work.
3. If the entire side of the work must be faced, it is good practice to use a paper feeler between the toolbit point and mandrel for setting the toolbit. This will prevent marring or scoring the surface of the mandrel.
4. When turning the outside diameter of work, always cut towards the large end of the mandrel.
5. On large diameter work, it is advisable to take light cuts to prevent the work from slipping on the mandrel or chattering.

ECCENTRICS

An *eccentric* (Fig. 9-98) is a shaft which may have two or more turned diameters parallel to each other, but not concentric with the normal axis of the work. Eccentrics are used in locking devices, in the feed mechanism on some shapers, and in the crank shaft of an automobile, etc., where it is necessary to *convert rotary motion into reciprocating motion*, or vice-versa.

The amount of eccentricity or *throw* of an eccentric is the distance that a set of centre holes has been offset from the normal work axis. If the centre holes were offset 5 mm from the work axis, the amount of throw would be 5 mm, but the total travel of the eccentric would be 10 mm.

There are three types of eccentrics which are generally cut on a lathe in the following ways.

a) When the throw enables all centres to be located on the ends of the workpiece.
b) When the throw is too small to allow all centres to be located on the workpiece at the same time.
c) When the throw is so great that all centres cannot be located on the workpiece.

Fig. 9-98   On an eccentric the axes are parallel but not in line

To Turn an Eccentric with a 10 mm or .375 in. Throw

1. Place the work in a chuck and face it to length. If the centre holes are to be removed later, leave the work 20 mm longer.
2. Place the work in a V-block on a surface plate and apply layout dye to both ends of the work.

Fig. 9-99   Locating the centres of an eccentric

3. Set a vernier height gauge to the top of the work and note the vernier reading.
4. Subtract half the work diameter from the reading and set the gauge to this dimension.
5. Scribe a centre line on both ends of the work.
6. Rotate the work 90° and scribe another centre line on both ends at the same height gauge setting (Fig. 9-99).
7. Lower or raise the height gauge setting 10 mm (or .375 in.) and scribe the lines for the offset centres on both ends.
8. Carefully centre punch the four scribed centres, and drill the centre holes in each end.
9. Mount the work in a lathe and turn the diameter with the true centres.
10. Set the work on the offset centres and turn the eccentric (centre section) to the required diameter.

To Cut an Eccentric with a Small Throw

This procedure should be followed when the centres are too close to be located on the workpiece at the same time.

To Cut an Eccentric with a Small Throw

1. Cut the work 20 mm longer than required.
2. Face the ends and drill one set of centre holes in the lathe.

3. Mount the work between centres and turn the large diameter to size.

4. Cut off the ends to remove the centre holes.

5. Lay out and drill a new set of centre holes, offsetting them from centre the required throw.

6. Turn the eccentric diameter to size.

To Turn an Eccentric with a Large Throw

1. Set the work on the normal centres and turn both ends to size.

2. Secure or make a set of support blocks as shown in Fig. 9-100. The hole in the

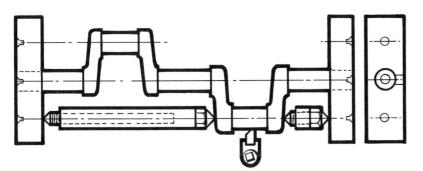

Fig. 9-100   The setup required for turning an eccentric with a large throw

support block should fit the turned ends of the work snugly. A set screw in each block is used to securely fasten the support blocks to the work. The number of centres required should be laid out and drilled in the support blocks (Fig. 9-100).

3. Align both support blocks parallel on the work and lock them in position.

4. Counterbalance the lathe to prevent undue vibration.

5. Turn the various diameters as required.

GRINDING ON A LATHE

Cylindrical and internal grinding may be done on a lathe if a proper grinding machine is not available. A toolpost grinder (Fig. 9-101), mounted on a lathe, may be used for cylindrical and taper grinding as well as angular grinding of lathe centres. An internal grinding attachment for the toolpost grinder permits the grinding of straight and tapered holes. Grinding should be done on a lathe only when no other machine is available, or when the cost of performing a small grinding operation on a part would not warrant setting up a regular grinding machine. Since the work should rotate in an opposite direction to the grinding wheel, the lathe must be equipped with a reversing switch.

To Cylindrical Grind in a Lathe

1. Thoroughly clean the ways of the lathe.

2. Cover the ways with cloth or canvas to protect them from the grinding dust.

3. Adjust the tailstock centre as required for parallel or taper grinding. When grinding tapers, the taper attachment may be set as required.

4. Mount a toolpost grinder on the compound rest and adjust the spindle to centre height.

5. Mount the proper grinding wheel on the grinder.

6. Place a small pan of water directly under the grinding wheel and workpiece to catch as much grinding dust as possible.

7. True and dress the grinding wheel. *CAUTION: WEAR SAFETY GLASSES.*

8. Set a fairly slow spindle speed (depending on the diameter of the workpiece).

9. Set the carriage feed to about 1.50 mm to 2.00 mm (or .060 in. to .080 in.), depending on the width of the wheel.

10. Mount the work in the lathe.

11. Start the lathe and be sure that the work is revolving in reverse.

Fig. 9-101   A toolpost grinder mounted on a lathe for cylindrical grinding

12. Start the grinder and carefully bring it up to the revolving workpiece until it sparks lightly.

13. Slowly feed the carriage along the work, by hand, to remove any high spots.

14. Move the carriage until the wheel is opposite the right end of the work.

15. Feed the grinder in 0.02 mm to 0.08 mm (or .001 in. to .003 in.) using the crossfeed.

    CAUTION: Do not take heavy cuts since the work will heat quickly and may distort.

16. Engage the automatic feed and grind the workpiece for the required length.

17. At the end of the cut, reverse the feed and take a cut in the opposite direction.

18. Check the diameter with a micrometer. Do not measure work when it is hot.

19. Grind the workpiece to within 0.05 mm (or .002 in.) of size.

20. Redress the grinding wheel.

21. Finish grind the work. After the last cut, let the grinding wheel move back and forth across the length of the ground surface without changing the feed. This will let the wheel spark out.

To Grind a Lathe Centre

1. Remove the chuck or drive plate from the lathe spindle.

2. Mount the lathe centre to be ground in the headstock spindle.

3. Set a slow spindle speed.

4. Swing the compound rest to 30° (Fig. 9-102) with the centre line of the lathe.

5. Protect the ways of the lathe with cloth or canvas and place a pan of water below the lathe centre.

6. Mount the toolpost grinder and adjust the centre of the grinding spindle to centre height.

7. Mount the proper grinding wheel, true and dress.

8. Start the lathe, with the spindle revolving in reverse.

Fig. 9-102   The compound rest set at 30° to grind a lathe centre

9. Start the grinder and adjust the grinding wheel until it sparks lightly against the revolving centre.

10. Lock the carriage in this position.

11. Feed the grinding wheel in 0.02 mm, using the crossfeed handle.

12. Move the grinder along the face of the centre using the compound rest feed.

13. Check the angle of the centre using a centre gauge, and adjust the compound rest if necessary.

14. Finish grind the centre.

NOTE: If a high finish is desired, polish the centre with abrasive cloth at a high spindle speed.

INTERNAL GRINDING ON A LATHE

Internal grinding may be performed on the lathe, using a toolpost grinder with an internal grinding attachment. Internal grinding of tapered holes may be done with the taper attachment or with the compound rest feed handle.

1. Mount the work in a chuck or on a faceplate.

2. Mount the toolpost grinder and internal attachment at centre height on the compound rest.

    NOTE: If a tapered hole is to be ground using the compound rest feed, the compound rest should be swivelled to the required angle before mounting the toolpost grinder.

3. Cover the ways of the lathe with a cloth.

4. Start the grinding wheel, true and dress.

5. Start the lathe with the spindle rotating in the same direction as for turning.

6. Move the grinding wheel into the hole and carefully adjust it out until it just touches the surface of the hole.

7. Move the crossfeed out 0.02 mm (or .001 in.) and take a pass across the work. Do not overlap the ends of the hole with more than half the width of the wheel to avoid bell-mouthing.

8. Take light cuts and continue to grind until the work is within 0.05 mm (or .002 in.) in size.

9. Take a few passes through the hole to allow the wheel to spark out.

10. Finish grind to size.

FORM TURNING ON A LATHE

It is often necessary to form irregular shapes or contours on a workpiece. Form turning may be done on a lathe by three methods.
a) freehand
b) form turning tool
c) hydraulic tracer attachment

TURNING A FREEHAND FORM OR RADIUS

Freehand form turning probably presents the greatest problem to the beginning lathe operator. In this operation, coordination of both hands is required and practice is important in mastering this skill.

To Turn a 15 mm Radius on the End of a Workpiece

1. Mount the workpiece in a chuck and face the end.
2. With the work revolving, mark a line 15 mm from the end using a pencil (Fig. 9-103A).

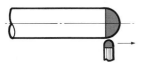

Fig. 9-103A   Turning a 12.7 mm radius on the end of a workpiece

3. Mount a round-nose turning tool on centre.
4. Start the lathe and adjust the toolbit in until it touches the diameter about 6 mm from the end.
5. Place one hand on the crossfeed handle and the other on the carriage handwheel.
6. Turn the carriage *handwheel* (*not the handle*) to feed the toolbit slowly towards the end of the work; at the same time, turn the crossfeed handle to move the tool into the work.
NOTE: It will take practice to coordinate the movement of the carriage in relation to the crossfeed. For the first 7.5 mm of the radius, the carriage

must be moved faster than the cross-feed handle. However, for the second 7.5 mm, the crossfeed handle must be moved faster than the carriage.
7. Back out the toolbit and move the carriage to the left.
8. Take successive cuts as in step #6 until the toolbit starts to cut close to the 15 mm line.
9. Test the radius with a 15 mm gauge.
10. If the radius is not correct, it may have to be recut. It is often possible to finish the cut to the required shape by filing.

The same procedure as step #6 is followed when cutting internal radii (Fig. 9-103B). It is always advisable to start at the large diameter, feeding along and in

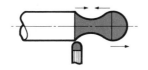

Fig. 9-103B   Turning a concave and convex radius on a workpiece

until the proper radius and diameter are obtained.

FORMING TURNING TOOLS

Smaller radii and contours are conveniently formed on a workpiece by a formed turning tool. The lathe toolbit is ground to the desired radius and used to form the contour on the workpiece. Toolbits may also be ground to produce a concave radius (Fig. 9-104A).

This method of forming radii and contours eliminates the need for checking

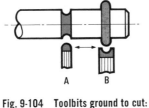

Fig. 9-104   Toolbits ground to cut:
A — A concave radius
B — a convex radius

with a gauge or template once the toolbit is ground to the desired shape. Duplicate contours may also be formed on several workpieces when the same toolbit is used.

When producing a convex radius, it is necessary to leave a collar of the desired size on the workpiece (Fig. 9-104B).

To produce a good finish by this method, the work should be revolved slowly. The tool should be fed into the work slowly while cutting oil is applied. To eliminate chatter during the cutting operation, the cutting tool should be moved slightly back and forth (longitudinally).

HYDRAULIC TRACER ATTACHMENT

When many duplicate parts, having several radii or contours which may be difficult to produce, are required, they may be easily made on a hydraulic tracer lathe or on a lathe equipped with a hydraulic tracer attachment (Fig. 9-105).

Hydraulic tracer lathes incorporate a means of moving the cross-slide by controlled oil pressure supplied by a hydraulic pump. A flat template of the desired contour of the finished piece, or a circular template identical to the finished piece, is mounted in an attachment on the lathe. Automatic control of the tool slide, and duplication of the part, is achieved by a stylus which bears against the template surface. As the carriage is fed along automatically, the stylus follows the contour of the template. The stylus arm actuates a control valve regulating the flow of oil into a cylinder incorporated in the tool slide base. A piston connected to the tool slide is moved in or out by the flow of oil to the cylinder. This movement causes the tool slide (and toolbit) to move in or out as the carriage moves along, duplicating the profile of the template on the workpiece.

ADVANTAGES OF A TRACER ATTACHMENT

a) Intricate forms, difficult to produce by other means, can be readily produced.

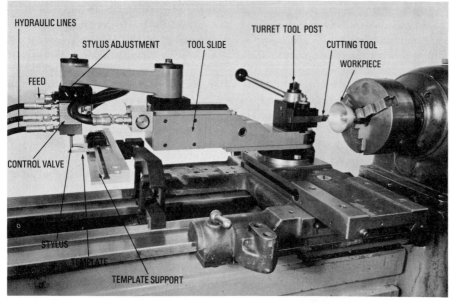

Courtesy Retor Developments Ltd.

Fig. 9-105 A hydraulic tracer attachment being used to machine an intricate form

b) Various forms, tapers, and shoulders can be produced in one cut.
c) Duplicate parts can be produced rapidly and accurately.
d) Accuracy and finish of the part does not depend on the skill of the operator.

Hints on the Use of a Tracer Attachment

1. The toolbit point and stylus should have the same form and radius.
2. The radius on the toolbit should be smaller than the smallest radius on the template.
3. The stylus must be set to the point on the template giving the smallest diameter of the work.
4. The centre line of the template must be parallel to the ways of the lathe.
5. The form of the template must be smooth.
6. No angle larger than 30°, or the equivalent radius, should be incorporated in the form of the template.
7. Duplicate parts produced between centres must be the same length and have the centre holes drilled to the same depth.
8. Duplicate parts held in a chuck should project the same distance from the chuck jaws.
9. The included angle of the tool point should be less than the smallest angle on the template.

TOOL FINISHES

In turning and boring operations, single-point cutting tools are used to produce cylindrical, tapered, or contoured surfaces. The accuracy and efficiency of these operations, and the quality of finish obtained, depend on a number of factors.

1. The *cutting tool* must:
   a) have the proper alloying elements to maintain a sharp cutting edge
   b) be sufficiently wear-resistant to prevent wearing of the cutting point
   c) have sufficient toughness to prevent chipping during the cutting operation
   d) be hard enough to prevent build-up at the cutting edge

The action of the cutting tool depends upon:
   a) the design of the cutting tool
   b) the cutting angles
   c) the speeds and feeds used
   d) the machinability of the metal
   e) the application of coolant
2. *The condition of the machine.* Machines with worn or loose bearings cannot be expected to produce the best results.
3. *The skill of the operator.* Knowledge of the machine and cutting principles is necessary to obtain good results.

The surface finish produced by any cutting tool may be analyzed and designated as to quality by comparing it to a known standard. A machine to measure the surface finish is the *profilometer* or *surface analyzer*. Surface finishes are indicated by ASA or CSA finish symbols. (See Chapter 3.)

LATHE QUESTIONS

1. List the operations which can be performed on a lathe.
2. How is the size of a lathe designated?

PARTS OF THE ENGINE LATHE

3. Name the four *main* units of a lathe.
4. State the purpose of the following:
   a) headstock spindle
   b) lead screw and feed rod
   c) quick-change gearbox
   d) split-nut lever
   e) feed change lever
   f) cross-slide
   g) compound rest

SETTING SPEEDS AND FEEDS

5. List three types of lathe drives.
6. Explain how speeds on a geared-head lathe are changed.
7. List the steps to set a feed of .010 in. (0.25 mm).
8. What is the purpose of:
   a) a shear pin?
   b) a slip clutch?

LATHE ACCESSORIES

9. Name the various types of lathe centres and state their purpose.
10. Describe the following and state their purpose.
    a) 3-jaw universal chuck
    b) 4-jaw independent chuck
    c) collet chuck
    d) magnetic chuck
    e) steady rest

CUTTING SPEEDS AND FEEDS

11. Define cutting speed and state how it is expressed.
12. Why is proper cutting speed important?
13. At what r/min should the lathe revolve to rough turn a piece of cast iron 101 mm in diameter when using a high speed steel toolbit?
14. Calculate the r/min to turn a piece of 3-3/4 in. diameter machine steel using a high speed steel toolbit.
15. Define lathe feed.
16. Define depth of cut.

LATHE TOOLHOLDERS

17. Describe three types of toolholders and state their purpose.
18. How does a carbide toolholder differ from a standard toolholder?

CUTTING TOOL MATERIALS

19. What properties should a cutting tool possess?
20. What elements are found in high-speed steel toolbits?
21. State the precaution which should be taken when grinding stellite toolbits.

CUTTING TOOL NOMENCLATURE

22. Make a neat, labelled sketch of a cutting tool.

LATHE TOOLBIT ANGLES AND CLEARANCES

23. State the purpose of the following:
    a) side cutting edge angle
    b) side relief angle
    c) end relief angle
    d) side rake angle
    e) back rake
24. Make neat sketches to illustrate the angles in question 23.

GRINDING LATHE CUTTING TOOLS

25. State the procedure for grinding a general purpose toolbit.

ALIGNMENT OF LATHE CENTRES

26. Name three methods of aligning centres.
27. List the steps required to align lathe centres to within 0.02 mm (or .001 in.) accuracy.

MOUNTING WORK BETWEEN CENTRES

28. Explain the procedure for setting up a cutting tool for turning.
29. List the main steps for mounting work between centres.

FACING BETWEEN CENTRES

30. State three purposes of facing a workpiece.
31. Explain how a facing toolbit is set up.

GRADUATED MICROMETER COLLARS

32. Name two classes of machines equipped with graduated collars and state the differences between them.
33. What precautions should be taken when setting a depth of cut?
34. How can the graduated collar be used to accurately face to length?
35. What is the value of one graduation on a metric graduated micrometer collar?
36. What size will a 75 mm diameter workpiece be after a 6.25 mm deep cut is taken from the work?

PARALLEL TURNING

37. What precaution must be taken before parallel turning?

38. Explain the procedure for setting an accurate depth of cut.
39. State the purpose of rough and finish turning.
40. How many cuts should be taken to turn a diameter to size?
41. What is the purpose of a light trial cut at the right-hand end of the work?

TURNING TO A SHOULDER

42. List the procedure for turning a square shoulder.

FILING AND POLISHING

43. List the precautions which should be taken when filing and polishing.

KNURLING

44. Define the process of knurling.
45. Explain how the knurling tool should be set up.
46. Why is it important not to disengage the feed during the knurling operation?

TAPERS

47. Define a taper.
48. Explain the difference between self-holding and steep tapers.
49. State the taper per foot for the following tapers:
    a) Morse
    b) Brown and Sharpe
    c) Jarno
    d) Standard taper pin
50. Describe the type D-1 and type L spindle nose and state where each is used.

TAPER CALCULATIONS

51. Explain what is meant by a metric taper of 1:50.
52. Calculate the large diameter of a 1:50 taper having a small diameter of 15 mm and a length of 75 mm.
53. Calculate the tailstock offset required to turn a 1:40 taper × 100 mm long on a workpiece 450 mm long. The small diameter is 25 mm.

54. Calculate the amount of setover for a 480 mm long guide bar to turn a 1:40 taper × 320 mm long on a workpiece. The small diameter of the taper is 37.5 mm.
55. Calculate the taper per foot and tailstock offset for a piece of work having:
    a) large diameter .938 in.
    b) small diameter .778 in.
    c) length of taper 3-3/16 in.
    d) length of work 8-1/2 in.

TAPER TURNING

56. Name three methods of offsetting the tailstock for taper turning.
57. List the advantages of a taper attachment.
58. List the main steps required to cut an external taper using the taper attachment.
59. Describe a taper micrometer and state its advantages.
60. Explain in point form how to fit an external taper.

MOUNTING AND REMOVING CHUCKS

61. Explain the procedure for mounting and removing a cam lock lathe chuck.
62. Why is it necessary that both the lathe spindle nose and the mating parts of a chuck be thoroughly cleaned before mounting?
63. Explain how to set up and true a piece of work in a 4-jaw chuck to within 0.02 mm (or .001 in.) accuracy.
64. How is a piece of work faced, in a chuck, to an accurate length?
65. What is the purpose of spotting; what methods may be used to perform this operation?

BORING

66. Define the boring operation.
67. Why should a hole be bored before reaming?

68. Explain the procedure for boring a 20 mm (or 3/4 in.) diameter hole.

REAMING

69. What is the purpose of reaming in a lathe?
70. What precautions should be taken when reaming in a lathe?
71. Calculate the r/min required to drill, bore, and ream a 13 mm (or 1/2 in.) hole in a 56 mm (or 2-1/4 in.) diameter piece of cast iron.

TAPPING

72. How is a tap started and guided so the thread will be true to the bored hole?

CUTTING OFF WORK IN A CHUCK

73. When cutting off work held in a chuck, how is chatter and jamming (galling) prevented?

FOLLOWER AND STEADY RESTS

74. State the purpose of a follower rest.
75. Explain how to set up a steady rest for turning a long shaft held between centres.
76. Describe a cathead and state when it is used.
77. Explain how a damaged centre hole may be trued.

THREADS

78. Define a thread.
79. List four general applications of threads.
80. Why was the ISO metric system of threads adopted?
81. Describe a thread designated as M 56 × 5.5.
82. Name five thread forms used in North America and state the proportions of each.
83. What are the principal differences between the American and Unified threads?

THREAD TERMINOLOGY

84. Define: pitch diameter, pitch, lead, root, crest.
85. How is the pitch designated for:
    a) Metric threads?
    b) UNC threads?
86. Why is the diameter of the blank for a rolled thread equal to the pitch diameter?
87. How may a right-hand thread be distinguished from a left-hand thread?

THREAD FITS AND CLASSIFICATIONS

88. Define: fit, allowance, tolerance, limits.
89. How are external UNC threads classified?
90. Name and describe three classifications of UNC fits.
91. How are thread fits designated for the ISO threads?

THREAD CALCULATIONS

92. For an M 20 × 2.5 thread, calculate:
    a) Pitch
    b) Depth
    c) Minor diameter
    d) Width of crest
    e) Width of root
93. Sketch a UNC thread and show the dimensions of the parts.
94. How does a Brown and Sharpe Worm thread differ from an Acme thread?
95. For a 1 in. — 8 NC thread, calculate:
    a) minor diameter
    b) width of toolbit point
    c) amount of compound rest feed
96. What is the purpose of the quick-change gearbox?
97. Describe a thread chasing dial and state its purpose.
98. The lead screw on an inch-designed lathe has 6 threads per inch; at what point or points on the thread chasing dial may the split-nut lever be engaged to cut the following threads: 8, 9, 11-1/2, 12?

THREAD CUTTING

99. List the main steps required to set up the lathe for cutting a 60° thread.
100. List the main steps required to cut a 60° thread.
101. It has been necessary to remove a partially threaded piece of work from the lathe and to finish it at a later time. Describe how to reset the threading tool to "pick up" the thread.

METRIC THREADS

102. a) What two change gears are required to cut a metric thread on a standard lathe?
     b) Where are these gears mounted?
103. Describe how a lathe (having a quick-change gearbox) is set up to cut a 2.5 mm thread.
104. What precaution should be taken when cutting a metric thread?

THREAD MEASUREMENT

105. Why is thread measurement and inspection an important aspect of the machine trade?
106. What is the difference between a screw thread micrometer and a thread comparator micrometer?
107. Make a sketch to illustrate how a thread is measured using the three-wire method.
108. Calculate the best wire size and the measurement over the wires for the following threads:
     a) 1/4 in. – 20 NC
     b) 5/8 in. – 11 NC
     c) 1-1/4 in. – 7 NC

MULTIPLE THREADS

109. What is the purpose of a multiple thread?
110. If the pitch of a multiple thread is 1/8 in., what will be the lead for a double start thread? A triple start thread?
111. List three methods by which multiple threads may be cut.

112. The end gear train on a lathe has a 42-tooth gear on the headstock spindle and a 35-tooth gear on the leadscrew (quick change gearbox drive spindle). These gears are connected by an idler gear having 120 teeth.
     a) List the steps required to set up a lathe and cut a 1 in. – 9 NC, 3-start thread.
     b) Calculate the following for this thread:
        i) pitch
        ii) lead
        iii) depth
        iv) measurement over the wires (three-wire method)

SQUARE THREADS

113. Name two factors that affect the helix angle of a thread.
114. Calculate the leading and following angles of a square threading toolbit required to cut a 1-1/2 in. – 6 square thread.
115. List the main steps required to cut a square thread.

ACME THREAD

116. If the width of the root of an Acme thread is .3707P at minimum depth, why is the Acme threading tool ground to .3707P – .0052?
117. Describe how an Acme thread may be measured.

INTERNAL THREADS

118. List the steps required to cut a 1-1/4 in. – 7 UNC thread 2 in. deep in a block of steel 3 in. × 3 in. × 3 in. Show all necessary calculations.

MANDRELS

119. State the purpose of a mandrel.
120. Draw a 1 in. (25 mm■) standard mandrel and include all specifications.
121. Name and describe four types of mandrels and state their purpose.

122. List the precautions that must be taken when using a mandrel (include mounting and turning).

ECCENTRICS

123. Define an eccentric and state its purpose.
124. Explain the difference between the throw and total travel of an eccentric.
125. A crankshaft, 150 mm long having equal length journals, is required to produce a travel of 40 mm on a piston. The journal (finished shaft) size is 25 mm.
     a) Describe how to lay out this eccentric.
     b) What size material would be required if 3 mm is allowed for "cleaning up"? This can be calculated easily with the aid of a sketch.
126. What precautions must be taken when turning an eccentric having a large throw?

GRINDING ON A LATHE

127. List eight important points to be observed when grinding on a lathe.
128. Outline the procedure for grinding a lathe centre.
129. In which direction should the work turn when grinding an external surface and an internal surface on a lathe?

FORM TURNING

130. Name three methods by which form turning may be done on a lathe.
131. Briefly describe the procedure for turning a 12 mm radius on the end of a workpiece.
132. What is a template?
133. What types of templates may be used with a tracer lathe?
134. List three advantages of a tracer lathe or tracer attachment.
135. List six points to observe when using a tracer lathe.

10 SHAPERS AND SLOTTERS

Courtesy The Cincinnati Shaper Co.

Shapers and slotters (vertical shapers) are used primarily to produce flat surfaces by means of single or multiple cutting tools. These machines use a reciprocating motion and produce a straight line cut on the work during the forward stroke. On the backward stroke, the tool returns to the starting position and the table (and work) is advanced either by automatic or hand feed the desired amount for the next cut. Figure 10-1A illustrates the cutting action of the shaper.

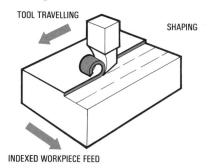

Fig. 10-1A   Cutting action of a shaper

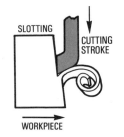

Fig. 10-1B   Cutting action of a slotter

The cutting action of the slotter (Fig. 10-1B) is similar to that of the shaper, except that the tool reciprocates vertically. The work may be fastened to a rotary table that can be fed in a circular, horizontal, and longitudinal direction for various types of operations.

SHAPERS

The most common type of shaper is the horizontal type, used primarily for producing flat, angular, and contour machined surfaces. These shapers are manufactured with either the crank type or the hydraulic driving mechanism. The size of a shaper is determined by the largest cube which can be machined on it. For example, a 30 cm shaper can machine a block 30 cm × 30 cm × 30 cm, and a 14 in. shaper can machine a block 14 in. × 14 in. × 14 in.

PRINCIPLE OF THE CRANK-TYPE SHAPER

There are several methods of driving the reciprocating shaper ram by mechanical means, the crank-type being the most commonly used. Fig. 10-3 shows the complete cycle of the crank-type mechanism, which is contained inside the column of the shaper (Fig. 10-2). The quick return of the ram on the back or noncutting stroke is obtained when the crank pin is travelling through 140° of the cycle. The forward or cutting stroke of the ram is made when the crank pin is in the upper portion of the vibrating (rocker) arm slot. In this position, the crank pin is farther from the fulcrum or pivot and exerts a powerful push on the lever arm and, therefore, on the ram. The crank pin passes through 220° of the cycle during the cutting stroke. As the crank pin passes centre and moves further down the vibrating arm slot, it begins the return movement of the arm and the ram. At this time, the crank pin is in the lower part of the slot and in the lower 140° arc of the circle. It is also much closer to the pivot pin. Therefore, the movement of the upper end of the vibrating arm to which the ram is attached is more rapid but less powerful than on the forward stroke, even though the large gear and its crank pin are moving at a steady rate throughout the cycle.

PRINCIPLE OF THE HYDRAULIC SHAPER

Hydraulic driven shapers are similar in nearly all respects to the crank type; only the drive principle is different (Fig. 10-5).

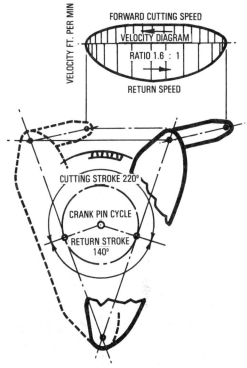

Fig. 10-3   The cycle of a crank-type shaper

Oil pressure is provided by a pump through the *reversing valve* to the right-hand end of the operating cylinder where it moves the piston which drives the ram forward for the cutting stroke. The return stroke is obtained by the reversing valve directing the flow of oil to the left-hand end of the operating cylinder. The length of the stroke can be controlled by setting the position of the reversing stops on the ram. The table feed is operated by a table feed cylinder and piston. The speed and feed changes are made by control valves which allow the setting of variable speeds and feeds while the machine is operating. The principle of a hydraulic shaper is dealt with in greater detail in Chapter 18.

The main advantages of a hydraulic shaper are:
a) It provides a uniform positive motion.
b) A wide range of speeds and feeds is available.

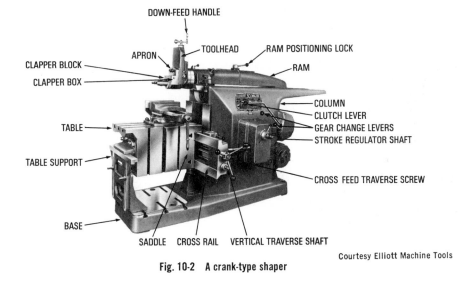

Courtesy Elliott Machine Tools

Fig. 10-2   A crank-type shaper

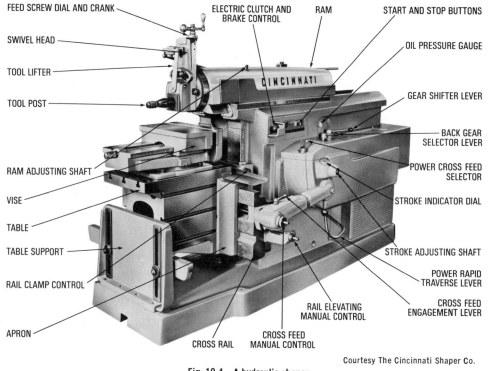

Fig. 10-4 A hydraulic shaper

Courtesy The Cincinnati Shaper Co.

c) Speeds and feeds are independent and constant during the cutting stroke.
d) The surface finish obtained is free from gear chatter marks.
e) The speeds and feeds can be readily adjusted without stopping the shaper.
f) Cutting speeds and feeds are shown on a dial; thus, calculation is eliminated.

SHAPER PARTS

Shaper parts are the same for all horizontal types. The *ram* is a semi-cylindrical form of heavy construction on which the toolhead is mounted. The *driving mechanism* which provides a reciprocating action to the ram may be of the crank or hydraulic type. Fastened to the *shaper toolhead* (Fig. 10-6) is the *apron* which consists of the *clapper box, clapper block, hinge pin,* and the *toolpost.* The hinged clapper block prevents the cutting tool from dragging on the return stroke.

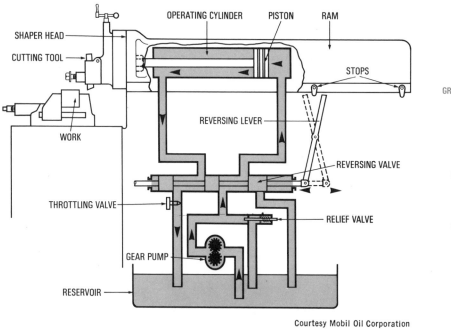

Courtesy Mobil Oil Corporation

Fig. 10-5 Hydraulic shaper principle

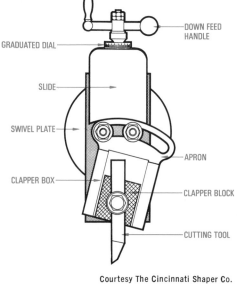

Courtesy The Cincinnati Shaper Co.

Fig. 10-6 Parts of a shaper toolhead

TABLE 10-1: SHAPER SPEEDS AND FEEDS

CUTTING TOOL	MACHINE STEEL				TOOL STEEL				CAST IRON				BRASS			
	Speed per min		Feed		Speed per min		Feed		Speed per min		Feed		Speed per min		Feed	
	m	ft.	mm	in.	m	ft.	mm	in.	m	ft.	mm	in.	m	ft.	mm	in.
H.S.S.	24	80	0.25	.010	15	50	0.38	.015	18	60	0.51	.020	48	160	0.25	.010
Carbide	46	150	0.25	.010	46	150	0.30	.012	30	100	0.30	.012	92	300	0.38	.015

SHAPER SPEEDS

To operate the shaper efficiently, it is necessary to calculate the speed at which the ram should operate. The speed depends on three factors: the type of material being cut, its length, and the type of cutting tool used. *Cutting speeds for materials are expressed in either metres per minute (m/min) or feet per minute (ft./min).* A list of recommended cutting speeds for various metals is shown in Table 10-1. Shaper speeds, however, are calculated in strokes per minute. To calculate the proper shaper speed, one should understand the theory of the cutting and return stroke.

CUTTING AND RETURN STROKE

Since the length of the cutting stroke is the same as that of the return stroke, the pin and crosshead fastened to the gear pass through 220° on the cutting stroke and only 140° on the return stroke; therefore, the ratio is 220:140 or about a 3:2 ratio (Fig. 10-3). That is, if 3 seconds are required for the cutting stroke, 2 seconds are needed for the return stroke. Thus the return stroke is called the *quick-return*. Since the sum of these figures is 5, the cutting stroke requires 3/5 of the time of a complete cycle, while the return stroke requires 2/5.

FORMULA FOR CALCULATING STROKES PER MINUTE

METRIC SPEED CALCULATIONS

When shaping a workpiece with metric dimensions, set the length of stroke to 3 cm longer than the workpiece, to allow for clearance at each end of the stroke. The number of strokes per minute is calculated as follows:

$$\text{Strokes per minute } (N) =$$
$$\frac{\text{Cutting speed in metres}}{\text{Length of strokes in metres}} \times \frac{3}{5}$$
$$N = \frac{CS \text{ (metres)}}{\text{Length of stroke (metres)}} \times 0.6$$

EXAMPLE: How many strokes per minute will be required to machine a piece of tool steel 33 cm long (*CS* 15)?
Length of stroke (*L*) = 33 + 3 cm

$$N = \frac{CS}{L} \times 0.6$$
$$= \frac{15}{0.36} \times 0.6$$
$$= 25 \text{ strokes per minute}$$

INCH SPEED CALCULATIONS

When the length of the stroke in inches and the number of strokes per minute are given, the product is equal to the total inches cut in one minute of the machine operating time. Since the recommended cutting speeds are stated in feet per minute and the length of the cutting stroke in inches, it is necessary to change the inches into feet by multiplying by 1/12. As the cutting stroke takes up 3/5 of the cycle, it is necessary to divide the above calculation by 3/5 (or multiply by 5/3) to arrive at the cutting strokes per minute. Instead of multiplying by 1/12 and then by 5/3 for every calculation, it is easier to use .14 or $\frac{1}{7}$ which is the result of 1/12 × 5/3.

Therefore, to calculate strokes per minute, divide the cutting speed of the metal by the length of the stroke × .14 or $\frac{1}{7}$

$$N = \frac{CS}{L \times .14}$$
OR
$$N = \frac{CS}{L \times \frac{1}{7}}$$
OR
$$N = \frac{CS \times 7}{L}$$

N = Number of strokes per minute
CS = Cutting speed of the material
     in feet per minute
L = Length of stroke in inches
NOTE: The length of the stroke is always the length of the work plus 1 in. for tool clearance.

EXAMPLE: Find the number of strokes per minute for a shaper to machine a piece of 11 in. long cast iron at 60 feet per minute.

$$N = \frac{CS \times 7}{L}$$

$$N = \frac{60 \times 7}{12}$$

$$= 35 \text{ strokes per minute}$$

SHAPER FEEDS

Shaper feed is defined as the distance the work is moved transversely toward the cutting tool for each forward stroke of the ram. Feed rate is an important factor in determining the time required for the machining operation and the surface finish produced. In order for metals to be machined efficiently in a shaper, the following factors must be considered when speeds and feeds are selected.

a) the type of material being cut
b) the condition of the shaper
c) the type of cut (roughing or finishing)
d) the type of cutting tool used
e) the surface finish required

The machinist must exercise a certain amount of judgment to arrive at the best feed rate.

The feed must be set so that the table and the workpiece are moved on the return stroke of the ram. If the feed is set to operate on the cutting (forward) stroke, the cutting tool will be damaged and the work surface will be rough and irregular.

As in most machining operations, it is important that metal be removed as quickly as possible during the roughing cut. Coarse feeds and light cuts are not as

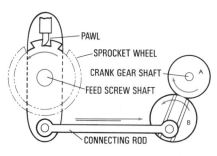

Fig. 10-7 Shaper table feed mechanism

efficient as fine feeds and deep cuts because a thick chip will not curl as readily and requires more power to drive the tool. Coarse feeds cause the metal to tear more readily, resulting in a rougher surface. It is good practice to set the feed to produce the desired surface finish and then gradually increase the depth of cut to the capacity of the machine. For finish cuts, a finer feed with a light cut is recommended. The purpose of roughing cuts is to remove excess material as quickly as possible; finishing cuts are used to produce the desired accuracy and the proper surface finish.

In crank type shapers, the amount and direction of feed are obtained by the principle illustrated in Fig. 10-7. Gear A is fastened to the crank-gear shaft. When the crank gear turns to produce the return stroke of the ram, gear A turns 140°. This turns gear B 140° and moves the connecting rod in the direction of the arrows. This in turn causes the pawl to turn the sprocket wheel, and since the sprocket wheel is keyed to the table feed screw shaft, this shaft also turns, moving the table on the return stroke. To vary the rate of feed, set the connecting rod closer to the centre of the T-slot on the feed driving mechanism for finer feeds and away from the centre for coarser feeds (Fig. 10-7). To disengage the feed, raise the pawl knob and turn it 90° to prevent the pawl from engaging the teeth in the sprocket wheel.

On hydraulic shapers, the feed direction and the amount of feed are regulated by control and reversing valves. The feed

is driven by a gear and a rack which are controlled by a hydraulic system. Feeds can be increased or decreased while the machine is running by adjustment of the valves.

VERTICAL FEED

Vertical feed on a shaper may be used for machining vertical or angular surfaces. Vertical feed (Fig. 10-8) may be operated manually by the downfeed screw on the toolhead or automatically by the power downfeed. The power feed is attached to the downfeed screw by a bevel gear drive, and on the return stroke of the ram, the feed mechanism indexes the amount of vertical feed per cut. Feeds used for flat or angular surfaces should always be operated on the return stroke. When a vertical surface is to be machined, the top of the clapper box should be swivelled away from the surface to be machined (Fig. 10-8). This will prevent the cutting tool from binding against the work on the return stroke.

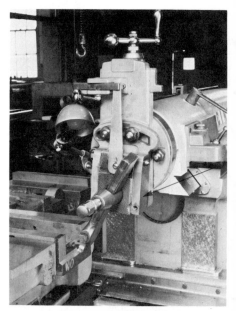

Courtesy The Cincinnati Shaper Co.

Fig. 10-8 Shaper vertical feed mechanism. Note: Clapper box swung for machining a vertical surface

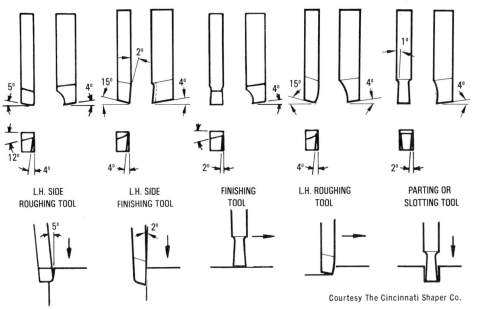

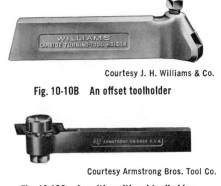

Courtesy J. H. Williams & Co.

Fig. 10-10B   An offset toolholder

Courtesy Armstrong Bros. Tool Co.

Fig. 10-10C   A multi-positional toolholder

Courtesy The Cincinnati Shaper Co.

Fig. 10-9   Recommended angles and tools for cutting steel

NOTE: The hole that accommodates the cutting tool in a shaper toolholder is parallel to the base, not inclined as in a lathe toolholder.

CARBIDE TOOLS

Carbide tools can be used efficiently only if the shaper can exceed a cutting speed of 30 m/min (or 100 ft./min). Greater efficiency may be obtained with carbide cutting tools on a hydraulic shaper because of the constant speed and feed rate which can be maintained. When using carbide cutting tools, the shaper should be equipped with a tool lifter (Fig. 10-14) to lift the tool clear of the work on the return stroke. This is necessary to prevent excessive tool wear and chipping of the cutting edge. Without these factors, it is not economical to use carbides instead of high-speed steel cutting tools.

Most materials are machined at cutting speeds two or three times faster with carbides, and the feeds are generally about the same as used with high-speed steel cutting tools. When machining with carbide cutting tools, it is more efficient to increase the cutting speed than the feed. A deep cut with a light feed is better than a light cut and a heavy feed because the chip pressure is distributed over a longer cutting edge. As the depth of cut is increased, the speed is decreased. Power consumed in shaping is directly proportional to the cutting speed.

CUTTING TOOLS

Shaping operations vary from producing a flat surface to producing contours, grooves, and various intricate shapes. To produce these surfaces, a wide variety of cutting tools ground at different shapes and angles is required. The shape of the cutting tool varies with the work, type of cut, and condition of the machine. Fig. 10-9 illustrates cutting tools with the recommended clearance angles for cutting steel.

The shaper toolbits must have cutting clearances as do lathe toolbits, even though the shaper tool is held in a vertical position and the lathe toolbit is held horizontally. Since the shaper tool does not feed sideways into the workpiece on the cutting stroke, about 2 to 4° *side clearance* is sufficient. The *front clearance* is usually about 4°. Too much front clearance will cause the toolbit to dull rapidly because of insufficient support behind the cutting edge. When insufficient front clearance is ground on the toolbit, the toolbit rubs and causes poor cutting action, leaving a rough surface finish.

Side clearance and side rake influence the true lip angle. The side rake for steel is generally from 10 to 20°; the side clearance of 2 to 8° depends upon the tool used and the hardness of the metal being machined. Cutting tools can be made from the solid shank type or from toolbits. They are ground for left-hand or right-hand cutting, depending upon the direction of cut. The left-hand cutting tool is perhaps the most commonly used because the operator can readily see the cutting action. The square-nose tool may be used for finishing cuts on cast iron and steel. Generally 0.25 mm to 0.40 mm for steel and 0.12 mm to 0.25 mm for cast iron should be left for finishing with this type of tool.

Toolholders used for shaping may be straight, offset, or multi-positional (Fig. 10-10A, B, C).

Courtesy J. H. Williams & Co.

Fig. 10-10A   A straight toolholder

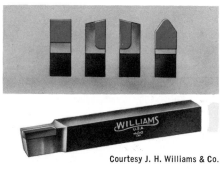

Courtesy J. H. Williams & Co.

Fig. 10-11   Brazed carbide shaper tools

Carbide cutting tools can be supplied in two common designs. *Brazed-on tips* (Fig. 10-11) are generally used for fine cuts and light duty work. *Replaceable inserts* (Fig. 10-12) are used for deep cuts, interrupted cuts, and large-area cuts. The latter is preferred to the brazed tool because it can be held more firmly and is easily replaced.

Courtesy Armstrong Bros. Tool Co.

Fig. 10-12   Replaceable carbide inserts and toolholder

CARBIDE TOOL NOMENCLATURE

A – side rake angle
B – side clearance angle
C – front clearance
D – back rake angle
E – side cutting edge angle
F – nose radius
G – land width
H – point on the cutting edge

Shaper and planer carbide tools have specified angles and design (Fig. 10-13) to eliminate tool damage and maintain tool life and surface finish. *Side clearance angle*

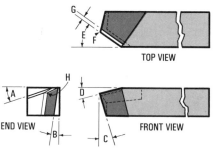

Fig. 10-13   Shaper carbide tool nomenclature

B is generally held to a minimum to provide the maximum support for the cutting edge without rubbing. Also, the *front clearance C* is approximately 4°, which provides a strong support to the cutting edge. The *back rake angle D*, used on most roughing tools for machining cast iron and steels, may vary between zero and 20° negative. This allows the cutting to start above the edge *H*, which is the weakest part of the tool, and protects the cutting edge against shock of starting and of intermittent cuts. On finishing tools, a 10 to 15° positive angle is often used so that tool chatter is avoided during light finishing cuts. A large cutting angle of 30 to 40°

should be used with as large a radius at *F* as possible, particularly on roughing tools. Machining with carbides can be economical if proper machining and tool practices are followed.

To Maintain Proper Tool Finishes Free from Chatter Marks

1. Check the cutting tool for proper clearance angles.
2. Inspect the cutting edge for dullness, radii, and fractured edge.
3. See that the work is fastened securely.
4. Reduce the speed and increase the feed.
5. Adjust the gibs on the table, ram, toolhead, and clapper block tapered pin to eliminate any play.
6. Avoid too much toolhead overhang and have the cutting tool as close to the toolpost screw as possible.

TOOL LIFTERS

The shaper feed operates on the return stroke, frequently causing tool wear, chipping, and riding marks on the machined surface. To prevent these conditions, a *tool lifter* (Fig. 10-14) is attached to the clapper block to raise the cutting edge of

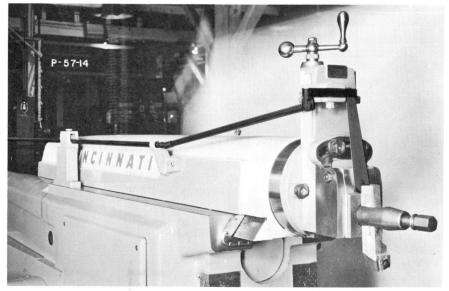

Courtesy The Cincinnati Shaper Co.

Fig. 10-14   A tool lifter raises the cutting tool on the return stroke

the tool from the work surface on the return stroke. Some advantages of tool lifters are:

a) They prevent cemented-carbide tools from chipping on the return stroke.

b) They clear grooving tools from a groove to prevent drag, wear, and chipping of the cutting edge.

c) They allow faster cutting speeds when shaping keyways, grooves, contours, gear teeth, and flat surfaces.

To Set the Length of the Shaper Stroke

1. Measure the length of the piece to be machined and add 25 mm to the length to allow clearance for the cutting tool.
2. Start the shaper and stop it when the ram is at the back end of the stroke.
3. Loosen the stroke regulator lock nut.
4. Adjust to the length required by turning the stroke regulator screw.
5. Tighten the stroke regulator lock nut.

NOTE: In Fig. 10-15 the *crosshead* that fits into the *vibrating arm* is the part moved by the stroke regulator screw away from the centre to lengthen the stroke and toward the centre to shorten it.

To Set the Position of the Shaper Stroke

To determine the position of the shaper stroke, the length of stroke is first set. The ram must then be adjusted so that its travel will machine the full length of the piece. For example, the length of stroke should be set to 32 cm long to allow 1 cm for clearance at each end for a workpiece 30 cm long. If a workpiece 8-1/2 in. long is to be machined, the stroke is set at 9-1/2 in., allowing 1/2 in. for clearance at each end.

1. Loosen the ram lock or clamp, with the ram at the back end of the stroke.
2. Adjust the ram by turning the ram adjusting screw.
3. Tighten the ram clamp to lock the ram in a fixed position.
4. Start the shaper and check the position of the ram to see if the cutting tool clears each end of the work.

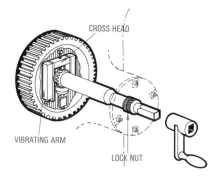

Fig. 10-15 The shaper stroke adjusting mechanism

ALIGNING THE SHAPER VISE

Most work machined in a shaper is held in a vise bolted to a table. The body of the vise can be swivelled on a base plate to any angular setting required. This method is especially useful for cutting angular surfaces. When work must be shaped parallel or at right angles to the direction of the cut, the vise jaw must be aligned. To accurately align the vise, a dial indicator is attached to the toolhead of the shaper and is passed over the entire length of the solid jaw. With this method, a vise may be aligned to within 0.02 mm accuracy.

Courtesy Kostel Enterprises Ltd.

Fig. 10-16 Aligning the shaper vise at 90° to the ram travel

To Align the Shaper Vise at 90° to the Ram Travel

1. Adjust the vise until the lines on the vise base and swivel plate are in line.
2. Tighten the clamping nuts lightly.

3. Set the dial indicator in the toolholder, and position it against the solid vise jaw or against a parallel held in the vise, Fig. 10-16.
4. Move the shaper ram by hand until the dial indicator registers approximately one-half revolution against the solid jaw of the vise.
5. Set the indicator bezel to zero.
6. Move the indicator along the length of the solid jaw or parallel by turning the crossfeed screw, and note the indicator reading.
7. Adjust the vise to one-half the amount registered on the indicator.
   NOTE: *Always* adjust the vise *away* from the indicator.
8. Tighten the clamping nuts, recheck the accuracy of the vise, and adjust if necessary.

To Align the Shaper Vise Parallel to the Ram Travel

1. Adjust the vise parallel to the ram travel by the lines on the vise base and swivel plate.
2. Tighten the clamping nuts lightly.
3. Adjust the length of the shaper stroke so that it is slightly shorter than the length of the shaper vise.
4. Set the dial indicator in the toolholder and position it on the solid jaw or on a parallel held in the vise.
5. Move the shaper table until the dial indicator registers approximately one-half revolution against the solid jaw or the parallel.
6. Set the indicator bezel to zero.
7. By hand, move the shaper ram along the length of the parallel or solid jaw and note the indicator reading.
   CAUTION: The indicator should not travel beyond the vise jaw or parallel.
8. Adjust the vise to one-half the amount registered on the indicator.
   NOTE: Always adjust the vise *away* from the indicator.
9. Tighten the clamping nuts, recheck the accuracy of the vise, and adjust if necessary.

To Test the Work Seat for Parallelism

1. Set up the indicator as shown in Fig. 10-17.
2. Place a set of parallels on the bottom of the vise.
3. Adjust the toolhead until the dial indicator registers approximately one-half revolution on one parallel.
4. Move the ram forward by hand for the length of the parallel and note the indicator reading.
5. With the crossfeed screw handle, move the vise to obtain a reading across the second parallel.

Fig. 10-17   Testing a work seat for parallelism

6. To correct any errors in alignment, remove the vise from the table, clean it, and remove burrs from all clamping surfaces on the vise and table.
7. Remount the vise on the table and test for accuracy.
   NOTE: If the shaper is equipped with a swivel or universal table, the table surface should be checked for alignment before the vise is removed.

SHAPER OPERATIONS

To Shape a Flat Surface

In Fig. 10-18, the toolhead is set up ready to shape a flat surface.
1. Clean the vise and remove all burrs from the workpiece.
2. Place parallels under the work if necessary, so that the machined surface will be approximately 5 mm above the vise jaws.

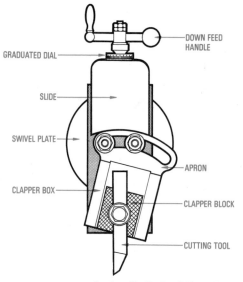

DOWN FEED HANDLE
GRADUATED DIAL
SLIDE
SWIVEL PLATE
APRON
CLAPPER BOX
CLAPPER BLOCK
CUTTING TOOL

Courtesy The Cincinnati Shaper Co.

Fig. 10-18   The correct method of clamping a tool

3. Mount the work in the centre of the vise.
4. At each end of the work, place a short paper feeler C between the work and parallels (Fig. 10-19).

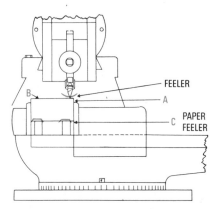

FEELER
A
C   PAPER FEELER
B

Fig. 10-19   The setup for machining a flat surface

5. Tighten the vise securely and tap the work lightly with a lead hammer until the paper feelers are tight.
6. Swing the toolhead apron to the right (Fig. 10-18) to allow the cutting edge to swing free of the work on the return stroke.

7. Set the length and position of the shaper stroke.
8. Set the shaper speed to the required number of strokes per minute.
9. Adjust the toolbit to the work surface by using a paper feeler.
10. Move the cutting tool clear of the work.
11. Set the depth of cut required by using the graduated downfeed screw collar.
12. Engage the automatic table feed, making sure that it feeds on the return stroke of the ram.

To Machine a Block Square and Parallel

To machine work in a shaper or milling machine vise so that it will be square and parallel, proceed as follows.
1. Set the work in the vise, preferably with one of the largest sides up, and machine side #1 (Fig. 10-20A).
   NOTE: Remove all burrs after machining each side.

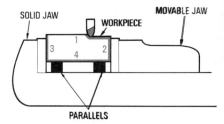

SOLID JAW   MOVABLE JAW
WORKPIECE
PARALLELS

Fig. 10-20A   Setup for shaping the first side. The stroke is set to cut the length rather than the width

2. Place side #1 against the solid jaw and a hold-down (round rod) between side #4 and the movable jaw so the work will be held flat against the solid

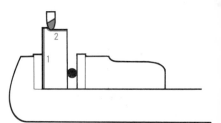

Fig. 10-20B   Setup for shaping the second side. Notice that the first side machined is placed against the solid jaw

jaw, and machine side #2 at right angles to #1 (Fig. 10-20B).

NOTE: The round bar should be in the centre of the amount of work being held in the vise.

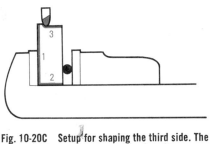

Fig. 10-20C   Setup for shaping the third side. The width should be correct in size after this operation

3. Place side #1 against the solid jaw and #2 at the bottom, with a round bar between side #4 and the movable jaw, and machine side #3 (Fig. 10-20C).

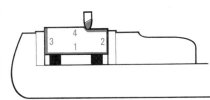

Fig. 10-20D   Setup for shaping the fourth side. The thickness should be correct after this operation

4. Place #4 side up as in Fig. 10-20D and machine it flat.

NOTE: With three finished surfaces, the round bar is not required in machining side #4.

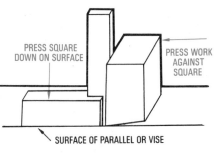

Fig. 10-20E   Method of setting up work for machining the ends

5. Use a square (Fig. 10-20E) to set up the work for machining the ends at right angles to the sides.

6. Check all surfaces with a square.

SHAPING WITH A HOLD-DOWN

Hold-downs are flat, wedge-shaped pieces of hardened steel generally used to hold thin pieces in a vise. They have a wide edge ground at an angle of approximately 8° and a narrow edge which may be ground straight or have a slight radius. The wide edge is placed against the vise jaw, and it forces or tips the narrow edge downward when the vise is tightened. Fig. 10-21 shows a hold-down being used to hold a thin workpiece for a machining operation.

Courtesy Atlas Press Co.

Fig. 10-21   Work set up in a vise using hold-downs

When the top surface of a workpiece must be machined parallel to the bottom surface, two hold-downs are used, one against each jaw and directly opposite each other. The action of the hold-down is to force the work against the parallels under the work, or to the base of the vise.

Procedure for Machining a Flat with One Hold-Down

1. Set the work in the vise on parallels with a machined side down.

NOTE: Use thin paper strips between each corner of the work and the parallels.

2. Place the machined edge against the solid jaw.

3. Hold the wide edge of the hold-down against the movable jaw with the thin edge against the edge of the work surface.

NOTE: The hold-down is generally placed at about the centre of the workpiece. The angle ground on the wide edge of the hold-down will force the work onto the parallel when the vise is tightened.

4. Tap the work *lightly* and retighten the work in the vise.

5. If the paper strips are not tight, remove the work and check all surfaces for burrs or cuttings.

6. Replace the work in the vise and again check to see that the work is seated firmly on the parallels.

NOTE: When thin workpieces are to be machined, it may be necessary to use two hold-downs, one against each vise jaw.

To Shape a Vertical Surface

When it is necessary to shape the ends of a long workpiece square with the sides, the work should be set up as in Fig. 10-22.

1. Align the vise at right angles to the ram.

2. Place a square on the bottom of the vise and align the toolhead (vertically) with the blade.

3. Place the work in the vise with the edge to be machined extending approximately 15 mm beyond the vise jaws.

4. Swing the top of the apron away from the surface being machined (Fig. 10-22). This will permit the cutting

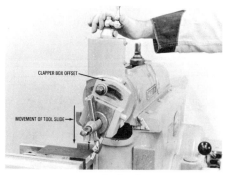

Fig. 10-22   The clapper box must be swivelled for making vertical cuts
Courtesy Kostel Enterprises Ltd.

tool to swing away from the work so that it will not bind on the return stroke.

5. Offset the toolholder enough to permit the cutting tool to machine the entire edge in one pass.

6. Set the length and position of the stroke.

7. Check to see that the toolhead clears the frame or work at the end of the vertical travel.

8. Set the depth of cut, using the crossfeed traverse crank.

9. Start the machine and feed the cutting tool down, on the return stroke, using the downfeed handle.

Courtesy Kostel Enterprises Ltd.

Fig. 10-23   Work set on an angle with the layout line parallel to the top of the vise

Fig. 10-24   The vise swivelled to cut an angle

MACHINING ANGULAR SURFACES

Most angular surfaces can be machined by setting the work on an angle in the vise (Fig. 10-23), swivelling the universal vise (Fig. 10-24), or by setting the toolhead to an angle and feeding the toolbit in the plane of the toolhead (Fig. 10-25).

To Swivel the Toolhead for Machining Angular Surfaces

To machine an angular surface, the toolhead must be swivelled from the vertical position to allow the downfeed screw to move the cutting tool on an angular plane (Fig. 10-25). Whenever the toolhead is swivelled, it is important to extend it to the full depth of cut so that the toolhead clears the shaper column on the return stroke. To produce an angle of 60° to the base, the toolhead must be adjusted to 30° from the vertical position. The clapper box should also be swivelled to the right (Fig. 10-25), to allow the tool to swing clear of the work on the return stroke of the ram. This prevents the tool from dragging, reduces damage to the cutting edge, and produces a better surface finish.

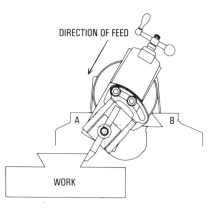

Fig. 10-25   Setting the toolhead to machine an angular surface

DOVETAILS

Dovetails may be produced by angular shaping, and are used to permit reciprocating motion between two elements of a machine. They are made up of combined external and internal dovetails (Fig. 10-26A and B). Dovetails are generally machined to a 30° or 35° angle from the vertical position. A *gib*, (Fig. 10-27) is used between the two dovetails to compensate for wear or side play and to permit a sliding fit between two mating surfaces.

Fig. 10-26A   An internal dovetail

Fig. 10-26B   An external dovetail

A gib is a narrow piece of metal machined to fit on one side of the internal dovetail. Gibs may be straight and can be adjusted by several set screws; or they may be tapered and adjusted from one end with an adjusting screw. The accuracy of a dovetail depends upon the angle to which it is machined, the tool finish, accurate calculations, and the measurement of the finished dovetail.

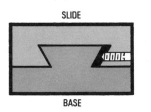

Fig. 10-27 An assembled dovetail showing a gib

To Shape a Dovetail

1. Accurately lay out the dovetail and lightly centre punch the layout lines.
2. Align the vise with a dial indicator.
3. Tighten the work in the centre of the vise.
4. Rough out the dovetails as in Fig. 10-28A and B.

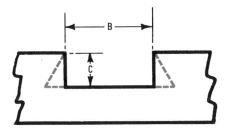

Fig. 10-28A Roughing out an internal dovetail

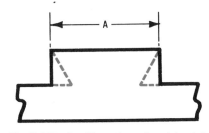

Fig. 10-28B Roughing out an external dovetail

5. Loosen the lock nuts and swivel the toolhead to the right, to the angle of the dovetail; or as in Fig. 10-25, to 30°.
6. With the use of a left-hand cutting tool, machine the angle, Fig. 10-29A and B.

Courtesy The Cincinnati Shaper Co.

Fig. 10-29A Shaping an internal dovetail

7. Set the toolhead to the left, and with a right-hand cutting tool machine the other angular surface.
   NOTE: The opposite angular surface may also be cut by swivelling the vise *exactly* 180° and leaving the toolhead set at the same angle.
8. Approximately 0.25 mm is left on the dovetail sides for fitting by means of scraping or grinding. If gibs are used between mating parts, the allowances are usually left on the internal dovetail.

Courtesy The Cincinnati Shaper Co.

Fig. 10-29B Shaping an external dovetail

9. Calculate the measurements between the rods, Fig. 10-30, and measure the dovetail for accuracy.

MEASURING A DOVETAIL

To measure a dovetail, the dimensions required are: the overall width A, the angle G, and the depth C, Fig. 10-30. With these dimensions, all other calculations can be obtained, with the exception of the sizes of the rods which should be used when measuring dovetails.

The most common method of measuring dovetails is by placing two cylindrical

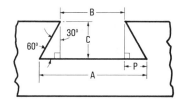

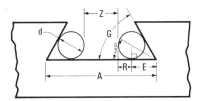

Fig. 10-30A Measuring an internal dovetail

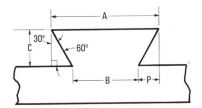

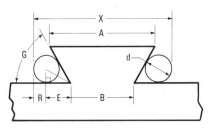

Fig. 10-30B Measuring an external dovetail

rods of the same diameter against the dovetail sides and measuring the distance over the rods. The dimensions between X and Z, Fig. 10-30, can be measured with calipers, verniers, micrometers or gauge blocks, depending on the accuracy required. In the case of an external dovetail, the measurement is taken over the rods, Fig. 10-30B, whereas for internal dovetails, the measurement is taken between the rods, Fig. 10-30A.

For external dovetails, Fig. 10-30B:

$$X = B + 2(E + R)$$
$$E = R \cot 1/2G$$
$$\therefore X = B + (2R \cot 1/2G + 2R)$$
$$= B + (d \cot 1/2G + d)$$
$$= B + d (\cot 1/2G + 1)$$

For internal dovetails, Fig. 10-30A:

$$Z = A - 2(E + R)$$
$$= A - d (\cot 1/2G + 1)$$

EXAMPLE 1 (inch):
The dimensions for the dovetails shown in Fig. 10-30A and B are:

$$B = 3.134$$
$$G = 60°$$
$$C = .750$$
$$d = .500$$

Calculate the distance X (distance over the rods) in Fig. 10-30B.

$$X = B + 2(E + R)$$
$$= B + d(\cot 1/2G + 1)$$
$$= 3.134 + 1/2 (\cot 30° + 1)$$
$$= 3.134 + 1/2 (1.732 + 1)$$
$$= 3.134 + \frac{2.732}{2}$$
$$= 3.134 + 1.366$$
$$= 4.500$$

By using the value for $2(E + R)$ in Table 10-2, the measurement over the rods may be easily calculated as follows:

$$X = B + 2(E + R)$$
$$= 3.134 + 1.366$$
$$= 4.500$$

NOTE: If "A" dimension is given, it is

		Values for Various Angles			
TABLE 10-2: CONSTANTS FOR MEASURING DOVETAILS					
Rod Diameter		45°	50°	55°	60°
METRIC RODS					
6 mm	$2(E + R)$	20.48	18.87	17.53	16.39
10 mm	$2(E + R)$	34.14	31.44	29.21	27.32
14 mm	$2(E + R)$	47.80	44.02	40.89	38.25
18 mm	$2(E + R)$	61.46	56.60	52.58	49.18
	$2P$	2.000(c)	1.678(c)	1.400(c)	1.155(c)
INCH RODS					
.250	$2(E + R)$	.853	.786	.730	.683
.375	$2(E + R)$	1.280	1.179	1.095	1.024
.500	$2(E + R)$	1.707	1.572	1.460	1.366
.750	$2(E + R)$	2.562	2.358	2.190	2.049
	$2P$	2.000(c)	1.678(c)	1.400(c)	1.155(c)

first necessary to calculate dimension "B" as follows:

$$B = A - 2P$$
$$P = C \cot G$$

EXAMPLE:
If dimension $A = 4.000$, then

$$B = 4.000 - 2(C \cot G)$$
$$B = 4.000 - 2(.750 \times .57735)$$
$$= 4.000 - 2(.433)$$
$$= 4.000 - .866$$
$$= 3.134$$

EXAMPLE 2 (metric):
Using Table 10-2, calculate the distance Z (distance between the rods) in Fig. 10-30A if:

$$B = 76 \text{ mm}$$
$$C = 18 \text{ mm}$$
$$d = 14 \text{ mm}$$
$$G = 60°$$

NOTE: If "B" dimension is given, it is first necessary to calculate dimension "A" as follows:

$$A = B + 2P$$
$$= 76 + 1.155 \ (c)$$

$$= 76 + 1.155 \ (18)$$
$$= 76 + 20.79$$
$$= 96.79 \text{ mm}$$

$$Z = A - 2(E + R)$$
$$= 96.79 - 38.25$$
$$= 58.54 \text{ mm}$$

CUTTING KEYWAYS AND GROOVES

A *keyway* is a groove cut on the inside of a hole in a gear, pulley or wheel. This groove receives a square, round, or rectangular piece of steel called a key. A keyseat cut into a shaft can be fitted with a key to provide a positive drive for a gear, pulley or wheel.

When cutting keyways, the tool is usually fed by hand on the return stroke. For cutting internal keyways, it is good practice to have the extension bar, Fig. 10-31, as short as possible to provide rigidity for the cutting tool. Keyways may be machined with the tool cutting on the bottom surface as shown in Fig. 10-32. Some machinists think that cutting upwards instead

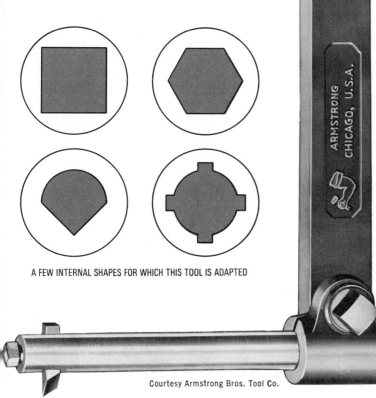

A FEW INTERNAL SHAPES FOR WHICH THIS TOOL IS ADAPTED

Courtesy Armstrong Bros. Tool Co.

Fig. 10-31 Extension bar for internal shaping

Courtesy The Cincinnati Shaper Co.

Fig. 10-32 Shaping an internal keyway in a gear

of downwards prevents tool chatter. It also prevents the cutting tool from raising on the forward stroke.

Shaping an Internal Keyway

1. Lay out the keyway at one end of the gear.
2. Align the vise with a dial indicator.
3. Set the apron and toolhead as in Fig. 10-32.
4. Mount the tool bar or shaper extension tool in the clapper block.
   NOTE: Use a strong, sturdy bar to avoid spring and chatter marks.
5. Set the length and position of the stroke. It is good practice to set the stroke a little longer (25 mm to 40 mm) on the return, to allow time to feed the depth of each cut.

Fig. 10-33 Aligning a keyway layout with a square

6. Set up the work in the centre of the vise and, with a square, align the centre line of the layout, Fig. 10-33.
7. Align the roughing tool, which is ground 0.8 mm less than the finished width, to the centre of the layout.
8. Take a trial cut until the toolbit *just* cuts on its full width and set the graduated dial on the downfeed screw at zero.
9. Apply cutting fluid and continue to feed the tool to the full depth, from 0.07 mm to 0.15 mm per cut, depending on the size of the keyway.
10. Finish the keyway to width by moving the table over, or by using a finishing tool ground to the correct width.

SHAPING A CONTOUR WITH A TRACER ATTACHMENT

Interchangeable manufacturing has brought about many changes in production. Although a shaper is generally not classified as a production-type machine,

Courtesy The Cincinnati Shaper Co.

Fig. 10-34 A tracer set up for contour shaping

transversely. This permits the machining of internal contour surfaces and intricate patterns necessary for tool and die work. The ram may be adjusted for the cutting of angular surfaces, slots, and keyways. A tracer attachment may easily be mounted on this machine for reproducing a number of intricate forms from a template.

Work machined on a vertical shaper or slotter is generally clamped to a table; however, smaller work may be held in a vise. Regardless of how the work is held, it is important that sufficient clearance be left between the bottom of the workpiece and the table or vise to allow for clearance of the cutting tool. The cutting tools used are different in that they must be suitable for internal cutting and must have clearance along the sides behind the cutting edges to prevent them from rubbing. Some of the more common slotter operations are illustrated in Fig. 10-35 (B, C, D).

with the use of a tracer attachment its cutting action can be controlled to produce contour surfaces on any number of objects.

Fig. 10-34 illustrates a tracer set up on a shaper to reproduce the contour form of a template onto a workpiece. The shaper toolhead may also be equipped with an automatic tracer attachment for reproducing any types of straight-line contour surfaces.

VERTICAL SHAPERS OR SLOTTERS

Vertical shapers or slotters, Fig. 10-35A, are generally used for cutting internal vertical surfaces which may be straight, angular, or contoured. This machine is especially valuable for making vertical internal cuts on die work, metal moulds, and metal patterns. The vertical ram has a rapid return stroke and operates on the same principle as the horizontal shaper. The length of the ram stroke can be adjusted to suit the workpiece being machined.

The work to be machined is fastened to a rotary table which may be rotated as well as being moved longitudinally and

Courtesy Rockford Machine Tool Co.

Fig. 10-35A A vertical shaper (slotter) cutting an internal surface

Courtesy Pratt & Whitney Inc.

Fig. 10-35B   Machining using a turret head

Courtesy Pratt & Whitney Inc.

Fig. 10-35C   Machining external grooves

Courtesy Rockford Machine Tool Co.

Fig. 10-35D   Form cutting with a tracer attachment

SHAPERS AND SLOTTERS QUESTIONS

SHAPERS

1. Explain briefly the cutting action of the shaper and slotter.
2. Why is the return stroke of the crank-type shaper faster than the cutting stroke?
3. Sketch the cycle for a crank-type shaper, indicating the path of each stroke.
4. How can the length of the stroke be controlled on a hydraulic shaper?
5. List the advantages of a hydraulic shaper.
6. Explain the purpose of the following shaper parts: apron, hinge pin, clapper block.

SPEEDS AND FEEDS

7. List the factors that determine the speed at which the shaper should operate.
8. a) How many strokes per minute should be used to provide a cutting speed of 18 m/min if the work is 250 mm long?
   b) Calculate the strokes per minute using a high-speed steel cutting tool for the following: bronze workpiece 7 in. long, cast iron 14 in. long, machine steel 10 in. long.
9. Calculate the number of strokes per minute to machine a piece of
   a) machine steel 13 cm long
   b) brass 29 cm long
   c) tool steel 50 cm long
10. What four main factors govern the selection of the feed?
11. Define: cutting speed, feed.
12. Explain why the feed should operate on the return stroke.
13. How is the feed regulated on a hydraulic shaper?

CUTTING TOOLS

14. Sketch a shaper cutting tool, show

the clearance angles, and explain why it differs from a lathe toolbit.
15. Why is it necessary to have a tool lifter on a shaper when using carbide cutting tools?
16. State four machine practices that help to prevent tool chatter.
17. Explain the advantages of a tool lifter.

TO SET THE LENGTH OF THE SHAPER STROKE

18. What information is required before setting the length of the stroke?
19. List the steps required to set the shaper stroke to machine a piece of work 10 cm long.

TO SET THE POSITION OF THE SHAPER STROKE

20. What parts of a shaper are used to set the position of the stroke?
21. Why is it important to set the position of stroke after the length has been set?
22. Why must the ram lock always be tightened before the shaper is started?

ALIGNMENT OF A VISE

23. In point form, list the steps necessary to align the vise jaws:
    a) parallel to the shaper stroke
    b) at 90° to the shaper stroke
24. Explain how the work seat may be tested for parallelism.

TO SHAPE A FLAT SURFACE

25. Explain why all cuttings and burrs must be removed before setting up work in a vise.
26. What size parallels should be selected when setting up work in a vise?
27. Why should paper feelers be used between the parallels and the work?
28. On what stroke should the automatic feed operate when shaping?

TO MACHINE A BLOCK SQUARE AND PARALLEL

29. How is the #1 surface selected?

30. Why is a hold-down or round rod used between the work and the movable jaw?
31. In what position should the round bar be set?
32. Make neat diagrams of the setups required to machine the four sides of a block square and parallel.

TO SHAPE A VERTICAL SURFACE

33. Why must the vise be aligned before shaping a vertical surface?
34. Explain how the toolhead, apron, and cutting tool should be set for shaping a vertical surface.

MACHINING ANGULAR SURFACES

35. List three methods of machining angular surfaces on a shaper.

36. What precaution should be taken when swivelling the toolhead?

DOVETAILS

37. Name three parts of a dovetail assembly.
38. Draw a neat sketch of a gib.
39. Explain how the apron should be set for shaping a dovetail.
40. Outline two methods for checking accuracy of the toolhead setting.
41. With the use of formulas or reference tables, calculate x and y for the following dovetails:

   a) $A = 4.125$ in. $d = .375$ in.
       $G = 55°$ $c = .875$ in.

   b) $A = 125$ mm $d = 18$ mm
       $G = 60°$ $c = 25$ mm

CUTTING KEYWAYS AND GROOVES

42. What is the difference between a keyway and a keyseat?
43. How can the keyway layout be centralized in a vise prior to cutting?
44. Explain how to shape an internal keyway in a gear.

VERTICAL SHAPERS

45. Name three main parts that are common to horizontal and vertical shapers.
46. Name four operations that can be performed on a vertical shaper.

11 MILLING MACHINES

Courtesy Cincinnati Milacron Inc.

NOTE: In this chapter, cam milling, woodruff keys, short lead helices, and rack indexing attachments are covered only in inch units, due to the lack of metric information and standards at the time of publication.

HORIZONTAL MILLING MACHINES

Milling machines are machine tools used to accurately produce one or more machined surfaces on a piece of material, *the workpiece*; this is done by one or more rotary milling cutters having single or multiple cutting edges. The workpiece is held securely on the *work table* of the machine or in a holding device clamped to the table. It is then brought into contact with a revolving cutter.

The milling machine is a versatile machine tool which can handle a variety of operations normally performed by other machine tools. It is used not only for the milling of flat and irregular shaped surfaces, but also for gear and thread cutting, drilling, boring, reaming, and slotting operations. Its versatility makes it one of the most important machine tools used in machine shop work.

In order to meet many different industrial requirements, milling machines are made in a wide variety of types and sizes. They are classified under the following headings:

a) *Manufacturing type*, in which the cutter height is controlled by vertical movement of the headstock.
b) *Special type*, designed for specific milling operations.
c) *Knee-and-column type*, in which the relationship between the cutter height and the work is controlled by vertical movement of the table.

MANUFACTURING TYPE MILLING MACHINES

Manufacturing type milling machines are used primarily for quantity production of identical parts. This type of machine may be either semi-automatic or fully automatic and is of simple but sturdy construction. Fixtures clamped to the table hold the workpiece for a variety of milling operations, depending upon the type of cutters or special spindle attachments used. Some of the distinctive features of manufacturing type machines are the *automatic cycle* of cutter and work approach, the *rapid movement* during the non-cutting part of the cycle, and the *automatic spindle stop*. After this machine has been set up, the operator is required only to load and unload the machine and start the automatic cycle controlled by cams and preset *trip dogs*.

Some of the more common manufacturing type milling machines are:

The plain manufacturing type (Fig. 11-1) has one horizontal spindle and one headstock. This machine is sometimes equipped with a reciprocating table cycle which permits feeding and rapid traversing in both directions. On this type of machine, *reciprocal milling* is possible. Two

Courtesy Cincinnati Milacron Inc.

Fig. 11-1   Plain manufacturing type milling machine

Courtesy Cincinnati Milacron Inc.

Fig. 11-2   Duplex manufacturing type milling machine

Courtesy Cincinnati Milacron Inc.

**Fig. 11-3   Small plain automatic knee-and-column
type milling machine**

identical fixtures may be mounted on opposite ends of the table. While work is
being machined at one end, a new piece
is being loaded into the fixture at the other
end.

The duplex manufacturing type (Fig. 11-2)
is similar to the plain type, except that it
has two horizontal spindles mounted in
two independently adjustable headstocks.
It can be used to perform two identical or
two different milling operations on one or
more pieces at the same time.

**The small plain automatic knee-and-
column type** (Fig. 11-3) is similar to the
plain horizontal mill. It is used for milling
small or medium size parts in different
quantities. The table is operated by power
and controlled automatically by trip dogs
mounted on the front of the table.

**The unit type automatic fixed bed milling
machine** (Fig. 11-4) consists of a group of
small size manufacturing milling machine
units mounted on a common base. As

Courtesy Cincinnati Milacron Inc.

Fig. 11-4   Unit type automatic fixed bed milling machine

many as four units can be mounted on one base for producing small parts at a high rate of speed.

The small plain automatic fixed bed type (Fig. 11-5) has complete automatic cycle control of the table by a cycle selector and trip dogs. The machine may also be equipped with *automatic rise and fall* of the spindle carrier, permitting quick and economical milling of surfaces on different levels or between obstructions.

Courtesy Cincinnati Milacron Inc.

Fig. 11-6   Tracer-controlled milling machine

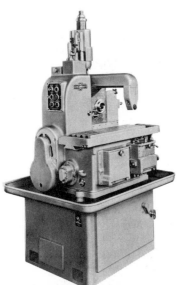

Courtesy Cincinnati Milacron Inc.

Fig. 11-5   Small plain automatic fixed bed milling machine

The tracer-controlled milling machine (Fig. 11-6) has a hydraulic or electrical circuit designed to automatically control the relative positions of the cutter and the workpiece by a tracer stylus riding on a cam, template, or model. This machine is used for efficient, accurate reproduction of curved or irregular surfaces. If the tracer is disengaged it can be used for standard milling operations.

SPECIAL TYPE MILLING MACHINES

These machines are designed for individual milling operations, and are used for

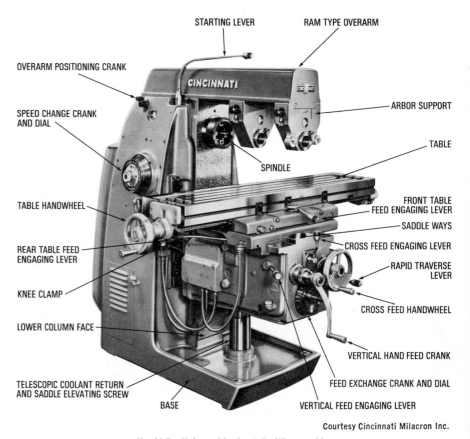

Courtesy Cincinnati Milacron Inc.

Fig. 11-7   Universal horizontal milling machine

only one particular job. They may be completely automatic and are used for production purposes when hundreds of thousands of similar pieces are to be machined.

KNEE-AND-COLUMN TYPE MILLING MACHINES

Machines in this class fall into three categories.
a) plain horizontal milling machines
b) universal horizontal milling machines
c) vertical milling machines

UNIVERSAL HORIZONTAL MILLING MACHINES

The universal horizontal milling machine is essential for advanced machine shop work, and the difference between this machine and the plain horizontal mill will be dealt with in this chapter.

Fig. 11-7 shows the parts of a universal horizontal mill. The only difference between this mill and the plain horizontal machine is the addition of a *table swivel housing* between the table and the saddle. This housing permits the table to be swivelled 45° in either direction in a horizontal plane for such operations as the milling of helical grooves in twist drills, milling cutters, and helical gears.

BACKLASH ELIMINATOR

A recent feature on most milling machines is the addition of a *backlash eliminator.* This device, when engaged, eliminates the backlash (play) between the nut and the table leadscrew, permitting the operation of *climb* (down) milling. Fig. 11-8 shows a diagrammatic sketch of the Cincinnati backlash eliminator.

The backlash eliminator works as follows. Two independent nuts are mounted on the lead screw. These nuts engage a common crown gear which in turn meshes with a rack. Axial movement of the rack is controlled by the backlash eliminator engaging knob located on the front of the saddle. By turning the knob "in," the nuts

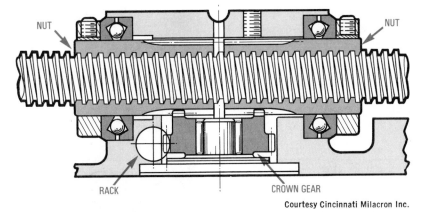

Courtesy Cincinnati Milacron Inc.

Fig. 11-8 Diagrammatic sketch of the Cincinnati backlash eliminator

are forced to move along the leadscrew in opposite directions, removing all backlash. The nuts-gear-rack arrangement is shown in Fig. 11-8.

MILLING PROCESSES

Although the majority of operations performed on a knee-and-column type machine are either plain milling or side milling, several other operations or combinations of operations may be performed.

STRADDLE MILLING

Straddle milling (Fig. 11-9) involves the use of two side milling cutters to machine the opposite sides of a workpiece parallel in one cut. The cutters are separated on the arbor by a spacer or spacers of the required length so that the distance between the inside faces of the cutters is equal to the desired size. An adjustable micrometer arbor spacer may be used to vary the distance between the two cutters and also

Courtesy Cincinnati Milacron Inc.

Fig. 11-9 Straddle milling

to compensate for the wear or the regrinding of the side milling cutters. Applications of straddle milling are the milling of square and hexagonal heads on bolts.

GANG MILLING

Gang milling (Fig. 11-10) is a fast method of milling and is used a great deal in production work. It is performed by using two or more cutters on the arbor to produce the desired shape. The cutters may be a combination of plain and side milling cutters. If more than one helical milling cutter is used, a right- and left-hand helix cutter should be used to offset the thrust created by this type of cutter and to minimize the possibility of chatter. If several cutters are used and the slots are to be the same size, it is important that the diameter and width of each cutter be the same.

Courtesy Cincinnati Milacron Inc.

Fig. 11-10   Gang milling

MILLING MACHINE ACCESSORIES

A wide variety of accessories, which greatly increase its versatility and productivity, is available for the milling machine. These accessories may be classed as *fixtures* or as *attachments*.

FIXTURES

A fixture (Fig. 11-11) is a work-holding device fastened to the table of a machine or to a machine accessory, such as a rotary

Courtesy Cincinnati Milacron Inc.

Fig. 11-11   Milling a workpiece held in a fixture

table. It is designed to hold workpieces that cannot be readily held in a vise or in production work when large quantities are to be machined. The fixture must be designed so that identical parts, when held in the fixture, will be positioned exactly and held securely. Fixtures may be constructed to hold one or several parts at one time and should permit the quick changing of workpieces. The work may be positioned by stops, such as pins, strips, or setscrews, and held in place by clamps, cam-lock levers, or setscrews.

To produce uniform workpieces, clean the chips and cuttings from a fixture before mounting a new workpiece.

MILLING MACHINE ATTACHMENTS

Milling machine attachments may be divided into three classes.

a) Those designed to hold cutters; these are attached to the main spindle of the machine. They are the *vertical*, *high speed*, *universal*, *rack milling*, and *slotting* attachments. These attachments are designed to increase the versatility of the machine.

b) Those designed specifically to hold the cutters, such as *arbors*, *collets*, and *adaptors*.

c) Those designed to hold the workpiece, such as a *vise*, *rotary table*, and *indexing or dividing head*.

VERTICAL MILLING ATTACHMENT

The *vertical milling attachment* (Fig. 11-12), which may be mounted on the face of the column or the overarm, enables a plain or universal milling machine to be used as a vertical milling machine. Angular surfaces may be machined by swinging the head, parallel to the face of the column, to any angle up to 45° on either side of the vertical position. On some models the head may be swung as much as 90° to either side. Vertical attachments enable the horizontal milling machine to be used for such operations as face milling, end milling, drilling, boring, and T-slot milling.

A modification of the vertical milling attachment is the *universal milling attachment* which may be swung in two planes, parallel to the column and at right angles to it, for the cutting of compound angles. The vertical and universal attachments are also manufactured in *high speed* models which permit the efficient use of small and medium size end mills and cutters for such operations as die sinking and key seating.

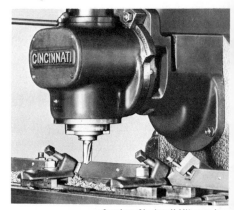

Courtesy Cincinnati Milacron Inc.

Fig. 11-12   Vertical milling attachment

RACK MILLING ATTACHMENT

The *rack milling attachment* (Fig. 11-13A) and the *rack indexing attachment* (Fig. 11-13B) are used to mill longer gear racks (flat gears) than could be cut with the standard horizontal milling machine. These attachments will be discussed later in the chapter with gear cutting accessories.

Courtesy Cincinnati Milacron Inc.

Fig. 11-13A   Rack milling attachment

Courtesy Cincinnati Milacron Inc.

Fig. 11-13B   Rack indexing attachment

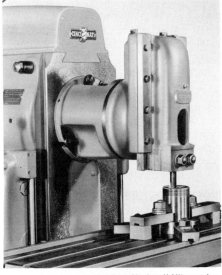

Courtesy Cincinnati Milacron Inc.

Fig. 11-14   Slotting attachment

SLOTTING ATTACHMENT

The *slotting attachment* (Fig. 11-14) converts the rotary motion of the spindle into reciprocating motion for cutting keyways, splines, templates, and irregularly shaped surfaces. The length of the stroke is controlled by an adjustable crank. The tool-slide may be swung to any angle in a plane parallel to the face of the column, making the slotting attachment especially valuable in die work.

ARBORS, COLLETS, AND ADAPTORS

Arbors, used for mounting the milling cutter, are inserted and held in the main spindle by a draw-bolt or a special quick-change adaptor (Fig. 11-15).

Shell end mill arbors may fit into the main spindle or the spindle of the vertical attachment. These devices permit face milling to be done either horizontally or vertically.

Collet adaptors are used for mounting drills or other tapered shank tools in the main spindle of the machine or the vertical milling attachment.

A *quick-change adaptor*, mounted in the spindle, permits such operations as drilling, boring, and milling without a change in the setup of the workpiece.

VISES

Milling machine vises are the most widely used work-holding devices for milling; they are manufactured in three styles.

Courtesy Cincinnati Milacron Inc.

Fig. 11-15   Arbors, collets, and adaptors

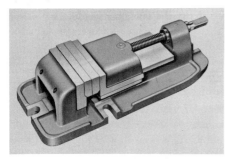

Courtesy Cincinnati Milacron Inc.

Fig. 11-16A   Plain vise

The *plain vise* (Fig. 11-16A) may be bolted to the table so that its jaws are parallel or at right angles to the axis of the spindle. The vise is positioned quickly and accurately by keys on the bottom which fit into the T-slots on the table.

Courtesy The Pedersen Company

Fig. 11-16B   Swivel base vise

Courtesy Cincinnati Milacron Inc.

Fig. 11-16C   Universal vise

The *swivel base vise* (Fig. 11-16B) is similar to the plain vise, except that it has a swivel base which enables the vise to be swivelled through 360° in a horizontal plane.

The *universal vise* (Fig. 11-16C) may be swivelled through 360° in a horizontal plane and may be tilted from zero to 90° in a vertical plane. It is used chiefly by toolmakers, mouldmakers, and diemakers, since it permits the setting of compound angles for milling.

INDEXING OR DIVIDING HEAD

This very useful accessory permits the cutting of bolt heads, gear teeth, and ratchets, etc. When connected to the leadscrew of the milling machine, it will revolve the work as required to cut helical gears and flutes in drills and reamers, etc. The dividing head will be fully discussed later in the chapter.

MILLING CUTTERS

The proper selection, use, and care of milling cutters must be practised if optimum results are to be achieved with the milling machine. The operator or apprentice must be able not only to determine the proper spindle speed for any cutter, but should also constantly observe how the milling machine performs with different cutters and clearances.

Milling cutters are manufactured in many types and sizes. Only the most commonly used cutter will be discussed.

PLAIN MILLING CUTTERS

Probably the most widely used milling cutter is the plain milling cutter which is a cylinder made of tool steel with teeth cut on the periphery; it is used to produce a *flat surface parallel to its axis*. These cutters may be of several types as shown in Fig. 11-17.

Light duty plain milling cutters (Fig. 11-17A) which are less than 20 mm (or 3/4 in.) wide usually have straight teeth;

those over 20 mm (or 3/4 in.) wide have a helix angle of about 25° (Fig. 11-17B).

A

B

Courtesy The Butterfield Division, Union Twist Drill Co.

C

Courtesy The Butterfield Division, Union Twist Drill Co.

D

Courtesy The Cleveland Twist Drill Co.

Fig. 11-17   Plain milling cutters

This type of cutter is used only for light milling operations since it has too many teeth to permit the chip clearance required for heavier cuts.

Heavy duty plain milling cutters (Fig. 11-17C) have fewer teeth than the light duty type, which provide for better chip clearance. The helix angle varies up to 45°. This greater helix angle on the teeth produces a smoother surface due to the shearing action, and reduces chatter. Less power is required with this type of cutter than with straight tooth and small helix angle cutters.

High helix plain milling cutters (Fig. 11-17D) have helix angles from 45° to over 60°. They are particularly suited to the milling of wide and intermittent surfaces in contour and profile milling. Although this type of cutter is usually mounted on the milling machine arbor, it is sometimes shank mounted with a pilot on the end, and used for milling elongated slots.

STANDARD SHANK TYPE HELICAL MILLING CUTTERS

Standard shank type helical milling cutters (Fig. 11-18), also called *arbor type cutters*, are used for milling forms from solid metal; for example, they are used when making yokes or forks. They are also used for removing inner sections from solids. They are inserted through a previously drilled hole, and supported at the outer end with type A arbor supports. Special spindle adaptors are used to hold these cutters.

SIDE MILLING CUTTERS

Side milling cutters (Fig. 11-19) are comparatively narrow cylindrical milling cutters with teeth on each side as well as on the periphery. They are used for cutting slots and for face and straddle milling operations. These cutters may have straight teeth (Fig. 11-19A) or staggered teeth (Fig. 11-19B). Staggered tooth cutters have each tooth set alternately to the

Courtesy The Butterfield Division, Union Twist Drill Co.

Fig. 11-18   Standard shank type helical milling cutter

right and left with an alternately opposite helix angle on the periphery. These cutters have free cutting action at high speeds and feeds. They are particularly suited for milling deep, narrow slots.

Half side milling cutters (Fig. 11-19C) are used when only one side of the cutter is required, as in end facing. These cutters are also made with interlocking faces so that two cutters may be placed side by side for slot milling. The interlocking type is more suited for slot cutting than the solid type staggered tooth cutter since the amount ground from the side of the cutter during regrinding may be compensated by a washer between the cutters. Half side milling cutters have considerable rake and, therefore, are able to take heavy cuts.

Courtesy The Butterfield Division, Union Twist Drill Co.

Fig. 11-19   Side milling cutters

Courtesy The Butterfield Division, Union Twist Drill Co.

Fig. 11-20   Face milling cutter

FACE MILLING CUTTERS

Face milling cutters (Fig. 11-20) are generally over 150 mm (or 6 in.) in diameter and have *inserted teeth* held in place by a wedging device. The teeth may be of high-speed steel, cast tool steel, or they may be tipped with sintered-carbide cutting edges. The corners of this type of cutter are bevelled; most of the cutting action occurs at these points and the periphery of the cutter. The face of the tooth removes a small amount of stock left by the spring of the work or cutter. To prevent chatter, only a small portion of the tooth face near the periphery is in contact with the work; the remainder is ground with a suitable clearance (8 to 10°).

This type of cutter is often used as a combination cutter, making the roughing and finishing cut in one pass. The roughing and finishing blades are mounted on the same body, with a limited number of finishing blades being set to a smaller diameter and extending slightly farther from the face than the roughing blades. The finishing blades have a slightly wider cutting face surface which creates a better finish.

Face milling cutters under 150 mm (or 6 in.) are called *shell end mills* (Fig. 11-21). They are solid, multiple-tooth cutters with teeth on the face and the periphery. They are usually held on a stub arbor which may be threaded or employ a key in the shank to drive the cutter. Shell end mills are more economical than large solid end mills because they are cheaper to replace when broken or worn out.

ANGULAR CUTTERS

Angular cutters have teeth that are neither parallel nor perpendicular to the cutting axis. They are used for milling angular surfaces, such as grooves, serrations, chamfers, reamer teeth, etc. They may be divided into two groups:

a) *Single angle milling cutters* (Fig. 11-22A) have teeth on the conical surface and may or may not have teeth on the flat side. The included angle between the flat face and the conical face designates the cutters, such as 45° or 60° angular cutter.

b) *Double angle milling cutters* (Fig. 11-22B) have two intersecting conical surfaces with cutting teeth on both. When these cutters have equal angles on both sides of the line at a right angle to the axis (symmetrical), they are designated by the size of the included angle. When the angles formed with this line are not the same (unsymmetrical), the cutters are designated by specifying the angle on either side of the plane or line, such as 12-48° double angle milling cutter.

Courtesy The Butterfield Division, Union Twist Drill Co.

Fig. 11-22A   Single angle milling cutter

Courtesy The Butterfield Division, Union Twist Drill Co.

Fig. 11-22B   Double angle milling cutter

Courtesy The Butterfield Division, Union Twist Drill Co.

Fig. 11-21   Shell end mill and adaptor

A Concave

B Convex

Fig. 11-23 Formed cutters

C Gear tooth

Courtesy The Butterfield Division, Union Twist Drill Co.

FORMED CUTTERS

Formed cutters (Fig. 11-23) incorporate the exact shape of the part to be produced, permitting exact duplication of irregularly shaped parts more economically than most other means. Formed cutters are particularly useful for the production of small parts. Each tooth of a formed cutter is identical in shape, and the clearance is machined on the full thickness of each tooth by the form or master tool in a cam controlled relieving machine. Examples of *form relieved cutters* are concave, convex, and gear cutters.

Formed cutters are sharpened by grinding the tooth face. Tooth faces are radial and may have positive, zero, or negative rake, depending on the cutter application. *It is imperative* that the original rake on the tooth be maintained so that the profiles of the tooth and of the work are not changed. If the tooth face rake is maintained exactly, the cutter may be resharpened until the teeth are too thin for use;

A

B

C

Courtesy The Butterfield Division, Union Twist Drill Co.

Fig. 11-24 Metal slitting saws

thus the exact, original shape of the tooth can be maintained. These cutters are sometimes produced with an angular face which causes a shearing action and reduces chatter during the cutting process. They are, however, more difficult to sharpen.

METAL SAWS

Metal slitting saws (Fig. 11-24) are basically thin plain milling cutters with sides relieved or "dished" to prevent rubbing or binding when in use. Slitting saws are made in widths from 0.8 mm to 5 mm and from 1/32 in. to 3/16 in. Because of their thin cross-section, they should be operated at approximately one-quarter to one-eighth of the feed per tooth used for other cutters. For nonferrous metals, their speed can be increased. Unless a special driving flange is used for slitting saws, it is *not* advisable to key the saw to the milling arbor. The arbor nut should be pulled up as tightly as possible *by hand only*. Since slitting saws are so easily broken, some operators find it desirable to "climb" or "down" mill when sawing. However, to overcome the play between the leadscrew and nut, the backlash eliminator should be engaged.

END MILLS

End mills have cutting teeth on the end as well as on the periphery and are fitted to the spindle by a suitable adaptor. They are of two types, the *solid end mill* in which the shank and the cutter are integral, and the *shell end mill* which, as previously stated, employs a separate shank.

Solid end mills, generally smaller than shell end mills, may have either straight or helical flutes. They are manufactured with straight and taper shanks and with two or more flutes. The two-flute type, sometimes called *slot drills* (Fig. 11-25A), have flutes which meet at the cutting end, forming two cutting lips across the bottom. These lips are of different lengths, one extending beyond the centre axis of the cutter. This arrangement eliminates the centre and permits the two-flute end mill to be

Fig. 11-25A   Two-flute end mill

Fig. 11-25B   Four-flute end mill

used in a milling machine for drilling a hole to start a slot that does not extend to the edge of the metal. When a slot is being cut with a two-flute end mill, the depth of cut should not exceed one-half the diameter of the cutter. When the four-flute end mill (Fig. 11-25B) is used for slot cutting, it is usually started at the edge of the metal.

T-SLOT CUTTER

The *T-slot cutter* (Fig. 11-26A) is used to cut the wide horizontal groove at the bottom of a T-slot after the narrow vertical groove has been machined with an end mill or a side milling cutter. It consists of a small side milling cutter with teeth on both sides and an integral shank for mounting, similar to an end mill.

Fig. 11-26A   T-slot cutter

DOVETAIL CUTTER

The *dovetail cutter* (Fig. 11-26B) is similar to a single angle milling cutter with an integral shank. Some dovetail cutters are manufactured with an internal thread and are mounted on a special threaded shank. They are used to form the sides of a dovetail after the tongue or the groove has

been machined with another suitable cutter, usually a side milling cutter. Dovetail cutters may be obtained with 45°, 50°, 55°, or 60° angles.

Fig. 11-26B   Dovetail cutter

WOODRUFF KEYSEAT CUTTERS

The *Woodruff keyseat cutter* (Fig. 11-26C) is similar in design to plain and side milling cutters. Smaller sizes up to approximately 2 in. (or 50 mm) in diameter are made with a solid shank and straight teeth; larger sizes are mounted on an arbor and have staggered teeth on both the sides and the periphery. They are used for milling semi-cylindrical keyseats in shafts.

Fig. 11-26C   Woodruff keyseat cutter

FLYCUTTERS

The *flycutter* (Fig. 11-27) is a single pointed cutting tool with the cutting end ground to the desired shape. It is mounted in a special adaptor or arbor. Since all the cutting is done with one tool, a fine feed must be used. Flycutters are used in experimental work and where the high cost of a special shaped cutter would not be warranted.

Fig. 11-27 Flycutter

MILLING CUTTER MATERIALS

In the milling process, as with most metal cutting operations, the cutting tool must possess certain qualities in order to function satisfactorily. Cutters must be harder than the metal being machined and strong enough to withstand pressures developed during the cutting operation. They must also be tough to resist the shock resulting from the contact of the tooth with the work. To maintain keen cutting edges, they must be able to resist the heat and abrasion of the cutting process.

Most milling cutters today are made of high-speed steel or tungsten carbide. Special purpose cutters, made in the plant for a special job, may be made from plain carbon steel.

High-speed steel, consisting of iron with various amounts of carbon, tungsten, chromium, molybdenum, and vanadium, is used for most solid milling cutters since it possesses all the qualities required for a milling cutter. In this steel, carbon is the hardening agent, while tungsten and molybdenum enable the steel to retain its hardness up to red heat. Vanadium increases the tensile strength and chromium increases the toughness and wear resistance.

When a higher rate of production is desired and when harder metals are being machined, cemented carbides replace high speed steel cutters. Cemented carbide cutters, although more expensive, may be operated from three to ten times faster than high-speed steel cutters. Cemented carbide tips may be either brazed to a steel body or held in place by means of a locking or clamping device (Fig. 11-28).

When cemented carbide cutters are to be used, care must be taken to select the proper type of carbide for the job. Straight tungsten carbide is used for machining cast iron, mild steel, most nonferrous alloys, and plastics. Tantalum carbide is used to machine low and medium carbon steels, and tungsten-titanium carbide is used for high carbon steels.

Although cemented carbides have many advantages as cutting tools, several disadvantages limit more extensive use.

a) Cemented carbide cutters are more costly to buy, maintain, and sharpen.

b) In order to use these cutters efficiently, machines must be rigid and have

Courtesy Cincinnati Milacron Inc.

Fig. 11-28 Milling cutters with cemented carbide tips

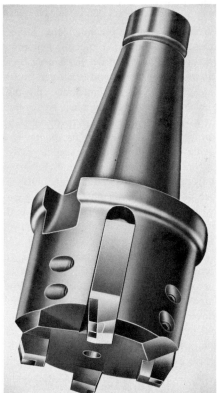

greater horsepower and speed than is required for high speed cutters.

c) Carbide cutters are brittle, and therefore the edges break easily if misused.

d) Special grinders with silicon carbide and diamond wheels are required to sharpen carbide cutters properly.

CUTTING SPEEDS

One of the most important factors affecting the efficiency of a milling operation is cutter speed. If the cutter is run too slowly, valuable time will be wasted, while excessive speed results in loss of time in replacing and regrinding cutters. Somewhere between these two extremes is the efficient *cutting speed* for the material being machined.

The cutting speed of a metal may be defined as *the speed, in metres per minute (or in surface feet per minute), at which the metal may be machined efficiently.* When the work is machined in a lathe, it must be turned at a specific number of revolutions per minute, *depending on its diameter*, to achieve the proper cutting speed. When work is machined in a milling machine, *the cutter* must be revolved at a specified number of revolutions per minute, *depending upon its diameter*, to achieve the proper cutting speed.

Since different types of metals vary in hardness, structure, and machinability, different cutting speeds must be used for each type of metal. The cutting speeds for the more common metals are shown in Table 11-1.

To get optimum use from a cutter, the proper speed at which the cutter should be revolved must be determined. When machining machine steel, the cutter would have to achieve a surface speed of about 30 m (or 90 feet) per minute. Since the diameter of the cutter affects this speed, it is necessary to consider its diameter in the calculation. The following example illustrates how the formula is developed.

EXAMPLE 1 (metric):

Calculate the speed required to revolve a 75 mm high-speed steel milling cutter when cutting machine steel (30 m/min).

1. First, determine the circumference of the cutter or the distance a point on the cutter would travel in one revolution.

   Circumference of cutter $= 75 \times 3.1416$

2. To determine the proper cutter speed or r/min it is necessary only to divide the cutting speed (in metres) by the circumference of the cutter (in metres).

$$r/min = \frac{\text{Cutting speed (in metres)}}{\pi D \text{ (in metres)}}$$

Since the cutter diameter is given in millimetres, it must first be changed to metres:

$$75 \div 1000 = 0.075 \text{ m}$$

$$r/min = \frac{30}{3.1416 \times 0.075}$$

$$= \frac{30}{0.2356}$$

$$= 127$$

If the problem had to be worked out in inches similar calculations would be involved, except that r/min would equal:

$$r/min = \frac{\text{cutting speed}}{\text{circumference}}$$

$$r/min = \frac{12 \times CS}{3.1416 \times D}$$

Since the cutting speed is given in feet per minute and the circumference is generally in inches, it is necessary to multiply the cutting speed by 12. Because of the difficulty of setting a machine to precise r/min, it is permissible to consider 3.1416 as dividing into 12 approximately 4 times.

The formula therefore becomes:

$$r/min = \frac{4 \times CS}{D}$$

Using either of these formulas, it is possible to calculate the proper cutter speed for any material and cutter diameter.

EXAMPLE 2 (inch):

At what speed should a 2 in. diameter carbide cutter revolve to mill a piece of cast iron ($CS = 150$)?

SOLUTION:

$$r/min = \frac{4 \times CS}{D}$$

$$= \frac{4 \times 150}{2}$$

$$= 300$$

TABLE 11-1
MILLING MACHINE CUTTING SPEEDS

MATERIAL	HIGH SPEED STEEL CUTTER		CARBIDE CUTTER	
	m/min	ft./min	m/min	ft./min
Machine steel	21–30	70–100	45–75	150–250
Tool steel	18–20	60–70	40–60	125–200
Cast iron	15–25	50–80	40–60	125–200
Bronze	20–35	65–120	60–120	200–400
Aluminum	150–300	500–1000	150–300	1000–2000

Although these formulas are helpful in calculating the cutter (spindle) speed, it should be remembered that they are approximate only, and the speed may have to be altered because of the hardness of the metal and/or the machine condition. Best results may be obtained if the following rules are observed.

1. For longer cutter life, use the lower cutting speeds in the recommended range.
2. Know the hardness of the material to be machined.
3. When starting a new job, use the lower range of the cutting speed and gradually increase to the higher range if conditions permit.
4. If a fine finish is required, reduce the feed rather than increase the cutter speed.
5. The use of coolant, properly applied, will generally produce a better finish and lengthen the life of the cutter, since it absorbs heat, acts as a lubricant, and washes chips away.

FEED

Milling machine feed may be defined as the distance in millimetres (or inches) per minute that the work moves into the cutter. On most milling machines, the feed is regulated in millimetres (or inches) per minute and is independent of the spindle speed. This arrangement permits faster feeds for larger, slowly rotating cutters.

The feed rate used on a milling machine depends upon a variety of factors, such as:

TABLE 11-2: RECOMMENDED FEED PER TOOTH (FOR HIGH SPEED STEEL CUTTERS)

Material	Face Mills		Helical Mills		Slotting and Side Mills		End Mills		Form-Relieved Cutters		Circular Saws	
	mm	in.	mm	in.	mm	in.	mm	in.	mm	in.	mm	in.
Aluminum	0.55	.022	0.45	.018	0.33	.013	0.28	.011	0.18	.007	0.13	.005
Brass & bronze (medium)	0.35	.014	0.28	.011	0.20	.008	0.18	.007	0.10	.004	0.08	.003
Cast iron (medium)	0.33	.013	0.25	.010	0.18	.007	0.18	.007	0.10	.004	0.08	.003
Machine steel	0.30	.012	0.25	.010	0.18	.007	0.15	.006	0.10	.004	0.08	.003
Tool steel (medium)	0.25	.010	0.20	.008	0.15	.006	0.13	.005	0.08	.003	0.08	.003
Stainless steel	0.15	.006	0.13	.005	0.10	.004	0.08	.003	0.05	.002	0.05	.002

Table 11.3 gives the same information for cemented carbide tipped cutters. Because of the machine condition and the often limited power of the machine, it is sometimes necessary to reduce the feed per tooth.

TABLE 11-3: RECOMMENDED FEED PER TOOTH (FOR CEMENTED CARBIDE TIPPED CUTTERS)

Material	Face Mills		Helical Mills		Slotting and Side Mills		End Mills		Form-Relieved Cutters		Circular Saws	
	mm	in.	mm	in.	mm	in.	mm	in.	mm	in.	mm	in.
Aluminum	0.50	.020	0.40	.016	0.30	.012	0.25	.010	0.15	.006	0.13	.005
Brass & bronze (medium)	0.30	.012	0.25	.010	0.18	.007	0.15	.006	0.10	.004	0.08	.003
Cast iron (medium)	0.40	.016	0.33	.013	0.25	.010	0.20	.008	0.13	.005	0.10	.004
Machine steel	0.40	.016	0.33	.013	0.23	.009	0.20	.008	0.13	.005	0.10	.004
Tool steel (medium)	0.35	.014	0.28	.011	0.20	.008	0.18	.007	0.10	.004	0.10	.004
Stainless steel	0.25	.010	0.20	.008	0.15	.006	0.13	.005	0.08	.003	0.08	.003

a) the depth and width of cut
b) the design or type of cutter
c) the sharpness of the cutter
d) the workpiece material
e) the strength and uniformity of the workpiece
f) the type of finish and accuracy required
g) the power and rigidity of the machine

As the work advances into the cutter, each successive tooth advances into the work an equal amount, producing chips of equal thickness. It is this thickness of the chips or the *feed per tooth*, along with the number of teeth in the cutter, which form the basis for determining the rate of feed. The ideal rate of feed may be determined as follows.

Feed = number of teeth in the cutter
$\times$ recommended feed per tooth
$\times$ r/min of the cutter

EXAMPLE 1 (metric):

Calculate the feed in millimetres per minute for a 75 mm diameter, 6 tooth helical milling cutter when machining a cast iron workpiece ($CS = 60$).

First calculate the r/min of the cutter.

$$r/min = \frac{CS \text{ (metres)}}{\text{Circumference of cutter (metres)}}$$
$$= \frac{60}{0.075 \times 3.1416}$$
$$= 255$$

Feed (mm/min)
$$= N \times \text{feed/tooth} \times r/min$$
$$= 6 \times 0.25 \times 255$$
$$= 382.5$$
$$= 383 \text{ mm/min}$$

EXAMPLE 2 (inch):

Calculate the proper feed for high speed helical milling cutter having 6 teeth and revolving at 90 r/min. The workpiece is machine steel and the recommended feed per tooth is .010 in.

Feed = No. of teeth $\times$ feed/tooth $\times$ r/min
$$= 6 \times .010 \times 90$$
$$= 5.4 \text{ in./min}$$

The calculated feeds given above would be possible only under ideal conditions. Under average operating conditions, it is suggested that the milling machine feed be set to approximately one-third or one-half the amount calculated. The feed can then be gradually increased to the capacity of the machine and the finish desired.

Tables 11-2 and 11-3 give suggested feed per tooth for various types of milling cutters for roughing cuts under average conditions. For finish cuts, the feed per tooth would be reduced to one-half or even one-third of the value shown.

One final consideration should be made concerning feed, that is, the direction in which the work is fed into the cutter.

The most commonly used method of feeding is to feed the work against the rotation direction of the cutter (*conventional or up milling*) (Fig. 11-29A). However, if the machine is equipped with a backlash eliminator (Fig. 11-8), certain types of work can best be milled by *climb milling* (Fig. 11-29B).

Although climb milling is not as widely used as conventional milling, it has certain advantages and disadvantages.

Advantages

a) It is particularly suited to the machining of thin and hard-to-hold parts since the workpiece is forced against the table or holding device by the cutter.
b) Work need not be clamped as tightly.
c) Consistent parallelism and size may be maintained, particularly on thin parts.
d) It may be used where break-out at the edge of the workpiece could not be tolerated.
e) It requires up to 20% less power to cut by this method.
f) It may be used when cutting off stock or when milling deep, thin slots.

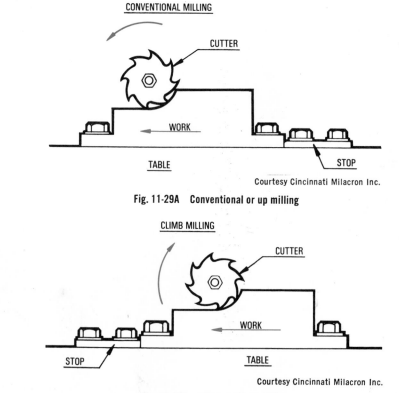

Courtesy Cincinnati Milacron Inc.

Fig. 11-29A Conventional or up milling

Fig. 11-29B Climb or down milling

Courtesy Cincinnati Milacron Inc.

Disadvantages

a) *This method cannot be used unless the machine has a backlash eliminator* and the table gibs have been tightened.

b) It cannot be used for machining castings or hot rolled steel since the hard outer scale will damage the cutter.

DEPTH OF CUT

Where a smooth accurate finish is desired, it is considered good milling practice to take a roughing and finishing cut. Roughing cuts should be deep, with a feed as heavy as the work and the machine will permit. Heavier cuts may be taken with helical cutters having fewer teeth than with those having many teeth. Cutters with fewer teeth are stronger and have a greater chip clearance than cutters with more teeth.

Finishing cuts should be light, with a finer feed than is used for roughing cuts. The depth of the cut should be at least 0.40 mm. Lighter cuts and extremely fine feeds are not advisable since the chip taken by each tooth will be thin and the cutter will often rub on the surface of the work, rather than bite into it, thus dulling the cutter. When a fine finish is required, the feed should be reduced rather than the cutter speeded up; more cutters are dulled by high speeds than by high feeds.

NOTE: To prevent damage to the finished surface, *never* stop the feed when the cutter is revolving over the workpiece. For the same reason, stop the cutter before returning the work to the starting position upon completion of the cut.

MILLING MACHINE SETUPS

To prolong the life of a milling machine and its accessories, and to produce accurate work, the following points should be carefully observed when making milling machine setups.

1. Prior to mounting any accessory or attachment check that both the machine surface and the accessory are free of dirt and chips.

2. Do not place the tools, cutters, or parts on the milling machine table. Place them on a piece of masonite, board, or a bench kept for this purpose to prevent their damaging the table or machined surfaces (Fig. 11-30).

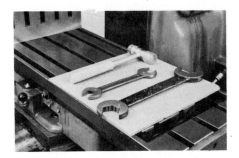

Fig. 11-30   Place tools on a piece of masonite or plywood to protect the machine table

3. When mounting cutters, be sure to use keys on all but slitting saws.

4. Check that the arbor spacers and bushings are clean and free of burrs.

5. When tightening the arbor nut take care to make it only hand tight with a wrench. NEVER USE A HAMMER ON THE NUT OR HOLDING DEVICE ON ANY MACHINE. The use of a hammer and wrench to tighten nuts will strip the threads and bend or damage the accessory or part.

6. When work is mounted in a vise, tap it into place with a LEAD or SOFT-FACED HAMMER and tighten the vise by hand.

Fig. 11-31   Indicating a universal milling machine table

ALIGNING THE TABLE ON A UNIVERSAL MILLING MACHINE

If the workpiece is to be machined accurately to a layout or have cuts made square or parallel to a surface, it is always good practice to align the table of a universal milling machine prior to aligning the vise or fixture.

NOTE: If a long keyway is to be milled in a shaft, it is of utmost importance to align the table. Care must be taken as to the method used for this job.

Procedure

1. Clean the table and the face of the column thoroughly.

2. Mount a dial indicator *on the table* by means of a magnetic base or any suitable mounting device (Fig. 11-31).

3. Move the table towards the column until the dial indicator registers approximately one-half a revolution and set the dial to zero.

4. Using the table feed handwheel, move the table along the width of the column. Note the reading on the dial indicator.

5. If there is any movement of the indicator hand, loosen the locking devices on the *swivel table housing*, adjust for half the difference of the needle movement, and lock the table housing.

6. *Recheck* the table for alignment and adjust if necessary.

NOTE: Always indicate from the table to the face of the column, never from the column to the table.

ALIGNING THE MILLING MACHINE VISE

Whenever accuracy is required on the workpiece, it is necessary to align the device which holds the workpiece. This may be a vise, angle plate, or a special fixture. Since most work is held in a vise, the alignment of this accessory will be outlined.

To Align the Vise Parallel to the Table Travel

1. Clean the surface of the table and the bottom of the vise.

Fig. 11-32A   Accurately aligning the vise parallel to the table travel

2. Mount and fasten the vise.
3. Swivel the vise until the solid jaw is approximately parallel with the table slots.
4. Mount a dial indicator to the arbor or to a cutter (Fig. 11-32A and 11-33A).
5. Adjust the table until the indicator registers about half a revolution against the solid jaw of the vise.
   NOTE: Make sure the solid jaw is clean and free of burrs.

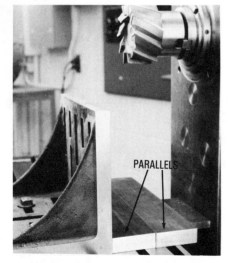

Fig. 11-32B   Aligning an angle plate parallel to the column

Fig. 11-33A   Accurately aligning the vise at right angles to the table travel

6. Set the bezel to zero.
7. Move the table along for the length of the jaw and note the reading of the indicator.
8. Loosen the nuts on the upper or swivel part of the vise.

Courtesy Kostel Enterprises Ltd.

Fig. 11-33B   Aligning an angle plate at right angles to the column

9. Adjust the vise to half the movement of the needle by tapping it by hand or with a *soft* hammer in the appropriate direction.
   NOTE: Never tap the vise so that the solid jaw moves against the indicator plunger. This will damage the indicator.
10. Tighten the vise at this setting.
11. *Recheck* and adjust if necessary.

Methods of aligning the vise at right angles to the travel of the table and methods of aligning an angle plate are shown in Figs. 11-32A and B, and 11-33A and B.

SAWING AND SLITTING

Metal slitting saws may be used for milling narrow slots and for cutting off work. Plain slitting saws, because of their thin cross-section, are rather fragile cutting tools, and if they are not used carefully they will break easily.

To get the maximum life from a slitting saw take the following precautions.

1. Never key a slitting saw on the arbor unless it is mounted in a special flanged mounting collar. If the slitting saw is keyed and jams in the work, it will rotate and cut through the key, and it will be difficult to remove the broken saw.
   NOTE: The arbor nut must be drawn up as tightly as possible by *hand* only.
2. When selecting a slitting saw, choose one with the smallest diameter that will permit adequate clearance between the arbor collars or supports and the clamping bolts, holding device, or workpiece.
3. Mount the saw close to the column face and have the outer arbor support as close as possible to the saw.
4. Always use a sharp cutter.
5. Be sure that the table gibs are drawn up to eliminate any play between the table and the saddle.
6. Operate saws at approximately one-quarter to one-eighth the feed per tooth used for side milling cutters.

7. When sawing or slitting fairly long or deep slots, it is advisable to climb mill to prevent the cutter from crowding sideways and breaking. The table should be fed carefully by hand and the backlash eliminator engaged.

THE INDEXING OR DIVIDING HEAD

The *indexing or dividing head* (Fig. 11-34) is one of the most important attachments for the milling machine. It is used to divide the circumference of a workpiece into equally spaced divisions when milling such items as gears, splines, squares, hexagons, etc. It may also be used to rotate the workpiece at a predetermined ratio to the table feed rate to produce cams and helical grooves on gears, drills, reamers, etc.

The universal dividing head set consists of the *headstock* with *index plates*, headstock *change gears* and *quadrant*, *universal chuck*, *footstock*, and the *centre rest*.

THE HEADSTOCK

A *swivelling block*, mounted in the *base*, enables the headstock to be tilted from 5° below the horizontal position to 10° beyond the vertical position. The side of the base and the block are graduated to indicate the angle of the setting. Mounted in the swivelling block is a *spindle*, with a *40-tooth worm wheel* attached, which meshes with a worm (Fig. 11-35). The worm, at right angles to the spindle, is connected to the *index crank*, the pin of which engages in the *index plate* (Fig. 11-36). A *direct indexing plate* is attached to the front of the spindle.

A 60° centre may be inserted into the front of the spindle and a *universal chuck* may be threaded onto the end of the spindle.

The *footstock* is used in conjunction with the headstock to support work held between centres or the end of work held in a chuck. The footstock centre may be adjusted longitudinally to accommodate various lengths of work and may be raised or lowered off centre. It may also be tilted out of parallel with the base when cuts are being made on tapered work.

Long slender work held between centres is prevented from bending by the *adjustable centre rest*.

Courtesy Cincinnati Milacron Inc.

Fig. 11-34   Universal dividing head set

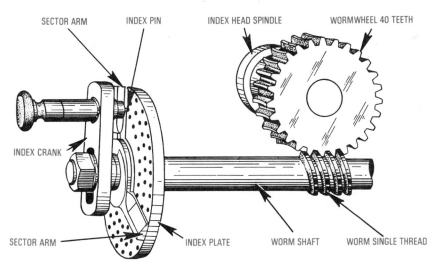

SECTOR ARM   INDEX PIN   INDEX HEAD SPINDLE   WORMWHEEL 40 TEETH

INDEX CRANK

SECTOR ARM   INDEX PLATE   WORM SHAFT   WORM SINGLE THREAD

Fig. 11-35   Section through dividing head showing the worm wheel and worm shaft

METHODS OF INDEXING

The main purpose of the indexing or dividing head is to accurately divide the workpiece periphery into any number of divisions. This may be accomplished by the following indexing methods: *direct*, *simple*, *angular*, and *differential*.

DIRECT INDEXING

Direct indexing is the simplest form of indexing. It is performed by first disengaging the worm shaft from the worm wheel by means of an eccentric device in the dividing head. Direct indexing is used for quick indexing of the workpiece when cutting flutes, hexagons, squares, etc.

The work is rotated the required amount and held in place by a pin which engages into a hole or slot in the *direct*

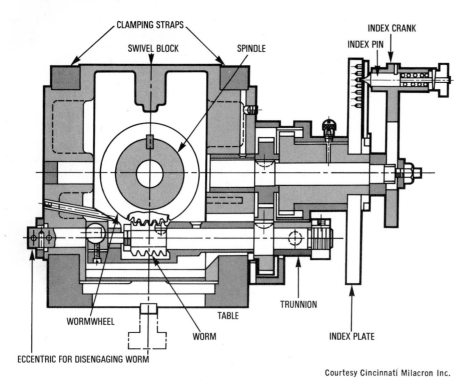

CLAMPING STRAPS

SWIVEL BLOCK   SPINDLE

INDEX CRANK
INDEX PIN

WORMWHEEL   TABLE   TRUNNION

WORM   INDEX PLATE

ECCENTRIC FOR DISENGAGING WORM

Courtesy Cincinnati Milacron Inc.

Fig. 11-36   Section through dividing head showing the spindle and index plate

indexing plate mounted on the end of the dividing head spindle. The direct indexing plate usually contains three sets of hole circles or slots: 24, 30, and 36. The number of divisions it is possible to index is limited to numbers which are factors of 24, 30, and 36. The common divisions that can be obtained by direct indexing are listed in Table 11-4.

EXAMPLE:

What direct indexing is necessary to mill 8 flutes on a reamer blank?

As the 24-hole circle is the only one divisible by 8 (the required number of divisions), it is the only circle which can be used in this case.

$$\text{Indexing} = \frac{24}{8} \text{ or 3 holes on a 24-hole circle.}$$

NOTE: NEVER count the hole or slot in which the index pin is engaged.

SIMPLE INDEXING

In *simple indexing*, the work is positioned by means of the crank, index plate, and sector arms. The worm, attached to the crank, must be engaged with the worm wheel on the dividing head spindle. Since there are 40 teeth on the worm wheel, one complete turn of the index crank will cause the spindle and the work to rotate 1/40 of a turn. Similarly, 40 turns of the crank will revolve the work one turn. Thus there is a ratio of 40:1 between the turns of the index crank and the dividing head spindle.

To calculate the indexing or the number of turns of the crank for most divisions, it is necessary only to divide 40 by the number of divisions to be cut.

$$\text{Indexing} = \frac{40}{\text{number of required divisions}}$$

$$\text{Indexing} = \frac{40}{N}$$

EXAMPLE:

The indexing required to cut 8 flutes would be:

$$\frac{40}{8} = 5 \text{ full turns of the index crank.}$$

If, however, it was necessary to cut 7 flutes, the indexing would be $\frac{40}{7} = 5\text{-}5/7$ turns. Five complete turns are easily made; however, the 5/7 of a turn involves the use of the index plate and sector arms.

INDEX PLATE AND SECTOR ARMS

The *index plate* is a circular plate provided with a series of equally spaced holes into which the index crank pin engages. The *sector arms* fit on the front of this plate and may be set to any portion of a complete turn.

To get 5/7 of a turn, choose any hole circle (Table 11-5) which is divisible by the denominator 7, such as 21, then take 5/7 of 21 = 15 holes on a 21-hole circle. Therefore, the indexing for seven flutes would be $\frac{40}{7} = 5\text{-}5/7$ turns or 5 complete turns plus 15 holes on the 21-hole circle. The procedure for cutting 7 flutes would be as follows:

Plate Hole Circles	TABLE 11-4: DIVISIONS POSSIBLE WITH DIRECT INDEXING												
24	2	3	4	—	6	8	—	—	12	—	—	24	—	—
30	2	3	—	5	6	—	—	10	—	15	—	—	30	—
36	2	3	4	—	6	—	9	—	12	—	18	—	—	36

1. Mount the proper index plate on the dividing head.

2. Loosen the index crank nut and set the index pin into a hole on the 21-hole circle.

3. Tighten the index crank nut and check to see that the pin enters the hole easily.

4. Loosen the set screw on the sector arm.

5. Place the narrow edge of the left arm against the index pin.

6. Count 15 holes on the 21-hole circle. *Do not include the hole in which the index crank pin is engaged.*

7. Move the right sector arm slightly beyond the 15th hole and tighten the sector arm set screw.

8. After the first flute has been cut, return the table to the original starting position.

9. Withdraw the index pin and turn the crank 5 turns plus the 15 holes indicated by the right sector arm. Release the index pin between the 14th and 15th holes, and gently tap it until it drops into the 15th hole.

10. Turn the sector arm *furthest from the pin* clockwise until it is against the index pin.
    NOTE: It is important that the arm *furthest from the pin* be held and turned. If the arm *next* to the pin were held and turned, the spacing between both sector arms would be increased when the other arm hit the pin. This could result in an indexing error which would not be noticeable until the work was completed.

11. Lock the dividing head; then continue machining and indexing for the remaining flutes. Whenever the crank pin is moved past the required hole, *remove the backlash* between the worm and worm wheel by turning the crank *counterclockwise* approximately one-half turn and then carefully *clockwise* until the pin engages into the proper hole.

TABLE 11-5: INDEX-PLATE HOLE CIRCLES		
Brown & Sharpe		**Cincinnati Standard Plate**
Plate 1	15-16-17-18-19-20	One side	24-25-28-30-34-37-
Plate 2	21-23-27-29-31-33		38-39-41-42-43
Plate 3	37-39-41-43-47-49	Other side	46-47-49-51-53-54-
			57-58-59-62-66

ANGULAR INDEXING

When the angular distance between divisions is given, instead of the number of divisions, the setup for simple indexing may be used; however, the method of calculating the indexing is changed.

One complete turn of the index crank turns the work 1/40 of a turn, or 1/40 of 360° which equals 9°.

When the angular dimension is given in *degrees*, the indexing is then calculated as follows:

Indexing in degrees

$$= \frac{\text{number of degrees required}}{9}$$

EXAMPLE 1:

Calculate the indexing for 45°.

$$\text{Indexing} = \frac{45}{9}$$

$$= 5 \text{ complete turns}$$

EXAMPLE 2:

Calculate the indexing for 60°.

$$\text{Indexing} = \frac{60}{9}$$

$$= 6\text{-}2/3$$

$$= 6 \text{ complete turns, 12 holes on an 18-hole circle}$$

If the dimensions are given in *degrees* and *minutes*, it will be necessary to convert the degrees into minutes (number of degrees × 60 minutes) and add the answer to the minutes required.

The indexing in minutes is calculated as follows:

Indexing in minutes

$$= \frac{\text{number of minutes required}}{540}$$

EXAMPLE 1:

Calculate the indexing necessary for 24 minutes.

$$\text{Indexing} = \frac{24}{540}$$

$$= \frac{4}{90}$$

$$= \frac{1}{22.5}$$

The indexing for 24 minutes would be one hole on the 22.5-hole circle. As the 23-hole circle is the nearest hole circle, the indexing would be one hole on the 23-hole circle. Since in this case there is a slight error (approximately one-half minute) in indexing, it is advisable to use this method only for a few divisions if extreme accuracy is required.

EXAMPLE 2:

Calculate the indexing for 24°30′.

Convert 24° into minutes
(24 × 60)   = 1440′

Add 30 minutes   =   30′

Total   = 1470′

$$\text{Indexing} = \frac{1470}{540}$$

$$= 2\text{-}13/18 \text{ turns}$$

$$= 2 \text{ complete turns plus 13 holes on an 18-hole circle}$$

When indexing for degrees and half degrees (30'), use the 18-hole circle (Brown & Sharpe).

$1/2°$ (30') = 1 hole on the 18-hole circle

$1°$ = 2 holes on the 18-hole circle

When indexing for $1/3°$ (20') and $2/3°$ (40'), the 27-hole circle should be used (Brown & Sharpe).

$1/3°$ (20') = 1 hole on the 27-hole circle

$2/3°$ (40') = 2 holes on the 27-hole circle

When indexing for minutes using a Cincinnati dividing head, note that one space on the 54-hole circle will rotate the work 10' ($1/54 \times 540$).

DIFFERENTIAL INDEXING

When it is impossible to calculate the required indexing by the simple indexing method, that is, when the fraction $\dfrac{40}{N}$ cannot be reduced to a factor of one of the available hole circles, it is necessary to use *differential indexing*.

With this method of indexing, the index plate must be revolved either forward or backward a part of a turn to attain the proper spacing or indexing.

In differential indexing, as in simple indexing, the index crank rotates the dividing head spindle. The spindle rotates the

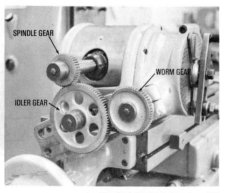

Courtesy Kostel Enterprises Ltd.

Fig. 11-37   Headstock geared for differential indexing

index plate, after the locking pin has been disengaged, by means of change gears connecting the dividing head spindle and the worm shaft (Fig. 11-37). The rotation of the plate may be either in the same direction (positive) or in the opposite direction (negative) of the index crank. This change of rotation is effected by an idler gear or gears in the gear train.

When it is necessary to calculate the indexing for a required number of divisions by the differential method, a number is chosen close to the required divisions which can be indexed by simple indexing.

To illustrate the principle of differential indexing, assume that the index crank has to be rotated 1/9 of a turn and there is only an 8-hole circle available.

If the crank is moved 1/9 of a turn, the index pin will contact the plate at a spot before the first hole on the 8-hole circle. The exact position of this spot would be the difference between 1/8 and 1/9 of a revolution of the crank. This would be

$$1/8 - 1/9 = \frac{9-8}{72} = 1/72 \text{ of a turn } less$$

than 1/8 of a turn, or 1/72 of a turn short of the first hole. Since there is no hole at this point into which the pin could engage, it is necessary to cause the plate to rotate backwards by means of change gears 1/72 of a turn in order that the pin will engage in a hole. At this point the index crank will be locked at exactly 1/9 of a turn.

The method of calculating the change gears (Fig. 11-37) required to rotate the plate the proper amount is as follows:

$$\text{Change gear ratio} = (A - N) \times \frac{40}{A}$$

$$= \frac{\text{driver (spindle) gear}}{\text{driven (worm) gear}}$$

A = approximate number of divisions

N = required number of divisions

When the approximate number of divisions is larger than the required number, the resulting fraction is plus and the index plate must move in the same direction as the crank (clockwise). This *positive rotation* is accomplished by using an idler gear. However, if the approximate number is smaller than the required number, the resulting fraction is minus and the index plate must move in a counterclockwise direction. This *negative rotation* requires the use of two idler gears. The numerator of the fraction represents the driving (spindle) gear or gears, while the denominator represents the driven (worm) gear or gears. The gearing may be either simple or compound and the rotation is as follows.

Simple gearing: 1 idler for a positive rotation of the index plate

2 idlers for a negative rotation of the index plate

Compound gearing: 1 idler for a negative rotation of the index plate

2 idlers for a positive rotation of the index plate

EXAMPLE:

Calculate the indexing and change gears required for 57 divisions.

The change gears supplied with the dividing head are as follows: 24, 24, 28, 32, 40, 44, 48, 56, 64, 72, 86, 100.

The available index plate hole circles are as follows:

Plate #1: 15, 16, 17, 18, 19, 20

Plate #2: 21, 23, 27, 29, 31, 33

Plate #3: 37, 39, 41, 43, 47, 49

Procedure

1. Indexing = $\dfrac{40}{N} = \dfrac{40}{57}$

   Since there is no 57-hole circle and since it is impossible to reduce this fraction to suit any hole circle, it is necessary to select an approximate number close to 57, for which simple indexing may be calculated.

2. Let the approximate number of divisions equal 56.

3. Indexing for 56 divisions $= \dfrac{40}{56} = \dfrac{5}{7}$ or

15 holes on the 21-hole circle.

4. Gear ratio $= (A - N) \times \dfrac{40}{A}$

$$= (56 - 57) \times \dfrac{40}{56}$$

$$= -1 \times \dfrac{40}{56}$$

$$= -\dfrac{5}{7}$$

Change gears $= -\dfrac{5}{7} \times \dfrac{8}{8}$

$$= -\dfrac{40 \text{ (spindle gear)}}{56 \text{ (worm gear)}}$$

Therefore, for indexing 57 divisions, a 40-tooth gear is mounted on the dividing head spindle, and a 56-tooth gear is mounted on the worm shaft. Since the fraction is a negative quantity and simple gearing is to be used, the index plate rotation is negative, or counterclockwise, and two idlers must be used. After the proper gears are installed, the simple indexing procedure for 56 divisions should be followed.

THE WIDE RANGE DIVIDING HEAD

Although simple or differential indexing is satisfactory for most indexing problems, there may be certain divisions which cannot be indexed by either of these methods. Cincinnati Milacron, Inc., manufactures a *wide range divider* (Fig. 11-38) that may be applied to a Cincinnati universal dividing head. With this attachment, it is possible to obtain divisions from 2 up to 400 000.

The wide range divider consists of a large index plate A (Fig. 11-38) sector arms, and crank B which engages in the plate A. This large plate contains 11-hole

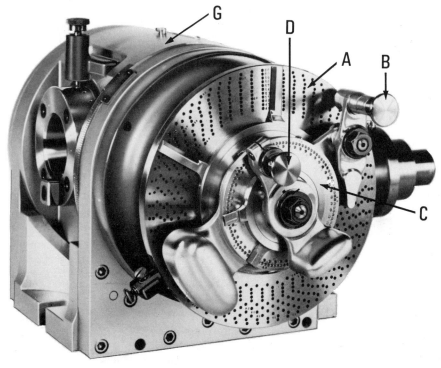

Courtesy Cincinnati Milacron Inc.

Fig. 11-38 Wide range dividing head

circles on each side. Mounted in front of the large index plate is a small index plate C containing a 54-hole and a 100-hole circle. The crank D operates through a reduction of gears having a ratio of 100:1. These gears are mounted in the housing G. The ratio between the worm (and the crank B) and the dividing head spindle is 40:1.

INDEXING FOR DIVISIONS

The ratio of the large index crank to the dividing head is 40:1, as in simple indexing. The ratio of the small index crank which drives the large crank by planetary gearing is 100:1. Therefore *one turn of the small crank* drives the index head spindle 1/100 of 1/40, or 1/4 000 of a turn. One hole on the 100-hole circle of the small index plate $C = 1/100 \times 1/4\,000$, or 1/400 000 of a turn. Therefore the formula for indexing *divisions*

with a wide range divider $= \dfrac{400\,000}{N}$ and is applied as follows.

As the ratio of the large index crank is 40:1, any numbers which divide into 40 (the two numbers to the left of the short vertical line) represent full turns of the large index crank. If a 100-hole circle is used with the large crank, *one hole* on this circle will produce 1/100 of 1/40, or 1/4 000 of a turn. Therefore, any numbers which divide into 4 000 (the two numbers to the left of the long vertical line) are indexed on the 100-hole circle of the large plate. The numbers to the right of the long vertical line are indexed on the 100-hole circle of the small plate. Thus for the 1 250 divisions, the indexing would be: 3 holes on the 100-hole circle of the large plate plus 20 holes on the 100-hole circle of the small plate.

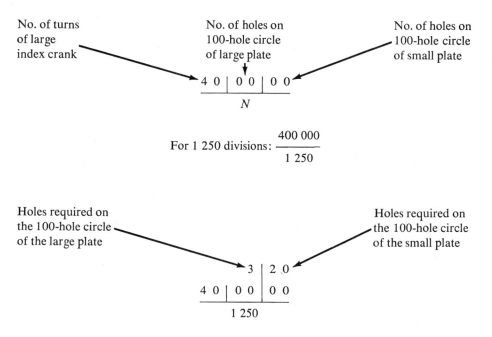

No. of turns of large index crank

No. of holes on 100-hole circle of large plate

No. of holes on 100-hole circle of small plate

$$\underline{4\ 0\ |\ 0\ 0\ |\ 0\ 0}_{N}$$

$$\text{For 1 250 divisions: } \frac{400\ 000}{1\ 250}$$

Holes required on the 100-hole circle of the large plate

Holes required on the 100-hole circle of the small plate

$$\frac{\ \ \ \ \ \ 3\ |\ 2\ 0}{4\ 0\ |\ 0\ 0\ |\ 0\ 0}_{1\ 250}$$

ANGULAR INDEXING WITH THE WIDE RANGE DIVIDER

The wide range divider is especially suited for accurate angular indexing. Indexing in degrees, minutes, and seconds is easily accomplished without the complicated calculations necessary with standard dividing heads.

For angular indexing, both the large and small index cranks are set on the 54-hole circle of each plate. Each space on the 54-hole circle of the large plate will cause the dividing head spindle to rotate 10 minutes (10'). Each space on the 54-hole circle of the small plate will cause the work to rotate 6 seconds (6"). Therefore, for indexing angles with a wide range divider, the following formulas are used.

$$\text{Degrees} = \frac{N}{9} \quad \text{(indexed on the large plate)}$$

$$\text{Minutes} = \frac{N}{10} \quad \text{(indexed on the large plate)}$$

$$\text{Seconds} = \frac{N}{6} \quad \text{(indexed on the small plate)}$$

EXAMPLE:
To index for an angle of 17°36'18".

1. $\text{Degrees} = \dfrac{17}{9}$

   $= 1\text{-}8/9 \text{ turns}$

   OR

   1 turn plus 48 holes on the 54-hole circle of the large index plate.

2. $\text{Minutes} = \dfrac{36}{10}$

   $= 3$ holes on a 54-hole circle of the large index plate, leaving a remainder of 6 minutes.

3. Convert the 6 minutes into seconds $(6 \times 60) = 360"$ and add it to the 18" still required.

4. $\text{Seconds} = \dfrac{378}{6}$

   $= 63$ holes on a 54-hole circle of the small plate

   OR

   1 turn and 9 holes on the 54-hole circle.

Therefore, to index for 17°36'18" would require 1 turn and 51 holes (48 + 3) on the 54-hole circle of the large plate plus 1 turn and 9 holes on the 54-hole circle of the small plate.

LINEAR GRADUATING

The operation of producing accurate spaces on a piece of flat stock, or that of *linear graduating*, is easily accomplished on the horizontal milling machine (Fig. 11-39).

Fig. 11-39 Linear graduating

In this process the work may be clamped to the table or held in a vise, depending on the shape and size of the part. Care must be taken to align the workpiece parallel with the table travel.

To produce an *accurate* longitudinal movement of the table, the dividing head spindle is geared to the leadscrew of the milling machine (Fig. 11-40).

If the dividing head spindle and the lead screw were connected with gears with equal number of teeth and the index crank turned one revolution, the spindle and leadscrew on an inch milling machine would revolve 1/40 of a revolution. This rotation of the leadscrew (having 4 tpi) would cause the table to move $1/40 \times 1/4$ (1 turn of the leadscrew) = 1/160 = .00625. Thus five turns of the index crank would move the table 5 × .00625, or 1/32 in.

The formula for calculating the indexing for linear graduations in thousandths

Fig. 11-40 Gearing for linear graduating

of an inch is $\dfrac{N}{.00625}$. Very small movements of the table, such as .001, may be obtained by applying the formula

$$\dfrac{.001}{.00625} = \dfrac{1}{6\text{-}1/4} \text{ turns (4/25 turn), or 4}$$

holes on the 25-hole circle.

If the leadscrew of a metric milling machine had a pitch of 5 mm, one turn of the index crank would move the table 1/40 of 5 mm, or 0.125 mm. Therefore it would require 4 complete turns of the index crank to move the table 0.5 mm.

The formula for calculating the indexing for linear graduations in millimetres is $\dfrac{N}{0.125}$. For a small movement of the table, such as 0.025 mm, apply the formula:

$$\dfrac{0.025}{0.125} = 1/5 \text{ turn, or 5 holes on a 25 hole}$$

circle.

Other suitable table movements may be obtained by using the appropriate hole circle and/or different change gears.

The point of the toolbit used for graduating is generally ground to a V shape, although other special forms may be desired. The tool is mounted vertically in a suitable arbor which is of sufficient length to extend the toolbit over the workpiece (Fig. 11-39).

The uniformity of the length of the lines is controlled by the *accurate* movement of the crossfeed handwheel or by stops suitably mounted on the ways of the knee.

When graduating is done, the starting point on the workpiece is positioned under the point of the *stationary*, vertical toolbit. The work is moved clear of the tool by the crossfeed handwheel and the proper depth is set by means of the vertical feed crank. The table is then locked in place. For a uniform width of lines to be maintained, the work must be held absolutely flat and the table height must never be adjusted.

GEARS AND GEAR CUTTING

DEVELOPMENT OF GEAR DRIVES

When it is required to transmit rotary motion from one shaft to another, several methods may be used, such as belts, pulleys, and gears. If the shafts are parallel to each other and quite a distance apart, a flat belt and large pulleys may be used to drive the second shaft, the speed of which may be controlled by the size of the pulleys.

When the shafts are closer together, such as in the case of the sensitive drill press, a V-belt, which tends to reduce the excessive slippage of a flat belt, may be used. Here the speed of the driven shaft may be controlled by means of stepped or variable speed pulleys. When the shafts are close together and parallel, some power may be transmitted by two rollers in contact, with one roller mounted on each shaft. Slippage is the main problem here, and the desired speed of the driven shaft could not be maintained.

The methods outlined are means by which power may be transmitted from one shaft to another, but the speed of the driven shaft may not be accurate in all cases due to slippage between the driving and driven members (belts, pulleys, or rollers). In order to eliminate slippage and produce a positive drive, gears are used.

GEARS AND GEARING

Gears are used to transmit power positively from one shaft to another by means of successively engaging teeth (in two gears). They are used in place of belt drives and other forms of friction drives when exact speed ratios and power transmission must be maintained. Gears may also be used to increase or decrease the speed of the driven shaft, thus decreasing or increasing the *torque* of the driven member.

Shafts in a gear drive or train are generally parallel. They may, however, be driven at any angle by means of suitably designed gears.

TYPES OF GEARS

Spur gears (Fig. 11-41) are generally used to transmit power between two parallel shafts. The teeth on these gears are straight and parallel to the shafts to which they are attached. When two gears of different sizes are in mesh, the larger is

Fig. 11-41   A spur gear and pinion are used for slower speeds

called the *gear* while the smaller is called the *pinion*. Spur gears are used where slow to moderate speed drives are required.

Internal gears (Fig. 11-42) are used where the shafts are parallel and the centres must be closer together than could be achieved with spur or helical gearing.

This arrangement provides for a stronger drive since there is a greater area of contact than with the conventional gear drive. It also provides speed reductions with a minimum of space requirement. Internal gears are used on heavy duty tractors where much torque is required.

Helical gears (Fig. 11-43) may be used to connect parallel shafts or shafts which are at an angle. Because of the progressive rather than intermittent action of the teeth, helical gears run more smoothly and quietly than spur gears. Since there is more than one tooth in engagement at any one time, helical gears are stronger than spur gears of the same size and pitch. However, special bearings (thrust bearings) are often required on shafts to overcome the end thrust produced by these gears as they turn.

On most installations where it is necessary to overcome end thrust, *herringbone gears* (Fig. 11-44) are used. This type of gear resembles two helical gears placed side by side, with one-half having a left-hand helix and the other half a right-hand helix. These gears have a smooth con-

Fig. 11-44   Herringbone gears eliminate end thrust on shafts

tinuous action and eliminate the need for thrust bearings.

When two shafts are located at an angle with their axial lines intersecting at 90°, power is generally transmitted by means of *bevel gears* (Fig. 11-45A). When the shafts are at right angles and the gears are of the same size, they are called *mitre gears* (Fig. 11-45B). However, it is not necessary that the shafts be only at right angles in order to transmit power. If the

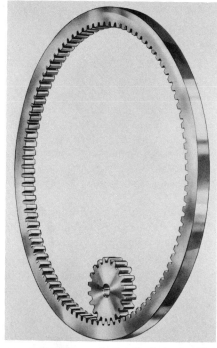

Fig. 11-42   Internal gears provide speed reductions with a minimum space requirement

A — For drives which are parallel to each other

**Fig. 11-43
Helical gears**

B — For drives which are at right angles to each other

Courtesy The Boston Gear Works

Fig. 11-45A Bevel gears transmit power at 90°

Courtesy The Boston Gear Works

Fig. 11-45B Driver and driven mitre gears are the same size

Courtesy General Motors Corp.

Fig. 11-45C Angular bevel gears are used for shafts which are not at right angles

Courtesy General Motors Corp.

Fig. 11-45D Hypoid gears are used in automotive drives

Courtesy The Boston Gear Works

Fig. 11-46 A worm and worm gear is used for speed reduction

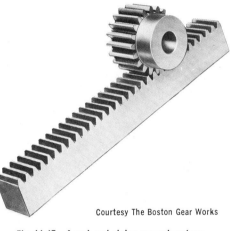

Courtesy The Boston Gear Works

Fig. 11-47 A rack and pinion converts rotary motion to linear motion

same plane and, therefore, do not intersect. Hypoid gears are used in automobile drives.

When shafts are at right angles and considerable reduction in speed is required, a *worm and worm gear* (Fig. 11-46) may be used. The worm which meshes with the worm gear may be a single or multiple start thread. A worm with a double-start thread will revolve the worm gear twice as fast as a worm with a single-start thread and the same pitch.

When it is necessary to convert rotary motion to linear motion, a *rack and pinion* (Fig. 11-47) may be used. The rack, which is actually a straight or flat gear, may have straight teeth to mesh with a spur gear, or angular teeth to mesh with a helical gear.

GEAR TERMINOLOGY

A knowledge of the more common gear terms is desirable to understand gearing and to make the calculations necessary to cut a gear. Most of these terms are applicable to either inch or metric gearing, although the method of calculating dimensions may differ. These methods are explained as applicable to the inch and metric gear cutting sections.

axes of the shafts intersect at any angle other than 90°, the gears are known as *angular bevel gears* (Fig. 11-45C). Bevel gears have straight teeth very similar to spur gears. Modified bevel gears having helical teeth are known as *hypoid gears* (Fig. 11-45D). The shafts of these gears, although at right angles, are not in the

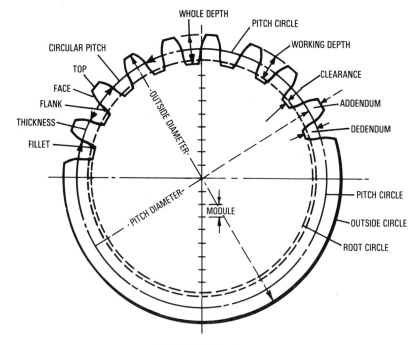

Fig. 11-48   Parts of a gear

Addendum is the radial distance between the pitch circle and the outside diameter or the height or the tooth above the pitch circle.

Centre distance is the shortest distance between the axes of two mating gears or the distance equal to one-half the sum of the pitch diameters.

Chordal addendum is the radial distance measured from the top of the tooth to a point where the chordal thickness and the pitch circle intersect on the edge of the tooth.

Chordal thickness is the thickness of the tooth measured at the pitch circle or the length of the chord which subtends the arc of the pitch circle.

Circular pitch is the distance from a point on one tooth to a corresponding point on the next tooth measured on the pitch circle.

Circular thickness is the thickness of the

tooth measured on the pitch circle; it is also known as the *arc thickness*.

Clearance is the radial distance between the top of one tooth and the bottom of the mating tooth space.

Dedendum is the radial distance from the pitch circle to the bottom of the tooth space. The dedendum is equal to the addendum plus the clearance.

Diametral pitch (inch gears) is the ratio of the number of teeth for each inch of pitch diameter of the gear. For example, a gear of 10 diametral pitch and a 3 in. *pitch diameter* would have 10 × 3, or 30, teeth.

Involute is the curved line produced by a point of a stretched string when it is unwrapped from a given cylinder (Fig. 11-49).

Linear pitch is the distance from a point on one tooth to the corresponding point on the next tooth of a gear rack.

Module (metric gears) is the pitch diameter of a gear divided by the number of teeth. It is an actual dimension, unlike diametral pitch which is a ratio of the number of teeth to the pitch diameter.

Outside diameter is the overall diameter of the gear which is the pitch circle plus two addendums.

Pitch circle is a circle which has the radius of half the pitch diameter with its centre at the axis of the gear.

Pitch circumference is the circumference of the pitch circle.

Pitch diameter is the diameter of the pitch circle which is equal to the outside diameter minus two addendums.

Pressure angle is the angle formed by a line through the point of contact of two mating teeth and tangent to the two *base circles* and a line at right angles to the centre line of the gears.

Root circle is the circle formed by the bottoms of the tooth spaces.

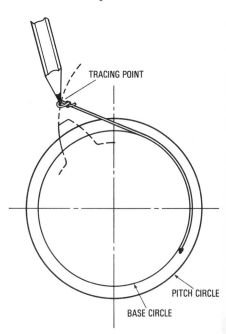

Fig. 11-49   Method of generating an involute

Root diameter is the diameter of the root circle.

Tooth thickness is the thickness of the tooth measured on the pitch circle.

Whole depth is the full depth of the tooth or the distance equal to the addendum plus the dedendum.

Working depth is the distance that a gear tooth extends into the tooth space of a mating gear which is equal to two addendums.

TABLE 11-6: RULES AND FORMULAS FOR SPUR GEARS

To Obtain	Knowing	Rule	Formula
Addendum	Circular pitch	Multiply the circular pitch by .3183.	$A = CP \times .3183$
Addendum	Diametral pitch	Divide 1 by the diametral pitch.	$A = \dfrac{1}{DP}$
Centre distance	Circular pitch	Multiply the number of teeth in both gears by the circular pitch, and divide the product by 6.2832.	$CD = \dfrac{(N + n) \times CP}{6.2832}$
Centre distance	Diametral pitch	Divide the total number of teeth in both gears by twice the diametral pitch.	$CD = \dfrac{N + n}{2 \times DP}$
Chordal (corrected) addendum	Pitch diameter Addendum Number of teeth	Subtract from 1 the cosine of the result of 90° divided by the number of teeth. Multiply this result by half the pitch diameter. To this product, add the addendum.	$CA = \left[\left(1 - \cos \dfrac{90}{N}\right) \dfrac{PD}{2} \right] + A$
Chordal thickness	Pitch diameter and Number of teeth	Divide 90 by the number of teeth; find the sine of this result and multiply by the pitch diameter.	$CT = \sin \dfrac{90}{N} \times PD$
Circular pitch	Centre to Centre distance	Multiply centre to centre distance by 6.2832, and divide the product by the total number of teeth in both gears.	$CP = \dfrac{CD \times 6.2832}{N + n}$
Circular pitch	Diametral pitch	Divide 3.1416 by the diametral pitch.	$CP = \dfrac{3.1416}{DP}$
Circular pitch	Pitch diameter and Number of teeth	Multiply pitch diameter by 3.1416 and divide by the number of teeth.	$CP = \dfrac{PD \times 3.1416}{N}$
Clearance	Circular pitch	Divide circular pitch by 20.	$Cl = \dfrac{CP}{20}$
Clearance	Diametral pitch	Divide .157 by the diametral pitch.	$Cl = \dfrac{.157}{DP}$
Dedendum	Circular pitch	Multiply the circular pitch by .3683.	$D = CP \times .3683$

Table 11-6: Continued

To Obtain	Knowing	Rule	Formula
Dedendum	Diametral pitch	Divide 1.157 by the diametral pitch.	$D = \dfrac{1.157}{DP}$
Diametral pitch	Circular pitch	Divide 3.1416 by the circular pitch.	$DP = \dfrac{3.1416}{CP}$
Diametral pitch	Number of teeth and Outside diameter	Add 2 to the number of teeth and divide the sum by the outside diameter.	$DP = \dfrac{N + 2}{OD}$
Diametral pitch	Number of teeth and Pitch diameter	Divide the number of teeth by the pitch diameter.	$DP = \dfrac{N}{PD}$
Number of teeth	Outside diameter and Diametral pitch	Multiply the outside diameter by the diametral pitch and subtract 2.	$N = OD \times DP - 2$
Number of teeth	Pitch diameter and Circular pitch	Multiply the pitch diameter by 3.1416 and divide by the circular pitch.	$N = \dfrac{PD \times 3.1416}{CP}$
Number of teeth	Pitch diameter and Diametral pitch	Multiply the pitch diameter by the diametral pitch.	$N = PD \times DP$
Outside diameter	Number of teeth and Circular pitch	Add 2 to the number of teeth and multiply the sum by the circular pitch. Divide this product by 3.1416.	$OD = \dfrac{(N + 2) \times CP}{3.1416}$
Outside diameter	Number of teeth and Diametral pitch	Add 2 to the number of teeth and divide the sum by the diametral pitch.	$OD = \dfrac{N + 2}{DP}$
Outside diameter	Pitch diameter and Diametral pitch	Add 2 to the pitch diameter and divide by the diametral pitch.	$OD = PD + \dfrac{2}{DP}$
Pitch diameter	Number of teeth and Circular pitch	Multiply the number of teeth by the circular pitch and divide by 3.1416.	$PD = \dfrac{N \times CP}{3.1416}$
Pitch diameter	Number of teeth and Diametral pitch	Divide the number of teeth by the diametral pitch.	$PD = \dfrac{N}{DP}$
Pitch diameter	Outside diameter and Number of teeth	Multiply the number of teeth by the outside diameter, and divide the product by the number of teeth plus two.	$PD = \dfrac{N \times OD}{N + 2}$

Table 11-6: Continued

To Obtain	Knowing	Rule	Formula
Tooth thickness	Circular pitch	Divide the circular pitch by 2.	$T = \dfrac{CP}{2}$
Tooth thickness	Circular pitch	Multiply the circular pitch by .5.	$T = CP \times .5$
Tooth thickness	Diametral pitch	Divide 1.5708 by the diametral pitch.	$T = \dfrac{1.5708}{DP}$
Whole depth	Circular pitch	Multiply the circular pitch by .6866.	$WD = CP \times .6866$
Whole depth	Diametral pitch	Divide 2.157 by the diametral pitch.	$WD = \dfrac{2.157}{DP}$

INCH GEARS AND GEAR CUTTING

INVOLUTE GEAR CUTTERS

Gear cutters are an example of formed cutters. This type of cutter is sharpened on the face and ensures exact duplication of the shape of the teeth, regardless of how far back the face of the tooth has been ground.

Gear cutters are available in many sizes ranging from 1 to 48 diametral pitch. Cutters for teeth smaller than 48 diametral pitch are available as special cutters. Comparative sizes of teeth ranging from 4 DP to 16 DP are shown in Fig. 11-50.

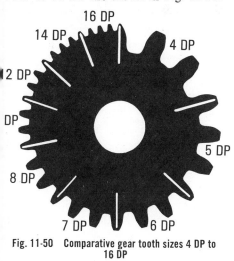

Fig. 11-50 Comparative gear tooth sizes 4 DP to 16 DP

When gear teeth are cut on any gear, a cutter must be chosen to suit both the diametral pitch and the number of teeth. The tooth space for a small pinion cannot be of the same shape as the tooth space for a large mating gear. The teeth on smaller gears must be more "curved" to prevent binding of meshing gear teeth. Therefore, sets of gear cutters are made in a series of slightly different shapes to permit the cutting of any desired number of teeth in a gear, with the assurance that the teeth will mesh properly with those of another gear of the *same diametral pitch.*

These cutters are generally made in sets of eight and are numbered from 1 to 8 (Fig. 11-51). Notice the gradual change in shape from the #1 cutter, which has almost straight sides, to the much more curved sides of the #8 cutter. As shown in Table 11-7, the #1 cutter is used for cutting any number of teeth in a gear from 135 teeth to a rack, while the #8 cutter will cut only 12 and 13 teeth. It should be noted that in order for gears to mesh, they must be of the same diametral pitch; the cutter number permits *only* a more accurate meshing of the teeth.

Some gear cutter manufacturers have augmented the set of eight cutters with seven additional cutters in half sizes, making a total 15 cutters in the set, num-

bered 1, 1-1/2, 2, 2-1/2, etc. In the half series, a #1-1/2 cutter would be used to cut from 80 to 134 teeth, while a 7-1/2 cutter would cut 13 teeth only (Table 11-7).

EXAMPLE:
A 10 DP gear and a pinion in mesh have 100 teeth and 24 teeth respectively. What cutters should be used to cut these gears?

TABLE 11-7: INVOLUTE GEAR CUTTERS	
Cutter Number	**Range**
1	135 teeth to a rack
1-1/2	80 to 134 teeth
2	55 to 134 "
2-1/2	42 to 54 "
3	35 to 54 "
3-1/2	30 to 34 "
4	26 to 34 "
4-1/2	23 to 25 "
5	21 to 25 "
5-1/2	19 and 20 "
6	17 to 20 "
6-1/2	15 and 16 "
7	14 to 16 "
7-1/2	13 teeth
8	12 to 13 teeth

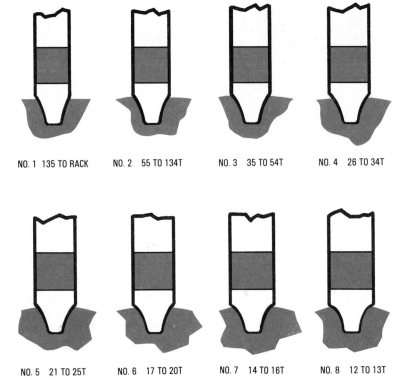

NO. 1 135 TO RACK   NO. 2 55 TO 134T   NO. 3 35 TO 54T   NO. 4 26 TO 34T

NO. 5 21 TO 25T   NO. 6 17 TO 20T   NO. 7 14 TO 16T   NO. 8 12 TO 13T

Courtesy The Butterfield Division, Union Twist Drill Co.

Fig. 11-51   Involute profiles for a set of gear cutters

Cutter Selection

Since the gears are in mesh, both must be cut with a 10 DP cutter.

A #2 cutter should be used to cut the teeth on the gear, since it will cut from 55 to 134 teeth.

A #5 cutter should be used to cut the pinion, since it cuts from 21 to 25 teeth.

TO CUT A SPUR GEAR

The procedure for machining a spur gear is outlined in the following example.

EXAMPLE:

A 52-tooth gear with an 8 diametral pitch is required.

Procedure

1. Calculate all the necessary gear data.

   i) Outside diameter $= \dfrac{N + 2}{DP}$

   $= \dfrac{54}{8}$

   $= 6.750$ in.

   ii) Whole depth of tooth $= \dfrac{2.157 \text{ in.}}{DP}$

   $= \dfrac{2.157 \text{ in.}}{8}$

   $= .2697$ in.

   iii) Cutter number $= 3$ (35 to 54 teeth)

   iv) Indexing (using Cincinnati standard plate)

   $= \dfrac{40}{N}$

   $= \dfrac{40}{52}$

   $= \dfrac{10}{13} \times \dfrac{3}{3}$

   $= \dfrac{30 \text{ holes on the}}{39 \text{-hole circle}}$

2. Turn the gear blank to the proper dimensions.

3. Press the gear blank firmly onto the mandrel.

   NOTE: If the blank was turned on a mandrel, be sure that it is tight because the heat caused by turning might have expanded the blank slightly.

4. Mount the index head and footstock, and check the alignment of the index centres (Fig. 11-52).

5. Set the dividing head so that the index pin fits into a hole on the 39-hole circle and the sector arms are set for 30 holes.

   NOTE: Do not count the hole in which the pin is engaged.

Courtesy Kostel Enterprises Ltd.

Fig. 11-52   Checking the alignment of the index centres with a dial indicator

6. Mount the mandrel (and workpiece), with the large end toward the indexing head, between the index centres.

   NOTE: i) The footstock centre should be adjusted up tightly into the mandrel and locked in position.

   ii) The dog should be tightened properly on the mandrel and the tail of the dog should not bind in the slot.

iii) The tail of the dog should then be locked in the driving fork of the dividing head by means of the set screws. This will ensure that there will be no play between the dividing head and the mandrel.

iv) The dog should be far enough from the gear blank to ensure that the cutter will not hit the dog when the gear is being cut.

7. Move the table close to the column to keep the setup as rigid as possible.

8. Mount an 8 DP — #3 cutter on the milling machine arbor over the approximate centre of the gear. Be sure to have the cutter rotating in the direction of the indexing head.

9. Centre the gear blank with the cutter by either of the following methods:

i) Place a square against the outside diameter of the gear (Fig. 11-53). With a pair of inside calipers or a rule, check the distance between the square and the side of the cutter. Adjust the table until the distances from both sides of the gear blank to the sides of the cutter are the same.

Courtesy Kostel Enterprises Ltd.

Fig. 11-53 Centring a gear cutter and the workpiece

ii) A more accurate method of centralizing the cutter is to use gauge blocks in lieu of the inside calipers or rule.

10. *LOCK THE CROSS SLIDE.*

11. Start the milling cutter and run the work under the cutter.

12. Raise the table until the cutter *just* touches the work. This can be done by using a chalk mark on the gear blank or a piece of paper between the gear blank and the cutter to indicate when the cutter is just touching the work.

13. Set the graduated feed collar on the vertical feed to zero.

14. Move the work clear of the cutter by means of the longitudinal feed handle and raise the table to about two-thirds the depth of the tooth (.180 in.); then *lock the knee clamp.*

NOTE: A special stocking cutter is sometimes used to rough out the teeth.

15. Slightly notch all gear teeth to check for correct indexing.

16. Rough out the first tooth and set the automatic feed trip dog after the cutter is clear of the work.

17. Return the table to the starting position.

NOTE: Clear the end of the work with the cutter.

18. Cut the remaining teeth and return the table to the starting position.

19. Loosen the knee clamp, raise the table to the proper depth of .270 in., and *lock the knee clamp.*

NOTE: It is advisable to remove the crank from the knee elevating shaft so that it will not be moved accidentally and change the setting.

20. Finish cut all teeth.

NOTE: After each tooth has been cut, the cutter should be stopped before the table is returned to prevent marring the finish on the gear teeth.

TABLE 11-8: RULES AND FORMULAS FOR METRIC MODULE SPUR GEARS			
TO OBTAIN	**KNOWING**	**RULE**	**FORMULA**
Addendum	Module	Addendum equals module	$A = M$
Circular pitch	Module	Multiply module by π	$CP = M \times 3.1416$
	Pitch diameter Number of teeth	Multiply pitch diameter by π and divide by number of teeth.	$CP = \dfrac{PD \times 3.1416}{N}$
	Outside diameter Number of teeth	Multiply outside diameter by π and divide by number of teeth minus 2.	$CP = \dfrac{OD \times 3.1416}{N - 2}$

Table 11-8: Continued on next page

TABLE 11-8 (cont'd)			
TO OBTAIN	**KNOWING**	**RULE**	**FORMULA**
Chordal thickness	Module and outside diameter	Divide 90° by the number of teeth. Find the sine of this angle and multiply by the pitch diameter.	$CT = PD \times \sin \dfrac{90}{N}$
	Module	Multiply module by π and divide by 2	$CT = \dfrac{M \times 3.1416}{2}$
	Circular pitch	Divide circular pitch by 2.	$CT = \dfrac{CP}{2}$
Clearance	Module	Multiply module by 0.166 mm.	$Cl = M \times 0.166$
Dedendum	Module	Multiply module by 1.166 mm.	$D = M \times 1.166$
Module	Pitch diameter and number of teeth	Divide pitch diameter by the number of teeth.	$M = \dfrac{PD}{N}$
	Circular pitch	Divide circular pitch by π.	$M = \dfrac{CP}{3.1416}$
	Outside diameter and number of teeth	Divide outside diameter by number of teeth + 2.	$M = \dfrac{OD}{N + 2}$
Number of teeth	Pitch diameter and module	Divide pitch diameter by the module.	$N = \dfrac{PD}{M}$
	Pitch diameter and circular pitch	Multiply pitch diameter by π and divide product by circular pitch.	$N = \dfrac{PD \times 3.1416}{CP}$
Outside diameter	Number of teeth and module	Add 2 to the number of teeth and multiply sum by module	$OD = (N + 2) \times M$
	Pitch diameter and module	Add 2 modules to pitch diameter.	$OD = PD + 2M$
Pitch diameter	Module and number of teeth	Multiply module by number of teeth.	$PD = M \times N$
	Outside diameter and module	Subtract 2 modules from outside diameter.	$PD = OD - 2M$

TABLE 11-8 (cont'd)			
TO OBTAIN	**KNOWING**	**RULE**	**FORMULA**
Pitch diameter	Number of teeth and outside diameter	Multiply number of teeth by outside diameter and divide product by number of teeth + 2.	$PD = \dfrac{N \times OD}{N + 2}$
Whole depth	Module	Multiply module by 2.166 mm.	$WD = M \times 2.166$
Centre to Centre distance	Pitch diameters	Divide the sum of the pitch diameters by 2.	$C/C \text{ Dist.} = \dfrac{PD_1 + PD_2}{2}$

METRIC GEARS AND GEAR CUTTING

Countries which have been using a metric system of measurement usually use the *module* system of gearing. The *module* of a gear equals the pitch diameter divided by the number of teeth ($M = \dfrac{PD}{N}$), whereas the diametral pitch of a gear is the ratio of the number of teeth to the pitch diameter ($DP = \dfrac{N}{PD}$). The diametral pitch of a gear is the *ratio of the number of teeth per inch of diameter* whereas *the module is an actual dimension*. Most of the terms used in diametral pitch gears remain the same for module gears; however, the method of calculating the dimensions has changed in some instances. Table 11-8 gives the necessary rules and formulas for metric spur gears.

METRIC MODULE GEAR CUTTERS

The most common metric gear cutters are available in modules ranging from 0.5 mm to 10 mm (Table 11-9). However, metric module gear cutters are available up to 75 mm. Any metric module size is available in a set of eight cutters, numbered from #1 to #8. The range of each cutter is reversed to those of diametral pitch cutters. For instance, a #1 metric module cutter will cut from 12 to 13 teeth; a #7 diametral pitch cutter will cut from 135 teeth to a rack. Table 11-9 shows the cutters available and the range of each cutter in the set.

TABLE 11-9: METRIC MODULE GEAR CUTTERS			
Module Size (mm)		**Milling Cutter Numbers**	
		Cutter No.	**for Cutting**
0.50	3.50		
0.75	3.75	1	12–13 Teeth
1.00	4.00		
1.25	4.50	2	14–16 Teeth
1.50	5.00	3	17–20 Teeth
1.75	5.50		
2.00	6.00	4	21–25 Teeth
2.25	6.50	5	26–34 Teeth
2.50	7.00		
2.75	8.00	6	35–54 Teeth
3.00	9.00	7	55–134 Teeth
3.25	10.00	8	135 Teeth to rack

EXAMPLE 1

A spur gear has a pitch diameter of 60 mm and 20 teeth.

Calculate:

a) module
b) circular pitch
c) addendum
d) outside diameter
e) dedendum
f) whole depth
g) cutter number

a) $M = \dfrac{PD}{N}$

$\quad = \dfrac{60}{20}$

$\quad = 3$ mm

b) $CP = M \times \pi$

$\quad = 3 \times 3.1416$

$\quad = 9.425$ mm

c) $A = M$

$\quad = 3$ mm

d) $OD = (N + 2) \times M$

$\quad = 22 \times 3$

$\quad = 66$ mm

e) $D = M \times 1.666$

$\quad = 3 \times 1.666$

$\quad = 4.998$ mm

f) $WD = M \times 2.166$

$\quad = 3 \times 2.166$

$\quad = 6.498$ mm

g) Cutter number (see Table 11-9).

$\quad = 3$

EXAMPLE 2

Two identical gears in mesh have a centre to centre distance of 120 mm. Each gear has 24 teeth.

Calculate:

a) pitch diameter
b) module
c) outside diameter
d) whole depth
e) circular pitch
f) chordal thickness

a) $PD = \dfrac{2 \times C/C \text{ (equal gears)}}{2}$

a) $\quad = \dfrac{2 \times 120}{2}$

$\quad = \dfrac{240}{2}$

$\quad = 120$ mm

b) $M = \dfrac{PD}{N}$

$\quad = \dfrac{120}{24}$

$\quad = 5$

c) $OD = (N + 2) \times M$

$\quad = 26 \times 5$

$\quad = 130$ mm

d) $WD = M \times 2.166$

$\quad = 5 \times 2.166$

$\quad = 10.83$ mm

e) $CP = M \times \pi$

$\quad = 5 \times 3.1416$

$\quad = 15.708$ mm

f) $CT = \dfrac{M \times \pi}{2}$

$\quad = \dfrac{5 \times 3.1416}{2}$

$\quad = 7.85$ mm

GEAR TOOTH MEASUREMENT

To ensure that the gear teeth are of the proper dimensions, they should be measured with a gear tooth vernier caliper. The caliper should be set to the corrected addendum, a dimension which may be found in most handbooks. Further information on the use of the gear tooth vernier caliper may be found in Chapter 3.

Gear sizes may also be accurately checked by measuring over wires or pins of a specific diameter, which have been placed in two diametrically opposite tooth spaces of the gear (Fig. 11-54A). For gears having an odd number of teeth, the wires are placed as nearly opposite as possible (Fig. 11-54B). A measurement taken over these wires is checked against tables found in most handbooks. These tables indicate the measurement over the wires

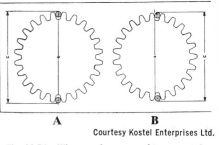

Fig. 11-54   Wires or pins are used to accurately check gear sizes

for any gear having a given number of teeth and a specific pressure angle. Since these tables are far too extensive to be printed in this book, the reader is asked to refer to any handbook for them.

In order to accurately measure inch gears, the diametral pitch and the number of teeth in the gear must be known. In order to measure metric gears, the module must be known. The wire or pin size to be used is determined as follows:

1. For external inch spur gears the wire or pin size is equal to 1.728 divided by the diametral pitch of the gear.

2. For internal inch spur gears, the wire size is equal to 1.44 divided by the diametral pitch of the gear.

3. Metric module gears are measured using a wire size equal to 1.728 multiplied by the module of the gear. The measurement over the wires should equal the value shown in the handbook tables multiplied by the module of the gear.

EXAMPLE (inch):

Determine the wire size and the measurement over the wires for a 10 diametral pitch external gear having 28 teeth and a 14.50° pressure angle.

Wire size $= \dfrac{1.728}{10}$

$\quad = .1728$ in.

By referring to handbook tables, the size over the wires for a gear having 28 teeth and a 14.50° pressure angle should be 30.4374 in. divided by the diametral pitch. Therefore the measurement over the wires should be

$$\frac{30.4374}{10}$$

$$= 3.0437 \text{ in.}$$

If the measurement is larger than this size, the pitch diameter is too large and the depth of cut will have to be increased. If it is less than the determined size, the gear is undersize. Gears having an odd number of teeth are calculated in a similar manner but using the proper tables for these gears.

HELICAL MILLING

The process of milling helical grooves, such as flutes in a drill, teeth in helical gears, or the worm thread on a shaft, is known as *helical milling*. It is performed on the universal milling machine by gearing the dividing head through the worm shaft to the leadscrew of the milling machine.

The term *spiral* is often used incorrectly in place of a *helix*.

A Helix is a theoretical line or path generated on a **cylindrical** surface by a cutting tool which is fed lengthwise at a uniform rate, while the cylinder is also rotated at a uniform rate (Fig. 11-55A).

The flutes on a drill or the threads on a bolt are examples of helices.

A Spiral is the path generated by a point moving at a fixed rate of advance along the surface of a **rotating cone or plane** (Fig. 11-55B). Threads on a wood screw and pipe threads are examples of conical spirals, while watch springs and scroll threads on a universal lathe chuck are examples of plane or flat spirals.

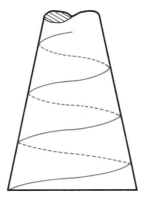

Fig. 11-55B   A spiral is produced on a conical surface

In order to cut either a metric or an inch helix, any two of the following must be known:

a) *The lead* of a helix is the longitudinal distance the helix advances axially in one complete revolution of the work.

b) *The angle of the helix* is formed by the intersection of the helix with the axis of the workpiece.

c) *The diameter (and circumference) of the workpiece.*

In comparing two different helices, it will be noticed that the greater the angle with the centre line, the shorter will be the lead. However, if the diameter is increased but the helix angle remains the same, the greater will be the lead. Thus it is evident that the lead of a helix varies with:

a) the diameter of the work

b) the angle of the helix

The relationship between the diameter (and circumference), the helix angle, and the lead is shown in Fig. 11-56. It will be noted that if the surface of the cylinder could be unwound to produce a flat surface, the helix would form the hypotenuse of a right-angled triangle, with the circumference forming the side opposite and the lead the side adjacent.

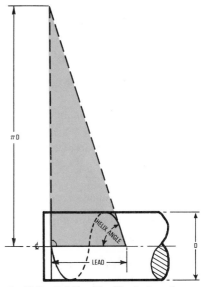

Fig. 11-56   Relationship of lead, circumference, and helix angle

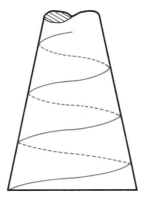

Fig. 11-55A   A helix will be generated if the work is turned and the tool moved along uniformly

CUTTING A HELIX

To cut a helix on a cylinder, the following steps are necessary:

1. Swing the table in the proper direction to the angle of the helix to ensure that a groove of the same contour as the cutter is produced.
2. The work must rotate one turn while the table travels lengthwise the distance equal to the lead. This is achieved by installing the proper change gears between the worm shaft on the dividing head, and on the milling machine leadscrew.

DETERMINING THE HELIX ANGLE

To ensure that a groove of the same contour as the cutter is produced, the table must be swung to the angle of the helix (Fig. 11-57A). The importance of this is shown in Fig. 11-57B.

Note that when the table is not swung (Fig. 11-57B), a helix having the proper lead but an improper contour will be generated. By referring to Fig. 11-56, it can easily be seen that the angle may be calculated as follows:

Tangent of the helix angle

$$= \frac{\text{circumference of the work}}{\text{lead of the helix}}$$

$$= \frac{3.1416 \times \text{diameter}}{\text{lead of the helix}}$$

EXAMPLE 1 (metric):
To what angle must a milling machine table be swivelled to cut a helix having a lead of 450 mm on a workpiece 40 mm in diameter?

Tangent of helix angle

$$= \frac{3.1416 \times \text{diameter (mm)}}{\text{lead of helix (mm)}}$$

$$= \frac{3.1416 \times 40}{450}$$

$$= 0.2796$$

$$= 15°31'$$

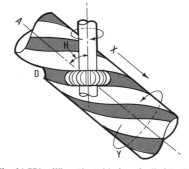

Fig. 11-57A When the table is swivelled to the correct helix angle, the exact profile of the cutter will be generated

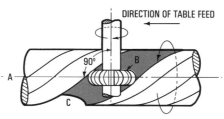

Fig. 11-57B An incorrect angle produces an incorrect profile

EXAMPLE 2 (inch):
To what angle must the milling machine table be swivelled to cut a helix having a lead of 10.882 in. on a piece of work 2 in. in diameter?

$$\text{Tangent of helix angle} = \frac{3.1416 \times D}{\text{lead of helix}}$$

$$= \frac{3.1416 \times 2}{10.882}$$

$$= \frac{6.2832}{10.882}$$

$$= .57739$$

$$\therefore \text{ Helix angle} = 30°$$

After the helix angle has been calculated, it is necessary to determine the *direction* in which to swivel the table to produce the proper hand of helix (that is, right- or left-hand).

DETERMINING THE DIRECTION TO SWING THE TABLE

In order to determine the hand of a helix, hold the cylinder on which the helix is cut in a horizontal plane with its axis running in a right-left direction.

If the helix slopes *down* and to the right, it is a right-hand helix (Fig. 11-58). A left-hand helix slopes *down* and to the left. When a *left-hand helix* is to be cut, the table of the milling machine must be swivelled in a clockwise direction (operator standing in front of the machine). A right-hand helix may be produced similarly by moving the right end of the table in towards the column or by moving it in a counterclockwise direction.

Fig. 11-58 The grooves of a right-hand helical cutter slope down and to the right

CALCULATING THE CHANGE GEARS TO PRODUCE THE REQUIRED LEAD

To cut a helix, it is necessary to have the work move lengthwise and rotate at the same time. The amount the work (and table) travels lengthwise as the work revolves one complete revolution is the *lead*. The rotation of the work is caused by gearing the worm shaft of the dividing head to the leadscrew of the machine (Fig. 11-59).

The pitch of the leadscrew on a metric milling machine is stated in millimetres. Most milling machine leadscrews have a 5 mm pitch and the dividing head has a ratio of 40 to 1. As the leadscrew revolves one turn, it would revolve the dividing

Courtesy Kostel Enterprises Ltd.

Fig. 11-59 Worm shaft and the leadscrew are connected for helical milling

head spindle 1/40 of a revolution. In order for the dividing head spindle (and work) to revolve one full turn, the leadscrew must make 40 complete revolutions. Therefore the lead of the machine would be 40 times the pitch of the leadscrew.

For metric calculations, the change gears required are calculated as follows:

$$\frac{\text{Lead of helix to be cut (mm)}}{\text{Lead of machine (mm)}}$$
$$= \frac{\text{product of driven gears}}{\text{product of driver gears}}$$

The normal change gears in a set are 24, 24, 28, 32, 36, 40, 44, 48, 56, 64, 72, 86, 100.

EXAMPLE:

Calculate the change gears required to cut a helix having a lead of 500 mm on a workpiece using a standard set of gears. The milling machine leadscrew has a pitch of 5 mm.

$$\frac{\text{Driven gears}}{\text{Driver gears}} = \frac{\text{lead of helix}}{\text{pitch of leadscrew} \times 40}$$
$$= \frac{500}{5 \times 40}$$
$$= \frac{500}{200}$$

$$= \frac{5}{2} \times \frac{20}{20}$$
$$= \frac{100}{40}$$

Driven gear $= 100$
Driver gear $= 40$

To cut a helix on an inch milling machine, it is necessary first to understand how to calculate the required change gears for any desired lead. Assume that the dividing head worm shaft is geared to the table leadscrew with equal gears (for example, both having 24-tooth gears). The dividing head ratio is 40:1, while a standard milling machine leadscrew has 4 threads/in. The leadscrew, as it revolves one turn, would revolve the dividing head spindle 1/40 of a revolution. In order for the dividing head spindle to revolve one turn, it would be necessary for the leadscrew to revolve 40 times. Thus the table would travel 40 × 1/4 in. or 10 in. while the work revolves one turn. Therefore, the lead of a milling machine is said to be 10 in. when the leadscrew (4 threads/in.) is connected to the dividing head (40:1 ratio) with equal gears.

In calculating the change gears required to cut any lead, the following formula may be used:

$$\frac{\text{Lead of helix to be cut}}{\text{Lead of machine (10 in.)}}$$
$$= \frac{\text{product of driven gears}}{\text{product of driver gears}}$$

The ratio of gears required to produce any lead on a milling machine having a leadscrew with 4 threads/in. is always equal to a fraction having the lead of the helix for the numerator and 10 for the denominator.

NOTE: The preceding formula may be inverted if preferred.

$$\frac{\text{Lead of the machine}}{\text{Lead of the helix}}$$

$$= \frac{\text{product of driver gears}}{\text{product of driven gears}}$$

EXAMPLE 1:

Calculate the change gears required to produce a helix having a lead of 25 in. on a piece of work. The available change gears have the following number of teeth: 24, 24, 28, 32, 40, 44, 48, 56, 64, 72, 86, 100.

SOLUTION:

Gear ratio

$$= \frac{\text{lead of helix (driven gears)}}{\text{lead of machine (driver gears)}}$$
$$= \frac{25}{10}$$

Since 10- and 25-tooth gears are not supplied with standard dividing heads, it is necessary to multiply the 25/10 ratio by a number that will suit the change gears available.

$$\text{Gear ratio} = \frac{25}{10} \times \frac{4}{4}$$
$$= \frac{100 \text{ (driven gear)}}{40 \text{ (driver gear)}}$$

As both 100-tooth and 40-tooth gears are available, simple gearing may be used.

EXAMPLE 2:

Calculate the change gears required to produce a helix having a lead of 27 in. The available change gears are as in Example 1.

SOLUTION:

Gear ratio

$$= \frac{\text{lead of helix (driven gears)}}{\text{lead of machine (driver gears)}}$$
$$= \frac{27}{10}$$

Since there are no gears in the set which are multiples of both 27 and 10, it is impossible to use simple gearing. Compound gearing must therefore be used, and it becomes necessary to factor the fraction $\dfrac{27}{10}$ as follows:

$$\text{Gear ratio} = \frac{27}{10}$$

$$= \frac{3}{2} \times \frac{9 \ (\text{driven})}{5 \ (\text{driver})}$$

It is now necessary to multiply both the numerator and denominator of each fraction by the same number in order to bring the ratio into the range of the gears available.

NOTE: This does not change the value of the fraction.

$$\frac{3 \times 16}{2 \times 16} = \frac{48}{32}$$

$$\frac{9 \times 8}{5 \times 8} = \frac{72}{40}$$

$$\text{The gear ratio} = \frac{48 \times 72 \ (\text{driven gears})}{32 \times 40 \ (\text{driver gears})}$$

∴ The driven gears are 48 and 72 and the driver gears are 32 and 40.

The gears would be placed in the train as follows (Fig. 11-59):

Gear on worm   72   (driven)
1st gear on stud   32   (driver)
2nd gear on stud   48   (driven)
Gear on leadscrew   40   (driver)

The preceding order is not absolutely necessary; the two driven gears may be interchanged and/or the two driver gears may be interchanged, *provided a driver is not interchanged with a driven gear.*

DIRECTION OF SPINDLE ROTATION

Fig. 11-59 illustrates the setup required to cut a right-hand helix. Note that the gear on the leadscrew and the worm gear revolve in the same direction. To cut a left-hand helix, the spindle must revolve in the opposite direction, and therefore an idler must be inserted as in Fig. 11-60. The idler in this case acts neither as a driven nor a

Courtesy Kostel Enterprises Ltd.

Fig. 11-60 A second idler reverses the direction of rotation

driver gear and is not considered in the calculation of the gear train. It acts merely as a means of changing the direction of rotation of the dividing head spindle. It should also be noted that the direction of spindle rotation for simple gearing will be opposite to that for compound gearing.

CUTTING SHORT LEAD HELICES

When it is necessary to cut leads smaller than those shown in most handbooks, it is advisable to disengage the dividing head worm and wormwheel and connect the change gears directly from the table leadscrew to the dividing head spindle, rather than to the worm shaft. This method permits machining leads to 1/40 of the leads shown in the handbook tables. Thus, if the machine is geared to cut a lead of 4.000 in. by connecting the worm shaft and the leadscrew, the same gearing would produce a lead of 1/40 × 4.000 in., or .100 in. when geared directly to the dividing head spindle.

PROBLEM:
A plain helical milling cutter is required to the following specifications:
Diameter: 4 in.
Number of teeth: 9
Helix: right hand
Helix angle: 25°
Rake angle: 10° positive radial rake
Angle of flute: 55°
Depth of flute: 1/2 in.

Length: 4 in.
Material: tool steel

Procedure

1. Turn blank to sizes indicated (Fig. 11-61).

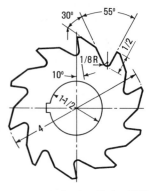

Courtesy Cincinnati Milacron Inc.

Fig. 11-61 Dimensions of a helical milling cutter (in inches)

2. Apply layout die to the end of the blank, and lay out as in Fig. 11-62A.
3. Lay out a line on periphery to indicate direction of the *right-hand* helix (Fig. 11-62B).

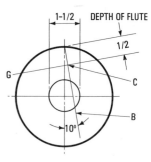

Courtesy Cincinnati Milacron Inc.

Fig. 11-62A Locating the first tooth on the cutter

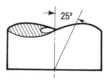

Courtesy Cincinnati Milacron Inc.

Fig. 11-62B Laying out the direction of the flute

4. Press the cutter blank firmly on the mandrel. If a threaded mandrel is used, be sure to tighten the nut securely.
5. Mount the dividing head and footstock.
6. Calculate the indexing for 9 divisions.

$$\text{Indexing} = \frac{40}{9}$$
$$= 4\text{-}4/9$$
$$= 4 \text{ turns, 8 holes on an}$$
18-hole circle

7. Set the sector arms to 8 holes on the 18-hole circle.
   NOTE: Do not count the hole in which the pin is engaged.
8. Disengage the index plate locking device.
9. Calculate the lead of the helix.

$$\text{Lead} = \frac{3.1416 \times D}{\tan \text{ helix angle}}$$
$$= 3.1416 \times D \cot \text{ helix angle}$$
$$(\text{since } \frac{1}{\tan} = \cot)$$
$$= 3.1416 \times 4 \times 2.1445$$
$$= 26.949 \text{ in.}$$

10. Consult any handbook for the change gears to cut the lead closest to 26.949 in. Obviously this is 27.
11. If a handbook is not available, change gears can be calculated for the closest lead which is 27 in.
12. Change gears required for 27 in. lead.

$$\frac{\text{Required lead}}{\text{Lead of machine}} = \frac{27}{10}$$
$$= \frac{9}{5} \times \frac{3}{2}$$
$$\frac{9 \times 8}{5 \times 8} = \frac{72}{40} \qquad \frac{3 \times 16}{2 \times 16} = \frac{48}{32}$$
$$\text{Change gears} = \frac{72 \times 48 \text{ (driven gears)}}{40 \times 32 \text{ (driver gears)}}$$

13. Mount the change gears, allowing a slight clearance between mating teeth.
14. Mount the work between the centres with the large end of the mandrel against the dividing head.
15. Swivel the table 25° in a counterclockwise direction.
16. Adjust the crossfeed handwheel until the table is about 1 in. (25 mm▪) from the face of the column. This is to ensure that the table clears the column when machining the cutter.
17. Swing the table back to "0."
18. Mount a 55° double-angle cutter so that it revolves towards the dividing head, and centre it approximately over the flute layout.
19. Rotate the blank until the flute layout is aligned with the cutter edge. This may be checked with a rule or straightedge (Fig. 11-63).

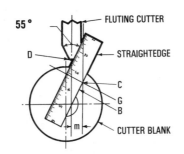

Courtesy Cincinnati Milacron Inc.

Fig. 11-63 Aligning the cutter blank with the cutter

20. Move the blank over, using the crossfeed for the distance of M (Fig. 11-63) or until the point C (Fig. 11-62A) is in line with the centre line of the cutter.
21. With the work clear of the cutter, set the depth to .500 in.
22. Rotate the table 25° and lock securely (right end in towards the column).
23. Carefully cut the first tooth space, checking the accuracy of the location and the depth.
24. Index for and cut the remaining flutes.
25. Remove the fluting cutter and mount a plain helical milling cutter.

26. Rotate the work (using the index crank) until a line at 30° to the side of the flute is parallel to the table (Fig. 11-62A). This may be checked by means of a surface gauge. The blank, however, may be rotated by indexing an amount equal to

$$90 - (30 + \frac{55}{2})$$
$$= 90 - 57.5$$
$$= 32.5° \ (32°30')$$

Indexing for 32°30':
$$32° \times 60' = 1920'$$
$$30' = 30'$$
$$32°30' = 1950'$$
$$= \frac{1950}{540}$$
$$= 3\frac{330}{540}$$
$$= 3\frac{11}{18}$$
$$= 3 \text{ turns} + 11 \text{ holes on the 18-hole circle}$$

27. Adjust the workpiece under the cutter.
28. With the cutter rotating, raise the table until the width of the land on the workpiece is about 1/32 in. (0.8 mm▪) wide.
29. Cut the secondary clearance (30° angle) on all teeth of the workpiece.

HELICAL MILLING CALCULATIONS (Metric)

For any helical milling calculations it is necessary to determine:
1. The angle at which the table must be swivelled to produce the proper helix angle.
2. The change gears required to revolve the work one turn as the work travels the distance of the lead.

For metric helices, these calculations are as follows:

1. Helix angle or angle to which to swivel the table.

Tangent ∠

$$= \frac{\text{circumference of workpiece}}{\text{lead of the helix}}$$

2. Change gears required.

$$\frac{\text{Driven gears}}{\text{Driver gears}}$$

$$= \frac{\text{lead of the helix}}{\text{pitch of the leadscrew} \times 40}$$

The normal change gears in a set are: 24, 24, 28, 32, 36, 40, 44, 48, 56, 64, 72, 86, 100.

EXAMPLE:

A lead of 480 mm is to be cut on a workpiece 40 mm in diameter. The leadscrew of the milling machine has a pitch of 5 mm. The dividing head has a ratio of 40:1 (40 turns of the crank are required to revolve the work one turn). Calculate the angle at which to set the table and the change gears necessary to produce the required lead:

a) *Helix angle*

Tan helix angle

$$= \frac{\text{circumference of work}}{\text{lead of helix}}$$

$$= \frac{40 \times 3.1416}{480}$$

$$= 0.26180$$

helix angle $= 14.67°$

b) *Change gears*

$$\frac{\text{Driven gears}}{\text{Driver gears}}$$

$$= \frac{\text{lead of the helix}}{\text{pitch of the leadscrew} \times 40}$$

$$= \frac{480}{5 \times 40}$$

$$= \frac{480}{200}$$

$$= \frac{12}{5} \quad \frac{(6 \times 2)}{(5 \times 1)}$$

$$\frac{6}{5} \times \frac{8}{8} = \frac{48}{40} \qquad \frac{2}{1} \times \frac{28}{28} = \frac{56}{28}$$

$$\text{Gears} = \frac{48}{40} \times \frac{56}{28}$$

Driven gears = 48 and 56

Driver gears = 40 and 28

RACK MILLING

A *rack*, in conjunction with a gear (pinion), is used to convert rotary motion into longitudinal motion. Racks are found on lathes, drill presses, and many other machines in a shop. A rack may be considered as a spur gear which has been straightened out so that the teeth are all in one plane. The circumference of the pitch circle of this gear would now become a straight line which would just touch the pitch circle of a gear meshing with the rack. Thus the pitch line of a rack is the distance of one addendum below the top of the tooth or $\dfrac{1}{DP}$ below the top of the tooth.

The pitch of a rack is measured in linear (circular) pitch, which is obtained by dividing 3.1416 by the diametral pitch:

$$\frac{3.1416}{DP}$$

The method used to cut a rack will depend generally on the length of the rack. If the rack is reasonably short (10 in. or less), it may be held in the milling machine vise in a position parallel to the cutter arbor. On short racks, the teeth may be

Courtesy Cincinnati Milacron Inc.

Fig. 11-64 Cutting the teeth on a helical rack using the rack milling and indexing attachments

cut by accurately moving the cross slide of the machine an amount equal to the circular pitch of the gear and then moving the table longitudinally to cut each tooth. If the rack is longer than the cross travel of the milling machine table, it must be held longitudinally on the table and is generally held in a special fixture.

The milling cutter is held in a *rack cutting attachment*. When cutting a straight tooth, the cutter is held at 90° to the position used when cutting a spur gear.

It is possible to mount slotting or narrow side milling cutters for milling operations that can be handled more easily by using the machine crossfeed.

RACK INDEXING ATTACHMENT

When cutting a rack using the rack milling attachment, the table is often moved (indexed) for each tooth by means of the *rack indexing attachment* (Fig. 11-64). This consists of an indexing plate with two diametrically opposed notches and a locking pin. Two change gears selected from a set of 14 are mounted as shown in Fig. 11-64. Different combinations of change gears permit the machine table to be moved accurately in increments, corresponding to the linear (circular) pitch of the rack, by making either a half turn or one complete turn of the plate. For indexing requiring one complete turn only, provision is made to close off one of the slots, thus preventing any error in indexing.

This attachment permits the indexing of all diametrical pitches from 4 to 32, as well as all circular pitches from 1/8 in. to 3/4 in., varying by 16ths. The following table movements can also be produced: 1/7 in., 1/6 in., 1/5 in., 2/7 in., 1/3 in., and 2/5 in.

HELICAL GEARING

Helical gearing requires a thorough knowledge of all the aspects of spur gearing, as well as the formulas and procedures used in helical milling. In helical (inch)

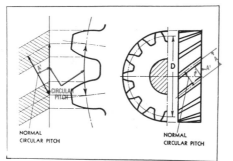

Fig. 11-65 Relationship between circular pitch and normal circular pitch

gear cutting two new terms are encountered: *normal circular pitch* and *normal diametrical pitch.*

The *normal circular pitch* is the distance from a point on one tooth to a corresponding point on the next tooth, measured on the pitch circle at right angles to the face of the tooth. The *circular pitch* is measured on the face of the gear in a plane at right angles to the axis of the gear. Fig. 11-65 illustrates the relationship between the circular pitch and the normal circular pitch. It will be noted that a right-angle triangle is formed, with a line representing the circular pitch as the hypotenuse and a line representing the normal circular pitch as the side opposite. By simple geometry, it may be proven that the angle a is equal to the angle a_1, which is the angle of the helix. Therefore, in the triangle illustrated in Fig. 11-65, the cos helix

$$\text{angle } a = \frac{\text{normal circular pitch}}{\text{circular pitch}}$$

Therefore, the relationship between normal circular pitch and circular pitch is exactly proportional to the length of these lines. The number of teeth in a helical and a spur gear of the same size and pitch will also be proportional to the length of these lines.

It is obvious that the circular pitch will increase as the helix angle increases; therefore, the greater the helix angle, the fewer the teeth in a helical gear as compared to a spur gear of the same pitch diameter and diametrical pitch.

Since most gearing is calculated on the diametral pitch system, it will be necessary to convert the circular pitch into diametral pitch terms. Referring to the spur gearing formulas, $DP = \dfrac{3.1416}{CP}$ or $CP = \dfrac{3.1416}{DP}$.

Since *normal diametral pitch* bears the same relation to *normal circular pitch* as *diametral pitch* does to *circular pitch*, the following formulas will apply:

$$NDP = \frac{3.1416}{NCP}$$

$$NCP = \frac{3.1416}{NDP}$$

Referring to Fig. 11-65, note that the cos helix angle $= \dfrac{NCP}{CP}$. This may be converted to diametral pitch as follows:

$$\text{Cos helix angle} = \frac{NCP}{CP}$$

$$= \frac{\left(\dfrac{3.1416}{NDP}\right)}{\left(\dfrac{3.1416}{DP}\right)}$$

$$= \frac{3.1416}{NDP} \times \frac{DP}{3.1416}$$

$$= \frac{DP}{NDP}$$

$\therefore$ cosine helix angle

$$= \frac{DP}{NDP}$$

Other formulas may be derived as follows:

$$NDP = \frac{DP}{\cos \text{ helix angle}}$$

$$DP = NDP \times \cos \text{ helix angle}$$

TABLE 11-10: RULES FOR CALCULATING INCH HELICAL GEARS

No. of Rule	To Find	Rule	Formula
1	Addendum	Divide 1 by the normal diametral pitch.	$A = \dfrac{1}{NDP}$
2	Cutter number	Divide the number of teeth by the cube of the cosine of the helix angle.	$CN = \dfrac{N}{(\cos \angle)^3}$
3	Helix angle of teeth	Divide the normal circular pitch by the circular pitch. The quotient equals the cosine of the helix angle.	$\cos \angle = \dfrac{NCP}{CP}$
4	Helix angle of teeth	Divide the diametral pitch by the normal diametral pitch. The quotient equals the cosine of the helix angle.	$\cos \angle = \dfrac{DP}{NDP}$
5	Helix angle of teeth	Divide the number of teeth by the product of the normal diametral pitch and the pitch diameter. The quotient equals the cosine of the helix angle.	$\cos \angle = \dfrac{N}{NDP \times PD}$
6	Lead of the helix	Divide the product of the number of teeth and the circular pitch by the tangent of the helix angle.	$Lead = \dfrac{N \times CP}{\tan \angle}$
7	Lead of the helix	Multiply the pitch diameter by 3.1416 times the cotangent of the helix angle.	$L = 3.1416 \times PD \cot \angle$
8	Normal diametral pitch	Divide the number of teeth by the cosine of the helix angle, add 2, and divide the sum by the outside diameter.	$NDP = \left(\dfrac{N}{\cos \angle} + 2 \right) \div OD$
9	Normal circular pitch	Multiply the circular pitch by the cosine of the helix angle.	$NCP = CP \cos \angle$
10	Outside diameter of gear blank	Add .6366 times the normal circular pitch to the pitch diameter.	$OD = .6366 \times NCP + PD$
11	Pitch diameter	Multiply the product of the circular pitch and the number of teeth by .3183.	$PD = .3183 \times CP \times N$
12	Pitch diameter	Multiply the product of the normal circular pitch and the number of teeth by .3183 and divide the product by the cosine of the helix angle.	$PD = \dfrac{.3183 \times NCP \times N}{\cos \angle}$
13	Pitch diameter	Divide the number of teeth by the product of the normal diametral pitch and the cosine of the helix angle.	$PD = \dfrac{N}{NDP \cos \angle}$
14	Thickness of tooth at pitch line	Divide 1.571 by the normal diametral pitch.	$T = \dfrac{1.571}{NDP}$
15	Whole depth of tooth	Divide 2.157 by the normal diametral pitch.	$WD = \dfrac{2.157}{NDP}$

TABLE 11-11: HELICAL GEAR CUTTER (INCH) NOMOGRAPH

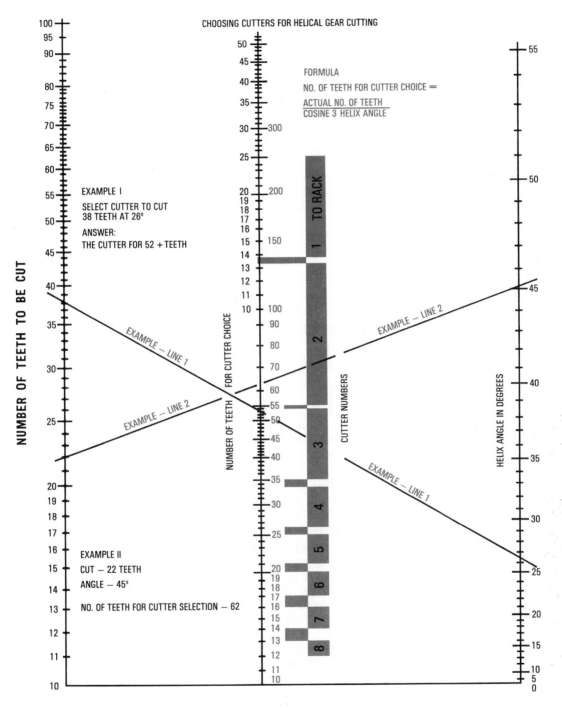

CHOOSING CUTTERS FOR HELICAL GEAR CUTTING

FORMULA

NO. OF TEETH FOR CUTTER CHOICE =

$$\frac{\text{ACTUAL NO. OF TEETH}}{\text{COSINE 3 HELIX ANGLE}}$$

EXAMPLE I

SELECT CUTTER TO CUT
38 TEETH AT 26°

ANSWER:
THE CUTTER FOR 52 + TEETH

EXAMPLE — LINE 1

EXAMPLE — LINE 2

EXAMPLE — LINE 2

EXAMPLE — LINE 1

EXAMPLE II

CUT — 22 TEETH

ANGLE — 45°

NO. OF TEETH FOR CUTTER SELECTION — 62

NUMBER OF TEETH TO BE CUT

NUMBER OF TEETH FOR CUTTER CHOICE

CUTTER NUMBERS

HELIX ANGLE IN DEGREES

TO RACK

Courtesy N. Durst

CUTTER SELECTION

The type of cutter used for cutting helical gears is the same as for spur gears. However, the diametral pitch of a spur gear, and the cutter, now becomes the normal diametral pitch of the helical gear. The thickness of the cutter at the pitch line for cutting helical gears should be equal to one-half the normal circular pitch.

When a spur gear is being cut, the number of the cutter used is dependent on the number of teeth being cut (Table 11-9). However, when a helical gear is being cut, this table does not apply since the shape of the tooth would be changed because of the helix angle of the gear teeth. To determine the proper cutter for machining a helical gear, it is necessary to consider the number of teeth being cut (Table 11-9). angle of the tooth. The cutter number may be determined by dividing the number of teeth by the cube of the cosine of the angle.

Thus the cutter number $= \dfrac{N}{(\cos a)^3}$

EXAMPLE:

Determine the cutter number required to cut 38 teeth on a helical gear having an angle of 45°.

Number of teeth for which to select the cutter $= \dfrac{N}{(\cos a)^3}$

$= \dfrac{38}{(.7071)^3}$

$= \dfrac{38}{.3534}$

$= 108$

Therefore, a #2 cutter would be used since it cuts from 55 to 134 teeth.

HELICAL GEAR CALCULATIONS AND FORMULAS

Many of the calculations and formulas that apply to spur gears also apply to helical gears. Others may be calculated from Table 11-10 as required. It is well to remember the following when making helical gears:

a) The diametral pitch of a spur gear is the normal diametral pitch of a helical gear.

b) The normal diametral pitch of the helical gear is the diametral pitch of the cutter.

c) The cutter number must be calculated using the formula:

Number of teeth for which to select a cutter $= \dfrac{N}{(\cos a)^3}$

The alignment chart (Table 11-11) will be found convenient when it is necessary to determine cutter numbers for helical gears.

By means of a straightedge, align the actual number of teeth in the left-hand column with the helix angle in the right-hand column. Read the cutter number from the centre column where the straightedge crosses the line.

METRIC HELICAL GEAR CALCULATIONS

Most metric module helical gear calculations are similar to those for diametral pitch helical gears and module spur gears. There are, however, certain changes which must be understood before any calculations are attempted. Refer to Fig. 11-65 to more clearly understand the following terms.

The *circular pitch* (CP) is the distance from one tooth to a corresponding point on the next tooth, measured on the pitch circle. The *real (pitch) module* (M) is calculated on the pitch circle.

The *normal circular pitch* (NCP) is the distance from one tooth to a corresponding point on the next tooth measured at right angles to the tooth face. The *normal (pitch) module* (nM) is calculated on this distance.

For all other calculations, see sections on metric spur gears and helical milling. Table 11-12 covers the rules and formulas for calculating metric module helical gears.

EXAMPLE:

It is required to cut a helical metric 5 (normal) module gear having 38 teeth. The pitch diameter of the gear is 200 mm. Calculate:

a) real module (M)
b) circular pitch (CP)
c) normal circular pitch (nCP)
d) addendum (A)
e) outside diameter (OD)
f) depth of tooth (WD)
g) helix angle ($\angle$)
h) lead (L)
i) indexing

SOLUTION:

a) $M = \dfrac{200}{38}$
   $= 5.263$ mm

b) $CP = M \times 3.1416$
   $= 5.263 \times 3.1416$
   $= 16.534$ mm

c) $nCP = nM \times 3.1416$
   $= 5 \times 3.1416$
   $= 15.708$ mm

d) $A = M$
   $= 5$ mm

e) $OD = PD + 2\,nM$
   $= 200 + 10$
   $= 210$ mm

f) $WD = nM \times 2.166$
   $= 10.83$ mm

g) $\cos \angle = \dfrac{nM}{M}$
   $= \dfrac{5}{5.2632}$
   $= 0.950$
   $= 18.186°$

h) $L = PD \times 3.1416 \times \cot \angle$
   $= 200 \times 3.1416 \times 3.0445$
   $= 1913$ mm

i) Indexing $= \dfrac{40}{N}$
   $= \dfrac{40}{38}$
   $= 1\text{-}2/38$
   $= 1\text{-}1/19$
   $= 1$ turn of crank $+ 1$ hole in the 19-hole circle

TABLE 11-12: RULES AND FORMULAS FOR METRIC MODULE HELICAL GEARS			
TO OBTAIN	**KNOWING**	**RULE**	**FORMULA**
Addendum (A)	Normal module	Addendum equals normal module	$A = nM$
Dedendum (D)	Normal module	Multiply normal module by 1.166	$D = nM \times 1.166$
Circular pitch (CP)	Module	Multiply the module by π	$CP = M \times 3.1416$
	Normal circular pitch Helix angle	Divide the normal circular pitch by the cosine of the helix angle.	$CP = \dfrac{nCP}{Cos \angle}$
	Normal module Helix angle	Multiply the normal module by π and divide the product by the cosine of the helix angle.	$CP = \dfrac{nM \times 3.1416}{Cos \angle}$
Normal Circular Pitch (nCP)	Normal module	Multiply normal module by π	$nCP = nM \times 3.1416$
	Circular pitch Helix angle	Multiply the circular pitch by the cosine of the helix angle.	$nCP = CP \times Cos \angle$
	Pitch diameter Helix angle Number of teeth	Multiply the pitch circumference by the cosine of the helix angle and divide the product by the number of teeth.	$nCP = \dfrac{PD \times 3.1416 \times Cos \angle}{N}$
Helix angle of Teeth ($<$)	Normal module Module	Normal module divided by the module equals the cosine of the helix angle.	$Cos \angle = \dfrac{nM}{M}$
	Number of teeth Normal module Pitch diameter	The number of teeth multiplied by the normal module and divided by the pitch diameter equals the cosine of the helix angle.	$Cos \angle = \dfrac{N \times nM}{PD}$
Lead of helix (L)	Pitch diameter Helix angle	Multiply the circumference of the pitch circle by the cotangent of the helix angle.	$L = PD \times 3.1416 \times Cot \angle$
	Number of teeth Module Helix angle	Multiply the number of teeth by the module times 3.1416. Multiply the product by the cotangent of the helix angle.	$L = N \times M \times 3.1416 \times Cot \angle$

		Table 11-12 cont'd	
TO OBTAIN	**KNOWING**	**RULE**	**FORMULA**
Normal module (nM)	Module Helix angle	Multiply the module by the cosine of the helix angle.	$nM = M \times \text{Cos } \angle$
	Normal circular pitch	Divide the normal circular pitch by π.	$nM = \dfrac{nCP}{3.1416}$
	Circular pitch Helix angle	Multiply the circular pitch by the cosine of the helix angle and divide the product by π.	$nM = \dfrac{CP \times \text{Cos } \angle}{3.1416}$
Module (M)	Normal module Helix angle	Divide normal module by the cosine of the helix angle.	$M = \dfrac{nM}{\text{Cos } \angle}$
	Circular pitch	Divide the circular pitch by π.	$M = \dfrac{CP}{3.1416}$
	Normal circular pitch Helix angle	Divide the normal circular pitch by π times the cosine of the helix angle.	$M = \dfrac{nCP}{3.1416 \times \text{Cos } \angle}$
Outside diameter (OD)	Pitch diameter Normal module	Add 2 normal modules to the pitch diameter.	$OD = PD + 2\,nM$
	Normal module Number of teeth Helix angle	Divide the normal module by the cosine of the helix angle and add 2 to the quotient. Multiply this number by the normal module.	$OD = nM \left(\dfrac{N}{\text{Cos } \angle} + 2 \right)$
Pitch diameter (PD)	Normal module Number of teeth	Multiply the number of teeth by the normal module and divide the product by the cosine of the helix angle.	$PD = \dfrac{N \times nM}{\text{Cos } \angle}$
Number of teeth (N)	Pitch diameter Circular pitch	Multiply the pitch diameter by π and divide the product by the circular pitch.	$N = \dfrac{PD \times 3.1416}{nCP}$
	Pitch diameter Module	Divide the pitch diameter by the module.	$N = \dfrac{PD}{M}$
	Pitch diameter Normal module Helix angle	Multiply the pitch diameter by the cosine of the helix angle and divide the product by the normal module.	$N = \dfrac{PD \times \text{Cos } \angle}{nM}$
Whole depth of Tooth (WD)	Normal module	Multiply the normal module by 2.166	$WD = nM \times 2.166$

TO MILL AN INCH HELICAL GEAR

The following problem will serve as a guide in making helical gear calculations. If the steps are followed in sequence, little difficulty should be encountered.

PROBLEM:

It is required to cut two mating helical gears having a 3:2 ratio, 12 diametral pitch, and 3.000 in. centre-to-centre distance.

CALCULATIONS

PITCH DIAMETERS

The sum of the pitch diameters is 3.000 in. × 2 = 6.000 in. Since the total of the ratios is 3 + 2 = 5, the large gear will occupy 3/5 of the total distance of the pitch diameters (6.000 in.), while the pinion will be 2/5 of the total distance.

PD of gear = 3/5 × 6.0 = 3.600 in.
PD of pinion = 2/5 × 6.0 = 2.400 in.
————————
6.000 in.
(proof)

NUMBER OF TEETH

$$N = DP \times PD$$

Number of teeth in gear = 3.6 × 12
= 43.2

Number of teeth in pinion = 2.4 × 12
= 28.8

Since it is impossible to cut 43.2 or 28.8 teeth, it is necessary to change the number of teeth in each gear to two whole numbers which have a 3:2 ratio. The teeth of the gear are cut at an angle, and there will be fewer teeth in a helical gear than in a corresponding spur gear. It is therefore necessary to select two whole numbers which are *less* than 43.2 and 28.8 and which have a ratio of 3:2.

The largest numbers under 43.2 and 28.8 having this ratio are 42 and 28. Therefore:

Number of teeth in gear = 42
Number of teeth in pinion = 28

Fig. 11-66   8 DP, 3:1 ratio

DIAMETRAL PITCH

$$DP = \frac{N}{PD}$$

Diametral pitch of gear = $\frac{42}{3.6}$
= 11.666 teeth

OR

Diametral pitch of pinion = $\frac{28}{2.4}$
= 11.666 teeth
(proof)

It has now been established that the diametral pitch, or the number of teeth per inch of pitch diameter of each gear, is 11.666. It is, however, required to use a 12 DP cutter which will cut 12 teeth per inch of pitch diameter. This will necessitate swinging the table to the proper helix angle to cut the gears.

HELIX ANGLE

$$Cos\ helix\ angle = \frac{DP}{NDP}$$

$$= \frac{11.666}{12}$$

$$= .97216$$

∴ helix angle = 13°33′

OUTSIDE DIAMETER

$$OD = PD + \frac{2}{DP}$$

Outside diameter of gear = $3.600 + \frac{2}{12}$
= 3.766 in.

Outside diameter of pinion = $2.400 + \frac{2}{12}$
= 2.566 in.

LEADS

Lead = PD × 3.1416 cot helix angle

Lead of gear = 3.6 × 3.1416 cot 13°33′
= 3.6 × 3.1416 × 4.1493
= 46.926 in.

Lead of pinion = 2.4 × 3.1416 × 4.1493
= 31.285 in.

CHANGE GEARS

The change gears may be determined from the tables supplied with the dividing head or most machinery handbooks. To determine the change gears for the gear having a lead of 46.926 in., check a handbook for the closest lead which is 46.880 in. The gears for this lead are as follows:

$$\frac{Driven\ gears}{Driver\ gears} = \frac{100 \times 72}{32 \times 48}$$

The error in this lead is 46.926 − 46.880 = .046 in. in approximately 47 in. Change gears for pinion having a lead of 31.285 in.; the closest lead is 31.270 in.

$$\frac{Driven\ gears}{Driver\ gears} = \frac{86 \times 64}{40 \times 44}$$

The error in this lead is 31.285 − 31.270 = .015 in. in approximately 31 in.

NOTE: If a chart or handbook is not available, the change gears may be calculated by *continued fractions* which are dealt with later in this chapter where the examples for this pinion are shown.

CUTTER NUMBER

Number of teeth in gear for which to select a cutter

$$= \frac{\text{number of teeth in gear}}{(\cos \text{ helix angle})^3}$$

$$= \frac{42}{(.97216)^3}$$

$$= 45.71 \text{ teeth}$$

A #3 cutter would be used since it will cut from 35 to 54 teeth.

Number of teeth in pinion for which to select a cutter

$$= \frac{28}{(.97216)^3}$$

$$= 30.47 \text{ teeth}$$

A #4 cutter would be selected since it will cut from 26 to 34 teeth.

The alignment chart (Table 11-11) may be used to determine the proper cutter number. This will eliminate the need to calculate the required number of the cutter.

CUTTING THE GEARS

The setup for cutting the gears is exactly the same as for helical milling. Having made all the necessary calculations for the gear and the pinion, list all the pertinent information, including the depth of tooth and indexing for both gears, on a separate sheet of paper as follows.

Procedure

1. Mount the dividing head at the end of the milling machine table.
2. Mount the work between centres.
3. Set the indexing crank and the sector arms.
4. Disengage the index plate locking device.
5. Mount the change gears as required.
6. Swing the table to the helix angle and in the proper direction.

   NOTE: When cutting mating helical gears for parallel shafts, it is always necessary to cut one gear with a left-hand helix and the other with a right-hand helix so that the gears will mesh.

7. Move the table, using the crossfeed handle, to within 25 mm of the column to ensure clearance between the table and column.
8. Swing the table back to zero.
9. Mount the cutter on the arbor over the approximate centre of the work.
10. Centre the work with the cutter.
11. Raise the table until the cutter just touches the work.
12. Set the vertical feed screw collar to zero.
13. With the work clear of the cutter, raise the table to the proper depth of the tooth.
14. Swing the table in the proper direction.

    NOTE: When the table is swung in the other direction to cut the opposite helix, it will be necessary to add an idler to the gear train in order to reverse the direction of rotation of the work.

15. Nick each tooth to ensure the proper indexing.
16. Cut all teeth.

    NOTE: Lower the table one full turn of the handwheel before returning it to the starting position to overcome backlash and so that the cutter will not damage the finish on the teeth.

HELICAL GEAR DATA		
	Gear	**Pinion**
DP	12	12
PD	3.600 in.	2.400 in.
OD	3.766 in.	2.566 in.
N	42	28
Cutter number	3	4
Indexing (Cincinnati plate)	20 holes on 21-hole circle	1 turn 9 holes on 21-hole circle
Depth of tooth	.1797 in.	.1797 in.
Helix angle	13°33' (right-hand)	13°33' (left-hand)
Direction to swing table	counterclockwise	clockwise
Lead	46.926 in.	31.285 in.
Change Gears – Worm gear	100	86
1st stud gear	32	40
2nd stud gear	72	64
Lead screw gear	48	44

CONTINUED FRACTIONS

Most handbooks contain a table of inch change gears for milling various inch leads. If there are no tables available or if the lead is not within the range shown in the tables, the change gears may be calculated by means of *continued fractions* or *successive quotients*.

To calculate the change gears by this method, it is necessary to form a fraction using the required lead and the lead of the machine.

PROBLEM:

Calculate the gears required to produce a lead of 5.189 in. on a helical gear. The lead of the milling machine is 10 in. The available change gears are as follows: 24, 24, 28, 32, 40, 44, 48, 56, 64, 72, 86, 100.

Procedure

1. Gear Ratio $= \dfrac{\text{required lead}}{\text{lead of machine}}$

   $= \dfrac{\text{product driven}}{\text{product drivers}}$

   $= \dfrac{5.189}{10}$

   $= \dfrac{5189}{10000}$

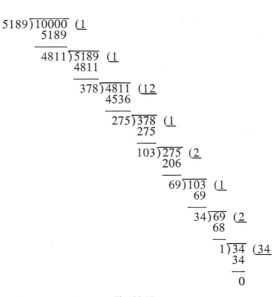

Fig. 11-67

2. Since this fraction cannot be factored, the required gears may be obtained by dividing the smaller number into the larger number to obtain the successive quotients. Continue to divide the remainder into the previous divisor until the remainder is zero (Fig. 11-67).

3. Arrange the successive quotients on a chart (Fig. 11-68). In the left-hand columns, place the figures 1 and 0 as in Fig. 11-69. The numbers are arranged in this way only when the gear ratio is a proper fraction, that is $\dfrac{5189}{10\,000}$, or when the lead of the helix is less than the lead of the machine.

   If the ratio is an improper fraction, such as that produced by the

1	1	12	1	2	1	2	34	QUOTIENTS
1	0							
0	1							
1	1	12	1	2	1	2	34	QUOTIENTS

Fig. 11-68

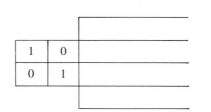

Fig. 11-69

Fig. 11-70

lead required for the larger helical gear, which has a lead greater than the lead of the machine, as in the foregoing problem $\left(\dfrac{15\,566}{10\,000}\right)$, the numbers must be arranged as in Fig. 11-70.

4. After the numbers have been arranged on the chart, the convergents are found by multiplying each quotient (A) by the number in the box (B), the upper row of convergents, which is located below and one square to the left of the quotient. To this product add the number in the next box to the left (C) (Fig. 11-71). The result is then placed in the convergent box below the quotient used (A).

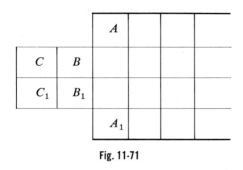

Fig. 11-71

		1	1	
1	0	1		

Fig. 11-72

		1	1	12	1	2	1	2	34	QUOTIENTS
1	0	1	1	13	14	41	55	151	5189	CONVERGENTS
0	1	1	2	25	27	79	106	291	10000	CONVERGENTS
		1	1	12	1	2	1	2	34	QUOTIENTS

Fig. 11-73

FOR EXAMPLE:
$A \times B + C$ (in the upper section)
$$= 1 \times 0 + 1$$
$$= 1$$

5. Move to the next quotient in the upper row and follow the same procedure. Continue this process until the original number (5189) is arrived at (Fig. 11-73).

6. Follow the same procedure for the lower set of convergents which should end with the original number (10 000). The calculation is proved correct when the original number appears in the runs of convergents. Examination of Fig. 11-73 reveals several sets of fractions in the convergent squares. These are really ratios which become more accurate as they move to the right until the original numbers finally appear.

7. Starting at the right, examine each ratio until one is found that will factor into a set of numbers which can be fitted into the range of change gears available. In this case (Fig. 11-73), the ratio or fraction is $\dfrac{14}{27}$.

8. Factor this fraction as follows:
$$\frac{14}{27} = \frac{7 \times 2}{9 \times 3}$$

9. These fractions may then be multiplied by a fraction having the value of 1 to suit the change gears available.
$$\frac{7}{9} \times \frac{8}{8} = \frac{56}{72}$$
$$\frac{2}{3} \times \frac{16}{16} = \frac{32}{48}$$

Therefore, the gears used to cut a lead reasonably close to 5.189 in. are:
$$\frac{56 \times 32}{72 \times 48} = \frac{\text{driven gears}}{\text{driver gears}}$$

It should be noted that the further to the right that the factorable fraction lies, the more accurate will be the lead produced by the gears.

CALCULATING THE ERROR IN THE LEAD

To calculate the error in the lead produced by these gears, proceed as follows.

$$\text{Lead produced} = \frac{56}{72} \times \frac{32}{48}$$
$$= \frac{14}{27} \times 10 \; \begin{array}{l}(\text{lead of}\\ \text{machine})\end{array}$$
$$= 5.185 \text{ in.}$$
$$\text{Desired lead} = 5.189$$
$$\text{Error} = 5.189 - 5.185$$
$$= .004 \text{ in.}$$

DETERMINING THE RATIO USING A SLIDE RULE

Another method of determining the convergents, $\dfrac{14}{27}$, is by means of the slide rule.

Procedure

1. Place 5.189 on the *C*-scale over 1 at the right end of the *D*-scale.

2. Carefully slide the cursor from the right end towards the left end until it reveals two factorable numbers which are exactly in line with each other. In this case, 14 on the *C*-scale is exactly in line with 27 on the *D*-scale.

BEVEL GEARING

Bevel gears are generally used to provide a positive drive between two intersecting shafts. The centres of these shafts must be in line, but not necessarily at right angles to each other. Bevel gear teeth are cut on the frustrum of a cone; thus the teeth are radial and point to the apex of the cone.

Correctly cut bevel gears have the same tooth form as spur gears. This shape will be maintained at any point on the tooth. However, the size of the tooth diminishes as the tooth tapers towards the apex of the cone. Because of this, bevel gears cannot be cut properly by using a standard involute formed gear cutter.

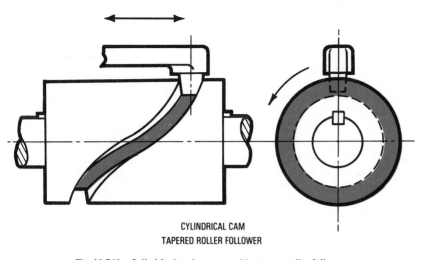

CYLINDRICAL CAM
TAPERED ROLLER FOLLOWER

Fig. 11-74A   Cylindrical or drum cam with a taper roller follower

CAMS AND CAM MILLING

A *cam* is a device generally applied to a machine to change rotary motion into straight line or reciprocating motion and to transmit this motion to other parts of the machine through a follower. The cam shaft on an automobile engine incorporates several cams which control the opening and closing of the intake and exhaust valves. Many machine operations, especially on automatic machines, are controlled by cams which transmit the desired motion to the cutting tool through a follower and some type of push rod.

Cams are also used to transform linear motion into a reciprocating motion of the follower. Cams of this type are called *plate*, or *bar*, cams or are often referred to as *templates*. Templates are often used on tracer type milling machines and lathes where parts must be produced to the profile of the template.

Cams may also be used as locking devices. Extensive applications are found in jig and fixture design and in quick locking clamps.

CAMS USED TO IMPART MOTION

Cams of this type are generally found on machines and may be of two types, the *positive* and the *non-positive*.

Positive type cams, such as the cylindrical and grooved plate (Fig. 11-74A and B), control the follower at all times. That is, the follower remains engaged in the groove on the face or the periphery of the cam and uses no other means to maintain engagement between the cam and the follower.

Examples of the non-positive type cams are the Plate, Toe and Wiper, and Crown (Fig. 11-74C, D, and E). In the non-positive types, the cam pushes the follower in a given direction and then depends on some external force, such as gravity or springs, to keep the follower bearing against the cam surface.

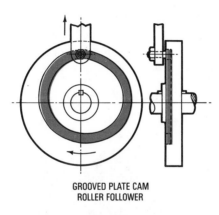

GROOVED PLATE CAM
ROLLER FOLLOWER

Fig. 11-74B   Grooved plate cam with a roller follower

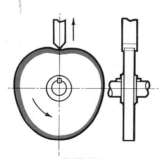

PLATE CAM
KNIFE-EDGE FOLLOWER

Fig. 11-74C   Plate cam with a knife-edge follower

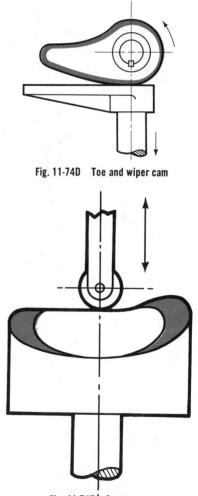

Fig. 11-74D   Toe and wiper cam

Fig. 11-74E   Crown cam

Followers may be of several types.

The roller type (Fig. 11-75A) has the least frictional drag and requires little or no lubrication.

The tapered roller type (Fig. 11-75 B) is used with grooved plate or cylindrical cams.

The flat, or plunger, type (Fig. 11-75C) is used to transmit large forces and requires lubrication.

The knife edge, or pointed, type (Fig. 11-75D) is used on more intricate cams as it permits sharp contours to be followed more readily than with a roller cam.

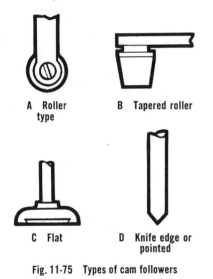

A Roller type

B Tapered roller

C Flat

D Knife edge or pointed

Fig. 11-75 Types of cam followers

CAM MOTIONS

There are three standard types of motions imparted by cams to followers and machine parts. These are:
a) uniform motion
b) harmonic motion
c) uniformly accelerated and decelerated motion

The *uniform motion* cam moves the follower at the same rate from the beginning to the end of the stroke. Since the movement starts from zero to full speed and ends in the same abrupt way, there is a distinct shock at the beginning and the end of the stroke. Machines using this type of cam must be rigid and sturdy enough to withstand this constant shock.

The *harmonic motion* cam provides a smooth start and stop to the cycle. It is used when uniformity of motion is not essential and where high speeds are required.

The *uniformly accelerated and decelerated* cam moves the follower slowly at first, then accelerates or decelerates at a uniform rate. It then gradually decreases in speed, permitting the follower to come to a slow stop before reversal takes place. This type is considered the smoothest of the three motions and is used on high-speed machines.

RADIAL CAM TERMS

A Lobe is a projecting part of the cam which imparts a reciprocal motion to the follower. Cams may have one or several lobes, depending on the application to the machine (Figs. 11-76 and 11-77).

Fig. 11-76 Single lobe uniform rise cam

Rise is the distance one lobe will raise or lower the follower as the cam revolves.

Lead is the total travel which would be imparted to the follower in one revolution of a uniform rise cam, having only one lobe in 360°. In Fig. 11-77, the lead for a double lobe cam is twice the lead of a single lobe cam having the same rise. It is the *lead* of the cam and not the rise that controls the gear selection in cam milling.

Fig. 11-77 Double lobe uniform rise cam

Uniform rise is the rise generated on a cam which moves inward at an even rate around the cam, assuming the shape of an Archimedes spiral. This is caused by uniform feed and rotation of the work when a cam is being machined.

CAM MILLING

In the majority of plate cams which do not have a uniform rise, the cam must be laid out and machined by incremental cuts. By this method, the blank is rotated through an angular increment and the cut is taken to the layout line or a predetermined point. This process is repeated until the outline of the cam is produced as closely as possible. The ridges left between each successive cut are then removed by filing and polishing (Fig. 11-78).

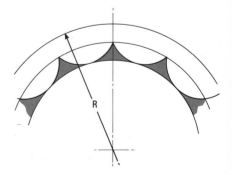

Fig. 11-78 Ridges left by incremental cuts

Courtesy Cincinnati Milacron Inc.

Fig. 11-79   Machine set up for cam milling using a short lead milling attachment

Uniform rise cams may be produced in the milling machine, with a vertical head, by the combined *uniform rotation* of the cam blank, held in the spindle of a dividing head and the *uniform feed* of the table.

When a cam is machined by this method, the work and the vertical head are usually swung at an angle so that the axis of the work and the axis of the mill are parallel (Fig. 11-79).

If the work and the vertical milling attachment are maintained in a vertical position, only a cam having the same lead for which the machine is geared can be cut. When the work and the vertical milling attachment are inclined, any desired lead may be produced, providing that the desired lead is *less* than the lead for which the machine is geared. In other words, the required lead to be cut on the cam must always be less than the forward feed of the table during one revolution of the work.

The principle involved in swinging the head is as follows. If an inch milling machine is set up to cut a cam and has equal gears on the dividing head and the lead screw, with the work and the vertical attachment in a vertical position (Fig. 11-80), the table would advance 10 in. while the work revolved one turn. An Archimedes spiral would be generated, and the cam would have a lead of 10 in. which is also a rise of 10 in. in 360°.

Rotate both the work and cutter so that they are parallel to the table and reading zero (Fig. 11-81). If a cut is taken, the work will move along the length of the end mill (which in this case would have to be 10 in.), and a circle having no lead would be generated.

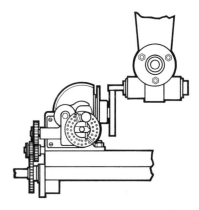

Fig. 11-81   Vertical attachment and work at zero

From these two examples, it can be seen that it is possible to mill any lead between zero and that for which the machine is geared, if the cutter and the work are inclined to any given angle between zero and 90°. If this method were not used, it would be necessary to have a different change gear combination for every lead to be cut. This would be impossible because of the large number of change gears required and the time required to change the gears for each different lead.

The calculations required to set the machine for cam cutting are as follows.

From the drawing determine the *lead* of the lobe or lobes of the cam; that is,

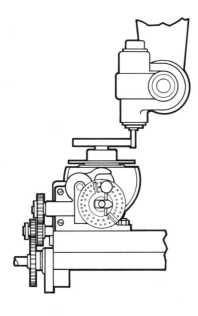

Fig. 11-80   Vertical head and work set at 90°

determine the amount of rise of each lobe if it were continued for the full circumference of the cam.

If the space occupied by the lobe is indicated in degrees on the drawing, the lead would be calculated as follows.

$$\text{Lead} = \frac{\text{rise of lobe in inches} \times 360}{\text{number of degrees of circumference occupied by the lobe}}$$

However, if the circumference is divided into 100 equal parts, it will be necessary to calculate the lead as follows.

$$\text{Lead} = \frac{\text{rise of lobe in inches} \times 100}{\text{percent of the circumference occupied by the lobe}}$$

EXAMPLE 1:
It is required to cut a uniform rise cam having a rise of .375 in. in 360°. Calculate the required lead, the inclination of the work, and the vertical head.

Procedure

Lead of cam = .375 in.
The machine and the dividing head should then be geared to .375 in. This is impossible, since the shortest lead which can be cut with regular change gears on a milling machine is generally .670 in.
NOTE: Any handbook will contain these milling tables.

To cut a lead of .375 in., it will be necessary to gear the machine to something more than .375 in.; in this case it will be .670 in. By consulting a handbook, it will be noted that the gears required for a .670 in. lead are 24, 86, 24, 100. It will also be necessary to swing the work and the vertical head to a definite angle. Fig. 11-82 illustrates how this is calculated.
In the diagram,

L = lead to which the machine is geared

H = *lead* of the cam

i = angle of inclination of the dividing head spindle in degrees

$$\text{Sin } i = \frac{H}{L}$$

Therefore, Sine angle of inclination

$$= \frac{\text{lead of cam}}{\text{lead of machine}}$$

$$\text{Sine angle} = \frac{.375}{.670}$$

$$= .55970$$

$$\text{Angle} = 34°2'$$

Fig. 11-82 illustrates that when the work travels along the distance L (.670), it will rotate one turn and reach a point on the cutter which is .375 in. higher than the starting point. This will produce a rise and a lead of .375 in. on the cam.

EXAMPLE 2:
It is required to cut a uniform rise cam having three lobes, each lobe occupying 120° and each having a rise of .150 in.

Procedure

1. Lead of cam $= \dfrac{.150 \times 360}{120}$
   $= .450$ in.

2. The smallest lead over .450 in. to which a machine can be geared $= .670$ in. (handbook)

3. Change gears required to produce a lead of .670 in.
   $$= \frac{24}{86} \times \frac{24}{100} \quad \frac{\text{(driven)}}{\text{(drivers)}}$$

4. Mount the dividing head, and connect the worm shaft and the lead screw with the above gears. *Disengage the index plate locking device.*

5. Scribe three marks 120° apart on the periphery of the cam.

6. Mount the work in the dividing head chuck.

7. Mount an end mill of sufficient length in the vertical attachment.

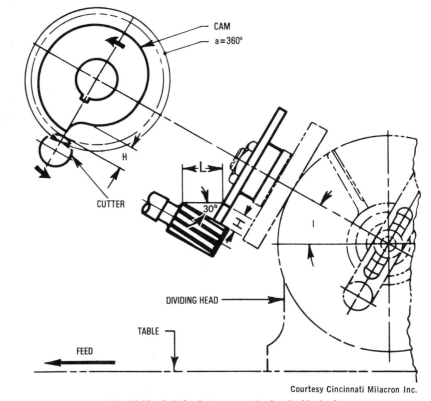

CAM
a = 360°
H
CUTTER
L
30°
H
DIVIDING HEAD
TABLE
FEED
i

Courtesy Cincinnati Milacron Inc.

Fig. 11-82   Relation between cam lead and table lead

8. Calculate the offset of the work and the vertical head.

$$\text{Sine} = \frac{.450}{.670}$$
$$= .67164$$
$$\therefore \text{Angle} = 42°12'$$

9. Swivel the dividing head to 42°12'.
10. Swivel the vertical milling attachment to 90° − 42°12' = 47°48'.
11. Centralize the work and the cutter.
12. Rotate work with the index crank until one scribed mark on the cam blank is exactly at the bottom dead centre.
13. Adjust the table until the cutter is touching the lower side of the work and the centre of the cutter is in line with the mark.
    NOTE: When the cutter is below the work, the setup will be more rigid and there will be no chance of chips obscuring any layout lines.
14. Set the vertical feed collar to zero.
15. Start the machine.
16. Using the index head crank, rotate the work one-third turn or until the second scribed line is in line with the forward edge of the cutter.
    NOTE: If the machine is geared to a lead over 2-1/2 in., the automatic feed may be used. If it is geared to a lead of less than 2-1/2 in., a short lead attachment should be used or the table should be fed along by means of the index head crank.
17. Lower the table slightly and disengage the gear train, or disengage the dividing head worm.
18. Return the table to the starting position.
19. Rotate the work until the next line on the circumference is in line with the centre of the cutter.
20. Re-engage the gear train or the dividing head worm.
21. Cut the second lobe.
22. Repeat steps 17, 18, 19, and 20, and cut the third lobe.

NOTE: When calculating the offset as in step 8, the lead of the machine is often set to the whole number nearest to *twice* the cam lead. When the lead of the machine is exactly twice the lead of the cam, the offset will always equal 30° because the lead of the machine, which is the hypotenuse (Fig. 11-82), is twice the lead of the cam. Thus the sine of the angle of inclination is equal to 1/2 or .500, which then makes the angle equal to 30°.

WORMS AND WORM GEARS

Worms and worm gears are used when a great ratio reduction is required between the driving and driven shafts. A worm is a cylinder on which is cut a single or multiple start Acme-type thread. The angle of this thread ranges from a 14.5° to 30° pressure angle. As the lead angle of the worm increases, the greater the pressure angle should be on the side of the thread. The teeth on a worm gear are machined on a peripheral groove which has a radius equal to half the root diameter of the worm. The drive ratio between a worm and worm gear assembly is one to the number of teeth in the worm gear. Thus if a worm gear had 50 teeth, the ratio would be 50:1, providing the worm had a single start thread. If it had a double start thread, the ratio would be 50:2, or 25:1.

TO MILL A WORM

Worms are often cut on a milling machine with a rack milling attachment and a thread milling cutter (Fig. 11-83). The

Fig. 11-83 Milling machine setup for machining a worm

setup of the cutter is similar to that for rack milling. The work is held between index centres and is rotated by suitable gears between the worm shaft and the lead screw of the milling machine. This is similar to the setup for helical milling. A short lead attachment is generally used when a worm is being milled because the thread usually has a short lead. If a short lead attachment is not available, the work may be rotated and the table moved lengthwise by means of the index crank on the dividing head.

Procedure

1. Calculate all dimensions of the thread, that is, lead, pitch, depth, and angle of thread.
   NOTE: The angle of the thread is calculated using the pitch diameter.
2. Mount the worm blank between the dividing head centres located at the end of the milling machine table.
3. Determine the proper gears for the lead, and mount them so that they connect the worm shaft and the lead screw.
4. Disengage the index plate locking device.
5. Mount the proper thread milling cutter on the rack milling attachment.
6. Swing the rack milling attachment to the required helix angle of the worm thread and in the proper direction for the lead of the worm.
7. Centre the work under the cutter.
8. Raise the work up to the cutter.
9. Move the work clear of the cutter, and raise the table to the required depth of thread.
10. Cut the thread using the automatic feed or by turning the index crank handle to feed the table.

CLUTCHES

Positive drive clutches are used extensively to drive or disconnect gears and shafts in machine gear boxes. The headstocks on most lathes use clutches, machined on the hubs of gears, to engage or disengage gears to provide different spindle speeds. The positive drive on this type of clutch is produced by means of interlocking teeth or projections on the driving and driven parts and does not rely on friction drive as in the case of friction type clutches.

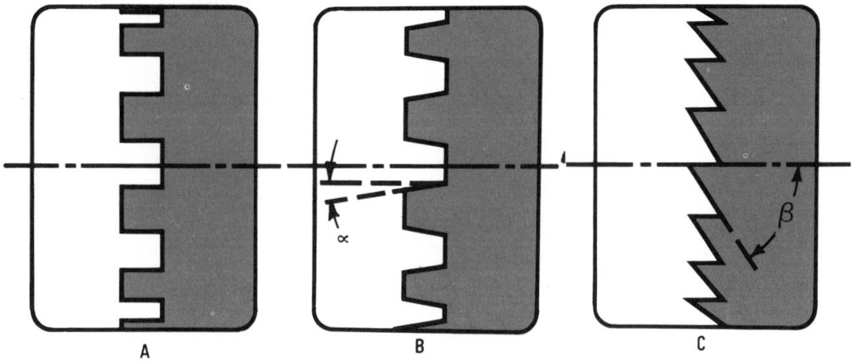

Three forms of positive drive clutches are shown in Fig. 11-84. The *straight tooth clutch* (Fig. 11-84A) permits rotation in either direction. This type is more difficult to engage since the mating teeth and grooves must be in perfect alignment before engagement is possible.

The *inclined tooth clutch* (Fig. 11-84B) provides an easier means of engaging or disengaging the driving and driven members because of an 8° or 9° angle machined on the faces of the teeth. Since this type of clutch tends to disengage more rapidly, it must be provided with a positive means of locking it in engagement. Clutches of this type permit the shafts to run in either direction without backlash.

The *saw tooth clutch* (Fig. 11-84C) permits drive in only one direction but is more easily engaged than the other two types of clutches. The angle of the teeth in this type is generally 60°.

To Machine a Straight Tooth Clutch Having Three Teeth

NOTE: This method applies to all clutches having an odd number of teeth.

1. Mount the dividing head on the milling machine table.
2. Mount a 3-jaw chuck in the dividing head.
3. Mount the workpiece in the chuck.
   NOTE: The spindle and the chuck of the dividing head may be positioned either horizontally or vertically. For this operation, it is assumed to be in a vertical position.
4. Set the sector arms to the proper indexing, that is, $\dfrac{40}{3} = 13\text{-}1/3$ turns $= 13$ turns and 13 holes on a 39-hole circle.

Fig. 11-84   Types of clutch teeth

Fig. 11-85   Adjusting work to the cutter

5. Mount a side milling cutter on the milling machine arbor. The cutter should be no wider than the narrowest or innermost part of the groove.
6. Set the proper spindle speed and table feed.
7. Start the cutter and adjust the work until the edge nearest the front of the machine *just* touches the inner side of the cutter (Fig. 11-85). Set the cross-feed graduated feed collar to zero.
8. Move the table longitudinally until the work is clear of the cutter.
9. Move the table laterally half the diameter of the work plus about 0.02 mm (or .001 in.) for clearance. Lock the saddle in this position.
10. Set the depth of cut, and lock the knee clamps.
11. Take a cut across the full width of the workpiece as in Fig. 11-86.
12. Return the table to starting position.
13. Index for the next tooth and take the second cut as shown in Fig. 11-87.
14. Return the table to starting position.
15. Index for the next tooth.
16. Take the third cut as shown in Fig. 11-88.

Fig. 11-87 Second cut

Fig. 11-86 First cut

Fig. 11-88 Three tooth clutch

To Machine a Straight Tooth Clutch Having Four Teeth

When machining a straight or inclined tooth clutch having an even number of teeth, it is necessary to machine one side of each tooth first and then machine the second side of each. This obviously requires more time; therefore, it is desirable that clutches be designed with an odd number of teeth to reduce machining time and the chance of error.

1. Mount the work as in the previous example and set the proper indexing, if required.
2. Start the cutter and adjust the workpiece until the edge nearest the front of the machine just touches the inner edge of the cutter (Fig. 11-85).
3. With the work clear of the cutter, move the saddle over half the diameter of the work plus the thickness of the cutter minus 0.02 mm (or .001 in.) for clearance.
4. Adjust the work until the cutter is over the centre hole of the clutch. It is advisable to cut from the centre to the outside of the clutch in order to minimize the vibration.
5. Set the depth and lock the knee clamp.
6. Take the first cut.
   NOTE: When cutting an even number of clutch teeth, it is absolutely necessary that the cut be made through one wall only.
7. Index for and cut the remaining teeth on the one side. (Indexing = 10 turns for each tooth.)
8. Revolve the work one-eighth of a turn (five turns of the index crank).
9. Touch the opposite side of the work to the other side of the cutter, that is, the outside of the cutter to the inner edge of the work.
10. Repeat operations 3, 4, 5, 6, and 7 until all the teeth are cut. If any pie-shaped pieces of metal remain in the tooth spaces, they must be removed with an additional cut through the centre of the space.

Courtesy Cincinnati Milacron Inc.

Fig. 11-89   Standard vertical milling machine

VERTICAL MILLING MACHINES

Much of the work on a milling machine is best done with a vertical milling attachment. The time involved in setting up a vertical attachment prevents the milling machine from being used for other milling operations at the same time; therefore, the vertical milling machine has become popular in industry. This machine offers versatility not found in any other machine. Some of the operations which can conveniently be carried out on these machines are: face milling, end milling, keyway cutting, dovetail cutting, T-slot and circular slot cutting, gear cutting, drilling, boring, and jig boring. Because of the machine construction (vertical spindle), many of the facing operations can be done with a fly cutter, which reduces the cost of cutters considerably. Also, since most cutters are much smaller than for the horizontal mill, the cost of the cutters for the same job is usually much less for a vertical milling machine.

The standard vertical milling machine (Fig. 11-89) has all the construction features of a plain horizontal milling machine, except that the cutter spindle is mounted in a vertical position. The spindle head on most vertical milling machines may be swivelled, which readily permits the machining of angular surfaces. The spindles on most vertical milling machines have a short travel, which facilitates step milling and the drilling and boring of holes.

The cutters used are of the end mill or shell end mill type. This type of machine is particularly suited to the use of the rotary table, permitting the machining of circular grooves and the positioning of holes which have been laid out with angular measurements.

The *ram type* vertical milling machine (Fig. 11-90) is a lighter type than the standard vertical machine. Because of its simplicity and the ease of setup, it has become increasingly popular. Machines of this type are generally used for lighter types of milling machine work.

PARTS OF THE RAM TYPE VERTICAL MILL

The base is made of ribbed cast iron. It may contain a coolant reservoir.

The column is often cast integrally with the base. The machined face of the column provides the ways for vertical movement of the knee. The upper part of the column is machined to receive a *turret* on which the overarm is mounted.

The overarm is round, or of the ram type, as illustrated in Fig. 11-90. It may be adjusted towards or away from the column to increase the capacity of the machine.

The head is attached to the end of the ram. Provision is made to swivel the head in one plane. On universal type machines, the head may be swivelled in two planes. Mounted on top of the head is the *motor* which provides drive to the *spindle*, usually through V-belts. Spindle speed

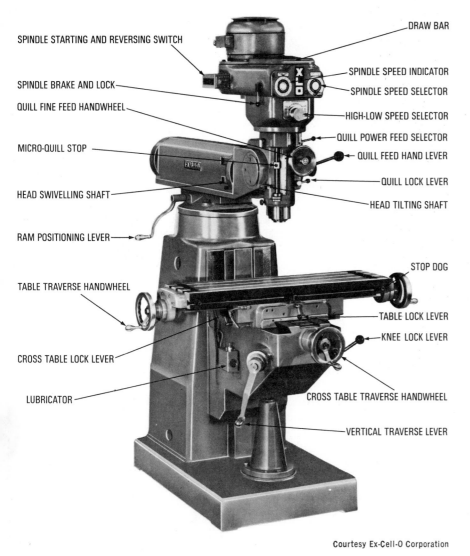

SPINDLE STARTING AND REVERSING SWITCH

SPINDLE BRAKE AND LOCK

QUILL FINE FEED HANDWHEEL

MICRO-QUILL STOP

HEAD SWIVELLING SHAFT

RAM POSITIONING LEVER

TABLE TRAVERSE HANDWHEEL

CROSS TABLE LOCK LEVER

LUBRICATOR

DRAW BAR

SPINDLE SPEED INDICATOR

SPINDLE SPEED SELECTOR

HIGH-LOW SPEED SELECTOR

QUILL POWER FEED SELECTOR

QUILL FEED HAND LEVER

QUILL LOCK LEVER

HEAD TILTING SHAFT

STOP DOG

TABLE LOCK LEVER

KNEE LOCK LEVER

CROSS TABLE TRAVERSE HANDWHEEL

VERTICAL TRAVERSE LEVER

Courtesy Ex-Cell-O Corporation

Fig. 11-90 Ram type vertical milling machine

changes are effected by means of a variable speed pulley and crank or by belt changes and a reduction gear. The spindle may be fed by means of a hand lever, a handwheel, or by automatic power feed. Most machines are equipped with a micrometer quill stop for precision drilling and boring to depth.

The knee moves up and down on the face of the column and supports the saddle and

the table. The knee in this type of machine does *not* contain the gears for the automatic feed as in the horizontal milling machine and the standard vertical milling machine. The automatic feed on most of these types of machines is not a standard feature and is usually added as an accessory. It is an external device and controls only the longitudinal feeds of the table. Most cutting on the vertical milling machine is done by end mill types of cutters; therefore, it is not necessary to swing the

table even when cutting a helix. As a result, vertical milling machines are equipped with plain tables only.

ALIGNING THE VERTICAL HEAD

Proper alignment of the head is of the utmost importance when machining holes or when face milling. If the head is not at an angle of 90° to the table, the holes will not be square with the work surface when the cutting tool is fed by hand or by automatic feeds. When face milling, the machined surface will be stepped if the head is not square with the table. Although all heads are graduated in degrees and some have vernier devices used for setting the head, it is well to check the spindle alignment as follows.

Procedure

1. Mount a dial indicator on a suitable rod, bent at 90° and held in the spindle (Fig. 11-91).
2. Position the indicator over the front of the table.
3. Carefully lower the spindle until the indicator button touches the table and the dial indicator registers about one-half revolution, then set the bezel to zero. Lock the spindle in place.
4. Carefully rotate the vertical mill spindle 180° by hand until the button bears on the back of the table. Compare the readings.
5. If there is any discrepancy in the readings, loosen the locking nuts on the swivel mounting and adjust the head until the indicator registers one half the difference between the two readings. Tighten the locking nuts.
6. Recheck the accuracy of the head and adjust if necessary.
7. Rotate the vertical mill spindle 90°, and set the dial indicator as in step 3.
8. Rotate the machine spindle 180°, and check the reading at the other end of the table.
9. If the two readings do not coincide, repeat step 5 until the readings are the same.

Fig. 11-91   Checking the spindle alignment with a dial indicator

10. Tighten the locking nuts on the swivel mount.
11. Recheck the readings and adjust if necessary.

NOTE: When readings are taken, it is important that the indicator button does not catch in the T-slots of the table. To prevent this, it is advisable to work from the high reading first and then rotate to the low reading. It should be apparent that the longer the rod used, the more accurate the setting will be.

ALIGNING THE VISE

When the vise is aligned on a vertical milling machine, the dial indicator may be attached to the quill or the head by any convenient means, such as clamps or magnetic base. The same method of alignment should be followed as was outlined earlier in this chapter for aligning the vise on a horizontal milling machine.

To Machine a Flat Surface

1. Clean the vise and mount the work securely in the vise, on parallels if necessary.
2. Check that the vertical head is square with the table.
3. If possible, select a cutter which will just overlap the edges of the work.

This will then require only one cut to be taken to machine the surface. If the surface to be machined is fairly narrow, an end mill slightly larger in diameter than the width of the work should be used. If the surface is large and requires several passes, a shell end mill or a suitable fly cutter should be used.

NOTE: It is not advisable to use a facing cutter which is too wide since the head may be thrown out of alignment if the cutter should jam.

4. Set the proper spindle speed for the size and type of cutter and the material being machined.
5. Tighten the quill clamps.
6. Start the machine, and adjust the table until the end of the work is under the edge of the cutter.
7. Raise the table until the work surface just touches the cutter. Move the work clear of the cutter.
8. Raise the table about 0.75 mm and take a trial cut for approximately 5 mm.
9. Move the work clear of the cutter, *stop the cutter*, and measure the work.
10. Raise the table the desired amount, and lock the knee clamp.

11. Mill the surface to size using the automatic feed if the machine is so equipped.

To Machine an Angular Surface

1. Lay out the angular surface.
2. Clean the vise.
3. Align the vise with the direction of the feed. This is of the utmost importance.
4. Mount the work on parallels in the vise.
5. Swivel the vertical head to the required angle (Fig. 11-92).
6. Tighten the quill clamp.
7. Start the machine and raise the table until the cutter touches the work. Carefully raise the table until the cut is of the desired depth.
8. Take a trial cut for about 12 mm.
9. Check the angle with a protractor.

Fig. 11-92   Setup to machine an angle

10. If the angle is correct, continue the cut.

NOTE: It is always advisable to feed the work into the rotation of the cutter, rather than with the rotation of the cutter which may draw the work into the cutter and cause damage to the work, the cutter, or both.

11. Machine to the required depth, taking several cuts if necessary.

Fig. 11-93   Machining an angle by adjusting the work

ALTERNATE METHOD

Angles may sometimes be milled by leaving the head in a vertical position and setting the work on an angle in the vise (Fig. 11-93). This will depend on the shape and size of the workpiece.

Procedure

1. Check that the vertical head is square with the table.
2. Clean the vise.

3. Lock the quill clamp.
4. Set the workpiece in the vise with the layout line parallel to the top of the vise jaws and about 5 mm above them.
5. Adjust the work under the cutter so that the cut will start at the narrow side of the taper and progress into the thicker metal.
6. Take successive cuts of about 3 mm to 4 mm, or until the cut is about 1 mm above the layout line.
7. Check to see that the cut and the layout line are parallel.
8. Raise the table until the cutter just touches the layout line.
9. Clamp the knee at this setting.
10. Take the finishing cut.

SETTING THE VERTICAL HEAD TO AN ACCURATE ANGLE

When it is necessary to machine an angle to extreme accuracy, the vertical head may be set by using a sine bar.

Procedure

1. Set an angle plate square on the machine table.
2. Make a gauge block buildup under a sine bar for the angle required.
3. Lightly fasten the sine bar to the angle plate.
4. Mount an indicator to the vertical head spindle.
5. Have the indicator registering approximately 0.75 mm (or .030 in.) on the sine bar surface.
6. By hand, feed the vertical head spindle along the length of the sine bar.
7. Adjust the head until there is no movement of the dial indicator.

NOTE: If the angular surface to be machined is small, it may be advisable to set the sine bar to the complement of the desired angle and cut with the bottom of the end mill.

TO MILL A COMPOUND ANGLE

The milling of a compound angle involves the swivelling of the vertical head in one

plane and the swinging of the vise to obtain the second angle.

CUTTING SLOTS AND KEYSEATS

Slots and keyseats with one or two blind ends may be cut in shafts more easily on a vertical milling machine, using a two- or three-fluted end mill, than with a horizontal mill and a side facing cutter.

Procedure

1. Lay out the position of the keyseat on the shaft, and scribe reference lines on the end of the shaft (Fig. 11-94).
2. Secure the workpiece in a vise on a parallel. If the shaft is long, it may be clamped directly to the table by placing it in one of the table slots or in V-blocks.

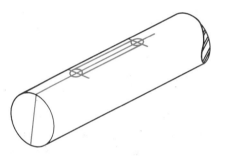

Fig. 11-94   Layout of a keyseat on a shaft

3. Using the layout lines on the end of the shaft, set up the shaft so that the keyseat layout is in the proper position on top of the shaft.
4. Mount a two- or three-fluted end mill of a diameter equal to the width of the keyseat, in the milling machine spindle.

NOTE: If the keyseat has two blind ends, a two- or three-lip end mill must be used, since they may be used as a drill to start the slot. If the slot is at one end of the shaft (one blind end only), a four-fluted end mill may be used, although a two- or three-lip end mill will give better chip clearance.

5. Centre the workpiece by carefully touching the cutter up to one side of

Fig. 11-95A   Setting the cutter to the side of the work

Fig. 11-95B   The cutter centred with the layout

Fig. 11-95C   Finished keyseat

the shaft (Fig. 11-95A). This may also be done by placing a piece of thin paper between the shaft and the cutter.

NOTE: Paper may be made to adhere to shafts or work surfaces by wetting it with coolant or oil before applying it to the surface. This eliminates the necessity of holding paper between the cutter and the work, thus making it a safer operation.

6. Lower the table until the cutter clears the workpiece.

7. Move the table over an amount equal to half the diameter of the shaft plus half the diameter of the cutter plus the thickness of the paper (Fig. 11-95B). For example, if a 5 mm slot is required in a 50 mm shaft and the thickness of the paper used is 0.02 mm the table would be moved over 25.00 mm + 2.50 mm + 0.02 mm = 27.52 mm.

8. If the keyseat being cut has two blind ends, adjust the work until the end of the keyseat is aligned with the edge of the cutter.

9. Feed the cutter down (or the table up) until the cutter *just* cuts to its full diameter. If the keyseat has one blind end only, the work is adjusted so that this cut is taken at the end of the work. The work would now be moved clear of the cutter.

10. Adjust the depth of cut to one-half the thickness of the key, and machine the keyseat to the proper length (Fig. 11-95C).

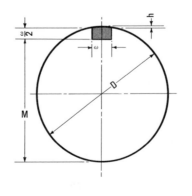

Fig. 11-96   Keyseat calculations

MEASURING THE DEPTH OF KEYSEATS

If the keyseat is at the end of a shaft, the proper depth of the keyseat is checked by measuring diametrically from the bottom of the keyseat to the opposite side of the shaft.

This distance may be calculated as follows (Fig. 11-96):

$$M = D - \left(\frac{W}{2} + h \right)$$
$$h = 0.5 \ \left(D - \sqrt{D^2 - W^2} \right)$$

M = the distance from the bottom of the keyseat to the opposite side of the shaft.

D = diameter of the shaft.

W = width of the keyseat.

h = height of the segment above the width of the keyseat.

PROBLEM:

Calculate the measurement M if the shaft is 50 mm in diameter and a 6 mm key is to be used.

$$h = 0.5 \quad \left(D - \sqrt{D^2 - W^2}\right)$$
$$= 0.5 \quad \left(50 - \sqrt{2500 - 36}\right)$$
$$= 0.5 \quad \left(50 - \left(\sqrt{2464}\right)\right)$$
$$= 0.5 \quad \left(50 - 49.64\right)$$
$$= 0.5 \quad \left(0.36\right)$$
$$= 0.18 \text{ mm}$$

$$M = D - \left(\frac{W}{2} + h\right)$$
$$= 50 - \left(\frac{6}{2} + 0.18\right)$$
$$= 50 - \left(3 + 0.18\right)$$
$$= 50 - 3.18$$
$$= 46.82 \text{ mm}$$

WOODRUFF KEYS

Woodruff keys are used when keying shafts and mating parts (Fig. 11-97). Woodruff keyseats are more quickly cut than are square keyseats, and the key should not require any fitting after the keyseat has been cut. These keys are semi-circular in shape and can be purchased in standard sizes. They can be conveniently made from round bar stock of the required diameter. Note that metric standards and information for woodruff keys and key cutters had not yet been decided at the time of publication.

Inch-designed woodruff keyseat cutters (Fig. 11-97) have shank diameters of 1/2 in. for cutters up to 1-1/2 in. in diameter. The shank is undercut adjacent to the cutter to permit the cutter to go into the proper depth. The sides of the cutter are slightly tapered towards the centre to permit clearance while cutting. Cutters over 2 in. in diameter are mounted on an arbor.

The size of the cutter is stamped on the shank. The last two digits of the number indicate the nominal diameter in eighths of an inch. The digit or digits preceding the last two numbers indicate the nominal width of the cutter in thirty-seconds of an

A

B

Fig. 11-97 Woodruff key and keyseat cutter

inch. Thus a cutter marked 608 would be 8 × 1/8, or 1 in. in diameter, and 6 × 1/32, or 3/16 in. wide. The key would be a semi-circular cross-section to fit the groove exactly.

To Cut a Woodruff Keyseat

1. Align the spindle of the vertical milling machine 90° to the table.
2. Lay out the position of the keyseat.
3. Set the shaft in the vise of the milling machine or on V-blocks.
4. Mount the cutter of the proper size in the spindle.
5. Start the cutter, and touch the bottom of the cutter to the top of the workpiece. Set the vertical graduated feed collar to zero.
6. Move the work clear of the cutter. Raise the table half the diameter of the work plus half the thickness of the cutter. Lock the knee at this setting.
7. Position the centre of the slot with the centre of the cutter. Lock the table in this position.
8. Touch the revolving cutter to the work. Use a strip of paper between the cutter and the work if desired. Set the cross-feed screw collar to zero.

9. Cut keyseat to the proper depth.
   NOTE: Keyseat proportions may be found in any handbook.

THE ROTARY TABLE

The *rotary table* or the *circular milling attachment* (Fig. 11-98) can be used on plain universal vertical milling machines and slotters. It may provide rotary motion to the workpiece in addition to the longitudinal and vertical motion provided by the machine. With this attachment, it is possible to cut radii, circular grooves, and circular sections not possible by other means. The drilling and boring of holes which have been designated by angular measurements, as well as other indexing operations, are easily accomplished with this accessory. This attachment is also suitable for use with the slotting attachment on a milling machine.

Rotary tables may be of two types: those having hand feed, and those having power feed. The construction of these is basically the same, the only exception being the automatic feed mechanism.

HAND FEED ROTARY TABLE CONSTRUCTION

The rotary table unit consists of a *base* which is bolted to the milling machine table. Fitting into the base is the *rotary table*, on the bottom of which is mounted a *worm gear*. A *worm shaft* mounted in the bases meshes with and drives the worm gear. The worm shaft may be quickly disengaged when rapid rotation of the table is required, as when setting work concentric with the table. A *handwheel* is mounted on the outer end of the worm shaft. The bottom edge of the table is graduated in half degrees. On most rotary table units, there is a *vernier scale* on the handwheel collar which permits setting to within two minutes of a degree. The table has T-slots cut into the top surface to permit the clamping of work.

A hole in the centre of the table accommodates test plugs to permit easy centring

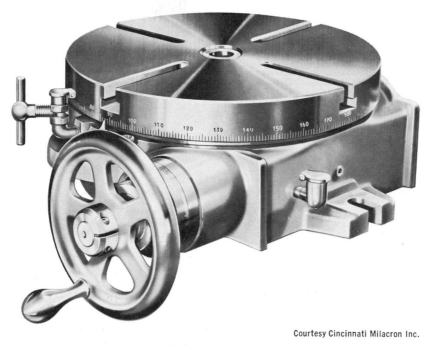

Courtesy Cincinnati Milacron Inc.

Fig. 11-98   A hand feed rotary table

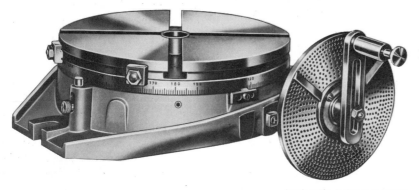

Courtesy The Pedersen Company

Fig. 11-99   Rotary table with an indexing attachment

of the table with the machine spindle. Work may be centred with the table by means of test plugs or arbors.

Some rotary tables use an *indexing attachment* in place of a handwheel (Fig. 11-99). This attachment is often supplied as an accessory to the standard rotary table. It not only serves the same purpose as a handwheel, but also permits the indexing of work with dividing head accuracy.

The worm and wormwheel ratio of rotary tables is not necessarily 40:1 as on most dividing heads. The ratio may be 72:1, 80:1, 90:1, 120:1, or any other ratio. Larger ratios are usually found on larger tables. The method of calculating the indexing is the same as for the dividing head except that the number of teeth in the wormwheel is used, rather than 40 as in the dividing head calculations.

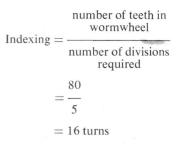

EXAMPLE:

Calculate the indexing for five equally spaced holes on a circular plate using a rotary table with an 80:1 ratio.

$$\text{Indexing} = \frac{\text{number of teeth in wormwheel}}{\text{number of divisions required}}$$

$$= \frac{80}{5}$$

$$= 16 \text{ turns}$$

Accurately spaced holes on circles and segments (such as clutch teeth and teeth in gears too large to be held between index centres) are some of the applications of this type of rotary table. This type may be supplied with a power feed mechanism.

The third type of rotary table has provision for power rotation of the table (Fig. 11-100). Here the worm shaft is connected to the milling machine lead screw drive gear by a special shaft and an end gear train. The rate of rotation is controlled by the feed mechanism of the milling machine. When operated by power, the rotation of the table may be controlled by the operator using a feed lever attached to the unit or by trip dogs located on the periphery of the table. The operation of the table may be controlled by the handwheel or the automatic feed lever as required.

This type of attachment is particularly suited for production work and continuous milling operations when large numbers of small identical parts are required. In this operation, the parts are mounted in suitable fixtures on the table, and the rotary feed moves the parts under the cutter. After the piece has passed beneath the cutter, the finished piece is removed and replaced with an unfinished workpiece.

To Centre the Rotary Table with the Vertical Mill Spindle

1. Square the vertical head with the machine table.

Courtesy Cincinnati Milacron Inc.

Fig. 11-100   Rotary table with power feed

2. Mount the rotary table on the milling machine.

3. Place a test plug in the centre hole of the rotary table.

4. Mount an indicator with a grasshopper leg in the machine spindle.

5. With the indicator just clearing the top of the test plug, rotate the machine spindle by hand and approximately align the plug with the spindle.

6. Bring the indicator into contact with the diameter of the plug, and rotate the spindle by hand.

7. Adjust the machine table by the longitudinal and crossfeed handles until the dial indicator registers no movement.

8. Lock the machine table and saddle, and recheck the alignment.

9. Readjust if necessary.

To Centre a Workpiece with the Rotary Table

Often it is necessary to perform a rotary table operation on several identical workpieces, each having a machined hole in the centre. To quickly align each workpiece, a special plug can be made to fit the centre hole of the workpiece and the hole in the rotary table. Once the machine spindle has been aligned with the rotary table, each succeeding piece can be aligned quickly and accurately by placing it over the plug.

If there are only a few pieces, which would not justify the manufacture of a special plug, or if the workpiece does not have a hole through its centre, the following method can be used to centre the workpiece on the rotary table.

1. Align the rotary table with the vertical head spindle.

2. Lightly clamp the workpiece to the rotary table in the approximate centre. *NOTE: Do not* move the crossfeed or longitudinal feed handles.

3. Disengage the rotary table worm mechanism.

4. Mount an indicator in the machine spindle or on the milling machine table, depending upon the workpiece.

5. Bring the indicator into contact with the surface to be indicated, and revolve the rotary table by hand.

6. With a soft metal bar, tap the work (away from the indicator movement)

until no movement is registered on the indicator in a complete revolution of the rotary table.

7. Clamp the workpiece tightly, and recheck the accuracy of the setup.

NOTE: If a centre punch mark must be aligned, a wiggler instead of an indicator is mounted in the milling machine spindle and the punch mark is positioned under the point of the wiggler.

RADIUS MILLING

When it is required to mill the ends on a workpiece to a certain radius or to machine circular slots having a definite radius, a sequence should be followed. Fig. 11-101 illustrates a typical setup.

Procedure

1. Align the vertical milling machine spindle at 90° to the table.

2. Mount a circular milling attachment (rotary table) on the milling machine table.

3. Centre the rotary table with the machine spindle using a test plug in the table and a dial indicator on the spindle.

Fig. 11-101   Milling a circular slot in a workpiece

4. Set the longitudinal feed dials and the crossfeed dial to zero.

5. Mount the work on the rotary table, aligning the centre of the radial cuts with the centre of the table. A special arbor may be used for this. Another method is to align the centre of the radial cut with a wiggler mounted in the machine spindle.

6. Move either the crossfeed or the longitudinal feed (whichever is more convenient) an amount equal to the radius required.

7. *Lock both the table and the saddle,* and remove the handles if convenient.

8. Mount the proper end mill.

9. Rotate the work, using the rotary table feed handwheel, to the starting point of the cut.

10. Set the depth of cut and machine the slot to the size indicated on the drawing, using hand or power feed.

MILLING A T-SLOT

T-slots are machined in the tops of machine tables and accessories to receive bolts for clamping workpieces. They are machined in two operations.

Procedure

1. Consult a handbook for the T-slot dimensions.

2. Lay out the position of the T-slot.

3. Square the vertical milling machine spindle with the machine table.

4. Mount the work on the milling machine. If the work is to be held in a vise, the vise jaw must be aligned with the table travel. If the work is clamped to the table, the position of the slot must be aligned with the table travel.

5. Mount an end mill having a diameter slightly larger than the diameter of the bolt body. The size of the end mill to be used is shown in the T-slot tables.

6. Machine the centre slot to the proper depth of the T-slot, using the end mill.

7. Remove the end mill, and mount the proper T-slot cutter.

8. Set the T-slot cutter to the depth of the bottom of the slot.

9. Machine the lower part of the slot.

MILLING DOVETAILS

Dovetails are used to permit reciprocating motion between two elements of a machine. They are composed of an external or an internal part and are adjusted by means of a gib. Dovetails may be machined on a vertical milling machine or on a horizontal mill equipped with a vertical milling attachment. A dovetail cutter is a special single-angle end mill type of cutter ground to the angle of the dovetail required.

Procedure for Milling an Internal Dovetail

1. Refer to Chapter 10 for the method of measuring a dovetail.

2. Check the measurements of the workpiece in which the dovetail is to be cut. Remove all burrs.

3. Lay out the position of the dovetail.

4. Mount the workpiece in a vise, clamp it on a rotary table, or if the work is long, bolt it directly to the machine table.

5. Indicate the side of the workpiece or the slot layout to see that it is parallel to the line of table travel.

6. Mount an end mill of a diameter narrower than the centre section of the dovetail (Fig. 11-102A).

7. Start the end mill, and touch up to the side of the work.

8. Set the crossfeed dial to zero.

9. Move the work over until the end mill is in the centre of the dovetail. In this case, it will be the distance from the side of the workpiece to the centre of the dovetail plus half the diameter of the cutter (plus the thickness of paper, if used).

10. Lock the saddle in this position, and set the crossfeed dial to zero.

11. Touch the edge of the cutter to the top of the work.

12. Move the work clear of the cutter, and set the depth of cut. Lock the knee in this position. Note the depth of this slot should be 0.75 mm to 1.25 mm

A   Centre section roughed out

B   Both sides of the dovetail machined

Fig. 11-102   Milling a dovetail

deeper than the bottom of the dovetail, to prevent drag and to provide clearance for dirt and chips between the mating dovetail parts.

13. Mill the channel to the width of the cutter (Fig. 11-102A).
14. Move the work over an amount equal to half the difference between the machined slot size and the size of the dovetail at the top. *Check for backlash.*
15. Take this finish cut along the one side of the work.
16. Check the width of the slot.
17. Move the work over to the finished width of the top of the dovetail. *Check for backlash.*
18. Cut the second side and check the width of the slot.
19. Return the saddle to zero.
20. Mount a dovetail cutter.
21. Set the depth for a roughing cut. This should be about 0.12 mm to 0.25 mm less than the finish depth.
22. Calculate the width of the dovetail at the bottom.
23. Move the work over 0.25 mm less than the finished size of this side. This will leave enough for the finish cut. Note the readings on the crossfeed dial.
24. Rough out the angle on the first side.
25. Move the work over to the other side the same amount from the centre line, and rough cut the other side.
26. Set the cutter to the proper depth.
27. Machine the bottom surface (both sides) of the dovetail to the finished depth.
28. Using two rods, measure the dovetail for size.
29. Move the table over half the difference between the rough dovetail and the finished size. *Check for backlash.*
30. Take the finish cut on one side.
31. Move the table over the required amount, and finish the other side (Fig. 11-102B).
32. Check the finished size of the dovetail.

NOTE: If the work is mounted centrally on a rotary table, it is possible to rotate the work a half turn (180°) after step #18 and take the same cuts on each side of the block for each successive step.

To Mill an External Dovetail

1. Centre the cutter over the dovetail position.
2. Remove as much material as possible from each side of the external dovetail, that is, cut it to the largest size of the dovetail. In this operation it will be necessary to note the readings from the centre line and remove the backlash for each side.
3. Mount a dovetail cutter, and centre it with the workpiece.
4. Move the work over one-half the width of the dovetail plus half the diameter of the cutter. Allow 0.25 mm for a finish cut.
5. Take this roughing cut.
6. Move the work over an equal amount to the other side of the centre line, taking up the backlash.
7. Rough cut the second side.
8. Adjust the work over, and take the finish cut on the one side.
9. Measure the dovetail using two rods.
10. Adjust for the finish cut on the second side, and take this cut.
11. Measure the width of the finished dovetail.

NOTE: If the work is mounted centrally on a rotary table, the work may be rotated a half turn and the same cuts taken on each side.

JIG BORING ON A VERTICAL MILLING MACHINE

If a jig borer is not available, the vertical milling machine may be used for jig boring purposes.

When the vertical milling machine is used for accurate hole location, the same setup, locating, and machining methods used in a jig borer apply. The coordinate system of hole location is used in each case. Since this topic is covered extensively in Chapter 12, the reader is advised to refer to this chapter before jig boring on the vertical milling machine.

Since the vertical milling machine does not have the same lead screw accuracy as a jig borer, it must have some external measuring system to ensure the accuracy of the table setting. Measuring rods and dial indicators, a vernier scale, or optical measuring devices, such as digital readout boxes, may be used for this purpose.

A **metric precision end measuring rod** set consists of two micrometer heads capable of measuring to an accuracy of 0.002 mm and a number of solid measuring rods.

A standard measuring rod set consists of two rods in the following lengths: 25, 50, 75, 150, and 300 millimetres. Other rods are available in lengths of 100, 125, 175, 200, 250, and 375 millimetres.

Inch precision end measuring rods (Fig. 11-103) are generally supplied in sets of 11 rods, including two micrometer heads capable of measuring from 4 to 5 in. to an accuracy of .0001. These micrometer heads are usually furnished with a red identifying ring on one and a black identifying ring on the other. One of these is used for longitudinal settings and the other for transverse settings. The solid rods are made of hardened and ground tool steel and have several concentric collars (Fig. 11-103C). The nine rods in a standard set are as follows: two in each of the following sizes: 1 in., 2 in., and 6 in. lengths, and one 12 in. rod. Other rods are available in 4 in., 5 in., 7 in., 8 in., 10 in., and 15 in. lengths. The rod ends (and the micrometer head ends) are hardened, ground, and precision lapped, providing extreme accuracy.

The rods are held in V-shaped troughs, one mounted on the milling machine table and the other on the saddle (Fig. 11-104). A stop rod is mounted at one end of the trough, while at the other end a long range dial indicator graduated in .0001 is mounted.

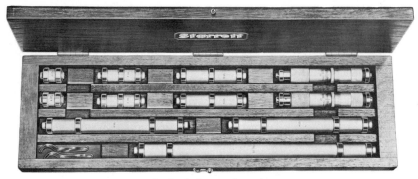

A   A set of measuring rods

B   Micrometer head

C   A 3″ measuring rod

Courtesy The L. S. Starrett Company

Fig. 11-103   Precision and measuring rods

Courtesy The L. S. Starrett Company

Fig. 11-104   Using measuring rods to accurately set the table position

The table is positioned accurately from the *X* and *Y* coordinates by adding (or subtracting) specified lengths or buildups of various rod combinations and micrometer settings.

To Position the Milling Machine Table Using Measuring Rods

1. Set the spindle to the edge of the work. See Chapter 12 for methods of locating an edge.
2. Clean the trough and ends of the stop rod and indicator rod.
3. Check the indicator for free operation.
4. Place the required number of rods, including the micrometer head, in the trough to take up the space between the stop rod and the indicator rod.
5. Adjust the micrometer until it has extended enough to cause the indicator needle to move a half turn.
6. Lock the table.
7. Set the indicator bezel to zero.
8. Increase the rod and micrometer buildup by the length of the measure-

ment between the side of the work-piece and the hole location.
9. Move the table along more than this required distance.
10. Insert the rods and the micrometer head.
11. Move the table back until the needle moves the half turn and registers zero.
12. Lock the table.
13. Recheck the setting and adjust if necessary.

DIGITAL READOUT BOXES

These electronically controlled measuring devices, suitably mounted on the table and the saddle, indicate the table travel to an accuracy of 0.002 mm (or .0001 in.). A digital readout box (Fig. 11-105) resembles the odometer on an automobile dashboard and indicates the distance travelled by a series of numbers visible through a glass front on the box. This arrangement permits quick and accurate setting of the machine table.

VERNIER SCALE

The milling machine may be equipped with scales on the table and saddle with pointers suitably mounted on the machine. The scales are generally graduated in increments of 2.0 mm or tenths of an inch. A vernier arrangement is mounted adjacent to the feed screw collars which permits the reading in 0.002 mm or .0001 in. *NOTE*: Settings on this machine must be made in one direction only in order to remove the backlash.

Vertical milling machines may be used to position holes without the use of any of the afore-mentioned equipment; however, this method is not too accurate.

The table is positioned by means of the graduated feed collars. This method may be used if the accuracy of the location must not be less than 0.05 mm or .002 in. In order to eliminate backlash, it is important that all settings be made in one direction only.

Courtesy Bendix Corporation

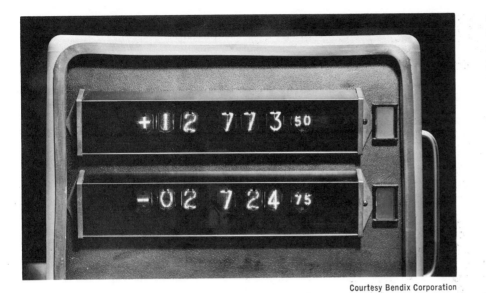

Fig. 11-105 A digital readout box

VERTICAL MILLING MACHINE ATTACHMENTS

The versatility of the vertical milling machine may be further increased by the use of the following attachments:

The *rack milling attachment* permits the machining of racks and broaches on the vertical mill. The spindle of this attachment is fitted into the spindle of the machine while the housing is clamped to the machine quill. It operates on the same principle as a rack milling attachment on the horizontal milling machine.

The *slotting attachment* (Fig. 11-106) is generally fitted to the back end of the overarm, which may be rotated 180° to permit the use of this device. The slotting attachment operates independently of the machine drive on most vertical milling machines. It provides a reciprocating motion to a single pointed tool by means of a motor driven eccentric. This attachment may be used for cutting keyways and slotting out small blanking dies.

DIE SINKING

One important application of the vertical milling machine is that of *die sinking*. Dies used in drop forging and die casting have impressions or cavities cut in them by means of die sinking. The operation of machining a die cavity on a vertical mill is generally done by hand control of the machine, using various end mill type cutters. This is usually followed by considerable filing, scraping, and polishing to produce the highly finished, properly curved, and contoured surfaces required on the die.

Complicated shapes and patterns on molds and dies are made more conveniently and accurately on a vertical milling machine equipped with tracer control. In addition to the regular cutting head, the machine is equipped with a tracer head.

On a tracer-controlled machine (Fig. 11-107), the form of a master or pattern is transferred to the workpiece by means of a hydraulic tracer unit actuated by a stylus

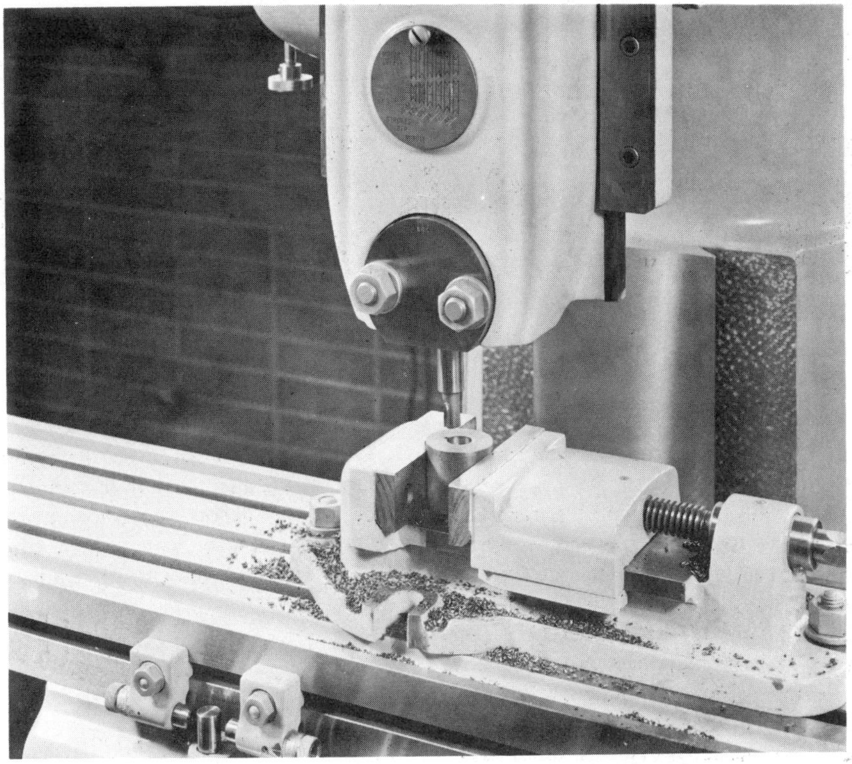

Courtesy Cincinnati Milacron Inc.

Fig. 11-106 Cutting an internal keyway with a slotting attachment

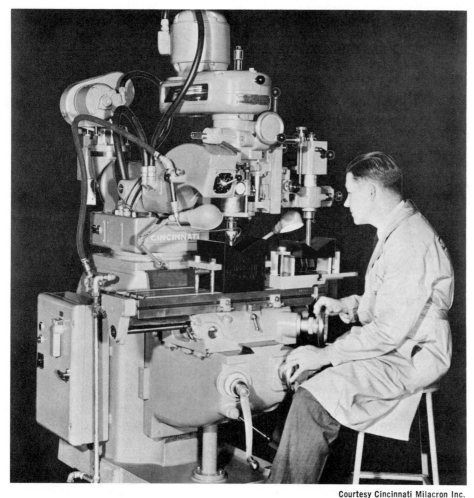

Courtesy Cincinnati Milacron Inc.

Fig. 11-107 A tracer-controlled vertical milling machine

or tracer finger. This contacts the master so that the cutter is moved up or down to coincide with the vertical or side travel of the stylus.

Since both the work and the master are fastened to the table, they both travel at the same rate. As the pattern moves under the stylus, the workpiece assumes the identical form of the master. Some machines may be equipped with ratio arms or devices, and the master can be made considerably larger than the finished workpiece. If a master is made 10 times larger, the arms on the machine are set at a 10:1 ratio and then the part is cut. An error of 0.20 mm on the master will only result in a 0.02 mm error on the workpiece.

Only a light pressure on the stylus, in contact with the master or template, is necessary to deflect the tracer arm and actuate the control valve which controls the movement of the cutting head.

HORIZONTAL MILLING MACHINE QUESTIONS

HORIZONTAL MILLING MACHINE

1. Name six operations that can be performed on a milling machine.

MANUFACTURING TYPE MILLING MACHINE

2. List four features of a manufacturing type milling machine.
3. Name, and describe briefly, six manufacturing type milling machines.

UNIVERSAL HORIZONTAL MILLING MACHINE

4. What is the difference between a plain horizontal and a universal horizontal milling machine?
5. What is the purpose of the backlash eliminator?
6. What is the difference between straddle and gang milling?

MILLING MACHINE ACCESSORIES AND ATTACHMENTS

7. What is the purpose of a fixture?
8. List three classes of milling machine attachments and give three examples of each.
9. Describe the purpose of the following devices:
   a) vertical milling attachment
   b) rack milling attachment
   c) slotting attachment
10. Name three methods of holding cutters on a milling machine.
11. What are the features of the:
    a) plain vise
    b) swivel base vise
    c) universal vise

MILLING CUTTERS

12. Describe three types of plain milling cutters and explain their uses.
13. Describe three types of side milling cutters, and state where each is used.
14. List two ways in which formed cutters differ from plain milling cutters.
15. What advantage has a two-flute end mill.
16. Name two materials which are used to make milling cutters.

17. Name five elements that may be added to iron or steel to produce high-speed steel, and state the purpose of each additive.
18. Discuss the advantages and disadvantages of cemented-carbide tools.

CUTTING SPEEDS

19. What two factors determine the r/min of the milling cutter?
20. At what maximum speed should a 3-1/2 in. cemented carbide milling cutter revolve to machine cast iron?
21. At what r/min should a 115 mm high-speed steel cutter revolve to machine a piece of tool steel?
22. What rules should be observed to obtain best results when using milling cutters?

FEEDS

23. List six factors which will determine the feed rate to be used.
24. Define "feed per tooth."
25. What feed, in millimetres per minute, is required for a 90 mm diameter, 4-tooth helical milling cutter to machine a piece of aluminum?
26. Determine the proper feed for a cemented-carbide face-milling cutter, 3 in. in diameter, which has eight teeth and is revolving at the maximum speed for machining cast iron.
27. Describe climb milling and illustrate by a neat sketch.
28. State five advantages of climb milling.
29. What are the limitations of climb milling?

DEPTH OF CUT

30. What is considered to be a proper roughing cut?
31. Why is a very light cut not desirable as a finish cut?
32. What precautions should be observed when finish milling to prevent damage to the surface of the workpiece?

MILLING MACHINE SETUPS

33. State five precautions that should be observed when setting up work on a milling machine.

ALIGNING THE TABLE AND VISE OF THE UNIVERSAL MILLING MACHINE

34. Why is the table alignment so important to most milling operations?
35. Why must the indicator be mounted on the table, and not the column or the arbor, when aligning a universal table?
36. By means of suitable sketches, show how the vise may be aligned:
    a) parallel to the line of longitudinal table travel
    b) at right angles to the milling machine column

SAWING AND SLITTING

37. List five of the most important precautions to be observed when using a slitting saw.

INDEXING OR DIVIDING HEAD

38. Describe the construction of the indexing or dividing head.
39. Name four methods of indexing that may be performed on the dividing head, and state when each may be used.
40. How does direct indexing differ from the other three methods mentioned in question 39?

SIMPLE INDEXING

41. Explain the principle of simple indexing.
42. Calculate the simple indexing, using a Brown and Sharpe dividing head, for the following divisions: 37, 41, 22, 34, and 120.
43. What procedure should be followed in order to set the sector arms for twelve holes on an 18-hole circle?

ANGULAR INDEXING

44. Explain the principle of angular indexing.
45. Calculate the indexing, using a Cincinnati dividing head, for the following angles: 21°, 37°, 21°30′, and 37°40′.

DIFFERENTIAL INDEXING

46. Describe the principle of differential indexing.
47. What is meant by positive rotation and negative rotation of the index plate?
48. Why does the use of idlers differ for simple and compound gearing?
49. Using a Brown and Sharpe dividing head, calculate the indexing and change gears for the following divisions: 53, 59, 101, and 175. A standard set of change gears, having the following numbers of teeth, is supplied: 24, 24, 28, 32, 40, 44, 48, 56, 64, 72, 86, 100.

WIDE RANGE DIVIDING HEAD

50. How does the wide range dividing head differ from a standard dividing head?
51. What two ratios are found in a wide range dividing head?
52. Calculate the indexing for (a) 1000 and (b) 1200 divisions, using the wide range dividing head.
53. Calculate the angular indexing for the following, using a wide range dividing head: 20°45′, 25°15′32″.

LINEAR GRADUATING

54. How are the dividing head and the milling machine geared for linear graduating?
55. Describe the principle of linear indexing.
56. a) What indexing would be required to move the table .003 in. when using equal gearing on the dividing head and the lead screw?

b) Calculate the indexing required to move the milling machine table 0.05 mm if the lead screw has a pitch of 5 mm.

57. a) How may the work be held for linear indexing?
    b) What type of tool is used and how is it held?

GEARS AND GEAR CUTTERS

58. List six types of gears, and state where each may be used.

59. Define the following gear terms, and state the formula used to determine each. Use the formulas involving diametral pitch where applicable, *not* circular pitch.
    a) pitch diameter
    b) diametral pitch
    c) addendum
    d) dedendum
    e) clearance
    f) outside diameter
    g) number of teeth

60. Calculate the pitch diameter, outside diameter, and whole depth of tooth for the following gears:
    a) 8 DP having 36 teeth
    b) 12 DP having 81 teeth
    c) 16 DP having 100 teeth
    d) 6 DP having 23 teeth
    e) 4 DP having 54 teeth

61. What cutter numbers would be used for cutting the gears in question 60?

62. Describe two methods of centring the gear blank with the cutter when machining a spur gear.

63. What precautions should be observed when mounting the gear blank between the index head and centres?

64. Compare the terms *module* and *pitch diameter*.

65. How does the metric module numbering system for gear cutters differ from that for diametral pitch systems?

66. For a 40-tooth spur gear, 240 mm in diameter, calculate:
    a) module
    b) circular pitch
    c) outside diameter
    d) addendum
    e) dedendum
    f) whole depth
    g) cutter number

GEAR TOOTH MEASUREMENT

67. State two methods of measuring gear teeth.

68. How is the wire size determined for:
    a) external gears?
    b) internal gears?

HELICAL MILLING

69. Define:
    a) helix
    b) spiral
    c) lead
    d) angle of helix

70. Make a sketch to illustrate the relationship between the lead, circumference, and helix angles.

71. List two factors which affect the lead of a helix.

72. To what angle must the table be swung to cut the following helices?
    a) lead 10.290 in., diameter of workpiece 3-1/4 in.
    b) lead 12.000 in., diameter of workpiece 2-3/4 in.
    c) lead = 600 mm
       work diameter = 100 mm
    d) lead = 232 mm
       work diameter = 25 mm

73. How may a right- and left-hand helix be recognized, and in which direction should the table be swivelled for each?

74. a) Calculate the change gears to cut the following leads:
    1) 6.000 in.
    2) 7.500 in.
    3) 9.600 in.
    4) 33.330 in.
    b) The lead screw of a milling machine has a pitch of 5 mm. The available change gears are 24,

24, 28, 32, 36, 40, 44, 48, 56, 64, 72, 86, 100. Calculate the change gears required for the following leads: 800 mm, 560 mm.

75. It is required to make a helical milling cutter having the following specifications:
    Diameter: 3.475 in.
    Helix: Left-hand
    Rake angle: 5° positive
    Depth of flute: .5 in.
    Material: tool steel
    Number of teeth: 7
    Helix angle: 20°
    Angle of flute: 55°
    Length: 3 in.
    Calculate:
    a) indexing
    b) lead
    c) change gears required to cut this lead

RACK MILLING

76. Define a rack and state its purpose.

77. A 10 DP gear is in mesh with a rack. The gear has 42 teeth. The rack is 1 in. thick from the top of the tooth to the bottom of the rack. Calculate the distance from the centre of the gear to the bottom of the rack.

78. Calculate the linear pitch of a 5-pitch rack; an 8-pitch rack; a 14-pitch rack.

HELICAL GEARING

79. Compare circular pitch to normal circular pitch. Illustrate by means of a suitable sketch.

80. a) The following information applies to helical gears having parallel shafts.

	Pitch	Ratio	Centre distance
1)	3	3:1	10.5 in.
2)	10	4:1	5.5 in.
3)	6	3:1	7.5 in.
4)	8	12:5	6.0625 in.

For the above gears and pinions calculate:
1) pitch diameter
2) number of teeth

3) diametral pitch
4) helix angle
5) outside diameter
6) lead
7) change gears
   Note: A standard set of change gears is supplied.
8) cutter number to be used

b) It is required to cut a 34 tooth helical metric 6 module gear with a 600 mm lead. The pitch diameter of the gear is 180 mm and the pitch of the lead screw is 5 mm. Calculate:
   1) Module
   2) Circular pitch
   3) Normal circular pitch
   4) Addendum
   5) Outside diameter
   6) Depth of tooth
   7) Helix angle
   8) Indexing

CONTINUED FRACTIONS

81. Using continued fractions, calculate the change gears required to produce the following leads, when a standard set of change gears is supplied: a) 20.570 in. b) 31.360 in. c) 9.778 in. d) 6.667 in.

CAMS AND CAM MILLING

82. Define a cam.
83. Name four types of cams.
84. Name four types of followers, and state where each is used.
85. List three cam motions, and describe the type of motion which is imparted to the follower in one revolution of the cam.
86. In a single-lobe cam and a double-lobe cam, what is the relationship of the lead to the rise?
87. Calculate:
    a) lead of cam
    b) the change gears required to produce this lead
    c) the angle at which to swing the dividing head
    d) the angle at which to swing the vertical head for each of the following examples of uniform rise:
       i) a single-lobe cam having a rise of .125 in. in 360°
       ii) a two-lobed cam, each lobe having a rise of .187 in. in 180°
       iii) a three-lobed cam, each lobe having a rise of .200 in. in 120°

WORMS AND WORM GEARS

88. Define a worm and worm gear, and state the purpose for which they are used.
89. Describe briefly how a worm is cut on a milling machine.

CLUTCHES

90. List three type of clutches, and state the application of each.
91. Why are clutches with an odd number of teeth preferred to those with an even number of teeth?
92. After the outside surface of a 75 mm diameter clutch blank has been touched up to a 12 mm wide side cutter, how far must the table be moved over when cutting
    a) a clutch having five teeth?
    b) a clutch having six teeth?

VERTICAL MILLING MACHINE QUESTIONS

93. Why has the vertical milling machine been so readily accepted by industry?
94. Name six operations which can be performed in a vertical mill.
95. Describe:
    a) a standard vertical mill
    b) a ram type vertical mill
96. State the purpose of the following parts:
    a) column
    b) overarm
    c) head
    d) knee

ALIGNING THE VERTICAL HEAD AND VISE

97. Why is it necessary to align the vertical head square with the table?
98. Describe briefly how the vertical head may be aligned with the table surface.
99. Why is it important that the vise be aligned with the table travel?
100. Describe one method of aligning the vise parallel to the table travel.

MACHINING A FLAT SURFACE

101. What precautions should be observed before machining a flat surface?
102. What type of cutter should be used when machining a large surface?
103. How can the edge of a flat piece be machined square with a flat finished surface?

MACHINING ANGULAR SURFACES

104. Describe briefly two methods of machining angular surfaces.
105. List the procedure for setting a vertical head to an accurate angle.
106. How should small angular surfaces be cut?
107. How can compound angles be machined on a vertical mill?

CUTTING SLOTS AND KEYWAYS

108. What type of cutter should be used to cut slots or keyways having one or two blind ends?
109. How can round work be held for machining slots and keyways?
110. Explain one method of aligning the end mill with the centre of a shaft.
111. How may the depth of a keyway be measured?
112. Calculate the measurement for a 12 mm wide keyseat from the bottom of a 50 mm diameter shaft to the bottom of the keyseat.
113. Describe a Woodruff key and state its purpose.
114. Explain the markings 810 found on a Woodruff key cutter.

115. Explain how a Woodruff key cutter may be centred with a shaft.

ROTARY TABLE

116. For what purpose may a rotary table be used?
117. Describe briefly the construction of a rotary table.
118. What is the purpose of the hole in the centre of a rotary table?
119. What common ratios are found on rotary tables?
120. Explain how power feed may be supplied to a rotary table.
121. Describe briefly how a rotary table may be centred with the vertical mill spindle.
122. Explain how a number of identical parts, having a hole in the centre, can be quickly aligned on a rotary table.
123. Describe briefly how a single workpiece would be centred on a rotary table.

RADIUS AND T-SLOT MILLING

124. Explain how a large radius may be cut using a rotary table.
125. What purpose do T-slots serve?
126. List the two operations necessary in order to cut a T-slot.

MILLING DOVETAILS

127. What is the purpose of a dovetail?
128. What is the procedure for machining the centre section of an internal dovetail?
129. Describe a dovetail cutter.
130. Explain how the first angular side of a dovetail is cut.
131. How can an internal dovetail be measured accurately for size?
132. Explain the advantages of using a rotary table when cutting dovetails.

JIG BORING ON A VERTICAL MILL

133. Name and describe three types of measuring systems used on vertical mills for jig boring.
134. How are measuring rods used on a vertical mill for locating a hole?
135. Name three methods of locating an edge.
136. How may a table be moved exactly 2.6836 in. from one location to another by using measuring rods?

VERTICAL MILLING MACHINE ATTACHMENTS

137. What is the purpose of the rack milling and slotting attachments?
138. How does a slotting attachment operate?
139. How can a vertical mill be used for various die sinking operations
    a) manually?
    b) automatically?
140. Explain the purpose of ratio arms or devices in die sinking.

12 THE JIG BORER AND JIG GRINDER

THE JIG BORER

The jig borer was developed primarily to overcome the toolmaker's perpetual problem of accurately locating and producing holes. The jig borer is especially useful in the manufacture of jigs and fixtures when there must be an accurate dimensional relationship between the locators aligning the workpiece and the bushing holes which are used to provide accurate hole locations. It is an invaluable machine tool in the manufacture of simple, compound, progressive, and lamination dies which re-

Courtesy Moore Special Tool Co. Inc.

quire great accuracy between a variety of locating parts. Holes in the punch pad and die plate, pilot holes, and bushing holes which align the stripper plate are obvious "naturals" for a jig borer. Such holes can be produced quickly and accurately. By interchanging the tools in the spindle of the jig borer, operations such as drilling, boring, reaming, and counterboring can be readily performed.

A jig borer, although similar to a vertical milling machine, is much more accurate and built closer to the floor so that the worker can operate it while he is in a seated position. The precision-ground lead screws controlling the table movements are capable of infinitely fine incremental divisions and permit simultaneous measurement and positioning to within an accuracy of 0.002 mm (or .0001 in.) over the table length. This machine must be not only rugged for the heavy cuts necessary for roughing purposes, but also sensitive for the more accurate finishing cuts.

Since the beginning of the machine age, the problem of locating holes accurately has plagued the toolmaker. Before the development of accurate locating and measuring machines, the toolmaker was faced with a tedious and costly, though reasonably accurate, method of locating holes. At that time, each problem of hole location involved three basic operations:

Locating: establishing the desired location of the hole on the workpiece.

Machining: removing material to produce a desired size hole in the required location.

Inspection: checking the location of the finished hole to see that it is within the acceptable limits of the desired location. Each of these basic operations can be performed by a variety of methods. The method used depends upon the nature of the job.

LOCATING

Locating, the first operation, is accomplished by three methods: layout, buttoning, or transfer.

LAYOUT

The *layout* operation consists of scribing lines on the workpiece to indicate the desired position of the finished hole. A prick-punch mark is necessary in order to mark the centre of the hole and to align it with the axis of the cutting tool.

a) *A combination square and scriber* provides the quickest but least accurate method of layout. The coarseness of the rule graduations and the angle of the scriber limit the accuracy attained.

b) *A surface gauge* is more accurate since it eliminates errors resulting from reading graduations and the variable scriber angle.

c) *A planer gauge* set to a micrometer is accurate, but not very handy.

293

d) *A height gauge* is more accurate and convenient than the previous three methods.

e) *Gauge blocks with a lapped scriber* (Fig. 12-1) provide the greatest accuracy, but even so the error of the final punch mark remains.

Courtesy Moore Special Tool Co. Inc.

Fig. 12-1   Using gauge blocks with a lapped scriber to scribe a line accurately

BUTTONING

Buttoning consists of mounting a cylindrical toolmaker's button on the workpiece in the desired hole location. A hole is drilled and tapped in the centre of the hole location, and the button is attached to the work with a screw. The clearance between the diameter of the screw and the hole in the button permits the button to be moved to the desired position; the screw is then tightened. The button must be aligned from two directions, a tedious and painstaking operation.

Tapping the button to location in one direction (Fig. 12-2) generally results in displacing it in the other direction. The final tightening of the screw tends to shift the button location, making it necessary to recheck the settings.

a) *A height gauge* is sometimes used to check the position of the button. This is more accurate than the layout method because the error of the prick-punch mark is eliminated.

b) *Gauge blocks*, used together with an indicator (Fig. 12-2), make it possible to locate a button to within ± 0.002 mm (or .0001 in.) accuracy.

Courtesy Moore Special Tool Co. Inc.

Fig. 12-2   Locating a button using gauge blocks and an indicator. This requires patience since the button must be aligned in two directions

TRANSFER

Transfer consists of using a hole in a matching or master workpiece to establish the location of the hole in another piece.

a) *Special transfer punches* having the same diameter as the existing hole are used to mark the desired location on the workpiece.

b) The original piece may be clamped to the work and used as a guide or jig while the workpiece is drilled.

c) The original piece may be clamped to the workpiece; the hole in the master is aligned by indicating. The accuracy attained is greater than the previous methods since the hole is finished by boring.

No matter how carefully a toolmaker works, there is bound to be a certain amount of inaccuracy introduced in methods used to work from a layout. If a drill press is used, the drill is guided by the prick-punch mark which limits accuracy. Work may be mounted on a lathe faceplate (Fig. 12-3) and aligned with the use of a "wiggler" or *pump centre* and indicator. This method of hole location is more accurate than using a drill press.

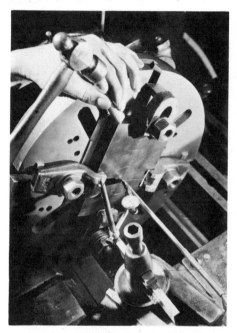

Courtesy Moore Special Tool Co. Inc.

Fig. 12-3   Picking up the location of a prick punch mark with a pump centre and indicator

MACHINING

Machining, the second operation, generally consists of three methods: drilling, single-point boring, or grinding. The type and condition of the machine will affect the accuracy of the hole location.

DRILLING

Drilling is the least accurate method of locating holes. Inaccurate prick-punch marks, improperly ground drills, and hard spots or flaws in the work material are some of the factors affecting the accuracy.

a) When *drilling from a layout*, a progression of drills must be used to open the hole to the desired size. Each drill used contributes a certain amount to the inaccuracy of the hole location.

b) Guiding a drill by means of a drill bushing or master hole is only a little more accurate than drilling since there must be a certain amount of clearance between the bushing and the revolving drill.

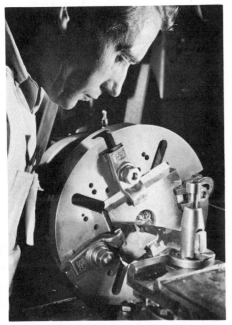

Courtesy Moore Special Tool Co. Inc.

Fig. 12-4 Single-point boring in a lathe represents the correct principle in the wrong machine

SINGLE-POINT BORING

Single-point boring is the most accurate method of machining a hole in soft material. This is a geometrically sound principle since the axis of the hole is generated from the axis of the machine spindle. However, even this method used on conventional machines is subject to error.

a) The most commonly used method of machining a hole to the correct location is doing it in a lathe (Fig. 12-4). The accuracy of this method is often

affected by factors such as loose spindle bearings, an unsymmetrical workpiece not carefully counterbalanced, and the clamping pressure required to resist both centrifugal force and the pressure of the cutting tool.

b) Even the use of a vertical milling machine, where the work is stationary and the cutting tool revolves, is subject to a certain amount of error. A vertical milling machine spindle is rarely accurate enough, and the squareness of the spindle to the table is questionable.

GRINDING

Grinding is used to finish a hole to size in a hardened workpiece (Fig. 12-5). This method is fairly accurate; however, the same factors present in boring apply to the grinding operation in the lathe. Another factor which must be considered is the error incurred in aligning the hole for the grinding operation.

Courtesy Moore Special Tool Co. Inc.

Fig. 12-5 The potential location accuracy attainable by grinding cannot be developed under makeshift conditions

INSPECTION

Inspection is the third operation and is always time-consuming. When an error is discovered, some doubt still exists as to whether the error is a result of the machining or the inspection operation.

The location of the finished hole is checked by measuring from a finished edge of the workpiece to the edge of the hole or to the diameter of a plug tightly fitted to the hole.

a) *Vernier calipers* may be used to measure the distance between holes (Fig. 12-6). Tightly fitting plugs may also be placed in the holes, and the distance between the holes measured with a micrometer.

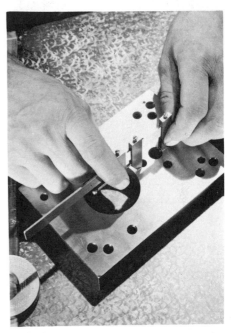

Courtesy Moore Special Tool Co. Inc.

Fig. 12-6 Measuring the distance between two holes with a vernier caliper

b) *An indicator* mounted on a surface or height gauge (Fig. 12-7) can be used to compare the location of a hole to a buildup of gauge blocks. It should be noted that the work must be placed on

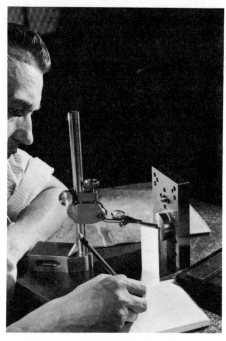

Courtesy Moore Special Tool Co. Inc.

Fig. 12-7   Measuring the distance from the edge of the work to a plug fitted in a hole

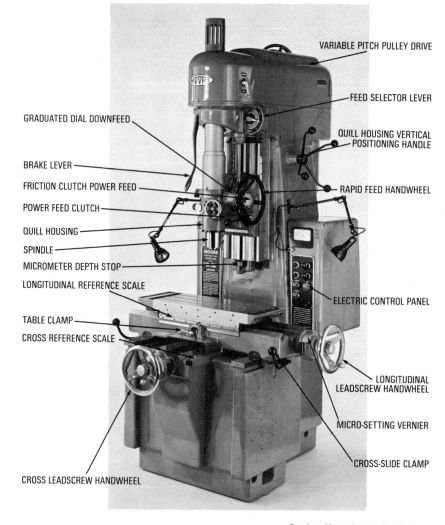

VARIABLE PITCH PULLEY DRIVE

FEED SELECTOR LEVER

QUILL HOUSING VERTICAL POSITIONING HANDLE

RAPID FEED HANDWHEEL

GRADUATED DIAL DOWNFEED

BRAKE LEVER

FRICTION CLUTCH POWER FEED

POWER FEED CLUTCH

QUILL HOUSING

SPINDLE

MICROMETER DEPTH STOP

LONGITUDINAL REFERENCE SCALE

TABLE CLAMP

CROSS REFERENCE SCALE

ELECTRIC CONTROL PANEL

LONGITUDINAL LEADSCREW HANDWHEEL

MICRO-SETTING VERNIER

CROSS-SLIDE CLAMP

CROSS LEADSCREW HANDWHEEL

Courtesy Moore Special Tool Co. Inc.

Fig. 12-8   A #3 Moore precision jig borer

an accurate surface plate and that all measurements must be taken from a finished edge of the workpiece.

Since the previous methods of accurately locating holes, which involved the operations of layout, machining, and inspection, were inaccurate and costly because of the time involved, it became necessary to develop a machine which could do this quickly and accurately. The *jig borer* (Fig. 12-8), first developed in 1917, now provides the toolmaker with a means of quickly and accurately locating holes to within an accuracy of 0.002 mm over 455 mm of length (or .00009 in. over 18 in.) of length. It is used to finish-bore holes in material left soft or to rough-bore holes in work which will later be hardened and jig ground.

JIG BORER PARTS

The *variable pitch pulley drive* is operated by pushing a button on the *electric control*

panel to provide the spindle with a variable speed range from 60 to 2250 revolutions per minute.

The *quill housing* can be raised or lowered to accommodate various sizes of work if first the *quill housing clamp* is loosened and then the *quill housing vertical positioning handle* is turned.

The *brake level* is manually operated to stop the rotation of the spindle. It is especially useful while various tools are being removed or replaced in the spindle. The *rapid feed handwheel* allows the

spindle to be raised or lowered rapidly by hand.

The *friction clutch* may be used to engage or disengage the handfeed of the quill. The *graduated downfeed dial*, by means of a vernier, reads the distance of vertical spindle travel in hundredths of a millimetre or in thousandths of an inch for inch-designed dials.

The *adjustable stop for hole depths* can be adjusted to allow the spindle to move to a predetermined depth for drilling or boring a hole.

3. Avoid inserting shanks too tightly, especially when the spindle is warmer than the inserted shank. When the shank warms up, it expands and may jam in the spindle.
4. When removing or replacing tools in the spindle, apply the brake firmly with the left hand. The wrench should be held carefully to prevent it from slipping out of the hand and damaging the machine table.

ACCESSORIES AND SMALL TOOLS

A wide variety of accessories enable a jig borer to meet three basic requirements: *accuracy, versatility,* and *productivity.* Only accessories concerned with drilling, boring, and reaming will be dealt with.

DRILLING

Key-type and keyless chucks are used to hold smaller-sized straight shank spotting tools, drills, and reamers. Special collets are used to hold larger straight-shank spotting tools, drills, and reamers. A set screw in the collet is tightened against a flat on the tool shank, providing a positive grip which eliminates twisting and scuffing of the tool shank.

BORING

Single-point boring, the most accurate method of attaining locational accuracy in jig boring, makes it necessary to have a wide variety of boring tools. The most commonly used boring tools are a solid boring bar, a swivel block boring chuck, a dovetail-offset boring chuck, and a DeVlieg microbore boring bar.

The solid boring bar (Fig. 12-10A) is fitted with an adjusting screw which, when adjusted, advances the toolbit over a relatively short range. Solid boring bars are rigid, making them especially useful in boring deep holes; a number of solid boring bars may be left set at a specific size for repetitive boring.

Courtesy Moore Special Tool Co. Inc.

Fig. 12-9   Replacing a tool into the jig borer spindle

The *spindle* revolves inside the quill and supplies drive for the cutting tools. An internal taper in the spindle allows a variety of tools to be rapidly and accurately interchanged.

The *reference scales* (longitudinal and crossfeed) serve as reference points in moving the table into position. They determine the position of the starting or reference point of the job.

The *graduated dials,* with micro-setting verniers on the *longitudinal* and *crossfeed screw handwheels,* allow the table to be positioned quickly and accurately to within 0.002 mm or to within .0001 in. for inch-graduated dials.

To Insert Shanks in the Spindle

Toolroom work, with a variety of hole sizes, requires frequent changing of tools (Fig. 12-9). The tapered hole in the spindle allows this to be done quickly and accurately if certain precautions are taken.

1. The taper shank on the tool being inserted and the hole in the spindle must be *perfectly clean*; otherwise the tapers will be damaged and inaccuracy will occur.
2. Protect the taper shanks from finger perspiration, especially if the shank will be in the machine for some time. This may cause both the shank and the spindle to rust.

Courtesy Moore Special Tool Co. Inc.

Fig. 12-10A   Solid boring bars

The swivel block boring chuck (Fig. 12-10B) provides a greater range of adjustment than other types in proportion to its diameter and better visibility to the operator while boring. One disadvantage of this type of chuck is that since the tool swings in an arc, the graduations for adjusting the tool travel vary depending upon the length of cutting tool used.

Courtesy Moore Special Tool Co. Inc.

Fig. 12-10B   Swivel block boring chuck

The dovetail offset boring chuck (Fig. 12-10C) is a versatile tool which permits the cutting tool to be moved outward at 90° to the spindle axis of the machine because of the dovetail slide. This allows the use of a wide variety of cutting tools without altering the value of the adjusting graduations. This chuck makes it possible to perform operations such as boring, counterboring, facing, undercutting, and machining outside diameters.

Courtesy Moore Special Tool Co. Inc.

Fig. 12-10C   Dovetail offset boring chuck

The DeVlieg microbore boring bar (Fig. 12-10D) is equipped with a micrometer vernier adjustment which permits the cutting tool to be accurately adjusted to within a tenth of a thousandth.

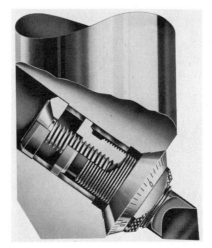

Courtesy DeVlieg Machine Co.

Fig. 12-10D   DeVleig microbore boring bars

SINGLE-POINT BORING TOOLS

Since single-point boring is the most accurate method of generating accurate hole location, a wide variety of cutting tools is available for this operation. The toolbits shown in Fig. 12-11 are generally used for small holes; however, with the necessary chuck attachments, larger holes may be bored. These toolbits are available in high-speed steel and also with brazed, cemented carbide tips.

Courtesy Moore Special Tool Co. Inc.

Fig. 12-11   Single-point boring toolbits

COLLETS AND CHUCKS

An assortment of collets and chucks (Fig. 12-12) is available for a jig borer spindle to hold straight-shank spotting tools, drills, and precision end cutting reamers.

REAMERS

Two types of reamers, the rose, or fluted, and the precision end cutting, are used in jig boring for bringing a hole to size quickly. The *rose*, or *fluted*, *reamer*, with a long flexible shank, is used after a hole has been bored and provides an accurate method of sizing a hole. If handled carefully and used to remove only about 0.02 mm to 0.08 mm (or .001 in. to .003 in.)

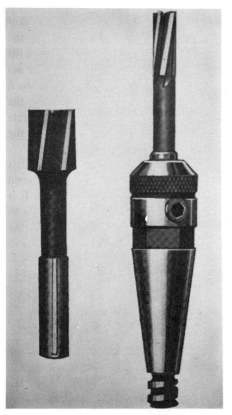

Fig. 12-12   A hardened and ground collet holding a precision end cutting reamer

these reamers maintain fairly accurate hole sizes.

Precision end cutting reamers, with short sturdy shanks (Fig. 12-12), provide the fastest method of locating and sizing holes to within an accuracy of $\pm$ 0.015 mm (or .0005 in.). The end cutting reamer, held rigidly and running true with the spindle, acts likes a boring tool and reamer, locating and sizing the hole at the same time. End cutting reamers eliminate the use of boring tools if the accuracy of the hole diameter and location does not require closer tolerance than $\pm$ 0.015 mm (or .0005 in.).

WORK-HOLDING DEVICES

A wide variety of work-holding devices is necessary to fasten work for jig boring. Parallel setup blocks, matched parallel set-up angle irons, matched box parallels, and extension parallels help to set up and align a variety of work shapes. To prevent machining into the table surface, most work held on a jig borer is mounted on parallels or another suitable device. *Bolts* and *strap clamps* (Fig. 12-13) provide an efficient and convenient method of holding most types of work. The heel rests for these clamps are made of brass to avoid marring the table and will build up to any height from approximately 10 to 300 mm.

The precision vise (Fig. 12-14) is a valuable accessory for holding work too small to be held with bolts and strap clamps. It has stepped jaws which serve as parallels and a V-slot for holding round work. The vise is mounted on a base plate which is ground square and parallel to the stationary jaw, allowing the vise to be aligned quickly and accurately against the straightedge of the machine.

Fig. 12-14   A precision vise

Fig. 12-15   Cylindrical work set up in V-blocks

V-blocks are used to support and align cylindrical workpieces. If the work is long enough to require the use of two V-blocks (Fig. 12-15), it is important that a

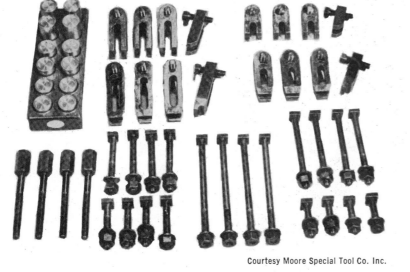

Fig. 12-13   Bolts, strap clamps, heel rests

matched set be used to ensure parallelism with the table surface. The work must also be aligned parallel with the table travel; indicate along the diameter of the cylinder and tap the V-blocks to correct any error.

The micro-sine plate (Fig. 12-16), based on the sine bar principle, is used to hold work for the machining of angular holes. It can be set to any angle from zero to 90° by the use of the proper gauge-block buildup. A clamp rod is used to prevent the micro-sine plate from moving during machining operations. The surface of the sine plate is large enough to allow the rotary table (Fig. 12-16) to be mounted for work requiring compound angular setups and spacings.

The rotary table (Fig. 12-16) can be mounted on the machine table and then used for spacing holes accurately in a circle. The table is accurately graduated around its circumference in half-degree divisions and, by means of a vernier on the handwheel dial, settings accurate to

within ±12″ or less can be made. When holes are required at 90° to the axis of the work, the *Moore Precision Rotary Table* is constructed so that it may be mounted in a vertical position on the table of the jig borer. A lapped bushing in the centre of the table may be used for aligning workpieces centrally. On some rotary tables, the handwheel can be removed and replaced with an index plate attachment. This is especially valuable where a large number of holes or graduations are required, since it eliminates errors resulting from calculation of the angles.

TO SET UP WORK

Several methods of setting up work are used in jig boring.

The most common are:

a) Setting the work parallel to the machine table and aligning one edge of the workpiece with the table travel.

b) Mounting the work on a sine plate for angular machining.

c) Mounting the work on a rotary table for the angular spacing of holes in a circle.

The most common type of workpiece is flat and rectangular and is one of the easiest to set up. The basic requirement for this type of work is that *two edges be accurately ground at right angles to each other.* This greatly assists in aligning the workpiece and also provides an accurate surface for aligning the centre of the spindle with an edge.

The work is usually placed on parallels to avoid cutting the table, and is fastened by means of bolts and strap clamps. It is important that the supporting parallels be directly under the clamps to prevent the work from being sprung or bowed, as in Fig. 12-17.

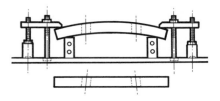

Fig. 12-17 The spring induced by improper clamping will result in holes machined out of square

The edge of the workpiece may be aligned with the table travel by setting one of the two ground edges against the straightedge of the machine. Should it be desirable to have the work closer to the centre of the table, parallel setup blocks or gauge blocks may be used between the straightedge and the work (Fig. 12-18). To ensure correct alignment, it is good practice to check the work with a dial indicator.

To Align the Work Edge with an Indicator

On work that does not allow the use of the straightedge, alignment may be accomplished by holding an indicator in the machine spindle (Fig. 12-19).

1. Clamp the work lightly to the table.
2. Hold the indicator shank in a collet or drill chuck in the machine spindle.

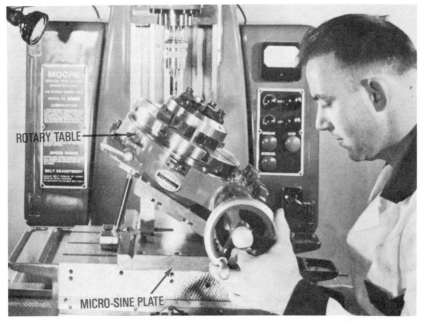

Fig. 12-16 Combining the micro-sine plate and the rotary table for compound angle setups and indexing spacing

Courtesy Moore Special Tool Co. Inc.

Fig. 12-18 Setup blocks spacing the work from the straightedge and parallel to the table travel

Courtesy Moore Special Tool Co. Inc.

Fig. 12-19 Aligning the edge of the work parallel with the table travel with an indicator

METHODS OF LOCATING AN EDGE

Once the work has been set parallel with the table travel, it is necessary to align the centre of the jig borer spindle to some reference or starting point. The reference points vary greatly and may include a hole, pin, boss, scribed line, slot or contour, or an edge. The two most commonly used reference points are a hole or an edge.

BACKLASH

When a reference point is being picked up, table dials set, or the table positioned, *the movement must always be made in the direction of the arrows on the dials* (Fig. 12-24) to eliminate errors as the result of *backlash*. If the crossfeed or longitudinal dial is turned past the required setting, it is necessary to back the dial away from the setting approximately one-quarter turn to eliminate backlash, and then reset it by turning it in the proper direction. When it is necessary to move the table backwards (in the opposite direction of the dial arrows), turn the dial past the setting required by at least one-quarter turn, and then make the final setting in the direction of the arrows.

PICKING UP AN EDGE WITH AN EDGEFINDER

The *edgefinder* (Fig. 12-20A) is a valuable accessory for picking up an edge. It is constructed so that the surface of the edgefinder which is held against the edge of the work is exactly in the centre of the slot used for indicating purposes.

1. Hold the edgefinder firmly against the work. On some workpieces, it may be possible to hold the edgefinder to the work with the aid of a clamp.
2. Adjust the indicator holder so that the indicator point just touches one edge of the slot.
3. Bring the indicator into contact with one side of the slot, and have it register approximately 0.25 mm to 0.50 mm.

3. Bring the indicator against the ground edge of the work and make it register approximately 0.50 mm (or .020 in.).
4. Turn the machine spindle slightly in each direction and stop when the indicator registers the highest reading. This establishes a 90° relationship between the indicator point and the work edge.
5. Set the indicator dial to zero.
6. Turn the jig borer table handwheel to move the workpiece edge past the indicator point. In this way, the indicator will show how much error there is in the work alignment.
7. Then gently tap the work until the indicator shows no movement while the work is moved past the indicator. *NOTE*: The work should *always be tapped away from the indicator*, not towards it, to prevent damage to the indicator.
8. When no indicator movement is shown, tighten the clamping nuts and *recheck the alignment* with the indicator.

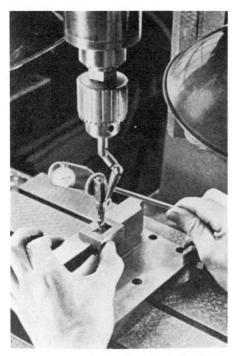

Fig. 12-20A   Picking up an edge with an edgefinder and indicator. The mirror assists in reading the indicator when it is turned away from the operator

4. Make sure that the indicator is at right angles to the edge by *slightly turning* the jig borer spindle backward and forward. Stop when the indicator registers its highest reading and *set the indicator dial to zero.*
5. Turn the machine spindle one-half turn, stopping when the indicator registers its highest reading on the other edge (Fig. 12-20A).
6. Turn the table handwheel in the direction of the arrow one-half the difference between the two indicator readings.
7. Repeat steps 4, 5, and 6 until both indicator readings are exactly the same.
8. When both indicator readings are identical, the centre of the machine spindle is located on the edge of the work.

Work may be quickly located to within 0.015 mm by means of a spring-loaded

edgefinder (Fig. 12-20B) mounted in a drill chuck or collet. This device, which has a movable head the same diameter as the shank, moves approximately 0.80 mm off centre when the edgefinder is rotated. As the edgefinder is brought against the edge of the workpiece, the eccentricity of the head decreases. When the head of the edgefinder runs concentric with the body, the edge of the workpiece will be half the diameter of the head from the centre line of the spindle.

Fig. 12-20B   Spring-loaded edgefinder

To Pick Up an Edge Without an Edgefinder

If an edgefinder is not available, it is still possible to pick up an edge fairly accurately by using the method illustrated in Fig. 12-21.

1. Mount the indicator into the machine spindle.
2. Adjust the indicator holder so that the indicator point is as close as possible to the centre of the machine spindle.
3. Bring the indicator into contact with the edge of the work, and have it register approximately 0.25 mm to 0.50 mm.
4. Make sure the indicator is at right angles to the edge by *slightly turning* the jig borer spindle backward and forward. Stop when the indicator registers its lowest reading and *set the indicator dial to zero.*
5. Raise the machine spindle to clear the top of the work and rotate the spindle 180° (one-half turn).

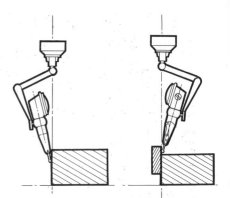

Fig. 12-21   Picking up an edge without an edgefinder. The indicator is set against the work, raised, rotated 180°, and set against a gauge block held against the edge

6. Place a gauge block against the work edge (Fig. 12-21), and turn the machine spindle slightly backward and forward. Stop when the indicator registers its lowest reading.
7. Turn the table handwheel in the direction of the arrow, one-half the difference between the two indicator readings.
8. Repeat steps 4, 5, 6, and 7 until both indicator readings are exactly the same.

To Locate with a Linefinder

A method which is not very accurate, but sometimes used to pick up an edge or a

Fig. 12-22   Picking up an edge with a linefinder

scribed line, is to locate with a *linefinder* or *wiggler*.

1. Mount the wiggler (Fig. 12-22) into a drill chuck held in the machine spindle.
2. Start the machine and make the wiggler run true by bringing a finger into contact with the wobbling point.
3. Move the table so that the point of the wiggler is as close as possible to the reference line or edge.
4. Use a magnifying glass so the final settings may be made as accurately as possible.

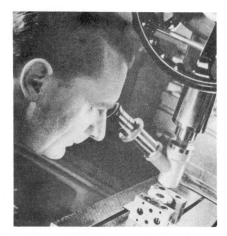

Courtesy Moore Special Tool Co. Inc.

Fig. 12-23   The Moore locating microscope permits optical pickups where conventional means are impractical

To Locate with a Microscope

There are times when the reference point on the work does not suit the pickup methods of an indicator or linefinder. When small or partial holes, irregular contours, slots, and punch marks are used as reference points, a *locating microscope* (Fig. 12-23) is used. This microscope has a 40 × magnification, great enough to permit 0.002 mm (.0001 in.) to be seen. The reticle reference on the microscope consists of a number of concentric circles and two pairs of crossed centre lines for picking up a wide variety of reference points.

THE COORDINATE LOCATING SYSTEM

The *coordinate* locating system is the most efficient method of establishing hole locations for jig boring operations. This system eliminates the tedious and often inaccurate methods of hole location, such as buttoning and layout. It also permits the best sequence of operations, such as spotting, drilling, and rough boring all holes on a workpiece before the finish boring operation. The coordinate locating system provides the best conditions for maintaining precision hole location in jig boring.

The two general types of coordinates used are:

a) *rectangular coordinates*, for dimensions given in straight lines
b) *polar coordinates*, used with the rotary table for holes on circles and showing angles and distances from a zero line or centre

RECTANGULAR COORDINATES

The rectangular coordinate system consists of establishing the relationship of the work to be jig bored to a pair of crossed ordinates, or *zero lines*. On the Moore jig borer, the zero lines are at the upper left-hand corner of the table. These crossed ordinates, sometimes referred to as the *x* and *y* axis, represent zero readings on both the crossfeed and longitudinal reference scales of the jig borer. Fig. 12-24 shows the relationship of the reference scales and the lead screw dials with the coordinate dimensions. (Most jig borers now in use only read in inches. Some of the newer machines on the market, however, are capable of providing readouts in both millimetres and inches.)

After the work is fastened to the table and the spindle aligned with *both edges* of the work, the reference scales (longitudinal and crossfeed) should be set to the nearest inch line. For example, if the crossfeed reference scale is set at 4.000 in. and the longitudinal reference scale is set

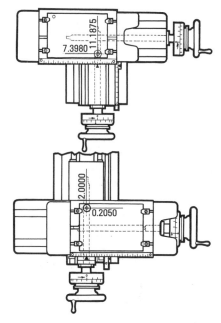

Courtesy Moore Special Tool Co. Inc.

Fig. 12-24   The relationship of the reference scales and dials with the coordinate dimensions (dimensions in inches)

at 6.000 in., the figures 4.000 in. and 6.000 in. are immediately written on the corresponding edge of the drawing in the correct relationship to the table movement.

Fig. 12-25 shows a conventionally dimensioned drawing where some of the dimensions are from an edge, while others are from hole to hole. Fig. 12-26 shows the same drawing dimensioned using the coordinate system. The 4.000 in. on the upper right-hand corner and the 6.000 in. on the upper left-hand corner correspond to the settings on the crossfeed and longitudinal reference scales. All dimensions are added to these two points and are labelled on the diagram correspondingly (Fig. 12-26). For example, the three holes on top are all .500 in. from the edge which now becomes 4.500 in. from the reference point on the scale. The distance between these three and the hole immediately below is .5625 in. which now becomes 5.0625 in. (4.000 + .500 + .5625) from the reference point.

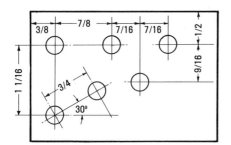

Courtesy Moore Special Tool Co. Inc.

Fig. 12-25   A conventionally dimensioned drawing (dimensions in inches)

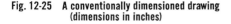
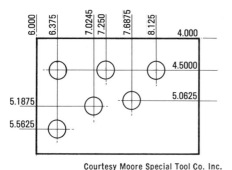

Courtesy Moore Special Tool Co. Inc.

Fig. 12-26   The same drawing with rectangular coordinates (dimensions in inches)

POLAR COORDINATES

This is the conventional dimensioning system used to indicate the location of holes on a circle which are all the same distance from a common centre. Such dimensions may be given either in the form of angles between holes, or by the number of equally spaced holes required on the circle. To convert the number of equally spaced holes into an angular value between each hole, divide this number into 360°. Great care must be taken in these calculations to avoid error, especially if the number is not evenly divisible into 360°.

Once polar coordinates are calculated, they lend themselves directly to use with the rotary table. Here also, if many holes that do not divide evenly into 360° are required, great care must be taken in the indexing of the rotary table since a small error between each hole can result in a sizable cumulative error. The example in

Fig. 12-27 shows the problems which can be encountered in calculating the angular spacing when the number is not evenly divisible into 360°.

The Woodworth tables (see Appendix) were developed by W. J. Woodworth and J. D. Woodworth to eliminate the problems and inaccuracies encountered in polar coordinates. The tables establish rectangular coordinates for each hole from an upper and left-hand tangent line, enabling holes to be accurately located without the use of a rotary table. A complete set of coordinate tables for up to 100 holes may be found in the book *Holes, Contours and Surfaces*, published by the Moore Special Tool Company, Bridgeport, Connecticut.

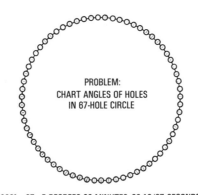

PROBLEM:
CHART ANGLES OF HOLES
IN 67-HOLE CIRCLE

360° ÷ 67 = 5 DEGREES 22 MINUTES 23-19/67 SECONDS
STARTING AT ZERO, ADD AND TABULATE AS FOLLOWS.

HOLE NO.	DEGREES	MINUTES	SECONDS
0	0		
1	5	22	23-19/67
ADD	5	22	23-19/67
2	10	44	46-38/67
ADD	5	22	23-19/67
3	16	7	9-57/67
ADD	5	22	23-19/67
4	21	29	33-9/67
ADD	5	22	23-19/67
5	26	51	56-28/67
ADD	5	22	23-19/67
6	32	14	19-47/67
	etc.	etc.	etc.

Courtesy W. J. & J. D. Woodworth

Fig. 12-27   Steps required to calculate angles between holes on a circle. To prevent cumulative error, each small fraction of an angle must be added every time

To Calculate Rectangular Coordinates Using Woodworth Tables

1. Determine the coordinates of line *A* (left tangent) and line *B* (upper tangent). These two coordinates would be taken from the reference scales on the jig borer table.
2. Multiply the *A* factor by the diameter of the circle for the location of each hole from the left tangent line (Fig. 12-28).
3. Add the result of the calculation to the coordinate of the *A* line.
4. Multiply the *B* factor by the diameter of the circle for the location of each hole from the upper tangent line (Fig. 12-28).
5. Add the result of the calculation to the coordinate of the *B* line.

PRE-FIGURING COORDINATES

In order to save operators' time and secure the greatest amount of production from a jig borer, many firms are supplying drawings where dimensions are already given in coordinate readings. In this way, after the job is clamped to the table, the operator is required only to set the reference scales to correspond to the starting point indicated on the drawing and proceed with the job. When coordinate dimensions are not supplied, it is good practice for the operator to convert all measurements into coordinate dimensions before proceeding with the job. This procedure will not only save time, but also prevent many errors occurring as a result of alternation between jig boring operations and locational calculations.

MAKING SETTINGS

Some jig borer manufacturers use measuring rods and indicators, while others, such as the Moore Special Tool Company, use accurate lead screws with vernier readings on the dial to move the table to the required location. Regardless of the system employed, it is important to remember to make *all locational settings* by turning the table handwheels *in one direction only* to avoid errors resulting from backlash. On Moore jig borers, this direction is indicated by an arrow on the crossfeed and longitudinal dials. Whenever it is necessary to move the table in the opposite direction, it is important that the table be moved past the setting by approximately one-quarter turn and then brought to the desired setting by the handwheel being turned in the direction of the arrows. This procedure will eliminate errors as a result of backlash.

Jig Boring Procedure

Because of the wide variety of work encountered in jig boring, no standard procedure would always apply. However, the following sequence should be followed whenever possible.

1. Set up and carefully align the work parallel to the table travel.
2. Align the centre of the machine spindle with the reference point on the work. Set the reference scales of the machine to the nearest major measurement line.
3. Calculate the coordinate location of all holes and mark them on the drawing of the workpiece.
4. Spot the location of all holes lightly with a centre drill or spotting tool.
5. Respot all the holes to a depth which will provide a good guide for future drilling operations. This operation is a means of rechecking the initial spotting operation to ensure that errors have not been made in reading the scale or dials.
6. Drill holes over 12 mm or 1/2 in. diameter to within 0.80 mm or 1/32 in. of finish size. For holes less than 12 mm or 1/2 in. diameter, drill to within 0.40 mm or 1/64 in. of finish size.

    NOTE: When drilling large holes, it is advisable to enlarge the hole in 6 mm (or 1/4 in.) steps to avoid undue drilling pressure which may move the work location.
7. Recheck the work alignment, as well as the alignment of the spindle with the reference points, to make sure it has not shifted during the roughing operation. If any error is evident, it will be necessary to repeat steps 1 and 2 before proceeding.
8. Rough bore all holes to within 0.08 mm to 0.12 mm (or .003 in. to .005

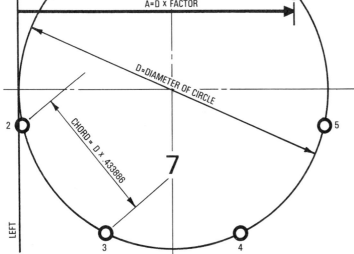

→	Factor for A		Factor for B		Angle of Hole		
					Degree	Minute	Second
1	.109084	1	.188255	1	51	25	42-6/7
2	.012536	2	.611261	2	102	51	25-5/7
3	.283058	3	.950484	3	154	17	8-4/7
4	.716942	4	.950484	4	205	42	51-3/7
5	.987464	5	.611261	5	257	8	34-2/7
6	.890916	6	.188255	6	308	34	17-1/7
7	.500000	7	.000000	7	360	0	0

Courtesy W. J. & J. D. Woodworth

Fig. 12-28   Rectangular coordinate factors and angles for seven evenly spaced holes

in.) of the size required. Work requiring precise accuracy should be allowed to return to *room temperature* before the finish boring operation.

9. Finish bore all holes to the required size.

10. Mount an indicator in the machine spindle and inspect the accuracy of the jig boring before removing the work from the machine.

NOTE: If the accuracy of the work is not required to closer tolerances than ±0.012 mm (or .0005 in.) a precision end cutting reamer may be used to finish the hole, a procedure which eliminates steps 8 and 9.

MEASUREMENT AND INSPECTION OF HOLES

MEASURING HOLE SIZE

A wide variety of instruments is available for measuring hole sizes to various accuracies.

An inside caliper may be adjusted to lightly contact the sides of the hole; this setting is then transferred to a micrometer (Fig. 12-29).

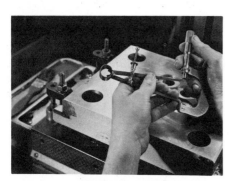

Courtesy Moore Special Tool Co. Inc.

Fig. 12-29   Transferring an inside caliper setting to a micrometer

Telescopic and small-hole gauges are used in the same manner as inside calipers. However, because they are more rigid, greater measuring accuracy is possible. Fig. 12-30 shows a telescopic gauge being used to measure the hole diameter.

Courtesy Moore Special Tool Co. Inc.

Fig. 12-30   A telescopic gauge used to measure hole size

A plug gauge (Fig. 12-31) is more accurate than either calipers or telescopic gauges for checking a hole diameter. It has a serious limitation in that it is effective only in checking a hole whose size is exactly that of the gauge. Since a plug gauge does not relate hole size in measurement units, it is impossible to determine how much material must still be removed from the hole.

Courtesy Moore Special Tool Co. Inc.

Fig. 12-31   A plug gauge is an accurate means of checking final hole size

Flat leaf taper gauges (Fig. 12-32) provide a rapid means of checking hole sizes, especially during the rough boring operation. The most common set consists of 36 leaf taper gauges, allowing holes from

.095 in. to 1.005 in. (2.41 mm to 25.53 mm■) to be measured. Each leaf taper gauge is 1-1/2 in. (38.1 mm) long, marked off in .001 in. (0.025 mm■) graduations, and has a range of .030 in. (0.08 mm). Because these gauges are tapered, they cannot determine whether a hole is bell-mouth or tapered and cannot measure to within a tenth of a thousandth.

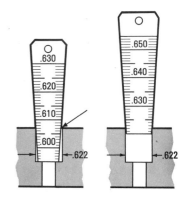

Courtesy Moore Special Tool Co. Inc.

Fig. 12-32   Hole size is read directly from the leaf taper gauge at the point of contact with the edges of the hole

Vernier calipers and various types of *inside micrometers* are instruments capable of measuring hole sizes accurately to within hundredths of a millimetre or thousandths of an inch. They are direct reading instruments and, therefore, do not require their settings to be transferred to another instrument.

The internal indicator gauge (Fig. 12-33) is an extremely accurate instrument, capable of measuring hole sizes to 0.002 mm (or .0001 in.). This gauge is set for a particular size against either a standard ring gauge or a micrometer, and then the indicator dial is revolved until the needle is on the zero line. The gauge is then inserted into the hole and the hole size is compared to the indicator setting. Errors, such as taper, bell-mouth, or out-of-roundness, are easily checked with this type of instrument.

Fig. 12-33 The internal indicator gauge provides extremely accurate measurements

INSPECTING HOLE LOCATION

After the work has been jig bored, it is important to verify the accuracy of the hole locations. Many methods of inspecting hole locations may be employed; the method chosen depends upon the accuracy required.

Fig. 12-34 An indicator mounted in the machine spindle for inspection purposes

It is good practice to use the *jig borer* to inspect the accuracy of hole locations before removing the work from the machine. This is one of the most accurate and convenient methods of inspection since the work is already set up in the machine. An *indicator* (Fig. 12-34) is mounted in the machine spindle and the original reference point is then picked up. From this reference point, the table is moved to the various hole locations, which are checked for accuracy by having the indicator entered into the hole and the machine spindle revolved. The accuracy of the hole location is shown by the amount the indicator needle varies. A locating microscope, mounted in the jig borer spindle, is especially valuable in inspecting locations given from reference points, such as small or partial holes, contours, or slots.

The advantages of using the jig borer for inspecting hole locations are:

a) The work is already set up, saving time and eliminating errors which could occur in setting up work again.

b) The same coordinate dimensions which were used for jig boring are used for inspection.

Fig. 12-35 The Moore measuring machine

c) The machine's measuring system is just as accurate as most measuring standards.

d) The indicator mounted in the machine spindle may be used to check the location, out-of-roundness, bell-mouth, or taper of a hole.

e) Work which was bored to polar coordinates can be inspected with the use of rectangular coordinates; the accuracy of rotary table calculations and settings will also be checked.

Vernier calipers (Fig. 12-6) provide a rapid, but not very accurate method of measuring the distance between two holes. The accuracy in using vernier calipers is subject to the following factors.

a) improper tension on the instrument

b) mistakes in reading the vernier caliper

c) errors in angular alignment which are not easily noticed

An outside micrometer may be used to measure the distance between tightly fitting plugs which have been inserted into the holes. The accuracy of this method is subject to the following factors.

a) holes being out-of-square with each other

b) looseness between the plug and the hole

c) burrs or dirt in the hole or on the plug

A fairly accurate method of inspecting hole location is by means of *gauge blocks and a dial indicator* (Fig. 12-7). The work is clamped to an angle plate with the finished edge resting on the surface plate, and the distance from the work edge to the hole surface or inserted plug is calculated. A gauge block buildup for the calculated dimension is set up and the dial indicator set to the blocks. The indicator is then passed over the surface of the plug or into the hole, comparing this location with the gauge block buildup.

Hole locations may be quickly checked by a *precision height gauge and dial indicator* as outlined in Chapter 3 (Fig. 3-48).

The measuring machine, specially developed for inspecting hole locations to less than 0.002 mm (or .0001 in.), is the most accurate instrument used for inspection purposes. The Moore measuring machine (Fig. 12-35) incorporates the same basic principles used in jig borers for accurately establishing hole locations.

JIG BORER QUESTIONS

1. For what purpose were jig borers developed?
2. For what type of work are they especially valuable?
3. Name the operations which can be performed on a jig borer.
4. Explain the difference between a jig borer and a vertical milling machine.
5. Name and briefly describe the three operations necessary for accurate hole location prior to the development of the jig borer.
6. Briefly describe two methods of locating, machining, and inspecting holes for accuracy.

JIG BORER PARTS

7. State the purpose of each of the following: quill housing, vertical positioning handle, brake lever, rapid feed handwheel, adjustable stop for hole depths, spindle.
8. What purpose do reference scales serve in jig boring?
9. Explain why longitudinal and cross-feed settings may be set quickly and accurately to 0.002 mm (or .0001 in.).
10. List three precautions that should be observed while inserting shanks in the machine spindle.

ACCESSORIES AND SMALL TOOLS

11. Name four common boring tools and explain the advantages of each.
12. Name two types of reamers used in jig boring and explain the advantages of each.

WORK-HOLDING DEVICES

13. Explain why a precision vise is a very valuable jig borer accessory.
14. How should a long, cylindrical piece of work be set up and aligned?
15. State the purpose of
    a) a micro-sine plate
    b) a rotary table
16. Explain how the versatility of the rotary table may be increased.

SETTING UP WORK

17. Name three methods of setting up work on a jig borer.
18. What requirements are necessary for rectangular work before it is set up in a machine? Explain why these are necessary.
19. What precautions should be observed for clamping?
20. Briefly describe two methods of aligning the edge of a workpiece parallel to the table travel.
21. Why should the work always be tapped away from an indicator, not towards it?

METHODS OF LOCATING AN EDGE

22. What must be done to eliminate errors resulting from backlash?
23. If the dial is turned past the required setting, how is backlash eliminated?
24. Name four methods used to pick up an edge or reference point.
25. Describe in detail the procedure to follow in picking up an edge with or without an edgefinder.
26. Describe a locating microscope and state the purpose for which it is used.

THE COORDINATE LOCATING SYSTEM

27. Define and state the purpose of the two types of coordinates.
28. Explain the principle of the coordinate locating system and how it is used in jig boring.
29. What purpose do the reference scales serve in the coordinate locating system?

30. Why are polar coordinates difficult to use in jig boring?

31. Explain the procedure for converting polar coordinates to rectangular coordinates using the Woodworth tables.

MAKING SETTINGS

32. Why should all locational settings be made in the same direction?

33. What must be done when it is necessary to move the table in the direction opposite to that used for locational settings?

JIG BORING PROCEDURE

34. Why is it advisable to calculate all the coordinate dimensions before proceeding with jig boring?

35. What is the purpose of respotting all holes after the initial spotting operation?

36. What precaution should be observed after the drilling operation to ensure accurate hole locations?

37. When is it advisable to use precision end cutting reamers?

MEASUREMENT AND INSPECTION OF HOLES

38. List four instruments used to measure hole size.

39. Describe two precision instruments which can accurately measure hole size.

40. State the advantages of using the internal indicator gauge for checking holes.

41. List the advantages of using the jig borer for inspection purposes.

42. Briefly explain two other methods used to inspect hole locations.

THE JIG GRINDER

The need for accurate hole locations in hardened material led to the development of the jig grinder in 1940. While it was originally developed to position and grind

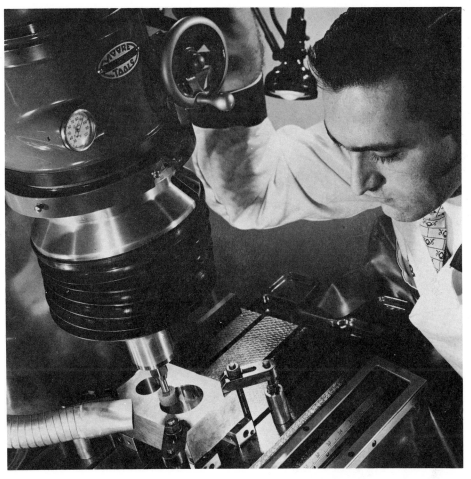

Courtesy Moore Special Tool Co. Inc.

accurately straight or tapered holes, many other uses have been found for the jig grinder over the years. The most important of these has been the grinding of contour forms which may include a combination of radii, tangents, angles, and flats (Fig. 12-36).

The advantages of jig grinding are:

a) Holes distorted during the hardening process can be accurately brought to correct size and position.

b) Holes and contours requiring taper or draft may be ground. Mating parts, such as punches and dies, can be finished to size, eliminating the tedious job of hand fitting.

c) Because more accurate fits and better surface finishes are possible, the service life of the part is greatly prolonged.

Courtesy Moore Special Tool Co. Inc.

Fig. 12-36   A flanged punch represents an ideal example of jig grinding

d) Many parts requiring contours can be made in a solid form, rather than in sections as was formerly necessary.

JIG GRINDER PARTS

The jig grinder (Fig. 12-37) is similar to a jig borer, both having precision-ground lead screws capable of positioning the table within 0.002 mm or .0001 in. accuracy over its entire length. Both are vertical spindle machines and employ the same basic cutting principle encountered in single-point boring. The main difference between these two machines is in the spindles.

The jig grinder is equipped with a high speed pneumatic turbine grinding spindle for holding and driving the grinding wheel. The spindle construction permits outfeed

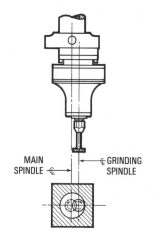

MAIN SPINDLE ℄ — ℄ GRINDING SPINDLE

Fig. 12-38   The grinding spindle may be offset from the main spindle. Lower view shows the planetary path of rotation

grinding (Fig. 12-38), and also the grinding of tapered holes (Fig. 12-39).

TAPER SETTING

The jig grinder spindle can be set to any angle up to 1.5° in either direction for the grinding of tapered holes. The spindle of this machine contains an inclinable guide sleeve which is pivoted at its lower

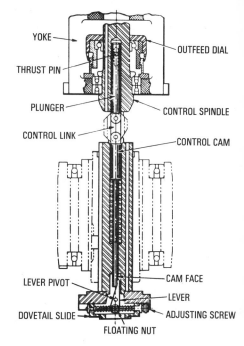

YOKE
OUTFEED DIAL
THRUST PIN
PLUNGER
CONTROL SPINDLE
CONTROL LINK
CONTROL CAM
CAM FACE
LEVER PIVOT
LEVER
DOVETAIL SLIDE
ADJUSTING SCREW
FLOATING NUT

Courtesy Moore Special Tool Co. Inc.

Fig. 12-40   Assembly for controlling size by outfeed. Dial setting outfeed is graduated in tenths

end on two diametrically opposed pivot pins (Fig. 12-39). By an adjustment of the taper-setting screws on the top of the

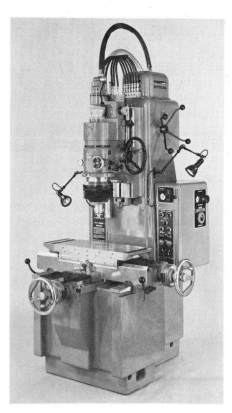

Courtesy Moore Special Tool Co. Inc.

Fig. 12-37   A #3 Moore jig grinder

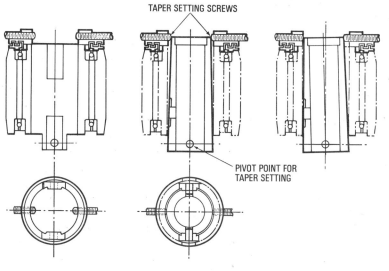

TAPER SETTING SCREWS

PIVOT POINT FOR TAPER SETTING

Fig. 12-39   Main spindle assembly

spindle, the inclinable guide sleeve can be set to an angle which can be read directly on the taper-setting plate.

GRINDING HEAD OUTFEED

A horizontal dovetail slide connects the grinding head to the main spindle of the jig grinder. The grinding head may be offset from the centre of the main spindle to grind various size holes. The amount of eccentricity (offset) of the grinding head can be *accurately* controlled by the internally threaded *outfeed dial* which is mounted on the nonrotating yoke at the top of the jig grinding spindle (Fig. 12-40). This dial is graduated in steps of .0001 in. (0.002 mm▪) permitting accurate control of the hole size during grinding.

Coarse adjustment of the grinding wheel position is attained by a fine pitch adjusting screw within the dovetail slide (Fig. 12-40). This coarse adjusting screw is accessible only when the machine spindle is stopped.

DEPTH MEASURING DEVICES

The Moore jig grinder has three distinct features for controlling and measuring the depth of holes (Fig. 12-41A and B).

a) The *adjustable positive stop* is on the left-hand end of the pinion shaft. Microadjustment can be made by a limiting screw.

b) The *graduated dial* on the downfeed handwheel indicates the travel of the quill. It can be set to zero at any position and reads the travel depth in steps of 0.02 mm (or .001 in.).

c) The *micrometer stop* (Fig. 12-41), fastened to the column of the grinder, controls hole depth.

DOWNFEED GRADUAL DIAL AND VERNIER

OUTFEED GRADUATED DIAL

ADJUSTABLE POSITIVE STOP

MICROMETER STOP

A   B

Courtesy Moore Special Tool Co. Inc.

Fig. 12-41 Depth measuring devices

DIAMOND DRESSING ARM

Jig grinders must rapidly dress grinding wheels without disturbing the setup and location of the grinding spindle.

The diamond dressing arm (Fig. 12-42) may be quickly swung into the approximate grinding wheel location and then locked into position. The final approach to the grinding wheel is done by a fine adjusting knurled screw which advances the diamond through the dressing arm.

Fig. 12-42   Dressing a wheel with the diamond dressing arm

Courtesy Moore Special Tool Co. Inc.

Fig. 12-43   Grinding a large hole using an extension plate

GRINDING METHODS

The removal of material from a hole with a conventional grinding wheel is carried out by two methods: *outfeed* and *plunge* grinding. Each method has its advantages, and at times both can be used effectively to grind the same hole. Small holes, less than 6.4 mm (or 1/4 in.) in diameter, can be effectively ground by using diamond-charged mandrels. Holes larger in diameter than the normal machine range can be ground effectively if an extension plate (Fig. 12-43) is used between the grinding spindle and the main spindle. With the use of an extension plate, holes up to 230 mm (or 9 in.) diameter may be ground.

OUTFEED GRINDING

Outfeed grinding is similar to internal grinding where the wheel is fed radially into the work with passes as fine as 0.002 mm or .0001 in. at a time. The cutting action takes place with the periphery of the grinding wheel. Outfeed grinding is generally used to remove small amounts of stock when high finish and accurate hole size are required.

PLUNGE GRINDING

Plunge grinding with a grinding wheel can be compared to the cutting action of a boring tool. The grinding wheel is fed radially to the desired diameter and then into the work. Cutting is done with the bottom corner of the wheel only. It is a rapid method of removing excess stock, and if the wheel is properly dressed, it produces satisfactory finishes for some jobs. The sharp cutting action which results from the small contact area of the wheel keeps the work cooler than outfeed grinding.

Diamond-charged mandrels (Fig. 12-45) are used instead of conventional grinding wheels for grinding holes less than 6.4 mm (or 1/4 in.) in diameter. These mandrels

Fig. 12-44   Hole size may be increased by 1/16 in. (1.59 mm) in one cut by plunge grinding

should be made of cold-rolled steel which has been turned to the correct size and shape in relation to the hole to be ground. The grinding end of the mandrel is placed in diamond dust and is tapped sharply with a small hardened hammer to embed the diamond dust in the mandrel surface.

DIAMOND CHARGED MANDREL

CEMENT

MOUNTED GRINDING WHEEL

Courtesy Moore Special Tool Co. Inc.

Fig. 12-45   The strength and rigidity of a diamond-charged mandrel exceed those of a mounted grinding wheel

The advantages of this tool over a conventional grinding wheel are:

a) Mandrels have maximum strength and rigidity.
b) Mandrels can be made the ideal diameter and length for each hole.

c) The velocity required for efficient grinding is approximately one-quarter of that for a wheel.
d) The cost per hole is less due to the greater efficiency.

GRINDING WHEELS

SELECTION

Selection of the proper wheel is necessary for satisfactory grinding performance. Since many factors influence the selection of the grinding wheel to be used, a few general principles are outlined.

1. The shank or mandrel of mounted wheels should be as short as possible to assure rigidity.

2. Wherever possible, the grinding wheel diameter should be approximately three-quarters of the diameter of the hole to be ground.

3. Widely spaced abrasive grains in the bond increase the penetrating power of the wheel.

4. When soft, low-tensile strength materials are being ground, a hard abrasive grain with a fairly strong or hard bond should be used.

5. For grinding high-alloy hardened steels, a hard abrasive grain in a soft or weak bond is recommended.

WHEEL SPEED

The majority of grinding wheels are operated most efficiently at about 1800 m/min. Diamond-charged mandrels used for small hole grinding should be operated at approximately 460 m/min. The spindle speed can be varied for the different types and diameters of wheels used; three grinding heads are available for the Moore jig grinder. With these heads, a range from 12 000 to 60 000 r/min is possible. The speed of each head may be varied within its range by adjustment of the pressure regulator which controls its air supply.

Fig. 12-46   The hand-held diamond dresser is convenient and effective

WHEEL DRESSING

For a grinding wheel to perform efficiently, it is important that it be dressed or trued properly. An improperly dressed wheel will tend to produce the following conditions.

a) poor surface finish on the hole
b) surface burns
c) holes which are out of round
d) taper or bell-mouth holes
e) locational error

Care in dressing a grinding wheel can prevent many of these undesirable conditions from developing. To develop the best cutting characteristics of the wheel, use the following recommended techniques for dressing a grinding wheel on a jig grinder.

1. While the wheel is running at a reduced rate, dress the top and bottom face with an abrasive stick held in the hand.

2. Dress the diameter of the wheel with a *sharp* diamond (Fig. 12-46).

3. Repeat steps 1 and 2 with the wheel at the proper operating speed.

4. Relieve the upper portion of the diameter (Fig. 12-47) so that approximately 6 mm or 1/4 in. of the cutting face remains.

5. The bottom face of the wheel should be concaved slightly with an abrasive stick for grinding to a shoulder or to the bottom of a hole.

Courtesy Moore Special Tool Co. Inc.

Fig. 12-47   The width of the wheel face is reduced to avoid excessive side pressure while grinding

In *outfeed grinding*, only the diameter of the wheel should be dressed when required. When *plunge grinding*, dress the bottom face of the wheel with an abrasive stick.

GRINDING ALLOWANCES

Many factors determine the amount of material which should be left in a hole for the jig grinding operation. Some of the more common factors are:
a) type of surface finish in the bored hole
b) size of the hole
c) material of the workpiece
d) distortions which occur during the hardening process

It is difficult to set specific rules on the amount of material which should be left for grinding, because of the many variable factors involved. However, general rules which would apply in most cases are as follows.
a) Holes up to 12 mm (or 1/2 in.) diameter should be 0.12 mm to 0.20 mm (or .005 in. to .008 in.) undersize for the grinding operation.
b) Holes over 12 mm (or 1/2 in.) diameter should be 0.25 mm to 0.40 mm (or .010 in. to .015 in.) undersize for the grinding operation.

SETTING UP WORK

When setting up work for jig grinding, take care to avoid distortion of the workpiece or machine table due to clamping pressures. Keep the following points in mind while mounting the work.
1. When bolts or strap clamps are used, keep the bolts as close as possible to the work.
2. Strap clamps should be placed exactly over the parallels supporting the work. Distortion of the work can occur if a strap clamp is tightened over a part of the work not supported by parallels.
3. Bolts should *not* be tightened any more than is required to hold the workpiece. There is less pressure exerted during jig grinding than during jig boring.
4. Do not clamp work too tightly in the precision vise since this may spring the stationary jaw, dislocating the aligned edge of the work.
5. Set up work on parallels high enough to allow the bottom of the hole being ground to be measured.

To Locate the Workpiece

The same basic methods as in jig boring are used to locate accurately a workpiece on the jig grinder; the straightedge, edge-finder, and indicator are used, for example. Distortion of the workpiece during the heat treating process may necessitate "juggling" during the setting-up process to ensure that all holes will "clean up." The workpiece may be set up parallel to the table travel by three methods.
a) Indicate an edge of the workpiece.
b) Set the work against the table straightedge; then check the alignment with an indicator.
c) On a heat-treated piece, indicate two or more holes and set up the work to suit the average location of a group of holes.

GRINDING SEQUENCE

When a series of holes in a workpiece must be accurately related to each other, consideration must be given to the sequence of grinding operations. The following sequence is suggested when a number of different holes are required, for example, straight, tapered, blind, or holes with shoulders.
1. Rough grind all holes first. When a high degree of accuracy is required, allow the work to cool to room

Courtesy Moore Special Tool Co. Inc.

Fig. 12-48   The taper angle is indicated on the taper setting plate

temperature before proceeding to finish grind.

2. Finish grind all holes which can be ground with the same grinding head. This avoids continually changing grinding heads.

3. Holes whose relationship to others is most important should be ground in one continuous period of time.

4. Grind holes with shoulders or steps only once to avoid making accurate depth settings twice.

TO GRIND A TAPERED HOLE

The grinder spindle can be set for grinding tapers in either direction by loosening one adjusting screw and tightening the other. For most taper hole grinding, it is accurate enough to set the grinder spindle to the degrees indicated on the taper setting plate (Fig. 12-48).

When an *extremely accurate* angular setting is required, the following steps are suggested.

1. Convert the angle into hundredths of a millimetre per 25 mm of length (or into thousandths taper per inch) by mathematical calculations.

2. Mount an indicator in the machine spindle.

3. Set an angle plate or master square on the machine table.

4. Move the indicator through 25 mm (or 1 in.) of vertical movement as read on the downfeed dial.

5. Set the adjusting screws until the desired taper is attained.
   NOTE: If the adjusting screws are too tight, they will bind the vertical movement of the spindle; if too loose, the machine may grind out of round.

By reversing this procedure, one can accurately reset the machine spindle for straight hole grinding.

Most tapered holes also have a straight section, and the taper is ground to a certain distance from the top. Sometimes it is difficult to observe exactly where the taper begins because of the high finish in the hole and the gradual advance of most

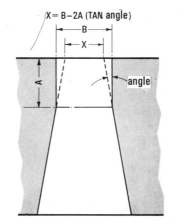

$$X = B - 2A \ (\text{TAN angle})$$

Courtesy Moore Special Tool Co. Inc.

Fig. 12-49   Formula for calculating X at the top of a tapered hole to produce the desired length of section A

tapers. Two methods are generally used to show where the tapered section begins.

a) Apply layout dye to the top portion of the hole with a pipe cleaner. The dye will be removed from the taper portion during the grinding operation, allowing the length of the straight hole to be measured.

b) On holes too small or difficult to see and measure, it is recommended that the taper be ground first to dimension X in Fig. 12-49. This involves the use of the formula in Fig. 12-49 in order to calculate what size the hole would be at dimension X. Once the tapered hole has been correctly ground to size, the straight hole is ground to the

proper diameter. This will automatically produce the proper length of the straight hole A.

TO GRIND SHOULDERED HOLES

Many times it is necessary to grind not only the diameter of a hole, but also the bottom of blind or shouldered holes. Grinding shouldered holes presents a few problems not encountered in straight or taper grinding, and the following suggestions are offered.

1. Select the proper size grinding wheel for the hole size (Fig. 12-50).

2. Make the bottom of the wheel slightly concave with an abrasive stick.

3. Set the depth stop so that the wheel just touches the bottom or shoulder of the hole.

4. Rough grind the sides and shoulder of the hole at the same time. This eliminates leaving a slight step near the bottom of the hole.

5. Dress the wheel and proceed to finish grind the hole.

Jig Grinding Hints

1. Calculate all coordinate hole locations first.

2. Clamp work just enough to hold it in place. Clamping too tightly may cause distortion.

3. Select a grinding wheel which is three-quarters the diameter of the hole to be ground.

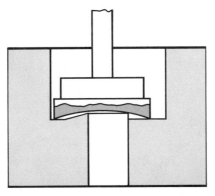

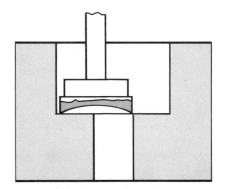

Fig. 12-50 Left: grinding wheel too large and cannot grind a flat surface

Right: wheel small enough to clear the opposite side of the hole

4. A wheel with widely spaced grains should be selected for rough grinding.
5. Relieve the wheel diameter so that only 6 mm of the cutting face remains.
6. Never use a glazed wheel for grinding.
7. Rough grind all holes by plunge grinding.
8. Allow the work to cool before finish grinding.
9. Finish grind holes with a freshly dressed wheel by outfeed grinding.

JIG GRINDER QUESTIONS

1. Why was the jig grinder developed?
2. State the advantages of jig grinding.
3. Explain the similarities and differences between a jig borer and a jig grinder.

JIG GRINDER PARTS

4. How is the jig-grinder spindle constructed to allow for the grinding of taper holes?
5. Explain how the grinding wheel may be positioned to the hole diameter.
6. What three methods may be used for controlling and measuring the depth of a hole?
7. Name two methods of dressing a wheel on a jig grinder.

GRINDING METHODS

8. Compare outfeed and plunge grinding.
9. How may large holes be ground on a jig grinder?
10. State the advantages of diamond-charged mandrels over grinding wheels for small hole grinding.

GRINDING WHEELS

11. List four general principles which should be observed in selecting a grinding wheel.
12. At what speed should the following be operated:
    a) grinding wheels?
    b) diamond-charged mandrels?
13. What undesirable conditions will an improperly dressed wheel cause?
14. Explain the procedure for dressing a grinding wheel.
15. What portion of the wheel is dressed for
    a) outfeed grinding?
    b) plunge grinding?

GRINDING ALLOWANCES

16. Name the factors which determine the amount of material that should be left in a hole for jig grinding.

17. State the grinding allowance which would apply in most cases for holes
    a) under 12 mm or 1/2 in.
    b) over 12 mm or 1/2 in. in diameter

SETTING UP WORK

18. Explain how bolts and clamps should be placed when setting up work.
19. Why is it important that bolts not be tightened too tightly?
20. Name three methods which are used to set up work parallel to the table travel.
21. Why is it necessary to sometimes "juggle" work during the setting-up process?

GRINDING SEQUENCE

22. List the sequence suggested when grinding a variety of holes.
23. Explain how the grinding head may be set to an accurate angle.
24. What would occur if the taper adjusting screws were too tight? too loose?
25. Name two methods which may be used to indicate where a taper begins in a hole.
26. Calculate the X dimension for a 4 mm diameter hole with a 5 mm straight section (see Fig. 12-49).
27. Explain the procedure for grinding shouldered holes.

13 ABRASIVES

In modern industry, the use of abrasives has contributed more to mass production than any other single factor. Only by means of abrasives and precision machinery has it been possible to produce the close tolerances and surface finishes required by industry.

In order to function properly, an abrasive must have certain characteristics.
a) It must be harder than the material being ground.
b) It must be strong enough to withstand grinding pressures.
c) It must be heat-resistant so that it does not become dull at grinding temperatures.
d) It must be friable (capable of fracturing) so that when the cutting edges become dull, they will break off and present new sharp surfaces to the material being ground.

TYPES OF ABRASIVES

Abrasives may be divided into two classes: *natural* and *artificial*.

Natural abrasives, such as sandstone, emery, quartz, and corundum, were used extensively prior to the early part of the 20th century. However, they have been almost totally replaced by manufactured abrasives with their inherent advantages. One of the best natural abrasives is diamond but, because of the high cost of industrial diamonds (bort), its use in the past was limited mainly to grinding cemented carbides and glass, and sawing concrete, marble, limestone, and granite. However, due to the introduction of synthetic or manufactured diamonds, industrial natural diamonds will become cheaper in cost and will be used on many more grinding applications.

Manufactured abrasives are used extensively because their grain size, shape, and purity can be closely controlled. This uniformity of grain size and shape, which ensures that each grain does its share of work, is not possible with natural abrasives.

There are several types of manufactured abrasives: *aluminum oxide, silicon carbide, boron carbide, cubic boron nitride, and manufactured diamond.*

ALUMINUM OXIDE

Aluminum oxide is probably the most important abrasive since about 75% of the grinding wheels manufactured are made of this material. It is generally used for high tensile strength materials including all ferrous metals except cast iron.

Aluminum oxide is manufactured with various degrees of purity for different applications, the hardness and brittleness augmenting with increasing purity. Regular aluminum oxide (Al_2O_3) is about 94.5% pure and is a tough abrasive capable of withstanding abuse. It is a greyish colour and is used for grinding strong, tough materials, such as steel, malleable and wrought iron, and tough bronzes.

ALUMINUM OXIDE

SILICON CARBIDE

Courtesy Lionite Abrasives Limited

Aluminum oxide of about 97.5% purity is more brittle and not as tough as the regular aluminum oxide. This grey abrasive is used in the manufacture of grinding wheels for centreless, cylindrical, and internal grinding of steel and cast iron.

The purest form of aluminum oxide for grinding wheels is a white material which produces a sharp cutting edge when fractured. It is used for grinding the hardest steels and stellite and for die and gauge grinding.

Fig. 13-1   Aluminum oxide is produced in an arc-type furnace

MANUFACTURE OF ALUMINUM OXIDE

Bauxite ore, from which aluminum oxide is made, is mined by the open-pit method in Arkansas and in the Guianas of South America. The bauxite ore is usually calcined (reduced to powder form) in a large furnace where most of the water is removed. The calcined bauxite is then loaded into a cylindrical, unlined steel shell about 1.5 m in diameter by 1.5 m deep (Fig. 13-1). This furnace is open at the top and lined with carbon bricks at the bottom. Two or three electrodes of carbon or graphite project into the open top of the furnace. During the operation, the outside of the furnace is cooled by a circumferential spray of water. The furnace is half filled with a mixture of bauxite, coke screenings, and iron borings in the proper proportions. The coke is used to reduce the impurities in the ore to their metals, which combine with the iron and sink to the bottom of the furnace. The electrodes are then lowered onto the top of the charge, a starting batch of coke screenings is placed between the electrodes, and the current is applied. The coke is rapidly heated to incandescence and the fusion of the bauxite starts. After a small amount of bauxite is fused it becomes the conductor and carries the current. After the fusion of the bauxite has begun, more bauxite and coke screenings are added, and the process continues until the shell is full. During the entire operation, the height of the electrodes is automatically adjusted to maintain a constant rate of power input. When the furnace is full, the power is shut off, and the furnace is allowed to cool for about 12 hours. The fused ingot is removed from the shell and allowed to cool for about a week. The ingot is broken up and fed into crushers; the material then is washed, screened, and graded to size.

SILICON CARBIDE

Silicon carbide is suited for grinding materials which have a low-tensile strength and high density, such as cemented carbides, stone, and ceramics. It is also used for cast iron and most nonferrous and non-metal materials. It is harder and tougher than aluminum oxide. Silicon carbide may vary in colour from green to black. Green silicon carbide is used mainly for grinding cemented carbides and other hard materials. Black silicon carbide is used for grinding cast iron and soft non-ferrous metals, such as aluminum, brass, and copper. It is also suitable for grinding ceramics.

MANUFACTURE OF SILICON CARBIDE

A mixture of silica sand and high purity coke is heated in an electric resistance furnace (Fig. 13-2). Sawdust is added to produce porosity in the finished product and to permit the escape of the large volume of gas formed during the operation. Sodium chloride (salt) is added to assist in removing some of the impurities.

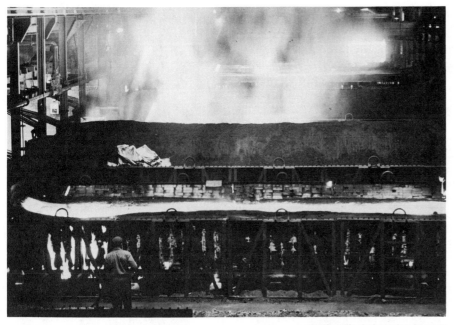

Courtesy The Carborundum Company

Fig. 13-2 Silicon carbide is produced in a resistance type furnace

The furnace is a brick-lined rectangle about 15.2 m long, 2.4 m wide, and 2.4 m high. It is open at the top. One or more electrodes protrude from each end of the furnace. The mixture of sand, coke, and sawdust is loaded into the furnace to the height of the electrodes. A granular core of coke is placed around the electrodes for the full length of the furnace. The core is covered with more sand, coke, and sawdust mixture and heaped to the top of the furnace. The current is then applied to the furnace and the voltage closely regulated to maintain the desired rate of power input. The time required for this operation is about 36 hours.

After the furnace has cooled for about 12 hours, the brick side walls are removed and the unfused mixture falls to the floor; the silicon carbide ingot can then cool more rapidly. After cooling for several days, the ingot is broken up and the silicon carbide removed. Care must be taken to remove the pure silicon carbide since the outer layer has not been properly fused and is not usable. The inner core sur-

rounding the electrodes is also unusable since it is only graphitized coke.

The resultant silicon carbide is then crushed, treated with acid and alkalis to remove any remaining impurities, screened, and graded to size.

BORON CARBIDE

One of the newer abrasives is boron carbide. It is harder than silicon carbide and, next to the diamond, it is the hardest material manufactured. Boron carbide is not suitable for use in grinding wheels and is used only as a loose abrasive and a relatively cheap substitute for diamond dust. Because of its extreme hardness, it is used in the manufacture of precision gauges and sand blast nozzles. Crush dressing rolls made of boron carbide have proven superior to tungsten carbide rolls for the dressing of grinding wheels on multi-form grinders. Boron carbide is also widely accepted as an abrasive used in ultrasonic machining applications.

MANUFACTURE OF BORON CARBIDE

Boron carbide is produced by dehydrated boric acid being mixed with high quality coke. The mixture is heated in a horizontal steel cylinder which is completely enclosed except for a hole in each end to accommodate a graphite electrode and vent holes to prevent the escape of the gases formed. The outside of the furnace is sprayed with water to prevent the shell from melting. During the heating process, air must be excluded from the furnace. This is done by dampening the mixture with kerosene which will volatize and expel the air from the furnace as it is heated. A high current at low voltage is applied for about 24 hours, after which the furnace is cooled. The resulting product, boron carbide, is a hard, black, lustrous material.

CUBIC BORON NITRIDE

One of the more recent developments in the abrasive field has been the introduction of cubic boron nitride. This man-made abrasive has hardness properties between silicon carbide and diamond. The crystal known as Borazon Ⓣ CBN (cubic boron nitride) was developed by the General Electric Company in 1969. This material is capable of grinding high speed steel with ease and accuracy, and is superior to diamond in many applications.

Cubic boron nitride is about twice as hard as aluminum oxide and is capable of withstanding high grinding temperatures (up to 1370°C) before breaking down. CBN is cool cutting and chemically resistant to all inorganic salts and organic compounds. Because of the extreme hardness of this material, grinding wheels made of CBN are capable of maintaining very close tolerances. These wheels require very little dressing and are capable of removing a constant amount of material across the face of a large work surface without having to compensate for wheel wear. Because of the cool cutting action of CBN wheels, there is little or no surface damage to the work surface.

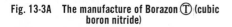
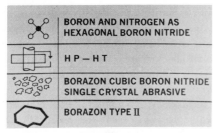

Fig. 13-3A   The manufacture of Borazon Ⓣ (cubic boron nitride)

Fig. 13-3B   Crystals of cubic boron nitride

Manufacture

Cubic boron nitride is synthesized in crystal form from hexagonal boron nitride ("white graphite") with the aid of a catalyst, heat, and pressure (Fig. 13-3A). The combination of extreme heat (1500°C) and a tremendous pressure (6895 mPa) on the hexagonal boron nitride and the catalyst produces a strong, hard, blocky, crystalline structure with sharp corners known as cubic boron nitride (Fig. 13-3B).

There are two types of cubic boron nitride:

Borazon CBN is an uncoated abrasive which can be used on plated mandrels and in metal bonded grinding wheels. This type of wheel is used for general purpose grinding and for internal grinding on hardened steel.

Borazon Type II CBN is nickel plated grains of cubic boron nitride used in resin bonds for general purpose dry and wet grinding of hardened steel. Uses of these wheels range from resurfacing blanking dies to the sharpening of high speed steel end mills.

MANUFACTURED DIAMONDS

Diamond, the hardest substance known to man, was primarily used in machine shop work for truing and dressing grinding wheels. Because of the high cost of natural diamonds, industry began to look to cheaper, more reliable sources. In 1954, the General Electric Company, after four years of research, produced Man-Made Ⓣ diamonds in their laboratory. In 1957, the General Electric Company, after more researching and testing, began the commercial production of these diamonds.

Many forms of carbon were used in experiments to manufacture diamonds. After much experimentation with various materials, the first success came when carbon and iron sulphide in a granite tube closed with tantalum discs were subjected to a pressure of 9650 MPa and temperatures between 1400°C and 2350°C. Various diamond configurations are produced by using other metal catalysts such as chromium, manganese, tantalum, cobalt, nickel or platinum in place of iron. The temperatures used must be high enough to melt the metal saturated with carbon and start the diamond growth.

DIAMOND TYPES

Because the temperature, pressure, and catalyst-solvent can be varied, it is possible to produce diamonds of various sizes, shapes, and crystal structure best suited to a particular need.

Type RVG Diamond

This manufactured diamond is an elongated, friable crystal with rough edges (Fig. 13-4A). The letters "RVG" indicate that this type may be used with a resinoid or vitrified bond and is used for grinding ultra-hard materials such as tungsten carbide, silicon carbide, and space-age alloys. The RVG Diamond may be used for wet and dry grinding.

Type MBG-II Diamond

This tough, blocky-shaped crystal is not as friable as the RVG type and is used in

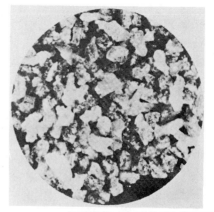

Fig. 13-4A   Type RVG is used to grind ultra-hard materials

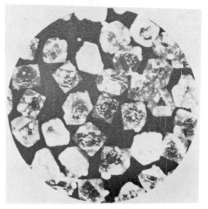

Fig. 13-4B   Type MBG -II is a tough crystal used in metal bond grinding wheels

Fig. 13-4C   Type MBS is a very tough, larger crystal used in metal bonded saws

metal-bonded grinding wheels (Fig. 13-4B). It is used for grinding cemented carbides, sapphires, and ceramics as well as in electrolytic grinding.

Type MBS Diamond

This is a blocky, extremely tough crystal with a smooth, regular surface which is not very friable (Fig. 13-4C). It is used in metal bonded saws (*MBS*) to cut concrete, marble, tile, granite, stone, and masonry materials.

Diamonds may be coated with nickel or copper to provide a better holding surface in the bond and to prolong the life of the wheel.

ABRASIVE PRODUCTS

After the abrasive has been produced, it is formed into products such as grinding wheels, coated abrasives, polishing and lapping powders, and abrasive sticks, all of which are used extensively in machine shops.

GRINDING WHEELS

Grinding wheels, the most important product made from abrasives, are composed of abrasive material held together with a suitable bond. The basic functions of grinding wheels in a machine shop are:

a) generation of cylindrical, flat, and curved surfaces
b) removal of stock
c) production of highly finished surfaces
d) cutting-off operations
e) production of sharp edges and points

For grinding wheels to function properly, they must be hard and tough, and the wheel surface must be capable of gradually breaking down to expose new sharp cutting edges to the material being ground.

The material components of a grinding wheel are the *abrasive grain* and the *bond*; however, there are other physical characteristics, such as *grade* and *structure*, that must be considered in grinding wheel manufacture and selection.

ABRASIVE GRAIN

The abrasive used in most grinding wheels is either *aluminum oxide* or *silicon carbide*. The function of the abrasive is to remove material from the surface of the work being ground. Each abrasive grain on the working surface of a grinding wheel acts as a separate cutting tool and removes a small metal chip as it passes over the surface of the work. As the grain becomes dull, it fractures and presents a new sharp cutting edge to the material. This fracturing action reduces the heat of friction which would be caused if the grain became dull, producing a relatively cool cutting action. As a result of hundreds of thousands of individual grains all working on the surface of a grinding wheel, a smooth surface can be produced on the workpiece.

One important factor to consider in grinding wheel manufacture and selection is the *grain size*. After the abrasive ingot, or pig, is removed from the electric furnace, it is crushed, and the abrasive grains are cleaned and sized by passing them through screens which contain a certain number of meshes, or openings, per inch. (Information on metric standards and grain size was not available at the time of publication.) A #8 grain size would pass through a screen having 8 meshes per linear inch and would be approximately 1/8 in. across. The sizing of the abrasive grain is rather an important operation since undersize grains in a wheel will fail to do their share of the work, while oversize grains will scratch the surface of the work.

Commercial grain sizes are classified as follows.

Very Coarse	Coarse	Medium
6	14	30
8	16	36
10	20	46
12	24	54
		60

A   8-grain size

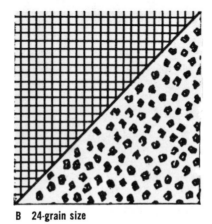

B   24-grain size

Fig. 13-5   Relative grain size

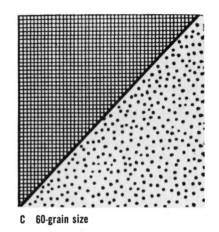

C   60-grain size

Courtesy The Carborundum Company

Fine	Very Fine	Flour Size
70	150	280
80	180	320
90	220	400
100	240	500
120		600

Relative grain sizes are shown in Fig. 13-5.

The factors affecting the selection of grains sizes are:

a) *The type of finish desired.* Coarse grains are best suited for rapid removal of metal. Fine grains are used for producing smooth and accurate finishes.

b) *The type of material being ground.* Generally coarse grains are used on soft material, while fine grains are used for hard materials.

c) *The amount of material to be removed.* Where a large amount of material is to be removed and surface finish is not important, a coarse-grain wheel should be used. For finish grinding, a fine-grain wheel is recommended.

d) *The area of contact between the wheel and the workpiece.* If the area of contact is wide, a coarse-grain wheel is generally used. Fine-grain wheels are used when the area of contact between the wheel and the work is small.

BOND TYPES

The function of the bond is to hold the abrasive grains together in the form of a wheel. There are six common bond types used in grinding wheel manufacture. They are: vitrified, resinoid, rubber, shellac, silicate, and metal.

Vitrified. Vitrified bond is used on most grinding wheels. It is made of clay or feldspar, which fuses at a high temperature and when cooled forms a glassy bond around each grain. Vitrified bonds are strong but break down readily on the wheel surface to expose new grains during the grinding operation. This bond is par-ticularly suited to wheels used for the rapid removal of metal. Vitrified wheels are not affected by water, oil, or acid and may be used in all types of grinding operations. Vitrified wheels should be operated between 1920 and 1980 m/min.

Resinoid bond. Synthetic resins are used as bonding agents in resinoid wheels. The majority of resinoid wheels generally operate at 2900 m/min; however, the modern trend is towards greater power and faster speeds for faster stock removal. Special resinoid wheels are manufactured to operate at speeds of 3810 to 6860 m/min for certain applications. These wheels are cool cutting and remove stock rapidly. They are used for cutting-off operations, snagging, and rough grinding, as well as for roll grinding.

Rubber bond. Rubber bonded wheels produce high finishes such as those required on ball bearing races. Because of the strength and flexibility of this wheel, it is used for thin cut-off wheels. Rubber bonded wheels are also used as regulating wheels on centreless grinders.

Shellac bond. Shellac bonded wheels are used for producing high finishes on parts such as cutlery, cam shafts, and paper-mill rolls. They are not suitable for rough or heavy grinding.

Silicate bond. Silicate bonded wheels are not used to any extent in industry. Silicate bond is used principally for large wheels and for small wheels where it is necessary to keep heat generation to a minimum. The bond (silicate of soda) releases the abrasive grains more rapidly than does the vitrified bond.

Metal bond. Metal bonds (generally nonferrous) are used on diamond wheels and for electrolytic grinding operations where the current must pass through the wheel.

GRADE

The grade of a grinding wheel may be defined as the degree of strength with which

A Weak bond posts

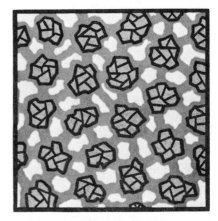

B Medium bond posts

C Strong bond posts

Courtesy The Carborundum Company

Fig. 13-6 Wheel grades

the bond holds the abrasive particles in the bond setting. If the bond posts are very strong (Fig. 13-6C), that is, if they retain the abrasive grains in the wheel during the grinding operation, the wheel is said to be of a hard grade. If the grains are released rapidly during the grinding operation, the wheel is classified as a soft grade (Fig. 13-6A).

The selection of the proper grade of wheel is important. Wheels which are too hard do not release the grains readily; consequently, the grains become dull and do not cut effectively. This is known as glazing. Wheels which are too soft release the grain too quickly, and the wheel will wear rapidly.

It is well to remember that all abrasive grains are hard, and the hardness of a wheel refers to grade (the strength of the bond) and not to the hardness of the grain. Wheel grade symbols are indicated alphabetically ranging from A (softest) to Z (hardest). The grade selected for a particular job depends on the following factors.

a) *Hardness of the material.* A hard wheel is generally used on soft material and soft grades on hard materials.

b) *Area of contact.* Soft wheels are used where the area of contact between the wheel and the workpiece is large. Small areas of contact require harder wheels.

c) *Condition of the machine.* If the machine is rigid, a softer grade of wheel is recommended. Light duty machines or machines with loose spindle bearings require harder wheels.

d) *The speed of the grinding wheel and the workpiece.* The higher the wheel speed in relation to the workpiece, the softer the wheel should be. Wheels which revolve slowly wear faster; therefore, a harder wheel should be used at slow speeds.

e) *Rate of feed.* Higher rates of feed require the use of harder wheels since the pressure on the grinding wheel is greater than with slower feeds.

f) *Operator characteristics.* An operator who removes the material quickly requires a harder wheel than one who removes the material more slowly. This is particularly evident in offhand grinding and where piece-work programs are involved.

STRUCTURE

The structure of a grinding wheel is the space relationship of the grain and bonding material to the voids that separate them. In brief, it is the density of the wheel.

If the spacing of the grains is close, the structure is dense (Fig. 13-7A). If the spacing of the grains is relatively wide, the structure is open (Fig. 13-7C).

Selection of the wheel structure depends on the type of work required. Wheels with open structures (Fig. 13-8) provide greater chip clearance than those with dense structures and remove material faster than dense wheels.

The structure of grinding wheels is indicated by numbers ranging from 1 (dense) to 15 (open). Selection of the proper wheel structure is affected by the following factors.

a) *The type of material being ground.* Soft materials will require greater chip clearance; therefore an open wheel should be used.

b) *Area of contact.* The greater the area of contact, the more open should be the structure to provide better chip clearance.

c) *Finish required.* Dense wheels will give a better, more accurate finish.

d) *Method of cooling.* Open structure wheels provide a better supply of coolant for machines using "through the wheel" coolant systems.

In summary, Table 13-1 will serve as a guide to the factors that must be considered in selecting a grinding wheel.

Courtesy The Carborundum Company

Fig. 13-7A   Dense grinding wheel structure

Courtesy The Carborundum Company

Fig. 13-7B   Medium grinding wheel structure

Courtesy The Carborundum Company

Fig. 13-7C   Open grinding wheel structure

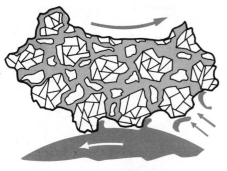

Courtesy The Carborundum Company

Fig. 13-8   An open structure wheel provides greater chip clearance

GRINDING WHEEL MANUFACTURE

Most grinding wheels used for machine shop operations are manufactured with vitrified bonds; therefore, the manufacture of only this type of wheel will be discussed. The main operations in the manufacture of vitrified grinding wheels are as follows.

Mixing. The correct proportions of abrasive grain and bond are carefully weighed and thoroughly mixed in a rotary power mixing machine (Fig. 13-9). A certain

Courtesy Cincinnati Milacron Inc.

Fig. 13-9   Mixing the abrasive grain and bond

percentage of water is added to moisten the mix.

Molding. The proper amount of this mixture is placed in a steel mold of the desired wheel shape and compressed in a hydraulic press (Fig. 13-10) to form a wheel slightly larger than the finished size. The amount of pressure used varies with the size of the wheel and the structure required.

Shaving. Although the majority of wheels are molded to shape and size, some machines require special wheel shapes and recesses. These are shaped or shaved to size in the green, or unburned, state on a shaving machine which resembles a potter's wheel.

Firing (burning). The "green" wheels are carefully stacked on cars and are moved slowly through a long kiln 75 to 90 m long. The temperature of the kiln is held at approximately 1260°C. This operation, which takes about five days, causes the bond to melt and form a glassy case around each grain; the product is a hard wheel.

Truing. The cured wheels are mounted in a special lathe and turned to the required size and shape by hardened-steel conical cutters, diamond tools, or special grinding wheels.

TABLE 13-1:
FACTORS TO BE CONSIDERED WHEN SELECTING A GRINDING WHEEL

Grinding Factors	Wheel Considerations				
	Abrasive Type	Grain Size	Bond	Grade	Structure
MATERIAL TO BE GROUND High or low tensile strength, hard, soft	X	X		X	X
TYPE OF OPERATION Cylindrical, centreless, surface, cut-off, snagging, etc.			X		
MACHINE CHARACTERISTICS Rugged, light, loose bearings				X	
WHEEL SPEED Slow, fast			X	X	
RATE OF FEED Slow, rapid				X	
AREA OF CONTACT Large, small		X		X	X
OPERATOR CHARACTERISTICS				X	
AMOUNT OF STOCK TO BE REMOVED Light cut, heavy cut	?		X	X	X
FINISH REQUIRED		X	X		X
USE OF COOLANT Wet or dry grinding			X	X	X

Courtesy Cincinnati Milacron Inc.

Fig. 13-10 Molding grinding wheels using a hydraulic press

Bushing. The arbor hole in a grinding wheel is fitted with a lead or plastic-type bushing to fit a specific spindle size. The edges of the bushing are then trimmed to the thickness of the wheel.

Balancing. To remove vibration which may occur while a wheel is revolving, each wheel is balanced. Generally, small, shallow holes are drilled in the "light" side of the wheel and filled with lead to assure proper balance.

Speed Testing. Wheels are rotated in a special, heavy, enclosed case and revolved at speeds at least 50% above normal operating speed. This ensures that the wheel will not break under normal operating speeds and conditions.

STANDARD GRINDING WHEEL SHAPES

Nine standard grinding wheel shapes have been established by the United States Department of Commerce, the Grinding Wheel Manufacturers, and the Grinding Machine Manufacturers. Dimensional sizes for each of the shapes have also been standardized. Each of these nine shapes is identified by a number as shown in Table 13-2.

MOUNTED GRINDING WHEELS

Mounted grinding wheels (Fig. 13-11) are driven by a steel shank mounted in the wheel. They are produced in a variety of shapes for use with jig grinders, internal grinders, portable grinders, toolpost grinders, and flexible shafts. They are manufactured in both aluminum oxide and silicon carbide types.

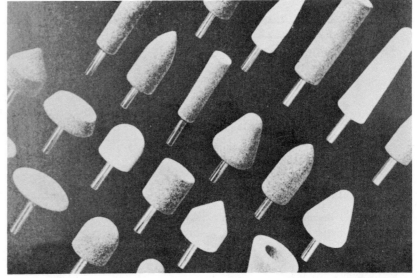

Courtesy The Carborundum Company

Fig. 13-11 A variety of mounted grinding wheels

GRINDING WHEEL MARKINGS

The standard marking system chart (Fig. 13-12) is used by the manufacturers to identify grinding wheels. This information is found on the blotter of all small- and medium-size grinding wheels. It is stenciled on the side of larger wheels.

The six positions shown in the standard sequence are followed by all manufacturers of grinding wheels. The prefix shown is a manufacturer's symbol and is not always used by all grinding wheel producers.

NOTE: This marking system is used only for aluminum oxide and silicon carbide wheels; it is not used for diamond wheels.

SELECTING A GRINDING WHEEL FOR A SPECIFIC JOB

From the foregoing information, the machinist should be able to select the proper wheel for the job required.

EXAMPLE 1:

It is required to rough surface grind a piece of SAE 1045 steel using a straight wheel. Coolant is to be used.

TABLE 13-2: COMMON GRINDING-WHEEL SHAPES AND APPLICATIONS

Shape	Name	Applications
	Straight (Type 1)	Cylindrical, centreless, internal, cutter, surface, and offhand grinding operations
	Cylinder (Type 2)	Surface grinding on horizontal and vertical spindle grinders
	Tapered (both sides) (Type 4)	Snagging operations. The tapered sides lessen the chance of the wheel's breaking.
	Recessed (one side) (Type 5)	Cylindrical, centreless, internal and surface grinders. The recess provides clearance for the mounting flange.
	Straight cup (Type 6)	Cutter and tool grinder and surface grinding on vertical and horizontal spindle machines
	Recessed (both sides) (Type 7)	Cylindrical, centreless, and surface grinders. The recesses provide clearance for mounting flanges.
	Flaring cup (Type 11)	Cutter and tool grinder. Used mainly for sharpening milling cutters and reamers
	Dish (Type 12)	Cutter and tool grinder. Its thin edge permits it to be used in narrow slots
	Saucer (Type 13)	Saw gumming, gashing milling cutter teeth

Type of Abrasive: Because steel is to be ground, *aluminum oxide* should be used.

Size of Grain: Since the surface is not precision-finished, a medium grain can be used — about *46 grit.*

Grade: A *medium*-grade wheel which will break down reasonably well should be selected. Use grade *J.*

Structure: Since this steel is of medium hardness, the wheel should be of medium density — about *7.*

Bond Type: Since the operation is standard surface grinding and since coolant is to be used, a *vitrified* bond should be selected.

After the various factors have been considered, an A46-J7-V grinding wheel

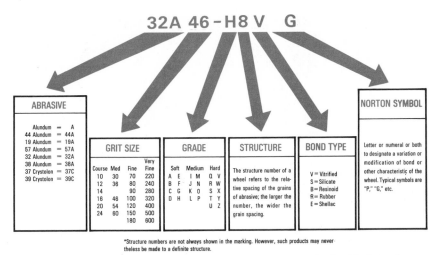

ABRASIVE			GRIT SIZE				GRADE			STRUCTURE	BOND TYPE	NORTON SYMBOL
Alundum	=	A					Soft	Medium	Hard	The structure number of a wheel refers to the relative spacing of the grains of abrasive; the larger the number, the wider the grain spacing.	V = Vitrified S = Silicate B = Resinoid R = Rubber E = Shellac	Letter or numeral or both to designate a variation or modification of bond or other characteristic of the wheel. Typical symbols are "P," "G," etc.
44 Alundum	=	44A					A E	I M	Q V			
19 Alundum	=	19A	Course	Med	Fine	Very Fine	B F	J N	R W			
57 Alundum	=	57A	10	30	70	220	C G	K O	S X			
32 Alundum	=	32A	12	36	80	240	D H	L P	T Y			
38 Alundum	=	38A	14		90	280			U Z			
37 Crystolon	=	37C	16	46	100	320						
39 Crystolon	=	39C	20	54	120	400						
			24	60	150	500						
					180	600						

32A 46 – H 8 V G

*Structure numbers are not always shown in the marking. However, such products may nevertheless be made to a definite structure.

Courtesy The Norton Company

Fig. 13-12   Straight grinding wheel marking system chart

should be selected to rough grind SAE 1045 steel.

NOTE: These specifications do not include the manufacturer's prefix or the manufacturer's records.

EXAMPLE 2:
It is required to finish grind a high-speed steel milling cutter on the cutter and tool grinder.

Type of Abrasive: Since the cutter is steel, an *aluminum oxide* wheel should be used.

Size of Grain: Since the milling cutter must have a smooth finish, a medium to fine grain should be used. About a *60 grit* is recommended for this type of operation.

Grade: It is important that a cool cutting wheel be used to prevent burning the cutting edge of the cutter. A wheel which breaks downs reasonably well will permit cool grinding. Use a medium-soft grade such as *J*.

Structure: In order to produce a smooth cut, a medium-dense wheel should be used. For this application, use a *#6*.

Bond Type: Because most cutter and tool grinders are designed for standard speeds, a *vitrified* bond should be used. When the speed is excessive for the wheel size, a *resinoid* bond should be used.

The wheel selected for this job (disregarding the manufacturer's prefix and records) should be A60-J6-V.

NOTE: If the cutter is chipped or if considerable metal must be removed to resharpen, it is advisable to first rough grind using a 46-grit wheel.

HANDLING AND STORAGE OF GRINDING WHEELS

Since all grinding wheels are breakable, proper handling and storage is important. Damaged wheels can be dangerous if used; therefore, the following rules should be observed.

1. Do not drop or bump grinding wheels.
2. Always store wheels properly on shelves or in bins provided. Flat and tapered wheels can be stored on edge, while large cup wheels and cylindrical wheels should be stored on the flat sides with a suitable layer of packing between each wheel.
3. Thin organic (resinoid and rubber) bonded wheels should be laid flat on a horizontal surface, away from excessive heat, to prevent warping.

4. Small cup and small internal grinding wheels may be stored separately in boxes, bins, or drawers.

INSPECTION OF WHEELS

After wheels have been received, they should be inspected to see that they have not been damaged in transit.

For further assurance that wheels have not been damaged, they should be suspended and tapped lightly with a screwdriver handle for small wheels (Fig. 13-13) or with a wooden mallet for larger wheels. If vitrified or silicate wheels are sound, they give a clear, metallic ring. Organic bonded wheels give a duller ring, and cracked wheels do not produce a ring. Wheels must be dry and free of sawdust before testing; otherwise the sound will be deadened.

Courtesy The Carborundum Company

Fig. 13-13   Testing a grinding wheel for cracks

DIAMOND WHEELS

Diamond wheels are used for grinding cemented carbides and hard vitreous materials, such as glass and ceramics.

Diamond wheels are manufactured in a variety of shapes, such as straight, cup, dish, and thin cut-off wheels.

Wheels of 12 mm (or 1/2 in.) diameter or less have diamond particles throughout the wheel. Wheels larger than 12 mm (or 1/2 in.) are made with a diamond surface on the grinding face only. The diamonds for this purpose are made in grain sizes ranging from 100 to 400. The proportions of the diamond and bond mixture vary with the application. This diamond concentration is identified by the letters A, B, or C. "C" concentration will contain four times the number of diamonds of a grinding wheel with an A concentration. This mixture is coated on the grinding face of the wheel in thicknesses ranging from 1/32 to 1/4 in. (0.79 to 6.35 mm■).

BONDS

There are three types of bonds available for diamond wheels: resinoid, metal, and vitrified.

Resinoid bonded wheels give a maximum cutting rate and require very little dressing. These wheels remain sharp for a long time and are well suited to grinding carbides.

A recent development in the manufacture of resinoid bonded diamond wheels has been the coating of the diamond particles with nickel plating by means of an electroplating process. This process is carried out before the diamonds are mixed with the resin. It reduces the tendency of the diamonds to chip and results in cooler-grinding, longer-lasting wheels.

Metal bonds, generally nonferrous, are particularly suited to offhand grinding and cutting-off operations. This type of wheel holds its form extremely well and does not wear on radius work or on small areas of contact.

Vitrified bonded wheels remove stock rapidly but require frequent cleaning with a boron carbide abrasive stick to prevent the wheel from loading. These wheels are particularly suited for offhand and surface grinding of cemented carbides.

DIAMOND WHEEL IDENTIFICATION

The method used to identify diamond wheels differs from that used for other grinding wheels (Fig. 13-14).

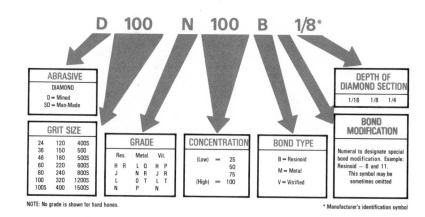

Courtesy The Norton Company of Canada Ltd.

Fig. 13-14   Diamond wheel identification

COATED ABRASIVES

Coated abrasives (Fig. 13-15) consist of a flexible backing (cloth or paper) to which abrasive grains have been bonded. Garnet, flint, and emery (natural abrasives) are being replaced by aluminum oxide and silicon carbide in the manufacture of coated abrasives. This is due to the greater toughness and the more uniform grain size and shape of manufactured abrasives.

Coated abrasives serve two purposes in the machine shop: metal grinding and polishing.

Metal grinding may be done on a belt or disc grinder and is a rapid, non-precision method of removing metal. Coarse grit coated abrasives are used for rapid removal of metal, whereas fine grits are used for polishing.

Emery, a natural abrasive which is black in appearance, is used to manufacture coated abrasives, such as emery cloth and emery paper. Since the grains are not as sharp as artificial abrasives, emery is generally used for polishing metal by hand.

Courtesy The Norton Company

Fig. 13-15   A variety of coated abrasives

SELECTION OF COATED ABRASIVES

ALUMINUM OXIDE

Aluminum oxide, brown in appearance, is used for high-tensile strength materials, such as steels, alloy steels, high carbon steels, and tough bronzes. Aluminum oxide is characterized by the long life of its cutting edges.

For *hand operations*, 60 to 80 grit is used for fast cutting (roughing), while 120 to 180 grit is recommended for finishing operations.

For *machine operations*, such as on belt and disc grinders, 36 to 60 grit is used for roughing, while 80 to 120 grit is recommended for finishing operations.

SILICON CARBIDE

Silicon carbide, bluish-black in appearance, is used for low-tensile strength materials, such as cast iron, aluminum, brass, copper, glass, and plastics. The selection of grit size for hand and machine operations is the same as for aluminum oxide coated abrasives.

ABRASIVES QUESTIONS

1. What characteristics must an abrasive have in order for it to function properly?

TYPES OF ABRASIVES

2. Name four natural abrasives.
3. What is "bort" and for what purpose is it used?
4. Name three manufactured abrasives and state why they are used extensively today.
5. For what purposes are aluminum oxide and silicon carbide abrasives used?
6. Describe the manufacture of aluminum oxide.
7. Describe the manufacture of silicon carbide.
8. How does the manufacture of boron carbide differ from that of the other manufactured abrasives?
9. List the uses for boron carbide.
10. List five advantages of cubic boron nitride grinding wheels.
11. Name two types of Borazon Ⓣ (cubic boron nitride) and state where each is used.

12. List three types of manufactured diamonds and state where each is used.
13. a) Name two materials used to coat the diamonds.
    b) What is the purpose of coating the diamonds?

GRINDING WHEELS

14. What are the basic functions of a grinding wheel?
15. Describe the function of each abrasive grain.
16. How is grain size determined and why is it important?
17. What factors affect the selection of the proper grain size?
18. What is the function of a bond and how does it affect the grade of a grinding wheel?
19. Name six types of bonds and state the purpose of each type in the manufacture of grinding wheels.
20. Why is the selection of the grade of wheel important to the grinding operation?
21. What factors should be considered when the grade of wheel is being selected for a particular job?
22. Define the structure of a grinding wheel and state how this is indicated.
23. What factors affect the selection of the proper wheel structure?

GRINDING WHEEL MANUFACTURE

24. Describe briefly the manufacture of a vitrified grinding wheel.

STANDARD GRINDING WHEEL SHAPES

25. Describe the following grinding wheels and state their purpose: Types 1, 5, 6, 11.

26. For what purpose are mounted grinding wheels used?

GRINDING WHEEL MARKINGS

27. Explain the meaning of the following grinding wheel markings: A80-G8-S, C-60-L4-V.
28. What wheel should be selected for grinding
    a) machine steel?
    b) cemented carbide?
    c) cast iron?

INSPECTION OF WHEELS

29. Explain why it is important to inspect a grinding wheel before it is mounted on a grinder.
30. How may grinding wheels be inspected?

DIAMOND WHEELS

31. For what purpose are diamond wheels used?
32. Explain "diamond concentration" in a grinding wheel.
33. Name three types of bonds used in diamond wheels and state the purpose of each.
34. Define the following diamond-wheel markings: D 120 – N 100 – B 1/8.

COATED ABRASIVES

35. Name the three common abrasives used in the manufacture of coated abrasives and state their purpose.
36. What grit size is recommended for
    a) hand operations?
    b) machine operations?

14 GRINDING MACHINES

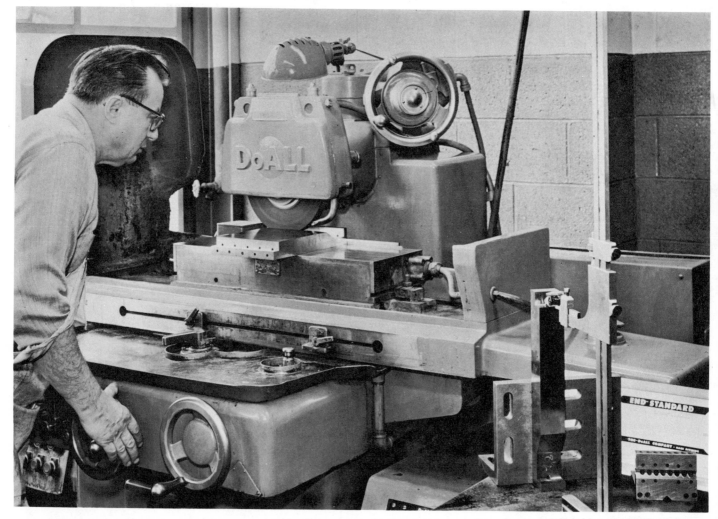

Courtesy DoALL Company

Grinding is one of the fastest-growing areas in the machine trade. Improved grinding machine construction has permitted the production of parts to extremely fine tolerances with improved surface finishes and accuracy. Because of the dimensional accuracy obtained by grinding, interchangeable manufacture has become commonplace in most industries.

Grinding has also, in many cases, eliminated the need for conventional machining. Often the rough part is finished in one grinding operation, thus eliminating the need for other machining processes. The role of grinding machines has changed over the years; initially they were used on hardened work and for truing hardened parts which had been distorted by heat treating. Today, grinding is applied extensively to the production of unhardened parts where high accuracy and surface finish are required. In many cases, modern grinding machines permit the manufacture of intricate parts faster and more accurately than other machining methods.

THE GRINDING PROCESS

In the grinding process the workpiece is brought into contact with a revolving grinding wheel. Each small abrasive grain on the periphery of the wheel acts as an individual cutting tool and removes a chip of metal (Fig. 14-1). As the abrasive grains become dull, the pressure and heat

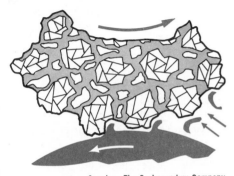

Courtesy The Carborundum Company

Fig. 14-1   Cutting action of the abrasive grain

created between the wheel and the workpiece cause the dull face to break away, leaving new sharp cutting edges.

Regardless of the grinding method used, whether it be cylindrical, centreless, or surface grinding, the grinding process is the same and certain general rules will apply in all cases.

1. Use a silicon carbide wheel for low tensile strength materials and an aluminum oxide wheel for high tensile strength materials.
2. Use a hard wheel on soft materials and a soft wheel on hard materials.
3. If the wheel is too hard, increase the speed of the work or decrease the speed of the wheel to make it act as a softer wheel.
4. If the wheel appears too soft or wears rapidly, decrease the speed of the work or increase the speed of the wheel, but not above its recommended speed.
5. A glazed wheel will affect the finish, accuracy, and metal removal rate. The main causes of wheel glazing are:

    i) The wheel speed is too fast.
    ii) The work speed is too slow.
    iii) The wheel is too hard.
    iv) The grain is too small.
    v) The structure is too dense, which causes the wheel to load.

6. If a wheel wears too quickly, the cause may be any of the following.

    i) The wheel is too soft.
    ii) The wheel speed is too slow.
    iii) The work speed is too fast.
    iv) The feed rate is too great.
    v) The face of the wheel is too narrow.
    vi) The surface of the work is interrupted by holes or grooves.

SURFACE GRINDING

Surface grinding is a technical term referring to the production of flat, contoured, and irregular surfaces on a piece of work which is passed against a revolving grinding wheel.

TYPES OF SURFACE GRINDERS

There are four distinct types of surface grinding machines (Fig. 14-2), all of which provide a means of holding the metal and bringing it into contact with the grinding wheel.

The horizontal spindle grinder with a reciprocating table (Fig. 14-2A) is probably the most common surface grinder for toolroom work. The work is reciprocated under the grinding wheel, which is fed down to provide the desired depth of cut. Feed is obtained by a transverse movement of the table at the end of each stroke.

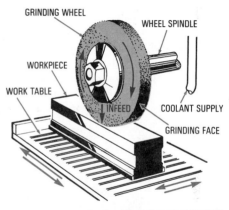

Courtesy The Carborundum Company

Fig. 14-2A   Horizontal spindle with reciprocating table

The horizontal spindle grinder with a rotary table (Fig. 14-2B) is often found in toolrooms for the grinding of flat circular parts. The surface pattern it produces makes it particularly suitable for grinding parts which must rotate in contact with each other. The work is held on the magnetic chuck of a rotating table and passed under a grinding wheel. Feed is obtained by the transverse movement of the wheelhead. This type of machine permits faster grinding of circular parts since the wheel is always in contact with the workpiece.

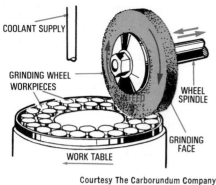

Courtesy The Carborundum Company

Fig. 14-2B Horizontal spindle with rotary table

The vertical spindle grinder with a rotary table (Fig. 14-2C) produces a finished surface by grinding with the face of the wheel rather than the periphery, as in horizontal spindle machines. The surface pattern appears as a series of intersecting arcs. Vertical spindle grinders have a higher metal removal rate than the horizontal type spindle machines. It is probably the most efficient and accurate form of grinder for the production of flat surfaces.

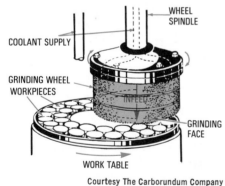

Courtesy The Carborundum Company

Fig. 14-2C Vertical spindle with rotary table

The vertical spindle grinder with a reciprocating table (Fig. 14-2D) grinds on the face of the wheel while the work is moved back and forth under the wheel. Because of its vertical spindle and greater area of contact between the wheel and the work, this machine is capable of heavy

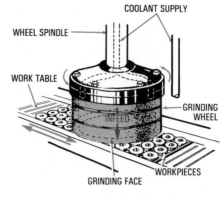

Courtesy The Carborundum Company

Fig. 14-2D Vertical spindle with reciprocating table

cuts. Material up to 12 mm thick may be removed in one pass on larger machines of this type. Provision is made on most of these grinders to tilt the wheelhead a few degrees from the vertical. This permits greater pressure where the rim of the wheel contacts the workpiece and results in faster metal removal. When the wheelhead is vertical and grinding is done on the face of the wheel, the surface pattern produced is a series of uniform intersecting arcs. If the wheelhead is tilted, it produces a semicircular pattern.

THE HORIZONTAL SPINDLE RECIPROCATING TABLE SURFACE GRINDER

The horizontal spindle reciprocating table surface grinder is the most commonly used, and will be discussed in detail. Machines of this type may be either hand or hydraulically operated (Fig. 14-3).

PARTS OF A HYDRAULIC SURFACE GRINDER

The *base* is generally of heavy cast iron construction. It usually contains the hydraulic reservoir and pump used to operate the table and power feeds. The top of the base has accurately machined ways to receive the saddle.

The *saddle* may be moved in or out across the ways, manually or by automatic feed.

The *table* is mounted on the top of the saddle. The ways for the table are at right angles to those on the base. Thus the table reciprocates across the upper ways on the saddle, while the saddle (and table) moves in or out on the ways of the base.

The *column*, mounted on the back of the frame, contains the ways for the *spindle housing* and *wheelhead*. The wheel feed handwheel provides a means of moving the wheelhead vertically to set the depth of cut.

The reciprocating action of the table may be controlled manually by the *table traverse handwheel* or by the *hydraulic control valve lever*.

The direction of the table is reversed when one of the *stop dogs* mounted on the side of the table strikes the *table traverse reverse lever*.

The table may be fed towards or away from the column manually by means of the *crossfeed handwheel* or automatically by the *power crossfeed control*. This operation moves the work laterally under the wheel.

GRINDING WHEEL CARE

In order to ensure the best results in any surface grinding operation, proper care of the grinding wheel must be taken.

1. When not in use, all grinding wheels should be properly stored.
2. Wheels should be tested for cracks prior to use.
3. Select the proper type of wheel for the job.
4. Grinding wheels should be properly mounted and operated at the recommended speed.

MOUNTING A GRINDING WHEEL

After the correct wheel has been selected for the job, proper mounting of the grinding wheel ensures the best grinding performance.

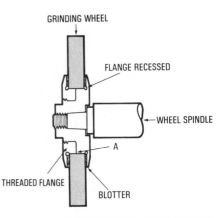

Courtesy "Precision Surface Grinding,"
Delmar Publishers Inc.

Fig. 14-4 A grinding wheel properly mounted on the grinding spindle

4. Tighten the wheel adaptor flanges only enough to hold the wheel firmly. If it is tightened too much, it may damage the flanges or break the wheel.

BALANCING A GRINDING WHEEL

Proper balance of a mounted grinding wheel is very important since improper balance will greatly affect the surface finish and accuracy of the work. Excessive imbalance creates vibrations which will damage the spindle bearings.

After the wheel has been mounted on the adaptor it should be balanced, if provision is made in the adaptor for balancing.

To Balance a Grinding Wheel

1. Mount the wheel and adaptor on the surface grinder and true the wheel with a diamond dresser.
2. Remove the wheel assembly and mount a special tapered balancing arbor in the hole of the adaptor.
3. Place the wheel and arbor on a balancing stand (Fig. 14-5) which has been levelled.
4. Allow the wheel to rotate until it stops. This will indicate that the heavy side is at the bottom. Mark this point with chalk.

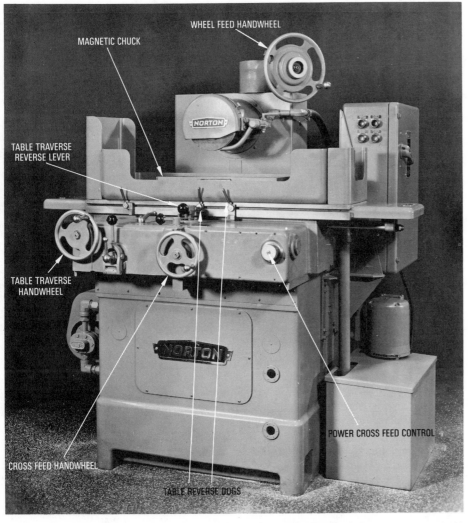

Courtesy The Norton Company of Canada Ltd.

Fig. 14-3 A hydraulic surface grinder

Procedure

1. Test the wheel to see that it is not cracked.
2. Clean the grinding wheel adaptor.
3. Mount the adaptor through the wheel and tighten the threaded flange (Fig. 14-4).
   i) Be sure that the blotter is on each side of the wheel prior to mounting. A perforated blotter should be used for through-the-wheel coolant. A rubber washer is sometimes used in place of the blotter on some grinders.
   ii) The wheel should be a good fit on the adaptor or spindle. If it is too tight or too loose, the wheel should not be mounted.
   iii) To comply with the Wheel Manufacturers' Safety Code, the diameter of the flanges should not be less than one-third the diameter of the wheel.

Courtesy "Precision Surface Grinding,"
Delmar Publishers Inc.

Fig. 14-5   A grinding wheel balancing stand

5. Rotate the wheel to three positions, 1/4, 1/2, and 3/4 of a turn, to check the balance. If the wheel moves from any of these positions, it is not balanced.

6. Loosen the set screws in the wheel counter balances, in the grooved recess of the flange, and move the counterbalances opposite the chalk mark (Fig. 14-6).

7. Check the wheel in the four positions mentioned in steps 4 and 5.

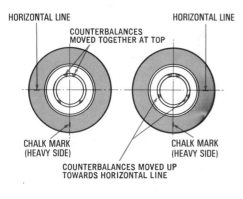

Courtesy Cincinnati Milacron Inc.

Fig. 14-6   Method of adjusting counterbalances to balance a grinding wheel

8. Move the counterbalances around the groove an equal amount on each side of the centre line and check for balance again.

9. Continue to move the balances away from the heavy side until the wheel remains stationary at any position.

10. Tighten the counterbalances in place.

TRUING AND DRESSING A GRINDING WHEEL

After mounting a grinding wheel, it is necessary to *true* the wheel to ensure that it will be concentric with the spindle. *Truing* a wheel is the operation of removing any high spots on the wheel, thereby causing it to run concentric with the spindle. Proper grinding practice requires that a wheel be trued before use.

Dressing a wheel is the operation of removing the dull grains and metal particles. This operation exposes sharp cutting edges of the abrasive grains to make the wheel cut better. A dull or glazed wheel should be dressed for the following reasons.

a) To reduce the heat generated between the work surfaces and the grinding wheel.

b) To reduce the strain on the grinding wheel and the machine.

c) To improve the surface finish and accuracy of the work.

d) To increase the rate of metal removal.

An industrial diamond, mounted in a suitable holder on the magnetic chuck, is generally used to true and dress a grinding wheel (Fig. 14-7A).

Fig. 14-7A   A diamond dresser in use

To True and Dress a Grinding Wheel

1. Check the diamond for wear and, if necessary, turn it in the holder to expose a sharp cutting edge to the wheel.

   NOTE: Most diamonds are mounted in the holder at an angle of 5 to 15° from the vertical to prevent the possibility of chatter and of the diamond digging into the wheel. It also permits the diamond to wear on an angle so that a sharp cutting edge may be obtained by merely turning the diamond in the holder.

2. Clean the magnetic chuck thoroughly with a cloth and wipe it with the palm of the hand to remove all grit and dirt.

3. Place a piece of paper, slightly larger than the base of the diamond holder, on the left-hand end of the magnetic chuck. This prevents scratching of the chuck when the diamond holder is being removed.

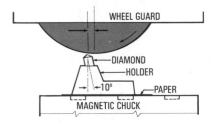

Fig. 14-7B   Proper positioning of the diamond dresser

4. Place the diamond holder on the paper, covering as many magnetic inserts as possible, and energize the chuck. The diamond should be pointing in the same direction as the grinding wheel rotation (Fig. 14-7B).

5. Raise the wheel above the height of the diamond.

6. Move the table longitudinally so that the diamond is offset approximately 5 mm to the left of the centre line of the wheel.

7. Adjust the table laterally so that the diamond is positioned under the high

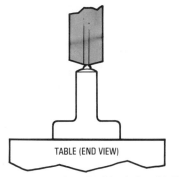

Fig. 14-8   Positioning the diamond under the high point of the wheel

point on the face of the wheel (Fig. 14-8). This is important since grinding wheels will wear more quickly on the edges of the wheel, leaving the centre of the face higher than the edges.

8. Start the machine and carefully lower the wheel until the high point touches the diamond.

9. Move the table laterally, using the crossfeed handwheel to feed the diamond across the face of the wheel.

10. Lower the grinding wheel about 0.02 mm to 0.05 mm (or .001 in. to .002 in.) per pass, and rough dress the face of the wheel until it is flat and has been dressed all around the circumference.

11. Lower the wheel 0.01 mm (or .0005 in.) and take several passes across the face of the wheel. The rate of crossfeed will vary with the structure of the wheel. A rule of thumb is to use a fast crossfeed with coarse wheels and a slow crossfeed for fine, closely spaced grains.

The following additional points may be helpful when truing or dressing a grinding wheel.

1. To minimize wear on the diamond the wheel may be rough dressed with an abrasive stick.

2. If coolant is to be used during the grinding operation, it is advisable to use coolant when dressing the wheel.

This will protect the diamond and the wheel from excessive heat.

3. A loaded wheel is indicated by a discolouration on the periphery or grinding wheel face. When dressing the wheel, sufficient material should be removed to completely remove any discolouration on the wheel face.

4. If rapid removal of metal is more important than the surface finish, do not finish dress the wheel. After the wheel has been rough dressed, some operators will take a final pass of 0.02 mm to 0.05 mm (or .001 in. to .002 in.) at a high rate of feed. The rough surface produced by this operation will remove the metal more rapidly than a finish-dressed wheel.

WORK-HOLDING DEVICES

THE MAGNETIC CHUCK

In some surface grinding operations the work may be held in a vise, on V-blocks, or bolted directly to the table. However, most of the ferrous work ground on a surface grinder is held on a *magnetic chuck* which is clamped to the table of the grinder.

Magnetic chucks may be of two types: the *electromagnetic chuck* and the *permanent magnetic chuck*.

The *electromagnetic chuck* uses electromagnets to provide the holding power. It has the following advantages.

a) The holding power of the chuck may be varied to suit the area of contact and the thickness of the work.

b) A special switch neutralizes the residual magnetism in the chuck, permitting the work to be removed easily from the chuck.

The *permanent magnetic chuck* provides a convenient means of holding most workpieces to be ground. The holding power is provided by means of permanent magnets. The principle of operation is the same for both electromagnetic and permanent magnetic chucks.

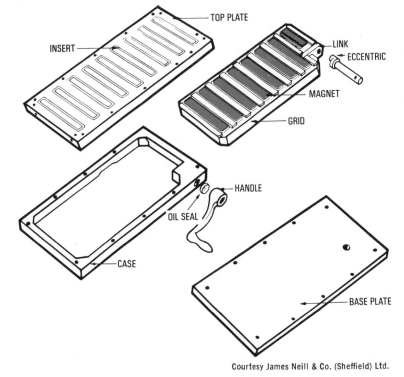

Fig. 14-9   Construction of a permanent magnetic chuck

PERMANENT MAGNETIC CHUCK CONSTRUCTION (Fig. 14-9)

The *base plate* provides a base for the chuck and a means of clamping it to the table of the grinder.

The *grid* or *magnetic pack* houses the *magnets* and the *grid conductor bars*. It is moved longitudinally by a handle when the chuck is placed in the "on" or "off" position.

The *case* houses the grid assembly and permits longitudinal movement of the grid. It also provides an oil reservoir for the lubrication of the moving parts.

The *top plate* contains *inserts* or *pole pieces* which are separated magnetically from the surrounding plate by means of white metal. This separation provides the poles necessary to conduct the magnetic lines of flux.

When the work is placed on the face of the chuck (top plate) and the handle moved to the "on" position (Fig. 14-10A) the grid conductor bars and the inserts in the top plate are in line. This permits the magnetic flux to pass through the work, holding it onto the top plate.

When the handle is rotated 180° to the "off" position (Fig. 14-10B), the grid assembly moves the grid conductor bars and the inserts out of line. In this position, the magnetic lines of flux enter the top plate and inserts, but not the work.

MAGNETIC CHUCK ACCESSORIES

Often it is not possible to hold all work in the chuck. The size, shape, and type of work will dictate how the work should be held for surface grinding. The holding power of a magnetic chuck is dependent on the size of the workpiece, the area of contact, and the thickness of the workpiece. A highly finished piece will be held better than a poorly machined workpiece.

Very thin workpieces will not be held too securely on the face of a magnetic chuck because there are too few magnetic lines of force entering the workpiece (Fig. 14-11A).

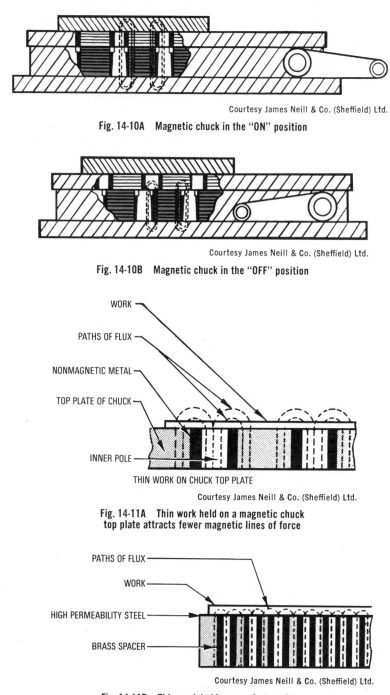

Courtesy James Neill & Co. (Sheffield) Ltd.

Fig. 14-10A   Magnetic chuck in the "ON" position

Courtesy James Neill & Co. (Sheffield) Ltd.

Fig. 14-10B   Magnetic chuck in the "OFF" position

WORK

PATHS OF FLUX

NONMAGNETIC METAL

TOP PLATE OF CHUCK

INNER POLE

THIN WORK ON CHUCK TOP PLATE

Courtesy James Neill & Co. (Sheffield) Ltd.

Fig. 14-11A   Thin work held on a magnetic chuck top plate attracts fewer magnetic lines of force

PATHS OF FLUX

WORK

HIGH PERMEABILITY STEEL

BRASS SPACER

Courtesy James Neill & Co. (Sheffield) Ltd.

Fig. 14-11B   Thin work held on an adaptor plate .

An *adaptor plate* (Fig. 14-11B) is used to securely hold thin work (less than 5 mm). This plate, with alternate layers of steel and brass, converts the wider pole spacing of the chuck to finer spacing with more but *weaker* flux paths. This method is particularly suited to small, thin pieces and reduces the possibility of distortion when grinding thin work.

Magnetic chuck blocks (Figs. 11-12A and B) provide a means of extending the flux paths to hold workpieces that cannot be held securely on the chuck face. V-blocks may be used to hold round or square stock for *light* grinding.

NOTE: Set the chuck blocks so that the maximum number of magnetic loops pass through the workpiece. They must also be

Sine chuck. When it is required to grind an angle on a workpiece, the work may be set up with a sine bar and clamped to an angle plate. Often a *sine chuck* (Fig. 14-13), which is a form of a magnetic sine plate, is used to hold the work. The build-up for the angles is the same as for the sine bar. Compound sine chucks, which have two plates hinged at right angles to each other, are available for grinding compound angles.

Courtesy The Taft-Peirce Manufacturing Company

Fig. 14-13   A compound sine chuck

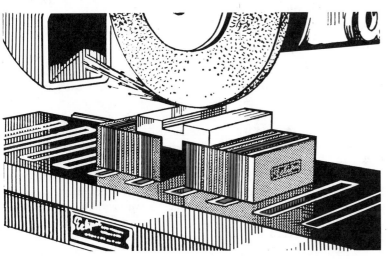

Courtesy James Neill & Co. (Sheffield) Ltd.

Fig. 14-12A,B   Applications of magnetic chuck blocks

placed so that the laminations are in line with the inner poles or inserts.

If the following points are observed magnetic chuck blocks will last longer.
1. Clean thoroughly before and after use.
2. Store in a covered wooden box.
3. Check frequently for accuracy and burrs.
4. If regrinding is necessary to restore accuracy, take light cuts with a dressed wheel. Use coolant when grinding to prevent the magnetic chuck blocks from heating (even slightly).

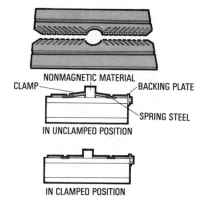

CLAMP — NONMAGNETIC MATERIAL — BACKING PLATE

SPRING STEEL

IN UNCLAMPED POSITION

IN CLAMPED POSITION

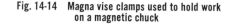

Courtesy Brown & Sharpe Mfg. Co.

Fig. 14-14   Magna vise clamps used to hold work on a magnetic chuck

Magna-vise clamps (Fig. 14-14) may be used when the workpiece does not have a large bearing area on the chuck, or when the work is non-magnetic. These magnetically actuated clamps consist of comb-like bars attached to a solid bar by a piece of spring steel. When work is held with these clamps, the solid bar of one clamp is placed against the backing plate of the magnetic chuck. The work is placed on the chuck surface between the toothed edges of two clamps as shown. The toothed edges on the bars in contact with the work should be above the magnetic chuck face. When the chuck is energized, the jaws of the clamps are brought down toward the face of the chuck, locking the work in place.

Double-faced tape is often used for holding thin, non-magnetic pieces on the chuck for grinding. The tape, having two adhesive sides, is placed between the chuck and the work, causing the work to be held securely enough for light grinding.

Special fixtures are often used to hold non-magnetic materials and odd shaped workpieces, particularly when a large number of workpieces must be ground.

GRINDING FLUIDS

Although work is ground dry in many cases, most machines have provision for applying grinding fluids or coolants. Grinding fluids serve four purposes.

a) *Reduction of grinding heat*, which affects work accuracy, surface finish, and wheel wear.

b) *Lubrication* of the surface between the workpiece and the grinding wheel, which results in a better surface finish.

c) *Removal of swarf* (small metal chips and abrasive grains) from the cutting area.

d) *Control of grinding dust*, which may present a health hazard.

TYPES OF GRINDING FLUIDS

a) *Soluble oil and water* when mixed form a milky solution which provides excellent cooling, lubricating, and rust-resistant qualities. This solution is generally applied by flooding the surface of the work.

b) *Soluble chemical grinding fluids and water* when mixed form a grinding fluid which may be used with flood cooling or "through-the-wheel" cooling systems. The chemical grinding fluid contains rust inhibitors and bactericides to minimize odours and skin irritation.

c) *Straight oil grinding fluids*, generally applied by the flood system, are used where high finish, accuracy, and long wheel life are required. These fluids have better lubricating qualities than the water-soluble fluids, but do not have as high heat dissipating capacity.

METHODS OF APPLYING COOLANTS

The flood system is probably the commonest form of coolant application. By this method, the coolant is directed onto the workpiece by a nozzle and is recirculated through a system containing a reservoir, a pump, a filter, and a control valve.

Through-the-wheel cooling provides a convenient and efficient method of applying coolant to the area being ground. The fluid is pumped through a tube and discharged into a dove-tailed groove in the wheel flange. Holes through the flange and corresponding holes in the wheel blotter permit the fluid to be discharged into the porous grinding wheel. The centrifugal force, created by the high speed rotation of the wheel, forces the fluid through the wheel onto the area of contact between the wheel and the work. Some machines have a coolant reservoir above the grinding wheel guard which feeds the coolant into the wheel flange groove by gravity.

The mist cooling system, which supplies coolant in the form of a mist, uses the atomizer principle. Air passes through a line containing a T-connection which leads to the coolant reservoir. The velocity of the air as it passes through the T-connection draws a small amount of coolant from the reservoir and discharges it through a small nozzle in the form of vapour. The nozzle is directed to the point of contact between the work and the wheel. The air and the vapour, as it evaporates, cause the cooling action. The force of the air also blows away the swarf.

SURFACE FINISH

The finish produced by a surface grinder is important, and the factors affecting it should be considered. Some parts that are ground do not require a fine surface finish, and time should not be spent producing fine finishes if not required.

The following factors affect the surface finish.

Material being ground. Soft materials such as brass and aluminum will not permit as high a finish as harder ferrous materials. A much finer finish can be produced on hardened steel workpieces than can be produced on soft steel or cast iron.

Amount of material being removed. If a large amount of material is to be removed, a coarse grit, open structure wheel should be used. This will not produce as fine a finish as a fine grit, dense wheel.

Grinding wheel selection. A wheel containing abrasive grains which are friable, or fracture easily, will produce a better finish than a wheel made up of tough grains. A fine grit, dense structure wheel produces a smoother surface than a coarse grit, open wheel. A grinding wheel which is too soft releases the abrasive grains too easily, causing them to roll between the wheel and the work, creating deep scratches in the work.

Grinding wheel dressing. An improperly dressed wheel will leave a pattern of scratches on the work. Care should be taken when finish dressing the wheel to move the diamond slowly across the wheelface. Always dress the wheel sufficiently to expose new abrasive grains and ensure that all glazing or foreign particles have been removed from the periphery of the wheel. New grinding wheels *which have not been properly balanced and trued* will produce a chatter pattern on the surface of the work.

Condition of the machine. A light machine or one with loose spindle bearings will not produce the accuracy and fine surface finish possible in a rigid machine with properly adjusted spindle bearings. Also, to ensure optimum accuracy and surface finish, the machine should be kept clean.

Feed. Coarse feeds tend to produce a rough finish. If "feed lines" persist when a fine feed is used, the wheel edges should be rounded slightly with an abrasive stick.

MOUNTING THE WORKPIECE FOR GRINDING

The size, shape, and type of work will determine the method by which the work should be held for surface grinding.

FLAT WORK OR PLATES

1. Remove all burrs from the surface of the work.
2. Clean the chuck surface with a clean cloth and wipe the palm of the hand over the surface to remove all dirt.
3. Place a piece of paper slightly larger than the workpiece, on the magnetic chuck face.
4. Place the work on top of the paper, and be sure to straddle as many magnetic inserts as possible.
5. If the workpiece is warped and rocks on the chuck face, it is advisable to shim the work where necessary to prevent rocking. This will avoid distortion when the work is removed from the magnetic chuck.
6. Turn the handle to the "on" position.
7. Check the work to see that it is held securely by trying to remove the workpiece.

THIN WORKPIECES

Thin workpieces tend to warp because of the heat created during the grinding operation. To minimize the amount of heat generated, it is advisable to mount the workpiece at an angle of approximately 15 to 30° from the side of the chuck. This reduces the length of time the wheel is in contact with the work, which in turn reduces the amount of heat generated per pass. If an adaptor is available, it should be used, and the work mounted at an angle.

SHORT WORKPIECES

Work which does not straddle three magnetic poles will generally not be held firmly enough for grinding. It is advisable to straddle as many poles as possible and to set parallels or steel pieces around the work to prevent it from moving during the grinding operation. The parallels or steel pieces should be slightly thinner than the workpiece to provide maximum support.

GRINDER SAFETY

When operating any type of grinder, it is important that certain basic, time-tested safety precautions be observed. Generally, the safest grinding practice is also the most efficient.

1. Before mounting a grinding wheel, ring test the wheel to check for defects.
2. Be sure that the grinding wheel is properly mounted on the spindle.
3. See that the wheel guard covers at least one-half the wheel.
4. Make sure that the magnetic chuck has been turned on, by trying to remove the work.
5. See that the grinding wheel clears the work before starting a grinder.
6. Be sure that the grinder is operating at the correct speed for the wheel being used.
7. When starting a grinder, always stand to one side of the wheel and make sure no one is in line with the grinding wheel in case of breakage.
8. Never attempt to clean the magnetic chuck or mount and remove work until the wheel has stopped completely.
9. ALWAYS wear safety glasses when grinding.

GRINDING OPERATIONS

The most common operation performed on a surface grinder is the grinding of flat (horizontal) surfaces. Regardless of the type of grinding operation, it is important that the correct wheel be mounted and the work held securely.

To Grind a Flat (Horizontal) Surface

1. Mount the work on a clean chuck, placing a piece of paper between the chuck and the workpiece.
2. Check to see that the work is held firmly.
3. Set the table reverse dogs so that the centre of the grinding wheel clears each end of the work by approximately 25 mm.

4. Set the crossfeed for the type of grinding operation – roughing cuts 0.75 mm to 1.25 mm (or .030 in. to .050 in.); finishing cuts 0.15 mm to 0.50 mm (or .005 in. to .020 in.).

5. Bring the work under the grinding wheel by hand, *having about 3 mm of the wheel over the work* (Fig. 14-15).

Courtesy Kostel Enterprises Ltd.

Fig. 14-15 The edge of the wheel should overlap the work by about 3 mm

6. Start the grinder and lower the wheelhead until the wheel just sparks the work.

7. The wheel may have been set on a low spot of the work. It is good practice, therefore, to always raise the wheel about 0.15 mm (or .005 in.).

8. Start the table travelling automatically and feed the entire width of the work under the wheel to check for high spots.

9. Lower the wheel for every cut until the surface is completed. Roughing cuts 0.15 mm to 0.40 mm (or .005 in. to .015 in.), finishing cuts 0.02 mm to 0.05 mm (or .001 in. to .002 in.).

10. Release the magnet and remove the workpiece, by raising one edge, to break the magnetic attraction. This will prevent scratching the chuck surface.

NOTE: Cutting fluid should be used whenever possible to aid the grinding action and keep the work cool.

Grinding the Edges of a Workpiece

Much work which is machined on a surface grinder must have the edges ground square and parallel so that these edges may be used for further layout or machining operations.

Work which is to be ground all over should be machined to about 0.25 mm (or .010 in.) over the finished size for each surface that must be ground. The large, flat surfaces are usually ground first which then permits them to be used as reference surfaces for further setups.

When the four edges of a workpiece must be ground, clamp the work to an angle plate so that two adjacent sides may be ground square without moving the workpiece.

Setting Up the Workpiece

1. Clean and remove all burrs from the workpiece, the angle plate, and the magnetic chuck.

2. Place a piece of paper which is slightly larger than the angle plate on the magnetic chuck.

3. Place one end of the angle plate on the paper (Fig. 14-16).

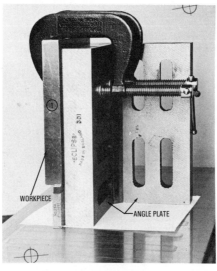

Courtesy Kostel Enterprises Ltd.

Fig. 14-16 The workpiece may be clamped to an angle plate for grinding the edges square

4. Place a flat-ground surface of the workpiece against the angle plate so that the top and one edge of the workpiece project about 12 mm beyond the edges of the angle plate (Fig. 14-16).

NOTE: Be sure that the one edge of the work does not project beyond the base of the angle plate. If the work is smaller than the angle plate, a suitable parallel must be used to bring the top surface beyond the end of the angle plate.

5. Hold the work firmly against the angle plate and turn on the magnetic chuck.

Courtesy Kostel Enterprises Ltd.

Fig. 14-17 A workpiece set up to grind the first edge

6. Clamp the work securely to the angle plate and set the clamps so that they will not interfere with the grinding operation.

NOTE: Place a thin piece of brass or aluminum between the clamp and the work to prevent marring the finished surface.

7. Turn off the magnetic chuck and carefully place the base of the angle plate on the magnetic chuck (Fig. 14-17).

8. Carefully place two more clamps on the end of the workpiece to hold the work securely.

Grinding the Edges of a Workpiece Square and Parallel

After the work has been properly set up on the magnetic chuck, the following procedure should be followed for grinding the four edges of the workpiece.

Courtesy Kostel Enterprises Ltd.

Fig. 14-18 Angle plate and work set for grinding the second edge of the workpiece at 90° to the first edge

1. Raise the wheelhead so that it is about 12 mm above the top of the work.
2. Set the table reverse dogs so that each end of the work clears the grinding wheel by about 25 mm.
3. With the work under the centre of the wheel, turn the crossfeed handle until *about 3 mm of the wheel overlaps the edge of the work* (Fig. 14-15).
4. Start the grinding wheel and lower the wheelhead until the wheel just sparks the work.
5. Move the work clear of the wheel with the crossfeed handle.
6. Raise the wheel about 0.10 mm to 0.25 mm (or .005 in. to .010 in.) in case the wheel had been set to a low spot on the work.
7. Check for further high spots by feeding the table by hand so that the entire length of the work passes under the wheel. Raise the wheel if necessary.
8. Engage the table reverse lever and grind the surface until all marks are removed. The depth of cut should be 0.07 to 0.17 mm (or .003 in. to .007 in.) for roughing cuts and 0.01 mm to 0.02 mm (or .0005 in. to .001 in.) for finishing cuts.

9. Stop the machine and remove the clamps from the right-hand end of the work.
10. Turn off the magnetic chuck and remove the angle plate and workpiece as one unit. Be careful not to jar the work setup.
11. Clean the chuck and the angle plate.
12. Place the angle plate (with the attached workpiece) on its end so that the surface to be ground is at the top (Fig. 14-18).
13. Fasten two clamps to the right-hand side of the workpiece and the angle plate.
14. Remove the original clamps from the top of the setup.
15. Repeat steps 1 to 8 and grind the second edge.
16. Remove the assembly from the chuck and remove the workpiece from the angle plate.

Grinding the Third and Fourth Edges

When two adjacent sides have been ground, they are then used as reference surfaces to grind the other two sides square and parallel.

Courtesy Kostel Enterprises Ltd.

Fig. 14-19 Work which is of a suitable shape and has sufficient bearing surface may be set on the chuck for finishing the remaining edges

1. Clean the workpiece, the angle plate, and the magnetic chuck thoroughly and remove any burrs.
2. Place a clean piece of paper on the magnetic chuck.
3. Place a ground edge of the workpiece on the paper.
   a) If the workpiece is at least 25 mm thick and long enough to span three magnetic poles on the chuck, no angle plate is required (Fig. 14-19).
   b) If the work is less than 25 mm thick and does not span three magnetic poles, it should be fastened to an angle plate (Fig. 14-20).

Courtesy Kostel Enterprises Ltd.

Fig. 14-20 An angle plate may be required to finish the third and fourth edges

   i) Place a ground edge on the paper and place an angle plate no higher than the workpiece against the workpiece.
      NOTE: A suitable parallel may be required to raise the edge of the work above the edge of the angle plate.
   ii) Turn on the chuck and carefully clamp the work to the angle plate.
4. Grind the third edge to the required size.
5. Repeat operations 1 to 3 and grind the fourth edge.

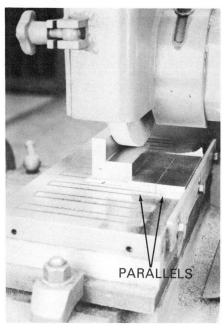

Courtesy Kostel Enterprises Ltd.

Fig. 14-21   Setup for vertical grinding

TO GRIND A VERTICAL SURFACE

Although most grinding performed on a surface grinder is the grinding of flat horizontal surfaces, it is often necessary to grind a vertical surface (Fig. 14-21). Extreme care must be taken in the setup of the workpiece when grinding the vertical surface. Before grinding a vertical

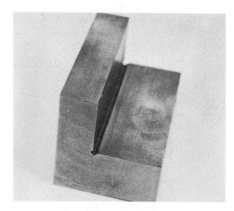

Fig. 14-22   Corner of work is relieved to provide clearance and prevent the corner of the wheel from breaking down

surface, it is necessary to relieve the corner of the work (Fig. 14-22) to ensure clearance for the edge of the wheel.

Procedure

1. Mount the proper grinding wheel; true, dress, and balance as required.
2. Dress the side of the wheel to give it a slight clearance (Fig. 14-23A and B).
3. Clean the surface of the magnetic chuck and mount the work.
4. With an indicator, align the edge of the work parallel to the table travel.

OR

Place the work against the stop bar of the magnetic chuck which has been

Fig. 14-23A   Dressing the side of the wheel for grinding a vertical surface

aligned. If the work cannot be set against the stop bar, parallels may be used to position the work on the magnetic chuck (Fig. 14-21).
5. Turn on the magnetic chuck and test to see that the work is held securely.
6. Set the reversing dogs, allowing sufficient table travel to permit clearance for the wheel at each end of the stroke.

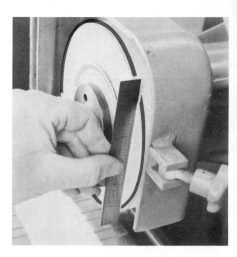

Fig. 14-23B   Side of wheel should be slightly concave for grinding a vertical surface

7. Bring the side of the wheel close to the vertical surface to be ground.
8. Lower the wheel to within 0.05 mm to 0.13 mm (or .002 in. to .005 in.) of the flat or horizontal surface which has been finish ground.
9. Start the table travelling *slowly* and feed the wheel until it just sparks the vertical surface.
10. Rough grind the vertical surface to within 0.05 mm (or .002 in.) of size by feeding the table in approximately 0.02 mm (or .001 in.) per pass.
11. Redress the side of the wheel if necessary.
12. Finish grind the vertical surface by feeding the table approximately 0.01 mm (or .0005 in.) per pass.

TO GRIND AN ANGULAR SURFACE

When it is necessary to grind an angular surface, the work may be held at an angle by a sine bar and angle plate (Fig. 14-24), a sine chuck (Fig. 14-25), or an adjustable angle vise (Fig. 14-26). When work is held by any of these methods, grinding is done with a flat dressed wheel.

Angular surfaces may also be ground by holding the work flat and dressing the grinding wheel to the required angle with a sine dresser (Fig. 14-27).

Fig. 14-24   Work may be set to a sine bar when an angle must be ground accurately

Fig. 14-28   Dressing a wheel using a parallel set at an angle

Fig. 14-25   Grinding an accurate angle using a sine chuck

Fig. 14-27   Dressing the wheel face to an angle using a sine dresser

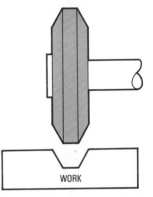

Courtesy "Precision Surface Grinding,"
Delmar Publishers Inc., Albany, N.Y.

Fig. 14-29   When form grinding, the wheel is dressed to the reverse profile

Contours and radii may be produced on the grinding wheel by means of a radius wheel dresser (Fig. 14-30A).

To Dress a Convex Radius on a Grinding Wheel

1. Mount the radius dresser (Fig. 14-30A) squarely on a clean magnetic chuck.

When a sine dresser is not available, a parallel set to the desired angle by means of a sine bar may be clamped to an angle plate. This setup is then placed on a magnetic chuck beneath the grinding wheel (Fig. 14-28).

FORM GRINDING

Form grinding refers to the production of curved and angular surfaces produced by means of a specially dressed wheel.

The reverse form or contour required on the workpiece is dressed on the grinding wheel (Fig. 14-29).

Fig. 14-26   Work held in an adjustable angle vise

Fig. 14-30A   A radius wheel dresser

2. Set both stops on the radius dresser so that it can only be rotated one-quarter of a turn. The two stops should be 90° apart.

3. Fasten the diamond height setting bar in the radius dresser. The bottom surface of the height setting bar is the centre of the radius dresser.

4. Place a gauge block buildup using wear blocks on each side, equal to the radius required on the grinding wheel, between the height setting bar and the diamond point.

5. Raise the diamond until it just touches the gauge blocks (Fig. 14-30B) and then lock it in this position. *NOTE*: When dressing a *concave radius*, the diamond point must be set *above* the centre of the radius dresser a distance equal to the radius desired.

Fig. 14-30B   Gauge block being used to set the diamond to the correct height for the radius to be dressed on a grinding wheel

6. Move the table longitudinally until the diamond is under the centre of the grinding wheel (Fig. 14-30A).

7. Lock the table to prevent longitudinal movement.

8. Rotate the arm of the radius dresser one-quarter of a turn, so that the diamond is in a horizontal position.

9. Start the machine and, using the cross-feed handle, bring the diamond in until it just touches the side of the grinding wheel.

10. Lock the table cross-slide in this position.

11. Stop the grinder and raise the wheel until it clears the diamond.

Fig. 14-30C   A convex radius being dressed on a grinding wheel

12. Start the grinder, and while slowly rotating the diamond back and forth through the 90° arc, lower the wheel until it just touches the diamond.

13. Feed the wheel down approximately 0.05 mm to 0.08 mm (or .002 in. to .003 in.) for every rotation of the dresser.

14. Continue to dress the radius until the periphery of the wheel just touches the diamond when it is in a vertical position. This indicates that the radius is completely formed (Fig. 14-30C).

15. Stop the grinder, raise the wheel and remove the radius dresser.

SPECIAL FORMS

When complex profiles are being ground on long production runs, the wheel may often be crush formed. A tool steel or carbide roll, having the desired form or contour of the finished workpiece, is forced

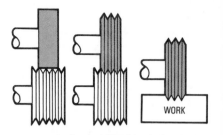

Courtesy "Precision Surface Grinding," Delmar Publishers Inc.

Fig. 14-31   Principle of crush form grinding

Courtesy "Precision Surface Grinding," Delmar Publishers Inc.

Fig. 14-32   Crush dressing a wheel to grind serrations with the roll mounted on the machine

into the slowly revolving grinding wheel (60 m/min–90 m/min). The grinding wheel assumes the reverse form of the crushing roll. The wheel is then used to grind the form or contour on the workpiece (Fig. 14-31). Grinding wheels may be crush formed to tolerances as close as ±0.05 mm (or .002 in.), and to radii as small as 0.12 mm (or .005 in.), depending on the grit size and structure of the wheel. As the wheel is used, it will gradually wear out of tolerance and the form must be redressed, using the crush roll. When the crush roll wears, as a result of many redressings, it must be reground to the original tolerance.

Some surface grinders are not designed for crush form dressing of the wheel. It is not advisable to perform crush form dressing on any machine equipped with a ball bearing spindle, since the bearings are subjected to a considerable load in crush dressing and may be damaged. Machines equipped with roller bearings have proven quite satisfactory for crush dressing operations.

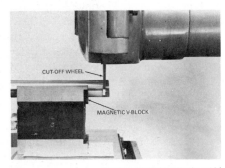

Courtesy Kostel Enterprises Ltd.

Fig. 14-33 Cutting off work, held in a magnetic V block, on a surface grinder

TABLE 14-1: SURFACE GRINDING PROBLEMS, CAUSES, AND REMEDIES

Grinding Problem	Cause	Possible Remedy
Burning or discolouration	Wheel too hard.	Use a softer, free cutting wheel. Decrease wheel speed. Increase work speed. Coarse dress the wheel. Take lighter cuts and dress wheel frequently. Use coolant directed at point of contact between the wheel and the work.
Burnished work surface (work is highly polished in irregular patches)	Wheel glazed.	Dress the wheel. Use a coarser grit wheel. Use a softer wheel. Use a more open structure wheel.
Chatter or wavy pattern	Wheel out of balance. Wheel out of round. Spindle bearing too loose. Wheel too hard. Glazing of wheel.	Rebalance. True and dress. Adjust or replace bearings. Use a softer wheel, coarser grit or more open structure. Increase table speed. Redress.
Scratches on the work surface	Grinding wheel is too soft. (Abrasive grains break off too readily and catch between the wheel and work surface.) Wheel is too coarse. Loose particles of swarf fall onto the work from the wheel guard. Dirty coolant carries dirt particles onto the work surface. Feed lines.	Use a harder wheel. Use a finer grit wheel. Clean the grinding wheel guard when changing a wheel. Clean the coolant tank and replace the coolant. Slightly round the edges of the wheel.

CUTTING-OFF OPERATIONS

The surface grinder may be used for cutting off hardened materials by using thin cut-off wheels. The work may be clamped in a fixture or vise and positioned below the wheel (Fig. 14-33). For thin, short pieces, the wheelhead may be fed straight down to cut off the work. If longer pieces are to be cut, the work is properly mounted and the table is reciprocated as in normal grinding while the wheel is fed down. Diamond wheels may also be mounted for cutting-off operations on carbides.

CYLINDRICAL GRINDERS

When the diameter of a workpiece must be ground accurately to size and to a high surface finish, it may be done on a *cylindrical* grinder. There are two types of machines suitable for cylindrical grinding – the *centre type* and the *centreless type* – each with its special applications.

CENTRE TYPE CYLINDRICAL GRINDERS

Work which is to be finished on a cylindrical grinder is generally held between centres, but may also be held in a chuck for certain types of work.

There are two types of cylindrical grinders (centre type), the *plain* and the *universal*. The plain type grinder is generally a manufacturing type of machine. The universal cylindrical grinder, Fig. 14-34, is more versatile, since both the wheelhead and headstock may be swivelled.

PARTS OF THE UNIVERSAL CYLINDRICAL GRINDER

The *base* is of heavy cast iron construction to provide rigidity. The top of the base is machined to form the *ways* for the table.

The *wheelhead* is mounted on a crossslide at the back of the machine. The ways on which it is mounted are at right angles to the table ways, permitting the wheelhead to be fed towards the table and the work, either automatically or by hand. On universal machines, the wheelhead may be swivelled to permit the grinding of steep tapers by plunge grinding.

The *table*, mounted on the ways, is driven back and forth by hydraulic or mechanical means. The reversal of the table is controlled by *trip dogs*. The table is composed of the *lower table* which rests on the ways, and the *upper table* which may be swivelled for grinding tapers and alignment purposes. The *headstock* and *footstock*, used to support work held between centres, are mounted on the table.

The *headstock* unit is mounted on the left end of the table and contains a motor for rotating the work. A dead centre is mounted in the headstock spindle. When work is mounted between centres, it is rotated on *two dead centres* by means of a dog and a drive plate which is attached to, and revolves with, the headstock spindle. The purpose of a dead centre in the headstock is to overcome any spindle inaccuracies (looseness, burrs, etc.) which may be transferred to the workpiece. Grinding work on two dead centres results in truer diameters which are concentric with the centre line of the work.

Work may also be held in a chuck which is mounted on the spindle nose of the headstock.

The *footstock* supports the right end of the work and is adjustable along the length of the table. The dead centre, on which the work is mounted, is spring loaded to provide the proper centre tension on the workpiece.

The *backrest or steadyrest* provides support for long, slender work and prevents it from springing. Outward and downward movement of the workpiece is prevented by means of adjustable supports in front of and below the workpiece. It may be positioned anywhere along the length of the table.

The *centre rest*, which resembles a lathe steadyrest, may be mounted at any point on the table. It is used to support the right end of the work when external grinding is confined to the end of the workpiece. Long workpieces on which internal grinding is to be performed are also supported on the end by the centre rest.

An *internal grinding attachment* may be mounted on the wheelhead on most machines for internal grinding. It is usually driven by a separate motor.

A *diamond wheel dresser* may be clamped to the table to dress the grinding wheel as required. On some types of grinders, diamond dressers may be permanently mounted on the footstock.

The *coolant system* is built into all cylindrical grinders to provide dust control, temperature control, and a better surface finish on the workpiece.

MACHINE PREPARATION FOR GRINDING

MOUNTING THE WHEEL

All precautions, such as wheel balancing and mounting procedures, used on surface grinders should be observed for cylindrical grinding.

To True and Dress the Wheel

1. Start the grinding wheel to permit the spindle bearings to warm up.

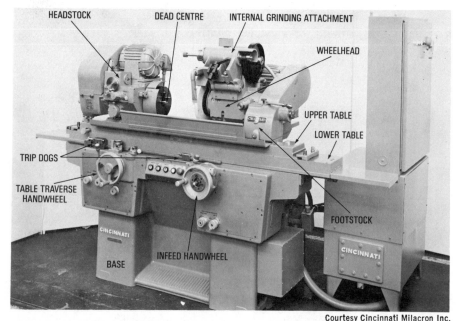

Courtesy Cincinnati Milacron Inc.

Fig. 14-34 Parts of a universal cylindrical grinder

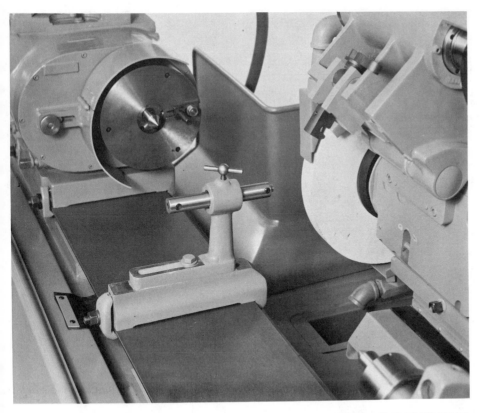

Courtesy Cincinnati Milacron Inc.

Fig. 14-35 Dressing a grinding wheel on a cylindrical grinder

2. Mount the proper diamond in the holder and clamp it to the table. The diamond should be mounted at an angle of 10 to 15° to the wheelface and should be held on or slightly below the centre line of the wheel (Fig. 14-35).

3. Adjust the wheel until the diamond almost touches the high point of the wheel, which is usually in the centre of the wheelface.

4. Turn on the coolant if this is to be used for the grinding operation.

5. Feed the wheel into the diamond about 0.02 mm (or .001 in.) per pass, and move it back and forth across the wheelface at a medium rate until the wheelface has been completely dressed.

6. Finish dress the wheel by using an infeed of 0.01 mm (or .0005 in.) and a slow traverse feed. When a very fine finish is required, the diamond should be traversed slowly across the wheelface for a few passes without any additional infeed.

To Parallel Grind an Outside Diameter

1. Lubricate the machine as required.

2. Start the grinding wheel to warm up the spindle bearings. This will ensure the utmost accuracy when grinding.

3. True and dress the grinding wheel if required.

4. Clean the machine centres and the centre holes of the work. If the grinder centres are damaged, they must be reground. On hardened steel workpieces, the centre holes should be honed or lapped to ensure the utmost accuracy.

5. Align the headstock and footstock centres with a test bar and indicator.

6. Lubricate the centre holes with a suitable lubricant.

7. Set the headstock and footstock for the proper length of work so that the centre of the work will be over the centre of the table.

8. Mount the work between centres with the dog mounted loosely on the left end of the work.

9. Tighten the dog on the end of the work and engage the drive plate pin in the fork of the dog.

10. Adjust the table dogs so that the wheel will overrun each end of the work by about one-third of the width of the wheelface. If grinding must be done up to a shoulder, the table traverse must be carefully set so that it reverses just before the wheel touches the shoulder.

11. Set the grinder to the proper speed for the wheel being used. Some machines are provided with a means of increasing the wheel speed as the wheel becomes smaller. If this is not done, the wheel will act softer and wear quickly.

12. Set the work speed for the diameter and type of material being ground. Proper work speed is very important. A slow speed causes heating and distortion of the work. High work speeds will cause the wheel to act softer and break down quickly.

13. Set the headstock spindle to rotate the work in an opposite direction to that of the grinding wheel. When grinding, the sparks should be directed down towards the table.

14. If the machine is so equipped, set the automatic infeed for each table reversal. Also set the dwell or "tarry" time which permits the wheel to clear itself at each end of the stroke.

15. Select and set the desired table traverse or speed. This should be such that the table will move one-half to two-thirds of the wheel width per revolution of the work. Finish grinding is done at a slower rate of table traverse.

16. Start the table and move the wheel up to the workpiece until it just sparks.
17. Engage the wheel feed clutch lever and grind until the work is cleaned up.
18. Check the work for taper and adjust if necessary.
19. Determine the amount of material to be removed and set the feed index (if the machine is so equipped) for this amount. The infeed of the wheel will stop automatically when the work is at the proper diameter.
20. Stop the machine with the wheel clear of the work and measure the size of the workpiece. If necessary, make a correction on the index setting and grind the piece to size.

TO GRIND A TAPERED WORKPIECE

Tapered work, held between centres, is ground in the same manner as parallel work, except that the table is swivelled to half the included angle of the taper. The taper should be checked for accuracy after the workpiece is cleaned up and the table adjusted if necessary.

Short steep tapers may be ground on work held in a chuck, or between centres, by swivelling the wheelhead to the desired angle and plunge grinding the tapered surface with the face of the wheel.

PLUNGE GRINDING

When a short tapered or parallel surface is to be ground on a workpiece, it may be plunge ground by feeding the wheel into the revolving work, with the table remaining stationary. The grinding wheel may be fed in automatically to the setting on the feed index. It then dwells for a suitable time to permit "spark out" and retracts automatically. In the case of tapered work, the wheelhead must be swung to half the included angle. When plunge grinding, the length of the surface to be ground must be no longer than the width of the grinding wheelface.

TABLE 14-2: CYLINDRICAL GRINDING FAULTS, CAUSES, AND REMEDIES

Fault	Cause	Possible Remedy
"Barber Pole" finish	Work loose on centres. Centres are a poor fit in the spindle.	Adjust centre tension. Use properly fitting centres.
Burnt work, cracked surfaces	Grinding wheel not trued. Grinding wheel too hard. Grinding wheel structure too dense. Incorrect bond. Grinding wheel too fast. Work revolving too slowly. Too heavy cut. Insufficient coolant. Wrong type of coolant. Dull diamond dresser.	True and dress the wheel. Use a softer wheel. Use a more open wheel. Consult manufacturer's handbook. Adjust the speed. Increase the speed. Reduce the depth of cut. Increase coolant supply. Try other type. Turn diamond in holder.
Chatter marks	Too heavy a cut. Grinding wheel too hard. Work too slender. Vibrations in machine. External vibrations transferred to machine.	Try a lighter cut. Use a softer wheel. Increase work speed. Reduce wheel speed. Use a steadyrest. Locate the vibrations and correct. Isolate the machine to prevent vibrations.
Diamond truing lines	Fast dressing feed. Diamond too sharp.	Slow dressing feed. Use a cluster type nib.
Feed lines	Wrong wheel structure. Improper traverse speed when finish grinding. Coolant not directed properly. Improperly adjusted steadyrest.	Change to suit. Change work speed and wheel speed. Adjust nozzle. Check and adjust.
Intermittent cutting action	Work too tight on centres. Work too hot. Work out of balance.	Adjust centre tension. Use coolant. Counterbalance as required.
Out-of-round work	Work centre holes damaged or dirty. Work loose on centres. Loose machine centres. Machine centres worn. Loose gibs on the table.	Hone and lap centres. Adjust the centre tension. Clean and reset. Regrind centres. Adjust the gibs.

Table 14-2: Continued

Fault	Cause	Possible Remedy
Rough finish	Wheel too coarse. Wheel too hard. Diamond too sharp. Wheel rough dressed. Table traverse too fast. Work speed too fast. Work springing.	Use a finer wheel. Use a softer wheel. Use a cluster type nib. Finish dress wheel. Slow to suitable feed. Slow to suitable speed. Use a steadyrest.
Wavy marks (long)	Wheel out of balance. Coolant has been directed against a stationary wheel.	Redress and balance wheel. Always shut off coolant well before stopping the wheel.
Wavy marks (short)	Vibrations caused by unmatched belts.	Replace belts with a matched set. Check motor and pulleys for balance.

INTERNAL GRINDERS

Internal grinding may be defined as the accurate finishing of holes in a workpiece by a grinding wheel. Although internal grinders were originally designed for hardened workpieces, they are now used extensively for finishing holes to size and accuracy in soft material.

Production internal grinding is done on internal grinders designed exclusively for this type of work. The wheel is fed into the work automatically until the hole reaches the required diameter. When the hole is finished to size, the wheel is withdrawn from the hole and automatically dressed before the next hole is ground.

Internal grinding may also be performed on the universal cylindrical grinder, the cutter and tool grinder, and the lathe. Since these machines are not designed primarily for internal grinding, they are not as efficient as the standard internal grinder. For most internal grinding operations, the work is rotated in a chuck mounted on the workhead spindle. Work may also be mounted on a face plate, collet chucks, or special fixtures. When work is too large to be rotated, internal diameters may be ground by using

a planetary grinder. In this operation, the grinding wheel is guided in a circular motion about the axis of the hole and is fed out to the required diameter. The work or the grinding head is fed parallel to the wheel spindle to provide a smooth, uniform surface.

INTERNAL GRINDING ON A UNIVERSAL CYLINDRICAL GRINDER

Although the universal cylindrical grinder is not designed primarily as an internal grinder, it is used extensively in toolrooms for this purpose. On most universal cylindrical grinders, the internal grinding attachment is mounted on the wheelhead column and is easily swung into place when required. One advantage of this machine is that the outside and inside diameters of a workpiece may often be finished in one setup. Although the grade of the wheel used for internal grinding will depend on the type of work and the rigidity of the machine, the wheels used for internal grinding are generally softer than those for external grinding, for the following reasons.

1. There is a larger area of contact between the wheel and the workpiece during the internal grinding operation.

2. A soft wheel requires less pressure to cut than a hard wheel; thus the spindle pressure and spring is reduced.

To Grind a Parallel Internal Diameter on a Universal Cylindrical Grinder

1. Mount the workpiece in a universal chuck, a collet chuck, or on a face plate. Care must be taken not to distort thin workpieces.
2. Swing the internal grinding attachment into place and mount the proper spindle in the quill. For maximum rigidity, the spindle should be as large as possible, with the shortest overhang.
3. Mount the proper grinding wheel, as large as possible, for the job.
4. Adjust the spindle height until its centre is in line with the centre axis of the hole in the workpiece.
5. True and dress the grinding wheel.
6. Set the wheelspeed to 1525-1980 m/min (5000-6500 sf/min).
7. Set the workspeed to 45 to 60 m/min (or 150 to 200 sf/min).
8. Adjust the table dogs so that *only* one-third of the wheel width overlaps the ends of the work at each end of the stroke. On blind holes, the dog should be set to reverse the table just as the wheel clears the undercut at the bottom of the hole.

   NOTE: In order to prevent "bell-mouthing," the wheel must *never* overlap the end of the work by more than one-half the width of the wheel.

9. Start the work and the grinding wheel.
10. Touch the grinding wheel to the diameter of the hole.
11. Turn on the coolant.
12. Grind until the hole just cleans up, feeding the wheel in no more than 0.05 mm (or .002 in.) per table reversal.
13. Check the hole size and set the automatic infeed (if the machine is so equipped) to disengage when the

work is roughed to within 0.02 mm (or .001 in.) of size.

14. Reset the automatic infeed to 0.005 mm (or .0002 in.) per table reversal.

15. Finish grind the work and let the wheel spark out.

16. Move the table longitudinally and withdraw the wheel and spindle from the workpiece.

17. Check the hole diameter and finish grind if necessary.

TO GRIND A TAPERED HOLE

When grinding tapered holes, the same procedures and precautions should be observed as for grinding parallel holes. However, the workhead must be set to one-half the included angle of the taper. It is *very* important that the centre lines of the grinding wheel and the hole be set at the same height in order to produce the correct taper.

CENTRELESS GRINDERS

The production of cylindrical, tapered, and multi-diameter workpieces may be achieved on a centreless grinder (Fig. 14-36A). As the name suggests, the work is not supported on centres but rather by a work rest blade, a regulating wheel, and a grinding wheel (Fig. 14-36B).

On a centreless grinder, the work is supported on the work rest blade, which is equipped with suitable guides for the type of workpiece. The rotation of the grinding wheel forces the workpiece onto the work rest blade and against the regulating wheel, while the regulating wheel controls the speed of the work and the longitudinal feed movement. To provide longitudinal feed to the work, the regulating wheel is set at a slight angle. The rate of feed may be varied by changing the angle and the speed of the regulating wheel. The regulating and grinding wheels rotate in the same direction, and the centre heights of these wheels are fixed. Because the centres are fixed, the diameter of the workpiece is controlled by the distance between

TABLE 14-3: INTERNAL GRINDING PROBLEMS, CAUSES, AND REMEDIES

Problem	Cause	Remedy
Bell-mouthed hole	Stroke is too long and wheel overlaps hole too much. Centre lines of workpiece and wheel spindle are at different heights.	Reduce overlap of wheel at each end of hole. Align the centres before setting up work.
Burning or discolouration of work	Wheel too hard. Insufficient coolant.	Use a softer wheel. Increase work speed. Decrease diameter of wheel. Use a narrower wheel. Coarse dress the wheel. Increase coolant supply and direct it at the point of grinding contact.
Chatter marks	Worn spindle bearings. Belt slipping. Defective belts. Wheel out of balance. Wheel not true. Wheel too hard. Incorrect work speed.	Adjust if possible or replace. Adjust tension. Replace the complete set of belts. Balance the wheel. True and dress. Use a softer wheel. Adjust.
Feed lines or spirals	Improper dressing. Wheel too hard. Edges of wheel too sharp. Feed too coarse. Wheelhead is tipped or swung.	Dress the wheel carefully using a sharp diamond. Use a softer wheel. Round edges slightly with an abrasive stick. Reduce feed on final passes. Align wheelhead and spindle.
Out-of-round hole	Work is distorted when mounting it in the chuck or holding device. Work overheated when rough grinding.	Use extreme care when mounting work. Reduce depth of cut and feed. If work is mounted on a face plate, loosen each clamp slightly and retighten evenly.
Scratches on ground surface	Wheel too soft and abrasive grains are caught between work surface and wheel. Improperly dressed wheel. Dirty coolant deposits particles between the wheel and the work. Wheel too coarse.	Use a harder wheel. Carefully dress the wheel. Clean coolant tank and replace coolant. Use a finer wheel.

Table 14-3: Continued

Problem	Cause	Remedy
Tapered hole	Workhead set at a slight angle. Wheel too soft to hold size. Feed too fast.	Align workhead. Use a harder wheel. Reduce feed.
Wheel glazing	Wheel too hard. Wheel too dense. Improper dressing.	Use a softer wheel. Increase work speed. Use a more open wheel. Use a sharp diamond and rough dress.
Wheel loading	Wheel too hard. Wheel too fine. Dirty coolant. Truing diamond is dull.	Use a softer wheel. Increase work speed. Increase traverse feed. Use coarser grain. Clean coolant system and replace coolant. Use a sharp diamond and coarse dress the wheel.

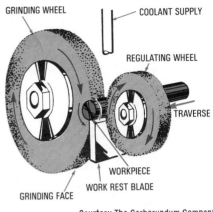

Fig. 14-36B   Principle of the centreless grinder

Courtesy The Carborundum Company

Courtesy Cincinnati Milacron Inc.

Fig. 14-36A   A centreless grinder

the wheels and the height of the work rest blade.

The higher the workpiece is placed above the centre lines of the wheels, the faster it will be ground cylindrical. However, there is a limit to the height at which it may be placed, since the work will eventually be lifted periodically from the work rest blade. There is one exception to placing the work above centre: when removing slight bends in long, small-diameter work, the centre of the piece is placed below the centre line of the wheels and the rate of traverse is high. This operation eliminates whipping and chattering that might result from bent work and is used primarily for straightening the workpiece. After the work has been straightened, it is ground in the normal manner above centres.

METHODS OF CENTRELESS GRINDING

There are three methods of centreless grinding: thru-feed, infeed, and endfeed.

THRU-FEED CENTRELESS GRINDING

Thru-feed centreless grinding (Fig. 14-37) consists of feeding the work between the

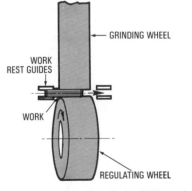

Courtesy Cincinnati Milacron Inc.

Fig. 14-37   Principle of thru-feed centreless grinding

grinding and regulating wheels. The cylindrical surface is ground as the work is fed by the regulating wheel past the grinding wheel. The speed at which the work is fed across the grinding wheel is controlled by the speed and angle of the regulating wheel.

INFEED CENTRELESS GRINDING

Infeed centreless grinding, a form of plunge grinding, is used when the work being ground has a shoulder or head (Fig. 14-38). Several diameters of a workpiece may be finished simultaneously by infeed grinding. Tapered, spherical, and other irregular profiles are ground efficiently by this method.

With infeed grinding, the work rest blade and the regulating wheel are clamped in a fixed relation to each other. The work is placed on the rest, against the regulating wheel, and is fed into the grinding wheel by moving the infeed lever through a 90° arc. When the lever is at the full end of the travel, the predetermined size has been reached and the part is the desired size. When the lever is reversed, the regulating wheel and work rest move back and the part is ejected either manually or automatically.

If the part to be ground is longer than the wheels, one end is supported on the work rest and the other on rollers mounted on the machine.

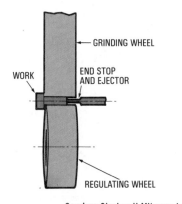

Courtesy Cincinnati Milacron Inc.

Fig. 14-38   Principle of infeed centreless grinding

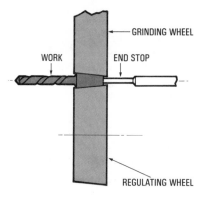

Courtesy Cincinnati Milacron Inc.

Fig. 14-39   Principle of endfeed centreless grinding

ENDFEED CENTRELESS GRINDING

The *endfeed method* (Fig. 14-39) is used mainly for grinding tapered work. The grinding wheel, the regulating wheel, and the work rest all remain in a fixed position. The work is then fed in from the front, manually or mechanically, up to a fixed stop. When the machine is prepared for endfeed grinding, the grinding wheel and the regulating wheel are often dressed to the required taper. In some cases where only a few parts are required, only the regulating wheel may be dressed.

ADVANTAGES OF CENTRELESS GRINDING

a) There is no limit to the length of work being ground.
b) There is no axial thrust on the workpiece, permitting the grinding of long workpieces which would be distorted by other methods.
c) For truing purposes, less stock is required on the workpiece than if the work is held between centres. This is due to the fact that the work "floats" in the centreless grinder. Work held between centres may run eccentrically and require more stock for truing up.
d) Because there is less stock to be removed, there is less wheel wear and less grinding time is required.

THE UNIVERSAL CUTTER AND TOOL GRINDER

The universal cutter and tool grinder (Fig. 14-40) is designed primarily for the grinding of cutting tools such as milling cutters, reamers, and taps. Its universal feature and various attachments permit a variety of other grinding operations to be performed. Other operations which may be performed are internal, cylindrical, taper and surface grinding, single-point tool grinding, and cutting-off operations. Most of the latter operations require additional attachments or accessories.

PARTS OF THE UNIVERSAL CUTTER AND TOOL GRINDER

The *base* is of heavy, cast iron, box-like construction that provides rigidity. The top of the base is machined to provide the *ways* (which are generally hardened) for the saddle.

The *wheelhead* is mounted on a column at the back of the base. It may be raised or lowered by the wheelhead handwheels located on either side of the base. The wheelhead may be swivelled through 360°. The wheelhead spindle is mounted in anti-friction bearings and is tapered and threaded at both ends to receive grinding wheel collets. The spindle speed may be varied by stepped pulleys to suit the size of the wheel being used.

The *saddle* is mounted on the ways of the base and is moved in and out by the crossfeed handwheels located at the front and back of the machine. The upper part of the saddle has machined and hardened ways at right angles to the ways on top of the base.

The *table* is composed of two units, the *upper* and *lower* table. The lower table, mounted on the upper ways of the saddle, rests and moves on anti-friction bearings. The upper table is fastened to the lower table and may be swivelled for grinding tapers. The table unit (upper and lower tables) may be moved longitudinally by three *table traverse knobs*, one located at

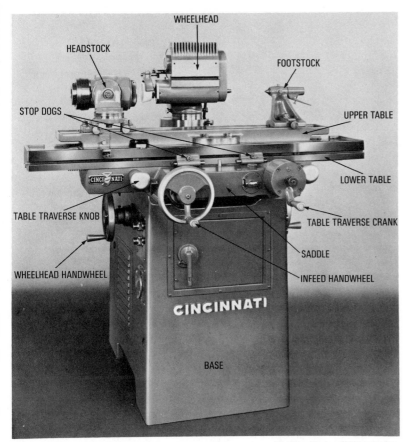

HEADSTOCK

WHEELHEAD

FOOTSTOCK

STOP DOGS

UPPER TABLE

LOWER TABLE

TABLE TRAVERSE KNOB

TABLE TRAVERSE CRANK

SADDLE

WHEELHEAD HANDWHEEL

INFEED HANDWHEEL

CINCINNATI

BASE

Courtesy Cincinnati Milacron Inc.

Fig. 14-40 A universal cutter and tool grinder

also used to align the cutter tooth on centre in some grinding setups.

The adjustable tooth rest supports the cutter tooth and may be fastened to the wheelhead or table, depending on the type of cutter being ground. Another form of tooth rest is the *universal micrometer flicker-type*, which has a micrometer adjustment for small vertical movements of the tooth rest.

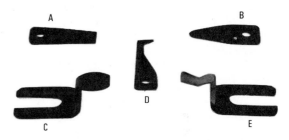

Fig. 14-41 Various shaped tooth rest blades

Plain tooth rest blades (Fig. 14-41A) are used for grinding straight tooth milling cutters.

Rounded tooth rest blades (Fig. 14-41B) are used for sharpening shell end mills, small end mills, taps, and reamers.

Offset tooth rest blades (Fig. 14-41C) are a universal type suitable for most applications, such as coarse pitch helical milling cutters and large face mills with inserted blades.

Hook or L-shaped tooth rest blades (Fig. 14-41D) are used for sharpening slitting saws, straight tooth plain milling cutters with closely spaced teeth, and end mills.

Inverted V-tooth rest blades (Fig. 14-41E) are used for grinding the periphery of staggered tooth cutters.

Cutter grinding mandrels and arbors (Fig. 14-42). It is most important when grinding a milling cutter to hold it in the same manner as it is held for milling. For example, shell end mills should be sharpened on the same arbor as that used for milling.

the front of the machine and two at the back. The table may also be traversed slowly by means of the *slow table traverse crank*. The table may be locked in place laterally and longitudinally with locking screws.

Stop dogs, mounted in a T-slot on the front of the table, control the length of the table traverse. Each dog has a positive stop pin on one side and a spring loaded plunger on the other. They are reversible to provide for a positive or a cushioned stop for the table, as desired.

ACCESSORIES AND ATTACHMENTS

The right- and left-hand tailstocks are mounted in the T-slot of the upper table and support the work for certain grinding operations. They may be placed at any point along the table.

The universal workhead (Fig. 14-40) or headstock is mounted on the table and used for supporting end mills and face mills for grinding. It may also be equipped with a pulley and motor (motorized headstock, Fig. 14-55) and used for cylindrical grinding. A chuck may be mounted in the workhead to hold work for internal and cylindrical grinding, as well as cutting-off operations (Fig. 14-56).

The centring gauge (Fig. 14-49A) is used to quickly align the tailstock centre with the centre of the wheelhead spindle. It is

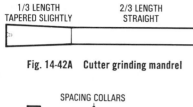

Fig. 14-42A   Cutter grinding mandrel

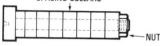

Fig. 14-42B   Cutter grinding arbor

Plain milling and side facing cutters, which are held on the standard milling machine arbor, should be held on a grinding mandrel (Fig. 14-42A) or a cutter grinding arbor (Fig. 14-42B).

A grinding mandrel rather than a lathe mandrel should be used to hold the cutter. This is necessary since a lathe mandrel will hold the cutter only at one end. The straight length of a grinding mandrel is a sliding fit into the cutter, and the slightly tapered end will hold the cutter securely for grinding.

Where considerable cutter grinding is done, a cutter grinder arbor will be found useful.

MILLING CUTTER NOMENCLATURE

To grind cutters correctly, the cutter parts and their function should be understood. Milling cutter parts are shown in Fig. 14-43A. A brief description of the various parts follows.

Primary clearance is the clearance ground on the land adjacent to the tooth face. It is the angle formed between the slope of the land and a line tangent to the periphery. Primary clearance prevents the land behind the cutting edge from rubbing on the work. The amount of primary clearance on a cutter will vary with the type of material being cut.

Secondary clearance is ground behind the primary clearance and gives additional

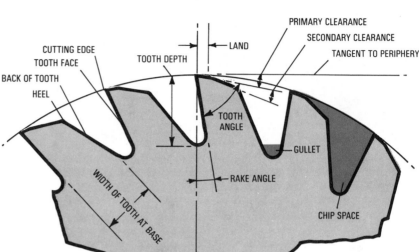

NOMENCLATURE OF A MILLING CUTTER

Fig. 14-43A   Nomenclature of a milling cutter

clearance to the cutter behind the tooth face. When grinding the clearance on a milling cutter, the primary clearance is always ground first. The secondary clearance is then used to control the width of the land.

The cutting edge is formed by the intersection of the face of the tooth with the land. On side milling cutters, the cutting edges may be on one or both sides as well as on the periphery. When the teeth are straight, the cutting edge engages along the full width of the tooth at the same moment. This creates a gradual buildup of pressure as the tooth cuts into the work and a sudden release of this pressure as the tooth breaks through, causing a vibration or chatter. This type of cutter produces a poor finish and does not retain its sharp cutting edge as long as a helical cutter does.

When the teeth are helical, the length of the cutting edge contacting the work varies with the helix angle. The number of teeth in contact with the work will vary with the size of the face being machined,

the number of teeth in the cutter, the cutter diameter, and the helix angle. Helical cutters produce a shearing action on the material being cut.

The helix angle, sometimes called the *shear angle*, is the angle formed by the angle of the teeth and the centre line of the cutter. It may be measured with a protractor or by bluing the edge of the cutter teeth and rolling the cutter against a straightedge over a sheet of paper (Fig. 14-43B). The marks left by the teeth can easily be measured in relation to the axis of the cutter to determine the helix angle.

The land is the narrow surface behind the cutting edge on the primary clearance produced when the secondary clearance is ground on the cutter. The width of the land varies from about 0.40 mm on small cutters to about 1.60 mm on large cutters. On face mills, the land is more correctly called the *face edge*.

The tooth angle is the included angle between the face of the tooth and the land caused by grinding the primary clearance.

Fig. 14-43B   A method of measuring the helix angle of a milling cutter

This angle should be as large as possible to provide maximum strength at the cutting edge and better dissipation of heat generated during the cutting process.

The tooth face is the surface on which the metal being cut forms a chip. This face may be flat, as in straight tooth plain milling cutters and inserted face tooth mills, or curved, as in helical milling cutters.

CUTTER CLEARANCE ANGLES

To perform efficiently, a milling cutter must be ground to the correct clearance angle. The proper clearance angle on a milling cutter may only be determined by the "cut and try" method. The clearance angle will be influenced by such factors as finish, the number of pieces per sharpening, the type of material, and the condition of the machine. Excessive primary clearance produces chatter, causing the cutter to dull quickly.

A general rule followed by a large machine tool manufacturer for grinding cutter clearance angles is: on high-speed steel cutters, 6° primary clearance plus an additional 6° for the secondary clearance. Thus the primary clearance is 6° and the secondary clearance is 12° when cutting machine steel. Carbide cutters used on machine steel are ground to 4° primary clearance plus an *additional* 4° (8°) for the secondary clearance.

Table 14-4 provides a "rule of thumb" for grinding cutter clearance angles on high-speed steel milling cutters. Table 14-5 gives the angles for carbide cutters. It should be remembered that this is a guide only. If the cutter does not perform satisfactorily with these angles, adjustments will have to be made to suit the job.

METHODS OF GRINDING CLEARANCE ON CUTTERS

Clearance may be ground on cutters by the following three methods. The type of cutter being ground will determine the method used.

CLEARANCE GRINDING

Clearance grinding (Fig. 14-44) produces a flat surface on the land. A 100 mm (or 4 in.) flared cup wheel is used for this method, and is offset slightly to permit long cutters to clear the opposite side of the wheel. When clearance grinding, the tooth rest may be set between the centre and the top of the wheel, but never below centre. The higher the tooth rest is placed, the less will be the clearance between the cutter and the opposite edge of the wheel. When clearance grinding, the tooth rest may be attached to the table or the wheelhead, depending on the type of cutter being ground. For straight tooth cutters, it may be mounted on the table, while for helical teeth, it must be mounted on the wheelhead.

TABLE 14-4: CLEARANCE ANGLES FOR HIGH-SPEED STEEL CUTTERS		
Material to be Machined	**Primary Clearance Angle**	**Secondary Clearance Angle**
High carbon and alloy steels	3°–5°	6°–10°
Machine steel	3°–5°	6°–10°
Cast iron	4°–7°	7°–12°
Medium and hard bronze	4°–7°	7°–12°
Brass and soft bronze	10°–12°	13°–17°
Aluminum, magnesium and plastics	10°–12°	13°–17°

TABLE 14-5: PRIMARY CLEARANCE ANGLES FOR CEMENTED CARBIDE CUTTERS									
Type of Cutter	**Periphery**			**Chamfer**			**Face**		
	Steel	**Cast Iron**	**Aluminum**	**Steel**	**Cast Iron**	**Aluminum**	**Steel**	**Cast Iron**	**Aluminum**
Face or side	4°–5°	7°	10°	4°–5°	7°	10°	3°–4°	5°	10°
Slotting	5°–6°	7°	10°	5°–6°	7°	10°	3°	5°	10°
Sawing	5°–6°	7°	10°	5°–6°	7°	10°	3°	5°	10°

Courtesy Cincinnati Milacron Inc.

Fig. 14-44   Setup for clearance grinding. The face of a flaring cup wheel is used to produce the clearance

HOLLOW GRINDING

The land produced by hollow grinding (Fig. 14-45) is concave. A 150 mm (or 6 in.) diameter dish wheel or a 150 mm (or 6 in.) diameter cut-off wheel is desirable. The cut-off wheel generally produces a better finish and breaks down more slowly, because of the resinoid bond. Since all grinding wheels break down in use, it is better to grind diagonally opposite teeth in rotation and to take light cuts. In hollow grinding, the wheel and cutter centres must be aligned. Then, clearance is obtained by raising or lowering the wheel, depending on the method used to set up the cutter.

CIRCLE GRINDING

Circle grinding (Fig. 14-46) provides only a minute amount of clearance and is used mainly for reamers. The reamer is mounted between centres and is rotated *backwards* so that the heel of the tooth contacts the wheel first. As the tooth rotates against the grinding wheel, the pressure of the wheel causes the cutter to spring back slightly as each cut progresses. Thus a very small amount of clearance is produced between the cutting edge and the heel of the tooth. The grinding wheel

Courtesy Cincinnati Milacron Inc.

Fig. 14-45   The periphery of the wheel is used for hollow grinding

Courtesy Cincinnati Milacron Inc.

Fig. 14-46   The work is revolved against the grinding wheel for circle grinding

should be set on centre when circle grinding. Secondary clearance must be obtained by clearance or hollow grinding. Circle grinding is also used to obtain concentricity of milling cutters prior to clearance or hollow grinding.

METHODS OF CHECKING CUTTER CLEARANCE ANGLES

There are three methods of determining tooth clearance on a milling cutter. They are as follows.

a) dial indicator
b) Brown and Sharpe cutter clearance gauge
c) Starrett cutter clearance gauge

TO CHECK CUTTER CLEARANCE WITH A DIAL INDICATOR

When a dial indicator is being used, clearance is determined by the movement of

the indicator from the front to the back of the cutter land (Fig. 14-47). The basic rule used to determine the clearance by this method is as follows.

For a land of 1.6 mm (or 1/16 in.) width, 1° of clearance is equivalent to 0.02 mm (or .001 in.) on the dial indicator. Thus 4° of clearance on a 1.6 mm (or 1/16 in.) land would register 0.10 mm (or .004 in.) on the dial indicator. The cutter diameter does not affect the measurement.

Courtesy Brown & Sharpe Mfg. Co.

Fig. 14-48A   Checking the cutter clearance with a Brown & Sharpe cutter clearance gauge

TO CHECK CUTTER CLEARANCE WITH A BROWN AND SHARPE CLEARANCE GAUGE

When the Brown and Sharpe clearance gauge is being used (Fig. 14-48A), the inside surfaces of the hardened arms (which are at 90°) are placed on top of two teeth of the cutter. The cutter is revolved sufficiently to bring the face of the tooth in contact with the angle ground on the end of the hardened centre blade. The clearance angle of the tooth should correspond with the angle marked on the end of the blade. Two gauge blades are furnished with each gauge, and are stamped at each end with the diameters of the cutters for which they are intended. This

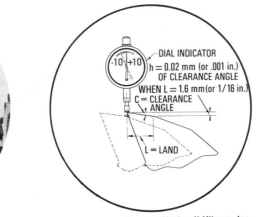

Courtesy Cincinnati Milacron Inc.

Fig. 14-47   Measuring the clearance angle with a dial indicator

inch cutter clearance gauge measures all cutters from 1/2 to 8 in. (13 to 205 mm) in diameter, except those with less than eight teeth.

CHECKING THE CUTTER CLEARANCE WITH A STARRETT CUTTER CLEARANCE GAUGE

The Starrett gauge (Fig. 14-48B) may be used to check the clearance on all types of inch cutters from 2 to 30 in. (50 to 760 mm■) in diameter, and on small cutters and end mills from 1/2 to 2 in. (12 to 50 mm■), providing the teeth are evenly spaced. This gauge consists of a frame graduated from 0 to 30°, a fixed foot, and a beam. An adjustable foot slides along the beam extension. A blade, which may be adjusted angularly and vertically, is used to check the angle of the land on a tooth.

Fig. 14-48B   Checking the clearance with a Starrett cutter clearance gauge

When in use, the feet are positioned on two alternate teeth of the cutter with the gauge at right angles to the tooth face. The adjustable blade is then lowered onto the top of the middle tooth and adjusted until the angle corresponds to the angle of the land being checked. The land angle is indicated on the protractor on the top of the frame.

CUTTER GRINDING OPERATIONS AND SETUPS

It is most important that milling cutters be ground properly, and to the correct clearance angles. Otherwise, the cutter will not cut efficiently and its life will be shortened considerably.

TO GRIND A PLAIN HELICAL MILLING CUTTER

Primary Clearance

1. Mount a parallel ground test bar between the tailstock centres and check the alignment with an indicator. This will ensure that the table travel is parallel to the grinding edge of the wheel.
2. Remove the test bar.
3. Mount a 100 mm (or 4 in.) flaring cup wheel (A 60-L 5-V BE) on the grinding head spindle so that the wheel rotates in a counterclockwise direction.
4. Adjust the machine so that the wheel revolves at the proper speed.
5. True the face of the wheel and dress the cutting edge so that it is no more than 1.6 mm (or 1/16 in.) wide.
6. Swivel the wheelhead to 89° so that the wheel will touch the cutter on the left side of the wheel only.
7. Using a centring gauge, adjust the wheelhead spindle to the height of the tailstock centres (Fig. 14-49A). Lock the wheelhead spindle.
8. Mount the cutter on a mandrel and place it temporarily between the footstock centres on the machine table.
9. Set up the tooth rest, on which an offset tooth rest blade has been mounted (Fig. 14-41C), on the wheelhead housing. Adjust the top of the tooth rest to approximately centre height.
10. Move the table until the cutter is near the tooth rest.
11. Adjust the tooth rest between two teeth at the approximate helix angle of the cutter teeth.

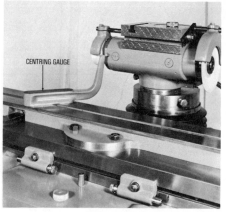

Courtesy Cincinnati Milacron Inc.
Fig. 14-49A   Aligning the wheelhead spindle and the footstock centre height

Fig. 14-49B   Centring the bearing point on the tooth rest

12. Chalk or blue the top of the tooth rest blade.
13. Move the cutter over the tooth rest blade and rotate it until the tooth rests on top of the blade.
14. While holding the tooth face against the rest, traverse the table back and forth to mark the point where the tooth bears on the tooth rest blade.
15. Remove the mandrel and cutter from between the centres.
16. Using the centring gauge, adjust the tooth rest so that the *centre* of the marked bearing point is at centre height and also in the centre of the grinding surface of the wheel (Fig. 14-49B). The tooth rest blade must

be as close to the wheel as possible without touching it.

NOTE: At this point, the centre of the grinding spindle, the footstock centres, and the bearing point on the tooth rest blade are in line.

17. Place a dog on the end of the grinding mandrel and mount the work between the tailstock centres.

18. Adjust a cutter tooth onto the top of the tooth rest blade.

19. Set the cutter clearance setting dial (Fig. 14-50) to zero and lock. Adjust the dog into the pin of the cutter clearance gauge.

Courtesy Cincinnati Milacron Inc.

Fig. 14-50 The cutter clearance dial indicates the amount of clearance being ground on the cutter

20. Set the wheelhead graduated collar to zero.

21. Loosen the wheelhead lock and the cutter clearance setting dial lock.

22. Holding the cutter tooth on the tooth rest blade, carefully *lower* the wheelhead until the required clearance is shown on the cutter clearance dial. When using a flaring cup wheel, the distance to lower the wheelhead may also be calculated by either of the following methods:

a) Distance = 0.0087 × clearance angle × diameter of cutter.

b) Distance = sine of the clearance

$$\text{angle} \times \frac{\text{diameter of cutter}}{2}$$

If the cutter is being hollow ground, the distance to lower the wheelhead is Distance = 0.0087 × clearance angle × diameter of wheel

23. Remove the dog from the end of the mandrel and unlock the table.

24. Adjust the table stops so that the wheel clears the cutter sufficiently at each end to permit indexing for the next tooth.

25. Start the grinding wheel.

26. Carefully feed the cutter in until it just touches the wheel.

27. Standing at the rear of the machine, turn the table traverse knob with the left hand. At the same time, with the right hand, hold the arbor firmly enough to keep the cutter tooth on the tooth rest.

28. Grind one tooth for the full length and return to the starting position, being careful *at all times* to keep the tooth tight against the tooth rest.

29. Traverse the table until the cutter is clear of the tooth rest and rotate the cutter until the diagonally opposite tooth comes in line with the tooth rest blade.

30. Grind this tooth without changing the infeed setting.

31. Check for taper by measuring both ends of the cutter with a micrometer.

32. Remove any taper, if necessary, by loosening the holding nuts on the upper table and adjusting the table.

33. Grind the remaining teeth.

34. Finish grind all teeth by using a 0.01 mm (or .0005 in.) depth of cut.

35. If the land is over 1.6 mm (or 1/16 in.) for larger cutters grind the secondary clearance.

To Grind the Secondary Clearance of a Plain Helical Milling Cutter

1. Reset the dog on the mandrel as in step #17 for grinding the primary clearance.

2. Loosen the clearance dial set screw.

3. Hold the cutter tooth against the tooth rest and lower the wheelhead until the required secondary clearance is shown on the clearance setting dial.

4. Lock the dial, remove the dog, and proceed to grind the secondary clearance in the same manner as for primary clearance.

5. Grind the secondary clearance until the land is the required width.

TO GRIND A STAGGERED TOOTH CUTTER

To grind the primary clearance on the periphery of a staggered tooth cutter (Fig. 14-51) proceed as follows.

1. Carry out steps 1 to 7 as for grinding primary clearance on a plain helical milling cutter.

2. Mount a staggered tooth cutter tooth rest blade (Fig. 14-41E) in the holder and mount the unit on the wheelhead.

3. Place the high point of the inverted V *exactly* in the centre of the width of the grinding wheel cutting face and at centre height.

4. Place the centring gauge on the table and adjust the wheelhead height until the highest point of the tooth rest blade is at centre height.

Courtesy Cincinnati Milacron Inc.

Fig. 14-51 Setup for clearance grinding a staggered-tooth cutter

TABLE 14-6: VERTICAL WHEELHEAD ADJUSTMENT FOR CUTTER CLEARANCE ANGLES

Cutter Diameter in Inches	Clearance Angle and Distance							
	4°		5°		6°		7°	
	mm	in.	mm	in.	mm	in.	mm	in.
½	0.45	.017	0.55	.022	0.65	.026	0.80	.031
¾	0.65	.026	0.85	.033	1.00	.040	1.15	.046
1	0.90	.035	1.10	.044	1.35	.053	1.55	.061
1¼	1.10	.044	1.40	.055	1.65	.066	1.95	.077
1½	1.35	.053	1.65	.066	2.00	.079	2.35	.092
1¾	1.55	.061	1.95	.076	2.35	.092	2.75	.108
2	1.75	.070	2.20	.087	2.65	.105	3.10	.123
2½	2.20	.087	2.75	.109	3.30	.131	3.90	.153
2¾	2.45	.097	3.05	.120	3.65	.144	4.25	.168
3	2.65	.105	3.30	.131	4.00	.158	4.65	.184
3½	3.10	.122	3.90	.153	4.65	.184	5.45	.215
4	3.55	.140	4.95	.195	5.35	.210	6.20	.245
4½	4.00	.157	5.00	.197	6.00	.237	7.00	.276
5	4.45	.175	5.55	.219	6.70	.263	7.80	.307
5½	4.85	.192	6.10	.241	7.35	.289	8.60	.338
6	5.35	.210	6.65	.262	8.00	.315	9.35	.368
6½	5.75	.226	7.20	.283	8.60	.339	10.05	.396
7	6.20	.244	7.45	.305	9.25	.365	10.80	.426
7½	6.60	.261	8.30	.326	9.95	.392	11.60	.457
8	7.05	.278	8.85	.348	10.60	.418	12.35	.487
8½	7.50	.296	9.40	.370	11.25	.444	13.20	.519
9	7.95	.313	9.95	.392	11.95	.470	13.90	.548
9½	8.40	.331	10.50	.413	12.60	.496	14.70	.579
10	8.85	.348	11.05	.435	13.25	.522	15.45	.609
11	9.70	.383	12.15	.479	14.55	.574	17.00	.670
12	10.60	.418	13.25	.522	15.90	.626	18.55	.731
13	11.50	.452	14.35	.566	17.25	.679	20.10	.792
14	12.35	.487	15.45	.609	18.55	.731	21.65	.853
15	13.25	.522	16.60	.653	19.90	.783	23.20	.914
16	14.15	.557	17.65	.696	21.20	.835	24.75	.974

NOTE: Metric cutter sizes were not available at the time of publication. Metric and inch wheelhead adjustments are approximate equivalents.

5. Mount the cutter between centres with the dog loosely on the mandrel and adjust the table until one cutter tooth rests on the blade. Lock the table in position.

6. Set the cutter clearance dial (Fig. 14-50) to zero and tighten the dog on the mandrel.

7. Loosen the cutter clearance dial lock and the wheelhead lock.

8. Lightly holding the cutter tooth onto the tooth rest blade, lower the wheelhead until the required clearance shows on the clearance setting dial.

9. Remove the clearance setting dog and unlock the table.

10. Set the stop dogs so that the wheel clears both sides of the cutter enough to allow indexing for the next tooth.

11. Start the grinding wheel.

12. Adjust the saddle until the cutter just touches the grinding wheel.

13. Grind one tooth and move the cutter clear of the tooth rest.

14. Rotate the next tooth, which is offset in the opposite direction, onto the tooth rest and grind it on the return stroke.

15. After grinding two teeth, check them with a dial indicator to see that they are the same height. If not, adjust the blade slightly toward the high side and grind the next two teeth. Repeat the process until the teeth are within 0.007 mm (or .0003 in.).

Secondary Clearance

Because it is necessary to provide adequate chip clearance when milling deep slots, a secondary clearance of 20 to 25° on staggered tooth cutters is recommended. It is also suggested that enough secondary clearance be ground to reduce the width of the land to approximately 0.80 mm (or 1/32 in.). This will permit regrinding of the primary clearance at least once without the need for grinding the secondary clearance.

To Grind the Secondary Clearance on a Staggered Tooth Cutter

1. Remove the tooth rest from the wheelhead and mount it on the table between the tailstocks. A universal micrometer flicker-type tooth rest and a straight blade (Fig. 14-52) should be used to permit the cutter to be rotated.

2. Place the centring gauge on the table and bring the *centre* of one tooth to centre height. Mark this tooth with layout dye or chalk.

3. Locate the dog on the clearance setting dial pin and tighten it on the mandrel.

4. Rotate the cutter to the desired amount of clearance using the clearance setting dial.

5. Adjust the tooth rest under, or on the side of, the marked tooth.

6. Swivel the table sufficiently to the right or the left (depending on the helix angle of the tooth being ground) to grind a straight land.

7. Grind the secondary clearance on this tooth until the land is 0.80 mm (or 1/32 in.) wide.

8. Grind all remaining teeth having the same slope or helix.

9. Swivel the table in the opposite direction and follow steps 6, 7, and 8 to set up and grind the remaining teeth.

Side Clearance

The side of the teeth of any milling cutter should not be ground unless absolutely necessary, since this reduces the width of the cutter. If the teeth must be ground, proceed as follows.

1. Mount the cutter on a stub arbor in the workhead (Fig. 14-52).

2. Mount a flaring cup wheel.

3. Tilt the workhead to the desired primary clearance angle. This is generally 2 to 4°. The secondary clearance is about 12°.

4. Place the centring gauge on the wheelhead and adjust one tooth of the cutter until it is on centre and level. Clamp the workhead spindle.

5. Mount the tooth rest on the workhead using a flicker-type rest and a plain blade.

6. Raise or lower the wheelhead so that the grinding wheel only contacts the tooth resting on the blade.

7. Grind the primary clearance on all teeth.

8. Tilt the workhead to the required angle for the secondary clearance and grind all teeth.

TO GRIND A FORM RELIEVED CUTTER

Unlike other types of milling cutters, form relieved cutters are ground on the face of the teeth rather than on the periphery; otherwise the form of the cutter will be changed when it is sharpened.

When grinding formed cutters for the first time, grind the backs of the teeth before grinding the cutting face, to ensure that all teeth are the same thickness. This

Courtesy Covel Mfg. Co.

Fig. 14-52 Setup for grinding the sides of the teeth on a milling cutter using a flicker-type tooth rest

is necessary because the locating pawl on the grinding fixture bears against *the back of the tooth* when the cutter is being ground.

Procedure

1. Swing the wheelhead so that the spindle is at 90° to the table travel.
2. Mount a dish wheel and the proper wheel guard.
3. Mount a gear cutter sharpening attachment on the table to the left of the grinding wheel (Fig. 14-53).

Courtesy Cincinnati Milacron Inc.

Fig. 14-53   Grinder set up to sharpen a form-relieved cutter

4. Place the gear cutter on the stud of the attachment so that the back of each tooth may be ground.
   NOTE: This operation is only necessary when the cutter is being sharpened for the first time.
5. Place the centring gauge on the wheelhead and adjust the wheelhead until the centre of the tooth face is on centre.
6. Move the table in until the back edge of a tooth is near the grinding wheel. At the same time, rotate the cutter until the back of the tooth is parallel with the face of the wheel (Fig. 14-54).
7. Engage the edge of the pawl on the face of the tooth and clamp the pawl in place (Fig. 14-54).
8. Grind the back of this tooth.
9. Move the table to the left so that the cutter is clear of the grinding wheel.

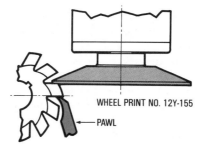

WHEEL PRINT NO. 12Y-155

PAWL

Courtesy Cincinnati Milacron Inc.

Fig. 14-54   Back of the tooth set parallel to the wheel and the pawl in place

10. Index the cutter so that the pawl will bear against the next tooth. Hold the tooth face against the pawl when grinding.
11. Grind the backs of all teeth.
12. Reverse the cutter on the stud and adjust the pawl against the back of the tooth, after the face of the tooth has been brought to bear against the centring gauge fastened to the attachment. Swing the centring gauge out of the way.
13. Adjust the saddle to bring the face of one tooth in line with the grinding wheel. After this time, adjust the saddle only to compensate for wheel wear.

14. Loosen one set screw and tighten the other to rotate the cutter against the grinding wheel.
15. Grind one tooth, traverse the table and index for the next tooth.
16. Grind all tooth faces.

CYLINDRICAL GRINDING

With the aid of a motorized workhead, the cutter and tool grinder may be used for cylindrical and plunge grinding. Work may be ground between centres or held in a chuck, depending on the type of work.

To Grind Work Parallel Between Centres

1. Mount the motorized workhead on the left end of the table (Fig. 14-55).
2. Examine the centres of the machine and the work to see that they are in good condition.
3. Using the centring gauge on the wheelhead, adjust the wheelhead to the tailstock centre height.
4. Mount a 150 mm (or 6 in.) straight grinding wheel on the wheelhead spindle so that the wheel rotates downwards at the front of the wheel. This will deflect the sparks downwards.

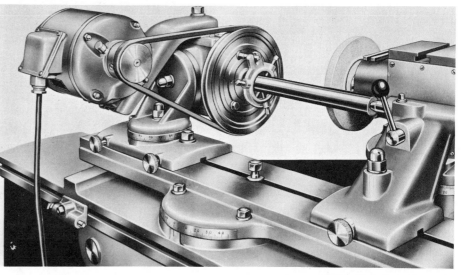

Courtesy The Pedersen Machine Co.

Fig. 14-55   Setup for cylindrical grinding on a cutter and tool grinder

5. Mount a parallel, hardened and ground test bar between centres.

6. Using a dial indicator, align the centres for height and then align the side of the bar parallel with the table travel. Remove the bar and indicator.

7. Mount the work between centres.

8. Set the stop dogs so that the wheel overlaps the work by one-third the width of the wheelface at each end.

9. Start the grinding wheel and workhead. The workpiece should revolve in the opposite direction to that of the grinding wheel.

10. Bring the revolving work up until it just touches the grinding wheel.

11. Traverse the table slowly and clean up the workpiece. The traverse speed should be such that the work travels approximately one-quarter the width of the wheel for each revolution of the work.

12. Measure each end of the workpiece for size and taper. If a taper exists, adjust as required.

13. After the work is parallel, set the crossfeed graduated collar to zero.

14. Feed the work into the grinding wheel approximately 0.02 mm (or .001 in.) per pass until the work is within 0.02 mm (or .001 in.) of finished size. Use 0.005 mm (or .0002 in.) cuts for finishing.

15. Feed in the work until the graduated collar indicates it is to the proper size.

    NOTE: Since work expands during grinding, it should never be checked for accurate size when warm.

16. Traverse the table several times to permit the wheel to spark out.

The same procedure is followed for taper grinding, except that the table must be swung to half the angle of the taper. After the work is cleaned up, the taper should be carefully checked for size and accuracy, and adjustments made as required. When taper grinding, it is most important that the centre height of the wheel and the workpiece be in line.

INTERNAL GRINDING

Light internal grinding may be performed on the tool and cutter grinder by mounting the internal grinding attachment on the wheelhead. The workpiece is held in a chuck mounted on the motorized workhead (Fig. 14-56).

1. Mount a test bar in the workhead spindle and align it both vertically and horizontally. When grinding a tapered hole, the workhead spindle must be aligned vertically and then swung to half the included angle of the taper.

2. Mount the internal grinding attachment on the workhead.

3. Centre the grinding wheel spindle using the centring gauge.

4. Mount the proper grinding wheel on the spindle.

5. Mount a chuck on the motorized workhead.

6. Mount the work in the chuck. Care must be taken not to distort the workpiece by gripping it too tightly.

7. Set the rotation of the workhead in an opposite direction to that of the grinding spindle.

8. Start the grinding wheel and the workpiece.

9. Carefully bring the wheel into the hole of the workpiece.

10. Set the table travel so that only one-third of the wheel overlaps the hole at each end.

11. Clan up the inside of the hole and check for size, parallelism, and bellmouthing. Correct as required.

12. Set the crossfeed graduated collar to zero and determine the amount of material to be removed.

13. Feed the grinding wheel in about 0.01 mm (or .0005 in.) per pass.

Courtesy Cincinnati Milacron Inc.

Fig. 14-56 Setup for internal grinding on a cutter and tool grinder

14. When work is close to the finished size, let the wheel spark out to improve the finish and remove the spring from the spindle.
15. Finish grind the hole to size.

GRINDING MACHINES QUESTIONS

GRINDING MACHINES AND PROCESS

1. Discuss how the role of grinding has contributed to interchangeable manufacture.
2. How has the role of grinding changed over the years?
3. Outline the action that takes place during a grinding operation.
4. List five important rules which apply to any grinding operation.

SURFACE GRINDING

5. Define surface grinding.
6. Name four different types of surface grinders and briefly outline the principle of each.

PARTS OF THE HYDRAULIC SURFACE GRINDER

7. Name five *main* parts of the hydraulic surface grinder.
8. Name and state the purpose of five controls found on the hydraulic surface grinder.

GRINDING WHEEL CARE

9. List four points to be observed in grinding wheel care.

TO MOUNT A GRINDING WHEEL

10. List the steps required to properly mount a grinding wheel.
11. Why is a blotter on each side of the wheel necessary when mounting a grinding wheel?

TO BALANCE A GRINDING WHEEL

12. Why is the proper balance of a grinding wheel essential?

13. Describe briefly the procedure for balancing a grinding wheel.

TO TRUE AND DRESS A GRINDING WHEEL

14. Define truing and dressing.
15. Why are most diamond dressers mounted at an angle of 10 to 15° to the base?
16. Explain how a grinding wheel should be finish dressed for:
    a) rough grinding
    b) finish grinding

WORK-HOLDING DEVICES

17. List the advantages and disadvantages of an electromagnetic chuck.
18. Describe the construction and operation of a permanent magnetic chuck.

MAGNETIC CHUCK ACCESSORIES

19. How are thin workpieces held for surface grinding? Why is this necessary?
20. What precautions must be observed when using magnetic chuck blocks?
21. Describe and state the purpose of magna-vise clamps.

GRINDING FLUIDS

22. State four purposes of grinding fluids.
23. Name three methods of applying coolant and briefly describe the method by which each is applied.

SURFACE FINISH

24. List any five factors that affect the surface finish on the part being ground. How do these factors affect the surface finish?

TO MOUNT THE WORKPIECE FOR GRINDING

25. Describe briefly the procedure for mounting the following for grinding:
    a) flat work
    b) short work

GRINDER SAFETY

26. How should a wheel be checked for defects?
27. Why is it necessary to see that no one is in line with the grinding wheel before starting the grinder?
28. List five grinder safety rules which you consider to be most important and explain the reason for the selection of each.

TO GRIND A FLAT SURFACE

29. Explain how the grinding wheel should be set to the surface of the work.
30. How should work be removed from a magnetic chuck?

GRINDING THE EDGES OF A WORKPIECE

31. Why are the edges of workpieces often ground square and parallel?
32. How much allowance should be left on a surface for grinding?
33. What precautions should be observed before mounting any workpiece or accessory on the magnetic chuck?
34. What precautions should be observed when mounting a workpiece on an angle plate for grinding two adjacent sides?
35. After the first side of a workpiece has been ground, how is the work set to grind the second side square to the first?
36. What precautions should be observed when setting the grinding wheel to the work surface?

TO GRIND A VERTICAL SURFACE

37. Outline briefly the procedure for grinding a vertical surface.
38. When grinding a vertical surface, why is it necessary first to relieve the corner between the two adjacent surfaces?
39. How is the grinding wheel dressed when grinding a vertical surface? Why is this necessary?

TO GRIND AN ANGULAR SURFACE

40. By what methods may work be held for grinding an angle when using a flat dressed wheel?
41. Name two methods of dressing a wheel to an angle.

FORM GRINDING

42. Name two methods of dressing contours and radii on grinding wheels.
43. Describe the principle of crush-form dressing.
44. On what types of surface grinders should crush-form dressing be performed?

SURFACE GRINDING PROBLEMS, CAUSES, AND REMEDIES

45. List three causes and three remedies for each of the following grinding problems:
    a) chatter or wavy pattern
    b) scratches on the work surface

CYLINDRICAL GRINDERS

46. Name two types of cylindrical grinders.
47. List the main parts of a cylindrical grinder and state the purpose of each.
48. What precautions should be observed when truing and dressing the grinding wheel of a cylindrical grinder?

TO PARALLEL GRIND THE OUTSIDE DIAMETER OF A WORKPIECE

49. List six precautions which must be taken to ensure the utmost accuracy when parallel grinding the outside diameter of a workpiece.

TO GRIND A TAPERED WORKPIECE

50. List three ways in which tapers may be ground on a universal cylindrical grinder.

CYLINDRICAL GRINDING FAULTS, CAUSES, AND REMEDIES

51. List three causes and three remedies for the following cylindrical grinding faults.
    a) burnt work
    b) chatter marks
    c) feed lines
    d) work out-of-round
    e) rough finish
    f) wavy marks

INTERNAL GRINDING

52. Describe internal grinding and name four machines on which it may be performed.

INTERNAL GRINDING ON A UNIVERSAL CYLINDRICAL GRINDER

53. Why are grinding wheels used for internal grinding generally softer than those used for external grinding?
54. What precautions must be taken when setting up and grinding a parallel hole in a workpiece?

TO GRIND A TAPERED HOLE

55. At what height should the grinding wheel be set when grinding a taper? Why is this necessary?

INTERNAL GRINDING PROBLEMS, CAUSES, AND REMEDIES

56. List four important problems encountered when internal grinding. State at least two causes and two remedies for each of the problems listed.

CENTRELESS GRINDING

57. Describe the principle of centreless grinding. Illustrate by means of a suitable sketch.
58. How is the work held when centreless grinding to make it cylindrical as quickly as possible?

METHODS OF CENTRELESS GRINDING

59. Name three methods of centreless grinding and illustrate each of these methods by a suitable labelled sketch.

60. List four advantages of centreless grinding.

PARTS OF THE UNIVERSAL CUTTER AND TOOL GRINDER

61. Name five main parts of the universal cutter and tool grinder.
62. How many controls are there for each of the following parts of the universal cutter and tool grinder?
    a) wheelhead
    b) saddle
    c) table
63. Name five accessories used with the universal cutter and tool grinder and state the purpose of each.
64. Sketch and name five types of tooth rest blades and indicate the purpose for which each is used.

CUTTER GRINDING MANDRELS AND ARBORS

65. Make a suitable sketch of a cutter grinding mandrel and a cutter grinding arbor.
66. How does a cutter grinding mandrel differ from a lathe mandrel?

MILLING CUTTER NOMENCLATURE

67. Make a suitable sketch of at least two teeth on a milling cutter and indicate the following parts:
    a) primary clearance angle
    b) secondary clearance angle
    c) cutting edge
    d) land
    e) tooth angle
    f) tooth face
68. Why are cutters with widely spaced teeth more efficient than those with closely spaced teeth?
69. What factors influence the cutter clearance angle?

METHODS OF GRINDING CLEARANCE ON MILLING CUTTERS

70. Name and describe briefly three methods of grinding clearance on cutting tools.

CHECKING CUTTING CLEARANCE WITH A DIAL INDICATOR

71. Describe the principle by which cutter clearance is checked using a dial indicator.
72. Name and describe two other methods of checking cutter clearance angles and state the limitations of each method.

CUTTER GRINDING OPERATIONS AND SETUPS

73. Describe how the tooth edge of a milling cutter is placed on centre.
74. Describe how the correct cutter clearance is set on the machine using the clearance setting dial.
75. Explain two methods to determine how far to lower the wheelhead, for the proper cutter clearance angle.
76. How far would the wheelhead be lowered to grind the proper clearance on the following cutters?
    a) 5° clearance angle on a 75 mm diameter cutter using a flaring cup wheel
    b) 8° clearance angle on a 65 mm diameter cutter using a flaring cup wheel
    c) 5° clearance angle on a 3 in. diameter cutter using a 6 in. straight wheel
77. List four precautions to be taken when grinding a helical milling cutter.
78. Where is the tooth rest mounted when grinding cutters having:
    a) helical teeth?
    b) straight teeth?

TO GRIND A STAGGERED TOOTH CUTTER

79. How does the grinding of a staggered tooth milling cutter differ from the grinding of a plain helical milling cutter?

TO GRIND A FORM RELIEVED CUTTER

81. On what surface are form relief cutters ground, when being sharpened? Explain why.
82. Why is it advisable to grind the backs of the teeth on a new gear cutter?
83. What type of grinding wheel is used for sharpening gear cutters?

CYLINDRICAL GRINDING

84. List the steps required to *set up* the cutter and tool grinder for cylindrical grinding.
85. Why is it advisable to permit the grinding wheel to spark out when cylindrical grinding?
86. How should the stop dogs be set when cylindrical grinding?
87. How fast should the table be traversed when cylindrical grinding on a cutter and tool grinder?
88. What precautions must be taken when setting up the machine for taper grinding?

INTERNAL GRINDING

89. What precautions should be taken when setting up the work for internal grinding?
90. List briefly the steps required to grind the inside diameter of a bushing using a cutter and tool grinder.

15 CARBIDE, CERAMIC AND DIAMOND CUTTING TOOLS

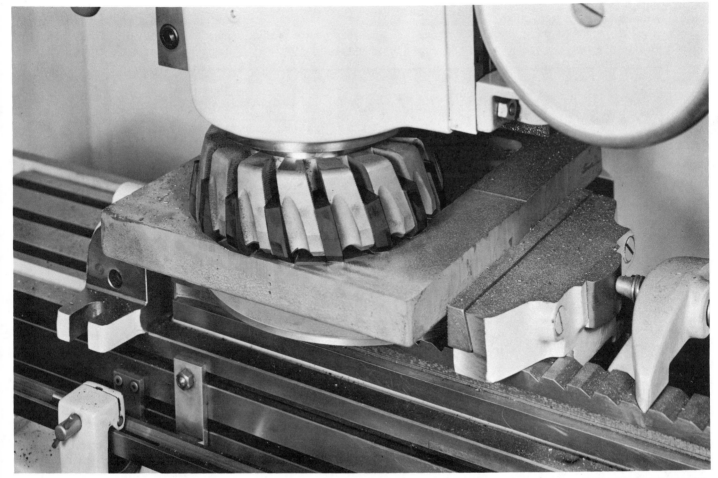

Courtesy Cincinnati Milacron Inc.

Single point cutting tools have always been widely used for metal removal, and man has continually attempted to find new cutting tool materials to increase production. Over the past 100 years, high-carbon steel, high-speed steel, cemented carbide, ceramic, and diamond cutting tools have been developed. During this time, the rate of cutting metal has increased from 3 to 4.5 m/min to as high as 3050 m/min in some cases. Cutting speeds of 90 to 305 m/min are quite common.

CARBIDE CUTTING TOOLS

Carbide was first used for cutting tools in Germany during World War I as a substitute for badly needed diamonds. During the 1930s, various additives were discovered which greatly improved the quality and performance of carbide tools. Since that time, various types of cemented (sintered) carbides have been developed to suit different materials and machining operations. Cemented carbides are similar to steel in appearance, but they are so hard that the diamond is almost the only material which will scratch them. They have been accepted widely by industry because they have good wear resistance and are capable of operating efficiently at cutting speeds ranging from 45 to 365 m/min. Carbide tools can machine metals at speeds that cause the cutting edge to become red hot without its losing its hardness or sharpness.

MANUFACTURE OF CEMENTED CARBIDES

Cemented carbides are products of the powder-metallurgy process; they consist primarily of minute particles of tungsten and carbon powders cemented together under heat by a metal of lower melting point, usually cobalt. Powdered metals such as tantalum, titanium, and niobium are also used in the manufacture of cemented carbides to provide cutting tools with various characteristics. The entire operation of producing cemented-carbide products is illustrated in Fig. 15-1.

BLENDING

Five types of powders are used in the manufacture of cemented-carbide tools: tungsten carbide, titanium carbide, tantalum carbide, niobium carbide, and cobalt. One or any combination of these carbide powders and cobalt (the binder) are blended together in different proportions, depending on the grade of carbide desired. This powder is mixed in alcohol;

Courtesy Canadian General Electric Co. Ltd.

Fig. 15-1   The process of manufacturing cemented carbide products

the mixing process takes anywhere from 24 to 190 hours. After the powder and alcohol have been thoroughly mixed, the alcohol is drained, and paraffin is added to simplify the pressing operation.

COMPACTION

After the powders have been thoroughly mixed, they must be moulded to shape and size. Five different methods may be used to compact the powder to shape (Fig. 15-2): the extrusion process, the hot press, the isostatic press, the ingot press, or the pill press. The green (pressed) compacts are soft and must be presintered to dissolve the paraffin and lightly bond the particles together so that they may be handled easily.

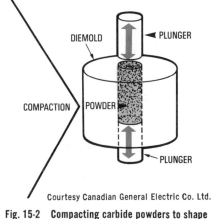

Courtesy Canadian General Electric Co. Ltd.

Fig. 15-2   Compacting carbide powders to shape and size

PRESINTERING

The green compacts are heated to about 900°C in a furnace under a protective atmosphere of hydrogen. After this operation, the carbide blanks have the consistency of chalk, and may be machined to the required shape and approximately 40% oversize to allow for the shrinkage which occurs during final sintering.

SINTERING

Sintering, the last step in the process, converts the presintered machined blanks into cemented carbide. Sintering is carried out in either a hydrogen atmosphere or a vacuum, depending on the grade of carbide manufactured, at temperatures between 1400 and 1500°C. During the sintering operation, the binder (cobalt) unites and cements the carbide powders into a dense structure of extremely hard carbide crystals.

CEMENTED CARBIDE APPLICATIONS

Because of the extreme hardness and good wear-resistance properties of cemented carbide, it has been used extensively in the manufacture of metal cutting tools. Drills, reamers, milling cutters, shaper and lathe cutting tools are only a few examples of uses for cemented carbides. These tools may be manufactured out of solid carbide, or may have cemented-carbide inserts, either brazed or held mechanically, on the cutting edge.

Cemented carbides were first used successfully in machining operations as lathe cutting tools. The majority of cemented-carbide tools in use are single-point cutting tools used on machines such as lathes, shapers, and milling machines.

TYPES OF CARBIDE LATHE CUTTING TOOLS

Cemented-carbide lathe cutting tools are available in two types: the brazed-tip type and the throwaway insert type.

Brazed-tip carbide tools. Cemented carbide tips can be brazed to steel shanks and are available in a wide variety of styles and sizes (Fig. 15-3). Brazed-tip carbide tools are rigid and are generally used for production turning purposes.

Throwaway inserts. Cemented carbide indexible throwaway inserts (Fig. 15-4) are made in a wide variety of shapes, such as triangular, square, diamond, round, etc. These inserts are held mechanically in a special holder (Fig. 15-5), and when one cutting edge becomes dull, it may be quickly indexed or turned in the holder and a new cutting edge will be presented. A triangular insert has three cutting edges on the top surface and three on the bottom, for a total of six cutting edges. When all six cutting edges are dull, the carbide insert is discarded and replaced with a new insert.

Courtesy Canadian General Electric Co. Ltd.

Fig. 15-3   A variety of brazed carbide tools

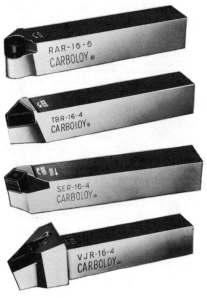

Courtesy Canadian General Electric Co. Ltd.

Fig. 15-4   A variety of indexible throwaway cemented carbide inserts

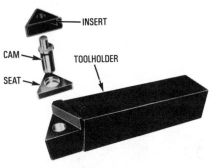

Courtesy Canadian General Electric Co. Ltd.

Fig. 15-5   A toolholder for indexible throwaway inserts

Cemented carbide throwaway inserts are becoming more popular than the brazed-tip carbide tools because:

a) Less time is required to change to a new cutting edge.

b) The amount of machine "down-time" is reduced considerably and production is thus increased.

c) The time normally spent in regrinding a tool is eliminated.

d) Faster speeds and feeds can be used with throwaway inserts.

e) The cost of diamond wheels, required for grinding carbide tools, is eliminated.

f) Throwaway inserts are cheaper than brazed-tip tools.

CEMENTED-CARBIDE INSERT IDENTIFICATION

The American Standards Association has developed a system by which throwaway inch inserts can be identified quickly and accurately. This system has been generally adopted by manufacturers of cemented-carbide inserts.

GRADES OF CEMENTED CARBIDES

There are two main groups of carbides from which various grades can be selected: the straight tungsten carbide grades and the crater resistant grades.

The straight tungsten carbide grades, containing only tungsten carbide and cobalt, are the strongest and most wear resistant. Generally they are used for machining cast iron and nonmetals. Tungsten carbide grades are not very satisfactory for steel because of their tendency to crater and to cause rapid tool failure as a result.

The size of the tungsten carbide particles and the percentage of cobalt used determine the qualities of tungsten carbide tools.

a) the finer the grain particles, the lower the tool toughness

b) the finer the grain particles, the higher the tool hardness

c) the higher the hardness, the greater the wear resistance

d) the lower the cobalt content, the lower the tool toughness

e) the lower the cobalt content, the higher the hardness

For maximum tool life, always select a tungsten carbide grade with the lowest cobalt content and the finest grain size possible which gives satisfactory performance without breakage.

Crater resistant grades contain titanium carbide and tantalum carbide in addition to the basic components of tungsten carbide and cobalt. These grades are used for machining most steels.

The additions of tantalum carbide and/or titanium carbide provide tools with various characteristics.

a) The addition of titanium carbide provides resistance to tool cratering. The higher the titanium content, the greater the resistance to cratering.

b) As the titanium carbide content is increased, the toughness of the tool is decreased.

c) As the titanium carbide content is increased, the abrasive wear resistance at the cutting edge is lowered.

d) Tantalum carbide additions have effects similar to tungsten carbide on the resistance to cratering and strength.

e) Tantalum carbide gives good crater resistance without affecting the abrasive wear resistance.

f) The addition of tantalum carbide increases the tool's resistance to deformation.

Because of the wide variety of cemented-carbide compositions available and the rapid development of new, improved types, no standard grade classification system has been developed. It is wise to follow the manufacturer's recommendations as to the type and grade of carbide for each specific application. A few general rules will assist in the selection of the proper cemented carbide grade.

1. Always use a grade with the lowest cobalt content and the finest grain size (strong enough to eliminate breakage).

2. To combat abrasive wear only, use straight tungsten carbide grades.

3. To combat cratering, seizing, welding, and galling, use titanium carbide grades.

4. For crater and abrasive wear resistance, use tantalum carbide grades.

5. For heavy cuts in steel, when heat and pressure might deform the cutting edge, use tantalum carbide grades.

TABLE 15-1: CEMENTED-CARBIDE INSERT IDENTIFICATION SYSTEM
(DIMENSIONS IN INCHES)

Code example: **T N G A – 4 4 3 A**

T — SHAPE

- R — Round
- S — Square
- T — Triangle
- L — Rectangle
- D — Diamond 55°
- C — Diamond 80°
- M — Diamond 86°
- P — Pentagon
- B — Parellelogram 82°
- A — Parallelogram 85°
- H — Hexagon
- O — Octagon

N — RELIEF ANGLE

- N — 0°
- A — 3°
- B — 5°
- C — 7°
- P — 10°
- D — 15°
- E — 20°
- F — 25°
- G — 30°

G — TOLERANCES

CUTTING POINT   THICKNESS

- A = ± .0002 .... ± .001
- B = ± .0002 .... ± .005
- C = ± .0005 .... ± .001
- D = ± .0005 .... ± .005
- E = ± .001 .... ± .001
- G = ± .001 .... ± .005
- **M = ± .002 ± .004 .... ± .005
- **U = ± .005 ± .012 .... ± .005
- R Blank with grind stock

A — *TYPE

- A — With hole
- B — With hole and one countersink
- C — With hole and two countersinks
- D — Smaller than 1/4 I.C. with hole
- E — Smaller than 1/4 I.C. without hole
- F — Clamp-on type with chipbreaker
- G — With hole and chipbreaker
- H — With hole, one countersink and chipbreaker
- J — With hole, two countersinks and chipbreaker

4 — SIZE

Number of 1/32nds on inserts less than 1/4 I.C.

Number of 1/8ths on inserts 1/4 I.C. and over.

Rectangle and Parallelogram Inserts require two digits:

1st Digit—Number of 1/8ths in width

2nd Digit—Number of 1/4ths in length.

4 — THICKNESS

Number of 1/32nds on inserts less than 1/4 I.C.

Number of 1/16ths on inserts 1/4 I.C. and over.

Use width dimension in place of I.C. on Rectangle and Parallelogram inserts.

3 — POINT RADIUS, FLATS

- 0 — Sharp corner
- 1 — 1/64 Radius
- 2 — 1/32 Radius
- 3 — 3/64 Radius
- 4 — 1/16 Radius
- 6 — 3/32 Radius
- 8 — 1/8 Radius

- A — Square Insert with 45° chamfer
- B — Square insert with 45° chamfer and 4° sweep angle, R.H. or Neg.
- C — Square insert with 45° chamfer and 4° sweep angle, L.H.
- D — Square insert with 30° chamfer, R.H. or Neg.
- E — Square insert with 15° chamfer, R.H. or Neg.
- F — Square insert with 5° chamfer, F.H. or Neg.
- G — Square insert with 30° chamfer, L.H.
- H — Square insert with 15° chamfer, L.H.
- J — Square insert with 5° chamfer, L.H.
- K — Square insert with 30° double chamfer
- L — Square insert with 15° double chamfer
- M — Square insert with 5° double chamfer
- N — Truncated triangle insert
- P — Flatted corner triangle, R.H. or Neg.
- R — Flatted corner triangle, L.H.

A — *FINISH

- A — Ground all over—light honed
- B — Ground all over—heavy honed
- C — Ground top and bottom only—light honed
- D — Ground top and bottom only—heavy honed
- E — Unground insert—honed
- F — Unground insert—not honed

*SHALL BE USED ONLY WHEN REQUIRED.   **EXACT TOLERANCE IS DETERMINED BY SIZE OF INSERT.

Courtesy Canadian General Electric Co. Ltd.

TOOL GEOMETRY

The geometry of cutting tools refers to the various angles and clearances machined or ground on the tool faces. Although the terms and definitions relating to single-point cutting tools vary greatly, the ones adopted by the ASME and currently in general use are illustrated in Fig. 15-6.

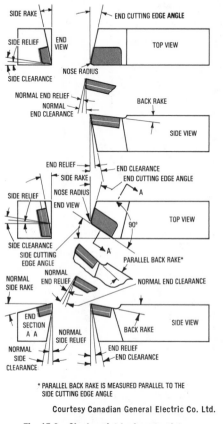

* PARALLEL BACK RAKE IS MEASURED PARALLEL TO THE SIDE CUTTING EDGE ANGLE

Courtesy Canadian General Electric Co. Ltd.

Fig. 15-6   Single point tool nomenclature

CUTTING TOOL TERMS

Front, or End, Relief (Clearance). The front relief, or clearance, allows the end of the cutting tool to enter the work. This clearance should be just enough to prevent the tool from rubbing. Too much front clearance will reduce the support under the point and cause rapid tool failure.

Side Relief (Clearance). This angle permits the side of the tool to advance into the work. Too little side relief, or clearance, will prevent the tool from cutting, and excessive heat will be generated by the rubbing action. Too much side clearance will weaken the cutting edge and cause it to chip.

Side Cutting Edge Angle. The angle of the side of the cutting edge that meets the work may be either positive or negative. A negative side cutting angle (Fig. 15-6) is preferred because it protects the point of the tool at both the start and the end of a cut; this is especially useful on work that has a hard abrasive scale.

Nose Radius. The nose radius strengthens the finishing point of the tool and improves the surface finish on the work. The nose radius of most cutting tools should be approximately twice the amount of feed per revolution. Too large a nose radius may cause chatter, while too small a radius weakens the point of the cutting tool.

TABLE 15-2: NOSE RADIUS NOMOGRAPH
TO OBTAIN MAXIMUM EFFICIENCY WITH CARBIDE TOOLS THE NOSE RADIUS SHOULD BE KEPT SMALL. USE CHART BELOW AS A GUIDE. USE STRAIGHTEDGE TO JOIN FEED WITH DEPTH OF CUT. USE NOSE RADIUS WHERE LINE CROSSES.

Feed per rev. (Inches)		Nose Radius (Inches)		Depth of Cut (Inches)	
	mm	mm	mm		mm
.050	1.3	4.8 3/16		1-1/4	32
.045	1.1	4.0 5/32	3.2 1/8	1-1/8	29
.040	1.0			1	25
.035	0.9	3.2 1/8	2.4 3/32	7/8	22
.030	0.8			3/4	19
.025	0.6	2.4 3/32	1.6 1/16	5/8	16
.020	0.5	1.6 1/16		1/2	12
.015	0.4		1.2 3/64	7/16	11
.010	0.3	1.2 3/64	0.8 1/32	3/8	10
.0075	0.2	0.8 1/32		5/16	8
.005	0.1		0.40 1/64	1/4	6
.0025	0.05	0.40 1/64		3/16	5
.000	0.00		0.13 to 0.40 .005 to .015	1/8	3
				1/16	1.6
				0	0.00

ECCENTRIC FORGINGS, INTERRUPTED OR SCALE CUTS

REGULAR CUTS IN CLEAN METAL

Courtesy Canadian General Electric Co. Ltd.

To obtain maximum efficiency with carbide tools, keep the nose radius as small as possible. Use Table 15-2 to find the proper nose radius for the depth of cut and feed being used.

Side Rake. The side rake angle should be as large as possible, without weakening the cutting edge, to allow the chips to escape readily (Fig. 15-7A). The amount of side rake will be determined by the type and grade of the cutting tool, the type of material being cut, and the feed per revolution. For difficult-to-machine metals, it may be advisable to use a small side rake angle or at times even negative side rake (Fig. 15-7B). Fig. 15-8 shows suggested side rakes for a variety of materials.

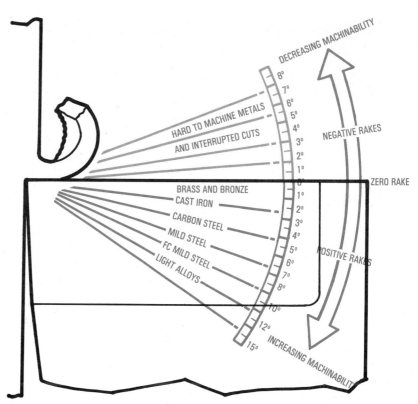

Courtesy A. C. Wickman Limited

Fig. 15-8   Recommended side rake angles for various materials

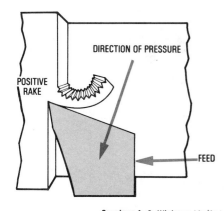

Courtesy A. C. Wickman Limited

Fig. 15-7A   Positive side rake angles

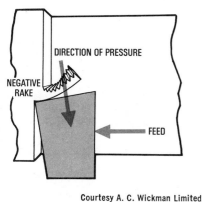

Courtesy A. C. Wickman Limited

Fig. 15-7B   Negative side rake angles

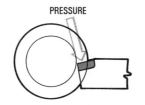

Fig. 15-9A   Negative back rake

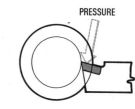

Fig. 15-9B   Positive back rake

Back Rake. The back rake angle is the angle formed between the top face of the tool and the top of the tool shank. It may be positive, negative, or neutral. When a tool has *negative back rake*, the top face of the tool slopes upward away from the point (Fig. 15-9A). Negative back rake protects the tool point from the cutting pressure and also from the abrasive action of hard materials and scale. When a tool has *positive back rake* (Fig. 15-9B), the top face of the tool slopes downward away from the point. This allows the chips to flow away freely from the cutting edge.

CEMENTED CARBIDE CUTTING TOOL ANGLES AND CLEARANCES

The angles and clearances of single point carbide tools vary greatly and generally depend on three factors.

a) the hardness of the cutting tool

TABLE 15-3: RECOMMENDED ANGLES FOR SINGLE-POINT CARBIDE TOOLS				
Material	End Relief (Front Clearance)	Side Relief (Side Clearance)	Side Rake	Back Rake
Aluminum	6 to 10°	6 to 10°	10 to 20°	0 to 10°
Brass, bronze	6 to 8°	6 to 8°	+8 to −5°	0 to −5°
Cast iron	5 to 8°	5 to 8°	+6 to −7°	0 to −7°
Machine steel	5 to 10°	5 to 10°	+6 to −7°	0 to −7°
Tool steel	5 to 8°	5 to 8°	+6 to −7°	0 to −7°
Stainless steel	5 to 8°	5 to 8°	+6 to −7°	0 to −7°
Titanium alloys	5 to 8°	5 to 8°	+6 to −5°	0 to −5°

NOTE: Use the lower range of these figures for hard-to-machine metals and interrupted cuts.

b) the workpiece material
c) the type of cutting operation

Table 15-3 lists recommended cutting tool angles and clearances for a variety of materials. These may have to be altered slightly to suit various conditions encountered while machining.

CUTTING SPEEDS AND FEEDS

Many variables influence the speeds, feeds, and depth of cut which should be used with cemented carbide tools. Some of the most important factors are:

a) the type and hardness of the work material
b) the grade and shape of the cutting tool
c) the rigidity of the cutting tool
d) the rigidity of the work and machine
e) the power rating of the machine

Table 15-4 gives the recommended cutting speeds and feeds for single point carbide tools. These should be used as a guide and may have to be altered slightly to suit the machining operation.

Table 15-5 illustrates the nomograph method of determining the cutting speed in feet per minute when the Brinell hardness of the steel is known.

MACHINING WITH CARBIDE TOOLS

To obtain maximum efficiency with cemented carbide cutting tools, certain precautions in machine setup and the cutting operation should be observed. The machine being used should be rigid, equipped with heat-treated gears, and have sufficient power to maintain a constant cutting speed. The work and cutting tool should be held as rigidly as possible to avoid chatter or keep it to a minimum.

Single point carbide cutting tools are more commonly used on a lathe, and therefore the setups and precautions for this machine will be outlined. The same basic precautions and setups should be applied when carbide tools are used on other machines.

Suggestions for Using Cemented Carbide Cutting Tools on a Lathe Work Setup

1. Work mounted in a chuck or other work-holding device must be held firmly enough to prevent it from slipping or chattering.
2. A revolving centre should be used in the tailstock for turning work between centres.
3. The tailstock spindle should be ex-

tended only a minimum distance and locked securely to ensure rigidity.
4. The tailstock should be clamped firmly to the lathe bed to prevent loosening.

Tool Geometry

1. Use a cutting tool with the proper rake and clearances for the material being cut.
2. Hone the cutting edge for good performance and longer tool life.
3. If the work permits, use a side cutting edge angle (Fig. 15-10A) large enough that the tool can be eased into the work. This helps to protect the nose of the cutting tool (weakest part) from shock and wear as it enters or leaves the work.

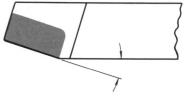

SIDE CUTTING EDGE ANGLE

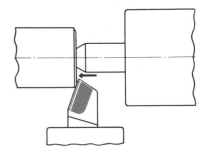

Courtesy Canadian General Electric Co. Ltd.

Fig. 15-10A A side cutting edge angle protects the point of the cutting tool

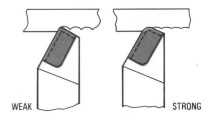

WEAK   STRONG

Courtesy Canadian General Electric Co. Ltd.

Fig. 15-10B A large nose radius strengthens the tool point and provides better surface finish

Material	Depth of Cut		Feed per Revolution		Cutting Speed	
	mm	in.	mm	in.	m/min	ft./min
Aluminum	0.15–0.40	.005–.015	0.05–0.15	.002–.005	215–305	700–1000
	0.50–2.30	.020–.090	0.15–0.40	.005–.015	135–215	450–700
	2.55–5.10	.100–.200	0.40–0.75	.015–.030	90–135	300–450
	7.60–17.80	.300–.700	0.75–2.30	.030–.090	30–60	100–200
Brass, bronze	0.15–0.40	.005–.015	0.05–0.15	.002–.005	215–245	700–800
	0.50–2.30	.020–.090	0.15–0.40	.005–.015	185–215	600–700
	2.55–5.10	.100–.200	0.40–0.75	.015–.030	150–185	500–600
	7.60–17.80	.300–.700	0.75–2.30	.030–.090	60–120	200–400
Cast iron (medium)	0.15–0.40	.005–.015	0.05–0.15	.002–.005	105–135	350–450
	0.50–2.30	.020–.090	0.15–0.40	.005–.015	75–105	250–350
	2.55–5.10	.100–.200	0.40–0.75	.015–.030	60–75	200–250
	7.60–17.80	.300–.700	0.75–2.30	.030–.090	25–45	75–150
Machine steel	0.15–0.40	.005–.015	0.05–0.15	.002–.005	215–305	700–1000
	0.50–2 30	.020–.090	0.15–0.40	.005–.015	170–215	550–700
	2.55–5.10	.100–.200	0.40–0.75	.015–.030	120–170	400–550
	7.60–17.80	.300–.700	0.75–2.30	.030–.090	45–90	150–300
Tool steel	0.15–0.40	.005–.015	0.05–0.15	.002–.005	150–230	500–750
	0.50–2.30	.020–.090	0.15–0.40	.005–.015	120–150	400–500
	2.55–5.10	.100–.200	0.40–0.75	.015–.030	90–120	300–400
	7.60–17.80	.300–.700	0.75–2.30	.030–.090	30–90	100–300
Stainless steel	0.15–0.40	.005–.015	0.05–0.15	.002–.005	115–150	375–500
	0.50–2.30	.020–.090	0.15–0.40	.005–.015	90–115	300–375
	2.55–5.10	.100–.200	0.40–0.75	.015–.030	75–90	250–300
	7.60–17.80	.300–.700	0.75–2.30	.030–.090	25–55	75–175
Titanium alloys	0.15–0.40	.005–.015	0.05–0.15	.002–.005	90–120	300–400
	0.50–2.30	.020–.090	0.15–0.40	.005–.015	60–90	200–300
	2.55–5.10	.100–.200	0.40–0.75	.015–.030	55–60	175–200
	7.60–17.80	.300–.700	0.75–2.30	.030–.090	15–40	50–125

TABLE 15-4: RECOMMENDED CUTTING SPEEDS AND FEEDS FOR SINGLE POINT CARBIDE TOOLS

Courtesy Canadian General Electric Co. Ltd.

NOTE: Millimetre and inch speeds are approximate equivalents.

4. Use the largest nose radius (Fig. 15-10B) which operating conditions will permit. Too large a nose radius causes chattering, while too small a nose radius causes the point to break down quickly. Use Table 15-2 to determine the correct nose radius to use for the amount of feed and depth of cut being used.

Tool Setup

1. Carbide tools should preferably be held in a sturdy, turret type holder (Fig. 15-11A). The amount of tool overhang should be just enough for chip clearance.

2. The cutting tool should be set exactly on centre; when it is above or below centre, the tool angles and clearances

TABLE 15-5: CARBIDE CUTTING SPEED NOMOGRAPH

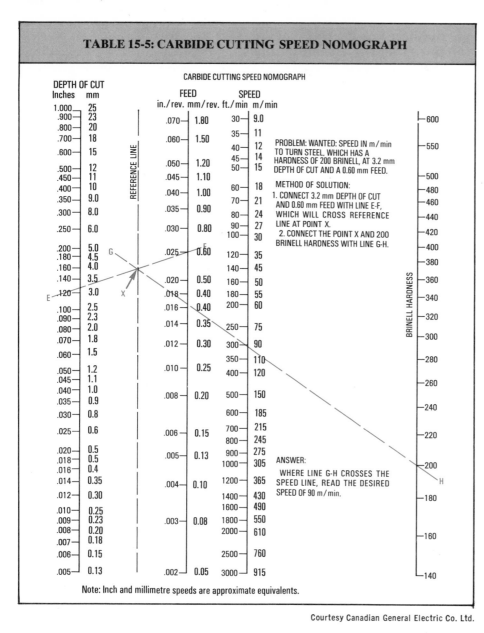

CARBIDE CUTTING SPEED NOMOGRAPH

PROBLEM: WANTED: SPEED IN m/min TO TURN STEEL, WHICH HAS A HARDNESS OF 200 BRINELL, AT 3.2 mm DEPTH OF CUT AND A 0.60 mm FEED.

METHOD OF SOLUTION:
1. CONNECT 3.2 mm DEPTH OF CUT AND 0.60 mm FEED WITH LINE E-F, WHICH WILL CROSS REFERENCE LINE AT POINT X.
2. CONNECT THE POINT X AND 200 BRINELL HARDNESS WITH LINE G-H.

ANSWER:
WHERE LINE G-H CROSSES THE SPEED LINE, READ THE DESIRED SPEED OF 90 m/min.

Note: Inch and millimetre speeds are approximate equivalents.

Courtesy Canadian General Electric Co. Ltd.

Courtesy Canadian General Electric Co. Ltd.

Fig. 15-11A   A carbide tool held "short" in a turret toolholder

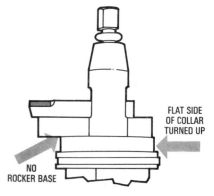

Courtesy Canadian General Electric Co. Ltd.

Fig. 15-11B   The tool shank is held in a horizontal plane

in relation to the job change and result in poor cutting action.

3. Carbide tools are designed to operate while the bottom of the tool shank is in a horizontal position (Fig. 15-11B).

4. If a rocker type toolpost is being used (Fig. 15-11C):
   i) Remove the rocker.
   ii) Invert the rocker base.
   iii) Shim the tool to the correct height.
   iv) Use a special carbide toolholder (having no rake) when machining with carbide tipped toolbits.

5. When setting up a carbide tool, always keep it away from the work and machine parts to avoid damaging the tool point.

FLAT SIDE OF COLLAR TURNED UP

NO ROCKER BASE

Courtesy Canadian General Electric Co. Ltd.

Fig. 15-11C   Remove rocker, invert rocker base, and shim tool to height when using a rocker type toolpost

Machine Setup

1. Always make sure that the machine has an adequate power rating for the machining operation and that there is no slippage in the clutch and belts.
2. Set the correct speed for the material being cut and the operation being performed.
   i) Too high a speed will cause rapid tool failure, while too low a speed will result in inefficient cutting action and poor production rates.
   ii) Use Table 15-4 or 15-5 to calculate the correct speed for the type of material being machined.
3. Set the machine at a feed which will give good metal removal rates and still provide the surface finish desired.
   i) Too light a feed causes rubbing which may result in hardening of the material being cut.
   ii) Too coarse a feed slows down the machine, creates excessive heat, and results in premature tool failure.

Cutting Operation

1. Never bring the tool point against work that is stationary; to do this will damage the cutting edge.
2. Always use the heaviest depth of cut possible for the machine and size of cutting tool.
3. Never stop a machine while the feed this will break the cutting edge. Always stop the feed and allow the tool to clear itself before stopping the machine.
4. Never continue to use a dull cutting tool.
5. A dull cutting tool may be recognized by:
   i) work being produced oversize and with a glazed finish
   ii) a rough and ragged surface finish
   iii) a change in the shape or colour of the chips
6. Apply cutting fluid only if:
   i) It can be applied under pressure.
   ii) It can be directed at the point of cutting and kept there at all times.

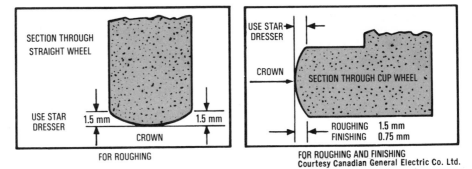

Fig. 15-12 A crown dressed on a silicon carbide wheel reduces heat when grinding carbide tools

Courtesy Canadian General Electric Co. Ltd.

GRINDING CEMENTED CARBIDE TOOLS

The efficiency of a cutting tool determines to a large extent the efficiency of the machine tool on which it is being used. A tool that has been improperly ground cannot perform well, and the cutting edge will soon break down. In order to grind cemented carbide cutting tools successfully, the type of grinding wheel used and the grinding procedure followed are important.

Grinding Wheels

1. An 80-grit, silicon carbide wheel should be used for rough grinding carbides.
2. A 100-grit silicon carbide wheel should be used for finish grinding carbides. The silicon carbide wheels should be dressed with a 1.5 mm crown (Fig. 15-12) to mimimize the amount of heat generated during grinding. These wheels should be used to grind only the carbide, not the steel tool shank.
3. Aluminum oxide grinding wheels should be used if it is necessary to grind the steel shank of a carbide tool.
4. Diamond grinding wheels (100 grit) are excellent for finish grinding of carbides for general work. Where high finishes on the tool and work are desired, a 220-grit diamond wheel is recommended.

Type of Grinder

1. A heavy duty grinder should be used for grinding carbides because the cutting pressures required to remove

Courtesy Canadian General Electric Co. Ltd.

Fig. 15-13 A carbide tool grinder equipped with an adjustable table and protractor

carbide are from five to ten times as great as when high-speed steel tools are ground.
2. The grinder should be equipped with an adjustable table and a protractor (Fig. 15-13) so that the necessary tool angles and clearances may be ground accurately.

Tool Grinding

1. Regrind the cutting tool to the same angles and clearances recommended by the manufacturer.
2. Use silicon carbide wheels for rough grinding. Diamond wheels should be used where high surface finishes are required.
3. When grinding, move the carbide tool back and forth over the grinding wheel face to keep the amount of heat generated to a minimum.
4. *Never quench carbide tools* which become hot during grinding; allow them to cool gradually. The shock of quenching carbide tools creates heat checks and results in rapid tool failure.

HONING

After carbide tools have been ground, it is important that the cutting edge be honed. The purpose of honing is to remove the fine, ragged edge left by the grinding wheel. This fine, nicked edge is fragile and will break down quickly under machining conditions. Honing often means the difference between tool success or failure.

1. A 320-grit silicon carbide or diamond hone is recommended for carbide tools.
2. On carbides used for cutting steel, a 45° chamfer (Fig. 15-14) 0.05 mm to 0.10 mm (.002 in. to .004 in.) wide should be honed on the cutting edge.
3. Carbide tools used for aluminum, magnesium, and plastics should not be chamfered with a hone. The fine, nicked edge should be honed to produce a sharp, keen cutting edge.

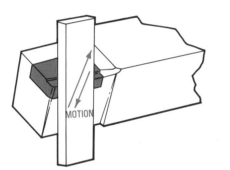

Courtesy Canadian General Electric Co. Ltd.

Fig. 15-14 Honing a slight chamfer on the cutting edge of a carbide tool will produce a stronger cutting edge

CEMENTED CARBIDE TOOL PROBLEMS

When problems occur while machining with carbide cutting tools, consult Table 15-6 for their possible causes and remedies. It is wise to change only one thing at a time until the problem is corrected. In this way, the real cause of the problem can be determined and steps taken to guard against its recurrence.

TABLE 15-6: CARBIDE TOOL PROBLEMS, CAUSES, AND REMEDIES

Problem	Cause	Remedy
Brazing failure and cracks	Improper braze material	Use the sandwich braze.
	Too much heat	Silver solder at 1400°.
	Improper cooling	Cool slowly.
	Tip not wiped on	Slide tip back and forth and tap gently.
	Contact surfaces dirty	Thoroughly clean both surfaces.
Built-up edge (on the tool)	Cutting speed too slow	Increase the speed.
	Insufficient rake angle	Increase rake angle.
	Wrong grade of carbide	Change to titanium and/or tantalum grade.
Chipped and broken cutting edge	Incorrect tool geometry	Increase side cutting edge angle. Decrease end cutting edge angle. Use a negative rake. Increase the nose radius. Decrease the relief angles.
	Improper carbide grade	Use a tougher grade.
	Cutting edge not honed	Hone cutting edge at 45°.
	Improper speed, feed or depth of cut	Change one or all as required.
	Too much tool overhang	Reduce overhang or use a larger shank.
	Lack of rigidity in setup or machine	Locate and correct.
	Machine stopped during cut	Disengage feed before stopping the machine.
Cratering	Improper grade	Select harder or crater resistant grade.
	Speed too high	Reduce the speed.
	Wrong tool geometry	Increase side rake.
Grinding cracks	Improper wheel	Select proper wheel.
	Wheel glazed	Dress often to a 1.5 mm crown.
	Tool quenched while hot	*Do not quench*; allow tool to cool slowly.
	Grinding carbide and steel shank with the same wheel	Relieve the steel shank with an aluminum oxide wheel first.
Tool wear (excessive)	Improper carbide grade	Select a wear resistant grade.
	Cutting speed too high	Reduce the speed.
	Feed too light	Increase the feed rate.
	Too little relief angle	Increase the relief angle.

CUBIC BORON NITRIDE (BORAZON) TOOLS

High-speed turning of hardened alloy steels and tough superalloys, which up until now has been impossible because of rapid cutting edge wear, is now possible with Borazon (CBN) indexible inserts.

Borazon CBN inserts are made by bonding a layer of polycrystalline cubic boron nitride to a cemented carbide base. The CBN layer is about 0.9 mm thick and the total thickness of the insert is about 5 mm. The CBN layer does the cutting, and the carbide provides a strong, tough, shock-resistant base for the cutting edge which can withstand temperatures up to 1000°C before breaking down.

The high-temperature resistance to oxidation makes it possible to machine superalloys which lose some strength at high temperatures, thus making them easier to machine.

In many cases, turning workpieces with CBN inserts has replaced some grinding operations, and in most cases it has proven much more satisfactory than carbides for those difficult-to-machine alloys. In certain test applications, carbide toolbits produced three pieces per cutting edge, whereas CBN inserts machined 1000 pieces per cutting edge.

Borazon CBN inserts produce good surface finishes – 0.62 to 1.6 μm. Out-of-roundness on tough alloys has been reduced from 0.03 mm to 0.05 mm, resulting in better accuracy. As a result of the good surface finishes and the geometric accuracy produced by Borazon CBN inserts, the amount of grinding required on workpieces has been reduced.

Although the application of CBN for indexible inserts is relatively new, CBN is becoming more popular and is being used for many machining applications.

CERAMIC CUTTING TOOLS

The first ceramic (cemented oxide) cutting tool inserts were put on the market in 1956; they were the result of many years of research. At first, these ceramic inserts were weak; inconsistent and unsatisfactory results were obtained because of lack of knowledge and improper use. Since then, the strength of ceramic cutting tools has nearly doubled and the uniformity and quality have greatly improved; they are now widely accepted by industry. Ceramic cutting tools are being used successfully in the machining of hard ferrous materials and cast iron; lower costs, increased productivity, and better results are being gained. In some operations, ceramic toolbits can be operated at approximately twice the speed of carbides. Ceramic tools have captured the imagination of everyone in the metal working industry interested in greater productivity and economy in machining operations.

MANUFACTURE OF CERAMIC TOOLS

Most ceramic or cemented oxide cutting tools are manufactured primarily from aluminum oxide. Bauxite (a hydrated alumina form of aluminum oxide) is chemically processed and converted into a denser, crystalline form called *alpha alumina*. Fine grains (micron size) are obtained from the precipitation of the alumina or from the precipitation of the decomposed alumina compound.

Ceramic tool inserts are produced by either *cold or hot pressing*. In cold pressing, the fine alumina powder is compressed into the required form and then sintered in a furnace at 1600°C to 1700°C. Hot pressing combines forming and sintering, pressure and heat being applied simultaneously. Certain amounts of titanium

Fig. 15-15 Ceramic toolbits are used at about twice the speed of carbides

oxide or magnesium oxide are added for certain types of ceramics to aid in the sintering process and to retard growth. After the inserts have been formed, they are finished with diamond-impregnated grinding wheels.

The most common ceramic cutting tool is the *throwaway insert* (Fig. 15-16A) which is fastened in a mechanical holder. Throwaway inserts are available in many styles, such as triangular, square, rectangular, and round. These inserts are indexible; when a cutting edge becomes dull, a sharp edge can be obtained by indexing (turning) the insert in the holder.

Courtesy The Carborundum Company

Fig. 15-16A Throwaway ceramic inserts are available in a variety of shapes

Cemented ceramic tools (Fig. 15-16B) are the most economical, especially if the tool shape must be altered from the standard shape. The ceramic insert is bonded to a steel shank with an epoxy glue. This method of holding the ceramic inserts almost eliminates the strains caused by clamping in mechanical holders.

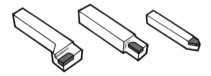

Courtesy The Carborundum Company

Fig. 15-16B Ceramic toolbits may be cemented to the toolshank

Cermets (ceramic metal combinations). Much research and experimentation has been done to reduce the brittleness of ceramics and to improve their qualities. Ceramic-metal combinations (cermets) are the most promising. Iron, chromium,

titanium, and other metals have been combined with aluminum oxide and boron carbide to form ceramic-metal cutting tools. Many combinations show definite advantages, and as they are improved, they will greatly assist in the machining of metals.

CERAMIC TOOL APPLICATIONS

Ceramic tools were intended to supplement rather than replace carbide tools. They are extremely valuable for specific applications and must be carefully selected and used. Ceramic tools can be used to replace carbide tools which wear rapidly in use, but should never be used to replace carbide tools which are breaking.

Ceramics are being used successfully for:

a) high-speed, single-point turning, boring, and facing operations, with continuous cutting action
b) finishing operations on ferrous and non-ferrous materials
c) light, interrupted finishing cuts on steel or cast iron; heavy, interrupted cuts on cast iron only if there is adequate rigidity in the machine and tool
d) machining castings when other tools break down, because of the abrasive action of sand, inclusions, or hard scale
e) cutting hard steels up to a hardness of Rockwell C 66, which previously could be machined only by grinding
f) any operation in which size and finish of the part must be controlled and in which previous tools have not proved satisfactory

FACTORS AFFECTING CERAMIC TOOL PERFORMANCE

As a result of an extensive research and testing program, several factors have been found which significantly affect the performance of ceramic tools. The following factors must be considered for optimum results to be derived from ceramic cutting tools.

1. Accurate and rigid machine tools are essential when ceramic tools are used. Machines with loose bearings, inaccurate spindles, slipping clutches, or any imbalance will result in the ceramic tools chipping and in premature failure.
2. The machine tool must be equipped with ample power and be capable of maintaining the high speeds necessary for ceramics.
3. The tool mounting and the toolholder rigidity are as important as the machine rigidity. An intermediate plate between the toolholder clamp and ceramic insert is recommended to distribute the clamping pressure.
4. The overhang of the tool should be kept to a minimum.
5. Negative rake inserts give the best results because less force is applied directly to the ceramic tip.
6. A large nose radius and a large side cutting edge angle on the ceramic insert reduces the tendency to chip.
7. Cutting fluids are generally not required because ceramics remain cool during the machining operation. If cutting fluids are required, a continuous and copious flow should be used to prevent thermal shock to the tool.

ADVANTAGES AND DISADVANTAGES OF CERAMIC TOOLS

ADVANTAGES

Ceramic cutting tools, when properly mounted in suitable holders and used on accurate rigid machines, offer many advantages.

a) Machining time is reduced because of the higher cutting speeds possible. Speeds ranging from 50 to 200% higher than those used for carbides are quite common.
b) High stock removal rates and increased productivity result because heavy depths of cut can be made at high surface speeds.

c) A ceramic tool used under proper conditions lasts from three to ten times longer than a carbide tool.

d) Ceramic tools retain their strength and hardness at high machining temperatures (in excess of 1100°C).

e) More accurate size control of the workpiece is possible because of the greater wear resistance of ceramic tools.

f) Ceramic cutting tools withstand the abrasion of sand and of inclusions found in castings.

g) A better surface finish is produced than is possible with other types of cutting tools.

h) Heat-treated materials as hard as Rockwell C 66 can be readily machined.

DISADVANTAGES

Although ceramic cutting tools have many advantages, they have the following limitations.

a) Ceramic tools are brittle and therefore tend to chip easily.

b) They are satisfactory for interrupted cuts only under ideal conditions.

c) The initial cost of ceramics is from 40 to 200% higher than that of carbides.

d) A more rigid machine is required than is necessary for other cutting tools.

e) Considerably more power is required for ceramics to cut efficiently.

CERAMIC TOOL GEOMETRY

The geometry of ceramic tools depends upon five main factors.

a) the material to be machined
b) the operation being performed
c) the condition of the machine
d) the rigidity of the work setup
e) the rigidity of the toolholding device

Although the final geometry of a ceramic cutting tool depends upon these five main factors, some general considerations can also be mentioned.

Rake Angles. Because of their brittleness, negative rake angles are generally preferred for ceramic tools. With the use of a negative rake angle, the shock of the cutting force is absorbed behind the tip and thus the cutting edge is protected. Negative rake angles from 2 to 30° are used for machining ferrous and non-ferrous metals. Positive rake angles are used for machining nonmetals such as rubber, graphite, and carbon.

Side Clearance. A side clearance angle is desirable for ceramic cutting tools whenever possible. The side clearance angle must not be too great, otherwise the cutting edge will be weakened and tend to chip.

Front Clearance. The front clearance angle should be only large enough to prevent the tool from rubbing on the workpiece. If this angle is too great, the ceramic tool becomes susceptible to chipping.

End Cutting Edge Angle. This angle governs the strength of the tool and the area of contact between the work and the end of the cutting tool. If properly designed, it will remove the crests resulting

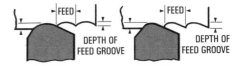

Courtesy The Carborundum Company

Fig. 15-17 The relationship of the nose radius and the end cutting edge angle to the surface finish produced

from feed lines (Fig. 15-17) and improve the surface finish.

Nose Radius. The nose radius (Fig. 15-17) has two important functions: to strengthen the weakest part of the tool, and to improve the surface finish of the workpiece. It should be as large as is possible without chatter or vibration resulting.

Cutting Edge Chamfer. A small chamfer, or radius, on the cutting edge is recommended for ceramic tools, especially on heavy cuts and hard materials. This strengthens and protects the cutting edge. A 0.05 mm to 0.20 mm (or .002 in. to .008 in.) radius, or chamfer, is recommended for machining steel. For heavy roughing cuts and hard materials, a 0.75 mm to 1.50 mm (or .030 in. to .060 in.) chamfer gives satisfactory results.

TABLE 15-7: SUGGESTED RAKE AND RELIEF ANGLES*		
Workpiece Material	**Rake Angles (degrees)**	**Relief Angles (degrees)**
Carbon and Alloy Steels: Annealed and heat-treated	Neg. 2 to 7	2 to 7
Cast Iron: Hard or chilled Gray or ductile	0 to Neg. 7	2 to 7
Nonferrous: Hard or soft	0 to Neg. 7	2 to 7
Nonmetallics: Wood, paper, green ceramics, fibre, asbestos, rubber, carbon, graphite	0 to Pos. 10	6 to 18

* For uninterrupted turning with tool point on centre line of workpiece.

Courtesy The Carborundum Company

TABLE 15-8: RECOMMENDED CUTTING SPEEDS FOR CERAMIC CUTTING TOOLS

Workpiece Material	Material Condition or Type	ROUGHING CUT		FINISHING CUT		Recommended Tool Geometry (Type of Rake Angle)	Recommended Coolant
		Depth > 1.60 mm Feed 0.40-0.75 mm	Depth > .062 Feed .015-.030	Depth < 1.60 mm Feed 0.25 mm	Depth < .062 Feed .010		
Carbon and Tool steels	Annealed	90–455	300–1500	185–610	600–2000	Neg.	None
	Heat-treated	90–305	300–1000	150–365	500–1200	Neg.	
	Scale	90–245	300–800			Neg. honed edge	
Alloy Steels	Annealed	90–245	300–800	120–425	400–1400	Neg.	None
	Heat-treated	90–245	300–800	90–305	300–1000	Neg. honed edge	
	Scale	90–185	300–600			Neg. honed edge	
High-Speed Steel	Annealed	30–245	100–800	30–305	100–1000	Neg.	None
	Heat-treated	30–185	100–600	30–385	100–600	Neg. honed edge	
	Scale	30–185	100–600			Neg. honed edge	
Stainless Steel	300 Series	90–305	300–1000	120–365	400–1200	Pos. and neg.	Sulphur base oil
	400 Series	90–305	300–1000	120–365	400–1200	Neg.	
Cast Iron	Gray iron	60–245	200–800	60–610	200–2000	Pos. and neg.	None
	Pearlitic	60–245	200–800	60–610	200–2000	Neg.	
	Ductile	60–185	200–600	60–427	200–1400	Neg.	
	Chilled	30–185	100–600	60–427	200–1400	Neg. honed edge	
Copper and Alloys	Pure	120–245	400–800	185–425	600–1400	Pos. and neg.	Mist coolant
	Brass	120–245	400–800	185–365	600–1200	Pos. and neg.	Mist coolant
	Bronze	45–245	150–800	45–305	150–1000	Pos. and neg.	Mist coolant
Aluminum Alloys*		120–610	400–2000	185–915	600–3000	Pos.	None
Magnesium Alloys		245–3050	800–10 000	245–3050	800–10 000	Pos.	None
Non-metallics	Green ceramics	90–185	300–600	150–305	500–1000	Pos.	None
	Rubber	90–305	300–1000	120–365	400–1200	Pos.	None
	Carbon	120–305	400–1000	185–610	600–2000	Pos.	None
Plastics		90–305	300–1000	120–365	400–1200	Pos.	None

* Alumina-based cutting rods have a tendency to develop a built-up cutting edge on certain aluminum alloys.   Courtesy A. C. Wickman Limited

CUTTING SPEEDS

When ceramics are used in machining, the highest cutting speed possible, considering the machine tool limitations, which gives reasonable tool life, should be used. There is less heat generated when machining is done with ceramics than with any other cutting tool, because there is a lower coefficient of friction between the chip, work, and tool surface. Since most of the heat generated escapes with the chip, the cutting speed can be from two to ten times as high as with other cutting tools. Table 15-8 lists the recommended speeds for various materials under ideal conditions. Should lower speeds be necessary to suit various machine or setup conditions, ceramic cutting tools will still perform well.

CERAMIC TOOL PROBLEMS

Ceramic tools remove metal faster than any other type of cutting tool and therefore should be selected carefully for the type of material and the operation. Some points to consider when selecting ceramic tools are:

a) The tool should be large enough for the job. It cannot be too large, but can easily be too small.

b) The style (tool geometry) should be right for the type of operation and material. A tool designed for one job is not necessarily right for another.

Some of the more common problems which occur with ceramic cutting tools and their possible causes are listed in Table 15-9.

GRINDING CERAMIC TOOLS

It is not generally recommended that ceramic tools be ground; however, with the proper care, these tools may be resharpened successfully. Resinoid-bonded, diamond-impregnated wheels are recommended for grinding ceramic tools. A coarse grit wheel should be used for rough grinding, while at least a 220-grit wheel should be used for finish grinding. Because ceramic tools are extremely notch-sensitive, all surfaces should be ground as smoothly as possible to avoid notches or grinding lines at the cutting edge. The cutting edge should be honed or lapped after grinding to remove any notches left by grinding, and to avoid the wedging action which would occur when the work material entered these notches.

FUTURE DEVELOPMENTS

The first problem that must be overcome before ceramics can assume their full potential is that of fatigue and fracture. Many new types of ceramic tools are expected to be developed as a result of the research being carried out for the aerospace industry. Titanium, tantalum, zirconium, carbide, nitride, and boride are some of the materials being combined to form new ceramic tools. It is possible that in the near future, various grades and types of ceramic tools will be developed for cutting different materials and for specific applications.

TABLE 15-9: CERAMIC TOOL PROBLEMS AND POSSIBLE CAUSES	
Problem	**Possible causes**
Chatter	a) tool not on centre b) insufficient end relief and/or clearance c) too much rake angle d) too much overhang or tool too small e) nose radius too large f) feed too heavy g) lack of rigidity in the tool or machine h) insufficient power or slipping clutch
Chipping	a) lack of rigidity b) saw-toothed or too keen a cutting edge c) chip breaker too narrow or too deep d) chatter e) scale or inclusions in the workpiece f) improper grinding g) too much end relief h) defective toolholder
Cracking or breaking	a) insert surfaces not flat b) insert not seated solidly c) stopping workpiece while tool is engaged d) worn or chipped cutting edges e) feed too heavy f) improperly applied coolant g) too much rake angle or end relief h) too much overhang or tool too small i) lack of rigidity in setup j) speed too slow k) too much variation in cut for size of tool l) chatter m) grinding cracks
Cratering	a) chip breaker set too close to the edge b) nose radius too large c) side cutting edge angle too great
Torn finish	a) lack of rigidity b) dull tool c) speed too slow d) chip breaker too narrow or too deep e) improper grinding
Wear	a) speed too high or feed too light b) nose radius too large c) improper grinding

DIAMOND CUTTING TOOLS

Diamond-tipped cutting tools are used to machine nonferrous and nonmetallic materials which require a high surface finish and extremely close tolerances. They are used primarily as finishing tools because they are brittle and do not resist shock or cutting pressure as well as carbide cutting tools. Single-point, diamond-tipped cutting tools are available in various shapes for turning, boring, grooving, and special forming.

The main advantages of diamond-tipped cutting tools are:

a) They can be operated at high cutting speeds and production can be increased to 10 to 15 times that of other cutting tools.

b) Surface finishes of 0.127 μm or less can be obtained easily. In many cases, the necessity of finishing operations on the workpiece is eliminated.

c) They are very hard and resist abrasion. Much longer runs are therefore possible on abrasive materials.

d) Closer tolerance work can be produced with diamond-tipped cutting tools.

e) Minute cuts, as low as 0.01 mm deep, can be taken from the inside or outside diameter.

f) Metallic particles do not build up (weld) on the cutting edge.

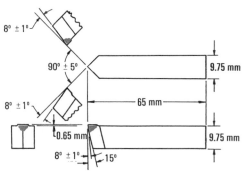

Courtesy Precision Diamond Tool Co.

Fig. 15-18 Diamond cutting tools are used efficiently for shallow cuts at very high speeds

USE OF DIAMOND CUTTING TOOLS

Some of the most successful applications of diamond cutting tools have been in the turning of metallic (non-ferrous) and non-metallic materials. The commonest of these materials are listed.

Metallic Materials

a) *light metals*, such as aluminum, dural-uminum, magnesium alloys, etc.

b) *soft metals*, such as copper, brass, and zinc alloys

c) *bearing metals*, such as bronze and babbitt

d) *precious metals*, such as silver, gold, and platinum

For these metallic materials, diamond tools can be expected to increase production from 10 to 15 times that possible with any other cutting tool.

Nonmetallic Materials

Some of the commonest materials machined with diamond cutting tools are hard and soft rubber, all types of plastics, carbon, graphite, and ceramics. In some cases, diamond tools will increase production 20 to 50 times that of carbide tools.

CUTTING SPEEDS AND FEEDS

In general, diamond-tipped cutting tools operate most efficiently with shallow cuts at high cutting speeds and fine feeds. They are not recommended for materials in which the temperature of the chip or the heat generated at the chip-tool interface exceeds 760°C. High cutting speeds, fine feeds, and shallow cuts are used, and the heat generated is entirely dissipated in the chip as it leaves the cutting edge. Low cutting speeds and heavy cuts create more heat and damage the diamond tip.

There is an ideal cutting speed for each type of material-machine combination. The minimum cutting speed for diamond tools should be 75 to 90 m/min. The conditions of the machine will determine the maximum cutting speed which can be used for each job. Cutting speeds as high

Courtesy Precision Diamond Tool Co.

Fig. 15-19 Diamond tipped cutting tool angles and clearances

	TABLE 15-10: DIAMOND CUTTING TOOL DATA					
Material	Cutting speed		Feed (per rev.)		Depth of Cut	
	m/min	ft./min	mm	in.	mm	in.
Metallic (nonferrous)	75–3 050	250–10 000	0.002–0.10	.000 8–.004	0.001–0.60	.000 5–.024
Nonmetallic	75–1 005	250–3 300	0.002–0.60	.000 8–.024	0.002–1.50	.000 8–.060

as 3050 m/min have been used for some applications. Table 15-10 lists the cutting-speed, feed, and depth of cut ranges for various material groups.

Hints on the Use of Diamond Tools

Diamond cutting tools will perform more efficiently and have longer life if the following hints and precautions are observed.

1. Diamond-tipped points should be designed with maximum included point angle and radius for added strength.
2. Diamond tools should always be handled with care, especially when setups are being made. The cutting edges should *never* be checked with a micrometer or bumped with a height gauge.
3. Diamond tools should always be stored in separate containers, with rubber protectors over the tips, so that they will not be fractured by coming into contact with other tools.
4. The machine tool should be as free of vibration as possible. Any vibration can result in tool failure.
5. A very rigid setup, with the diamond tip set exactly on centre, should be used.
6. The work should be roughed out with a carbide tool. This step will establish an even work surface and bring the work close to size.
7. Diamond tools should always be fed into the work while the work is revolving. Never stop a machine during a cut.
8. Interrupted cuts, especially on hard metals, will shorten tool life.

FUTURE DEVELOPMENTS

Much research and testing remains to be done in order to establish the exact role the diamond-tipped cutting tool will play in the future. It is reasonable to assume that as new and exotic materials are developed and as close tolerances and high surface finishes are required, the use of diamond cutting tools will increase. When, in the future, machine tools are designed for high-speed machining, it is felt that diamond cutting tools will be used to precision finish steel parts.

CARBIDE, CERAMIC, AND DIAMOND CUTTING TOOLS QUESTIONS

1. Explain why the cutting rate of metal has increased during the past 100 years.

CARBIDE CUTTING TOOLS

2. State four reasons why cemented carbide tools have been widely accepted by industry.

MANUFACTURE OF CEMENTED CARBIDES

3. Name five powders used in the manufacture of cemented carbides.
4. What purpose does cobalt serve?
5. Describe the process of compaction.
6. What is the purpose of presintering?
7. Describe the sintering process.

CEMENTED CARBIDE APPLICATIONS

8. Why is cemented carbide used extensively in the manufacture of cutting tools?
9. Name two types of cemented carbide lathe cutting tools, and state the advantages of each.
10. Identify the following throwaway insert: SNG – 321 – A.

GRADES OF CEMENTED CARBIDES

11. Describe straight tungsten carbide tools, and state the purpose for which they are used.
12. Explain how the size of the tungsten carbide particles and the percentage of cobalt affect the grade of carbide.
13. How does the addition of titanium carbide affect the cutting tool?
14. What properties does the addition of tantalum carbide provide?
15. List four important rules to observe for selecting a cemented carbide grade.

TOOL GEOMETRY

16. Define and state the purpose of:
   a) front or end relief
   b) side relief
   c) side rake
17. What is the purpose of the side cutting edge angle?
18. State the purpose of the nose radius on a cutting tool. How large should it be?
19. Name two types of back rake and state the purpose of each.

20. What three factors determine the angles and clearances of single point carbide tools?

CUTTING SPEEDS AND FEEDS

21. Name four important factors that influence the speed, feed, and depth of cut for carbide tools.
22. Use Table 15-5 to determine what cutting speed should be used for:
    a) taking a 3/32 in. depth of cut on 260 Brinell steel with a .015 in. feed.
    b) a cut 1.50 mm deep on 300 Brinell steel using a 0.20 mm feed.

MACHINING WITH CARBIDE TOOLS

23. List two important precautions that should be observed when work is being set up on a lathe.
24. Why should the cutting edge of a carbide tool be honed?
25. What occurs if the nose radius on the cutting tool is
    a) too large?
    b) too small?
26. Using Table 15-2, determine the necessary radius for a carbide tool taking:
    a) a 1/4 in. deep cut at .020 in. feed.
    b) a 3.2 mm depth of cut using a 0.40 mm feed.
27. How should carbide tools be set up for machining?
28. Explain how carbide tools should be set up in a rocker type toolpost.
29. What precautions should be taken when setting up a machine for cutting with carbide tools?
30. Discuss the effects of:
    a) too light feed
    b) too coarse feed

31. Why should a machine never be stopped while the tool is engaged in a cut?
32. Explain how a dull cutting tool may be recognized.

GRINDING CEMENTED CARBIDE TOOLS

33. What type of grinding wheels are used to grind carbide tools?
34. How should silicon carbide wheels be dressed? Explain why.
35. List three important points that should be observed in the grinding of carbide tools.
36. Why is it important not to quench carbide tools?
37. What is the purpose of honing carbide tools?
38. How should carbide tools used for steel be honed?

CEMENTED CARBIDE TOOL PROBLEMS

39. List the factors that would cause the following problems:
    a) cratering
    b) grinding cracks
    c) chipped or broken cutting edge

MANUFACTURE OF CERAMIC TOOLS

40. Briefly explain how cemented oxide cutting tools are manufactured.
41. Name three types of ceramic tools, and state the advantages of each.

CERAMIC TOOL APPLICATIONS

42. Name four important applications for ceramic tools.
43. List four main factors which affect the performance of ceramic tools.

ADVANTAGES AND DISADVANTAGES OF CERAMIC TOOLS

44. Name five advantages of ceramic tools.

45. What are the disadvantages of using ceramic cutting tools?

CERAMIC TOOL GEOMETRY

46. List five factors that determine the geometry of ceramic tools.
47. Fully explain the rake angle of ceramic tools.
48. Define "cutting edge chamfer" and state its purpose.

CUTTING SPEEDS

49. Explain why high cutting speeds can be used with ceramic tools.

CERAMIC TOOL PROBLEMS

50. What two points should be kept in mind when ceramic tools are being selected?
51. List the factors that may cause the following problems.
    a) chipping
    b) chatter
    c) wear

GRINDING CERAMIC TOOLS

52. Explain how ceramic tools should be ground.
53. What is the purpose of honing?

DIAMOND CUTTING TOOLS

54. List four main advantages of diamond cutting tools.
55. Explain where diamond cutting tools may be used successfully.

CUTTING SPEEDS AND FEEDS

56. What speeds, feeds, and depth of cut should be used for diamond tools? Explain why.
57. Why should the diamond tool be as rigid as possible and the machine free of vibration?

16 CUTTING FLUIDS

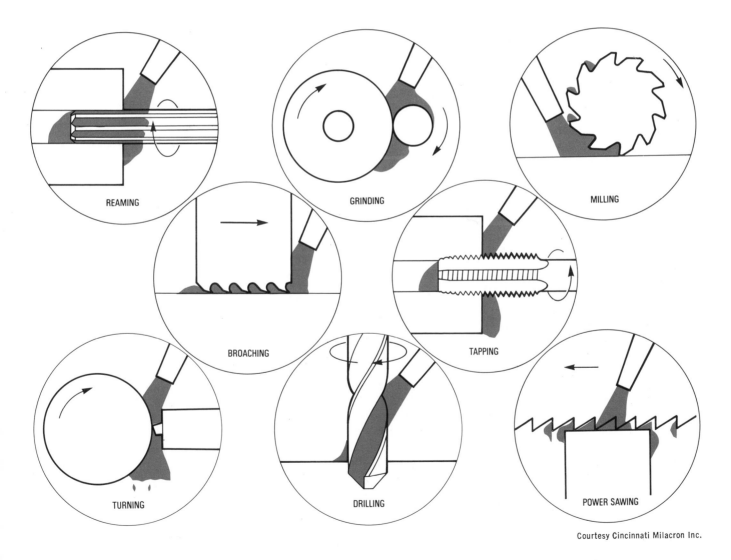

REAMING

GRINDING

MILLING

BROACHING

TAPPING

TURNING

DRILLING

POWER SAWING

Courtesy Cincinnati Milacron Inc.

Cutting fluids are essential in most metal-cutting operations. During a machining process, considerable heat and friction are created by the plastic deformation of metal occurring in the shear zone when the chip slides along the chip-tool interface. This heat and friction cause metal to adhere to the cutting edge of the tool and the tool may break down; the result is a poor finish and inaccurate work.

The use of cutting fluids is not new, some types having been used for hundreds of years. Centuries ago it was discovered that water dripped onto a grindstone kept the stone from glazing and a better surface finish was produced on the part being ground. The major problem was that the water caused the part being ground to rust. About 100 years ago, machinists found that wiping tallow on parts before machining helped to produce smoother and more accurate parts. Tallow, the forerunner of cutting fluids, lubricated but did not cool. Lard oils, developed later, lubricated well and had some cooling properties, but became rancid quickly.

Machinists experimented; they added rust inhibitors to water. The new cutting fluid cooled well because water is the best possible coolant; however, it failed to lubricate the work. In the early 20th century, soaps were added to water to improve cutting, prevent rust, and provide some form of lubrication.

In 1936, the development of soluble oils was a great improvement over the previously used cutting oils. These milky-white emulsions combined the high cooling ability of water with the lubricity of petroleum oil. Although economical, they had relatively poor rust control and tended to become rancid.

Chemical cutting fluids were introduced about 1944. They contained relatively little oil, being dependent upon chemical agents for lubrication and friction reduction. The chemical emulsions mix easily with water and reduce as well as remove the heat created during machining. Chemical cutting fluids are rapidly increasing in popularity because they provide good rust resistance, do not become rancid quickly, and have good cooling and lubricating qualities.

PURPOSE AND ADVANTAGES

During a machining process, considerable heat and friction are created. The correct selection and application of cutting fluids can prevent these results by effectively cooling the work and reducing the friction. Cutting fluids cool and lubricate the tool and workpiece. Their use can result in the following economic advantages.

a) *Reduction of tool costs.* Cutting oils reduce tool wear; they last longer and less time is spent in resharpening and resetting.

b) *Increased speed of production.* Because cutting oils help reduce heat and friction, higher cutting speeds can be used for machining operations.

c) *Reduction of labour costs.* As cutting tools last longer and require less regrinding when cutting oils are used, there is less stoppage of production, reducing the labour cost per part.

d) *Reduction of power costs.* Since friction is reduced by a cutting fluid, less power is required for machining operations and a corresponding saving in power costs is possible.

CHARACTERISTICS OF A GOOD CUTTING FLUID

For a cutting fluid to function effectively, it should possess the following desirable characteristics.

a) *Good cooling capacity,* to reduce the cutting temperature, increase tool life and production, and improve dimensional accuracy.

b) *Good lubricating qualities,* to prevent metal from adhering to the cutting edge, forming a built-up edge, resulting in a poor surface finish.

c) *Rust resistance.* It should not cause stain, rust, or corrosion to the workpiece or machine.

d) *Stability (long life),* both in storage and in use.

e) *Resistance to rancidity.* It should not become rancid easily.

f) *Nontoxic.* It should not cause skin irritation to the operator.

g) *Transparent,* so that the operator can clearly see the work during machining.

h) *Relatively low viscosity,* to permit the chips and dirt to settle quickly.

i) *Nonflammable.* It should not burn easily, and should preferably be noncombustible. In addition, it should not smoke excessively, form gummy deposits which may cause machine slides to become sticky, or clog the circulating system.

TYPES OF CUTTING FLUIDS

The need for a cutting fluid which possesses as many of the desirable characteristics of a good cutting fluid as possible has resulted in the development of many different types. The most commonly used cutting fluids are either aqueous- (water-) based solutions or cutting oils. These fluids fall into three categories: cutting oils, emulsifiable oils, and chemical (synthetic) cutting fluids.

CUTTING OILS

Cutting oils are classified under two types: active or inactive. These terms relate to the oil's chemical activity or ability to react with the metal surface at elevated temperatures to protect it and improve the cutting action.

Active cutting oils may be defined as those that will darken a copper strip immersed in it for three hours at a temperature of 100°C. These oils are generally used when steel is being machined and may be either dark or transparent. Dark oils usually contain more sulphur than the transparent types and are considered better for heavy-duty jobs.

Active cutting oils fall into three general categories.

a) *Sulphurized mineral oils* contain from 0.5 to 0.8% sulphur. They are generally light-coloured, transparent, and have good cooling, lubricating, and anti-weld properties. They are useful for the cutting of low-carbon steels and tough, ductile metals. Sulphurized mineral oils stain copper and its alloys, and, therefore, are not recommended for these metals.

b) *Sulfo-chlorinated mineral oils* contain up to 3% sulphur and 1% chlorine. These oils prevent excessive built-up edges from forming and prolong the life of the cutting tool. Sulfo-chlorinated mineral oils are more effective than sulphurized mineral oils in cutting tough low-carbon and chrome-nickel alloy steels. They are extremely valuable in cutting threads in soft, draggy steel.

c) *Sulfo-chlorinated fatty oil blends* contain more sulphur than the other types and are effective cutting fluids for heavy-duty machining.

Inactive cutting oils may be defined as those which will not darken a copper strip immersed in it for three hours at 100°C. The sulphur contained in an inactive oil is the natural sulphur of the oil and has no chemical value in the cutting fluid's function during machining. These fluids are termed inactive because the sulphur is so firmly attached to the oil that very little is released to react with the work surface during the cutting action.

Inactive cutting oils fall into four general categories.

a) *Straight mineral oils*, because of their low viscosity, have faster wetting and penetrating factors. They are used for the machining of non-ferrous metals, such as aluminum, brass, and magnesium, where lubricating and cooling properties are not essential. Straight mineral oils are also recommended for use in cutting leaded (free machining) metals and the tapping and threading of white metal.

b) *Fatty oils*, such as lard and sperm oil, once widely used, find limited applications as cutting fluids today. They are generally used for severe cutting operations on tough non-ferrous metals where a sulphurized oil might cause discoloration.

c) *Fatty and mineral oil blends* are combinations of fatty and mineral oil, resulting in better wetting and penetrating qualities than straight mineral oils. These factors result in better surface finishes on both ferrous and non-ferrous metals.

d) *Sulphurized fatty-mineral oil blends* are made by sulphur being combined with fatty oils and then mixed with certain mineral oils. Oils of this type provide excellent anti-weld properties and lubricity when cutting pressures may be high and tool vibration excessive. Most sulphurized fatty-mineral oil blends can be used when non-ferrous metals are cut to produce high surface finishes. They may also be used on machines when ferrous and non-ferrous metals are machined at the same time.

EMULSIFIABLE (SOLUBLE) OILS

An effective cutting fluid should possess high heat conductivity; neither mineral nor fatty oils are very effective as coolants. Water is the best cooling medium known; however, used as a cutting fluid, water alone would cause rust and have little lubricating value. By adding a certain percentage of soluble oil to water, it is possible to add rust resistance and lubrication qualities to the excellent cooling capabilities of water.

Emulsifiable, or soluble, oils are mineral oils containing a soap-like material (emulsifier) which makes them soluble in water. These emulsifiers break the oil into minute particles and keep them separated in the water for a long period of time. Emulsifiable, or soluble, oils are supplied in concentrate form. From *one to five*

parts of this concentrate are added to *100 parts* of water. Lean mixtures are used for light machining operations and when cooling is essential. Denser mixtures are used when lubrication and rust prevention are essential.

Soluble oils, because of their good cooling and lubricating qualities, are used when machining is done at high cutting speeds, at low cutting pressure, and when considerable heat is generated.

Emulsifiable, or soluble, oils are manufactured in three types for various machining conditions.

a) *Emulsifiable mineral oils* are mineral oils to which various compounds have been added to make the oil soluble in water. These oils are low in cost, provide good cooling and lubrication qualities, and are widely used for general cutting applications.

b) *Super-fatted emulsifiable oils* are emulsifiable mineral oils to which some fatty oil has been added. These mixtures provide better lubrication qualities and are, therefore, used for tougher machining operations. Often these soluble oils are used when aluminum is machined.

c) *Extreme-pressure emulsifiable oils* contain sulphur, chlorine, and phosphorus, as well as fatty oils, to provide the added lubrication qualities required for tough machining operations. Extreme-pressure oils are generally mixed with water at the rate of *one part* oil to *twenty parts* water.

CHEMICAL CUTTING FLUIDS

Chemical cutting fluids, sometimes called *synthetic fluids*, have been widely accepted since they were first introduced about 1945. They are stable, pre-formed emulsions which contain very little oil and mix easily with water. Chemical cutting fluids depend upon chemical agents for lubrication and friction reduction. Some types of chemical cutting fluids contain *extreme-pressure* (EP) lubricants which react with freshly machined metal under the heat and pressure of a cut to form a solid lubricant. Fluids containing extreme-pressure lubricants reduce both the *heat of friction* between the chip and tool face and the *heat caused by plastic deformation* of the metal.

The chemical agents found in most synthetic fluids include the following.

a) *amines* and *nitrites* for rust prevention
b) *nitrates* for nitrite stabilization
c) *phosphates* and *borates* for water softening
d) *soaps* and *wetting agents* for lubrication
e) *phosphorus, chlorine,* and *sulphur compounds* for chemical lubrication
f) *glycols* to act as blending agents
g) *germicides* to control bacteria growth

As a result of the chemical agents which are added to the cooling qualities of water, synthetic fluids provide the following advantages.

a) good rust control
b) resistance for long periods of time to becoming rancid
c) reduction of the amount of heat generated during a cutting action
d) excellent cooling qualities
e) longer durability than cutting or soluble oils
f) nonflammable, nonsmoking
g) non toxic
h) easy separation from the work and chips, which makes them clean to work with
i) quick settling of grit and fine chips so they are not recirculated in the cooling system
j) no clogging of the machine cooling system due to detergent action of the fluid

Chemical cutting fluids are manufactured in three types: *true solution fluids, wetting agent types,* and *wetting agent types with extreme-pressure lubricants.*

a) *True solution fluids* contain mostly rust inhibitors and are used primarily to prevent rust and provide rapid heat removal in grinding operations. These are generally clear solutions (sometimes a dye is added to colour the water) and are mixed *one part* solution to *50 to 250 parts* water, depending on the application.

Some of the true solution types have a tendency to form hard, crystalline deposits when the water evaporates. These deposits may interfere with the operation of chucks, slides, and moving parts.

b) *Wetting agent types* contain agents which improve the wetting action of water, providing more uniform heat dissipation and anti-rust action. They also contain mild lubricants, water softeners, and anti-foaming agents.

Wetting type chemical cutting fluids are versatile; they have excellent lubricating qualities and provide rapid heat dissipation. They can be used when machining is done with either high-speed-steel or carbide cutting tools.

c) *Wetting-agent types with extreme pressure lubricants* are similar to wetting-agent types, but have chlorine, sulphur, or phosphorus additives to provide extreme pressure or boundary lubrication effects. They are used for tough machining jobs with either high-speed steel or carbide cutting tools.

CAUTION: Although chemical cutting fluids have been widely accepted and used for many types of metal cutting operations, there are certain precautions which should be observed regarding their use. Chemical cutting fluids are generally used on ferrous metals; however, many aluminum alloys can be machined successfully with them. Most chemical cutting fluids are not recommended for use on alloys of magnesium, zinc, cadmium, or lead. Certain types of paint (generally poor quality) may be affected by some chemical cutting fluids which may mar the machine's appearance and allow paint to get into the coolant. Before changing to any type of cutting fluid, it is wise to contact suppliers for the right cutting fluid for the machining operation and the metal being cut.

FUNCTIONS OF A CUTTING FLUID

The prime functions of a cutting fluid are to provide both cooling and lubrication. In addition, good cutting fluids prolong the cutting-tool life, possess good resistance to becoming rancid, and provide rust control.

COOLING

Laboratory tests have proved that the heat produced during machining has a definite bearing on cutting tool wear. Temperature reduction of the cutting tool is important to tool life. Even a small reduction in temperature will result in a large extension in the life of the cutting tool. For example, if the tool temperature were reduced only 30°C, from 510 to 480°C, the cutting-tool life would be increased five times, from 19.5 to 99 minutes.

There are two sources of heat generated during a cutting action.

a) The plastic deformation of the metal which occurs immediately ahead of the cutting tool accounts for approximately two-thirds to three-quarters of the heat generated.
b) The friction resulting from the chip sliding along the cutting-tool face also produces heat.

To date, water has been found to be the most effective agent for reducing the heat generated during machining. Since water alone causes rusting, soluble oils or chemicals which prevent rust and provide other essential qualities are added to make it a good cutting fluid.

An abundant supply of cutting fluid should be applied to the machining area at a very low pressure. This will assure that the machining area will be well covered and that little splashing will occur. The flow of the cutting fluid will help to wash away the chips from the machining area.

LUBRICATING

The lubricating function of a cutting fluid is as important as its cooling function. Heat is generated by the plastic deformation of the metal and by the friction between the chip and tool face. The plastic deformation of metal occurs along the shear plane (Fig. 16-1). Any way of shortening the length of the shear plane would result in a reduction in the amount of heat that is generated.

The only known method of shortening the length of the shear plane for any given shape of a cutting tool and work material is to reduce the friction between the chip and tool face. Fig. 16-2 illustrates a chip sliding along the face of the cutting tool. The enlarged illustration shows the irregularities on the tool face which create areas of friction and tend to cause a built-up

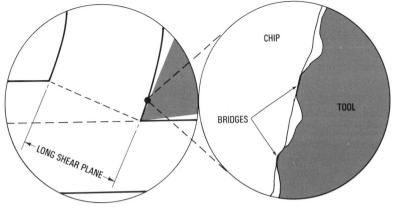

Courtesy Cincinnati Milacron Inc.

Fig. 16-2 A long shear plane results in great heat in the shear zone

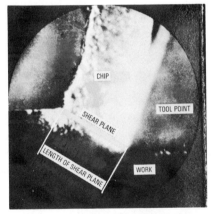

Courtesy Cincinnati Milacron Inc.

Fig. 16-1   During the cutting action the metal is deformed along the shear plane, producing heat

edge to form. Note also that because of this friction there is a long shear plane and a small shear angle. Most heat is created at the cutting edge when there is a small shear angle and a long shear plane.

Fig. 16-3 illustrates the same depth of cut as Fig. 16-2, but shows cutting fluid being used to reduce the friction at the chip-tool interface. As soon as the friction is reduced, the shear plane becomes shorter, and the area where plastic deformation

occurs is correspondingly smaller. Therefore, by reduction of the friction at the chip-tool interface, both sources of heat (plastic deformation and friction at the chip-tool interface) can be reduced.

The effective life of a cutting tool can be greatly lengthened if the friction and the resultant heat that is generated are reduced. When steel is machined, the temperature and pressure at the chip-tool interface may reach 540°C and 1 380 000 kPa respectively. Under such conditions, some oils and other liquids tend to vaporize or be squeezed out from between the chip and tool. Extreme-pressure (EP) lubricants are used to reduce the amount

of heat-producing friction. The EP chemicals of synthetic fluids combine chemically with the sheared metal of the chip to form solid compounds. These solid compounds or lubricants can withstand high pressure and temperature and allow the chip to slide up the tool face easily even under these conditions.

CUTTING TOOL LIFE

Heat and friction are the prime causes of cutting-tool breakdown. Decreasing the amount of heat and friction created during a machining operation can greatly increase the life of a cutting tool. Laboratory tests have proved that if the temperature

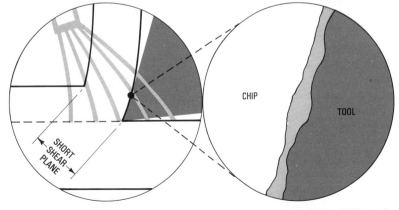

Courtesy Cincinnati Milacron Inc.

Fig. 16-3 Cutting fluid used to reduce friction results in a short shear plane

at the chip-tool interface is reduced by as little as 10°C, the life of the cutting tool increases five-fold. As a result, when cutting fluids are used, faster speeds and feeds can be used; increased production and a reduction in the cost per piece result.

During a cut, pieces of metal tend to weld themselves to the tool face, causing a built-up edge to form (Fig. 16-4). If the built-up edge becomes large and flat along the tool face, the effective rake angle of the cutting tool is decreased and more power is required to cut the metal. The built-up edge keeps breaking off and reforming; the result is a poor surface finish, excessive flank wear, and cratering of the tool face. Almost all the roughness of a machined surface is caused by tiny fragments of metal which have been left behind by the built-up edge.

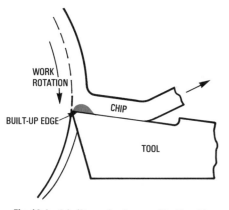

Fig. 16-4   A built-up edge is caused by the chip fragments pressure-welding to the cutting tool face

The use of an effective cutting fluid affects the action of a cutting tool in the following ways.

a) It lowers the heat created by the plastic deformation of the metal; thereby it increases cutting tool life.
b) The friction at the chip-tool interface is decreased; the resultant heat is reduced.
c) Less power is required for machining because of the reduced friction.
d) It prevents a built-up edge from forming; longer tool life is the result.

e) The surface finish of the work is greatly improved.

RUST CONTROL

Cutting fluids used on machine tools should prevent rust from forming; otherwise the parts of machines and the workpieces will be damaged. Cutting oil prevents rust from forming but does not cool as effectively as water. Water is the best and most economical coolant, but causes parts to rust unless rust inhibitors are added.

Rust is oxidized iron, or iron that has reacted chemically with oxygen, water, and minerals in the water. Water alone on a piece of steel or iron acts as a medium for the electro-chemical process to start causing corrosion or rust.

Chemical cutting fluids contain rust inhibitors which prevent the electrochemical process of rusting. Some types of cutting fluids form a *polar film* on all metals they contact which prevents rusting. This polar film (Fig. 16-5) consists of negatively charged, long, thin molecules which are attracted and firmly bond themselves to the metal. This invisible film, only molecules thick, is sufficient to prevent the electro-chemical action of rusting. Other types of cutting fluids contain rust inhibitors which form an insulating blanket known as a *passivating film* on the

metal surface. These inhibitors combine chemically with the metal and form a nonporous, protective coating which prevents rust.

RANCIDITY CONTROL

When lard oil was the only cutting fluid used, after a few days it would start to spoil and give off an offensive odour. This rancidity is caused by bacteria and microscopic organisms growing and multiplying almost anywhere and eventually causing bad odours to form. Today, any cutting fluid that has an offensive smell is termed *rancid*.

Most cutting fluids contain bactericides which control the growth of bacteria and make the fluid more resistant to rancidity. The bactericide, which is added to the fluid by the manufacturers, must be strong enough to control the growth of bacteria, but weak enough not to be harmful to the skin of the operator.

APPLICATION OF CUTTING FLUIDS

Cutting tool life and the machining operation are greatly influenced by the way that the cutting fluid is applied. It should be supplied in a copious stream under low pressure so that the work and cutting tool

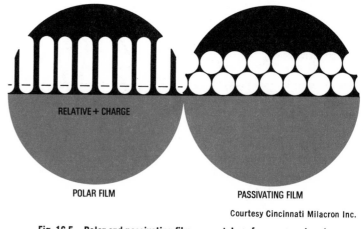

RELATIVE + CHARGE

POLAR FILM   PASSIVATING FILM

Courtesy Cincinnati Milacron Inc.

Fig. 16-5   Polar and passivating films on metal surfaces prevent rust

are well covered. The rule of thumb is that the inside diameter of the supply nozzle should be about three-quarters the width of the cutting tool. The fluid should be directed to the area where the chip is being formed to reduce and control the heat created during the cutting action and to prolong tool life.

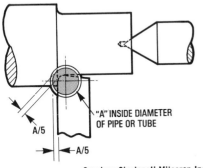

Fig. 16-6 Cutting fluid supplied by one nozzle for general turning and facing operations

LATHE TYPE OPERATIONS

On horizontal type turning and boring machines, cutting fluid should be applied to that portion of the cutting tool which is producing the chip. For general turning and facing operations, cutting fluid should be supplied directly over the cutting tool, close to the zone of chip formation (Fig. 16-6). In heavy-duty turning and facing operations, it is recommended that cutting fluid be supplied by two nozzles, one directly above and the other directly below the cutting tool (Fig. 16-7).

DRILLING AND REAMING

The most effective method of applying cutting fluids for these operations is to use "oil-feed" drills and hollow-shank reamers. Tools of this type transmit the cutting fluid directly to the cutting edges and at the same time flush the chips out of the hole (Fig. 16-8). When conventional drills and reamers are used, an abundant supply of fluid should be applied to the cutting edges.

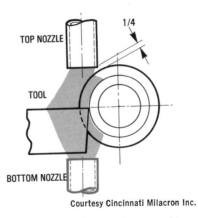

Fig. 16-7 Bottom and top nozzles are used to supply cutting fluid for heavy-duty turning operations

MILLING

In *slab milling*, cutting fluid should be directed to both sides of the cutter by fan-shaped nozzles approximately three-quarters the width of the cutter (Fig. 16-9).

For *face milling*, a ring type distributor (Fig. 16-10) is recommended in order to completely flood the cutter. Keeping each tooth of the cutter immersed in cutting fluid at all times can increase cutter life almost 100%.

GRINDING

Cutting fluid is very important in a grinding operation; it cools the work and keeps the grinding wheel clean. Cutting fluid

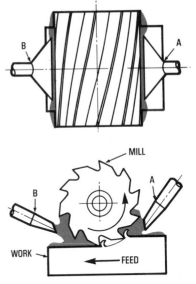

Fig. 16-9 Cutting fluid being supplied to both sides of the cutter in slab milling

should be applied in large quantities and under very little pressure.

a) *Surface Grinding*. Three methods may be used to apply the cutting fluid for surface grinding operations.

   i) The *flood method* is most commonly used and consists of a steady flow of cutting fluid being applied through a nozzle. Because of the reciprocating table action, most surface-grinding operations

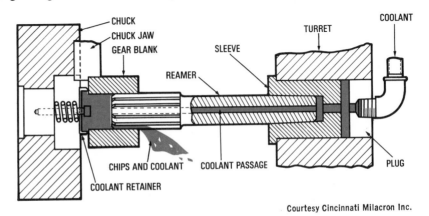

Fig. 16-8 Cutting fluid being supplied through a hole in the centre of the reamer

TABLE 16-1: RECOMMENDED CUTTING FLUIDS FOR VARIOUS MATERIALS

Material	Drilling	Reaming	Threading	Turning	Milling
Aluminum	Soluble oil Kerosene Kerosene & lard oil	Soluble oil Kerosene Mineral oil	Soluble oil Kerosene & lard oil	Soluble oil	Soluble oil Lard oil Mineral oil Dry
Brass	Dry Soluble oil Kerosene & lard oil	Dry Soluble oil	Soluble oil Lard oil	Soluble oil	Dry Soluble oil
Bronze	Dry Soluble oil Mineral oil Lard oil	Dry Soluble oil Mineral oil Lard oil	Soluble oil Lard oil	Soluble oil	Dry Soluble oil Mineral oil Lard oil
Cast iron	Dry Air jet Soluble oil	Dry Soluble oil Mineral lard oil	Dry Sulphurized oil Mineral lard oil	Dry Soluble oil	Dry Soluble oil
Copper	Dry Soluble oil Mineral lard oil Kerosene	Soluble oil Lard oil	Soluble oil Lard oil	Soluble oil	Dry Soluble oil
Malleable iron	Dry Soda water	Dry Soda water	Lard oil Soda water	Soluble oil	Dry Soda water
Monel metal	Soluble oil Lard oil	Soluble oil Lard oil	Lard oil	Soluble oil	Soluble oil
Steel alloys	Soluble oil Sulphurized oil Mineral lard oil	Soluble oil Sulphurized oil Mineral lard oil	Sulphurized oil Lard oil	Soluble oil	Soluble oil Mineral lard oil
Steel, machine	Soluble oil Sulphurized oil Lard oil Mineral lard oil	Soluble oil Mineral lard oil	Soluble oil Mineral lard oil	Soluble oil	Soluble oil Mineral lard oil
Steel, tool	Soluble oil Sulphurized oil Mineral lard oil	Soluble oil Sulphurized oil Lard oil	Sulphurized oil Lard oil	Soluble oil	Soluble oil Lard oil

Courtesy Cincinnati Milacron Inc.

NOTE: Chemical cutting fluids can be used successfully for most of the above cutting operations. These concentrates are diluted with water in proportions ranging from 1 part cutting fluid to 15 and as high as 100 parts of water, depending upon the metal being cut and the type of machining operation. When using chemical cutting fluids, it is wise to follow the manufacturer's recommendations for use and mixture.

can be greatly improved if the fluid is supplied through two nozzles as in Fig. 16-9.

ii) *Through-the-wheel* is a method in which the coolant is fed to a special wheel flange and is forced to the periphery of the wheel and to the area of contact by centrifugal force.

Courtesy Cincinnati Milacron Inc.

Fig. 16-10 Cutting fluid being applied by a ring-type distributor for a face milling operation

iii) *Mist spray*, where the coolant is siphoned from a reservoir by a stream of air and a fine spray is directed through a nozzle to the area of contact.

b) *Cylindrical Grinding*. For cylindrical grinding operations, it is important that the entire contact area between the wheel and work be flooded with a steady stream of clean, cool cutting

Courtesy Cincinnati Milacron Inc.

Fig. 16-11 Cutting fluid being applied to contact zone during cylindrical grinding

fluid. A fan-shaped nozzle (Fig. 16-11) somewhat wider than the wheel should be used to direct the cutting fluid.

c) *Internal Grinding*. During internal grinding, the cutting fluid must flush the chips and the abrasive wheel particles out of the hole being ground. Because internal grinding practices call for using as large a wheel as possible, it is sometimes difficult to get enough cutting fluid into the hole. A compromise must be made between the grinding wheel size and the amount of fluid entering the hole. As much fluid as possible should be applied during internal grinding operations.

CUTTING FLUID QUESTIONS

1. What is the function of a modern cutting fluid?
2. Briefly trace the development of cutting fluids.

PURPOSE AND ADVANTAGES

3. Explain the causes of heat and friction during a machining process.
4. Name four economical advantages which result from applying correct cutting fluids.

CHARACTERISTICS OF A GOOD CUTTING FLUID

5. List six *important* characteristics that a good cutting fluid should possess.

TYPES OF CUTTING FLUIDS

6. Name three categories into which cutting fluids fall.
7. Describe active and inactive cutting oils.
8. What type of cutting oil should be used for the following:
   a) tough, ductile metals?
   b) heavy-duty machining?
   c) non-ferrous metals?
   d) threading white metal?
9. Describe the composition of an emulsifiable oil and state its advantages.

10. State the purpose of:
    a) emulsifiable mineral oil
    b) extreme-pressure emulsifiable oil
11. Discuss and state six important advantages of chemical cutting fluids.
12. State the purpose of:
    a) true solution fluids
    b) wetting-agent types with extreme-pressure lubricants

FUNCTIONS OF A CUTTING FLUID

13. Name five functions of a cutting fluid.
14. Discuss the importance of lubricating and cooling as applied to cutting fluids.
15. Explain how a cutting fluid can change the length of the shear plane.
16. For what purpose are extreme-pressure lubricants used?
17. What occurs at the cutting tool face during a cut?
18. What is the main cause of surface roughness?
19. How does the application of cutting fluid affect the cutting tool?
20. Why is the control of rust important?
21. Describe a *polar film*, a *passivating film*.
22. Define *rancidity* and state the purpose of bactericides.

APPLICATION OF CUTTING FLUIDS

23. What is the general recommendation for applying cutting fluids?
24. How should cutting fluid be applied for lathe operations?
25. State two methods of applying cutting fluid when drilling or reaming is done.
26. Explain how cutting fluid should be applied for:
    a) slab milling
    b) face milling
    c) cylindrical grinding
27. Describe three methods of applying cutting fluid for surface-grinding operations.
28. Why is it sometimes difficult to apply cutting fluid during internal grinding operations?

17 METALLURGY

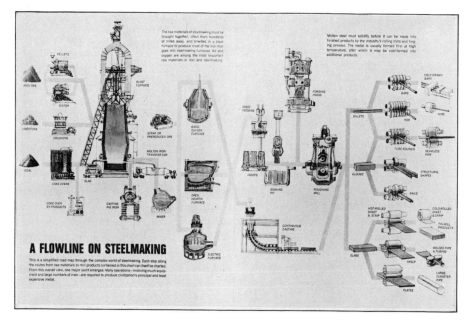

Courtesy American Iron & Steel Institute

Understanding the properties and heat treatment of metals has become increasingly important to machinists during the past two decades. Study of metal properties and development of new alloys have facilitated reduction in mass and increase in strength of machines, automobiles, aircraft, and many present-day commodities.

The most commonly used metals today are ferrous metals, or those which contain iron. The composition and properties of ferrous materials may be changed by the addition of various alloying elements during manufacture, to impart the desired qualities to the material. Cast iron, ma-

chine steel, carbon steel, alloy steel, and high-speed steel are all ferrous metals, each having different properties.

PHYSICAL PROPERTIES OF METALS

To better understand the use of the various metals, one should be familiar with the following terms:

Brittleness (Fig. 17-1A) is that property of a metal which permits no permanent distortion before breaking.

Cast iron is a brittle metal; it will break rather than bend under shock or impact.

Courtesy Linde Division, Union Carbide Corporation

Fig. 17-1A   Brittle metals will not bend but break easily

Ductility (Fig. 17-1B) is the ability of the metal to be permanently deformed without breaking. Metals such as copper and machine steel, which may be drawn into wire, are ductile materials.

Courtesy Linde Division, Union Carbide Corporation

Fig. 17-1B   Ductile metals are easily deformed

Elasticity (Fig. 17-1C) is the ability of a metal to return to its original shape after any force acting upon it has been removed. Properly heat-treated springs are good examples of elastic materials.

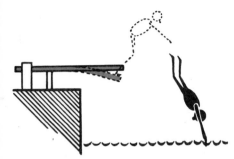

Courtesy Linde Division, Union Carbide Corporation

Fig. 17-1C   Elastic metals return to their original shape after the load is removed

Hardness (Fig. 17-1D) may be defined as the resistance to forceable penetration or plastic deformation.

Courtesy Linde Division, Union Carbide Corporation

Fig. 17-1D   Hard metals resist penetration

Malleability (Fig. 17-1E) is that property of a metal which permits it to be hammered or rolled into other sizes and shapes.

Courtesy Linde Division, Union Carbide Corporation

Fig. 17-1E   Malleable metals may be easily formed or shaped

Bruce
Dawes

Tensile strength (Fig. 17-1F) is the maximum amount of pull that a material will withstand before breaking. It is expressed as the number of pounds per square inch (on inch testers) or in kilograms per square centimetre (on metric testers) of pull required to break a bar having a one square inch or one square centimetre cross section.

Fig. 17-1F   Tensile strength: the amount that a metal will resist a direct pull

Toughness is the property of a metal to withstand shock or impact. Toughness is the opposite condition to brittleness.

MANUFACTURE OF FERROUS METALS

PIG IRON

Production of pig iron in the blast furnace (Fig. 17-2) is the first step in the manufacture of cast iron or steel.

RAW MATERIALS

Iron ore is the chief raw material used to make iron and steel. The main sources of iron ore in North America are at Steep Rock, the Ungava district near the Quebec-Labrador border, and the Mesabi range, situated at the western end of Lake Superior. The most important iron ores are:

Hematite which contains about 70% iron and varies in colour from black to brick-red.

Limonite is a brownish ore similar to hematite, but contains water. When the water has been removed by roasting, the ore resembles hematite.

Magnetite, a rich, black ore, contains a higher percentage of iron than any other ore, but is not found in large quantities.

Taconite, a low grade ore containing about 25% to 30% iron, must be specially treated before it is suitable for reduction into iron.

PELLETIZING PROCESS

Low grade iron ores are uneconomical to use in the blast furnace and, as a result, go through a pelletizing process, where most of the rock is removed and the ore is brought to a higher iron concentration. Some steelmaking firms are now pelletizing most ores to reduce transportation costs and the problems of pollution and slag disposal at the steel mills.

The crude ore is crushed and ground into a powder and passed through magnetic separators where the iron content is increased to about 65%. This high grade material is mixed with clay and formed into pellets about 12 mm to 20 mm in diameter in a pelletizer. The pellets at this stage are covered with coal dust and sintered (baked) at 1290°C. The resultant hard, highly concentrated pellets will remain intact during transportation and loading into the blast furnace.

Coal, after being converted to coke, is used to supply the heat to reduce the iron ore. The burning coke produces carbon monoxide which removes the oxygen from the iron ore and reduces it to a spongy mass of iron.

Limestone is used as a flux in the production of pig iron to remove the impurities from the iron ore.

MANUFACTURE OF PIG IRON

In the blast furnace (Fig. 17-2) iron ore, coke, and limestone are fed into the top of the furnace by means of a skip car. Hot air at about 540°C is fed into the bottom of the furnace through the bustle pipe and tuyeres. After the coke is ignited, the hot air makes it burn vigorously. Carbon monoxide, produced by the burning coke, combines with the oxygen in the iron ore, reducing it to a spongy mass of iron. The

pressure nozzle

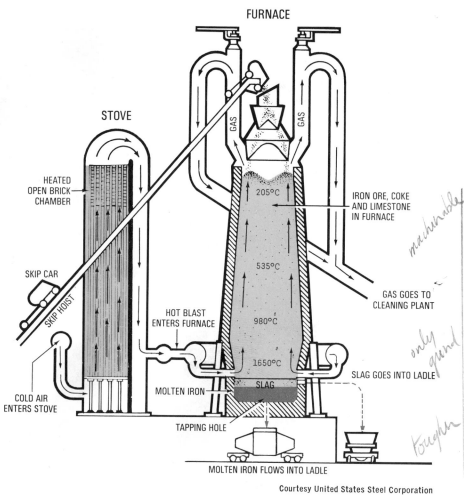

Fig. 17-2   A blast furnace produces pig iron

fuel is ignited and air is forced in near the bottom to aid combustion. When the iron is melted, it settles to the bottom of the furnace and is then tapped into ladles. The molten iron is poured into sand molds of the required shape and the metal assumes the shape of the mold. After the metal has cooled, the castings are removed from the molds.

The principal types of cast iron castings are:

Gray iron castings, made from a mixture of pig iron and steel scrap, are the most widely used. They are made into a wide variety of products including bathtubs, sinks, and parts for automobiles, locomotives, and machinery.

Chilled iron castings are made by pouring molten metal into metal molds so that the surface cools rapidly. The surface of such castings becomes very hard, and the castings are used for crusher rolls or other products requiring a hard, wear-resistant surface.

Alloyed castings contain certain amounts of alloys such as chromium, molybdenum, nickel, etc. Castings of this type are used extensively by the automobile industry.

iron gradually seeps down through the charge and collects in the bottom of the furnace. During this process, the decomposed limestone acts as a flux and unites with the impurities (silica and sulphur) in the iron to form a slag, which also seeps to the bottom of the furnace. Since the slag is lighter, it floats on the top of the molten iron. Every six hours, the furnace is tapped. The slag is drawn off first and then the molten iron is poured into ladles. The iron may be further processed into steel or cast into *pigs*, which are used by foundries in the manufacture of castings.

The manufacture of pig iron is a continuous process, and the blast furnaces are shut down only for repair or rebricking.

MANUFACTURE OF CAST IRON

Most of the pig iron manufactured in a blast furnace is used to make steel. However, a considerable amount is used to manufacture cast iron products. Cast iron is manufactured in a cupola furnace which resembles a huge stove pipe (Fig. 17-3).

Layers of coke, solid pig iron, and scrap iron are charged into the top of the furnace. After the furnace is charged, the

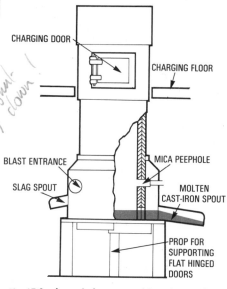

Fig. 17-3   A cupola furnace used to make cast iron

[handwritten notes at top: "knurled steel chip. readable machinable like steel. not general scrap! Bolts - hngs 5 or 6 days."]

Malleable castings are made from a special grade of pig iron and foundry scrap. After these castings have solidified, they are annealed in special furnaces. This makes the iron malleable and resistant to shock.

MANUFACTURE OF STEEL

Before molten pig iron from the blast furnace can be converted into steel, most of the impurities must be burned out. This process may be carried out in one of four types of furnaces: the *open hearth furnace*, the *Bessemer converter*, the *basic oxygen process furnace*, and the *electric furnace*.

OPEN HEARTH PROCESS

For several decades, the open hearth furnace was the "work horse" of the steel industry. At one time, almost 90% of the steel produced in North America was made in the open hearth furnace. Although many steel companies still use the modified open hearth furnace, this process is gradually giving way to more efficient methods of producing steel. The furnace is a large, rectangular, brick structure, 12 m to 15 m long and 4.5 m to 5.0 m wide (Fig. 17.4). The *hearth* is a large dish-shaped structure about 65 cm to 90 cm deep. Above each end of the hearth is a *burner* and an inlet for hot air from the *checkers*, which are large chambers filled with firebrick placed in a checkerboard fashion.

When the furnace is charged, limestone is put in and steel scrap is then added. After the scrap has been melted, molten pig iron is poured into the hearth. Large tongues of flame, produced by the union of fuel and the hot gas from the checkers, sweep over the molten metal from the right side (Fig. 17-4) and burn the impurities out of it. The burned gases from this operation are drawn off through the checkers on the left side and heat these checkers. At intervals of about 10 to 15 minutes, the direction of the air and the flame are

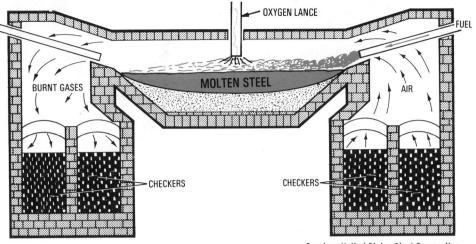

Courtesy United States Steel Corporation

Fig. 17-4   Schematic cross-section of an open hearth furnace

reversed and pass from left to right over the molten metal. During this operation, the limestone unites with the impurities and rises to the top as slag.

After seven to twelve hours, the furnace is tapped and the molten steel is run into a ladle which is just large enough to hold the batch (heat) of steel; the slag overflows through a spout in the ladle. Alloying materials, such as silicon, manganese, or other elements, are then added to the molten steel to give it the desired properties. The steel is poured, or *teemed*, into ingot molds and after solidification the ingots are removed from the molds and transferred to soaking pits. Here they are brought to a uniform temperature prior to rolling into the desired shapes and sizes. Open hearth furnaces have a capacity of up to about 500 t of steel at one heat.

Since the introduction of the basic oxygen furnace, steelmakers have found that the addition of oxygen to any steelmaking process will increase production considerably. Consequently, many open hearth furnaces have been updated with the addition of an oxygen lance, Fig. 17-4, which directs almost pure oxygen at a high velocity onto the top of the molten steel in the hearth. The oxygen burns the impurities out of the steel much quicker than was

possible by the straight open hearth process. As a result of this modification, the production of these furnaces has been greatly increased.

BASIC OXYGEN PROCESS

One of the newest developments in steelmaking is the basic oxygen process.

The basic oxygen furnace (Fig. 17-5) resembles a Bessemer converter, but does not have the air chamber and tuyeres at the bottom to admit air through the charge. Instead of air being forced through the molten metal, as in the Bessemer process, a high pressure stream of pure oxygen is directed onto the top of the molten metal.

The furnace is tilted and is first charged with scrap metal (about 30% of the total charge). Molten pig iron is poured into the furnace, after which the required fluxes are added. An oxygen lance with a water cooled hood is then lowered into the furnace until the tip is within 150 cm to 250 cm above the surface of the molten metal, depending on the blowing qualities of the iron and the type of scrap used. The oxygen is turned on and flows at the rate of 140 to 170 m^3/min at a pressure of 965 kPa to 1100 kPa.

The force of the oxygen starts a high temperature churning action and burns

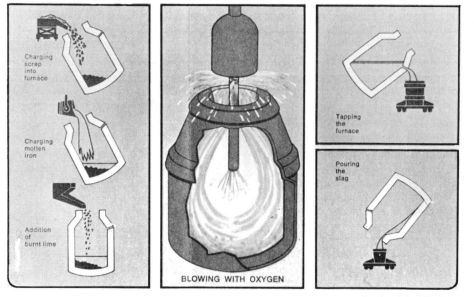

BLOWING WITH OXYGEN

Courtesy Inland Steel Co.

Fig. 17-5   The basic oxygen process

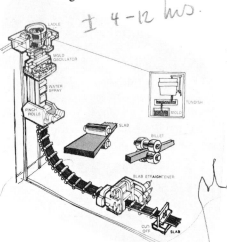

of the furnace, it takes from four to twelve hours to make a heat of steel. When the metal is ready to be tapped, the furnace is tilted forward and the steel flows into a large ladle. From the ladle, the steel is teemed into ingots.

Courtesy American Iron & Steel Institute

Fig. 17-7   The continuous casting process for making steel blooms or slabs

out the impurities. After all the impurities have been burned out, there will be a noticeable drop in the flame and a definite change in sound. The oxygen is then shut off and the lance removed.

The furnace is now tilted (Fig. 17-5) and the molten steel flows into a ladle. The required alloys are added, after which the molten metal is teemed into ingots. The refining process takes only about 50 minutes and about 270 t of steel can be made per hour.

ELECTRIC FURNACE

The electric furnace (Fig. 17-6) is used primarily to make fine alloy and tool steels. The heat, the amount of oxygen, and the atmospheric condition can be regulated at will in the electric furnace; this furnace is therefore used to make steels that cannot be readily produced in any other way.

Carefully selected steel scrap, containing smaller amounts of the alloying elements than are required in the finished steel, is loaded into the furnace. The three carbon electrodes are lowered until an arc jumps from them to the scrap. The heat

generated by the electric arcs gradually melts all the steel scrap. Alloying materials such as chromium, nickel, tungsten, etc., are then added to make the type of alloy steel required. Depending upon the size

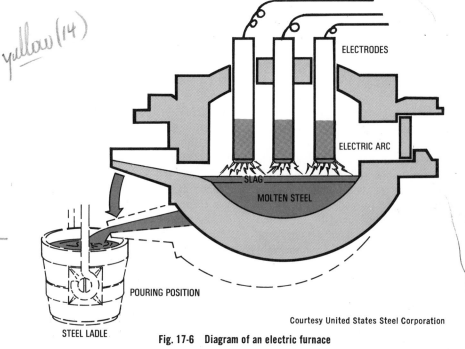

ELECTRODES

ELECTRIC ARC

SLAG

MOLTEN STEEL

POURING POSITION

STEEL LADLE

Courtesy United States Steel Corporation

Fig. 17-6   Diagram of an electric furnace

cold rolled changes   *won't change as much*

STEEL PROCESSING

After the steel has been properly refined in any of the furnaces, it is tapped into ladles where alloying elements and deoxidizers may be added. The molten steel may then be teemed (poured) into *ingots* weighing as much as 18 t, or it may be formed directly into slabs by the *continuous casting process*.

The steel is teemed (poured) into ingot molds and allowed to solidify. The ingot molds are then removed or *stripped* and the hot ingots are placed in soaking pits at 1200°C for up to 1.5 hours to make them a uniform temperature throughout. The ingots are then sent to the rolling mills where they are rolled and reduced in cross-section to form blooms, billets, or slabs.

The molten steel may also be converted into slabs or blooms by the *continuous casting process* (Fig. 17-7). Here, up to 180 t is poured into a tundish or reservoir at the top of the machine. The molten metal flows from the tundish to an oscillating mold, where a solid skin is formed on the outside of the metal due to the cooling action of the mold. The metal moves down through the cooling system and the skin becomes thicker. As the metal proceeds from the mold, further cooling action solidifies it throughout and the slab is moved to a straightener by means of pinch rolls. The continuous slab is then cut

into desired lengths by a travelling acetylene torch.

After the metal has been made into blooms or slabs by either of the forementioned processes, it is further rolled into billets and then, while still hot, into the desired shape, such as round, flat, square, hexagonal, etc. (Fig. 17-8). These rolled products are known as *hot rolled steel* and are easily identified by the bluish black scale on the outside.

Hot rolled steel may be further processed into *cold rolled* or *cold drawn steel* by removing the scale in an acid bath and passing the metal through rolls or dies of the desired shape and size.

Vacuum Processing of Molten Steel

Steel used in space and nuclear projects is often processed and solidified in a vacuum to remove oxygen, nitrogen, and hydrogen, and thus produce a high quality steel.

aircraft

CHEMICAL COMPOSITION OF STEEL

Although iron and carbon are the main elements in steel, certain other elements may be present in varying quantities. Some are present because they are difficult to remove, and others are added to impart certain qualities to the steel. The elements found in plain carbon steel are carbon,

manganese, phosphorus, silicon, and sulphur.

Carbon is the element which has the greatest influence on the property of the steel, since it is the hardening agent. The hardness, hardenability, tensile strength, and wear resistance will be increased as the percentage of carbon is increased up to about 0.83%. After this point has been reached, additional carbon does not noticeably affect the hardness of the steel, but increases wear resistance and hardenability.

Manganese, when added in small quantities (0.30% to 0.60%) during the manufacture of steel, acts as a deoxidizer or purifier. Manganese helps to remove the oxygen which, if it remained, would make the steel weak and brittle. Manganese also combines with sulphur, which in most cases is considered an undesirable element in steel. The addition of manganese increases the strength, toughness, hardenability, and shock resistance of steel. It will also slightly lower the critical temperature and increase ductility.

When manganese is added in quantities above 0.60%, it is considered an alloying element and will impart certain properties to the steel. When 1.5% to 2% manganese is added to high-carbon steel it will produce deep-hardening, nondeforming steel, which must be quenched in oil. Hard, wear-resistant steels, suitable for use in power shovel scoops, rock crushers, and grinding mills, are produced when up to 15% manganese is added to high-carbon steel.

Phosphorus is generally considered an undesirable element in carbon steel when present in amounts over 0.6%, since it will cause the steel to fail under vibration or shock. This condition is termed "cold-shortness". Small amounts of phosphorus (about 0.2%) tend to eliminate blow holes and decrease shrinkage in the steel. Phosphorus and sulphur may be added to low carbon steel (machine steel) to improve the machinability.

page 9 yellow

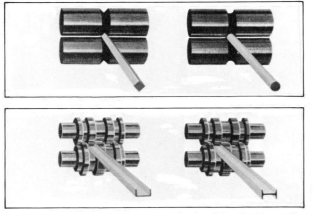

Fig. 17-8   Various shapes of steel are produced by rolling

screws etc.   fine na   *screw machines*

electric motors stator. bigger units good quality

Silicon, present in most steels in amounts from 0.10% to 0.30%, acts as a deoxidizer and makes steel sound when it is cast or hot worked. Silicon, when added in larger amounts (0.60% to 2%) is considered an alloying element. It is never used alone or simply with carbon; some deep hardening element, such as manganese, molybdenum, or chromium, is usually added with silicon. When added as an alloying element, silicon increases the tensile strength, toughness, and hardness penetration of steel.

Sulphur, generally considered an impurity in steel, causes the steel to crack during working (rolling or forging) at high temperatures. This condition is known as "hot-shortness." Sulphur may be added purposely to low-carbon steel in quantities ranging from 0.07% to 0.30%, to increase its machinability. Sulphurized, free-cutting steel is known as *screw stock* and is used in automatic screw machines.

CLASSIFICATION OF STEEL

Steel may be classified into two groups, *carbon steels* and *alloy steels*.

PLAIN CARBON STEELS

Plain carbon steels may be classified as those which contain only carbon and no other major alloying element. They are divided into three categories: low-carbon steel, medium-carbon steel, and high-carbon steel.

Low-carbon steel contains from 0.02% to 0.30% carbon by mass. Because of the low carbon content, this type of steel cannot be hardened, but can be casehardened. *Machine steel* and *cold-rolled steel*, which contain from 0.08% to 0.30% carbon, are the most common low-carbon steels. These steels are commonly used in machine shops for the manufacture of parts that do not have to be hardened. Such items as bolts, nuts, washers, sheet steel, and shafts are made of low-carbon steel.

Medium-carbon steel contains from 0.30% to 0.60% carbon and is used where greater tensile strength is required. Because of the higher carbon content, this steel can be hardened, which makes it ideal for steel forgings. Tools such as wrenches, hammers, and screwdrivers are drop forged from medium-carbon steel and later heat treated.

High-carbon steel, also known as tool steel, contains over 0.60% carbon and may range as high as 1.7%. This type of steel is used for cutting tools, punches, taps, dies, drills, and reamers. It is available in hot-rolled stock or in finish-ground flat stock and drill rod.

ALLOY STEELS

Often certain steels are needed which have special characteristics that a plain carbon steel would not possess. It is then necessary to choose an *alloy steel*.

Alloy steel may be defined as steel containing other elements, in addition to carbon, which produce the desired qualities in the steel.

The addition of alloying elements may impart one or more of the following properties to the steel.

a) increase in tensile strength
b) increase in hardness
c) increase in toughness
d) alteration of the critical temperature of the steel
e) increase in wear abrasion
f) red hardness
g) corrosion resistance

EFFECTS OF THE ALLOYING ELEMENTS

The following elements such as chromium, cobalt, manganese, molybdenum, nickel, phosphorus, silicon, sulphur, tungsten, and vanadium may be added to steel to give it the desired properties.

The properties imparted to the steel by these elements are given in Table 17-1.

HEAT TREATING EQUIPMENT

The heat treating of metal is carried out in specially controlled furnaces which may employ gas, oil, or electricity to provide the heat. These furnaces must also be equipped with certain safety devices, as well as control and indicating devices to maintain the temperature required for the job. All furnace installations should be equipped with a fume hood and exhaust fan to take away any fumes resulting from the heat treating operation or in case of gas installation, to exhaust the gas fumes.

In most gas installations, the exhaust fan, when running, will actuate the air switch in the exhaust duct. The air switch in turn operates a solenoid valve which permits the main gas valve to be opened. Should the exhaust fan fail for any reason, the air switch will also fail and the main gas supply will close down.

The furnace temperature is controlled by a thermocouple and an indicating pyrometer (Fig. 17-9). After the furnace has been started, the desired temperature is set on the indicating pyrometer. This pyrometer is connected on one side to a thermocouple, and on the other side to a solenoid valve which controls the flow of gas to the furnace.

The thermocouple is made up of two dissimilar metal wires twisted together and welded at the end. The thermocouple is generally mounted in the back of the furnace in a refectory tube to prevent damage and oxidation to the thermocouple wires.

As the temperature in the furnace rises, the thermocouple becomes hot, and due to the dissimilarity of the wires, a small electrical current is produced. This current is conducted to the pyrometer on the wall and causes the pyrometer needle to indicate the temperature of the furnace. When the temperature in the furnace reaches the amount set on the pyrometer, a solenoid valve connected to the gas supply is actuated and the flow of gas to the furnace

TABLE 17-1: THE EFFECT OF ALLOYING ELEMENTS ON STEEL

Effect	Carbon	Chromium	Cobalt	Lead	Manganese	Molybdenum	Nickel	Phosphorus	Silicon	Sulphur	Tungsten	Vanadium
Increases tensile strength	X	X			X	X	X					
Increases hardness	X	X										
Increases wear resistance	X	X			X		X				X	
Increases hardenability	X	X			X	X	X					X
Increases ductility					X							
Increases elastic limit		X				X						
Increases rust resistance		X					X					
Increases abrasion resistance		X			X							
Increases toughness		X				X	X					X
Increases shock resistance		X					X					X
Increases fatigue resistance												X
Decreases ductility	X	X										
Decreases toughness			X									
Raises critical temperature		X	X								X	
Lowers critical temperature					X		X					
Causes hot shortness										X		
Causes cold shortness								X				
Imparts red hardness			X			X					X	
Imparts fine grain structure					X							X
Reduces deformation					X		X					
Acts as deoxidizer					X				X			
Acts as desulphurizer					X							
Imparts oil hardening properties		X			X	X	X					
Imparts air hardening properties					X	X						
Eliminates blow holes									X			
Creates soundness in casting										X		
Facilitates rolling and forging					X					X		
Improves machinability				X						X		

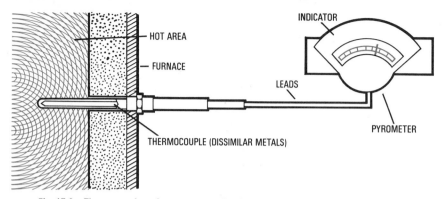

Fig. 17-9   Thermocouple and pyrometer used to indicate and control the temperature of a heat-treating furnace

is restricted. When the furnace temperature drops below the temperature indicated on the pyrometer, the solenoid valve opens, permitting a full flow of gas.

TYPES OF FURNACES

For most heat treating operations, it is advisable to have a *low-temperature furnace* capable of temperatures up to 700°C,

a *high-temperature furnace* capable of temperatures up to 1370°C, and a *pot type furnace*. The pot type furnace may be used for hardening and tempering by immersing the part to be heat treated in the molten heat treating medium, which may be salt or lead. Cyanide-type mixtures are used for casehardening operations. One advantage of this type of furnace is that the parts, when being heated, do not come

in contact with the air. This eliminates the possibility of oxidation or scaling. The temperature of the pot furnace is controlled by the same method as the high-temperature and low-temperature furnaces.

HEAT TREATMENT TERMS

Before one gets involved in the theory of heat treating, it is well to study and understand a few terms connected with this topic.

Heat treatment – the heating and subsequent cooling of metals to produce the desired mechanical properties.

Decalescence point – that temperature at which carbon steel, when being heated, transforms from pearlite to austenite; this is generally at about 720°C for 0.83% carbon steel.

Recalescence point – that temperature at which carbon steel, when being slowly cooled, transforms from austenite to pearlite.

Lower critical temperature point – the lowest temperature at which steel may be quenched in order to harden it. This temperature coincides with the decalescence point.

Upper critical temperature point – the highest temperature at which steel may be quenched in order to attain maximum hardness and the finest grain structure.

Critical range – the temperature range bounded by the upper and the lower critical temperatures.

Hardening – the heating of steel above its lower critical temperature and quenching in the proper medium (water, oil, or air) to produce martensite.

Tempering (Drawing) – reheating hardened steel to a desired temperature below its lower critical temperature, followed by any desired rate of cooling. Tempering removes the brittleness and toughens the

A   Low temperature   B   High temperature   C   Pot type

Courtesy Charles A. Hones Inc.

Fig. 17-10   Types of heat treating furnaces

steel. Steel in this condition is called tempered martensite.

Annealing (Full) – heating metal to just above its upper critical point for the required period of time, followed by slow cooling in the furnace, lime, or sand. Annealing will soften the metal, relieve the internal stresses and strains, and improve its machinability.

Process annealing – heating the steel to just below the lower critical temperature, followed by any suitable cooling method. This process is often used on metals which have been work-hardened. Process annealing will soften it sufficiently for further cold working.

Normalizing – heating the steel to just above its upper critical temperature and cooling it in still air. Normalizing is done to improve the grain structure and remove the stresses and strains. In general, it brings the metal back to its normal state.

Spheroidizing – the heating of steel to just below the lower critical temperature for a prolonged period of time followed by cooling in still air. This process produces a grain structure with globular-shaped particles (spheroids) of cementite rather than the normal needle-like structure, which improves the machinability of the metal.

Alpha iron – the state in which iron exists below the lower critical temperature. In this state, the atoms form a body-centred cube.

Gamma iron – the state in which iron exists in the critical range. In this state the molecules form face-centred cubes. Gamma iron is nonmagnetic.

Pearlite – a laminated structure of ferrite (iron) and cementite (iron carbide); usually the condition of steel before heat treatment.

Cementite – a carbide of iron (Fe_3C), which is the hardener in steel.

Austenite – a solid solution of carbon in iron which exists between the lower and upper critical temperatures.

Martensite – the structure of fully hardened steel obtained when austenite is quenched. Martensite is characterized by its needle-like pattern.

Tempered martensite – the structure obtained after martensite has been tempered. Tempered martensite was formerly known as *troosite* and *sorbite*.

Eutectoid steel – steel containing just enough carbon to dissolve completely in the iron when the steel is heated to its critical range. Eutectoid steel contains from 0.80% to 0.85% carbon. This may be likened to a saturated solution of salt in water.

Hypereutectoid steel – steel containing more carbon than will completely dissolve in the iron when the steel is heated to the critical range. This is similar to a supersaturated solution.

Hypoeutectoid steel – containing less carbon than can be dissolved by the iron when the steel is heated to the critical range. Here there is an excess of iron. This is similar to an unsaturated solution.

SELECTION OF TOOL STEEL

The proper selection and proper heat treatment of a tool steel are both essential if the part being made is to perform efficiently. Many problems may arise in the selection and heat treatment of the tool steel.

a) The steel may not be tough or strong enough for the job requirements.
b) It may not offer sufficient abrasion resistance.
c) It may not have sufficient hardening penetration.
d) It may warp during heat treatment.

Because of these problems, the steel producers have been forced to manufacture many types of alloy steels to cover the range of most jobs.

To select the correct steel for a job, consult the handbook provided by the steel company for the specifications and application of the various steels it produces. This handbook will also outline the proper heat treatment of the particular material chosen. These instructions should be carefully followed.

Tool steels are generally classified as *water hardening, oil hardening, air hardening,* or *high-speed steels*. They are usually identified by each manufacturer by a trade name such as Alpha 8, Keewatin, Nutherm, or Nipigon, which are some of the trade names of the Atlas Steel Company products.

WATER HARDENING TOOL STEEL

Water hardening tool steels generally contain from 0.50% to 1.3% carbon, along with small amounts (about 0.20%) of silicon and manganese. The addition of silicon facilitates the forging and rolling of the material, while manganese helps to make the steel more sound when it is first cast into the ingot. Further addition of silicon (above 0.20%) will reduce the grain size and increase the toughness of water hardening steel.

Most water hardening steels achieve the maximum hardness for a depth of about 3 mm; the inner core remains softer, but still tough. Chromium or molybdenum is sometimes added to increase the hardenability (hardness penetration), toughness, and wear resistance of water hardening steels. Water hardening steels are heated to around 790°C to 815°C during the hardening process. These steels are used where a dense, fine-grained outer casing with a tough inner core is required. Typical applications are drills, taps, reamers, punches, jig bushings, and dowel pins.

The problems connected with water hardening steels are those of distortion and cracking when the material is quenched. Should these problems occur, it would then be wise to select an oil hardening steel.

OIL HARDENING STEELS

A typical oil hardening steel contains about 0.90% carbon, 1.6% manganese, and 0.25% silicon.

The addition of manganese in quantities of 1.5% or more increases the hardenability (hardness penetration) of the steel up to about 25 mm from each surface. During the quenching of steels with a higher manganese content, the hardening is so rapid that a less severe quenching medium (oil) must be used. The use of oil as a quenching medium retards the cooling rate and reduces the stresses and strains in the steel which cause warping and cracking. Chromium and nickel, in varying quantities, may be added to oil hardening steel to increase its hardness and wear resistance. Higher hardening temperatures, from 815°C to 845°C, are required for these latter alloy steels.

Often, due to the intricate shape of the part, it may not be possible to eliminate warping or cracking during the quench, and it will be necessary to select an air hardening steel for the particular part. Typical applications of oil hardening steels are: blanking, forming, punching dies, precision tools, broaches, and gauges.

AIR HARDENING STEELS

Due to the slower cooling rate of air hardening steels, the stresses and strains which cause cracking and distortion are kept to a minimum. Air hardening steels are also used on parts having large cross-sections, where full hardness throughout could not be obtained by using water or oil hardening steels.

A typical air hardening steel will contain about 1.00% carbon, 0.70% manganese, 0.20% silicon, 5.00% chromium, 1.00% molybdenum, and 0.20% vanadium. Air hardening steels require higher hardening temperatures, from 870°C to 970°C, depending on the composition.

Typical applications of this steel are: large blanking dies, forming, trimming and coining dies, rolls, long punches, precision tools and gauges.

HIGH SPEED STEELS

High speed steels are used in the manufacture of cutting tools such as drills, reamers, taps, milling cutters, and lathe cutting tools. The analysis of a typical high speed steel could be as follows: 0.72% carbon, 0.25% manganese, 0.20% silicon, 4% chromium, 18% tungsten, and 1% vanadium. Tools of this type will retain their hardness and cutting edges even when operating at red heat.

During heat treatment, high speed steels must be preheated slowly to 815°C to 870°C in a neutral atmosphere and then transferred to another furnace and quickly brought up to 1260°C to 1315°C. They are generally quenched in oil, but small, intricate sections may be air cooled.

CLASSIFICATION OF STEEL

In order to ensure that the composition of various types of steel remains constant and that a certain type of steel will meet the required specifications, the Society of Automotive Engineers and the American Iron and Steel Institute have devised methods of identifying different types of steel. These numerical systems are similar and both are widely used in industry.

THE SAE-AISI CLASSIFICATION SYSTEMS

The systems designed by the Society of Automotive Engineers and the American Iron and Steel Institute are similar in most respects. They both use a series of four or five numbers to designate the type of steel.

The first digit, in these series, indicates the predominant alloying element. The last two digits (or sometimes three in certain corrosion or heat resisting alloys) indicate the average carbon content in points (hundredths of one percent).

The main difference in the two systems is that the AISI system indicates the steel-making process used by the following prefixes:

A – basic open hearth alloy steel
B – acid-Bessemer carbon steel

C – basic open hearth carbon steel
D – acid-open hearth carbon steel
E – electric furnace steel

In the classification charts, the various types of steels are indicated by the first number in the series as follows:

1. carbon   5. chromium
2. nickel   6. chromium-vanadium
3. nickel-chrome   8. triple alloy
4. molybdenum   9. manganese-silicon

Table 17-2 indicates the SAE-AISI classification of the various steels and alloys. The number seven does not appear on the chart. It formerly represented tungsten steel which is no longer listed in this chart since it is now considered a special steel.

Examples of Steel Identification

Determine the types of steel indicated by the following numbers: 1015, A2340, 4170.

> 1015 – 1 indicates plain carbon steel
> – 0 indicates there are no major alloying elements
> – 15 indicates that there is between 0.10% and 0.20% carbon content
> *NOTE*: This steel would naturally contain small quantities of manganese, phosphorus, and sulphur.
>
> A2360 – A indicates an alloy steel made by the basic open hearth process.
> – 23 indicates the steel contains 3.5% nickel (see Table 17-2).
> – 60 indicates 0.60% carbon content.
>
> 4170 – 41 indicates a chromium-molybdenum steel.
> – 70 indicates 0.70% carbon content.

HEAT TREATMENT OF CARBON STEEL

The proper performance of a steel part depends not only on the correct selection of steel, but also upon the correct heat

TABLE 17-2: SAE CLASSIFICATION OF STEELS

CARBON STEELS	1xxx
Plain Carbon	10xx
Free-Cutting (Resulphurized Screw Stock)	11xx
Free-Cutting, Manganese	X13xx
HIGH-MANGANESE	T13xx
NICKEL STEELS	2xxx
0.50% Nickel	20xx
1.50% Nickel	21xx
3.50% Nickel	23xx
5.00% Nickel	25xx
NICKEL-CHROMIUM STEELS	3xxx
1.25% Nickel, 0.60% Chromium	31xx
1.75% Nickel, 1.00% Chromium	32xx
3.50% Nickel, 1.50% Chromium	33xx
3.00% Nickel, 0.80% Chromium	34xx
Corrosion- and Heat-Resisting Steels	30xxx
MOLYBDENUM STEELS	4xxx
Chromium-Molybdenum	41xx
Chromium-Nickel-Molybdenum	43xx
Nickel-Molybdenum	46xx and 48xx
CHROMIUM STEELS	5xxx
Low-Chromium	51xx
Medium-Chromium	52xxx
CHROMIUM-VANADIUM STEELS	6xxx
TRIPLE ALLOY STEELS (Nickel, Chromium, Molybdenum)	8xxx
MANGANESE-SILICON STEELS	9xxx

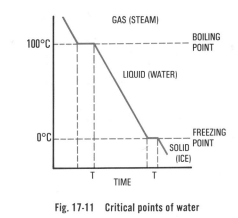

Fig. 17-11 Critical points of water

process were reversed and the steam cooled, it would form water at 100°C and ice at 0°C. These points (0°C and 100°C) where the water transforms to another state are known as the critical points of water.

Steel, like water, has critical points which, when determined, will lead to successful heat treatment of the metal.

TO DETERMINE THE CRITICAL POINTS OF 0.83% CARBON STEEL

A simple experiment may be performed to illustrate the critical points and the changes that take place in a piece of carbon steel when heated and slowly cooled.

Procedure
1. Select a piece of 0.83% (eutectoid) carbon steel about 40 mm × 40 mm × 50 mm long and drill a small hole in the end for most of the length.

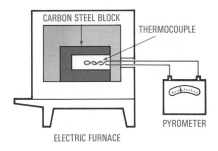

Fig. 17-12 Setup to determine the critical points of steel

treating procedure and an understanding of the theory behind it. When steel is heated from room temperature to the upper critical temperature and then quenched, several changes take place in the steel. These may be more easily understood if the changes which take place in water, from the frozen state until it is transformed into steam, are considered.

By referring to Fig. 17-11, it is noted that water exists as a solid at or below 0°C (freezing point). If the ice is heated, the temperature will remain 0°C until the ice completely melts. If the water is heated further, it will turn into steam at 100°C. Again the water remains at this temperature for a short time before turning into steam. It should also be noticed that if the

2. Insert a thermocouple in the hole as shown and seal the end of the hole with fireclay.

3. Place the block in a furnace and run the thermocouple wire to a voltmeter (Fig. 17-12).

4. Light the furnace and set the temperature for about 775°C on the pyrometer.

5. Plot the readings of the voltmeter needle at regular time intervals (Fig. 17-13).

6. When the furnace reaches 775°C, shut it down and let it cool.

7. Continue to plot the readings until the temperature in the furnace drops to approximately 540°C.

OBSERVATIONS AND CONCLUSIONS

Steel, at room temperature, consists of laminated layers of ferrite (iron) and cementite (iron carbide). This structure is called pearlite (Fig. 17-14A and B). As the steel is heated from room temperature, the curve climbs uniformly until a temperature of about 725°C is reached. At

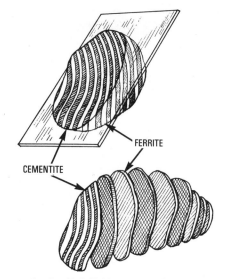

CEMENTITE

FERRITE

Courtesy Linde Division, Union Carbide Corporation

Fig. 17-14A   A pearlite grain is composed of alternate layers of iron (ferrite) and iron carbide (cementite)

Courtesy Linde Division, Union Carbide Corporation

Fig. 17-14B   A photomicrograph of high carbon steel. The pearlite grains are surrounded by iron carbide shown as white lines between the grains

this point, Ac (Fig. 17-13), the temperature of the steel drops slightly although the temperature of the furnace is rising.

The point Ac indicates the *decalescence point*, and it is here that several changes take place in the steel.

a) If the steel were observed in the furnace at this time, it would be noticed that the dark shadows in the steel disappear.

b) The steel would be nonmagnetic when tested with a magnet.

c) These changes were caused by a change in the atomic structure of the steel. The atoms rearrange themselves from body-centred cubes (Fig. 17-15A) to face-centred cubes (Fig. 17-15B). When the atoms are rearranged, the energy (heat) required for this change is drawn from the metal; thus a slight drop in the temperature of the workpiece is recorded at the decalescence point. The layers of iron carbide completely dissolve in the iron to form a solid solution known as *austenite*. Thus the decalescence point marked the transformation point from *pearlite* to *austenite*, or from body-centred cubes to face-centred cubes.

d) It is at this point that the steel, if quenched in water, would also show the first signs of hardening.

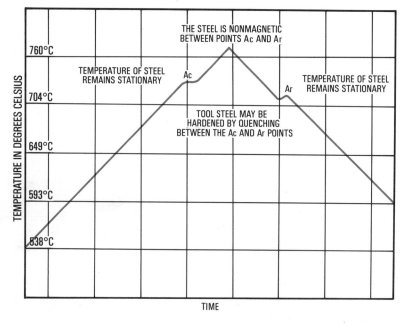

Fig. 17-13   Graph to illustrate the critical points of steel

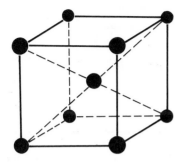

Fig. 17-15A   Arrangements of atoms in a body-centred cube

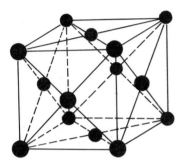

Fig. 17-15B   Arrangement of atoms in a face-centred cube

e) If the steel could be examined under a microscope, it would be noticed that the grain structure starts to get smaller. As the curve progresses upwards past Ac, the grain size would become progressively smaller until the upper critical temperature (775°C) were reached.

As the steel cools, the curve would continue uniformly down and the grain size would gradually get larger until the point Ar, at about 705°C, is reached. This is the *recalescence point* and here the needle on the voltmeter would show a slight rise in temperature, although the furnace is cooling. This process is obviously the reverse of the phenomenon which occurs at the decalescence point; the austenite reverts to pearlite, the atoms rearrange themselves into body-centred cubes, and the steel again becomes magnetic.

Another experiment, which demonstrates the decalescence and recalescence points, is as follows.

Decalescence Point

1. Place a magnet on a firebrick.
2. Select a 12 mm to 16 mm round piece of 0.90 to 1.00 carbon steel.
3. Place a can of cold water under the magnet ends.
4. Heat the piece held to the magnet using a small flame.
   NOTE: Do not allow the flame to come in contact with the magnet.
5. The steel will drop into the water and become hardened when the temperature reaches its critical point.

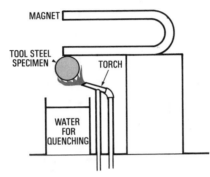

Fig. 17-16   Decalescence point experiment

Recalescence Point

1. Remove the can of water from under the magnet.
2. Place a flat plate under the work held on the magnet.
3. Heat the steel until it drops from the magnet on to the plate.
4. When the steel cools, it will become attracted by the magnet.

Summary

When the steel loses its magnetic value (decalescence point), it drops into the water and the change in the steel is trapped or stopped. The steel then hardens because it does not have time to revert to another state.

Conversely, when the steel is not quenched but is allowed to cool gradually from the decalescence point, it regains its magnetic value when it has cooled slightly (recalescence point). The steel

does not change from magnetic to non-magnetic; it merely acquires temporary characteristics of being attracted or *not* attracted to the magnet.

HARDENING OF 0.83% CARBON STEEL

Once the critical temperature of a steel has been determined, the proper quenching temperature, which is about 27°C over the upper critical temperature, can be determined. Not all steels have the same critical temperature; Fig. 17-17 indicates that the critical temperature of a steel drops as the carbon content increases up to 0.83%, after which it does not change. As a result, steels containing over 0.83% carbon (hypereutectoid) only need be heated to just above the lower critical temperature Ac_1 (Fig. 17-17) to obtain maximum hardness. This makes it possible to use a lower hardening temperature for hypereutectoid steels, thus decreasing the possibility of warping. The increase in the carbon content beyond 0.83% will not increase the hardness of the steel; however, it does increase the wear resistance of the steel considerably.

In order for the steel to be hardened properly, it must be heated uniformly to about 27°C above the upper critical temperature and held at this temperature long enough to allow sufficient carbon to dissolve and form a solid solution which permits maximum hardness. At this point the steel will have the smallest grain size and, when quenched, will produce the maximum hardness.

The critical temperature of a steel is also affected by alloying elements such as manganese, nickel, chromium, cobalt, and tungsten.

QUENCHING

When steel has been properly heated throughout, it is quenched in brine, water, or oil (depending on the type of steel), to cool it rapidly. During this operation, the austenite is transferred into *martensite*, a hard brittle metal. Because the steel is cooled rapidly, the austenite is prevented

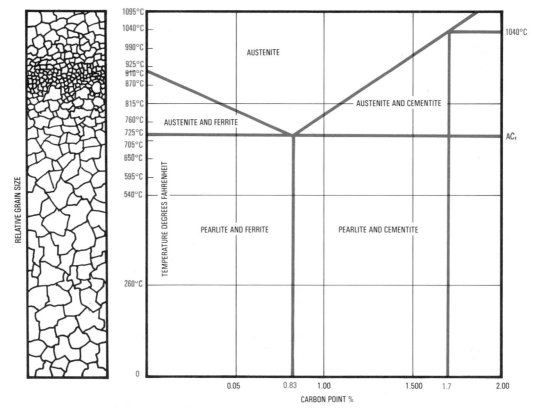

Fig. 17-17   Iron-carbide diagram illustrating the relationship between the carbon content of steel and the critical temperatures

from passing through the recalescence point (Ar), as in the case of slow cooling, and the small grain size of the austenite is retained in the martensite (Fig. 17-18).

The rate of cooling affects the hardness of steel. If a water hardening steel is quenched in oil, it cools more slowly and does not attain the maximum hardness. On the other hand, if an oil hardening steel is cooled too quickly by quenching it in water, it may crack. Cracking may also occur when the quenching medium is too cold.

The method of quenching greatly affects the stresses and strains set up in the metal, which cause warping and cracking. For this reason, long flat pieces should be held vertically above the quenching medium and plunged straight into the liquid. After immersion, the part should be moved around in a figure eight motion. This keeps the liquid at a uniform temperature

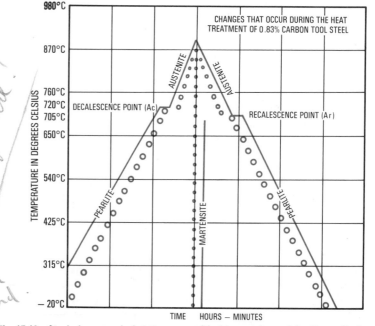

Fig. 17-18   Steel when quenched at the upper critical temperature retains the smallest grain size

and prevents air pockets forming on the steel, which would affect the uniformity of hardness.

METCALF'S EXPERIMENT

This simple experiment demonstrates the effect that various degrees of heat have on the grain structure, hardness, and strength of tool steel.

1. Select a piece of SAE 1090 (tool steel) about 12 mm diameter and about 100 mm long.
2. With a sharp pointed tool, cut shallow grooves approximately 12 mm apart.
3. Number each section (Fig. 17-19A).

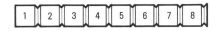

Fig. 17-19A   Test bar for Metcalf's experiment

4. Heat the bar with an oxyacetylene torch, bringing number 1 section to a white heat.
5. Keep number 1 section at white heat, and heat sections 4 and 5 to a cherry red. *DO NOT* apply heat to sections 6 to 8.
6. Quench in cold water or brine.
7. Test each section with the edge of a file for hardness.
8. Break off the sections and examine the grain structure under a microscope.

RESULTS

Sections 1 and 2 have been overheated. They break easily and the grain structure is very coarse.

Section 3 requires more force to break and the grain structure is somewhat finer.

Sections 4 and 5 have the greatest strength and resistance to shock. These sections have the finest grain structure.

Sections 6 to 8, where the metal was underheated, require greatest force to break, and bending occurs. It will be noted that the grain structure becomes coarser toward section 8. This section is the original structure of unheated steel (pearlite).

Courtesy Kostel Enterprises Ltd.

Fig. 17-19B   Tool steel overheated

Courtesy Kostel Enterprises Ltd.

Fig. 17-19C   Tool steel heated to proper temperature

Courtesy Kostel Enterprises Ltd.

Fig. 17-19D   Tool steel underheated

TEMPERING

Tempering is the process of heating a hardened carbon or alloy steel below its lower critical temperature and cooling it by quenching in a liquid or in air. This operation removes many of the stresses and strains set up when the metal was hardened. Tempering imparts toughness to the metal, but decreases the hardness and tensile strength. The tempering process modifies the structure of the martensite, changing it to *tempered martensite* which is somewhat softer and tougher than martensite. Tempered martensite was formerly known as *troostite* and *sorbite*.

The tempering and drawing temperature is not the same for each type of steel, and is affected by several factors:

a) the toughness required for the part
b) the hardness required for the part
c) the carbon content of the steel
d) the alloying elements present in the steel

The hardness obtained after tempering depends on the temperature used and the length of time the workpiece is held at this temperature. Generally, hardness decreases and the toughness increases as the temperature is increased (Fig. 17-20.)

As the length of the tempering time is increased for a specific part, the hardness of the metal decreases. On the other hand, if the tempering time is too short, the stresses and strains set up by hardening are not totally removed and the metal will be brittle. The cross-sectional size of the workpiece affects its tempering time. The tempering time and temperatures for various steels are always supplied in the steel manufacturer's handbook; these recommended times and temperatures should be followed to obtain the best results.

TEMPERING COLOURS

When a piece of steel is heated from room temperature to a red heat, it passes through several colour changes, caused by the oxidation of the metal. These

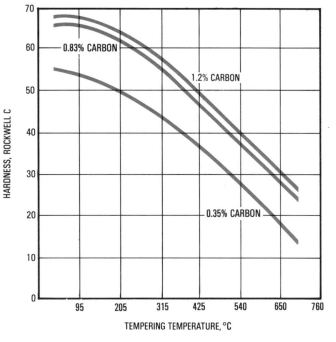

Fig. 17-20   Tempering temperatures

TABLE 17-3: TEMPERING COLOURS AND APPROXIMATE TEMPERATURES FOR CARBON STEEL

Colour	Celsius temperature	Use
Pale yellow	220°	Lathe tools, shaper tools.
Light straw	230°	Milling cutters, drills, reamers.
Dark straw	245°	Taps and dies.
Brown	255°	Scissors, shear blades.
Brownish purple	265°	Axes and wood chisels.
Purple	275°	Cold chisels, centre punches.
Bright blue	295°	Screw drivers, wrenches.
Dark blue	315°	Wood saws.

colour changes indicate the approximate temperature of the metal and are often used as a guide when tempering (Table 17-3).

ANNEALING

SPS

Annealing is a heat treating operation used to soften metal and to improve its ma-chinability. Annealing also relieves the internal stresses and strains caused by previous operations, such as forging or rolling.

Procedure

1. Set the pyrometer approximately 13°C above the upper critical temperature and start the furnace (Fig. 17-21A).
2. Place the part in the furnace. After the required temperature has been reached, allow it to soak for one hour per 25 mm of workpiece thickness.
3. Shut off the furnace and allow the part to cool slowly in the furnace; or re-move the part from the furnace and pack it immediately in lime or ashes.

NORMALIZING

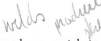

Normalizing is performed on metal to remove internal stresses and strains, and to improve its machinability.

Procedure

1. Set the pyrometer approximately 13°C above the upper critical temperature of the metal and start the furnace (Fig. 17-21A).
2. Place the part in the furnace. After the required temperature has been reached, allow the workpiece to soak for one hour per 25 mm of thickness.
3. Remove the part from the furnace and allow it to cool slowly in still air. Thin workpieces may cool too rapidly and may harden if normalized in air. It may be necessary to pack them in lime to retard the cooling rate.

SPHEROIDIZING

Spheroidizing is a process of heating metal for an extended period to just below the lower critical temperature. This process produces a special kind of grain structure whereby the cementite particles become spherical in shape. Spheroidizing is generally done on high carbon steel to im-prove the machinability.

take out hard spots

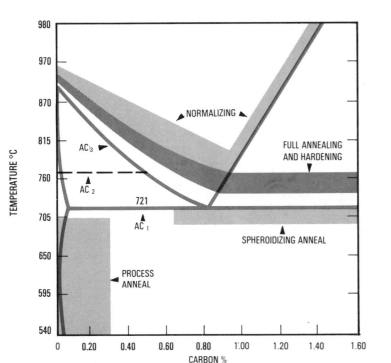

Fig. 17-21A Temperature ranges for various heat treating operations

CARBURIZING

Carburizing is a process whereby low carbon steel, when heated with some carbonaceous material, absorbs carbon into its outer surface. The depth of penetration depends on the time, the temperature, and the carburizing material used. Carburizing may be performed by three methods: pack carburizing, liquid carburizing, and gas carburizing.

Pack carburizing is generally used when a depth of penetration of 1.5 mm or more is required. The parts to be carburized are packed with a carbonaceous material such as activated charcoal in a sealed steel box.

Procedure

1. Place a 25 mm to 40 mm layer of carbonaceous material in the bottom of a steel box which will fit into the furnace.
2. Place the parts to be carburized in the box leaving about 40 mm between parts.
3. Pack the carburizer around the parts and cover the parts with about 40 mm of material.
4. Tap the sides of the box to settle the material and to pack it around the workpieces. This will exclude most of the air.
5. Place a metal cover over the box and seal around the joint with fireclay.
6. Place the box in the furnace and bring the temperature up to about 925°C.
7. Leave the box in the furnace long enough to give the required penetration. The rate of penetration is generally about 0.18 mm to 0.20 mm/h. However, the proper time (and temperature) for any depth of penetration is usually given in the literature supplied by the manufacturer of the carburizing material. (See Fig. 17-22).

Procedure

1. Set the pyrometer approximately 13°C below the lower critical temperature of the metal and start the furnace (Fig. 17-21).
2. Place the part in the furnace and allow it to soak for several hours at this temperature.
3. Shut down the furnace and let the part cool slowly to about 540°C.
4. Remove the part from the furnace and cool it in still air.

CASEHARDENING METHODS

When hardened parts are required, they may be made from carbon steel and heat treated to the specifications. Often these parts can be made more cheaply from machine steel and then casehardened. This process produces a hard outer case with a soft inner core, which is often preferable to through-hard parts made from carbon steel. Casehardening may be performed by several methods, such as carburizing, carbonitriding, and nitriding processes.

Fig. 17-21B A casehardened piece of machine steel

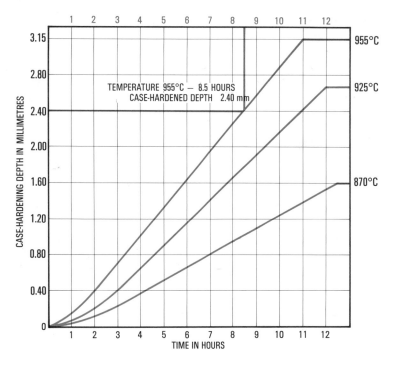

Fig. 17-22 Relationship between temperature and time to the depth of case

8. Shut down the furnace and leave the box in the furnace until it cools. This may take 12 to 16 hours.

9. Remove the box from the furnace and take out the parts and clean them. *NOTE*: The surfaces of the workpieces have now been transformed into a thin layer of carbon steel which is soft, due to the slow cooling of the parts in the carburizing material.

10. Heat the parts to the proper critical temperature in a furnace and quench in oil or water, depending on the shape of the parts and the hardness required. The parts are now surrounded with a hard layer of carbon steel and have a soft inner core.

Liquid carburizing is generally used to produce a thin layer of carbon steel on the outside of low-carbon steel parts. The parts are not usually machined after liquid carburization.

Procedure

1. Place the carburizing material into a pot furnace and heat until it becomes molten and reaches the recommended temperature.

2. Preheat the parts to be carburized to approximately 425°C in the low temperature drawing furnace. This eliminates the possibility of an explosion when the parts are immersed in the molten liquid.

3. Suspend the parts in the liquid carburizer and leave them for the time required to give the desired penetration. The depth of penetration (depending on the temperature of the liquid) may be from 0.40 mm to 0.50 mm for the first hour and about 0.25 mm for each succeeding hour.

4. Use dry tongs to remove the parts and quench immediately in water.

CAUTION:

Since most liquid carburizers contain cyanide, extreme care must be taken when using these materials.

1. Avoid letting *any moisture* come into contact with the liquid carburizer. This will cause an explosion.

2. Heat the jaws of the tongs before using to remove any moisture or oil.

3. Avoid inhaling the fumes; they are toxic.

4. Wear protective clothing (gloves, face and arm shields) when removing and quenching parts.

Gas carburizing, like pack carburizing, is used on parts where over 1.5 mm depth of case is required, and where it is necessary to machine the parts after carburizing. This method is generally done by specialized heat treating firms since it requires special types of furnaces.

The workpieces are heated to a carburizing temperature in a gas atmosphere. The parts are placed in a sealed drum into which natural gas or propane is introduced and circulated. The gas exhausts at one end of the drum and is burned to prevent air from entering the chamber. The exterior of the drum is heated by a source such as gas or oil. In this process the carbon from the gas is absorbed by the workpiece.

The parts remain in the drum for the time required to give the desired penetration. Depths of 0.50 mm to 0.75 mm are obtained in about four hours at a temperature of 925°C. The parts may then be removed and quenched or allowed to cool, after which they are reheated to the critical temperature and quenched.

CARBONITRIDING PROCESSES

Carbonitriding is a process whereby both carbon and nitrogen are absorbed by the surface of a steel workpiece when it is heated to the critical temperature to produce a hard, shallow outer case. Carbonitriding may be done by liquid or gas methods.

Cyaniding (liquid carbonitriding). This process uses a salt bath composed of cyanide-carbonate-chloride salts with varying amounts of cyanide, depending on the application. Liquid cyaniding is generally carried out in a pot-type furnace, and since cyanide fumes are poisonous, extreme care must be taken when using this method.

The parts are suspended in a liquid cyanide bath which must be at a temperature above the lower critical point of the steel being used. The depth of penetration when using this method is about 0.12 mm to 0.25 mm in one hour at 845°C. A depth of about 0.40 mm may be obtained in two hours at the same temperature. The parts may then be quenched in water or oil, depending on the steel being used. After the parts have been hardened, they should be thoroughly washed to remove all traces of the cyanide salt.

Carbonitriding (gas cyaniding) is carried out in a special furnace similar to the gas carburizing furnace. The workpieces are put into the inner drum of the furnace. A mixture of ammonia and a carburizing gas is introduced into and circulated through this chamber, which is heated externally to a temperature of 730°C to 925°C. During this process, the workpieces absorb carbon from the carburizing gas and nitrogen from the ammonia.

The parts are removed from the furnace and quenched in oil, which gives the part maximum hardness and minimum distortion. The depth of case produced by this method is relatively shallow. Depths of about 0.75 mm are obtained in four to five hours at a temperature of 925°C.

NITRIDING PROCESSES 100% better performance

Nitriding is used on certain alloy steels to provide maximum hardness. Most carbon alloy steels can only be hardened to about 62 Rockwell C by conventional means, whereas readings of 70 Rockwell C may be obtained on certain vanadium

production tools, more life!

and chromium alloy steels using a nitriding process. Nitriding may be done in a protected atmosphere furnace or in a salt bath. cutting tools - hand tap

Gas nitriding. The parts to be nitrided are placed in an airtight drum, which is heated externally to a temperature of 480°C to 620°C. Ammonia gas is circulated through the chamber. The ammonia, at this temperature, decomposes into nitrogen and hydrogen. The nitrogen penetrates the outer surface of the workpiece and combines with the alloying elements to form hard nitrides. Gas nitriding is a slow process requiring approximately 48 hours to obtain a case depth of 0.50 mm. Because of the low operating temperatures used in this process, and since no quenching of the part is required, there is little or no distortion. This method of increasing hardness is used on parts that have been hardened and ground. No further finishing is required on such parts.

Salt bath nitriding. Nitriding may also be carried out in a salt bath containing nitriding salts. The hardened part is suspended in the molten nitriding salt, which is held at a temperature from 480°C to 595°C depending on the application. Parts such as high-speed taps, drills, and reamers are often nitrided to increase surface hardness, which improves durability.

SURFACE HARDENING OF MEDIUM-CARBON STEELS

When selected areas of a part are to be surface hardened, to increase wear resistance and retain a soft inner core, the part must have a medium carbon content. It may be surface hardened by flame hardening or induction hardening, depending on the size of the part and its application. In both processes, the steel must contain carbon, since no external carbon is added as in other casehardening methods.

INDUCTION HARDENING

In this process, the part is surrounded by a coil through which a high frequency electrical current is passed. The current heats the surface of the steel to above the critical temperature in a few seconds. An automatic spray of water, oil, or compressed air is used to quench and harden the part, which is held in the same position as for heating. Since only the surface of the metal is heated, the hardness is localized at the surface. The depth of hardness is governed by the current frequency and heating cycle duration.

The current frequencies vary from 1 kHz to 2 MHz. Higher frequencies produce shallow hardening depths. Lower frequencies produce hardening depths up to 6 mm.

Induction hardening may be used for the selective hardening of gear teeth, splines, crank shafts, camshafts, and connecting rods.

FLAME HARDENING

Flame hardening is used extensively to harden ways on lathes and other machine tools, as well as gear teeth, splines, crank shafts, etc.

The surface of the metal is heated very rapidly to above the critical temperature and is hardened quickly by a quenching spray. Large surfaces such as lathe ways are heated by a special oxy-acetylene torch which is moved automatically along the surface, followed by a quenching spray. Smaller parts are placed under the flame, and spray quenched automatically.

Flame-hardened parts should be tempered immediately. Large surfaces are tempered by a special low tempering torch which follows the quenching nozzle as it moves along the work. The depth of flame hardening varies from 1.6 mm to 6.4 mm, depending on the speed at which the surface is brought up to the critical temperature.

TESTING OF METALS

After heat treating, certain tests may be performed to determine the properties of the metal. These tests fall into two categories:

a) *non-destructive testing*, whereby the test may be performed without damaging the sample

b) *destructive testing*, whereby a sample of the material is broken to determine the qualities of the metal

HARDNESS TESTING

This is the most common form of non-destructive testing, and is used to determine the hardness of a metal. Hardness in steel may be defined as its capacity to resist wear and deformation. The term hardness applied to metal is relative, and indicates some of its properties. For example, if a piece of steel is hardened, the tensile strength increases, but the ductility of the steel is reduced. If the hardness of a metal is known, the properties and performance of the metal can be predicted accurately.

Two types of testing machines are used to measure the hardness of a metal.

a) Those which measure the depth of penetration made by a penetrator under a known load. Rockwell, Brinell, and Vickers hardness testers are examples of this type.

b) Those which measure the height of rebound of a small mass dropped from a known height. The scleroscope employs this principle.

ROCKWELL HARDNESS TESTER

The Rockwell hardness tester (Fig. 17-23) indicates the hardness value by the depth that a penetrator advances into the metal under a known pressure. When testing hard materials, a 120° conical diamond penetrator (brale) is used. A 1.6 mm (or 1/16 in.) diameter ball is used as a penetrator for soft materials (Fig. 17-24A).

Rockwell hardness numbers are designated by various letters and numbers. The scales are indicated by the letters A, B, C, and D. The C-scale, which is the outside scale on the dial, is used in conjunction with the 120° diamond penetrator and a 150 kg major load for testing hardened metals. The B-scale, or the red inner scale, is read when the 1.6 mm (or 1/16 in.) ball penetrator is used along with the 100 kg load for testing soft metals. The other letters A and D are special scales and are not used as often as the B and C scales. Rockwell superficial hardness scales are used when testing the hardness of thin materials and casehardened parts.

To Perform a Rockwell C Hardness Test

Although the various makes of Rockwell-type testers may differ slightly in construction, they all operate on the same principle.

1. Select the proper penetrator for the material to be tested. Use a 120° diamond for hardened materials. Use a 1.6 mm (or 1/16 in.) ball for soft steel, cast iron, and non-ferrous metals.

2. Mount the proper anvil for the shape of the part being tested.

3. Remove the scale or oxidation from the surface on which the test is to be made. Usually an area of about 12 mm diameter is sufficient.

4. Place the workpiece on the anvil and apply the minor load (10 kg) by turning the handwheel until the small needle is in line with the red dot on the dial.

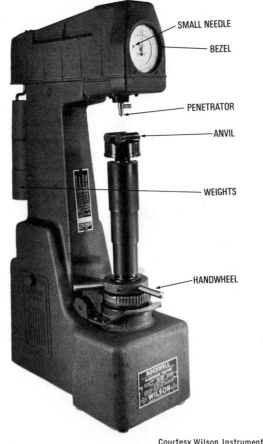

SMALL NEEDLE
BEZEL
PENETRATOR
ANVIL
WEIGHTS
HANDWHEEL

Courtesy Wilson Instrument Division, American Chain and Cable Company

Fig. 17-23   Rockwell hardness tester showing various anvils

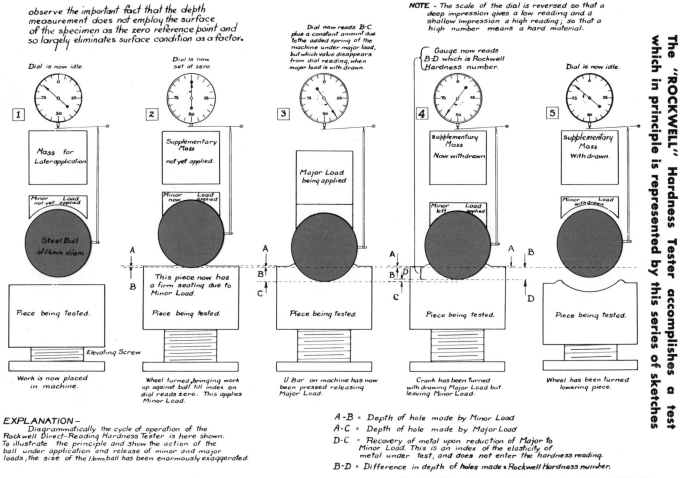

observe the important fact that the depth measurement does not employ the surface of the specimen as the zero reference point and so largely eliminates surface condition as a factor.

NOTE - The scale of the dial is reversed so that a deep impression gives a low reading and a shallow impression a high reading; so that a high number means a hard material.

The "ROCKWELL" Hardness Tester accomplishes a test which in principle is represented by this series of sketches

Dial is now idle.

1

Mass for Later application

Minor Load not yet applied

Steel Ball of 1.6mm diam.

Piece being tested.

Elevating Screw

Work is now placed in machine.

Dial is now set at zero

2

Supplementary Mass not yet applied.

Minor Load now applied

A

B

This piece now has a firm seating due to Minor Load.

Piece being tested.

Wheel turned, bringing work up against ball till index on dial reads zero. This applies Minor Load.

Dial now reads B-C plus a constant amount due to the added spring of the machine under major load, but which value disappears from dial reading, when major load is with drawn.

3

Major Load being applied

A
B
C

Piece being tested.

U Bar on machine has now been pressed releasing Major Load.

Gauge now reads B-D which is Rockwell Hardness number.

4

supplementary Mass Now withdrawn

Minor Load left applied

A   B
B   D
C

D

Piece being tested.

Crank has been turned withdrawing Major Load but leaving Minor Load.

Dial is now idle.

5

supplementary Mass Withdrawn.

Minor Load withdrawn

A   B

D

Piece being tested.

Wheel has been turned lowering piece.

EXPLANATION –
Diagrammatically the cycle of operation of the Rockwell Direct-Reading Hardness Tester is here shown. To illustrate the principle and show the action of the ball under application and release of minor and major loads, the size of the 1.6mm ball has been enormously exaggerated.

A–B = Depth of hole made by Minor Load
A–C = Depth of hole made by Major Load
D–C = Recovery of metal upon reduction of Major to Minor Load. This is an index of the elasticity of metal under test, and does not enter the hardness reading.
B–D = Difference in depth of holes made = Rockwell Hardness number.

Courtesy Wilson Instrument Division, American Chain and Cable Company

Fig. 17-24A   Operating principle of a Rockwell hardness tester—steel ball type

5. Adjust the bezel (outer dial) to zero.
6. Apply the major load (150 kg).
7. After the large hand stops, remove the major load.
8. When the hand ceases to move backwards, note the hardness reading on the C-scale (black). This reading indicates the difference in penetration of the brale between the minor and major loads (Fig. 17-24B).
9. Release the minor load and remove the specimen.

NOTE: For accurate results, two or three readings should be taken and averaged. If either the brale or the anvil has been removed and replaced, a "dummy run" should be made to properly seat these parts before performing a test. A test piece of known hardness should be tested occasionally to check the accuracy of the instrument.

BRINELL HARDNESS TESTER

The Brinell hardness tester is operated by pressing a 10 mm hardened steel ball under a load of 3000 kg into the surface of the specimen and measuring the diameter of the impression with a microscope. When the diameter of the impression and the applied load is known, the Brinell hardness number (BHN) can be obtained from Brinell hardness tables. The Brinell hardness value is determined by dividing the area of the impression (in square millimeters) by the load in kilograms which was applied to the penetrator.

A standard load of 500 kg is used for testing non-ferrous metals. The impression made in softer metals is larger and the Brinell hardness number is lower.

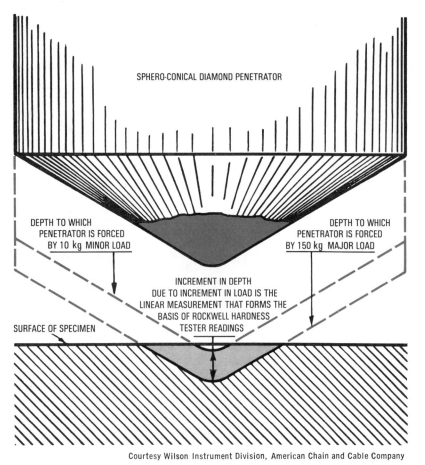

SPHERO-CONICAL DIAMOND PENETRATOR

DEPTH TO WHICH PENETRATOR IS FORCED BY 10 kg MINOR LOAD

DEPTH TO WHICH PENETRATOR IS FORCED BY 150 kg MAJOR LOAD

INCREMENT IN DEPTH DUE TO INCREMENT IN LOAD IS THE LINEAR MEASUREMENT THAT FORMS THE BASIS OF ROCKWELL HARDNESS TESTER READINGS

SURFACE OF SPECIMEN

Courtesy Wilson Instrument Division, American Chain and Cable Company

Fig. 17-24B   Operating principle of a Rockwell hardness tester—diamond cone type

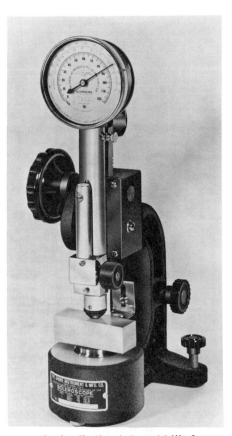

Courtesy The Shore Instrument & Mfg. Company

Fig. 17-25B   Dial recording scleroscope

SCLEROSCOPE HARDNESS TESTER

The scleroscope hardness tester is operated on the principle that a small diamond tipped hammer, when dropped from a fixed height, will rebound higher from a hard surface than from a softer one. The height of the rebound is converted to a hardness reading.

Scleroscopes are available in several models. On some models, the hardness reading is taken directly from the vertical barrel or tube (Fig. 17-25A). On others, the hardness numbers are marked on the dial (Fig. 17-25B). These models may also show the corresponding Brinell and Rockwell numbers.

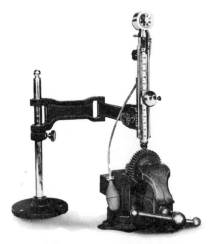

Courtesy The Shore Instrument & Mfg. Company

Fig. 17-25A   Vertical scale scleroscope

DESTRUCTIVE TESTING

There is a close relationship between the various properties of a metal; for example, the tensile strength of a metal increases as the hardness increases, and the ductility decreases as the hardness increases. Thus the tensile strength of a metal may be determined with reasonable accuracy if the hardness and the composition of the metal are known. A more accurate method of determining the tensile strength of a material is that of tensile testing. The tensile strength, or the maximum amount of pull (force) that a material can withstand before breaking, is determined on a tensile testing machine (Fig. 17-26).

A sample of the metal is pulled or stretched in a machine until the metal

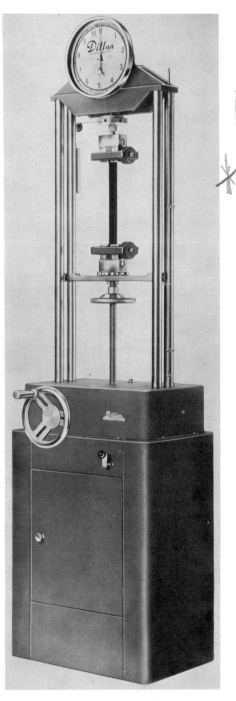

Courtesy W. C. Dillon & Co. Inc.

Fig. 17-26 A tensile testing machine

fractures. This test indicates not only the tensile strength, but also the elastic limit, the yield point, the percentage of area reduction, and the percentage of elongation of the material.

Tensile Testing Using Inch Equipment

The tensile strength of a material is expressed in terms of pounds per square inch and is calculated as follows:

Tensile strength

$$= \frac{\text{load in pounds}}{\text{area in square inches}}$$

Machines capable of extremely high tension loads are required to test a steel sample having a cross-sectional area of 1 square inch. For this reason, most samples are reduced to a definite cross-sectional area which can be used conveniently in calculating the tensile strength. For example, most samples are machined to .505 diameter (Fig. 17-27A) which is .2 square inches. Smaller tensile testing machines use a sample that has been machined to .251 diameter (Fig. 17-27B) which is an area of 1/20 square inch.

The tensile strength of these samples is as follows:

smooth!

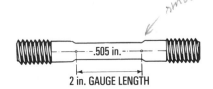

Fig. 17-27A Test sample .505 in. diameter

2 in. GAUGE LENGTH

blended radius or premature failure

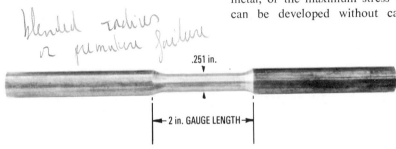

Fig. 17-27B Test sample .251 in. diameter

Load 10 000 pounds using .505 diameter sample (.2 square inch)

$$\text{Tensile strength} = \frac{10\ 000}{.2}$$
$$= 50\ 000 \text{ pounds per square inch (psi)}$$

Load 3 000 pounds using .251 diameter sample (1/20 square inch)

$$\text{Tensile strength} = \frac{3\ 000}{1/20}$$
$$= 60\ 000 \text{ pounds per square inch (psi)}$$

To Determine the Tensile Strength of Steel

1. Turn a sample of the steel to be tested to the dimensions shown in Fig. 17-27, and place on it two centre punch marks exactly 2 in. apart.
2. Mount the specimen in the machine (Fig. 17-28A), and make sure that the jaws grip the sample properly by jogging the motor switch until the black needle just starts to move. Remove any tension by reversing the motor.
3. Turn the red hand back until it bears against the black hand on the dial.
4. Set a pair of dividers to the centre punch marks on the sample (2 in.).
5. Start the machine and apply the load to the specimen.
6. Observe and record the readings at which there are any changes in the uniform movement of the needle.
   NOTE: At this time it is possible to determine the elastic limit of the metal, or the maximum stress which can be developed without causing

Fig. 17-28A   Specimen mounted ready for testing

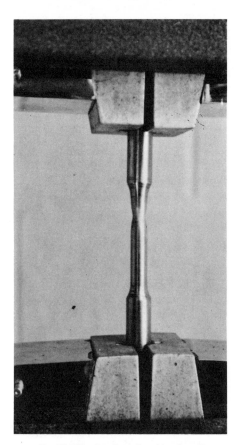

Fig. 17-28B   Specimen "necking down"

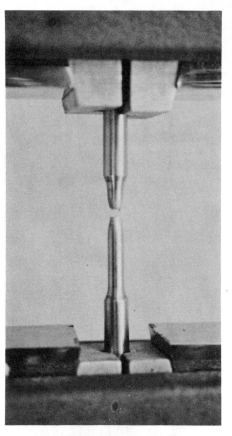

Fig. 17-28C   Fractured specimen

permanent deformation. This is done by checking the distance between the two centre punch marks with the pre-set dividers. Increased loads must be applied to the specimen and removed several times. After each load has been removed check that the distance between the centre punch marks remains at 2 in. When this distance increases even slightly, the elastic limit of the metal has been reached. An *extensometer* may also be used to indicate the elastic limit.

7. Continue to exert the pull on the sample until it "necks down" (Fig. 17-28B) and finally breaks (Fig. 17-28C). From this procedure, several properties of the metal may be determined (Fig. 17-29).

8. Remove the sample pieces, place the broken ends together and clamp them in this position.

9. Measure the distance between the centre punch marks to determine the amount of elongation.

10. Measure the diameter of the specimen at the break to determine the reduction in diameter.

OBSERVATIONS (refer to Fig. 17-29)

a) The needle continued to move uniformly until about 3 600 pounds showed on the scale, after which it slowed down slightly. The point at which it began to slow down indicated the *proportional limit*. It is here that

the metal reached its *elastic limit* and no longer returned to its original size or shape. At this point, the stress and strain were no longer proportional and the curve changed.

The *yield point* was reached just beyond the proportional limit and here the metal started to stretch or yield; the strain increased without a corresponding stress increase.

b) The needle continued to move slowly up to about 6 300 pounds and then it remained stationary.

c) After a short time, the metal began to show a reduction in diameter (necking down) at which time the needle began to show a rapid drop. The highest travel of the needle indicated the *ultimate strength* or the *tensile strength*

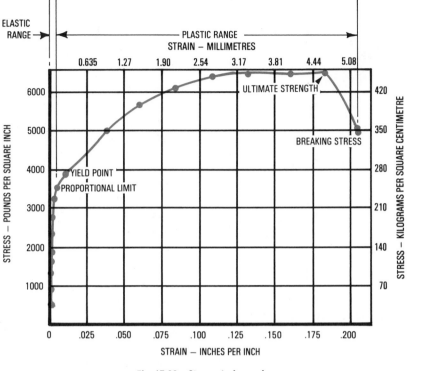

Fig. 17-29   Stress-strain graph

of the metal. This was the maximum pull to which a metal may be subjected before breaking.

d) The needle continued to move backwards (leaving the red hand stationary) and suddenly the metal broke at the point where it had "necked down." The point at which it broke is known as the *breaking stress*.

e) The position of the red hand was at 6 300 pounds. This indicated the load required to break a cross-sectional area of 1/20 in. The ultimate strength of the metal or the tensile strength was 6 300 × 20 = 126 000 pounds.

f) When the pieces were placed back together, clamped, and measured, the distance between the centre punch marks was about 2.185 in. This was an elongation of about 9%.

g) When the diameter of the metal at the fracture was measured, it was found

to be .170 in. This indicated a reduction in area of .080 in. or about 32%.

Tensile Testing Using Metric Equipment

Metric tensile testers are graduated in kilograms per square centimetre and the cross-sectional area of the sample is calculated in square centimetres or square millimetres. Metric extensometers are graduated in millimetres.

The calculations involved in determining the tensile strength, percentage elongation, and area of reduction are the same as for inch calculations.

Although not the accepted SI unit of pressure, most metric tensile testing machines available and in use at the time of publication were graduated in kg/cm². For conversion to kilopascals, use the formula $1 \text{ kg/cm}^2 = 95.01 \text{ kPa}$.

Example

A sample piece is 1.3 cm in diameter. The

ultimate pull exerted on it during a tensile test was 4650 kg. What was the tensile strength of this metal?

Tensile strength (kg/cm²)

$$= \frac{\text{Load in kilograms}}{\text{Area in square centimentres}}$$

$$= \frac{4650}{1.327}$$

$$= 3504 \text{ kg/cm}^2$$

Percentage of Elongation

If the punch marks were 50 mm apart at the start of the pull and 54 mm after the sample was broken, what was the percentage elongation?

% elongation

$$= \frac{\text{amount of elongation}}{\text{original length}} \times 100\%$$

$$= \frac{4}{50} \times 100\%$$

$$= 8\%$$

Percentage Reduction of Area

The original diameter was 1.3 cm and after breaking, the diameter was 0.95 cm. What was the percentage of area of reduction?

$$\text{Amount of reduction} = 1.3 - 0.95$$

$$= 0.35 \text{ cm}$$

$$\% \text{ of reduction} = \frac{0.35}{1.3} \times 100\%$$

$$= 27\%$$

IMPACT TESTS

The toughness of a metal, or its ability to withstand a sudden shock or impact, may be measured by the *Charpy impact test* or the *Izod test*.

In both tests a 10 mm square specimen is used which may be notched or grooved, depending on the test used.

Both tests use a swinging pendulum of a fixed mass, which is raised to a standard height, depending on the type of specimen. The pendulum is released and as it swings through an arc, it strikes the specimen in the pendulum's path.

In the Charpy test (Fig. 17-30), the specimen is mounted in a fixture and supported at both ends. The V or notch is placed on the side opposite to the direction of the pendulum's swing. When the pendulum is released, the knife-edge strikes the sample in the centre, reducing the travel of the pendulum. The difference in height of the pendulum at the beginning and end of the stroke is shown on the gauge and this indicates the amount of energy used to fracture the specimen.

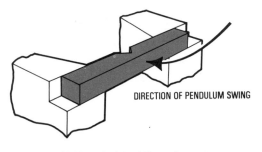

DIRECTION OF PENDULUM SWING

Fig. 17-30   Principle of Charpy impact test

The Izod test (Fig. 17-31) is similar in principle to the Charpy test. One end of the work is gripped in a clamp with the notched side toward the direction of the pendulum's swing. The amount of energy required to break the specimen is recorded on the scale.

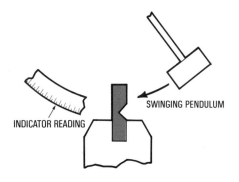

INDICATOR READING

SWINGING PENDULUM

Fig. 17-31   Principle of Izod impact test

Courtesy Ametek Testing Equipment

Fig. 17-32   Impact testing machine

NON-FERROUS METALS AND ALLOYS

Nonferrous metals, as the name implies, contain little or no iron and are generally nonmagnetic. Since all pure non-ferrous metals do not offer the qualities required for industrial applications, they are often combined to produce alloys having the desired qualities for a particular job. The most widely used non-ferrous metals for industrial use are aluminum, copper, lead, magnesium, nickel, tin, and zinc.

ALUMINUM

Aluminum is a light, soft, white metal produced from bauxite ore. It is resistant to atmospheric corrosion and is a good conductor of electricity and heat. It is malleable and ductile, and can easily be machined, forged, rolled, and extruded. It has a low melting point of about 660°C and can be cast easily. It is used extensively in transportation vehicles of all types, the construction industry, transmission line, cooking utensils, and hardware.

Aluminum is not generally used in a pure state, since it is too soft and weak. It is alloyed with other metals to form strong alloys used extensively in industry.

ALUMINUM BASE ALLOYS

Duralumin, an alloy of 95% aluminum and 4% copper, 0.05% manganese, and 0.05% magnesium, is widely used in the aircraft and transportation industries. This is a natural-aging alloy, i.e., it hardens as it ages. Due to this peculiarity, duralumin must be kept at a sub-zero temperature until ready for use. When it is brought to room temperature, the hardening process begins.

Other alloys contain varying amounts of copper, magnesium, and manganese.

Aluminum-Manganese alloys have good formability, good resistance to corrosion, and good weldability. These alloys are used for utensils, gasoline and oil tanks, pressure vessels, and piping.

Aluminum-Silicon alloys are easily forged and cast. They are used for forged automotive pistons, intricate castings, and marine fittings.

Aluminum-Magnesium alloys have good corrosion resistance and moderate strength. They are used for architectural extrusions, automotive gas and oil lines.

Aluminum-Silicon Magnesium alloys have excellent corrosion resistance, are heat treatable, and are easily worked and cast. They are used for small boats, furniture, bridge railings, and architectural applications.

Aluminum-Zinc alloys contain zinc, magnesium, and copper with smaller amounts of manganese and chromium. They have high tensile strength, good corrosion resistance, and may be heat treated. They are used for aircraft structural parts when great strength is required.

COPPER

Copper is a heavy, soft, reddish-coloured metal refined from copper ore (copper sulphide). It has high electrical and thermal conductivity, good corrosion resistance, strength, and is easily welded, brazed, or soldered. It is very ductile and is easily drawn into wire and tubing. Since copper work-hardens readily, it must be heated at about 650°C and quenched in water to anneal.

Because of its softness, copper does not machine well. The long chips produced in drilling and tapping tend to clog the flutes of the cutting tool and must be cleared frequently. Sawing and milling operations require cutters with good chip clearance. Coolant should be used to minimize heat and aid the cutting action.

COPPER BASE ALLOYS

Brass, an alloy of copper and zinc, has good corrosion resistance, and is easily formed, machined, and cast. There are several forms of brass. *Alpha* brasses containing up to 36% zinc are suitable for cold working. *Alpha + beta* brasses containing 54% to 62% copper are used in hot working of this alloy. Small amounts of tin or antimony are added to alpha brasses to minimize the pitting effect of salt water on this alloy.

Brass alloys are used for water and gasoline line fittings, tubing, tanks, radiator cores, and rivets.

Bronze, the term which originally referred to an alloy of copper and tin, has now been extended to include all alloys except copper-zinc alloys, which contain up to 12% of the principal alloying element.

Phospor-Bronze contains about 90% copper, 10% tin and a very small amount of phosphorus, which acts as a hardener. This metal has high strength, toughness, and corrosion-resistance, and is used for lock washers, cotter pins, springs, and clutch discs.

Silicon-Bronze (a copper-silicon alloy) contains less than 5% silicon and is the strongest of the work-hardenable copper alloys. It has the mechanical properties of mild steel and the corrosion resistance of copper. It is used for tanks, pressure vessels, and hydraulic pressure lines.

Aluminum-Bronze (a copper-aluminum alloy) contains between 4% and 11% aluminum. Other elements such as iron, nickel, manganese, and silicon are added to aluminum bronzes. Iron (up to 5%) increases the strength and refines the grain. Nickel, when added (up to 5%), has similar effects to iron. Silicon (up to 2%) improves machinability. Manganese promotes soundness in casting.

Aluminum-bronzes have good corrosion resistance and strength, and are used for condenser tubes, pressure vessels, nuts, and bolts.

Beryllium-Bronze (copper and beryllium), containing up to about 2% beryllium, is easily formed in the annealed condition. It has high tensile strength and fatigue strength in the hardened condition. Beryllium-bronze is used for surgical instruments, bolts, nuts, and screws.

LEAD

Lead is a soft, heavy metal, has a bright, silvery colour when freshly cut, but turns grey quickly when exposed to air. It has a low melting point, low strength, low electrical conductivity, and high corrosion resistance. It is used extensively in the chemical and plumbing industries. Lead is also added to bronzes, brasses, and mild steel to improve the machinability of these metals.

LEAD ALLOYS

Antimony and *tin* are the most common alloying elements of lead. *Antimony* when added to lead (up to 14%) increases its strength and hardness. This alloy is used for battery plates and cable-sheathing.

The most common lead-tin alloy is solder, which may be composed of 40% tin and 60% lead, or 50% of each. Antimony is sometimes added as a hardener.

Lead-tin-antimony alloys are used as type metals in the printing industry.

MAGNESIUM

Magnesium is a light-weight element which, when alloyed, produces a light, strong metal used extensively in the aircraft and missile industries. Magnesium plates are used to prevent corrosion by salt water in underwater fittings on ship hulls. Magnesium rods, when inserted in galvanized domestic water tanks, will prolong the life of the tank. Other uses for this metal are in photographic flash bulbs and thermite bombs.

NICKEL

Nickel, a whitish metal, is noted for its resistance to corrosion and oxidation. It is used extensively for electroplating, but its most important application is in the manufacture of stainless and alloy steels.

NICKEL ALLOYS

Nickel-Chromium-Iron base alloys (containing about 60% nickel, 16% chromium, and 24% iron) are widely used for electric heating elements in toasters, percolators, and water heaters.

Monel metal containing about 60% nickel, 38% copper and small amounts of manganese or aluminum, is a tough, ductile metal with good machining qualities. It is corrosion-resistant, nonmagnetic, and is used in valve seats, chemical marine pumps, and in nonmagnetic aircraft parts.

Hasteloy, containing about 87% nickel, 10% silicon, and 3% copper, is widely used in the chemical industry because of its non-corrosive qualities.

Inconel, a strong, tough alloy, containing about 76% nickel, 16% chromium, and

8% iron, is used in food processing equipment, milk pasteurizers, exhaust manifolds for aircraft, and in heat treating furnaces and equipment.

TIN

Pure tin has a silvery-white appearance, good corrosion resistance, and melts at about 230°C. It is used as a coating on other metals, such as iron, to form tin plate.

TIN ALLOYS

As already mentioned, tin when alloyed with lead forms solder.

Babbitt is an alloy containing tin, lead, and copper.

Pewter, another tin base alloy, is composed of 92% tin and 8% antimony and copper.

ZINC

Zinc is a coarse, crystalline, brittle metal used mainly for die casting alloys and as a coating for sheet steel, chain, wire, screws and piping. Zinc alloys, containing approximately 90% to 95% zinc, 5% aluminum, and small amounts of copper or magnesium, are widely used in the die casting field to produce automotive parts, building hardware, padlocks, and toys.

BEARING METALS

Bearing metals may be divided into two groups: leaded bronzes and babbitt.

LEADED BRONZES

The composition of bronze bearings varies according to their use. Bearings used to support heavy loads contain about 80% copper, 10% tin, and 10% lead. For lighter loads and faster speeds, the lead content is increased. A typical bearing of this type might contain 70% copper, 5% tin, and 25% lead.

BABBITT

Babbitt bearing materials may be divided into two groups: lead base and tin base.

Lead-base babbitt may contain 75% lead, 10% tin, and 15% antimony, depending upon the application. A small amount of arsenic is often added to permit the bearing to carry heavier loads. Applications of lead-base babbitt bearings are in automotive connecting rods, main and crankshaft bearings, and diesel engine bearings.

Tin-base babbitt may contain up to 90% tin with copper and antimony added, to 65% tin, 15% antimony, 2% copper, and 18% lead. Since tin has become less plentiful, tin-base babbitts are used in high grade bearing applications such as steam turbines.

METALLURGY QUESTIONS

1. What effect has the study of metals had on modern living?

PHYSICAL PROPERTIES OF METALS

2. Compare hardness, brittleness, and toughness.

MANUFACTURING OF PIG IRON

3. Briefly describe the manufacture of pig iron.

MANUFACTURING OF CAST IRON

4. Explain how cast iron is manufactured.
5. Name four types of cast iron and state one purpose for each.

THE OPEN HEARTH PROCESS

6. What is the purpose of the checkers in an open hearth furnace?
7. How are the impurities removed from the molten metal in an open hearth furnace?
8. What modification has been made to most open hearth furnaces and what has been its result?

THE BESSEMER PROCESS AND THE BASIC OXYGEN PROCESS

9. What are the chief differences between the Bessemer and the Basic Oxygen Process?
10. Briefly describe the Basic Oxygen Process.

THE CHEMICAL COMPOSITION OF STEEL

11. What effect does carbon in excess of 0.83% have on the steel?
12. What is the purpose of adding small quantities of manganese to steel?
13. What effect will the addition of larger quantities of manganese (1.5 to 2.0%) have on steel?
14. Why is phosphorus considered an undesirable element in steel?
15. How will steel be affected by the addition of silicon
    a) in small amounts?
    b) in large amounts?
16. Why is sulphur considered an undesirable element in steel?
17. Why are sulphur and phosphorus sometimes added to steel?

CLASSIFICATION OF STEEL

18. State the carbon content of and two uses for:
    a) low carbon steel
    b) high carbon steel
19. List six properties that alloying elements may impart to steel.

HEAT TREATING EQUIPMENT

20. Describe a thermocouple and explain how it functions.
21. Sketch a furnace installation showing the furnace, thermocouple, and pyrometer.
22. What is the purpose of:
    a) the pyrometer?
    b) the solenoid valve?
    c) the air switch?

HEAT TREATMENT TERMS

23. What is the difference between the decalescence point and the recalescence point of a piece of steel?
24. At what point in relation to the upper and lower critical temperatures are the following heat treating operations performed?
    a) hardening   d) normalizing
    b) tempering   e) spheroidizing
    c) annealing
25. What is the difference between hypereutectoid and hypoeutectoid steel?

WATER HARDENING TOOL STEEL

26. State two problems which often occur with water hardening steel.

OIL HARDENING TOOL STEEL

27. Why is oil used to advantage as a quenching medium?

AIR HARDENING STEELS

28. What are the advantages of air hardening steels?
29. What elements will give red hardness quality to a high speed steel toolbit?
30. Explain the difference in the hardening procedures between plain-carbon steel and high-speed steel.

THE SAE AND AISI AND CLASSIFICATION SYSTEMS

31. How does the AISI system differ from the SAE system of identifying steel?
32. What is the composition of the following steels?
    a) 2340
    b) 1020
    c) E4340

HEAT TREATMENT OF CARBON STEEL

33. Explain how the critical points of water are determined.
34. List five changes that take place in steel when it is heated to (and above) the decalescence point from room temperature.

35. Describe the changes that take place in a piece of steel when it is cooled to the recalescence point from the upper critical temperature.

HARDENING OF 0.83% CARBON STEEL

36. What is the advantage of using hypereutecoid steel?
37. To what temperature should steel be heated prior to quenching, in order to produce the best results?

QUENCHING

38. Name two quenching media and state the purpose of each.
39. Describe the proper method of quenching long, thin workpieces.

TEMPERING

40. What is the purpose of tempering a piece of steel?
41. What factors will affect the temperature at which a piece of steel is tempered?
42. What will happen to the steel if the tempering time is
    a) too long?
    b) too short?

ANNEALING, NORMALIZING, SPHEROIDIZING

43. What is the difference between annealing, normalizing, and spheroidizing?

CARBURIZING

44. Describe briefly how pack carburizing is performed.
45. What precautions should be observed when using the liquid carburizing process?
46. Describe the gas carburizing process.

CARBONITRIDING PROCESSES

47. Explain the difference between the carburizing and the carbonitriding processes.

48. Draw a chart to compare all case hardening methods. List the methods vertically in the left-hand column and use the following headings for the other columns: Depth of penetration, Temperature, Time, Casehardening Medium used, Advantages.

SURFACE HARDENING OF CARBON STEELS

49. What type of steel must be used for the flame hardening and induction hardening processes?

INDUCTION HARDENING

50. Describe briefly the induction hardening principle.

FLAME HARDENING

51. Why is it desirable to temper parts immediately after flame hardening?
52. How may this be done on large surfaces?

TESTING OF METALS

53. Explain the difference between nondestructive and destructive testing.
54. What information can be determined by hardness testing?

ROCKWELL HARDNESS TESTER

55. Name two scales which are found on a Rockwell-type hardness tester and state the penetrator used in each case.
56. Briefly describe how a Rockwell C hardness test is performed.

BRINELL HARDNESS TESTER

57. Compare the principles of the Brinell hardness tester and the Rockwell hardness tester.

SCLEROSCOPE

58. Describe the principle of the scleroscope.

DESTRUCTIVE TESTING

59. What effect does hardening have on the tensile strength and ductility of a metal?
60. Explain the principle of tensile testing.
61. What other properties may be determined by a tensile test?
62. How is the tensile strength of a metal calculated?
63. Explain the procedure for performing a tensile test.
64. How may the elastic limit of a metal be determined?
65. Define: proportional limit, yield point, ultimate strength, breaking stress.
66. a) A sample piece of steel has a diameter of 1.25 cm. The ultimate pull exerted in the test was 4600 kg. What was the tensile strength of the metal?
    b) The centre punch marks, originally 5 cm apart, were 5.6 cm apart after the break occurred. What was the percentage elongation?
    c) If the diameter after breaking was 0.92 cm, what was the percentage reduction in area?
67. Describe the principle of impact testing.

NONFERROUS METALS AND ALLOYS

68. Define a nonferrous metal.
69. Name four nonferrous metals commonly used as base metals in alloys.
70. Name four aluminum-base alloys and state one application of each.
71. Name two types of brasses and state the composition of each.
72. What is the difference between brass and bronze alloys?
73. Why is lead added to steel?
74. Where are magnesium alloys used extensively?
75. Name three nickel-base alloys and state two applications of each.
76. Name two tin-base alloys.
77. For what purpose are zinc alloys used extensively?
78. What are the three metals used for bearing alloys?
79. What is the basic difference between bronze and babbitt?
80. Explain the use of the following:
    a) lead-base babbitt
    b) tin-base babbitt

18 HYDRAULICS

A hydraulic system is a method of transmitting force or motion by applying pressure on a confined liquid. It can be used to substitute liquid linkage between moving parts for mechanical linkages such as shafts, gears, connecting rods, etc. The science of hydraulics dates back several thousand years when dams, sluice gates, and waterwheels were used to control water flow for domestic use and irrigation purposes.

Hydraulic power is used in nearly every phase of industry. Machine tools, cars, airplanes, jacks, missiles, and boats are only a few of the areas where hydraulics is applied. Hydraulic systems, because of their extreme versatility, are adaptable to almost every type of machine tool. They are generally used to provide reciprocating motions of feed mechanisms. In some cases, where the distance of travel would require a long cylinder, *rotary hydrostatic motors* may be used to provide a drive for a rack and pinion.

The wide acceptance of hydraulic applications in the machine tool industry is due to the following characteristics of fluids.

a) A fluid is one of the most versatile means of transmitting power and modifying motion.

b) A fluid is infinitely flexible, yet as unyielding as steel, due to its incompressibility.

c) It adjusts readily to changes in diameter and shape.

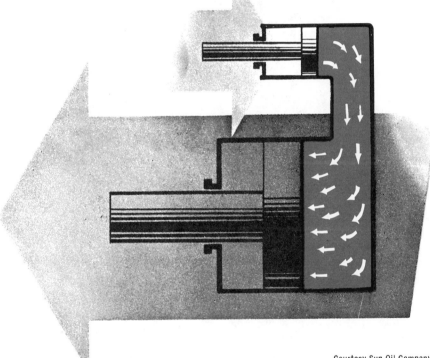

Courtesy Sun Oil Company

d) It can be divided to perform work in different areas simultaneously. The hydraulic brake system in an automobile is an example of this.

No other medium combines the same degree of accuracy, positiveness and flexibility of control, with the ability to transmit a maximum of motion in a minimum of bulk and mass. Oil is the fluid most frequently used in hydraulic systems, because it has all these characteristics. Oil also lubricates and gives anticorrosion properties to the mechanical parts of the system.

FUNDAMENTAL HYDRAULIC CIRCUIT

All hydraulic systems are basically simple, with six essential elements (Fig. 18-1).

a) A reservoir for the oil supply.

427

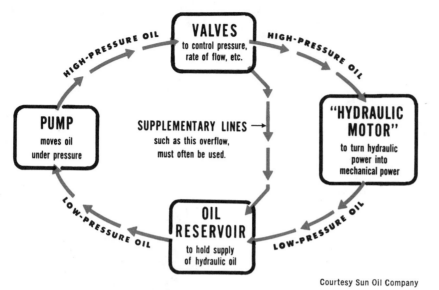

Fig. 18-1   A fundamental hydraulic circuit

f) Relief valves prevent overloads which may cause extensive damage.

g) Power costs and friction losses can be held to a minimum.

h) All moving parts in the system are constantly lubricated by the hydraulic oil.

i) The operation of a hydraulic system is comparatively quiet.

j) Rapid reversals at the end of each reciprocating stroke, such as on a shaper or surface grinder, are cushioned (smooth and shockless).

k) Component parts can be located close to the moving members because the power is transmitted through pipes which can run in any direction.

l) Intricate operations can be made almost completely automatic.

b) A pump to move the oil under pressure.

c) One or more control valves to regulate the flow.

d) A piston and cylinder (hydraulic motor) to convert hydraulic power into mechanical power.

e) Pipe or tubing to connect the various parts.

f) Hydraulic fluid, which is the "life blood" of the system.

There is no such thing as an all-hydraulic system. At certain points in any hydraulic circuit, mechanical devices must be used to control the fluid. A hydraulic system is a collection of mechanical elements joined together by *fluid connecting rods* and in many cases by *fluid levers*.

ADVANTAGES OF HYDRAULIC SYSTEMS

The development of suitable hydraulic oils and the precision tolerances maintained by manufacturers have led to the wide use of hydraulics in machine tool manufacture. The reason for this widespread use is that hydraulic power transmission offers many advantages.

a) A complex combination of cams, gears, levers, etc., can often be re-

placed by a simpler combination of pumps, valves, lines, and hydraulic motors.

b) Speeds and feeds can be varied infinitely without stopping the machine.

c) Smooth, steady cutting action, with a minimum amount of chatter or vibration, is easily obtained.

d) Even, positive motion is provided at all loads.

e) The rate of oil pressure or flow can easily be controlled by simple valves.

THE HYDRAULIC PRINCIPLE

The extensive use of hydraulics is due to the fact that liquids possess two properties which make them especially useful in power transmission. Liquids cannot be compressed and they have the ability to multiply force. In the 17th century, the French scientist Pascal studied the physical properties of liquids and formulated the basic law of hydraulics. Pascal's Law states that: *pressure at any one point in a static liquid is the same in every direction,*

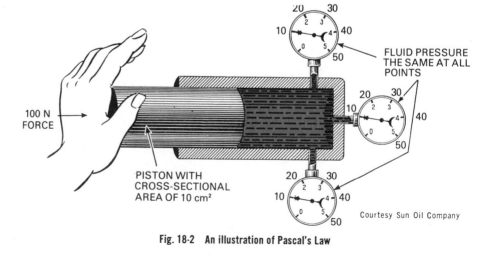

Fig. 18-2   An illustration of Pascal's Law

and pressure exerted on an enclosed liquid is transmitted undiminished in every direction, and acts with equal force on equal areas (Fig. 18-2).

The two types of hydraulic systems are the *hydrostatic* and the *hydrodynamic*. A basic comparison of these two principles is shown in Figs. 18-3A and B.

HYDROSTATIC PRINCIPLE

Most industrial systems work on the hydrostatic principle which can be easily understood by referring to Fig. 18-2.

Suppose a piston with a cross-sectional area of 10 cm² is tightly fitted in a liquid-filled cylinder. If a 100 N force is applied to the piston, a pressure of 10 kPa is created and this pressure is transmitted to all points in the cylinder. If there were no variations of pressure in the cylinder due to gravity, frictional losses, etc., a gauge installed anywhere in the cylinder would record a pressure of 10 kPa (Fig. 18-2).

The hydrostatic principle is often used to increase force or pressure. This can best be understood by connecting the piston-cylinder combination in Fig. 18-2 to a piston-cylinder combination which has a cross-sectional area of 50 cm² (Fig. 18-4A). By applying a 5 N force on the small piston, this 5 N force is transmitted to the 50 cm² piston area, creating a total force of 25 N (Fig. 18-4A). This increase in force is gained at the expense of the distance moved. For example, it would be

Fig. 18-3B   The dynamic principle; the force of a sledge hammer is used on the wedge to split the log

Courtesy Sun Oil Company

necessary to move the small piston 10 cm in order to move the large piston 2 cm. By applying pressure on the large piston, it is possible to reduce the total force and increase the distance the small piston moves.

Nearly all industrial hydraulic systems using the hydrostatic principle have pumps which apply constant pressure to the fluid. By using various devices to control the pressure, rate, and direction of flow, extremely flexible and versatile machines can be designed.

HYDRODYNAMIC PRINCIPLE

Dynamic force uses *kinetic energy* stored in a moving body to perform work. A log can be split *dynamically* by hitting the wedge with a sledge hammer (Fig. 18-3B). The amount of work performed depends on the speed and mass of the sledge hammer. Increasing either, or both, increases the amount of force exerted.

Hydraulic fluid can be used dynamically by directing a stream of fluid against a paddle wheel (Fig. 18-4B). Through impact, much of the kinetic energy of the moving fluid is conveyed to the paddle wheel. Hydraulic couplings and torque converters work on the hydrodynamic principle.

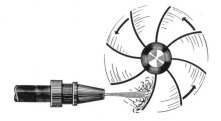

Courtesy Sun Oil Company

Fig. 18-4B   Hydrodynamic force is used to turn a paddle wheel

Courtesy Sun Oil Company

Fig. 18-3A   The static principle; a heavy mass is used to split a log

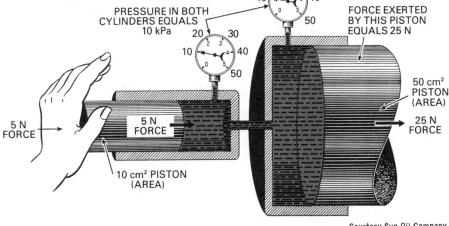

PRESSURE IN BOTH CYLINDERS EQUALS 10 kPa

FORCE EXERTED BY THIS PISTON EQUALS 25 N

5 N FORCE

5 N FORCE

10 cm² PISTON (AREA)

50 cm² PISTON (AREA)

25 N FORCE

Courtesy Sun Oil Company

Fig. 18-4A   Hydrostatic principle is used to increase force or pressure

HYDRAULIC SYSTEM COMPONENTS

Certain basic parts must be used in every hydraulic system; other parts are sometimes used to refine the system or to cope with special conditions. Each basic part will be discussed in detail, to show how a hydraulic system operates.

OIL RESERVOIR

Every hydraulic system requires a reservoir for storing the oil used in the system. A separate tank (Fig. 18-5) is generally used for large hydraulic systems. On smaller machines, the oil reservoir may be incorporated in the base of the machine. The built-in reservoirs are generally compact, but are hard to get at and difficult to clean.

PUMPS

The pump is an important part of a hydraulic system; its purpose is to transmit force by causing oil to flow. A simple example of a hydraulic pump may be found in the hydraulic brake system of a car. By depressing the brake pedal, the piston in the master brake cylinder moves toward the discharge end, causing the fluid under pressure to flow to the four wheel cylinders. By applying force at one end, this force is transmitted from one point (the brake pedal) to four points (the wheel cylinders). As soon as the brake shoes contact the brake drums, oil stops flowing. The primary purpose of the master cylinder, which is a very simple pump, is to transmit force hydraulically. In more complex hydraulic systems, the pump must provide a steady flow of liquid under pressure. Therefore the pump must provide a means of transmitting both force and motion.

Some of the more common types of pumps used in hydraulic systems will be described.

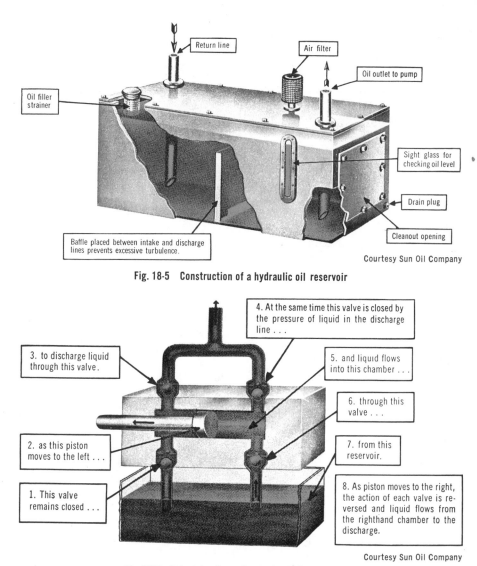

Fig. 18-5 Construction of a hydraulic oil reservoir

Courtesy Sun Oil Company

Fig. 18-6 Principle of a reciprocating hydraulic pump

Courtesy Sun Oil Company

Reciprocating pumps (Fig. 18-6) have limited use because the oil pulsates too much to provide smooth operation. However, by using several multi-piston types, a fairly steady flow can be provided. Reciprocating pumps are quite rugged and work well under adverse conditions such as low temperatures.

Gear pumps (Fig. 18-7) are simple in design. Because of their almost nonpulsating flow, they are well suited to applications requiring smooth operation. Simple gear pumps have spur gears; however, for quieter and smoother operation, some types contain helical or herringbone gears.

Internal gear pumps (Fig. 18-8) are basically the same as gear pumps except that they have an internal gear. They are generally not as efficient as gear pumps, and lose their efficiency rapidly as soon as mating parts become worn.

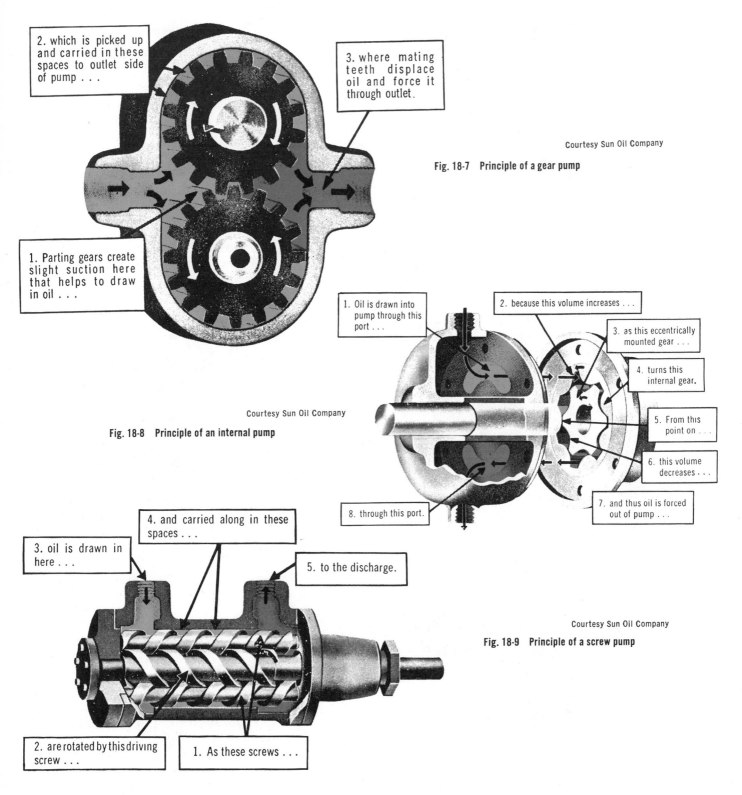

2. which is picked up and carried in these spaces to outlet side of pump . . .

3. where mating teeth displace oil and force it through outlet.

1. Parting gears create slight suction here that helps to draw in oil . . .

Courtesy Sun Oil Company

Fig. 18-7   Principle of a gear pump

Courtesy Sun Oil Company

Fig. 18-8   Principle of an internal pump

1. Oil is drawn into pump through this port . . .

2. because this volume increases . . .

3. as this eccentrically mounted gear . . .

4. turns this internal gear.

5. From this point on . . .

6. this volume decreases . . .

7. and thus oil is forced out of pump . . .

8. through this port.

4. and carried along in these spaces . . .

3. oil is drawn in here . . .

5. to the discharge.

Courtesy Sun Oil Company

Fig. 18-9   Principle of a screw pump

2. are rotated by this driving screw . . .

1. As these screws . . .

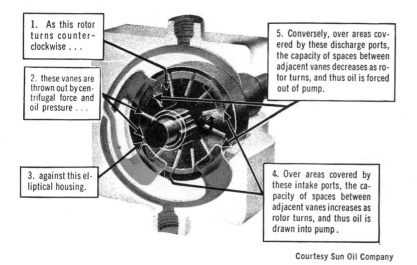

1. As this rotor turns counter-clockwise . . .

2. these vanes are thrown out by centrifugal force and oil pressure . . .

3. against this elliptical housing.

5. Conversely, over areas covered by these discharge ports, the capacity of spaces between adjacent vanes decreases as rotor turns, and thus oil is forced out of pump.

4. Over areas covered by these intake ports, the capacity of spaces between adjacent vanes increases as rotor turns, and thus oil is drawn into pump.

Courtesy Sun Oil Company

Fig. 18-10   Principle of a vane pump

Screw pumps (Fig. 18-9) are usually used to transfer oil from one point to another. They are seldom used to provide hydraulic power. Screw pumps are simple, rugged, and capable of operating at high speeds.

Vane pumps (Fig. 18-10) are used extensively to provide hydraulic power because they produce a reasonably steady flow. Wear of parts does not affect the efficiency of these pumps greatly, since the vanes can always maintain close contact with the ring in which they rotate.

Radial-Piston pumps (Fig. 18-11) are compact, rugged, and used in applications requiring a flexible source of hydraulic power. Through the use of ring-shifting mechanisms, the output of radial-piston pumps can be varied between zero and full volume.

Centrifugal pumps (Fig. 18-12) provide a nonpulsating flow and are used in moving large quantities of oil. This pump cannot be overloaded because the oil in the pump begins to rotate with the rotor as soon as the output pressure becomes too great. The output pressure is difficult to control; therefore centrifugal pumps are not generally used to provide hydraulic power.

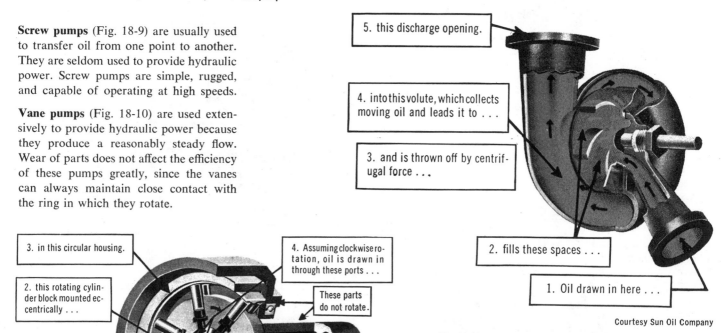

5. this discharge opening.

4. into this volute, which collects moving oil and leads it to . . .

3. and is thrown off by centrifugal force . . .

2. fills these spaces . . .

1. Oil drawn in here . . .

Courtesy Sun Oil Company

Fig. 18-12   Principle of a centrifugal pump

3. in this circular housing.

2. this rotating cylinder block mounted eccentrically . . .

4. Assuming clockwise rotation, oil is drawn in through these ports . . .

These parts do not rotate.

1. Pump pistons reciprocate as they are carried around by . . .

5. and discharged through these ports.

Courtesy Sun Oil Company

Fig. 18-11   Principle of a radial-piston pump

VALVES

Once the pump begins to move the oil under pressure, valves are usually required to *control pressure* and *to direct and control oil flow*. Valves were the only method of controlling flow and pressure until recently. Successful pumps have been developed during the past few years which are proving popular because they have the means of varying both the flow and pressure. However, valves are still the most important devices for providing flexibility in a hydraulic system, and a few of the more common types will be discussed.

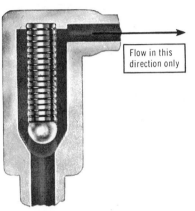

Courtesy Sun Oil Company

Fig. 18-13   A ball valve permits flow in one direction only

Ball valves (Fig. 18-13) are used in small reciprocating pumps and in small oil lines to permit oil flow in one direction only. Ball valves are usually spring-loaded and will open when the pressure in the system becomes greater than pressure exerted by the spring. Spring-loaded ball valves are often used as pressure relief valves. They are placed in a line connecting the hydraulic pump with the oil reservoir to prevent the buildup of excessive pressure in the system.

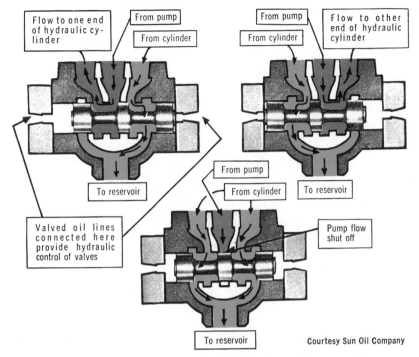

Courtesy Sun Oil Company

Fig. 18-15   The spool valve controls the flow of the oil to and from the cylinders

Rotary valves (Fig. 18-14) are used to control the direction of oil flow. They are generally used as pilot valves to control the movement of spool valves. The extra ports and passages in the rotating part of the valve allow the oil flow in several lines to be controlled by one valve. In a hydraulic surface grinder the reciprocating and crossfeed table movements are controlled by one rotary valve.

Spool valves (Fig. 18-15) are used extensively, because of their quick positive action, to control the direction of oil flow.

Spool valves are versatile and can control flow through several parts of a hydraulic system. The mating surfaces of this type of valve must be accurately machined and fitted to prevent leakage and to ensure efficient operation. Oil grooves are often machined around the pistons to keep the

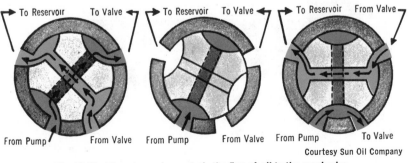

Courtesy Sun Oil Company

Fig. 18-14   The rotary valve controls the flow of oil to the spool valve

Courtesy Sun Oil Company

Fig. 18-16   A cock valve

spool centred and lubricated. Spool valves can be operated mechanically, electrically, or hydraulically.

Cock valves (Fig. 18-16) are simple valves used to bleed cylinders, eliminate air pockets, and control the operation of pressure gauges. They are generally built in small sizes and are used in systems using moderate pressure.

Needle valves (Fig. 18-17) provide a means of regulating oil flow precisely. They are operated manually and can be used in any position from fully opened to

fully closed. Their design prevents an abrupt change in oil flow; they are therefore often used in lines connecting sensitive devices which could be damaged by a sudden surge of pressure.

HYDRAULIC MOTOR

A hydraulic motor, generally a simple piston-and-cylinder combination, converts the oil flow into mechanical motion. Hydraulic motors alone can produce only two types of motion: straight-line (piston and cylinder type) and rotary (torque converter). When more complex motions are required, mechanical elements must be used in conjunction with the hydraulic motor.

The *piston motor* (Fig. 18-18) is the most commonly used hydraulic motor. Its design is simple and it can be made to withstand any pressure. When oil flows into the cylinder from the right side, the piston is moved to the left a certain distance in a given time. When the oil flow is reversed, the piston moves to the right at a slow rate because, with no piston rod to take up some of the cylinder volume, more oil must flow into the cylinder to move the piston the same distance. This

type of piston motor, commonly called a *differential piston motor* (Fig. 18-18), is often used in machines which require a powerful working stroke and a fast, but less powerful return stroke.

THE HYDRAULIC SYSTEM

A hydraulic system is produced when the various components such as reservoir, pump, valve, and motor are combined and joined together with the necessary pipe, tubing, and fittings. The hydraulic system illustrated in Fig. 18-19 is quite simple; however, when it becomes necessary to vary speeds, motions, etc., in a fixed or variable sequence, the complexity of the system increases. The most complex system still contains the basic components found in a simple system.

Two types of hydraulic systems, the *constant volume* and the *variable volume*, are generally used.

Constant-volume systems contain pumps which have a fixed output. The pump operates whenever the machine is in operation. If the full flow of oil delivered by the pump is not required in the system, it is bypassed through valves back to the oil reservoir.

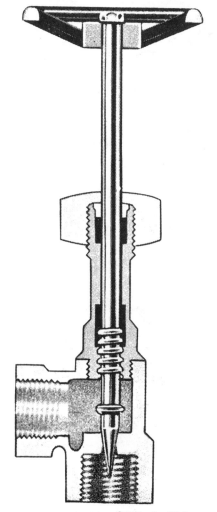

Courtesy Sun Oil Company

Fig. 18-17   A needle valve

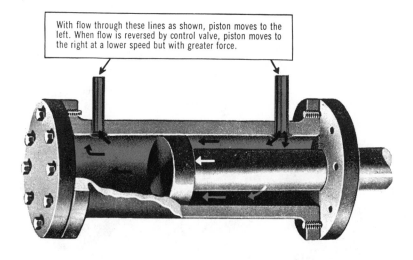

With flow through these lines as shown, piston moves to the left. When flow is reversed by control valve, piston moves to the right at a lower speed but with greater force.

Courtesy Sun Oil Company

Fig. 18-18   A simple hydraulic piston motor

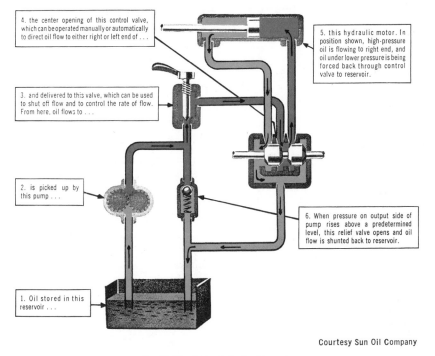

4. the center opening of this control valve, which can be operated manually or automatically to direct oil flow to either right or left end of . . .

3. and delivered to this valve, which can be used to shut off flow and to control the rate of flow. From here, oil flows to . . .

2. is picked up by this pump . . .

1. Oil stored in this reservoir . . .

5. this hydraulic motor. In position shown, high-pressure oil is flowing to right end, and oil under lower pressure is being forced back through control valve to reservoir.

6. When pressure on output side of pump rises above a predetermined level, this relief valve opens and oil flow is shunted back to reservoir.

Courtesy Sun Oil Company

Fig. 18-19   A simple hydraulic system

Variable-volume systems contain pumps whose output can be varied to suit different requirements. Combinations of mechanical, electrical, and pneumatic controls may be used to regulate the flow of oil. Variable-volume systems generally do not require certain bypass and flow-control valves which are needed in a constant-volume system. Variable-volume systems are widely used when the output power and speed vary over a wide range.

Many machine tools use both the constant-volume and the variable-volume systems. Each system may be used individually to operate different parts of a machine, or they may be combined to alternately control certain portions of the operating cycle. Examples of a few hydraulic systems found on machine tools will be explained in the following section.

CONSTANT-VOLUME SYSTEM

The shaper (Fig. 18-20) is an example of a constant-volume system applied to a

machine tool. A brief explanation of how this system operates follows.

a) The gear pump develops moderate oil pressure which it transmits through piping and a reversing valve to the operating cylinder.

b) The oil acts against the piston, moving it and the shaper ram forward on its cutting stroke.

c) As the piston moves forward, the oil ahead of the piston is expelled and returns to the reservoir.

d) At the end of the cutting stroke, a stop engages the reversing lever, which actuates a reversing valve, causing the oil to flow in the opposite direction.

e) This reversal of oil flow moves the piston and the shaper ram back to its starting position.

f) At the end of the return stroke, a second stop engages the reversing lever, actuating the reversing valve and again reversing the oil flow.

g) The length of the shaper stroke can be controlled by adjusting the position of the stops.

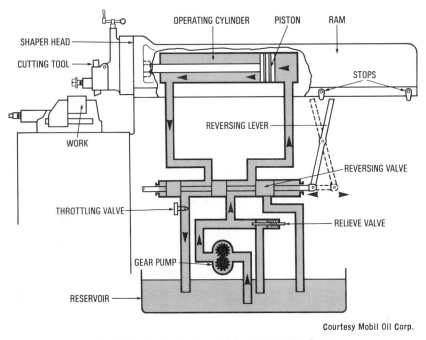

SHAPER HEAD

CUTTING TOOL

OPERATING CYLINDER   PISTON   RAM

STOPS

WORK

REVERSING LEVER

REVERSING VALVE

THROTTLING VALVE

RELIEVE VALVE

GEAR PUMP

RESERVOIR

Courtesy Mobil Oil Corp.

Fig. 18-20   Constant-volume hydraulic system of a shaper

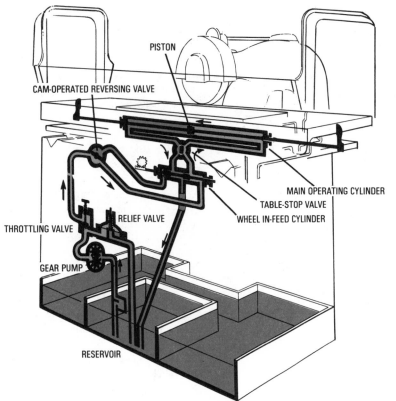

Fig. 18-21   Constant-volume hydraulic system of a surface grinder

Courtesy Mobil Oil Corp.

h) The speed of the forward (cutting) stroke can be controlled by a throttling valve which regulates the flow of oil back to the reservoir.

The operation of the constant-volume hydraulic system of a surface grinder (Fig. 18-21) is as follows.

a) A constant-volume or a constant-discharge gear pump delivers moderate oil pressure through various valves to the main operating cylinder.

b) The oil acts on the piston to reciprocate the worktable.

c) Excess oil pressure is released through a spring-loaded relief valve and returns to the reservoir.

d) At each reversal of the worktable, cams actuate the reversing valve, directing the oil through a wheel-infeed cylinder, then alternately to op-

posite ends of the main operating cylinder.

e) The wheel-infeed cylinder also actuates the ratchet mechanism of the wheel feed.

f) The rate of table travel is controlled by adjusting the throttling valve.

VARIABLE-VOLUME SYSTEM

The milling machine requires a slow feed during the cutting stroke, followed by a rapid return stroke which requires very little oil pressure. The lock-feed hydraulic system of a milling machine using three pumps is illustrated in Fig. 18-22. A brief explanation of the operation of this system follows.

a) The simple gear pump draws oil from the reservoir and supplies it at low pressure to the booster pump.

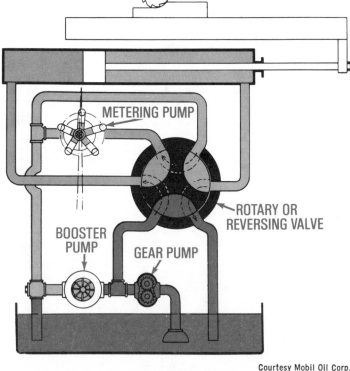

Courtesy Mobil Oil Corp.

Fig. 18-22   Variable-volume system of a manufacturing type milling machine

b) Oil from the booster pump, now under high pressure, travels through a reversing valve to one end of the working cylinder.

c) As the piston moves forward, the machine table, attached to the piston, also moves at a slow, steady rate.

d) A variable-discharge metering pump, connected to both ends of the cylinder, draws a specific amount of oil from the cylinder *ahead* of the motion of the piston.

e) The metering pump holds back and regulates the advance of the piston, which determines the rate of table travel.

f) When the reversing valve is actuated, the discharge and suction ports of the metering pump are interconnected.

g) The booster pump then discharges oil into the reservoir and the gear pump supplies low pressure oil to the cylinder for the rapid return stroke.

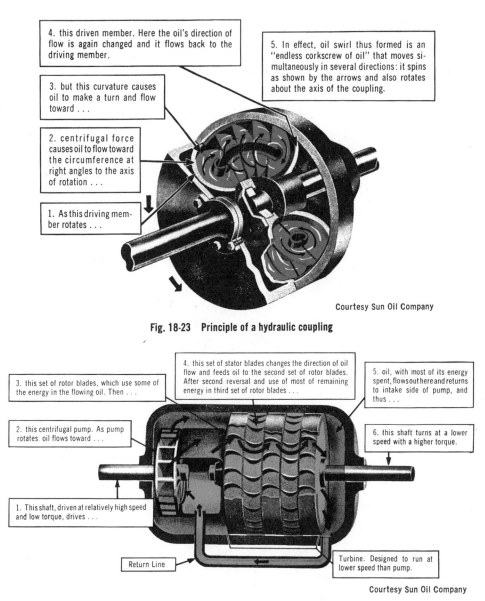

4. this driven member. Here the oil's direction of flow is again changed and it flows back to the driving member.

3. but this curvature causes oil to make a turn and flow toward . . .

2. centrifugal force causes oil to flow toward the circumference at right angles to the axis of rotation . . .

1. As this driving member rotates . . .

5. In effect, oil swirl thus formed is an "endless corkscrew of oil" that moves simultaneously in several directions: it spins as shown by the arrows and also rotates about the axis of the coupling.

Courtesy Sun Oil Company

Fig. 18-23   Principle of a hydraulic coupling

3. this set of rotor blades, which use some of the energy in the flowing oil. Then . . .

2. this centrifugal pump. As pump rotates, oil flows toward . . .

1. This shaft, driven at relatively high speed and low torque, drives . . .

4. this set of stator blades changes the direction of oil flow and feeds oil to the second set of rotor blades. After second reversal and use of most of remaining energy in third set of rotor blades . . .

5. oil, with most of its energy spent, flows out here and returns to intake side of pump, and thus . . .

6. this shaft turns at a lower speed with a higher torque.

Return Line

Turbine. Designed to run at lower speed than pump.

Courtesy Sun Oil Company

Fig. 18-24   Principle of a hydraulic torque converter

HYDRAULIC COUPLINGS AND TORQUE CONVERTERS

In the past few years, great strides have been made in perfecting two *hydrodynamic* devices: the hydraulic coupling, and the hydraulic torque converter. Hydraulic couplings and hydraulic torque converters are not new, but have only recently come into widespread use because of refinements in both.

A hydraulic coupling, sometimes called a fluid clutch (Fig. 18-23), is used to join two mechanisms hydraulically. An engine or motor at the power-input end may be joined hydraulically to another mechanism at the output end, without the use of mechanical connections. A hydraulic coupling transfers the torque (twist) delivered to it very smoothly, and at the same time protects the mechanisms against damage from vibration or shock loads.

A hydraulic torque converter, sometimes called a hydraulic gearbox (Fig. 18-24), is both a clutch and transmission source. It provides a means of coupling two mechanical elements and also of varying the ratio of the input torque to the output torque. Hydraulic torque converters provide a smooth flow of power, along with high torque at low speed, low torque at high speed, or any combination of the two within the capacity of the equipment.

HYDRAULIC OIL REQUIREMENTS

A hydraulic system contains an assembly of valves, cams, operating cylinders, etc., which all have close fitting tolerances. To obtain maximum efficiency from the system and protect the intricate moving parts, it is important that the proper oil be selected for use in hydraulic systems.

A hydraulic oil must perform two important functions:

a) It must transmit power efficiently.
b) It must lubricate adequately.

For a hydraulic oil to perform these two important functions satisfactorily, it must have the following characteristics.

a) *Proper viscosity*, to assure a ready flow of oil at all times, and to minimize leakage.
b) *Film strength and lubricity*, to provide adequate lubrication between closely fitted sliding parts.
c) *Resistance to oxidation*, to prevent intricate moving parts from damage due to oxidation of the oil (sludge formation).
d) *Resistance to emulsification*, to separate quickly from any water which may enter the system.
e) *Resistance to corrosion and rusting*, to prevent damage to the closely fitting parts.
f) *Resistance to foaming*, to free itself readily of air drawn into the hydraulic system.

VISCOSITY

Viscosity is one of the most important qualities that a hydraulic oil must possess. Viscosity should be thought of as a measure of the resistance of oil to flow. Low viscosity oils flow freely; high viscosity oils flow sluggishly. The viscosity of oil changes with the temperature; low temperatures cause the oil to flow sluggishly, while heat causes the oil to run freely.

The viscosity of oil has a direct bearing on the efficient transmission of power and the adequate lubrication of the parts in a hydraulic system. If hydraulic oil does not have the right viscosity, it cannot perform satisfactorily. Viscosity of an oil affects the operation of a hydraulic system in the following ways.

1. If an oil is too light (low viscosity), it usually results in:
   a) excessive leakage
   b) lower efficiency at the pump
   c) increased wear on parts
   d) loss of oil pressure
   e) lack of positive hydraulic control
   f) lower overall efficiency
2. If an oil is too heavy (high viscosity), it usually results in:
   a) increased pressure drop
   b) higher oil temperatures
   c) sluggish operation
   d) lower mechanical efficiency
   e) higher power consumption

FILM STRENGTH AND LUBRICITY

When parts of the hydraulic pump, cylinder, and control valves become worn, loss of pressure, leakage, and less accurate control may result. An important quality of a hydraulic oil should be its ability to minimize wear under the *thin-film* or *boundary lubrication* conditions that exist between the closely fitted sliding parts. A suitable oil maintains strong films that resist being squeezed out or pushed aside.

Both light (low viscosity) and heavy (high viscosity) oils have anti-wear or film-strength qualities. High viscosity oils have these qualities to a greater extent than low viscosity oils. Heavy oils, because of their greater resistance to leakage, tend to resist displacement from lubricated surfaces better than light oils. Therefore, an oil with as high a viscosity as possible, which fulfills all other requirements, should be used to minimize wear.

RESISTANCE TO OXIDATION

Hydraulic oil comes into contact with warm air in the reservoir. Because of this contact, the oil tends to oxidize, that is, combine chemically with the oxygen of the air. The tendency to oxidize is greatly increased at high operating temperatures and pressures, and by excessive agitation or splashing of oil.

A slight oxidation is not harmful, but if an oil has poor resistance to this chemical change, oxidation may become too great. If this occurs, substantial amounts of both soluble and insoluble oxidation products are created and the oil gradually increases in viscosity.

Insoluble oxidation products may be deposited in the form of gum and sludge in the oil passages, pump parts, and valve parts, where it will restrict the flow of oil. This may slow down the movement of pump vanes, spool and piston type valves, and cause seated valves to leak.

RESISTANCE TO EMULSIFICATION

Regardless of the precautions taken, some water gets into hydraulic systems through leaks and the condensation of atmospheric moisture. Most of the condensation occurs above the oil in the reservoir as the machine cools during idle periods. Any appreciable amount of water in a hydraulic system will promote rusting and decrease the lubricating value of the oil. This will eventually cause leakage, erratic pump action, and a breakdown in the system.

Where the percentage of water in a system is high, it is very important to use a hydraulic oil that has the ability to separate quickly and completely from the water. Oils that have exceptionally high oxidation resistance retain good water-separating abilities for a long time.

RESISTANCE TO CORROSION AND RUSTING

Water and oxygen can cause rusting of ferrous metal parts in a hydraulic system. Air is always present, oxygen is available, and some water is usually present; these conditions promote rusting. The danger of rusting is greatest when the machine is idle and surfaces usually covered with oil are left unprotected.

Rusting causes surface deterioration of metal parts, and rust particles may eventually be carried into the hydraulic system. This contributes to the formation of sludge-like deposits which can cause serious abrasions and interfere with the operation of cylinders, valves, and pumps.

To guard against rusting, it is important that a hydraulic system be kept as free from water as possible. High-quality hydraulic fluids contain a rust inhibitor which forms a film that resists displacement by water, thereby protecting the surfaces from contact with the water.

RESISTANCE TO FOAMING

Oil in a hydraulic system usually dissolves a certain amount of air, which causes a foaming (bubbling) action. Air can enter a system by oil falling from a considerable height into the reservoir, through leaks, or by suction of the pump. A hydraulic system can absorb the amount of air bubbles normally present; however, if an excessive amount of air is present and the bubbles persist at operating temperatures, pumping will be noisy and irregular, and the action of motors and controls will be erratic.

Foaming can be controlled by taking the following precautions.
1. Use of a premium-quality hydraulic oil which has good resistance to foaming.
2. The oil returning from the system should not fall from a great height into the reservoir.
3. Vent valves should be installed at high points in the hydraulic system.
4. The reservoir should be properly designed to allow the air to free itself readily at the oil surface.

HYDRAULICS QUESTIONS

1. Define hydraulics.
2. List four reasons why hydraulic applications have found wide acceptance in the machine tool industry.

THE FUNDAMENTAL HYDRAULIC CIRCUIT

3. Name the six essential elements of a hydraulic system.

ADVANTAGES OF HYDRAULIC SYSTEMS

4. List six important advantages of hydraulic power transmission.

THE HYDRAULIC PRINCIPLE

5. Name the two important properties that liquids possess.
6. State and illustrate Pascal's Law.
7. Explain the hydrostatic principle and state the purpose for which it is used.
8. Compare the hydrostatic and the hydrodynamic principles. Illustrations should be used to supplement the answer.
9. What hydraulic components operate on the hydrodynamic principle?

HYDRAULIC SYSTEM COMPONENTS

10. Give an example of a simple hydraulic pump and explain how it operates.
11. What purpose does a pump serve in a hydraulic system?
12. Describe briefly the operation of the following.
    a) gear pumps
    b) vane pumps
    c) radial-piston pumps
13. What purpose do valves serve in a hydraulic system?
14. For what purpose are the following used?
    a) ball valves
    b) rotary valves
    c) spool valves
    d) needle valves
15. Explain how a simple hydraulic motor operates.

THE HYDRAULIC SYSTEM

16. Compare a constant-volume and a variable-volume hydraulic system.
17. Explain briefly the operation of the constant-volume hydraulic system of a surface grinder.
18. Explain briefly the operation of the variable-volume hydraulic system of a milling machine.

HYDRAULIC COUPLINGS AND TORQUE CONVERTERS

19. State the purpose of a hydraulic coupling and briefly explain its operation.
20. State the purpose of a hydraulic torque converter and explain how it operates.

HYDRAULIC OIL REQUIREMENTS

21. What two important functions must a hydraulic oil perform?
22. List six characteristics that a hydraulic oil should possess in order to perform satisfactorily.
23. Discuss the importance of viscosity.
24. What would happen if either too light or too heavy an oil were used in a hydraulic system?
25. What effect does oxidation have on a hydraulic system?
26. Explain how water may enter a hydraulic system.
27. What effect does water have on a hydraulic system?
28. Discuss the effects of rusting and explain how it can be controlled.
29. What effect does foaming have on a hydraulic system?
30. How can foaming be minimized?

19 SPECIAL PROCESSES

Electro-chemical machining uses electrical and chemical energy as cutting tools

ELECTRICAL MACHINING PROCESSES

With the introduction of unique mechanisms and exotic materials in recent years, it has been found necessary to develop new methods of efficiently machining metals. Parts made out of cemented carbide or difficult-to-machine metals were previously shaped by the costly process of diamond wheel grinding. *Electro-chemical machining, electrical discharge machining,* and *electrolytic grinding* are three methods which have been developed recently. All remove metal by some form of electrical discharge.

ELECTRO-CHEMICAL MACHINING

Electro-chemical machining, more commonly called ECM, differs from conventional metal cutting techniques in that electrical and chemical energy are used as the cutting tools. This process machines metal easily, regardless of the work hardness, and is characterized by its "chipless" operation. A non-rotating tool the shape of the cavity required is the *cutting tool;* therefore square or difficult-to-machine shapes can easily be cut in a workpiece. The wear on the cutting tool is hardly noticeable since the tool *never* touches the work. Electro-chemical machining is particularly suitable for producing round through holes, square through holes, round or square blind holes, simple cavities which have straight, parallel sides, and planing operations. ECM is especially valuable when metals that exceed a hardness of 42 Rockwell C (400 BHN) are

machined. Sharp corners, flat bottom sections, or true radii are difficult to maintain because of the slight overcut which occurs during this process. A significant advantage of ECM is that the surfaces and edges of workpieces are not deformed and are left burr-free.

THE PROCESS

For years, metal in a solution has been transferred from one metal to another by means of electro-plating baths. Since ECM evolved from this process, it may be wise to examine the electro-plating principle (Fig. 19-1).

a) Two bars of unlike metal are immersed in an electrolyte solution.
b) One bar is fastened to a negative lead on a battery while the other is fastened to the positive lead.
c) When the circuit is closed, direct current passes through the electrolyte between the two bars of metal.
d) Chemical reaction transfers metal from one bar to the other.

Electro-chemical machining differs from the plating process in that an electro-chemical reaction dissolves metal *from a workpiece* into an electrolyte solution. A direct current is passed through an electrolyte solution between the electrode tool (the shape of the cavity desired), which is negative, and the workpiece, which is positive. This causes metal to be removed ahead of the electrode tool as the tool is fed towards the work. Chemical reaction caused by the direct current in the electrolyte dissolves the metal from the workpiece (Fig. 19-2).

The *electrode* for ECM is not a simple bar of metal, but a precision insulated tool which has been made to a specific shape and exact size. The electrode (tool) and workpiece, although located within 0.05 mm to 0.08 mm, never contact each other. The *electrolyte solution* is a controlled, swiftly flowing stream which carries the current. The *direct current* used may at times be as high as 1550 A/cm² of work material. All these factors affect the successful operation of the electro-chemical machining process and will be discussed in greater detail.

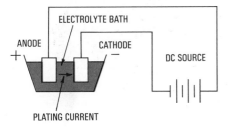

Fig. 19-1   Principle of a simple plating bath

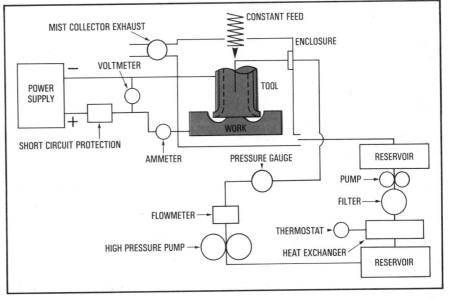

Courtesy Cincinnati Milacron Inc.

Fig. 19-2   Schematic diagram of a typical electro-chemical machining system

THE ELECTROLYTE

The electrolyte is a solution of water to which salt, mineral acid, caustic-potash, or caustic soda has been added to increase the electrical conductivity. A weak supply of the electrolyte solution will result in two disadvantages:

a) Metal removal rates will be low.

b) Excessive heat at the machining area will destroy the effectiveness of the solution.

Electrical energy which starts a chemical reaction in the electrolyte solution results in the formation of gas between the tool and workpiece and dissolves metal from the workpiece. The gas escapes into the atmosphere while the dissolved metal is carried away in the solution. As there is some resistance to current flow and chemical reactions occur, heat is generated in the machining area. The electrolyte is introduced into the machining area in great quantities to dissipate the heat and wash away the dissolved metal. Filters placed in an electro-chemical machining system remove the dissolved metal from the electrolyte and ensure a fresh flow of solution to the machining area.

The electrolyte is introduced to the machining area *through* the electrode tool; therefore, the amount of flow is affected by the electrode length, diameter, and shape. As much flow as possible is desirable, and some applications have been known to use as much as 760 *l*/min at pressures up to 2070 kPa.

THE ELECTRODE

The *electrode tool*, which is always the *negative terminal* of the electrical circuit, is an insulated tool made to the size and shape of the cavity desired. The electrolyte solution is fed to the machining area by a hole through the centre of the electrode. Because it is necessary that the electrolyte flow completely around the electrode and allowance be made for the overcut which occurs during the ECM process, the tool is made approximately 0.12 mm per side

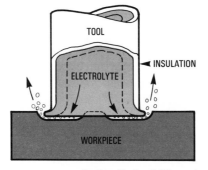

Courtesy Cincinnati Milacron Inc.

Fig. 19-3   Electrolyte flowing through the electrode tool

smaller than the hole it produces. The periphery of the electrode is insulated (Fig. 19-3) to prevent the sides from cutting as the tool extends deeper into the hole.

One of the chief purposes of the electrode tool is to impart its shape to the workpiece. For example, a square electrode will produce a square hole, while a round hole is produced by a round electrode. The shape of the cavity which can be produced through ECM is limited only by the shape which can be cut on the electrode. The material used to make the electrode tool should possess the following characteristics.

a) It must be machinable.

b) It must be rigid.

c) It must be a good conductor of electricity.

d) It must be able to resist corrosion.

Copper, brass, and stainless steel have generally been found to be good electrode materials for electro-chemical machining.

Copper, an excellent conductor of electricity, is not recommended for manufacturing electrodes for thin-walled sections or deep holes. Because of its softness and tendency to bend, it is difficult to machine long or thin sections.

Brass, while not as good a conductor of electricity as copper, can be used for electrode material with good results. The greater strength of brass, its ease in machining, and its lower cost make it an ideal material for most electrodes.

Stainless steel is used when large volume flow and high pressures of electrolyte are necessary. It is stronger than the other two materials; however, its high initial cost and difficulties encountered in machining limit its use as an electrode material.

METAL REMOVAL

In the electro-chemical process, the distance between the electrode and the work (the machining gap) (Fig. 19-3) is important. In order to encourage efficient electrical transmission, the tool and the work must be as close as possible to each other yet never come into contact. For most conditions, this gap will vary from 0.02 mm to 0.07 mm (or .001 in. to .003 in.). Because of the high current levels used, serious damage to both the electrode tool and the work will occur if there is any physical contact between them.

The rate of metal removal is directly proportional to the current passing between the tool and the workpiece. Current densities ranging from a minimum of 155 A/cm^2 to a maximum of 1550 A/cm^2

Courtesy Cincinnati Milacron Inc.

Fig. 19-4   Electro-chemical machining applications

have been used in ECM applications. The use of high current will result in a high rate of metal removal, while low current will result in a low rate of metal removal.

The amount of overcut (the difference between the tool size and the hole produced) depends upon various cutting conditions and may vary from 0.20 mm to 0.30 mm (.008 in. to .012 in.). Once the amount of overcut is known for a given tool, hole sizes will be repeated to within at least 0.04 mm to 0.01 mm of roundness.

The rate of penetration varies with the type of operation being performed, the type of work material, the cross-section of the electrode, and the current density used. ECM rates of penetration may vary from 6.4 mm to 11 mm (or .250 in. to .430 in.).

ADVANTAGES OF ECM

Electro-chemical machining is one of the metal cutting processes which has contributed to the machining of space-age metals. Some of its characteristics and advantages are:

a) Metal of any hardness can be machined.
b) It competes with drilling and some through-hole milling operations, especially if the work exceeds 42 Rockwell C hardness.
c) No heat is created during the machining process; therefore, there is no work distortion.
d) It machines metal without tool rotation.
e) Tool wear is insignificant as the tool never touches the work.
f) Because the tool never touches the work, thin fragile sections can be machined without distortion.
g) The workpiece is left burr-free.
h) Intricate forms, difficult to machine by other processes, can be produced easily (Fig. 19-4).
i) It is suitable for production type work where multiple holes or cavities may be machined at the same time.
j) Surface finishes of 0.60 μm (or 25 microinches) or less may be obtained.

ELECTRO-CHEMICAL MACHINING QUESTIONS

1. How does ECM differ from conventional machining techniques?
2. Describe briefly the process of ECM.
3. Name four suitable electrolytes.
4. Explain fully the purpose of the electrolyte solution.
5. Explain what part the electrolyte plays in the electro-chemical machining process.
6. What are the characteristics of a good electrode tool?
7. Name three electrode materials suitable for ECM and state the advantage of each.
8. Define: a) machining gap
           b) overcut
           c) rate of penetration
9. State seven main advantages of electro-chemical machining.

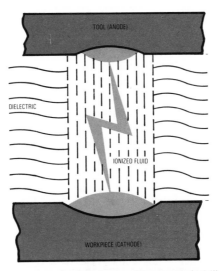

Courtesy "American Machinist"

A controlled spark removes metal during electrical discharge machining

ELECTRICAL DISCHARGE MACHINING

Electrical discharge machining, commonly known as EDM, is a process that is used to remove metal through the action of an electrical discharge of short duration and high current density between the tool and the workpiece. This principle of removing metal by an electric spark has been known for quite some time. In 1889, Paschen explained the phenomenon and devised a formula which would predict its arcing ability in various materials. The EDM process can be compared to a miniature version of a lightning bolt striking a surface, creating a localized intense heat, and melting away the work surface.

Electrical discharge machining has proved especially valuable in the machining of super-tough, electrically conductive materials such as the new space-age alloys. These metals would have been difficult to machine by conventional methods, but EDM has made it relatively simple to machine intricate shapes that would be impossible to produce with conventional cutting tools. This machining process is continually finding further applications in the metal cutting industry.

PRINCIPLE OF EDM

Electrical discharge machining is a controlled metal-removal technique whereby an electric spark is used to cut (erode) the workpiece, which takes a shape opposite to that of the cutting tool or electrode (Fig. 19-5). The *cutting tool (electrode)* is made from electrically conductive material, usually carbon. The electrode, made to the shape of the cavity required, and the workpiece are both submerged in a *dielectric fluid*, which is generally a light lubricating oil. This dielectric fluid should be a nonconductor (or poor conductor) of electricity. A *servo mechanism* maintains a gap of approximately 0.02 mm between the electrode and the work, preventing them from coming into contact with each other. A *direct current* of low voltage and

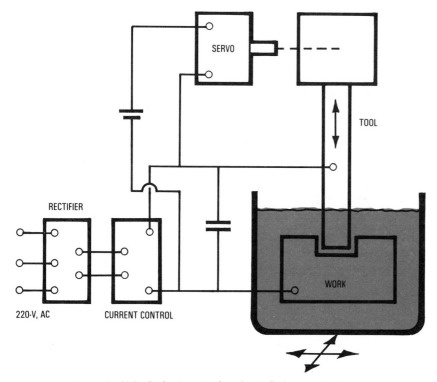

Fig. 19-5 Basic elements of an electro-discharge system

high amperage is delivered to the electrode at the rate of approximately 20 000 Hz. These electrical energy impulses become sparks which jump the gap (Fig. 19-6) between the electrode and the workpiece through the dielectric fluid. Intense heat is created in the localized area of the spark impact; the metal melts and a small particle of molten metal is expelled from the surface of the workpiece. The dielectric fluid, which is constantly being circulated, carries away the eroded particles of metal and also assists in dissipating the heat caused by the spark.

TYPES OF ELECTRICAL DISCHARGE CIRCUITS

Several types of electrical discharge power supply have been used for EDM. Although there are many differences between them, each type is used for the same basic purpose, that is, the precise, economical removal of metal by electric spark erosion.

The following types of electrical power supplies have been used.

a) resistance-capacitance power supply
b) pulse-type power supply
c) rotary impulse generator power supply
d) static impulse generator power supply

The resistance-capacitance and the pulse-type direct current power supplies are most commonly used; therefore, only these two will be explained in greater detail.

Resistance-capacitance power supply, also known as the *relaxation-type power supply,* was widely used on the first EDM machines. It is still the power supply used on many of the machines of foreign manufacture.

As illustrated in Fig. 19-7A, the capacitor is charged through a resistance from a direct current voltage source that is generally fixed. As soon as the voltage across the capacitor reaches the breakdown value of the dielectric fluid in the gap, a spark occurs. A relatively high voltage (125 V), high capacitance of over 100 μF (microfarads) for roughing cuts, low spark frequency, and high amperage are characteristics of the resistance-capacitance power supply.

In resistance-capacitance circuits, an increase in metal removal rates depends more on larger amperage and capacitance than on increasing the number of discharges per second. The combination of low frequency, high voltage, high capacitance, and high amperage results in:

a) a rather coarse surface finish
b) large overcut around the electrode (tool)
c) larger metal particles being removed and more space being required to flush out particles

The advantages of the resistance-capacitance power supply are:

a) The circuit is simple and reliable.
b) It works well at low amperages, especially with milliampere currents required for holes under 0.12 mm (.005 in.) in diameter.

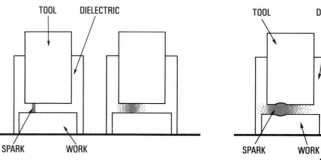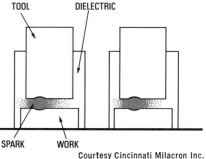

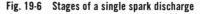
Courtesy Cincinnati Milacron Inc.

Fig. 19-6 Stages of a single spark discharge

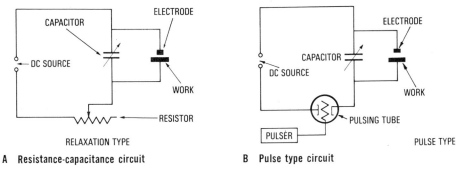

A   Resistance-capacitance circuit   **B**   Pulse type circuit

Courtesy Cincinnati Milacron Inc.

Fig. 19-7   Electro-discharge power supply circuits

Pulse type power supply is used almost exclusively by American manufacturers. It is similar to the resistance-capacitance type; however, vacuum tubes or solid state devices are used to achieve an extremely fast pulsing switch effect (Fig. 19-7B). The pulse width and intervals may also be accurately controlled by switching devices. The switching is extremely fast and the discharges per second are 10 or more times greater than with the resistance-capacitance power supply at low frequencies. The results of more discharges per second are illustrated in Fig. 19-8. With more discharges per second, and using the same current (10 A), it is clear that smaller craters are created, producing a finer surface finish while still maintaining the same metal removal rate.

Pulse type power supply circuits are usually operated on low voltages (70 to 80 V), high frequency (sparks at the rate of 260 000 Hz), low capacitance (50 μF or less), and low energy spark levels.

The main advantages of the pulse-type circuit are:

a) It is extremely versatile and can be accurately controlled for roughing and finishing cuts.

b) Better surface finish is produced as less metal is removed per spark since there are many sparks per unit of time.

c) There is less overcut around the electrode (tool).

THE ELECTRODE

The *electrode* in electrical discharge machining is formed to the shape of the cavity desired. As in conventional machining, some materials have better cutting and wearing qualities than others. Electrode materials must, therefore, have the following characteristics.

a) Be good conductors of electricity and heat.

b) Be easily machined to shape at a reasonable cost.

c) Produce efficient metal removal from the workpiece.

d) Resist deformation during the erosion process.

e) Exhibit low electrode (tool) wear rates.

Much experimentation has been carried out to find a good, economical material for the manufacture of electrical discharge machining electrodes. Tungsten carbide, copper tungsten, silver tungsten, yellow brass, copper, chrome-plated materials, graphite, and zinc alloys are some of the materials which have found certain applications as electrode materials. None of these electrode materials has general purpose application; each machining operation dictates the selection of the electrode material. *Yellow brass* has been used primarily as electrode material for pulse-type circuits because of its good machinability, electrical conductivity, and relatively low cost. *Copper* produces better results in the resistance-capacitance circuits where higher voltages are employed.

High-density and high-purity carbon, or *graphite*, is a relatively new electrode material which is gaining wide acceptance. It is commercially available in various shapes and sizes, is relatively inexpensive, can be machined easily, and makes an excellent electrode. Its tool wear rate is much less and its high metal removal rate is almost double that of any other metal. Development of superior graphite electrodes has increased the use of graphite electrodes because of their low cost and ease of fabrication.

THE ELECTRICAL DISCHARGE MACHINING PROCESS

The use of electrical discharge machining is increasing as more and more applications are found for this process. As new, important technological advances in equipment and application techniques become available, more industries are adopting the process. It is necessary, therefore, to discuss the various aspects of electrical discharge machining in more detail.

THE SERVO MECHANISM

It is important that there is no physical contact between the electrode (tool) and the workpiece; otherwise arcing will occur, causing damage to both the electrode and the workpiece. Electrical discharge machines are equipped with a servo control mechanism that automatically maintains a constant gap of approximately 0.02 mm (or .001 in.) between the electrode and the workpiece. The mechanism also advances the tool into the workpiece as the operation progresses and senses and corrects any shorted condition by rapidly retracting and returning the tool. Precise control of the gap is essential to a successful machining operation. If the gap is too large, ionization of the dielectric fluid does not occur and machining cannot take place. If the gap is too small, the tool and workpiece may weld together.

Precise gap control is accomplished by a circuit in the power supply comparing the average gap voltage to a preselected reference voltage. The difference between the two voltages is the input signal which tells the servo mechanism how far and how fast to feed the tool and when to retract it from the workpiece.

When chips in the spark gap reduce the voltage below a critical level, the servo mechanism causes the tool to withdraw until the chips are flushed out by the dielectric fluid. The servo system should not be too sensitive to "short lived" voltages caused by chips being flushed out; otherwise the tool would be constantly retracting, thereby seriously affecting machining rates.

Servo feed control mechanisms can be used to control the vertical movement of the electrode (tool) for sinking cavities. It can also be applied to the table of the machine for work requiring horizontal movement of the electrode (tool).

CUTTING CURRENT (AMPERAGE)

The EDM power supply provides the direct current electrical energy for the electrical discharges which occur between the tool and the workpiece. As the pulse-type power supply is the more commonly used in North America, only the characteristics of this type will be discussed.

CHARACTERISTICS OF PULSE TYPE CIRCUITS

a) low voltages (normally about 70 V which drop to about 20 V after the spark is initiated)
b) low capacitance (about 50 μF or less)
c) high frequencies (usually 20 000 to 30 000 Hz but may be as high as 260 000)
d) low energy spark levels

THE DISCHARGE PROCESS

Upon application of sufficient electrical energy between the electrode (cathode) and the workpiece (anode), the dielectric

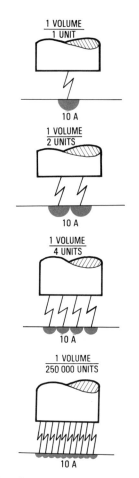

Fig. 19-8 Effects on cratering and surface finish using various frequencies of spark discharge

fluid changes into a gas, allowing a heavy discharge of current to flow through the ionized path and strike the workpiece. The energy of this discharge vaporizes and decomposes the dielectric fluid surrounding the column of electric conduction. As the conduction continues, the diameter of the discharge column expands and the current increases. The heat between the electrode and the work surface causes a small pool of molten metal to be formed on the work surface. When the current is stopped, usually only for microseconds, the molten metal particles solidify and are washed away by the dielectric fluid.

These electrical discharges occur at the rate of 20 000 to 30 000 Hz between the

electrode and the workpiece. Each discharge removes a minute amount of metal. Since the voltage during discharge is constant, the amount of metal removed will be proportional to the amount of charge between the electrode and the work. For fast metal removal, high amounts of current should be delivered as quickly as possible to melt the maximum amount of metal. This, however, produces large craters in the workpiece, resulting in rough surface finish. To obtain smaller craters and therefore finer surface finishes, smaller charges of energy can be used. This results in slower stock removal rates. If the current is maintained but the number of hertz is increased, this also results in smaller craters and better surface finish. The surface finish is proportional to the number of electrical discharges (cycles) per second (Fig. 19-8).

THE DIELECTRIC FLUID

The dielectric fluid used in the electrical discharge process serves several main functions.

a) Helps to initiate the spark between the electrode and the workpiece.
b) Confines the spark path to a narrow channel.
c) Serves as an insulator between the tool and the workpiece.
d) Flushes away the metal particles to prevent shorting.
e) Acts as a coolant for both the electrode and the workpiece.

TYPES OF DIELECTRICS

Many types of fluids have been used as dielectrics, resulting in various rates of metal removal. They must be able to ionize (vaporize) and deionize rapidly and have a low viscosity that will allow them to be pumped through the narrow machining gap. The most commonly used EDM fluids, proven to be satisfactory dielectrics, have been various petroleum products, such as light lubricating oils, transformer oils, silicon-base oils, and kerosene. These all perform reasonably well, especially with graphite electrodes, and are reasonable in cost. In certain cases, dielectrics such as carbon tetrachloride and certain compressed gases have been used.

The selection of the dielectric is important to the electrical discharge machining process since it affects the metal removal rate and electrode wear. Industry is continually searching for new and better dielectric fluids for this process. A fluid consisting of triethylene glycol, water, and monoethyl ether of ethylene glycol has been used in research with superior results, especially with metallic electrodes. It is quite likely that many new dielectric fluids will be developed to improve the electrical discharge machining process.

METHODS OF CIRCULATING DIELECTRICS

The dielectric fluid must be circulated under constant pressure if it is to flush away efficiently the metal particles and assist in the machining process. The pressure used generally begins with 35 kPa and is increased until optimum cutting is attained. Too much dielectric fluid will remove the chips before they can assist in the cutting action and thereby cause slower machining rates. Too little pressure will not remove the chips quickly enough and thereby cause short circuits.

Four methods are generally used to circulate the dielectric fluid. All methods must use fine filters in the system to remove the metal particles so that they are not recirculated.

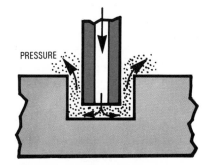

Fig. 19-9A Circulating dielectric fluid down through the electrode

Down through the electrode (Fig. 19-9A): A hole or holes are drilled through the electrode, and the dielectric fluid is forced through the electrode and between it and the workpiece. This rapidly washes away the metal particles from the machining area. On cavities, a small standing slug or core remains which must be ground away after the machining operation has been completed.

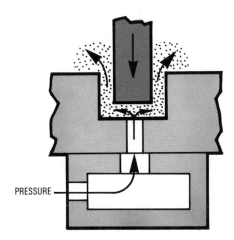

Fig. 19-9B Circulating dielectric fluid up through the workpiece

Up through the workpiece (Fig. 19-9B): Another common method is to cause the fluid to be circulated up through the workpiece. This type of flushing is limited to through-hole cutting applications and to cavities having holes for core or ejector pins.

Vacuum flow (Fig. 19-9C): A negative pressure (vacuum) is created in the gap which causes the dielectric to flow through the normal 0.02 mm (or .001 in.) clearance between the electrode and the workpiece. The flow can be either up through a hole in the electrode or down through a hole in the workpiece. Vacuum flow has several advantages over other methods in that it improves machining efficiency, reduces smoke and fumes, and helps to reduce or eliminate taper in the workpiece.

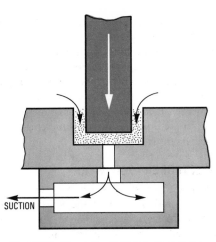

Fig. 19-9C Circulating fluid down through the workpiece by suction

Vibration (Fig. 19-9D): A pumping and sucking action is used to cause the dielectric to disperse the chips from the spark gap. The vibration method is especially valuable for very small holes, deep holes, or blind cavities where it would be impractical to use other methods.

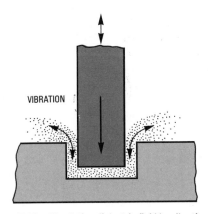

Fig. 19-9D Circulating dielectric fluid by vibration

METAL REMOVAL RATES

Metal removal rates for EDM are somewhat slower than with conventional machining methods. The rate of metal removal is dependent upon the following factors.

a) amount of current in each discharge

b) frequency of the discharge

c) electrode material
d) workpiece material
e) dielectric flushing conditions

The normal metal removal rate is approximately 16 cm³ of work material per hour for every 20 A of machining current. However, metal removal rates of up to 245 cm³/h are possible for roughing cuts with special power supplies.

ELECTRODE (TOOL) WEAR

During the discharge process, the electrode (tool) as well as the workpiece is subject to wear or erosion. As a result, it is difficult to hold close tolerances as the tool gradually loses its shape during the machining operation. At times it is necessary to use as many as five electrodes to produce a cavity of the required shape and tolerance. For through-hole operations, stepped electrodes are often used to produce roughing and finishing cuts in one pass.

The rate at which the tool wears is fortunately considerably less than that of the workpiece. An *average wear ratio* of the workpiece to the electrode is 3 to 1 for metallic tools, such as copper, brass, zinc alloys, etc. With graphite electrodes, this wear ratio can be greatly improved to 10 to 1.

Much development and research remains to be done to reduce the wear ratio of the electrode. *Reverse polarity machining*, a relatively new development, promises to be a major breakthrough in reducing electrode wear. With this method, molten metal from the workpiece is deposited on a graphite electrode about as fast as the electrode is worn away. Thus minute electrode wear is continually being replaced by a deposit of the work material. Reverse polarity machining operates best on low spark discharge frequencies and high amperage. It improves the metal removal rates and greatly reduces electrode wear.

OVERCUT

Overcut is the amount the cavity in the

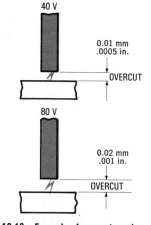

Fig. 19-10   Example of overcut produced by different voltages in EDM

workpiece is cut larger than the electrode used in the machining process. The distance between the surface of the work and the surface of the electrode (overcut) is equal to the length of the sparks discharged, which is constant over all areas of the electrode.

The amount of overcut in EDM ranges from 0.005 mm to 0.18 mm (or .0002 in. to .007 in.) and is dependent upon the amount of gap voltage. As illustrated in Fig. 19-10, the overcut distance increases with the increased gap voltage. Therefore, the amount of overcut can be controlled fairly accurately. The amount of overcut is generally varied to suit the metal removal rate and the surface finish required, which in turn determines the size of the chip removed.

Most manufacturers of EDM machines provide overcut charts to show the amount of clearance produced with various currents. The charts make it possible to accurately determine the electrode size required to machine an opening to within 0.002 mm (or .0001 in.).

The size of the chips removed is an important factor in setting the amount of overcut because:

a) Chips in the space between the electrode and the work serve as conductors for the electrical discharges.

b) Large chips produced with higher amperages require a larger gap to enable them to be flushed out effectively.

Therefore, overcut depends upon the gap voltage and the chip size, which vary with the amperage used.

SURFACE FINISH

In the last few years, major advances have been made with regard to the surface finishes that can be produced. With the low metal removal rates, surface finishes of 0.05 μm to 0.10 μm (or 2 to 4 microinches to .000 004 in.) are possible. With high metal removal rates (as much as 245 cm³/h) finishes of 25 μm (1000 microinches) are produced.

The type of finish required determines the number of amperes which can be used, the capacitance, frequency, and the voltage setting. For fast metal removal (roughing cuts), high amperage, low frequency, high capacitance, and minimum gap voltage are required. For slow metal removal (finish cut) and good surface finish, low amperage, high frequency, low capacitance, and the highest gap voltage are required.

ADVANTAGES OF THE EDM PROCESS

Electrical discharge machining has many advantages over conventional machining processes.

a) Any material that is electrically conductive can be cut, regardless of its hardness. It is especially valuable for cemented carbides and the new supertough space age alloys that are extremely difficult to cut by conventional means.

b) Work can be machined in a hardened state, thereby overcoming the deformation caused by the hardening process.

c) Broken taps or drills can readily be removed from workpieces.

d) It does not create stresses in the work material since the tool (electrode) never comes in contact with the work.

e) The process is burr-free.

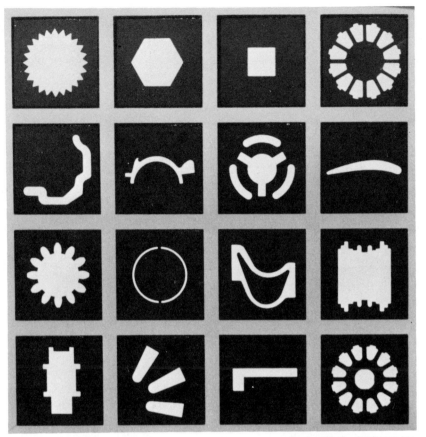

Courtesy Cincinnati Milacron Inc.

Fig. 19-11A   Examples of work produced by electro-discharge machining

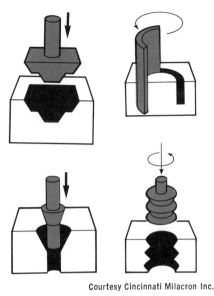

Courtesy Cincinnati Milacron Inc.

Fig. 19-11B   Tool movement required to produce various shaped cavities

d) Rapid electrode wear can become costly in some types of EDM equipment.
e) Electrodes smaller than 0.07 mm (or .003 in.) in diameter are impractical.
f) The work surface is damaged to a depth of 0.005 mm (or .0002 in.), but it is easily removed.
g) A slight case hardening occurs. This, however, may be classed as an advantage in some cases.

CONCLUSION

Since electrical discharge machining was first put to practical application, its use has been expanding by virtue of its ability to perform economically jobs which are extremely difficult or impossible to perform by conventional machining methods. Research and development are continuing to improve tool wear ratios, to increase metal removal rates without the surface finish suffering, and to improve power supplies and machine tool components. Wider recognition of this process and its possibilities will lead to increasing the importance of electrical discharge machining (EDM) in the future.

f) Thin, fragile sections can be easily machined without deforming.
g) Secondary finishing operations are generally eliminated for many types of work.
h) The process is automatic in that the servo mechanism advances the electrode into the work as the metal is removed.
i) One person can operate several EDM machines at one time.
j) Intricate shapes, impossible to produce by conventional means, are cut out of a solid with relative ease (Fig. 19-11A).
k) Better dies and molds can be produced at lower costs.

l) A die punch can be used as the electrode to reproduce its shape in the matching die plate, complete with the necessary clearance.

LIMITATIONS

Electrical discharge machining has found many applications in the machine trade; however, it does have some limitations.
a) The metal removal rates are low.
b) The material to be machined must be electrically conductive.
c) Cavities produced are slightly tapered, but can be controlled for most applications to as little as 0.002 mm (or .0001 in.) in every 6 mm (or 1/4 in.).

ELECTRICAL DISCHARGE MACHINING QUESTIONS

1. Describe briefly the principle of electrical discharge machining.
2. Explain the operation and advantages of the pulse-type power supply.
3. List the characteristics of a good electrode material.
4. Explain why graphite is gaining wide acceptance an an electrode material.
5. What is the purpose of the servo mechanism, and how does it operate?
6. Briefly explain what occurs during the discharge process.
7. What purpose does a dielectric serve?
8. Discuss the four methods of circulating dielectric fluids, and state the advantages of each method.
9. What factors affect the metal removal rate?
10. Explain the principle of reverse polarity machining.
11. Define *overcut*, and explain how it can be controlled.
12. What surface finishes are possible by EDM, and how are these achieved?
13. List six main advantages of the EDM process.
14. Name four limitations of electrical discharge machining.

ELECTROLYTIC GRINDING

Electrolytic grinding has been a boon to the machining of thin, fragile metal products and tough, difficult-to-machine space age alloys. In electrolytic grinding, the metal is removed from the work surface by a combination of electro-chemical action and the action of a metal-bonded abrasive grinding wheel. Approximately 90% of the metal removed from the work surface is the result of this electro-chemical deplating action, while the remaining 10% is "wiped away" by the grinding wheel. The electrolytic grinding process is very similar to the process used for electrochemical machining.

Courtesy Cincinnati Milacron Inc.

A carbide-tipped cutter being sharpened by electrolytic grinding

THE ELECTROLYTIC GRINDING PROCESS

The metal-bonded grinding wheel and the electrically conductive workpiece are both connected to a *direct current* power supply and are separated by the protruding abrasive particles of the wheel. An electrolytic grinding solution (electrolyte) is injected into the gap between the wheel and the work, completing the electrical circuit and producing the necessary deplating action which decomposes the work material. This decomposed material is removed by the action of the revolving grinding wheel and is washed away in the solution. In electrolytic grinding, the wheel never comes into actual contact with the work material.

THE GRINDING WHEEL

A special type of grinding wheel is used for the electrolytic grinding process. Metal-bonded, electrically conductive, abrasive grinding wheels are essential for this operation. Brass, bronze, and copper-bonded wheels which can be dressed to various forms are common in electrolytic grinding. The grinding wheel is the cathode ($-$) of the electrical circuit. The wheel spindle is connected to a *direct current* power supply through a set of contact brushes and is isolated from the rest of the machine by an insulating sleeve (Fig. 19-12). Metal-bonded diamond wheels are recommended for the grinding of tungsten carbides. Metal-bonded aluminum oxide wheels are used for grinding all other electrically conductive materials.

The wheel abrasive performs an important function in the electrolytic grinding process. The abrasive particles, protruding approximately 0.01 mm to 0.02 mm beyond the metal-bonded wheel, act as nonconductive spacers, maintaining the necessary gap between the wheel and the workpiece. They also provide thousands of little pockets which are filled with electrolyte solution which completes the electrical circuit. The accuracy of the working gap (the distance between the metal bond of the wheel and the workpiece) is determined by the amount these

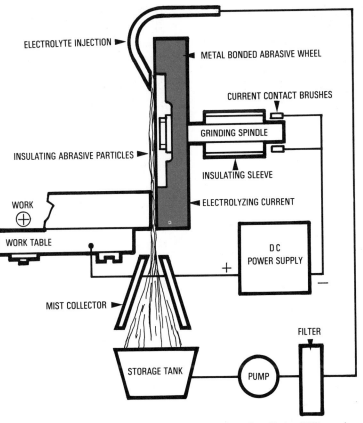

ELECTROLYTE INJECTION

METAL BONDED ABRASIVE WHEEL

CURRENT CONTACT BRUSHES

GRINDING SPINDLE

INSULATING ABRASIVE PARTICLES

INSULATING SLEEVE

WORK

ELECTROLYZING CURRENT

WORK TABLE

DC POWER SUPPLY

MIST COLLECTOR

FILTER

STORAGE TANK

PUMP

Courtesy Cincinnati Milacron Inc.

Fig. 19-12   Electrolytic grinding principle

abrasive particles protrude from the wheel (cathode).

TRUING

It is important that the grinding wheel run true within 0.01 mm to maintain grinding accuracy and also to provide maximum passage for the electrolyte solution to achieve maximum stock removal. Metal-bonded aluminum oxide wheels can be dressed or trued with a single-point diamond or a commercial brake truing attachment. Diamond wheels should be trued by the use of a dial indicator. After each dressing or truing operation, the electrolytic machining process is reversed by reversing the electrical leads on the power supply, causing a deplating action of the metal wheel bond. This removes a slight amount of the metal wheel bond and causes the abrasive particles to protrude.

THE WORKPIECE

The work, which must be electrically conductive, is the anode (+) of the circuit. It is electrically connected to the *direct current* power supply through the table of the machine (Fig. 19-12). Any material, even tungsten carbide and the difficult-to-machine space-age alloys, can be readily ground by this process, providing that the material is an electrical conductor.

THE CURRENT

A direct current of relatively low voltage (approximately 4 to 16 V) and high amperage (300 to 1 000 A or higher) is used in the electrolytic grinding process. The amount of current flow depends upon the size of the area on which the cutting action is occurring. A rule of thumb for stock removal rates is 0.15 cm³ (or .010 cubic inches) per minute for every 100 A of electrolytic grinding current. Each work material has a saturation point which limits the current it can accept. Machine tool manufacturers of electrolytic grinders generally provide charts with their machines showing the stock removal rates for various materials.

THE ELECTROLYTE

The electrolyte, generally a saline solution, serves two important functions:
a) Acts as a current conductor between the work and the wheel.
b) Chemically combines with the decomposed work material.

As the current flows from the workpiece (positive pole) through the electrolytic solution to the grinding wheel (negative pole), pockets of the solution act as electro-chemical cells decomposing the work surface. The current combines with the electrolyte to form a soft oxide film on the work surface which will not allow the current to flow. The wiping action of the revolving grinding wheel removes these oxides, allowing the current to flow again. The rate of this decomposition is in direct proportion to the amount of current flowing from the work to the wheel.

As the solution becomes contaminated with metal particles, it is flushed away into a storage tank, then passed through filters to remove these particles. A freshly filtered solution is necessary for efficient electrolytic grinding. An uneven supply of the electrolyte will result in excessive wheel wear, while a weak supply retards the metal removal rates.

The machine surfaces coming into contact with the electrolyte must be chrome plated to overcome the corrosive action of the electrolytic solution.

SURFACE FINISH

The surface finish obtained by electrolytic grinding ranges from 0.2 μm to 0.5 μm (8 to 20 microinches) when steels and various alloys are ground. As a rule, the higher the alloy, the better the surface finish obtainable. When surface or traverse grinding tungsten carbide, a surface finish of 0.25 μm to 0.3 μm (or 10 to 12 microinches) may be expected. A surface finish 0.2 μm to 0.25μm (8 to 10 microinches) is generally the rule when plunge grinding carbides. These surface finishes can be obtained at maximum stock removal rates with no finish cut required.

ELECTROLYTIC GRINDING METHODS

Grinding methods such as cylindrical, form, plunge, surface, traverse, etc., all lend themselves to electrolytic grinding. With all types of grinding methods, one important fact must be kept in mind, that is, the area of work-wheel contact along the cutting path of the wheel should never exceed 20 mm under normal conditions. If it is necessary to exceed this 20 mm dimension, a much slower feed rate must be used or the electrolyte must be supplied to the grinding area by auxiliary methods.

CYLINDRICAL GRINDING

All the advantages of electrolytic grinding apply to this form of grinding, except high stock removal rates. The reason for the lower stock removal is that the area of contact between the work and wheel is small, allowing little current to flow. It is recommended that plunge grinding be used to rough out work to within a few hundredths of a millimetre of size and then that work be finished by traverse grinding.

FORM GRINDING

Metal-bonded aluminum oxide wheels are usually employed for form grinding operations. They are easily formed to the desired shape by a conventional diamond truing attachment. Formed diamond wheels for grinding carbides are expensive to change from form to form and difficult to true. Therefore, metal-bonded abrasive wheels are generally used for the production grinding of carbides.

PLUNGE GRINDING

When an area is plunge ground, there is no traverse motion of the wheel, and the wheel is fed straight into the surface. Either the face or the side of the wheel may be used for plunge grinding. Single point tools, face milling cutters, straight side milling cutters, and any other single plane surfaces within the range of the wheel sizes may be effectively ground by this method. Fine manual feeds should be used for grinding individual pieces, while automatic feeds are recommended for production grinding.

SURFACE GRINDING

Since the area of contact in surface grinding varies with the depth of cut for each wheel diameter, the full depth of cut per pass is recommended for maximum results. Always use the largest wheel possible, depending on the capacity of the machine. The rate of traverse is not dependent upon the width of the wheel as long as there is sufficient current available. Whenever possible, automatic power feeds are advisable since too slow a feed rate results in excessive overcut and too fast a feed results in excessive wheel wear. At no time should the work and wheel contact exceed 20 mm. Machine tool manufacturers generally supply feed rate charts with their machines. The charts consider grinding current, wheel size, depth of cut, and area of contact.

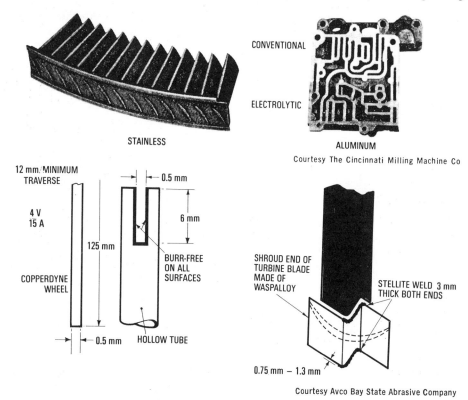

STAINLESS

CONVENTIONAL

ELECTROLYTIC

ALUMINUM

Courtesy The Cincinnati Milling Machine Co

12 mm/MINIMUM TRAVERSE

4 V 15 A

125 mm

COPPERDYNE WHEEL

0.5 mm

0.5 mm

6 mm

BURR-FREE ON ALL SURFACES

HOLLOW TUBE

SHROUD END OF TURBINE BLADE MADE OF WASPALLOY

STELLITE WELD 3 mm THICK BOTH ENDS

0.75 mm – 1.3 mm

Courtesy Avco Bay State Abrasive Company

Fig. 19-13   Examples of types of electrolytic grinding

TRAVERSE GRINDING

Most cutter sharpening operations are performed by traverse grinding with a cup or flare type wheel. Helical side milling cutters and others that are impractical to plunge grind are sharpened by this method.

Edge grinding with cup wheels is impractical as the work-wheel contact is small and allows little current to flow. For efficiency in traverse grinding, the wheel is swivelled slightly or an angle of 1 to 2° is dressed on the wheel surface to increase the area of work-wheel contact. Traverse feed rates depend upon the swivel angle, width of the wheel face, and the amount of current available.

ADVANTAGES OF ELECTROLYTIC GRINDING

Electrolytic grinding offers many advantages over conventional machining methods for metal removal.

a) It saves wheel costs, especially in metal-bonded diamond wheels, since only 10% of the metal is removed by abrasive action.

b) There is a high ratio of stock removal in relation to the wheel wear.

c) Higher production rates are possible because of the longer runs between wheel truing.

d) No heat is generated during the grinding operation: therefore, there is no burning or heat distortion of the work.

e) The process is burr-free, thereby eliminating deburring operations.

f) Thin, fragile workpieces can be ground without distortion since the wheel never touches the work.

g) Tungsten carbide and super-tough alloys can be ground quickly and with ease.

h) Exotic materials, such as zirconium, beryllium, etc., can be cut regardless of their hardness, fragility, or thermal sensitivity.

i) Dissimilar metals can be ground, providing they are electrically conductive.

j) Cutters may be reground in one pass, eliminating the necessity of finishing cuts.

k) No stresses are created in the work material.

l) No work hardening occurs during this process.

DISADVANTAGES OR LIMITATIONS

While there are many advantages of electrolytic grinding, there are also some disadvantages or limitations.

a) Only electrically conductive work can be ground.

b) Grinding wheels, especially the metal-bonded diamond wheels, are more expensive.

c) Inside corners cannot be ground sharper than a 0.25 mm to 0.40 mm (or .010 in. to 0.15 in.) radius because of the overcut occurring during the electrochemical action.

d) Accuracy is possible to within 0.01 mm (or .0005 in.) only.

e) The electrolytic solution is corrosive; therefore, machine parts coming into contact with the electrolyte must be chrome plated.

f) The wheel contact should not exceed 20 mm.

CONCLUSION

At present, this method of electrical machining simplifies production methods and provides savings in both machining time and grinding wheel costs. As new types of metal-bonded wheels, power supplies, and electrolyte are developed, this grinding process should find many more applications.

ELECTROLYTIC GRINDING QUESTIONS

1. Describe briefly the electrolytic grinding process.

2. Describe the type and function of the electrolytic grinding wheel.

3. What purpose does the wheel abrasive serve in electrolytic grinding?

4. Discuss the importance and operation of truing a grinding wheel.

5. What function does the workpiece serve in the electrolytic grinding circuit?

6. What type of current is used for this process?

7. Name two functions of the electrolyte solution.

8. Explain what occurs to the electrolyte when the current flows.

9. What surface finishes are possible to obtain by electrolytic grinding?

10. Discuss plunge and surface grinding.

11. Name eight main advantages of the electrolytic grinding process.

12. List four disadvantages of electrolytic grinding.

Energy from explosives being used to form large shapes

HIGH ENERGY METAL FORMING

Forming large metal parts has become important as a result of the missile and aerospace program. Small parts may be easily formed to shape in conventional presses; however, these presses do not have the capacity or the force necessary to form materials with higher elastic strength or large parts made of common material. Formed parts as large as 3 m in diameter were required by the aerospace program; to produce them in conventional presses would have been economically impractical due to the cost and size of the press that would be required.

High energy rate (explosive) forming has received considerable attention in recent years because of its ability to apply great amounts of pressure (as much as 700 MPa or higher) by controlled explosions to form metal to shape. In this type of metal forming, only the cavity part of the die is required, and the force created by the controlled explosion replaces the die punch. Although there are many variations of explosive forming, only chemical explosive, electric spark discharge, and electromagnetic will be briefly discussed to give the reader an insight into the principles involved.

EXPLOSIVE FORMING

Chemical explosives have proved to be a compact and relatively inexpensive source of high energy. Only a small amount of explosive is required to create a large force to form metal to shape. For example, 60 g of explosives in a 1.5 m diameter water tank can produce the same force as a hydraulic press rated at 14 000 MPa. If 2250 g of explosives were used, this would far exceed the capacity of any existing press.

The Process
1. The workpiece (blank) to be formed is clamped to the top of the die cavity by a clamping ring (Fig. 19-14).

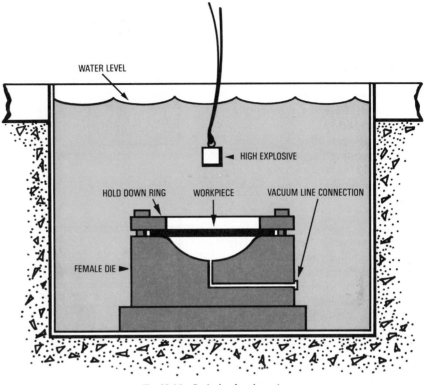

Fig. 19-14   Explosive forming setup

2. The explosive is mounted over the blank at a predetermined distance away from its surface.
3. The entire assembly is lowered into a water tank.
4. A vacuum is created in the die (the space between the workpiece and the die cavity) (Fig. 19-14).
5. The explosive charge is set off.
6. The shock wave which is created causes the metal to form to the shape of the die cavity.

The detonation of the exposive under water creates a shock wave that strikes the workpiece, forcing the metal into contact with the die. The pressures exerted on the work are high; however, the intensity and duration of the pressure can be controlled so that only slightly more energy than required is exerted. If too much pressure is exerted, it may cause the workpiece to rupture.

ADVANTAGES

Many advantages are offered by the use of explosives for forming large metal sections.
a) Since only one-half the die is required, the cost of die manufacture is reduced.
b) The cost of the equipment required is relatively low.
c) Parts difficult or impossible to form by mechanical means can be formed.
d) A better surface finish on the work is created than is possible by conventional die sets.
e) Better forming accuracy is possible because there is little or no springback in the workpiece.
f) Annealing operations required for deep forming by conventional means are eliminated.

LIMITATIONS AND DISADVANTAGES

Certain limitations or disadvantages must

be considered when using explosives to form metals.

a) Employees must be trained in the safe use of explosives.

b) Insurance rates are generally higher because of the use of explosives.

c) The forming must be done in a remote area, which increases transportation and handling costs.

d) Elevated temperatures which could assist in forming the workpiece cannot be used because of the cooling effects of water.

CONCLUSION

The use of explosives has provided industry with a relatively inexpensive method of forming large metal parts. This process should be considered for parts difficult or impossible to form by conventional means or if costs are lower.

ELECTRIC SPARK DISCHARGE FORMING

Shock waves, comparable to those produced by explosives, created by an underwater electrical discharge of high voltage have been used successfully for metal forming. The amount of electrical energy required for forming workpieces depends upon the following factors:

a) diameter and depth of the die cavity

b) distance from the spark to the surface of the water

c) width of the spark gap

d) thickness of the workpiece

Electrospark forming cannot and was not intended to compete with conventional presses in the forming of simple parts. It is generally used for forming parts which would be difficult or impossible to manufacture by conventional methods. Operations such as forming, blanking, piercing, embossing, flaring, trimming, and forming tubular parts either by expansion or contraction are possible with electrospark forming.

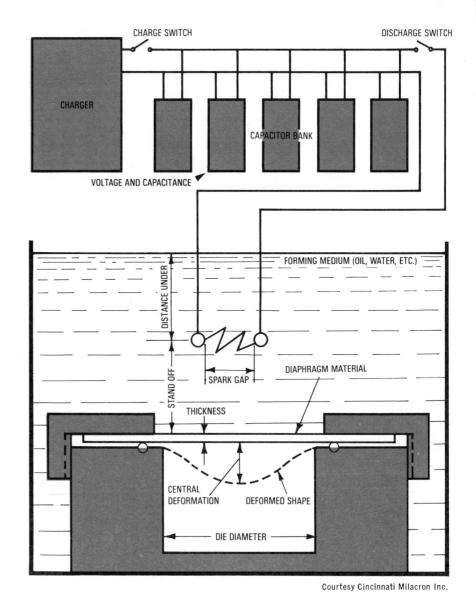

Courtesy Cincinnati Milacron Inc.

Fig. 19-15   Electrospark forming principle

The Process

1. The piece to be formed is fastened securely to the top of the die by means of a clamp ring (Fig. 19-15).

2. The die is then submerged in water.

3. A vacuum is created in the die cavity.

4. The electrodes are positioned at a predetermined distance above the workpiece (Fig. 19-15).

5. The stored energy from the high voltage capacitor bank is released between the submerged electrodes.

6. The spark discharge between the electrodes creates a shock wave, causing the workpiece to form to the shape of the die cavity.

The release of high energy between the submerged electrodes heats and vaporizes a thin channel of water, rapidly expanding it and creating a shock wave. When this shock wave reaches the workpiece, there is an imbalance of forces on the workpiece caused by low pressure in the die cavity as a result of the vacuum and high pressure of the shock wave. Because of this imbalance of forces, the work is forced in the direction of the low pressure and assumes the shape of the die cavity.

Often the path of the spark is controlled by connecting the space between the two electrodes with a thin wire. During discharge, the spark is confined to a specific path; however, the wire is vaporized and must be replaced for each part formed.

CONCLUSION

Most advantages and disadvantages listed for explosive forming apply also to electrospark forming. The differences between the two processes are:

a) The cost of the equipment required to initiate the discharge is considerably higher than with explosive forming.

b) Electrospark forming is a much safer process and does not have to be performed in a remote area.

c) Higher production rates are possible.

d) The path of the discharge can be more accurately controlled.

e) The amount of discharge is limited to the capacity of the electrical power bank.

ELECTROMAGNETIC FORMING

Electromagnetic forming is one of the newest methods of high energy metal forming. The magnetic field of force, created by passing a high current through a coil around either the outside or inside of a workpiece, is used to form parts to the desired shape. The best results with this method of high energy metal forming have been obtained when forming parts made of copper and aluminum which are good electrical conductors. Electromagnetic forming is primarily used for swaging or expanding tubular shapes. It may also be

used for embossing, punching, forming, and shrinking operations (Fig. 19-16).

The Process

In electromagnetic forming, the electrical energy from the capacitor bank (Fig. 19-17) is passed through a coil rather than between two electrodes as is the case in electrospark forming. A large magnetic field builds up around the coil, inducing a voltage in the workpiece. The resultant high current builds up its own magnetic field. These two magnetic fields of force are opposite in direction and repel each other, causing the deformation of the workpiece. If the coil is placed on the inside of a tubular workpiece, the magnetic force will cause the workpiece to bulge and assume the shape of the die cavity. Workpieces may be shrunk onto formed mandrels by placing the coil around the outside of the piece to be formed (Fig. 19-17). Field shaping coils may be used to concentrate the magnetic field of force when irregular shapes must be formed.

Experiments have been conducted using variations of electrical energy. The best results for electromagnetic forming have been obtained with a capacitor bank of low voltage and high capacitance. The amount of work deformation increases in relation to the amount of stored electrical energy released. Deformation of the workpiece decreases when the distance between the coil and the work is increased. Parts

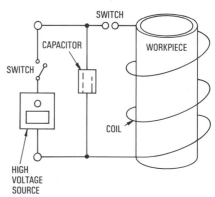

Courtesy Cincinnati Milacron Inc.

Fig. 19-16   Examples of electromagnetic forming

Fig. 19-17   Electromagnetic forming principle

made of poor or nonconductive materials can be formed by placing a conductive foil around or inside the parts to be formed. The foil acts as would a good electrically conductive material and causes the workpiece to assume the shape of the die cavity or formed mandrel.

ELECTROMAGNETIC FORMING FACTORS

Although electromagnetic forming is a relatively new method of metal forming, it has proven invaluable for many operations which were difficult or impossible to perform by other methods. The following factors must be carefully considered since they affect the efficiency of the electromagnetic forming process.

a) The amount of electrical energy employed must be sufficient to completely form the part.
b) The coil should be designed so that it is stronger than the part to be formed; otherwise, the electromagnetic force may deform the coil rather than the workpiece.
c) The size of the wire and the number of turns in the coil are very important because they determine the strength of the electromagnetic field which can be created. The coil must be placed at a specific distance from the part to be formed.
d) The electrical conductivity of the work material is an important factor in this process.
e) The thickness of the work material determines the location of the coil and the amount of electrical energy required.

ADVANTAGES

In electromagnetic forming, the size of the work that can be formed is controlled by the amount of electrical power that can be directed to the forming coil. However, it has certain advantages over other methods of high energy forming.

a) The amount of electrical energy can be accurately controlled.

b) An equal amount of force is applied to all areas of the part.
c) No forces are set up unless a part is in the magnetic field.
d) The work may be preheated because no water or liquid is required for the forming process.
e) There are no moving parts in the forming equipment.
f) The operation can be automated.
g) Forming can be performed in a vacuum or in an inert atmosphere.
h) It provides a low cost method of assembling where bands of metal must be formed around other parts.

CONCLUSION

Electromagnetic forming, although a relatively new process, has been used for a great variety of industrial applications ranging from the aerospace program to the assembly of electronic components. As electromagnetic pulse equipment of greater capacities becomes available, this method of metal forming should assume more importance in manufacturing processes.

HIGH ENERGY METAL FORMING QUESTIONS

1. Explain why high energy metal forming has become increasingly important in recent years.
2. Name three methods of explosive forming.
3. Explain briefly what occurs when a chemical explosive is detonated under water.
4. Name four advantages of explosive forming.
5. What are the disadvantages or limitations in using explosives for forming metals?
6. How does electric spark discharge forming differ from explosive forming?
7. Describe briefly the process of electric spark discharge forming.
8. Explain what occurs when high energy is released between two submerged electrodes.
9. Why is it necessary to create a vacuum in the die cavity for explosive and electric spark discharge forming?
10. On what principle does electromagnetic forming operate?
11. List four important factors which should be considered for electromagnetic forming.
12. Name five advantages of electromagnetic forming.

NUMERICAL CONTROL

Numerical control is one of the most exciting developments in the metalworking industry of the past century. It promises to have the same revolutionary effect on manufacturing as the advent of the automobile had on the country's economy. Since the latter half of the 1950s, its use for the accurate control of metal cutting machines has increased at a tremendous rate throughout the world.

Numerical control may be defined as a method of accurately controlling the movement of machine tools by a series of *programmed numerical data* which activates the motors of the machine tool. There is nothing complex or magical about this system. It is based on the simple fundamental that combines automatic measurement of the amount a machine table slide will move with a series of programmed instructions.

A basic form of numerical control has existed since the first blueprint or sketch of a part was dimensioned by a draftsman. The numbers on a blueprint convey the information to the machine operator who proceeds to transform these numbers into manual movements of the machine tool. The numerically controlled machines are supplied with detailed information regarding the part by means of punched cards or tape. The machine decodes this punched information and electronic devices activate the various motors on the machine

Courtesy Cincinnati Milacron Inc.

A five-axis, numerically controlled milling machine being used to produce aircraft structural members

tool, causing them to follow specific instructions. The measuring and recording devices incorporated into numerically controlled machine tools assure that the part being manufactured will be accurate. Numerically controlled machines eliminate the possibility of human error which existed before their development.

Numerical control is really an efficient method of reading blueprints and conveying this information to the motors which control the speeds, feeds, and various motions of the machine tool. The designer's information is transferred to punched cards or tape which is put into the machine tool reader. These punched cards or tape may be compared to the roll of punched paper used to operate the keys of a player-type piano and produce music. Each hole on the paper roll corresponds to a key

(note) on the player piano keyboard. As air passes through the hole, it moves a key on the keyboard, producing a note. On numerically controlled tape reading devices, air could also be used to decode the

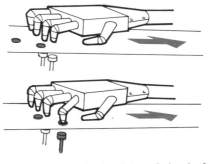

Courtesy Coleman Engineering Co.

Fig. 19-18   Mechanical fingers read tape information

tape information; however, small mechanical wires (fingers) (Fig. 19-18) or beams of light are generally used. The fingers or beams of light are connected to an electrical circuit. Each time a hole in the tape appears beneath the finger or beam of light, a specific circuit is activated, sending signals to start or stop motors (which positions the work) and control various functions of the machine tool.

MEASUREMENT FUNDAMENTALS

Accurate measurement is fundamental to the numerical control of machine tools. The workpiece or cutting tool must be moved a definite distance in one direction before the machining operation is performed. The distances moved must be accurately measured by some method that the numerical control system will understand.

There are many methods of measurement, but all consist of comparing the distance to be measured to some known standard. On a milling machine the distance the table is moved may be measured by a scale mounted beside the table or slide. In most cases, however, the table is positioned by turning the lead screw a specific number of turns, depending upon the distance the table is to be moved. As the lead screw has a certain pitch (or number of threads per inch) and was manufactured to a standard, the number of turns is transformed into a specific distance.

In numerical control systems, accurate measurement is achieved by the amount the lead screw has been rotated in accordance with the information on the tape or card. The degree of accuracy obtained will depend on the type of numerical control system being used.

TYPES OF NUMERICAL CONTROL SYSTEMS

Open loop and *closed loop* are the two main types of control systems used for numerical control machine tools.

OPEN LOOP SYSTEM

In the *open loop system* (Fig. 19-19), the tape is fed into a *tape reader* which decodes the information punched on the tape and stores it until the machine is ready to use it and then converts it into electrical pulses or signals. These signals are sent to the *control unit* which energizes the *servo control units*. The servo control units direct the *servo motors* to perform certain functions according to the information supplied by the tape. The amount each servo motor will move depends upon the number of electrical pulses it receives from the servo control unit. Precision lead screws, usually having 10 threads per inch (25.4 mm■) are used on numerical control machines. If the servo motor connected to the lead screw receives 1000 electrical pulses, the machine slide will move 1 in. (25.4 mm■). Therefore one pulse will cause the machine slide to move .001 in. (0.0254 mm■). This type of system is fairly simple; however, since there is no means of checking whether the servo motor has performed its function correctly, it is not generally used where an accuracy greater than .001 in. (0.025 mm■) is required. The open loop system may be compared to a gun crew who have made all the calculations necessary to hit a distant target, but do not have an observer to confirm the accuracy of the shot.

CLOSED LOOP SYSTEM

The *closed loop system* (Fig. 19-20) can be compared to the same gun crew who now have an observer to confirm the accuracy of the shot. The observer relays the information regarding the accuracy of the shot to the gun crew, who then make the necessary adjustments to hit the target.

The closed loop system is similar to the open loop system with the exception that a *feedback unit* (Fig. 19-20) is introduced in the electrical circuit. This feedback unit, generally called a *transducer*, compares the amount the machine table has been moved by the servo motor with the signal sent by the control unit. The control unit instructs the servo motor to make

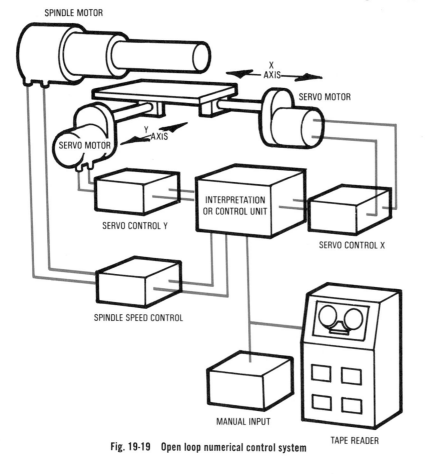

Fig. 19-19   Open loop numerical control system

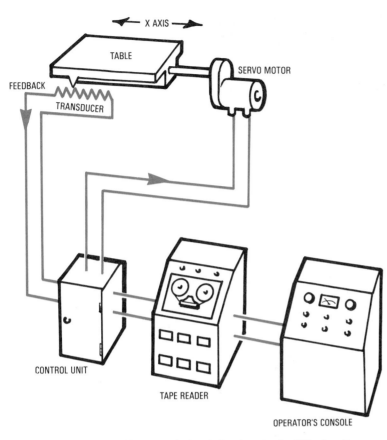

Fig. 19-20   Closed loop numerical control system showing "X" axis only

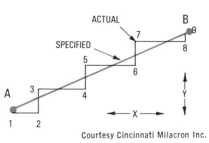

Courtesy Cincinnati Milacron Inc.

Fig. 19-21A   A comparison of point-to-point control and straight cut control (Red)

CONTINUOUS PATH OR CONTOURING CONTROL

When contours are being machined, the control unit must direct the path of the cutting tool at all times. If a machining operation, for example, a straight line cut, must be performed between points *A* and *B*, additional devices must be added to the system. Much more detailed signals are sent to the machine slide so that each step it takes to get from points *A* to *B* is minute. The *continuous path* or *straight cut system* would follow the specified path *AB* illustrated in Fig. 19-21A at a controlled rate, producing a straight line cut. A computer is essential for the continuous path system because of the large number of coordinates required to guide the machine tool on a straight line path.

By further upgrading the continuous path system, the path a machine follows can be controlled to form any type of contour. The complex part illustrated in Fig. 19-21B is an example of the types of forms which can be machined easily on a contouring system. This system also requires the use of a computer because the time it would take to calculate all the necessary coordinates would be prohibitive.

INPUT MEDIA

With the development of numerical control, a variety of input media was used to convey the information from the blueprint to the machine. The most common types of input media used were magnetic tape, punched cards, and punched tape.

whatever adjustments are necessary until both the signal from the control unit and the one from the servo unit are equal. In the closed loop system, 10 000 electrical pulses are required to move the machine slide 1 in. (25.4 mm■). Therefore, on this type of system, one pulse will cause .0001 in. (0.0025 mm■) movement of the machine slide. Closed loop numerical control systems are very accurate because the accuracy of the command signal is recorded and there is an automatic compensation for error.

TYPES OF CONTROL

There are two types of controls available which position and control the cutting tool and the workpiece during the machining operation. These are *point-to-point* control

and the *continuous path or contouring control*. The type of work to be performed on a machine will determine the type of control that should be purchased.

POINT-TO-POINT POSITIONING

With this type of control, the machine slide is instructed to go from point A to point B. The path taken by the machine slide between these two points does not matter since the operations required must be performed only at points A and B. The tool slide moves from point A to B in a series of small steps (Fig. 19-21A). As illustrated, there is a difference between the specified and the actual path of the machine slide. The point-to-point commands are ideal for drilling, boring, and tapping operations.

Courtesy Cincinnati Milacron Inc.

Fig. 19-21B   A complex part produced by a contouring system

MAGNETIC TAPE

Usually 1 in. (25.4 mm■) wide tape is used, and on a 4 in. (100 mm) length as many as 2000 pieces of information can be included. One major disadvantage of this input media is that it can be affected by nearby electrical transformers or disturbances which could remove some of the information on the tape.

PUNCHED CARDS

Some numerical control systems employ 80 or 90 column punched cards which can carry a great deal of information. As many as 120 cards per minute can be decoded by the card reader. The disadvantage of the card system is that cards can become bent and will not process through the reader. If not handled with extreme care, the sequence of the cards could be altered.

PUNCHED TAPE

Because each different type of input media required different types of systems to convey the blueprint information to the machine tool, the Electronics Industries Association decided to standardize the numerical control input media. A 1 in. (25.4 mm■), 8-channel punched tape was selected as a standard since it offered a number of advantages over the magnetic tape and punched cards.

STANDARD PUNCHED TAPE

Since the 1 in. (25.4 mm■) wide, 8-channel tape using the Binary Coded Decimal system (BCD) has been selected as a standard by the Electronics Industries Association, it will be discussed in greater detail. The following section will give the reader a better understanding of what types are available, how the numerical information from the blueprint is transferred to the tape, and the method of reading tapes.

TYPES OF TAPES

Standard numerical control tapes which have a continuous row of sprocket holes for feeding purposes (Fig. 19-22) are manufactured from a number of different materials.

1. *Paper*: Tapes made of paper are available in a variety of colours and may be purchased oiled or non-oiled. The oiled tapes are recommended because they help to lubricate the punches in the special tape typewriter which is used to punch the holes in the tape. Paper tape is inexpensive; however, it is not recommended for shop use if more than a few pieces are to be machined since it tears easily. Paper tapes are usually used for file purposes.

2. *Mylar*: Tapes made of mylar (a type of plastic) laminated between two strips of paper have provided a sturdy tape which is almost impossible to tear. Although it is more expensive than the plain paper tapes, it is highly recommended for shop use because of its sturdy quality. Aluminized mylar tapes are recommended for light source tape readers; however, they are slightly more expensive than the paper mylar type.

3. *Foil*: Foil tapes are sturdy but not generally recommended because they are very hard on the punches of the tape preparation equipment.

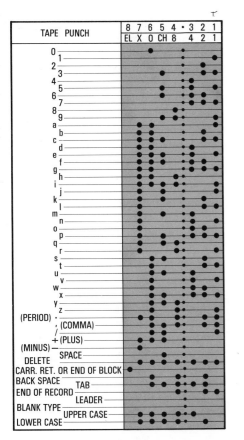

TAPE PUNCH	8	7	6	5	4	•	3	2	1
	EL	X	O	CH	8		4	2	1

Courtesy Cincinnati Milacron Inc.

Fig. 19-22 Electronics Industries Association standard coding for a 1 in. wide 8-channel tape

TAPE CODING

The Electronics Industries Association adopted the *Binary Coded Decimal System* for standardizing information punched on tapes used for numerical control. The standard coding system used for the 1 in. (25.4 mm■) wide, 8-channel tape is illustrated in Fig. 19-22.

The numbers 1 to 8 on the top of the tape represent only the number of each channel and have no relationship to the holes punched in the tape.

a) *The sprocket holes* between channels 3 and 4 are used to drive the tape through the machine. The sprocket holes are set off-centre so that it is im-

possible to put the reverse side of the tape into the machine.

b) *Channels 1, 2, 3 and 4* are used for *numerical data*, such as dimensions, speeds, feeds, etc.

c) *Channel 5*, marked CH, is called the *parity check*. An odd number of holes must appear in each row; otherwise the tape reader will stop the machine. If an even number of holes must be punched in one row to get the correct information on the tape, an additional hole must be punched in channel 5. The odd parity check checks for any errors or mechanical failures in the tape preparation.

d) *Channel 6* always represents a "zero."

e) *Channel 7*, marked X, is used to select a letter to identify various machine operations and is not used for dimensions. Each letter (a to z) in the left-hand, vertical column (Fig. 19-22) represents a certain machine function or operation, such as drilling, boring, reaming, etc. When channels 6 and 7 are punched together, in conjunction with channels 1, 2, 3, or 4, operations "a" to "i" will be selected. When only channel 7 is punched, in conjunction with channels 1, 2, 3, or 4, operations "j" to "r" will be selected. If only channel 6 is punched, in conjunction with channels 1, 2, 3, or 4, operations "s" to "z" will be selected.

f) *Channel 8*, marked EL (or EOB), represents the *end of a line or block* of information. It must always be at the beginning of a tape and at the end of each block of information.

The *TAB* code, punched in channels 2, 3, 4, 5, and 6, is used to separate each operation or dimension. The remaining codes in Fig. 19-22 beginning with a "." (a period) and ending with *lower case* are all acceptable codes used in numerical control tapes.

EXAMPLES OF PUNCHED INFORMATION

1. Assume that the numerical value of 1 must be recorded. A hole must be punched in channel 1 because it has a numerical value of 1.

2. Assume that the numerical value of 5 must be recorded. A hole must be punched in channels 3 and 1 because channel 3 has a numerical value of 4 and channel 1 has a numerical value of 1. These two totalled equal a numerical value of 5.

   NOTE: Since only two holes are punched across this row, an extra hole must be punched in the parity check channel (5) as the tape reader will not recognize an even number of holes (Fig. 19-22). If a hole is not punched in the parity check channel, the tape reader will stop the machine.

3. Operation "g" would be recorded by punching holes in channels 1, 2, 3, 6, and 7.

TAPE FORMAT

Each block of information must contain five complete words or pieces of information. If five complete words are not included in each block, the tape reader will not recognize the information on the tape, and therefore will not activate the control unit. Fig. 19-23 shows a punched tape containing one complete block of information consisting of five complete words. From left to right, the information punched on the tape is as follows:

1. A hole is punched in channel 8, which represents the end or the beginning of a line or block of information.

2. The *first word* of the block represents the number of the operation. H001 represents the first operation on the tape.

   The *letter H* is recorded by punching holes in channels 4, 6, and 7 (Fig. 19-23).

   The *two zeros* are recorded by punching channel 6 in two successive rows.

   The *1* is recorded by punching channel 1 which has a numerical value of 1.

3. The *TAB* code is used to separate each word into a block of information.

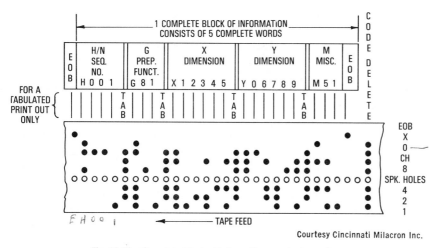

Fig. 19-23 Complete block of information punched on a tape

Courtesy Cincinnati Milacron Inc.

4. The *second word* in the block represents the type of operation to be performed. G81 is a drill cycle on Cincinnati Milacron Numerical Control systems.

The *letter G* is recorded by punching channels 1, 2, 3, 6, and 7.

The *8* is recorded by punching channel 4 which has a numerical value of 8.

The *1* is recorded by punching channel 1 which has a numerical value of 1.

5. The *third word* represents the distance the table slide must move from the *x*-axis. The information contained in the third word of Fig. 19-23 is X12345. As standard tapes on closed loop systems program all dimensions to ten-thousandths of an inch, the machine will move 1.2345 in from the *x*-axis.

6. The *fourth word* represents the distance the table slide must move from the *y*-axis. In Fig. 19-23, Y06789 represents a table movement of 0.6789 in. from the *y*-axis.

7. The *fifth word* represents a miscellaneous machining function. M51 would select the proper cam so that the hole in the workpiece is drilled to the required depth.

TAPE PREPARATION

A special tape data punching machine, similar to a typewriter, is used to punch information on the numerical control tape. A programmer reviews the part drawing, determines the sequence of operations required, and records this information on a program sheet. A typist transfers the information contained on the program sheet to the tape using a special tape punching machine (Fig. 19-24). To ensure that the typist has not made an error in punching the information on the tape, a second typist may also type the same program. These two tapes are then compared, and if they are identical, it is assumed the program is correct. On some types of tape punching machines, the finished tape may be run back through the machine, which makes a duplicate tape and at the same time produces a typed copy of the program. The typed copy of the program can be compared with the original program to determine its accuracy.

NUMERICAL CONTROL OPERATION

Although numerical control systems differ greatly in detail and complexity according to the manufacturer, all have basically the same elements. Regardless of the type of input media used, all operate a machine tool the same way. A complete sequence of operations beginning with the programmer transferring the information from a blueprint to a program sheet until the finished part is removed from the machine is illustrated in Fig. 19-24.

1. The programmer reviews the blueprint of the part to be machined, determines the sequence of operations required, and lists the particulars about each operation on a program sheet (Fig. 19-24A).

2. A typist transfers the information contained on the program sheet to the tape using a special tape punching machine (Fig. 19-24B). Generally two tapes are made by two different typists, and these are compared to ensure that no error has been made.

3. The punched tape and a copy of the program sheet are then handed to the machine operator. After positioning the part to be machined on the machine table according to the instructions contained on the program sheet, he threads the tape into the tape reader (Figs. 19-24C and 19-25).

4. The tape reader which automatically advances the tape is then started.

5. As each block of information is decoded by the tape reader, it sends the necessary information to the *cycle control*.

6. After the end of each machining operation, the *feedback switch* informs the cycle control that the previous operation has been completed.

7. The cycle control instructs the *command memory unit* to transfer the tape instructions for the next operation to the *indexer* (Fig. 19-24F).

8. The indexer starts the servo motors, which in turn move the machine table slides the required amount.

ADVANTAGES

Numerical control has been applied to a variety of machines and has gained wide acceptance by industry. Machine tools such as lathes, turret drills, milling, and boring machines are some of the more

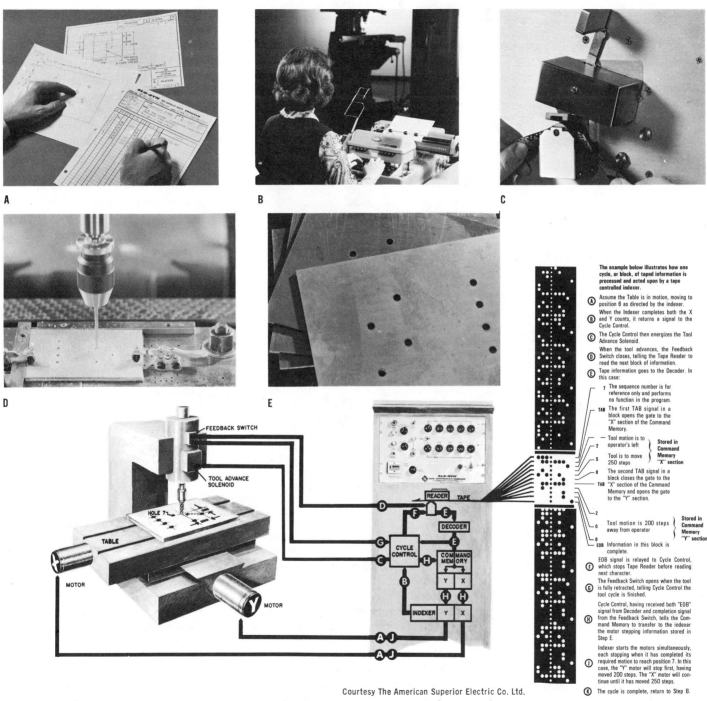

The example below illustrates how one cycle, or block, of taped information is processed and acted upon by a tape controlled indexer.

(A) Assume the Table is in motion, moving to position 6 as directed by the indexer.

(B) When the Indexer completes both the X and Y counts, it returns a signal to the Cycle Control.

(C) The Cycle Control then energizes the Tool Advance Solenoid.

(D) When the tool advances, the Feedback Switch closes, telling the Tape Reader to read the next block of information.

(E) Tape information goes to the Decoder. In this case:

7 The sequence number is for reference only and performs no function in the program.

TAB The first TAB signal in a block opens the gate to the "X" section of the Command Memory.

— Tool motion is to operator's left
2
5 Tool is to move 250 steps
0 } Stored in Command Memory "X" section

TAB The second TAB signal in a block closes the gate to the "X" section of the Command Memory and opens the gate to the "Y" section.

2
0 Tool motion is 200 steps away from operator
0 } Stored in Command Memory "Y" section

EOB Information in this block is complete.

(F) EOB signal is relayed to Cycle Control, which stops Tape Reader before reading next character.

(G) The Feedback Switch opens when the tool is fully retracted, telling Cycle Control the tool cycle is finished.

(H) Cycle Control, having received both "EOB" signal from Decoder and completion signal from the Feedback Switch, tells the Command Memory to transfer to the indexer the motor stepping information stored in Step E.

(J) Indexer starts the motors simultaneously, each stopping when it has completed its required motion to reach position 7. In this case, the "Y" motor will stop first, having moved 200 steps. The "X" motor will continue until it has moved 250 steps.

(K) The cycle is complete, return to Step B.

FEEDBACK SWITCH
TOOL ADVANCE SOLENOID
HOLE 7
TABLE
MOTOR
Y MOTOR
READER   TAPE
DECODER
CYCLE CONTROL
COMMAND MEMORY
Y   X
INDEXER
Y   X

A   B   C   D   E

Courtesy The American Superior Electric Co. Ltd.

Fig. 19-24   Numerical control sequence of operations

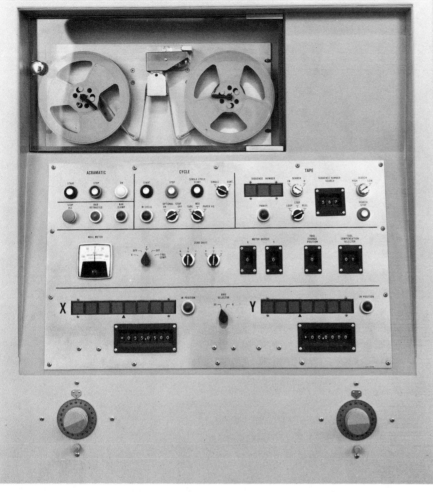

Courtesy Cincinnati Milacron Inc.

Fig. 19-25   Cincinnati Milacron Acromatic tape control reader

j) Once the program and tooling have been tested, the equipment does not require a highly skilled operator.

DISADVANTAGES

a) The initial cost of numerical control machines is higher than that of conventional machines.
b) Personnel trained in electronics are required to service the equipment.
c) Additional floor space is required for this equipment.
d) Personnel must be trained in the programming and operation of this equipment.

CONCLUSION

Numerical control has provided industry with a method of increasing productivity while maintaining a high degree of accuracy. Many changes have been made in machining procedures, resulting in a decrease in manufacturing costs. Refinements of numerical control systems will see this method applied to many other manufacturing processes.

NUMERICAL CONTROL QUESTIONS

1. Define and state the fundamentals of numerical control.
2. What methods may be used to permit the punched information to be decoded?
3. What purpose do transducers serve in a numerical control system?
4. Briefly define an open loop system.
5. In the closed loop system, how many electrical pulses are required to move the machine slide 1 in. (25.4 mm■).
6. How many electrical pulses would be required to move a machine slide 1/4 in. in an open loop system?
7. Explain the difference between an open loop and a closed loop system.
8. What is meant by point-to-point and continuous path commands?

common types of equipment which employ numerical control. The following are some of the advantages of numerical control equipment.

a) The machine has greater flexibility since one machine can act as a drill, mill, and turret lathe.
b) Once the program has been set up, there is over a 20 to 30% increase in production.
c) The reliability of the system eliminates the human error associated with manual operation, thereby reducing scrap loss.
d) Special jigs and fixtures usually required for positioning are eliminated since the machine can locate positions quickly and accurately.
e) The time required for setting up and locating the workpiece is reduced.
f) Complex operations can be performed with ease.
g) Single parts or production runs can be made with minimum effort and cost.
h) The program can be quickly changed by inserting a new tape in the machine.
i) Inspection costs are reduced because of the reliability of the system.

9. Name three types of input media and state their advantages.

10. State the advantages of paper and mylar tapes.

11. What feature on standard tape prevents it from being mounted incorrectly in a machine?

12. Explain a parity check and state its purpose.

13. What holes must be punched on a tape to signify operation "j9"?

14. Explain the purpose of the TAB and EL code.

15. By means of a suitable sketch, show what holes must be punched to indicate the following block of information on a tape.
    a) operation number: a26
    b) drilling operation: G81
    c) x-dimension: 2.6783
    d) y-dimension: .250
    e) drilling depth: 1.060

16. How is tape checked prior to its initial use to ensure its accuracy?

17. Describe briefly each step in a numerical control sequence of operations.

18. List six important advantages of numerical control.

19. Prepare a program sheet for a tape which could be used on a machine for locating the position of each hole in Fig. 19-26.

20. Make a drawing of a numerical control tape and indicate the position of the punch marks for the bottom row of holes.

POWDER METALLURGY

Powder metallurgy is the process of producing metal parts by:

a) Blending powdered metals and alloys.

b) Compressing the powders in a die which is the shape of the part to be produced.

c) Subjecting the shaped form to elevated temperatures (sintering) which causes the metal particles to "weld" together and form a solid part.

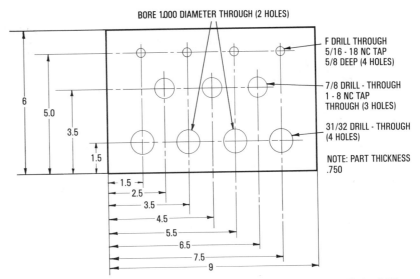

BORE 1.000 DIAMETER THROUGH (2 HOLES)

F DRILL THROUGH
5/16 - 18 NC TAP
5/8 DEEP (4 HOLES)

7/8 DRILL - THROUGH
1 - 8 NC TAP
THROUGH (3 HOLES)

31/32 DRILL - THROUGH
(4 HOLES)

NOTE: PART THICKNESS
.750

Courtesy Cincinnati Milacron Inc.

Fig. 19-26   Typical part drawing from which a numerical control tape is prepared (dimensions in inches)

HISTORY

The process of fabricating useful objects by forming metal powders is not new. The ancient Egyptians practised a form of powder metallurgy, and since that time man has continually experimented to perfect the process. Since World War I, research and development of this process have made considerable progress. Today powder metallurgy is used to produce cams, gears, self-oiling bearings, light filaments, levers, cemented carbide tools,

Courtesy The Powder Metallurgy Parts Mfg. Association

Gears being produced in a hydraulic press by the powder metallurgy process

Fig. 19-27   Examples of parts produced by powder metallurgy

a) Handling of molten metals is not involved.

b) Machining or finishing operations are rarely required.

c) It permits rapid mass production of steel and other high melting metal shapes.

d) Beryllium, molybdenum, and tungsten parts can be produced easily, when this would be impractical or uneconomical by other methods.

e) It permits combinations of metal and nonmetals as well as alloys which are not possible by any other method.

f) It permits accurate control over the density or the porosity of the finished part.

THE POWDER METALLURGY PROCESS

A part made by the powder metallurgy process begins with metal powders and goes through four main stages before it becomes a finished product (Fig. 19-29).

automotive filters, etc., which were previously produced by conventional machining methods (Fig. 19-27).

COMPARISON OF THE POWDER METALLURGY PROCESS

Powder metallurgy is a radical departure from the conventional machining process. With conventional machining methods, a piece of steel or bar stock larger than the finished part is selected and the required form is machined. The material cut away in the machining process is in the form of steel chips which are considered *scrap loss* (Fig. 19-28). In powder metallurgy, the correct types of powders are blended together and formed into the required shape in a die. Since machining is not required, scrap loss is minute as only the required amount of powder is used for each part.

The unique features of the powder metallurgy process are:

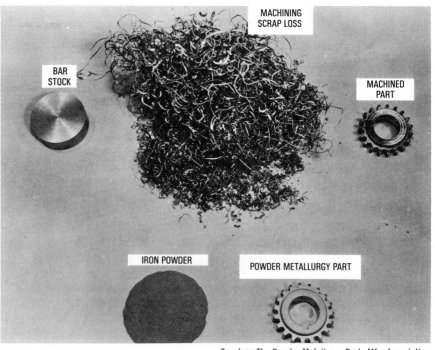

Fig. 19-28   Comparison of conventional machining and powder metallurgy processes

These include securing raw powders, blending, compacting, and sintering.

RAW POWDERS

Almost any type of metal can be produced in powder form; however, only a few have the desired characteristics and properties necessary for economical production. Iron and copper base powders are the two main types which lend themselves well to the powder metallurgy process. Aluminum, nickel, silver, and tungsten powders are not widely used; however, they have some important applications.

Some of the more common methods of manufacturing powders are:

a) *Atomization* or metal spraying is a means of producing powders from low temperature metals, such as aluminum, lead, tin, and zinc. This process produces powder particles, irregular in shape.

b) *Electrolytic deposition* is the common method used to produce copper, iron, silver, and tantalum powders.

c) *Granulation* is used to convert a few metals into powder. The metal is stirred rapidly while it is being cooled. This process depends upon the formation of oxides on the metal particles during stirring.

d) *Machining* produces coarse powders and is primarily used for producing magnesium powders.

e) *Milling* involves using various types of crushers, rollers, or presses to break the metal into powders.

f) *Reduction* is used to transform metal oxides to powder form by contact with gas at temperatures below their melting point. Cobalt, iron, molybdenum, nickel, and tungsten powders are produced by the reduction process.

g) *Shotting* is the operation of passing molten metal through an orifice or sieve and having the particles drop into water. Most metals can be powdered by this method; however, the particles are generally large.

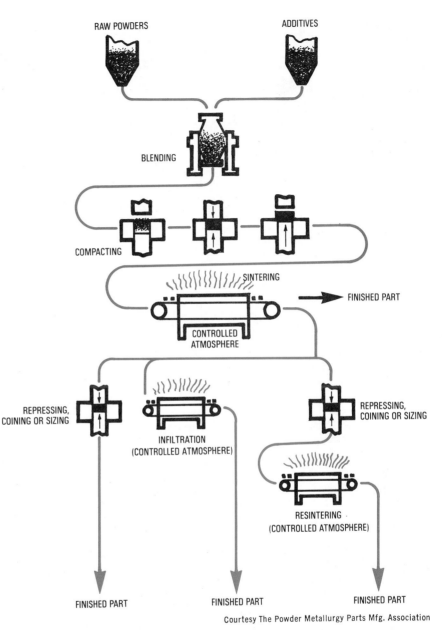

Courtesy The Powder Metallurgy Parts Mfg. Association

Fig. 19-29 The powder metallurgy process

BLENDING

The powder for a specific product must be carefully selected to ensure economical production and so that the finished part will have the required characteristics. The following information regarding the powder should be considered during its selection.

a) shape of the powder particle
b) particle size
c) flowability (its ability to flow readily)
d) compressibility (its ability to maintain a form)

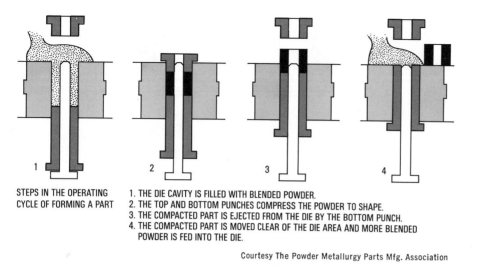

STEPS IN THE OPERATING
CYCLE OF FORMING A PART

1. THE DIE CAVITY IS FILLED WITH BLENDED POWDER.
2. THE TOP AND BOTTOM PUNCHES COMPRESS THE POWDER TO SHAPE.
3. THE COMPACTED PART IS EJECTED FROM THE DIE BY THE BOTTOM PUNCH.
4. THE COMPACTED PART IS MOVED CLEAR OF THE DIE AREA AND MORE BLENDED
   POWDER IS FED INTO THE DIE.

Courtesy The Powder Metallurgy Parts Mfg. Association

Fig. 19-30   Steps in compacting metal powders to shape

e) sintering ability (its ability to fuse or bond together)

Once the correct powders have been selected, the mass of each is carefully determined in the proportion required for the finished component, and a die lubricant, such as powdered graphite, zinc stearate, or stearic acid, is added. The purpose of this lubricant is to assist the flow of powder in the die, prevent scoring of the die walls, and permit easy ejection of the compressed part. This composition is then carefully mixed or blended (Fig. 19-30) to ensure homogeneous grain distribution in the finished product.

COMPACTING (BRIQUETTING)

The powder blend is then fed into a precision die which is the shape and size of the finished product. The die generally consists of a die shell, an upper punch, and a lower punch (Fig. 19-30). These dies are usually mounted on hydraulic or mechanical presses where pressures from about 14 kPa to as much as 1400 MPa are used to compress the powder. Soft powder particles can be pressed or keyed together readily and therefore do not require as high a pressure as the harder particles. The density and hardness of the finished product increases with the amount of pressure used to compact or briquette the powder. However, it should be kept in mind that for every case there is an optimum pressure above which very little improvement in qualities and properties can be obtained.

SINTERING

After compacting, the "green part" must be heated sufficiently in order to effect permanent cohesion of the metal particles into a solid. This operation of heating is known as *sintering*. The parts are passed through controlled protective atmosphere furnaces which are maintained at a temperature approximately one-third below the melting point of the principal powder. The carefully controlled atmosphere and temperature during the sintering operation permits particle bonding and recrystallization across the particle interfaces. Most sintering is done in a hydrogen atmosphere, producing parts with no scaling or discolouration.

The temperature within the furnaces varies from 870°C to 1500°C depending on the type of metal powder being sintered. The time required to sinter a part varies, depending on its shape and size; normally, however, it is from 15 to 45 min.

The purpose of the sintering operation is to bond the powder particles together to form a strong homogeneous part having the desired physical characteristics.

FINISHING OPERATIONS

After sintering, most parts are ready for service. However, some parts requiring very close tolerances or other qualities may require some additional operations, such as sizing and repressing, impregnation, infiltration, plating, heat treating, and machining.

SIZING AND REPRESSING

Parts requiring close tolerances or increased density must be *sized* or *repressed*. This involves putting the part into a die which is similar to the one used for compacting and repressing it. This operation improves the surface finish, the dimensional accuracy, increases the density, and gives added strength to the part.

IMPREGNATION

This is the process of filling the pores of a sintered part with a lubricant or nonmetallic material. Oilite bearings are a good example of a part impregnated with oil to overcome the necessity for constant lubrication and maintenance. Parts may be impregnated by a vacuum process or by soaking the parts in oil for several hours.

INFILTRATION

This is the process of filling the pores of a part with a metal or alloy having a lower melting point than the sintered piece. The purpose of this operation is to increase the density, strength, hardness, impact resistance, and ductility of the manufactured part.

Slugs of the material to be infiltrated are placed on the compacted parts and passed through the sintering furnace. Because of its lower melting point, the infiltrated material melts and penetrates the pores of the compacted part by capillary action.

Courtesy The Powder Metallurgy Parts Mfg. Association

Fig. 19-31 Examples of products available through powder metallurgy

PLATING, HEAT TREATING, MACHINING

Depending on the type of material, its application, and requirements, some powder metallurgy parts may be plated, heat treated, machined, brazed, or welded.

ADVANTAGES OF POWDER METALLURGY

The use of powder metallurgy is increasing rapidly, with many parts being made better and more economically than with previous manufacturing methods. Some of the advantages of the powder metallurgy process are:

a) Close dimensional tolerances of plus or minus 0.02 mm (or .001 in.) and smooth finishes can be obtained without costly secondary operations.

b) Complex or unusually shaped parts, which would be impractical to obtain by any other method, can be produced.

c) It is capable of producing porous bearings and cemented carbide tools.

d) The pores of a part can be infiltrated with other metals.

e) Surfaces of great wear resistance can be produced.

f) The porosity of the product can be accurately controlled.

g) Products made of extremely pure metals can be produced.

h) There is little waste in this process.

i) The operation can be automated and employ unskilled labour, keeping costs low.

j) The physical properties of the product can be minutely controlled.

k) Duplicate parts are accurate and unvarying.

l) Powders made from difficult-to-machine alloys can be formed into parts which would be difficult to produce by machining processes.

DISADVANTAGES OF POWDER METALLURGY

Although there are many advantages of the powder metallurgy process, there are also certain disadvantages or limitations.

a) Metal powders are quite expensive and must be carefully stored to avoid deterioration.

b) The cost of the presses and furnaces is high, and therefore it is not practical for short-run jobs.

c) The size of the part which can be produced is controlled by the capacity of the press available and the compression ratio of the powders.

d) Parts requiring sharp corners or abrupt changes in thickness are very difficult to produce.

e) Parts requiring internal threads, grooves, or undercuts are impossible to produce.

f) Some of the low temperature melting powders may cause difficulties during the sintering operation.

Powder Metallurgy Part Design Rules

1. The shape of the part must permit it to be ejected from the die. The following cannot be molded and must be machined later: undercuts, grooves, internal threads, diamond knurls, holes at right angles, and reverse tapers.

2. Avoid part designs that would require powder to flow into thin walls, narrow splines, or sharp corners. Parts with these characteristics can be produced only with extreme difficulty and should be avoided whenever possible.

3. The die should be designed to provide the maximum strength to all the components.

4. The length of the part should not be longer than 2-1/2 times the diameter.
5. The part should be designed with as few steps or diameters as possible.

POWDER METALLURGY QUESTIONS

1. List the three steps in the powder metallurgy process.
2. Name six products which are produced by powder metallurgy.
3. Compare conventional machining methods with powder metallurgy, and list four unique features of the process.
4. Name and briefly describe four methods of producing metal powders.
5. Describe the process of blending and state its importance to the finished product.
6. Describe the compacting operation with regard to the type of die used, pressures required, and the qualities obtained.
7. Fully describe and state the purposes of sintering.
8. Define and state the purpose of:
   a) sizing and repressing
   b) impregnation
   c) infiltration
9. List six important advantages of powder metallurgy.
10. State four disadvantages or limitations of powder metallurgy.

APPENDIX OF TABLES

TABLE 1: DECIMAL INCH, FRACTIONAL INCH, AND MILLIMETRE EQUIVALENTS					
Decimal inch	Fractional inch	Millimetre	Decimal inch	Fractional inch	Millimetre
.015625	1/64	0.397	.515625	33/64	13.097
.03125	1/32	0.794	.53125	17/32	13.494
.046875	3/64	1.191	.546875	35/64	13.891
.0625	1/16	1.588	.5625	9/16	14.288
.078125	5/64	1.984	.578125	37/64	14.684
.09375	3/32	2.381	.59375	19/32	15.081
.109375	7/64	2.778	.609375	39/64	15.478
.125	1/8	3.175	.625	5/8	15.875
.140625	9/64	3.572	.640625	41/64	16.272
.15625	5/32	3.969	.65625	21/32	16.669
.171875	11/64	4.366	.671875	43/64	17.066
.1875	3/16	4.762	.6875	11/16	17.462
.203125	13/64	5.159	.703125	45/64	17.859
.21875	7/32	5.556	.71875	23/32	18.256
.234375	15/64	5.953	.734375	47/64	18.653
.25	1/4	6.350	.75	3/4	19.05
.265625	17/64	6.747	.765625	49/64	19.447
.28125	9/32	7.144	.78125	25/32	19.844
.296875	19/64	7.541	.796875	51/64	20.241
.3125	5/16	7.938	.8125	13/16	20.638
.328125	21/64	8.334	.828125	53/64	21.034
.34375	11/32	8.731	.84375	27/32	21.431
.359375	23/64	9.128	.859375	55/64	21.828
.375	3/8	9.525	.875	7/8	22.225
.390625	25/64	9.922	.890625	57/64	22.622
.40625	13/32	10.319	.90625	29/32	23.019
.421875	27/64	10.716	.921875	59/64	23.416
.4375	7/16	11.112	.9375	15/16	23.812
.453125	29/64	11.509	.953125	61/64	24.209
.46875	15/32	11.906	.96875	31/32	24.606
.484375	31/64	12.303	.984375	63/64	25.003
.5	1/2	12.700	1.	1	25.400

TABLE 2:

CONVERSION OF INCHES TO MILLIMETRES						CONVERSION OF MILLIMETRES TO INCHES					
Inches	Milli-metres	Inches	Milli-metres	Inches	Milli-metres	Milli-metres	Inches	Milli-metres	Inches	Milli-metres	Inches
.001	0.025	.290	7.37	.660	16.76	0.01	.0004	0.35	.0138	0.68	.0268
.002	0.051	.300	7.62	.670	17.02	0.02	.0008	0.36	.0142	0.69	.0272
.003	0.076	.310	7.87	.680	17.27	0.03	.0012	0.37	.0146	0.70	.0276
.004	0.102	.320	8.13	.690	17.53	0.04	.0016	0.38	.0150	0.71	.0280
.005	0.127	.330	8.38	.700	17.78	0.05	.0020	0.39	.0154	0.72	.0283
.006	0.152	.340	8.64	.710	18.03	0.06	.0024	0.40	.0157	0.73	.0287
.007	0.178	.350	8.89	.720	18.29	0.07	.0028	0.41	.0161	0.74	.0291
.008	0.203	.360	9.14	.730	18.54	0.08	.0031	0.42	.0165	0.75	.0295
.009	0.229	.370	9.40	.740	18.80	0.09	.0035	0.43	.0169	0.76	.0299
.010	0.254	.380	9.65	.750	19.05	0.10	.0039	0.44	.0173	0.77	.0303
.020	0.508	.390	9.91	.760	19.30	0.11	.0043	0.45	.0177	0.78	.0307
.030	0.762	.400	10.16	.770	19.56	0.12	.0047	0.46	.0181	0.79	.0311
.040	1.016	.410	10.41	.780	19.81	0.13	.0051	0.47	.0185	0.80	.0315
.050	1.270	.420	10.67	.790	20.07	0.14	.0055	0.48	.0189	0.81	.0319
.060	1.524	.430	10.92	.800	20.32	0.15	.0059	0.49	.0193	0.82	.0323
.070	1.778	.440	11.18	.810	20.57	0.16	.0063	0.50	.0197	0.83	.0327
.080	2.032	.450	11.43	.820	20.83	0.17	.0067	0.51	.0201	0.84	.0331
.090	2.286	.460	11.68	.830	21.08	0.18	.0071	0.52	.0205	0.85	.0335
.100	2.540	.470	11.94	.840	21.34	0.19	.0075	0.53	.0209	0.86	.0339
.110	2.794	.480	12.19	.850	21.59	0.20	.0079	0.54	.0213	0.87	.0343
.120	3.048	.490	12.45	.860	21.84	0.21	.0083	0.55	.0217	0.88	.0346
.130	3.302	.500	12.70	.870	22.10	0.22	.0087	0.56	.0220	0.89	.0350
.140	3.56	.510	12.95	.880	22.35	0.23	.0091	0.57	.0224	0.90	.0354
.150	3.81	.520	13.21	.890	22.61	0.24	.0094	0.58	.0228	0.91	.0358
.160	4.06	.530	13.46	.900	22.86	0.25	.0098	0.59	.0232	0.92	.0362
.170	4.32	.540	13.72	.910	23.11	0.26	.0102	0.60	.0236	0.93	.0366
.180	4.57	.550	13.97	.920	23.37	0.27	.0106	0.61	.0240	0.94	.0370
.190	4.83	.560	14.22	.930	23.62	0.28	.0110	0.62	.0244	0.95	.0374
.200	5.08	.570	14.48	.940	23.88	0.29	.0114	0.63	.0248	0.96	.0378
.210	5.33	.580	14.73	.950	24.13	0.30	.0118	0.64	.0252	0.97	.0382
.220	5.59	.590	14.99	.960	24.38	0.31	.0122	0.65	.0256	0.98	.0386
.230	5.84	.600	15.24	.970	24.64	0.32	.0126	0.66	.0260	0.99	.0390
.240	6.10	.610	15.49	.980	24.89	0.33	.0130	0.67	.0264	1.00	.0394
.250	6.35	.620	15.75	.990	25.15	0.34	.0134	....	....	....	....
.260	6.60	.630	16.00	1.000	25.40						
.270	6.86	.640	16.26	....	....						
.280	7.11	.650	16.51	....	....						

Courtesy Automatic Electric Company

TABLE 3: LETTER DRILL SIZES

Letter	mm	in.	Letter	mm	in.
A	5.9	.234	N	7.7	.302
B	6.0	.238	O	8.0	.316
C	6.1	.242	P	8.2	.323
D	6.2	.246	Q	8.4	.332
E	6.4	.250	R	8.6	.339
F	6.5	.257	S	8.8	.348
G	6.6	.261	T	9.1	.358
H	6.7	.266	U	9.3	.368
I	6.9	.272	V	9.5	.377
J	7.0	.277	W	9.8	.386
K	7.1	.281	X	10.1	.397
L	7.4	.290	Y	10.3	.404
M	7.5	.295	Z	10.5	.413

TABLE 4: NUMBER DRILL SIZES

No.	mm	inch	No.	mm	inch	No.	mm	inch
1	5.80	.2280	34	2.80	.1110	66	0.84	.0330
2	5.60	.2210	35	2.80	.1100	67	0.81	.0320
3	5.40	.2130	36	2.70	.1065	68	0.79	.0310
4	5.30	.2090	37	2.65	.1040	69	0.74	.0292
5	5.20	.2055	38	2.60	.1015	70	0.71	.0280
6	5.20	.2040	39	2.55	.0995	71	0.66	.0260
7	5.10	.2010	40	2.50	.0980	72	0.64	.0250
8	5.10	.1990	41	2.45	.0960	83	0.61	.0240
9	5.00	.1960	42	2.40	.0935	74	0.57	.0225
10	4.90	.1935	43	2.25	.0890	75	0.53	.0210
11	4.90	.1910	44	2.20	.0860	76	0.51	.0200
12	4.80	.1890	45	2.10	.0820	77	0.46	.0180
13	4.70	.1850	46	2.05	.0810	78	0.41	.0160
14	4.60	.1820	47	2.00	.0785	79	0.37	.0145
15	4.60	.1800	48	1.95	.0760	80	0.34	.0135
16	4.50	.1770	49	1.85	.0730	81	0.33	.0130
17	4.40	.1730	50	1.80	.0700	82	0.32	.0125
18	4.30	.1695	51	1.70	.0670	83	0.31	.0120
19	4.20	.1660	52	1.60	.0635	84	0.29	.0115
20	4.10	.1610	53	1.50	.0595	85	0.28	.0110
21	4.00	.1590	54	1.40	.0550	86	0.27	.0105
22	4.00	.1570	55	1.30	.0520	87	0.25	.0100
23	3.90	.1540	56	1.20	.0465	88	0.24	.0095
24	3.90	.1520	57	1.10	.0430	89	0.23	.0091
25	3.80	.1495	58	1.05	.0420	90	0.22	.0087
26	3.70	.1470	59	1.05	.0410	91	0.21	.0083
27	3.70	.1440	60	1.00	.0400	92	0.20	.0079
28	3.60	.1405	61	0.99	.0390	93	0.19	.0075
29	3.50	.1360	62	0.97	.0380	94	0.18	.0071
30	3.30	.1285	63	0.94	.0370	95	0.17	.0067
31	3.00	.1200	64	0.92	.0360	96	0.16	.0063
32	2.95	.1160	65	0.89	.0350	97	0.15	.0059
33	2.85	.1130						

TABLE 5: TAP DRILL SIZES

Nominal Diameter mm	Thread Pitch mm	Tap Drill Size mm	Nominal Diameter mm	Thread Pitch mm	Tap Drill Size mm
1.60	0.35	1.20	20.00	2.50	17.50
2.00	0.40	1.60	24.00	3.00	21.00
2.50	0.45	2.05	30.00	3.50	26.50
3.00	0.50	2.50	36.00	4.00	32.00
3.50	0.60	2.90	42.00	4.50	37.50
4.00	0.70	3.30	48.00	5.00	43.00
5.00	0.80	4.20	56.00	5.50	50.50
6.30	1.00	5.30	64.00	6.00	58.00
8.00	1.25	6.80	72.00	6.00	66.00
10.00	1.50	8.50	80.00	6.00	74.00
12.00	1.75	10.20	90.00	6.00	84.00
14.00	2.00	12.00	100.00	6.00	94.00
16.00	2.00	14.00			

TABLE 6: ISO METRIC PITCH & DIAMETER COMBINATIONS

Nominal Dia. (mm)	Thread Pitch (mm)	Nominal Dia. (mm)	Thread Pitch (mm)
1.6	0.35	20	2.5
2	0.40	24	3.0
2.5	0.45	30	3.5
3	0.50	36	4.0
3.5	0.60	42	4.5
4	0.70	48	5.0
5	0.80	56	5.5
6.3	1.00	64	6.0
8	1.25	72	6.0
10	1.50	80	6.0
12	1.75	90	6.0
14	2.00	100	6.0
16	2.00		

TABLE 7: TAP DRILL SIZES
AMERICAN NATIONAL FORM THREAD

NC National Coarse			NF National Fine		
Tap Size	Threads per inch	Tap Drill Size	Tap Size	Threads per inch	Tap Drill Size
# 5	40	#38	# 5	44	#37
# 6	32	#36	# 6	40	#33
# 8	32	#29	# 8	36	#29
#10	24	#25	#10	32	#21
#12	24	#16	#12	28	#14
1/4	20	# 7	1/4	28	# 3
5/16	18	F	5/16	24	I
3/8	16	5/16	3/8	24	Q
7/16	14	U	7/16	20	25/64
1/2	13	27/64	1/2	20	29/64
9/16	12	31/64	9/16	18	33/64
5/8	11	17/32	5/8	18	37/64
3/4	10	21/32	3/4	16	11/16
7/8	9	49/64	7/8	14	13/16
1	8	7/8	1	14	15/16
1-1/8	7	63/64	1-1/8	12	1-3/64
1-1/4	7	1-7/64	1-1/4	12	1-11/64
1-3/8	6	1-7/32	1-3/8	12	1-19/64
1-1/2	6	1-11/32	1-1/2	12	1-27/64
1-3/4	5	1-9/16			
2	4-1/2	1-25/32			

NPT NATIONAL PIPE THREAD					
1/8	27	11/32	1	11-1/2	1-5/32
1/4	18	7/16	1-1/4	11-1/2	1-1/2
3/8	18	19/32	1-1/2	11-1/2	1-23/32
1/2	14	23/32	2	11-1/2	2-3/16
3/4	14	15/16	2-1/2	8	2-5/8

The major diameter of an NC or NF number size tap or screw $= (N \times .013) + .060$

EXAMPLE: The major diameter of a #5 tap equals

$(5 \times .013) + .060 = .125$ diameter

TABLE 8:

THREE WIRE THREAD MEASUREMENT
(60° Metric Thread)

$$M = PD + C \qquad PD = M - C$$

M = Measurement over wires
PD = Pitch diameter
C = Constant

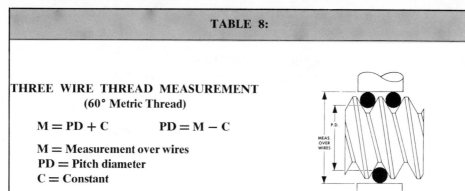

Pitch		Best Wire Size		Constant	
mm	Inches	mm	Inches	mm	Inches
0.2	.00787	0.1155	.00455	0.1732	.00682
0.225	.00886	0.1299	.00511	0.1949	.00767
0.25	.00934	0.1443	.00568	0.2165	.00852
0.3	.01181	0.1732	.00682	0.2598	.01023
0.35	.01378	0.2021	.00796	0.3031	.01193
0.4	.01575	0.2309	.00909	0.3464	.01364
0.45	.01772	0.2598	.01023	0.3897	.01534
0.5	.01969	0.2887	.01137	0.4330	.01705
0.6	.02362	0.3464	.01364	0.5196	.02046
0.7	.02756	0.4041	.01591	0.6062	.02387
0.75	.02953	0.4330	.01705	0.6495	.02557
0.8	.03150	0.4619	.01818	0.6928	.02728
0.9	.03543	0.5196	.02046	0.7794	.03069
1.0	.03937	0.5774	.02273	0.8660	.03410
1.25	.04921	0.7217	.02841	1.0825	.04262
1.5	.05906	0.8660	.03410	1.2990	.05114
1.75	.06890	1.0104	.03978	1.5155	.05967
2.0	.07874	1.1547	.04546	1.7321	.06819
2.5	.09843	1.4434	.05683	2.1651	.08524
3.0	.11811	1.7321	.06819	2.5981	.10229
3.5	.13780	2.0207	.07956	3.0311	.11933
4.0	.15748	2.3094	.09092	3.4641	.13638
4.5	.17717	2.5981	.10229	3.8971	.15343
5.0	.19685	2.8868	.11365	4.3301	.17048
5.5	.21654	3.1754	.12502	4.7631	.18753
6.0	.23622	3.4641	.13638	5.1962	.20457
7.0	.27559	4.0415	.15911	6.0622	.23867
8.0	.31496	4.6188	.18184	6.9282	.27276
9.0	.35433	5.1962	.20457	7.7942	.30686
10.0	.39370	5.7735	.22730	8.6603	.34095

TABLE 9: MORSE TAPERS

ANGLE OF KEY 8° 19' = TAPER 1-3/4 IN 12

Number of taper	Diameter of plug at small end	Diameter at end of socket	Whole length of shank	Shank depth	Depth of hole	Standard plug depth	Thickness of tongue	Length of tongue	Diameter of tongue	Width of keyway	Length of keyway	End of socket to keyway	Taper per foot
	D	A	B	S	H	P	t	T	d	w	L	K	
0	.252	.356	2-11/32	2-7/32	2-1/32	2	5/32	1/4	.235	.160	9/16	1-15/16	.6246
1	.369	.475	2-9/16	2-7/16	2-3/16	2-1/8	13/64	3/8	.343	.213	3/4	2-1/16	.5986
2	.572	.700	3-1/8	2-15/16	2-5/8	2-9/16	1/4	7/16	17/32	.260	7/8	2-1/2	.5994
3	.778	.938	3-7/8	3-11/16	3-1/4	3-3/16	5/16	9/16	23/32	.322	1-3/16	3-1/16	.6023
4	1.020	1.231	4-7/8	4-5/8	4-1/8	4-1/16	15/32	5/8	31/32	.478	1-1/4	3-7/8	.6232
5	1.475	1.748	6-1/8	5-7/8	5-1/4	5-3/16	5/8	3/4	1-13/32	.635	1-1/2	4-15/16	.6315
6	2.116	2.494	8-9/16	8-1/4	7-3/8	7-1/4	3/4	1-1/8	2	.760	1-3/4	7	.6256
7	2.750	3.270	11-1/4	11-5/8	10-1/8	10	1-1/8	1-3/8	2-5/8	1.135	2-5/8	9-1/2	.6240

Note: All measurements are in inches

TABLE 10: STANDARD MILLING MACHINE TAPER

Milling Machine Spindles	Milling Machine Arbors

3.500 Taper per ft.

3.500 Taper per ft.

Taper No.	A	B	C	D	L	N	Q	R	S	T	U	V	W
30	1.250	2.7493	.685 .692	21/32	2-7/8	1.250	1/2 – 13	.673 .675	13/16	1	2	2-3/4	1/16
40	1.750	3.4993	.997 1.005	21/32	3-7/8	1.750	5/8 – 11	.985 .987	1	1-1/8	2-5/16	3-3/4	1/16
50	2.750	5.0618	1.559 1.568	1-1/16	5-1/2	2.750	1 – 8	1.547 1.549	1	1-3/4	3-1/2	5-1/8	1/8
60	4.250	8.718	2.371 2.381	1-3/8	8-5/8	4.250	1-1/4 – 7	2.359 2.361	1-3/4	2-1/4	4-1/4	8-5/16	1/8

Note: All measurements are in inches

TABLE 11: TAPERS AND ANGLES					
Taper per Foot	**Included Angle**		**With Centre Line**		**Taper per Inch**	**Taper per Inch from Centre Line**
	Degree	Minute	Degree	Minute		
1/8	0	36	0	18	.010416	.005208
3/16	0	54	0	27	.015625	.007812
1/4	1	12	0	36	.020833	.010416
5/16	1	30	0	45	.026042	.013021
3/8	1	47	0	53	.031250	.015625
7/16	2	05	1	02	.036458	.018229
1/2	2	23	1	11	.041667	.020833
9/16	2	42	1	21	.046875	.023438
5/8	3	00	1	30	.052084	.026042
11/16	3	18	1	39	.057292	.028646
3/4	3	35	1	48	.062500	.031250
13/16	3	52	1	56	.067708	.033854
7/8	4	12	2	06	.072917	.036458
15/16	4	28	2	14	.078125	.039063
1	4	45	2	23	.083330	.041667
1-1/4	5	58	2	59	.104166	.052083
1-1/2	7	08	3	34	.125000	.062500
1-3/4	8	20	4	10	.145833	.072917
2	9	32	4	46	.166666	.083333
2-1/2	11	54	5	57	.208333	.104166
3	14	16	7	08	.250000	.125000
3-1/2	16	36	8	18	.291666	.145833
4	18	56	9	28	.333333	.166666
4-1/2	21	14	10	37	.375000	.187500
5	23	32	11	46	.416666	.208333
6	28	04	14	02	.500000	.250000

Courtesy Morse Twist Drill & Machine Co.

TABLE 12: ALLOWANCES FOR FITS		
RUNNING FITS		
Shaft Diameter	For Shafts with Speeds Under 600 r/min Ordinary Working Conditions	For Shafts with Speeds Over 600 r/min. Heavy Pressure – Severe Working Conditions
Up to 1/2	−.0005 to −.001	−.0005 to −.001
1/2 to 1	−.00075 to −.0015	−.001 to −.002
1 to 2	−.0015 to −.0025	−.002 to −.003
2 to 3-1/2	−.002 to −.003	−.003 to −.004
3-1/2 to 6	−.0025 to −.004	−.004 to −.005
SLIDING FITS		
Shaft Diameter	For Shafts with Gears, Clutches or Similar Parts which Must be Free to Slide	
Up to 1/2	−.0005 to −.001	
1/2 to 1	−.00075 to −.0015	
1 to 2	−.0015 to −.0025	
2 to 3-1/2	−.002 to −.003	
3-1/2 to 6	−.0025 to −.004	
PUSH FITS		
Shaft Diameter	For Light Service where Part is Keyed to Shaft and Clamped Endwise – No Fitting	With Play Eliminated – Part Should Assemble Readily – Some Fitting and Selecting May be Required
Up to 1/2	Standard to −.00025	Standard to +.00025
1/2 to 3-1/2	Standard to −.0005	Standard to +.0005
3-1/2 to 6	Standard to −.00075	Standard to +.00075
DRIVING FITS		
Shaft Diameter	For Permanent Assembly of Parts so Located that Driving Cannot be Done Readily	For Permanent Assembly and Severe Duty and Where There is Ample Room for Driving
Up to 1/2	Standard to +.00025	+.0005 to +.001
1/2 to 1	+.00025 to +.0005	+.0005 to +.001
1 to 2	+.0005 to +.00075	+.0005 to +.001
2 to 3-1/2	+.0005 to +.001	+.00075 to +.00125
3-1/2 to 6	+.0005 to +.001	+.001 to +.0015
FORCED FITS		
Shaft Diameter	For Permanent Assembly and Very Severe Service – Hydraulic Press Used for Larger Parts	
Up to 1/2	+.00075 to +.001	
1/2 to 1	+.001 to +.002	
1 to 2	+.002 to +.003	
2 to 3-1/2	+.003 to +.004	
3-1/2 to 6	+.004 to +.005	

Note: All measurements are in inches

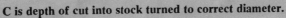

TABLE 13: RULES FOR FINDING DIMENSIONS OF CIRCLES, SQUARES, ETC.

D is diameter of stock necessary to turn shape desired.

E is distance "across flats," or diameter of inscribed circle.

C is depth of cut into stock turned to correct diameter.

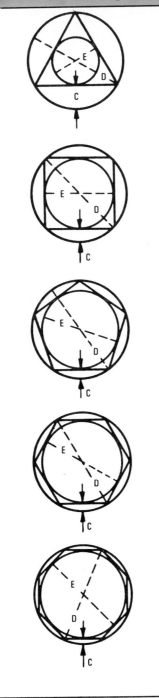

Triangle

E   = side × .57735

D   = side × 1.1547 = 2E

Side = D × .866

C   = E × .5 = D × .25

Square

E   = side = D × .7071

D   = side × 1.4142 = diagonal

Side = D × .7071

C   = D × .14645

Pentagon

E   = side × 1.3764 = D × .809

D   = side × 1.7013 = E × 1.2361

Side = D × .5878

C   = D × .0955

Hexagon

E   = side × 1.7321 = D × .866

D   = side × 2   = E × 1.1547

Side = D × .5

C   = D × .067

Octagon

E   = side × 2.4142 = D × .9239

D   = side × 2.6131 = E × 1.0824

Side = D × .3827

C   = D × .038

Courtesy Morse Twist Drill & Machine Co.

TABLE 14: HARDNESS CONVERSION CHART

10 mm Ball 3000 kg	120° Cone 150 kg	1/16 in. Ball 100 kg	Model C	Mpa	10 mm Ball 3000 kg	120° Cone 150 kg	1/16 in. Ball 100 kg	Model C	Mpa
Brinell	Rockwell C	Rockwell B	Shore Scleroscope	Tensile Strength	Brinell	Rockwell C	Rockwell B	Shore Scleroscope	Tensile Strength
800	72	.....	100	....	276	30	105	42	938
780	71	.....	99	....	269	29	104	41	910
760	70	.....	98	....	261	28	103	40	889
745	68	.....	97	2530	258	27	102	39	876
725	67		96	2460	255	26	102	39	862
712	66		95	2413	249	25	101	38	848
682	65		93	2324	245	24	100	37	820
668	64		91	2248	240	23	99	36	807
652	63		89	2193	237	23	99	35	793
626	62		87	2110	229	22	98	34	779
614	61		85	2062	224	21	97	33	758
601	60		83	2013	217	20	96	33	738
590	59		81	2000	211	19	95	32	717
576	57		79	1937	206	18	94	32	703
552	56		76	1862	203	17	94	31	689
545	55		75	1848	200	16	93	31	676
529	54	......	74	1786	196	15	92	30	662
514	53	120	72	1751	191	14	92	30	648
502	52	119	70	1703	187	13	91	29	634
495	51	119	69	1682	185	12	91	29	627
477	49	118	67	1606	183	11	90	28	621
461	48	117	66	1565	180	10	89	28	614
451	47	117	65	1538	175	9	88	27	593
444	46	116	64	1510	170	7	87	27	579
427	45	115	62	1441	167	6	87	27	565
415	44	115	60	1407	165	5	86	26	558
401	43	114	58	1351	163	4	85	26	552
388	42	114	57	1317	160	3	84	25	538
375	41	113	55	1269	156	2	83	25	524
370	40	112	54	1255	154	1	82	25	517
362	39	111	53	1234	152	.....	82	24	510
351	38	111	51	1193	150	.....	81	24	510
346	37	110	50	1172	147	.....	80	24	496
341	37	110	49	1158	145	.....	79	23	490
331	36	109	47	1124	143	.....	79	23	483
323	35	109	46	1089	141	.....	78	23	476
311	34	108	46	1055	140	.....	77	22	476
301	33	107	45	1020	135	.....	75	22	462
293	32	106	44	993	130	.....	72	22	448
285	31	105	43	965	....	.....	......	.....	....

TABLE 15: SOLUTIONS FOR RIGHT-ANGLED TRIANGLES

$$\text{Sine} \angle = \frac{\text{Side opposite}}{\text{Hypotenuse}}$$

$$\text{Cosine} \angle = \frac{\text{Side adjacent}}{\text{Hypotenuse}}$$

$$\text{Tangent} \angle = \frac{\text{Side opposite}}{\text{Side adjacent}}$$

$$\text{Cosecant} \angle = \frac{\text{Hypotenuse}}{\text{Side opposite}}$$

$$\text{Secant} \angle = \frac{\text{Hypotenuse}}{\text{Side adjacent}}$$

$$\text{Cotangent} \angle = \frac{\text{Side adjacent}}{\text{Side opposite}}$$

Knowing		Formulas to find	
	Sides a & b	$c = \sqrt{a^2 - b^2}$	$\sin B = \dfrac{b}{a}$
	Side a & angle B	$b = a \times \sin B$	$c = a \times \cos B$
	Sides a & c	$b = \sqrt{a^2 - c^2}$	$\sin C = \dfrac{c}{a}$
	Side a & angle C	$b = a \times \cos C$	$c = a \times \sin C$
	Sides b & c	$a = \sqrt{b^2 + c^2}$	$\tan B = \dfrac{b}{c}$
	Side b & angle B	$a = \dfrac{b}{\sin B}$	$c = b \times \cot B$
	Side b & angle C	$a = \dfrac{b}{\cos C}$	$c = b \times \tan C$
	Side c & angle B	$a = \dfrac{c}{\cos B}$	$b = c \times \tan B$
	Side c & angle C	$a = \dfrac{c}{\sin C}$	$b = c \times \cot C$

TABLE 16: SINE BAR CONSTANTS (5 in. BAR)
(Multiply Constants by Two for a 10 in. Sine Bar)

Min.	0°	1°	2°	3°	4°	5°	6°	7°	8°	9°	10°	11°	12°	13°	14°	15°	16°	17°	18°	19°	Min.
0	.00000	.08725	.17450	.26170	.34880	.43580	.52265	.60935	.69585	.78215	.86825	.95405	1.0395	1.1247	1.2096	1.2941	1.3782	1.4618	1.5451	1.6278	0
2	.00290	.09015	.17740	.26460	.35170	.43870	.52555	.61225	.69875	.78505	.87110	.95690	.0424	.1276	.2124	.2969	.3810	.4646	.5478	.6306	2
4	.00580	.09310	.18030	.26750	.35460	.44155	.52845	.61510	.70165	.78790	.87395	.95975	.0452	.1304	.2152	.2997	.3838	.4674	.5506	.6333	4
6	.00875	.09600	.18320	.27040	.35750	.44445	.53130	.61800	.70450	.79080	.87685	.96260	.0481	.1332	.2181	.3025	.3865	.4702	.5534	.6361	6
8	.01165	.09890	.18615	.27330	.36040	.44735	.53420	.62090	.70740	.79365	.87970	.96545	.0509	.1361	.2209	.3053	.3893	.4730	.5561	.6388	8
10	.01455	.10180	.18905	.27620	.36330	.45025	.53710	.62380	.71025	.79655	.88255	.96830	1.0538	1.1389	1.2237	1.3081	1.3921	1.4757	1.5589	1.6416	10
12	.01745	.10470	.19195	.27910	.36620	.45315	.54000	.62665	.71315	.79940	.88540	.97115	.0566	.1417	.2265	.3109	.3949	.4785	.5616	.6443	12
14	.02035	.10760	.19485	.28200	.36910	.45605	.54290	.62955	.71600	.80230	.88830	.97405	.0594	.1446	.2293	.3137	.3977	.4813	.5644	.6471	14
16	.02325	.11055	.19775	.28490	.37200	.45895	.54580	.63245	.71890	.80515	.89115	.97690	.0623	.1474	.2322	.3165	.4005	.4841	.5672	.6498	16
18	.02620	.11345	.20065	.28780	.37490	.46185	.54865	.63530	.72180	.80800	.89400	.97975	.0651	.1502	.2350	.3193	.4033	.4868	.5699	.6525	18
20	.02910	.11635	.20355	.29070	.37780	.46475	.55155	.63820	.72465	.81090	.89685	.98260	1.0680	1.1531	1.2378	1.3221	1.4061	1.4896	1.5727	1.6553	20
22	.03200	.11925	.20645	.29365	.38070	.46765	.55445	.64110	.72755	.81375	.89975	.98545	.0708	.1559	.2406	.3250	.4089	.4924	.5755	.6580	22
24	.03490	.12215	.20940	.29655	.38360	.47055	.55735	.64400	.73040	.81665	.90260	.98830	.0737	.1587	.2434	.3278	.4117	.4952	.5782	.6608	24
26	.03780	.12505	.21230	.29945	.38650	.47345	.56025	.64685	.73330	.81950	.90545	.99115	.0765	.1615	.2462	.3306	.4145	.4980	.5810	.6635	26
28	.04070	.12800	.21520	.30235	.38940	.47635	.56315	.64975	.73615	.82235	.90830	.99400	.0793	.1644	.2491	.3334	.4173	.5007	.5837	.6663	28
30	.04365	.13090	.21810	.30525	.39230	.47925	.56600	.65265	.73905	.82525	.91120	.99685	1.0822	1.1672	1.2519	1.3362	1.4201	1.5035	1.5865	1.6690	30
32	.04655	.13380	.22100	.30815	.39520	.48210	.56890	.65550	.74190	.82810	.91405	.99970	.0850	.1700	.2547	.3390	.4228	.5063	.5893	.6718	32
34	.04945	.13670	.22390	.31105	.39810	.48500	.57180	.65840	.74480	.83100	.91690	1.0016	.0879	.1729	.2575	.3418	.4256	.5091	.5920	.6745	34
36	.05235	.13960	.22680	.31395	.40100	.48790	.57470	.66130	.74770	.83385	.91975	.0054	.0907	.1757	.2603	.3446	.4284	.5118	.5948	.6772	36
38	.05525	.14250	.22970	.31685	.40390	.49080	.57760	.66415	.75055	.83670	.92260	.0082	.0935	.1785	.2631	.3474	.4312	.5146	.5975	.6800	38
40	.05820	.14540	.23265	.31975	.40680	.49370	.58045	.66705	.75345	.83960	.92545	1.0110	1.0964	1.1813	1.2660	1.3502	1.4340	1.5174	1.6003	1.6827	40
42	.06110	.14835	.23555	.32265	.40970	.49660	.58335	.66995	.75630	.84245	.92835	.0139	.0992	.1842	.2688	.3530	.4368	.5201	.6030	.6855	42
44	.06400	.15125	.23845	.32555	.41260	.49950	.58625	.67280	.75920	.84530	.93120	.0168	.1020	.1870	.2716	.3558	.4396	.5229	.6058	.6882	44
46	.06690	.15415	.24135	.32845	.41550	.50240	.58915	.67570	.76205	.84820	.93405	.0196	.1049	.1898	.2744	.3586	.4423	.5257	.6085	.6909	46
48	.06980	.15705	.24425	.33135	.41840	.50530	.59200	.67860	.76495	.85105	.93690	.0225	.1077	.1926	.2772	.3614	.4451	.5285	.6113	.6937	48
50	.07270	.15995	.24715	.33425	.42130	.50820	.59490	.68145	.76780	.85390	.93975	1.0253	1.1106	1.1955	1.2800	1.3642	1.4479	1.5312	1.6141	1.6964	50
52	.07565	.16285	.25005	.33715	.42420	.51105	.59780	.68435	.77070	.85680	.94260	.0281	.1134	.1983	.2828	.3670	.4507	.5340	.6168	.6991	52
54	.07855	.16580	.25295	.34010	.42710	.51395	.60075	.68720	.77355	.85965	.94550	.0310	.1162	.2011	.2856	.3698	.4535	.5368	.6196	.7019	54
56	.08145	.16870	.25585	.34300	.43000	.51685	.60355	.69010	.77645	.86250	.94835	.0338	.1191	.2039	.2884	.3726	.4563	.5395	.6223	.7046	56
58	.08435	.17160	.25875	.34590	.43290	.51975	.60645	.69300	.77930	.86540	.95120	.0367	.1219	.2068	.2913	.3754	.4591	.5423	.6251	.7073	58
60	.08725	.17450	.26170	.34880	.43580	.52265	.60935	.69585	.78215	.86825	.95405	1.0395	1.1247	1.2096	1.2941	1.3782	1.4618	1.5451	1.6278	1.7101	60

Courtesy Brown & Sharpe Mfg. Co.

Table 16 continued

TABLE 16: SINE BAR CONSTANTS (5 in. BAR)
(Multiply Constants by Two for a 10 in. Sine Bar)

Min.	20°	21°	22°	23°	24°	25°	26°	27°	28°	29°	30°	31°	32°	33°	34°	35°	36°	37°	38°	39°	Min.
0	1.7101	1.7918	1.8730	1.9536	2.0337	2.1131	2.1918	2.2699	2.3473	2.4240	2.5000	2.5752	2.6496	2.7232	2.7959	2.8679	2.9389	3.0091	3.0783	3.1466	0
2	.7128	.7945	.8757	.9563	.0363	.1157	.1944	.2725	.3499	.4266	.5025	.5777	.6520	.7256	.7984	.8702	.9413	.0114	.0806	.1488	2
4	.7155	.7972	.8784	.9590	.0390	.1183	.1971	.2751	.3525	.4291	.5050	.5802	.6545	.7280	.8008	.8726	.9436	.0137	.0829	.1511	4
6	.7183	.8000	.8811	.9617	.0416	.1210	.1997	.2777	.3550	.4317	.5075	.5826	.6570	.7305	.8032	.8750	.9460	.0160	.0852	.1534	6
8	.7210	.8027	.8838	.9643	.0443	.1236	.2023	.2803	.3576	.4342	.5100	.5851	.6594	.7329	.8056	.8774	.9483	.0183	.0874	.1556	8
10	1.7237	1.8054	1.8865	1.9670	2.0469	2.1262	2.2049	2.2829	2.3602	2.4367	2.5126	2.5876	2.6619	2.7354	2.8080	2.8798	2.9507	3.0207	3.0897	3.1579	10
12	.7265	.8081	.8892	.9697	.0496	.1289	.2075	.2855	.3627	.4393	.5151	.5901	.6644	.7378	.8104	.8821	.9530	.0230	.0920	.1601	12
14	.7292	.8108	.8919	.9724	.0522	.1315	.2101	.2881	.3653	.4418	.5176	.5926	.6668	.7402	.8128	.8845	.9554	.0253	.0943	.1624	14
16	.7319	.8135	.8946	.9750	.0549	.1341	.2127	.2906	.3679	.4444	.5201	.5951	.6693	.7427	.8152	.8869	.9577	.0276	.0966	.1646	16
18	.7347	.8162	.8973	.9777	.0575	.1368	.2153	.2932	.3704	.4469	.5226	.5976	.6717	.7451	.8176	.8893	.9600	.0299	.0989	.1669	18
20	1.7374	1.8189	1.8999	1.9804	2.0602	2.1394	2.2179	2.2958	2.3730	2.4494	2.5251	2.6001	2.6742	2.7475	2.8200	2.8916	2.9624	3.0322	3.1012	3.1691	20
22	.7401	.8217	.9026	.9830	.0628	.1420	.2205	.2984	.3755	.4520	.5276	.6025	.6767	.7499	.8224	.8940	.9647	.0345	.1034	.1714	22
24	.7428	.8244	.9053	.9857	.0655	.1447	.2232	.3010	.3781	.4545	.5301	.6050	.6791	.7524	.8248	.8964	.9671	.0369	.1057	.1736	24
26	.7456	.8271	.9080	.9884	.0681	.1473	.2258	.3036	.3807	.4570	.5327	.6075	.6816	.7548	.8272	.8988	.9694	.0392	.1080	.1759	26
28	.7483	.8298	.9107	.9911	.0708	.1499	.2284	.3061	.3832	.4596	.5352	.6100	.6840	.7572	.8296	.9011	.9718	.0415	.1103	.1781	28
30	1.7510	1.8325	1.9134	1.9937	2.0734	2.1525	2.2310	2.3087	2.3858	2.4621	2.5377	2.6125	2.6865	2.7597	2.8320	2.9035	2.9741	3.0438	3.1125	3.1804	30
32	.7537	.8352	.9161	.9964	.0761	.1552	.2336	.3113	.3883	.4646	.5402	.6149	.6889	.7621	.8344	.9059	.9764	.0461	.1148	.1826	32
34	.7565	.8379	.9188	.9991	.0787	.1578	.2362	.3139	.3909	.4672	.5427	.6174	.6914	.7645	.8368	.9082	.9788	.0484	.1171	.1849	34
36	.7592	.8406	.9215	2.0017	.0814	.1604	.2388	.3165	.3934	.4697	.5452	.6199	.6938	.7669	.8392	.9106	.9811	.0507	.1194	.1871	36
38	.7619	.8433	.9241	.0044	.0840	.1630	.2414	.3190	.3960	.4722	.5477	.6224	.6963	.7694	.8416	.9130	.9834	.0530	.1216	.1893	38
40	1.7646	1.8460	1.9268	2.0070	2.0867	2.1656	2.2440	2.3216	2.3985	2.4747	2.5502	2.6249	2.6987	2.7718	2.8440	2.9153	2.9858	3.0553	3.1239	3.1916	40
42	.7673	.8487	.9295	.0097	.0893	.1683	.2466	.3242	.4011	.4773	.5527	.6273	.7012	.7742	.8464	.9177	.9881	.0576	.1262	.1938	42
44	.7701	.8514	.9322	.0124	.0920	.1709	.2492	.3268	.4036	.4798	.5552	.6298	.7036	.7766	.8488	.9200	.9904	.0599	.1285	.1961	44
46	.7728	.8541	.9349	.0150	.0946	.1735	.2518	.3293	.4062	.4823	.5577	.6323	.7061	.7790	.8512	.9224	.9928	.0622	.1307	.1983	46
48	.7755	.8568	.9376	.0177	.0972	.1761	.2544	.3319	.4087	.4848	.5602	.6348	.7085	.7815	.8535	.9248	.9951	.0645	.1330	.2005	48
50	1.7782	1.8595	1.9402	2.0204	2.0999	2.1787	2.2570	2.3345	2.4113	2.4874	2.5627	2.6372	2.7110	2.7839	2.8559	2.9271	2.9974	3.0668	3.1353	3.2028	50
52	.7809	.8622	.9429	.0230	.1025	.1814	.2596	.3371	.4138	.4899	.5652	.6397	.7134	.7863	.8583	.9295	.9997	.0691	.1375	.2050	52
54	.7837	.8649	.9456	.0257	.1052	.1840	.2621	.3396	.4164	.4924	.5677	.6422	.7158	.7887	.8607	.9318	3.0021	.0714	.1398	.2072	54
56	.7864	.8676	.9483	.0283	.1078	.1866	.2647	.3422	.4189	.4949	.5702	.6446	.7183	.7911	.8631	.9342	.0044	.0737	.1421	.2095	56
58	.7891	.8703	.9510	.0310	.1104	.1892	.2673	.3448	.4215	.4975	.5727	.6471	.7207	.7935	.8655	.9365	.0067	.0760	.1443	.2117	58
60	1.7918	1.8730	1.9536	2.0337	2.1131	2.1918	2.2699	2.3473	2.4240	2.5000	2.5752	2.6496	2.7232	2.7959	2.8679	2.9389	3.0091	3.0783	3.1466	3.2139	60

Courtesy Brown & Sharpe Mfg. Co.

Table 16 continued

TABLE 16: SINE BAR CONSTANTS (5 in. BAR)
(Multiply Constants by Two for a 10 in. Sine Bar)

Min.	40°	41°	42°	43°	44°	45°	46°	47°	48°	49°	50°	51°	52°	53°	54°	55°	56°	57°	58°	59°	Min.
0	3.2139	3.2803	3.3456	3.4100	3.4733	3.5355	3.5967	3.6567	3.7157	3.7735	3.8302	3.8857	3.9400	3.9932	4.0451	4.0957	4.1452	4.1933	4.2402	4.2858	0
2	.2161	.2825	.3478	.4121	.4754	.5376	.5987	.6587	.7176	.7754	.8321	.8875	.9418	.9949	.0468	.0974	.1468	.1949	.2418	.2873	2
4	.2184	.2847	.3499	.4142	.4774	.5396	.6007	.6607	.7196	.7773	.8339	.8894	.9436	.9967	.0485	.0991	.1484	.1965	.2433	.2888	4
6	.2206	.2869	.3521	.4163	.4795	.5417	.6027	.6627	.7215	.7792	.8358	.8912	.9454	.9984	.0502	.1007	.1500	.1981	.2448	.2903	6
8	.2228	.2890	.3543	.4185	.4816	.5437	.6047	.6647	.7235	.7811	.8377	.8930	.9472	4.0001	.0519	.1024	.1517	.1997	.2464	.2918	8
10	3.2250	3.2912	3.3564	3.4206	3.4837	3.5458	3.6068	3.6666	3.7254	3.7830	3.8395	3.8948	3.9490	4.0019	4.0536	4.1041	4.1533	4.2012	4.2479	4.2933	10
12	.2273	.2934	.3586	.4227	.4858	.5478	.6088	.6686	.7274	.7850	.8414	.8967	.9508	.0036	.0553	.1057	.1549	.2028	.2494	.2948	12
14	.2295	.2956	.3607	.4248	.4879	.5499	.6108	.6706	.7293	.7869	.8433	.8985	.9525	.0054	.0570	.1074	.1565	.2044	.2510	.2963	14
16	.2317	.2978	.3629	.4269	.4900	.5519	.6128	.6726	.7312	.7887	.8451	.9003	.9543	.0071	.0587	.1090	.1581	.2060	.2525	.2978	16
18	.2339	.3000	.3650	.4291	.4921	.5540	.6148	.6745	.7332	.7906	.8470	.9021	.9561	.0089	.0604	.1107	.1597	.2075	.2540	.2992	18
20	3.2361	3.3022	3.3672	3.4312	3.4941	3.5560	3.6168	3.6765	3.7351	3.7925	3.8488	3.9039	3.9579	4.0106	4.0621	4.1124	4.1614	4.2091	4.2556	4.3007	20
22	.2384	.3044	.3693	.4333	.4962	.5581	.6188	.6785	.7370	.7944	.8507	.9058	.9596	.0123	.0638	.1140	.1630	.2107	.2571	.3022	22
24	.2406	.3065	.3715	.4354	.4983	.5601	.6208	.6805	.7390	.7963	.8525	.9076	.9614	.0141	.0655	.1157	.1646	.2122	.2586	.3037	24
26	.2428	.3087	.3736	.4375	.5004	.5621	.6228	.6824	.7409	.7982	.8544	.9094	.9632	.0158	.0672	.1173	.1662	.2138	.2601	.3052	26
28	.2450	.3109	.3758	.4396	.5024	.5642	.6248	.6844	.7428	.8001	.8562	.9112	.9650	.0175	.0689	.1190	.1678	.2154	.2617	.3066	28
30	3.2472	3.3131	3.3779	3.4417	3.5045	3.5662	3.6268	3.6864	3.7448	3.8020	3.8581	3.9130	3.9667	4.0193	4.0706	4.1206	4.1694	4.2169	4.2632	4.3081	30
32	.2494	.3153	.3801	.4439	.5066	.5683	.6288	.6883	.7467	.8039	.8599	.9148	.9685	.0210	.0722	.1223	.1710	.2185	.2647	.3096	32
34	.2516	.3174	.3822	.4460	.5087	.5703	.6308	.6903	.7486	.8058	.8618	.9166	.9703	.0227	.0739	.1239	.1726	.2201	.2662	.3111	34
36	.2538	.3196	.3844	.4481	.5107	.5723	.6328	.6923	.7505	.8077	.8636	.9184	.9720	.0244	.0756	.1255	.1742	.2216	.2677	.3125	36
38	.2561	.3218	.3865	.4502	.5128	.5744	.6348	.6942	.7525	.8096	.8655	.9202	.9738	.0262	.0773	.1272	.1758	.2232	.2692	.3140	38
40	3.2583	3.3240	3.3886	3.4523	3.5149	3.5764	3.6368	3.6962	3.7544	3.8114	3.8673	3.9221	3.9756	4.0279	4.0790	4.1288	4.1774	4.2247	4.2708	4.3155	40
42	.2605	.3261	.3908	.4544	.5169	.5784	.6388	.6981	.7563	.8133	.8692	.9239	.9773	.0296	.0807	.1305	.1790	.2263	.2723	.3170	42
44	.2627	.3283	.3929	.4565	.5190	.5805	.6408	.7001	.7582	.8152	.8710	.9257	.9791	.0313	.0823	.1321	.1806	.2278	.2738	.3184	44
46	.2649	.3305	.3950	.4586	.5211	.5825	.6428	.7020	.7601	.8171	.8729	.9275	.9809	.0331	.0840	.1337	.1822	.2294	.2753	.3199	46
48	.2671	.3326	.3972	.4607	.5231	.5845	.6448	.7040	.7620	.8190	.8747	.9293	.9826	.0348	.0857	.1354	.1838	.2309	.2768	.3213	48
50	3.2693	3.3348	3.3993	3.4628	3.5252	3.5866	3.6468	3.7060	3.7640	3.8208	3.8765	3.9311	3.9844	4.0365	4.0874	4.1370	4.1854	4.2325	4.2783	4.3228	50
52	.2715	.3370	.4014	.4649	.5273	.5886	.6488	.7079	.7659	.8227	.8784	.9329	.9861	.0382	.0891	.1386	.1870	.2340	.2798	.3243	52
54	.2737	.3391	.4036	.4670	.5293	.5906	.6508	.7099	.7678	.8246	.8802	.9347	.9879	.0399	.0907	.1403	.1886	.2356	.2813	.3257	54
56	.2759	.3413	.4057	.4691	.5314	.5926	.6528	.7118	.7697	.8265	.8820	.9364	.9896	.0416	.0924	.1419	.1902	.2371	.2828	.3272	56
58	.2781	.3435	.4078	.4712	.5335	.5947	.6548	.7138	.7716	.8283	.8839	.9382	.9914	.0433	.0941	.1435	.1917	.2387	.2843	.3286	58
60	3.2803	3.3456	3.4100	3.4733	3.5355	3.5967	3.6567	3.7157	3.7735	3.8302	3.8857	3.9400	3.9932	4.0451	4.0957	4.1452	4.1933	4.2402	4.2858	4.3301	60

TABLE 17A: COORDINATE FACTORS AND ANGLES
3-HOLE DIVISION

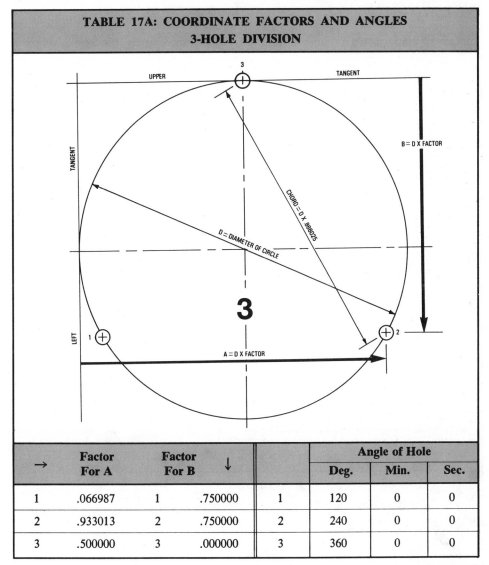

→	Factor For A		Factor For B	↓		Angle of Hole		
						Deg.	Min.	Sec.
1	.066987	1	.750000		1	120	0	0
2	.933013	2	.750000		2	240	0	0
3	.500000	3	.000000		3	360	0	0

Courtesy W. J. Woodworth and J. D. Woodworth

TABLE 17B: COORDINATE FACTORS AND ANGLES
4-HOLE DIVISION

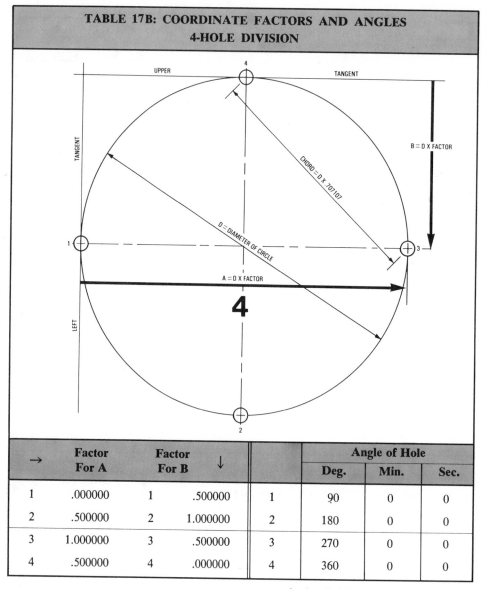

→	Factor For A		Factor For B ↓		Angle of Hole		
					Deg.	Min.	Sec.
1	.000000	1	.500000	1	90	0	0
2	.500000	2	1.000000	2	180	0	0
3	1.000000	3	.500000	3	270	0	0
4	.500000	4	.000000	4	360	0	0

Courtesy W. J. Woodworth and J. D. Woodworth

TABLE 17C: COORDINATE FACTORS AND ANGLES
5-HOLE DIVISION

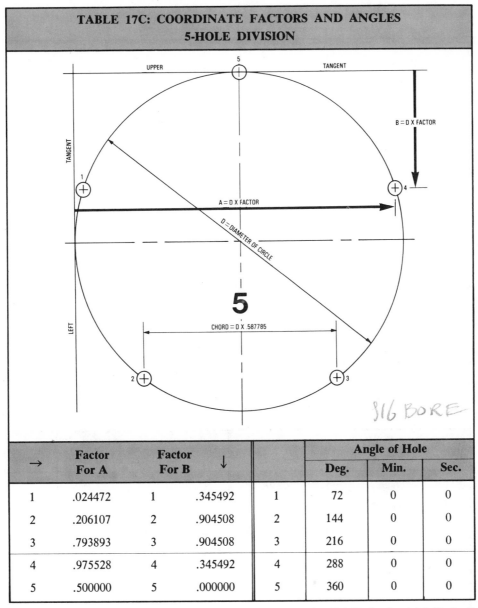

→	Factor For A	Factor	↓		Angle of Hole		
		For B			Deg.	Min.	Sec.
1	.024472	1	.345492	1	72	0	0
2	.206107	2	.904508	2	144	0	0
3	.793893	3	.904508	3	216	0	0
4	.975528	4	.345492	4	288	0	0
5	.500000	5	.000000	5	360	0	0

Courtesy W. J. Woodworth and J. D. Woodworth

TABLE 17D: COORDINATE FACTORS AND ANGLES
6-HOLE DIVISION

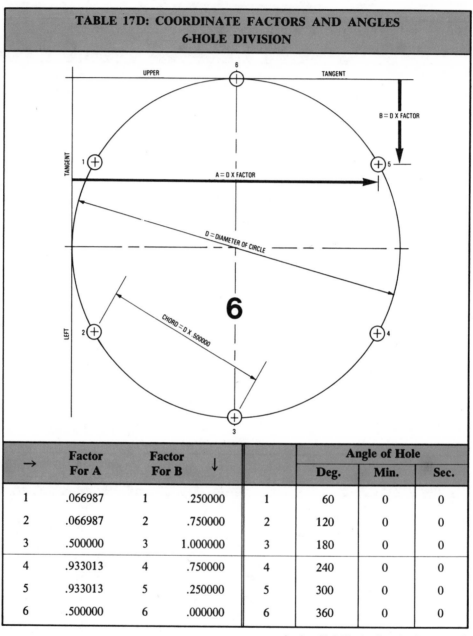

→	Factor For A		Factor For B ↓		Angle of Hole		
					Deg.	Min.	Sec.
1	.066987	1	.250000	1	60	0	0
2	.066987	2	.750000	2	120	0	0
3	.500000	3	1.000000	3	180	0	0
4	.933013	4	.750000	4	240	0	0
5	.933013	5	.250000	5	300	0	0
6	.500000	6	.000000	6	360	0	0

Courtesy W. J. Woodworth and J. D. Woodworth

TABLE 17E: COORDINATE FACTORS AND ANGLES
7-HOLE DIVISION

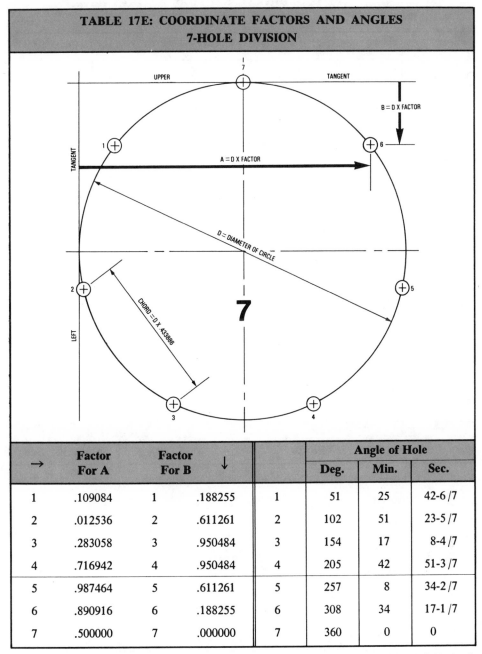

→	Factor For A		Factor For B	↓		Angle of Hole		
						Deg.	Min.	Sec.
1	.109084	1	.188255		1	51	25	42-6/7
2	.012536	2	.611261		2	102	51	23-5/7
3	.283058	3	.950484		3	154	17	8-4/7
4	.716942	4	.950484		4	205	42	51-3/7
5	.987464	5	.611261		5	257	8	34-2/7
6	.890916	6	.188255		6	308	34	17-1/7
7	.500000	7	.000000		7	360	0	0

Courtesy W. J. Woodworth and J. D. Woodworth

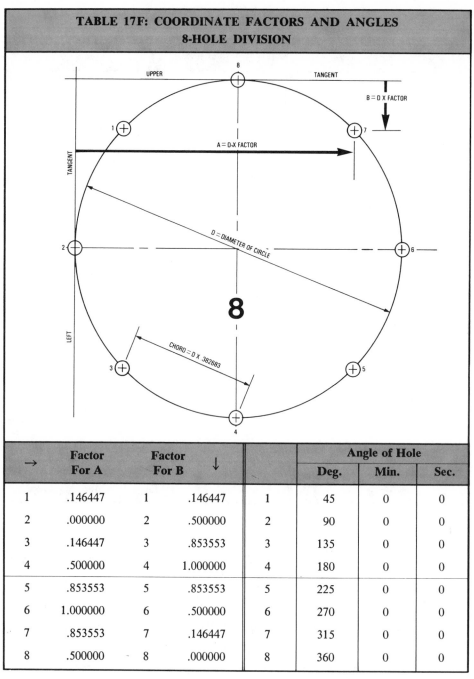

TABLE 17F: COORDINATE FACTORS AND ANGLES
8-HOLE DIVISION

→	Factor For A		Factor For B ↓			Angle of Hole		
						Deg.	Min.	Sec.
1	.146447	1	.146447		1	45	0	0
2	.000000	2	.500000		2	90	0	0
3	.146447	3	.853553		3	135	0	0
4	.500000	4	1.000000		4	180	0	0
5	.853553	5	.853553		5	225	0	0
6	1.000000	6	.500000		6	270	0	0
7	.853553	7	.146447		7	315	0	0
8	.500000	8	.000000		8	360	0	0

Courtesy W. J. Woodworth and J. D. Woodworth

TABLE 17G: COORDINATE FACTORS AND ANGLES
9-HOLE DIVISION

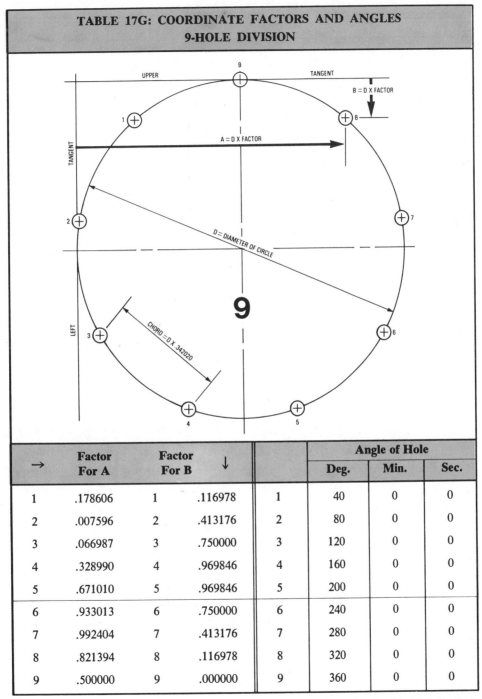

→	Factor For A		Factor For B ↓		Angle of Hole		
					Deg.	Min.	Sec.
1	.178606	1	.116978	1	40	0	0
2	.007596	2	.413176	2	80	0	0
3	.066987	3	.750000	3	120	0	0
4	.328990	4	.969846	4	160	0	0
5	.671010	5	.969846	5	200	0	0
6	.933013	6	.750000	6	240	0	0
7	.992404	7	.413176	7	280	0	0
8	.821394	8	.116978	8	320	0	0
9	.500000	9	.000000	9	360	0	0

Courtesy W. J. Woodworth and J. D. Woodworth

TABLE 17H: COORDINATE FACTORS AND ANGLES
10-HOLE DIVISION

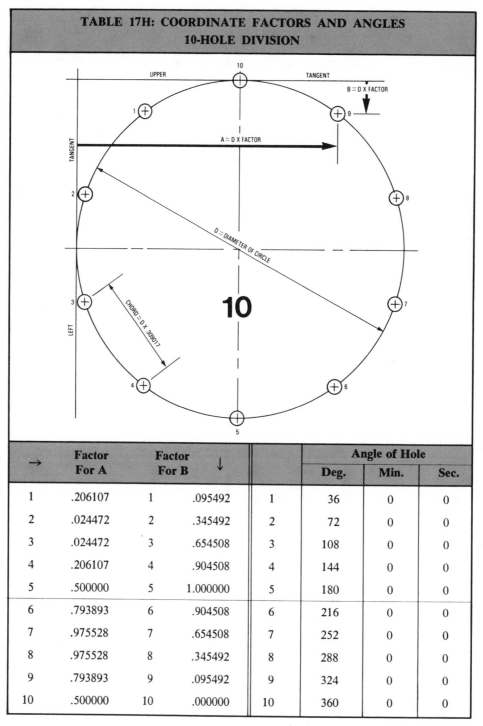

→	Factor For A		Factor For B ↓		Angle of Hole		
					Deg.	Min.	Sec.
1	.206107	1	.095492	1	36	0	0
2	.024472	2	.345492	2	72	0	0
3	.024472	3	.654508	3	108	0	0
4	.206107	4	.904508	4	144	0	0
5	.500000	5	1.000000	5	180	0	0
6	.793893	6	.904508	6	216	0	0
7	.975528	7	.654508	7	252	0	0
8	.975528	8	.345492	8	288	0	0
9	.793893	9	.095492	9	324	0	0
10	.500000	10	.000000	10	360	0	0

Courtesy W. J. Woodworth and J. D. Woodworth

TABLE 17I: COORDINATE FACTORS AND ANGLES
11-HOLE DIVISION

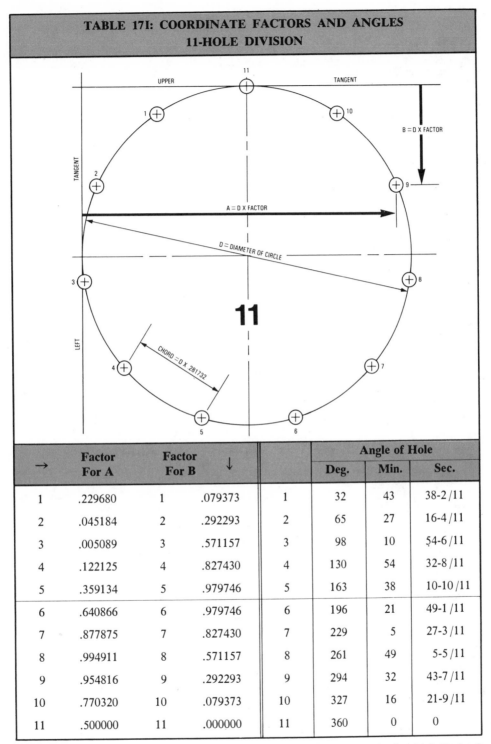

	Factor For A		Factor For B ↓		Angle of Hole		
→					Deg.	Min.	Sec.
1	.229680	1	.079373	1	32	43	38-2/11
2	.045184	2	.292293	2	65	27	16-4/11
3	.005089	3	.571157	3	98	10	54-6/11
4	.122125	4	.827430	4	130	54	32-8/11
5	.359134	5	.979746	5	163	38	10-10/11
6	.640866	6	.979746	6	196	21	49-1/11
7	.877875	7	.827430	7	229	5	27-3/11
8	.994911	8	.571157	8	261	49	5-5/11
9	.954816	9	.292293	9	294	32	43-7/11
10	.770320	10	.079373	10	327	16	21-9/11
11	.500000	11	.000000	11	360	0	0

Courtesy W. J. Woodworth and J. D. Woodworth

NATURAL TRIGONOMETRIC FUNCTIONS

′	0°						1°					
′	sin	cos	tan	cot	sec	cosec	sin	cos	tan	cot	sec	cosec
0	.00000	1.0000	.00000	Infinite	1.0000	Infinite	.01745	.99985	.01745	57.290	1.0001	57.299
1	.00029	.0000	.00029	3437.7	.0000	3437.7	.01774	.99984	.01775	56.350	.0001	56.359
2	.00058	.0000	.00058	1718.9	.0000	1718.9	.01803	.99984	.01804	55.441	.0001	55.450
3	.00087	.0000	.00087	1145.9	.0000	1145.9	.01832	.99983	.01833	54.561	.0002	54.570
4	.00116	.0000	.00116	859.44	.0000	859.44	.01861	.99983	.01862	53.708	.0002	53.718
5	.00145	1.0000	.00145	687.55	.0000	687.55	.01891	.99982	.01891	52.882	.0002	52.891
6	.00174	.0000	.00174	572.96	.0000	572.96	.01920	.99981	.01920	52.081	.0002	52.090
7	.00204	.0000	.00204	491.11	.0000	491.11	.01949	.99981	.01949	51.303	.0002	51.313
8	.00233	.0000	.00233	429.72	.0000	429.72	.01978	.99980	.01978	50.548	.0002	50.558
9	.00262	.0000	.00262	381.97	.0000	381.97	.02007	.99980	.02007	49.816	.0002	49.826
10	.00291	0.99999	.00291	343.77	.0000	343.77	.02036	.99979	.02036	49.104	.0002	49.114
11	.00320	.99999	.00320	312.52	.0000	312.52	.02065	.99979	.02066	48.412	.0002	48.422
12	.00349	.99999	.00349	286.48	.0000	286.48	.02094	.99978	.02095	47.739	.0002	47.750
13	.00378	.99999	.00378	264.44	.0000	264.44	.02123	.99977	.02124	47.085	.0002	47.096
14	.00407	.99999	.00407	245.55	.0000	245.55	.02152	.99977	.02153	46.449	.0002	46.460
15	.00436	.99999	.00436	229.18	.0000	229.18	.02181	.99976	.02182	45.829	.0002	45.840
16	.00465	.99999	.00465	214.86	.0000	214.86	.02210	.99975	.02211	45.226	.0002	45.237
17	.00494	.99999	.00494	202.22	.0000	202.22	.02240	.99975	.02240	44.638	.0002	44.650
18	.00524	.99999	.00524	190.98	.0000	190.99	.02269	.99974	.02269	44.066	.0002	44.077
19	.00553	.99998	.00553	180.93	.0000	180.93	.02298	.99974	.02298	43.508	.0003	43.520
20	.00582	.99998	.00582	171.88	.0000	171.89	.02326	.99973	.02327	42.964	.0003	42.976
21	.00611	.99998	.00611	163.70	.0000	163.70	.02356	.99972	.02357	42.433	.0003	42.445
22	.00640	.99998	.00640	156.26	.0000	156.26	.02385	.99971	.02386	41.916	.0003	41.928
23	.00669	.99998	.00669	149.46	.0000	149.47	.02414	.99971	.02415	41.410	.0003	41.423
24	.00698	.99997	.00698	143.24	.0000	143.24	.02443	.99970	.02444	40.917	.0003	40.930
25	.00727	.99997	.00727	137.51	.0000	137.51	.02472	.99969	.02473	40.436	.0003	40.448
26	.00756	.99997	.00756	132.22	.0000	132.22	.02501	.99969	.02502	39.965	.0003	39.978
27	.00785	.99997	.00785	127.32	.0000	127.32	.02530	.99968	.02531	39.506	.0003	39.518
28	.00814	.99997	.00814	122.77	.0000	122.78	.02559	.99967	.02560	39.057	.0003	39.069
29	.00843	.99996	.00844	118.54	.0000	118.54	.02589	.99966	.02589	38.618	.0003	38.631
30	.00873	.99996	.00873	114.59	.0000	114.59	.02618	.99966	.02618	38.188	.0003	38.201
31	.00902	.99996	.00902	110.89	.0000	110.90	.02647	.99965	.02648	37.769	.0003	37.782
32	.00931	.99996	.00931	107.43	.0000	107.43	.02676	.99964	.02677	37.358	.0003	37.371
33	.00960	.99995	.00960	104.17	.0000	104.17	.02705	.99963	.02706	36.956	.0004	36.969
34	.00989	.99995	.00989	101.11	.0000	101.11	.02734	.99963	.02735	36.563	.0004	36.576
35	.01018	.99995	.01018	98.218	.0000	98.223	.02763	.99962	.02764	36.177	.0004	36.191
36	.01047	.99994	.01047	95.489	.0000	95.495	.02792	.99961	.02793	35.800	.0004	35.814
37	.01076	.99994	.01076	92.908	.0000	92.914	.02821	.99960	.02822	35.431	.0004	35.445
38	.01105	.99994	.01105	90.463	.0001	90.469	.02850	.99959	.02851	35.069	.0004	35.084
39	.01134	.99993	.01134	88.143	.0001	88.149	.02879	.99958	.02880	34.715	.0004	34.729
40	.01163	.99993	.01164	85.940	.0001	85.946	.02908	.99958	.02910	34.368	.0004	34.382
41	.01193	.99993	.01193	83.843	.0001	83.849	.02937	.99957	.02939	34.027	.0004	34.042
42	.01222	.99992	.01222	81.847	.0001	81.853	.02967	.99956	.02968	33.693	.0004	33.708
43	.01251	.99992	.01251	79.943	.0001	79.950	.02996	.99955	.02997	33.366	.0004	33.381
44	.01280	.99992	.01280	78.126	.0001	78.133	.03025	.99954	.03026	33.045	.0004	33.060
45	.01309	.99991	.01309	76.390	.0001	76.396	.03054	.99953	.03055	32.730	.0005	32.745
46	.01338	.99991	.01338	74.729	.0001	74.736	.03083	.99952	.03084	32.421	.0005	32.437
47	.01367	.99991	.01367	73.139	.0001	73.146	.03112	.99951	.03113	32.118	.0005	32.134
48	.01396	.99990	.01396	71.615	.0001	71.622	.03141	.99951	.03143	31.820	.0005	31.836
49	.01425	.99990	.01425	70.153	.0001	70.160	.03170	.99950	.03172	31.528	.0005	31.544
50	.01454	.99989	.01454	68.750	.0001	68.757	.03199	.99949	.03201	31.241	.0005	31.257
51	.01483	.99989	.01484	67.402	.0001	67.409	.03228	.99948	.03230	30.960	.0005	30.976
52	.01512	.99988	.01513	66.105	.0001	66.113	.03257	.99947	.03259	30.683	.0005	30.699
53	.01542	.99988	.01542	64.858	.0001	64.866	.03286	.99946	.03288	30.411	.0005	30.428
54	.01571	.99988	.01571	63.657	.0001	63.664	.03315	.99945	.03317	30.145	.0005	30.161
55	.01600	.99987	.01600	62.499	.0001	62.507	.03344	.99944	.03346	29.882	.0005	29.899
56	.01629	.99987	.01629	61.383	.0001	61.391	.03374	.99943	.03375	29.624	.0006	29.641
57	.01658	.99987	.01658	60.306	.0001	60.314	.03403	.99942	.03405	29.371	.0006	29.388
58	.01687	.99986	.01687	59.266	.0001	59.274	.03432	.99941	.03434	29.122	.0006	29.139
59	.01716	.99985	.01716	58.261	.0001	58.270	.03461	.99940	.03463	28.877	.0006	28.894
60	.01745	.99985	.01745	57.290	.0001	57.299	.03490	.99939	.03492	28.636	.0006	28.654
′	cos	sin	cot	tan	cosec	sec	cos	sin	cot	tan	cosec	sec
	89°						88°					

2°						3°						′
sin	cos	tan	cot	sec	cosec	sin	cos	tan	cot	sec	cosec	′
.03490	.99939	.03492	28.636	1.0006	28.654	.05234	.99863	.05241	19.081	1.0014	19.107	60
.03519	.99938	.03521	28.399	.0006	28.417	.05263	.99861	.05270	18.975	.0014	19.002	59
.03548	.99937	.03550	28.166	.0006	28.184	.05292	.99860	.05299	18.871	.0014	18.897	58
.03577	.99936	.03579	27.937	.0006	27.955	.05321	.99858	.05328	18.768	.0014	18.794	57
.03606	.99935	.03608	27.712	.0006	27.730	.05350	.99857	.05357	18.665	.0014	18.692	56
.03635	.99934	.03638	27.490	.0007	27.508	.05379	.99855	.05387	18.564	.0014	18.591	55
.03664	.99933	.03667	27.271	.0007	27.290	.05408	.99854	.05416	18.464	.0015	18.491	54
.03693	.99932	.03696	27.056	.0007	27.075	.05437	.99852	.05445	18.365	.0015	18.393	53
.03722	.99931	.03725	26.845	.0007	26.864	.05466	.99850	.05474	18.268	.0015	18.295	52
.03751	.99930	.03754	26.637	.0007	26.655	.05495	.99849	.05503	18.171	.0015	18.198	51
.03781	.99928	.03783	26.432	.0007	26.450	.05524	.99847	.05532	18.075	.0015	18.103	50
.03810	.99927	.03812	26.230	.0007	26.249	.05553	.99846	.05562	17.980	.0015	18.008	49
.03839	.99926	.03842	26.031	.0007	26.050	.05582	.99844	.05591	17.886	.0016	17.914	48
.03868	.99925	.03871	25.835	.0007	25.854	.05611	.99842	.05620	17.793	.0016	17.821	47
.03897	.99924	.03900	25.642	.0008	25.661	.05640	.99841	.05649	17.701	.0016	17.730	46
.03926	.99923	.03929	25.452	.0008	25.471	.05669	.99839	.05678	17.610	.0016	17.639	45
.03955	.99922	.03958	25.264	.0008	25.284	.05698	.99837	.05707	17.520	.0016	17.549	44
.03984	.99921	.03987	25.080	.0008	25.100	.05727	.99836	.05737	17.431	.0016	17.460	43
.04013	.99919	.04016	24.898	.0008	24.918	.05756	.99834	.05766	17.343	.0017	17.372	42
.04042	.99918	.04045	24.718	.0008	24.739	.05785	.99832	.05795	17.256	.0017	17.285	41
.04071	.99917	.04075	24.542	.0008	24.562	.05814	.99831	.05824	17.169	.0017	17.198	40
.04100	.99916	.04104	24.367	.0008	24.388	.05843	.99829	.05853	17.084	.0017	17.113	39
.04129	.99915	.04133	24.196	.0008	24.216	.05872	.99827	.05883	16.999	.0017	17.028	38
.04158	.99913	.04162	24.026	.0009	24.047	.05902	.99826	.05912	16.915	.0017	16.944	37
.04187	.99912	.04191	23.859	.0009	23.880	.05931	.99824	.05941	16.832	.0018	16.861	36
.04217	.99911	.04220	23.694	.0009	23.716	.05960	.99822	.05970	16.750	.0018	16.779	35
.04246	.99910	.04249	23.532	.0009	23.553	.05989	.99820	.05999	16.668	.0018	16.698	34
.04275	.99908	.04279	23.372	.0009	23.393	.06018	.99819	.06029	16.587	.0018	16.617	33
.04304	.99907	.04308	23.214	.0009	23.235	.06047	.99817	.06058	16.507	.0018	16.538	32
.04333	.99906	.04337	23.058	.0009	23.079	.06076	.99815	.06087	16.428	.0018	16.459	31
.04362	.99905	.04366	22.904	.0009	22.925	.06105	.99813	.06116	16.350	.0019	16.380	30
.04391	.99903	.04395	22.752	.0010	22.774	.06134	.99812	.06145	16.272	.0019	16.303	29
.04420	.99902	.04424	22.602	.0010	22.624	.06163	.99810	.06175	16.195	.0019	16.226	28
.04449	.99901	.04453	22.454	.0010	22.476	.06192	.99808	.06204	16.119	.0019	16.150	27
.04478	.99900	.04483	22.308	.0010	22.330	.06221	.99806	.06233	16.043	.0019	16.075	26
.04507	.99898	.04512	22.164	.0010	22.186	.06250	.99804	.06262	15.969	.0019	16.000	25
.04536	.99897	.04541	22.022	.0010	22.044	.06279	.99803	.06291	15.894	.0020	15.926	24
.04565	.99896	.04570	21.881	.0010	21.904	.06308	.99801	.06321	15.821	.0020	15.853	23
.04594	.99894	.04599	21.742	.0010	21.765	.06337	.99799	.06350	15.748	.0020	15.780	22
.04623	.99893	.04628	21.606	.0011	21.629	.06366	.99797	.06379	15.676	.0020	15.708	21
.04652	.99892	.04657	21.470	.0011	21.494	.06395	.99795	.06408	15.605	.0020	15.637	20
.04681	.99890	.04687	21.337	.0011	21.360	.06424	.99793	.06437	15.534	.0021	15.566	19
.04711	.99889	.04716	21.205	.0011	21.228	.06453	.99791	.06467	15.464	.0021	15.496	18
.04740	.99888	.04745	21.075	.0011	21.098	.06482	.99790	.06496	15.394	.0021	15.427	17
.04769	.99886	.94774	20.946	.0011	20.970	.06511	.99788	.06525	15.325	.0021	15.358	16
.04798	.99885	.04803	20.819	.0011	20.843	.06540	.99786	.06554	15.257	.0021	15.290	15
.04827	.99883	.04832	20.693	.0012	20.717	.06569	.99784	.06583	15.189	.0022	15.222	14
.04856	.99882	.04862	20.569	.0012	20.593	.06598	.99782	.06613	15.122	.0022	15.155	13
.04885	.99881	.04891	20.446	.0012	20.471	.06627	.99780	.06642	15.056	.0022	15.089	12
.04914	.99879	.04920	20.325	.0012	20.350	.06656	.99778	.06671	14.990	.0022	15.023	11
.04943	.99878	.04949	20.205	.0012	20.230	.06685	.99776	.06700	14.924	.0022	14.958	10
.04972	.99876	.04978	20.087	.0012	20.112	.06714	.99774	.06730	14.860	.0023	14.893	9
.05001	.99875	.05007	19.970	.0012	19.995	.06743	.99772	.06759	14.795	.0023	14.829	8
.05030	.99873	.05037	19.854	.0013	19.880	.06772	.99770	.06788	14.732	.0023	14.765	7
.05059	.99872	.05066	19.740	.0013	19.766	.06801	.99768	.06817	14.668	.0023	14.702	6
.05088	.99870	.05095	19.627	.0013	19.653	.06830	.99766	.06846	14.606	.0023	14.640	5
.05117	.99869	.05124	19.515	.0013	19.541	.06859	.99764	.06876	14.544	.0024	14.578	4
.05146	.99867	.05153	19.405	.0013	19.431	.06888	.99762	.06905	14.482	.0024	14.517	3
.05175	.99866	.05182	19.296	.0013	19.322	.06918	.99760	.06934	14.421	.0024	14.456	2
.05204	.99864	.05212	19.188	.0013	19.214	.06947	.99758	.06963	14.361	.0024	14.395	1
.05234	.99863	.05241	19.081	.0014	19.107	.06976	.99756	06993	14.301	.0024	14.335	0
cos	sin	cot	tan	cosec	sec	cos	sin	cot	tan	cosec	sec	′
87°						86°						

Courtesy Bethlehem Steel Corporation

NATURAL TRIGONOMETRIC FUNCTIONS

	4°						5°						
′	sin	cos	tan	cot	sec	cosec	sin	cos	tan	cot	sec	cosec	′
0	.06976	.99756	.06993	14.301	1.0024	14.335	.08715	.99619	.08749	11.430	1.0038	11.474	60
1	.07005	.99754	.07022	14.241	.0025	14.276	.08744	.99617	.08778	11.392	.0038	11.436	59
2	.07034	.99752	.07051	14.182	.0025	14.217	.08773	.99614	.08807	11.354	.0039	11.398	58
3	.07063	.99750	.07080	14.123	.0025	14.159	.08802	.99612	.08837	11.316	.0039	11.360	57
4	.07092	.99748	.07110	14.065	.0025	14.101	.08831	.99609	.08866	11.279	.0039	11.323	56
5	.07121	.99746	.07139	14.008	.0025	14.043	.08860	.99607	.08895	11.242	.0039	11.286	55
6	.07150	.99744	.07168	13.951	.0026	13.986	.08889	.99604	.08925	11.205	.0040	11.249	54
7	.07179	.99742	.07197	13.894	.0026	13.930	.08918	.99601	.08954	11.168	.0040	11.213	53
8	.07208	.99740	.07226	13.838	.0026	13.874	.08947	.99599	.08983	11.132	.0040	11.176	52
9	.07237	.99738	.07256	13.782	.0026	13.818	.08976	.99596	.09013	11.095	.0040	11.140	51
10	.07266	.99736	.07285	13.727	.0026	13.763	.09005	.99594	.09042	11.059	.0041	11.104	50
11	.07295	.99733	.07314	13.672	.0027	13.708	.09034	.99591	.09071	11.024	.0041	11.069	49
12	.07324	.99731	.07343	13.617	.0027	13.654	.09063	.99588	.09101	10.988	.0041	11.033	48
13	.07353	.99729	.07373	13.563	.0027	13.600	.09092	.99586	.09130	10.953	.0041	10.998	47
14	.07382	.99727	.07402	13.510	.0027	13.547	.09121	.99583	.09159	10.918	.0042	10.963	46
15	.07411	.99725	.07431	13.457	.0027	13.494	.09150	.99580	.09189	10.883	.0042	10.929	45
16	.07440	.99723	.07460	13.404	.0028	13.441	.09179	.99578	.09218	10.848	.0042	10.894	44
17	.07469	.99721	.07490	13.351	.0028	13.389	.09208	.99575	.09247	10.814	.0043	10.860	43
18	.07498	.99718	.07519	13.299	.0028	13.337	.09237	.99572	.09277	10.780	.0043	10.826	42
19	.07527	.99716	.07548	13.248	.0028	13.286	.09266	.99570	.09306	10.746	.0043	10.792	41
20	.07556	.99714	.07577	13.917	.0029	13.235	.09295	.99567	.09335	10.712	.0043	10.758	40
21	.07585	.99712	.07607	13.146	.0029	13.184	.09324	.99564	.09365	10.678	.0044	10.725	39
22	.07614	.99710	.07636	13.096	.0029	13.134	.09353	.99562	.09394	10.645	.0044	10.692	38
23	.07643	.99707	.07665	13.046	.0029	13.084	.09382	.99559	.09423	10.612	.0044	10.659	37
24	.07672	.99705	.07694	12.996	.0029	13.034	.09411	.99556	.09453	10.579	.0044	10.626	36
25	.07701	.99703	.07724	12.947	.0030	12.985	.09440	.99553	.09482	10.546	.0045	10.593	35
26	.07730	.99701	.07753	12.898	.0030	12.937	.09469	.99551	.09511	10.514	.0045	10.561	34
27	.07759	.99698	.07782	12.849	.0030	12.888	.09498	.99548	.09541	10.481	.0045	10.529	33
28	.07788	.99696	.07812	12.801	.0030	12.840	.09527	.99545	.09570	10.449	.0046	10.497	32
29	.07817	.99694	.07841	12.754	.0031	12.793	.09556	.99542	.09599	10.417	.0046	10.465	31
30	.07846	.99692	.07870	12.706	.0031	12.745	.09584	.99540	.09629	10.385	.0046	10.433	30
31	.07875	.99689	.07899	12.659	.0031	12.698	.09613	.99537	.09658	10.354	.0046	10.402	29
32	.07904	.99687	.07929	12.612	.0031	12.652	.09642	.99534	.09688	10.322	.0047	10.371	28
33	.07933	.99685	.07958	12.566	.0032	12.606	.09671	.99531	.09717	10.291	.0047	10.340	27
34	.07962	.99682	.07987	12.520	.0032	12.560	.09700	.99528	.09746	10.260	.0047	10.309	26
35	.07991	.99680	.08016	12.474	.0032	12.514	.09729	.99525	.09776	10.229	.0048	10.278	25
36	.08020	.99678	.08046	12.429	.0032	12.469	.09758	.99523	.09805	10.199	.0048	10.248	24
37	.08049	.99675	.08075	12.384	.0032	12.424	.09787	.99520	.09834	10.168	.0048	10.217	23
38	.08078	.99673	.08104	12.339	.0033	12.379	.09816	.99517	.09864	10.138	.0048	10.187	22
39	.08107	.99671	.08134	12.295	.0033	12.335	.09845	.99514	.09893	10.108	.0049	10.157	21
40	.08136	.99668	.08163	12.250	.0033	12.291	.09874	.99511	.09922	10.078	.0049	10.127	20
41	.08165	.99666	.08192	12.207	.0033	12.248	.09903	.99508	.09952	10.048	.0049	10.098	19
42	.08194	.99664	.08221	12.163	.0034	12.204	.09932	.99505	.09981	10.019	.0050	10.068	18
43	.08223	.99661	.08251	12.120	.0034	12.161	.09961	.99503	.10011	9.9893	.0050	10.039	17
44	.08252	.99659	.08280	12.077	.0034	12.118	.09990	.99500	.10040	9.9601	.0050	10.010	16
45	.08281	.99656	.08309	12.035	.0034	12.076	.10019	.99497	.10069	9.9310	.0050	9.9812	15
46	.08310	.99654	.08339	11.992	.0035	12.034	.10048	.99494	.10099	9.9021	.0051	9.9525	14
47	.08339	.99652	.08368	11.950	.0035	11.992	.10077	.99491	.10128	9.8734	.0051	9.9239	13
48	.08368	.99649	.08397	11.909	.0035	11.950	.10106	.99488	.10158	9.8448	.0051	9.8955	12
49	.08397	.99647	.08426	11.867	.0035	11.909	.10134	.99485	.10187	9.8164	.0052	9.8672	11
50	.08426	.99644	.08456	11.826	.0036	11.868	.10163	.99482	.10216	9.7882	.0052	9.8391	10
51	.08455	.99642	.08485	11.785	.0036	11.828	.10192	.99479	.10246	9.7601	.0052	9.8112	9
52	.08484	.99639	.08514	11.745	.0036	11.787	.10221	.99476	.10275	9.7322	.0053	9.7834	8
53	.08513	.99637	.08544	11.704	.0036	11.747	.10250	.99473	.10305	9.7044	.0053	9.7558	7
54	.08542	.99634	.08573	11.664	.0037	11.707	.10279	.99470	.10334	9.6768	.0053	9.7283	6
55	.08571	.99632	.08602	11.625	.0037	11.668	.10308	.99467	.10363	9.6493	.0053	9.7010	5
56	.08600	.99629	.08632	11.585	.0037	11.628	.10337	.99464	.10393	9.6220	.0054	9.6739	4
57	.08629	.99627	.08661	11.546	.0037	11.589	.10366	.99461	.10422	9.5949	.0054	9.6469	3
58	.08658	.99624	.08690	11.507	.0038	11.550	.10395	.99458	.10452	9.5679	.0054	9.6200	2
59	.08687	.99622	.08719	11.468	.0038	11.512	.10424	.99455	.10481	9.5411	.0055	9.5933	1
60	.08715	.99619	.08749	11.430	.0038	11.474	.10453	.99452	.10510	9.5144	.0055	9.5668	0
′	cos	sin	cot	tan	cosec	sec	cos	sin	cot	tan	cosec	sec	′
	85°						84°						

	6°						7°						
′	sin	cos	tan	cot	sec	cosec	sin	cos	tan	cot	sec	cosec	′
0	.10453	.99452	.10510	9.5144	1.0055	9.5668	.12187	.99255	.12278	8.1443	1.0075	8.2055	60
1	.10482	.99449	.10540	.4878	.0055	.5404	.12216	.99251	.12308	.1248	.0075	.1861	59
2	.10511	.99446	.10569	.4614	.0056	.5141	.12245	.99247	.12337	.1053	.0076	.1668	58
3	.10540	.99443	.10599	.4351	.0056	.4880	.12273	.99244	.12367	.0860	.0076	.1476	57
4	.10568	.99440	.10628	.4090	.0056	.4620	.12302	.99240	.12396	.0667	.0076	.1285	56
5	.10597	.99437	.10657	9.3831	.0057	9.4362	.12331	.99237	.12426	8.0476	.0077	8.1094	55
6	.10626	.99434	.10687	.3572	.0057	.4105	.12360	.99233	.12456	.0285	.0077	.0905	54
7	.10655	.99431	.10716	.3315	.0057	.3850	.12389	.99229	.12485	.0095	.0078	.0717	53
8	.10684	.99428	.10746	.3060	.0057	.3596	.12418	.99226	.12515	7.9906	.0078	.0529	52
9	.10713	.99424	.10775	.2806	.0058	.3343	.12447	.99222	.12544	.9717	.0078	.0342	51
10	.10742	.99421	.10805	9.2553	.0058	9.3092	.12476	.99219	.12574	7.9530	.0079	8.0156	50
11	.10771	.99418	.10834	.2302	.0058	.2842	.12504	.99215	.12603	.9344	.0079	7.9971	49
12	.10800	.99415	.10863	.2051	.0059	.2593	.12533	.99211	.12633	.9158	.0079	.9787	48
13	.10829	.99412	.10893	.1803	.0059	.2346	.12562	.99208	.12662	.8973	.0080	.9604	47
14	.10858	.99409	.10922	.1555	.0059	.2100	.12591	.99204	.12692	.8789	.0080	.9421	46
15	.10887	.99406	.10952	9.1309	.0060	9.1855	.12620	.99200	.12722	7.8606	.0080	7.9240	45
16	.10916	.99402	.10981	.1064	.0060	.1612	.12649	.99197	.12751	.8424	.0081	.9059	44
17	.10944	.99399	.11011	.0821	.0060	.1370	.12678	.99193	.12781	.8243	.0081	.8879	43
18	.10973	.99396	.11040	.0579	.0061	.1129	.12706	.99189	.12810	.8062	.0082	.8700	42
19	.11002	.99393	.11069	.0338	.0061	.0890	.12735	.99186	.12840	.7882	.0082	.8522	41
20	.11031	.99390	.11099	9.0098	.0061	9.0651	.12764	.99182	.12869	7.7703	.0082	7.8344	40
21	.11060	.99386	.11128	8.9860	.0062	.0414	.12793	.99178	.12899	.7525	.0083	.8168	39
22	.11089	.99383	.11158	.9623	.0062	.0179	.12822	.99174	.12928	.7348	.0083	.7992	38
23	.11118	.99380	.11187	.9387	.0062	8.9944	.12851	.99171	.12958	.7171	.0084	.7817	37
24	.11147	.99377	.11217	.9152	.0063	.9711	.12879	.99167	.12988	.6996	.0084	.7642	36
25	.11176	.99373	.11246	8.8918	.0063	8.9479	.12908	.99163	.13017	7.6821	.0084	7.7469	35
26	.11205	.99370	.11276	.8686	.0063	.9248	.12937	.99160	.13047	.6646	.0085	.7296	34
27	.11234	.99367	.11305	.8455	.0064	.9018	.12966	.99156	.13076	.6473	.0085	.7124	33
28	.11262	.99364	.11335	.8225	.0064	.8790	.12995	.99152	.13106	.6300	.0085	.6953	32
29	.11291	.99360	.11364	.7996	.0064	.8563	.13024	.99148	.13136	.6129	.0086	.6783	31
30	.11320	.99357	.11393	8.7769	.0065	8.8337	.13053	.99144	.13165	7.5957	.0086	7.6613	30
31	.11349	.99354	.11423	.7542	.0065	.8112	.13081	.99141	.13195	.5787	.0087	.6444	29
32	.11378	.99350	.11452	.7317	.0065	.7888	.13110	.99137	.13224	.5617	.0087	.6276	28
33	.11407	.99347	.11482	.7093	.0066	.7665	.13139	.99133	.13254	.5449	.0087	.6108	27
34	.11436	.99344	.11511	.6870	.0066	.7444	.13168	.99129	.13284	.5280	.0088	.5942	26
35	.11465	.99341	.11541	8.6648	.0066	8.7223	.13197	.99125	.13313	7.5113	.0088	7.5776	25
36	.11494	.99337	.11570	.6427	.0067	.7004	.13226	.99121	.13343	.4946	.0089	.5611	24
37	.11523	.99334	.11600	.6208	.0067	.6786	.13254	.99118	.13372	.4780	.0089	.5446	23
38	.11551	.99330	.11629	.5989	.0067	.6569	.13283	.99114	.13402	.4615	.0089	.5282	22
39	.11580	.99327	.11659	.5772	.0068	.6353	.13312	.99110	.13432	.4451	.0090	.5119	21
40	.11609	.99324	.11688	8.5555	.0068	8.6138	.13341	.99106	.13461	7.4287	.0090	7.4957	20
41	.11638	.99320	.11718	.5340	.0068	.5924	.13370	.99102	.13491	.4124	.0090	.4795	19
42	.11667	.99317	.11747	.5126	.0069	.5711	.13399	.99098	.13520	.3961	.0091	.4634	18
43	.11696	.99314	.11777	.4913	.0069	.5499	.13427	.99094	.13550	.3800	.0091	.4474	17
44	.11725	.99310	.11806	.4701	.0069	.5289	.13456	.99090	.13580	.3639	.0092	.4315	16
45	.11754	.99307	.11836	8.4489	.0070	8.5079	.13485	.99086	.13609	7.3479	.0092	7.4156	15
46	.11783	.99303	.11865	.4279	.0070	.4871	.13514	.99083	.13639	.3319	.0092	.3998	14
47	.11811	.99300	.11895	.4070	.0070	.4663	.13543	.99079	.13669	.3160	.0093	.3840	13
48	.11840	.99296	.11924	.3862	.0071	.4457	.13571	.99075	.13698	.3002	.0093	.3683	12
49	.11869	.99293	.11954	.3655	.0071	.4251	.13600	.99071	.13728	.2844	.0094	.3527	11
50	.11898	.99290	.11983	8.3449	.0071	8.4046	.13629	.99067	.13757	7.2687	.0094	7.3372	10
51	.11927	.99286	.12013	.3244	.0072	.3843	.13658	.99063	.13787	.2531	.0094	.3217	9
52	.11956	.99283	.12042	.3040	.0072	.3640	.13687	.99059	.13817	.2375	.0095	.3063	8
53	.11985	.99279	.12072	.2837	.0073	.3439	.13716	.99055	.13846	.2220	.0095	.2909	7
54	.12014	.99276	.12101	.2635	.0073	.3238	.13744	.99051	.13876	.2066	.0096	.2757	6
55	.12042	.99272	.12131	8.2434	.0073	8.3039	.13773	.99047	.13906	7.1912	.0096	7.2604	5
56	.12071	.99269	.12160	.2234	.0074	.2840	.13802	.99043	.13935	.1759	.0097	.2453	4
57	.12100	.99265	.12190	.2035	.0074	.2642	.13831	.99039	.13965	.1607	.0097	.2302	3
58	.12129	.99262	.12219	.1837	.0074	.2446	.13860	.99035	.13995	.1455	.0097	.2152	2
59	.12158	.99258	.12249	.1640	.0075	.2250	.13888	.99031	.14024	.1304	.0098	.2002	1
60	.12187	.99255	.12278	8.1443	.0075	8.2055	.13917	.99027	.14054	7.1154	.0098	7.1853	0
′	cos	sin	cot	tan	cosec	sec	cos	sin	cot	tan	cosec	sec	′
	83°						82°						

NATURAL TRIGONOMETRIC FUNCTIONS

′	8° sin	8° cos	8° tan	8° cot	8° sec	8° cosec	9° sin	9° cos	9° tan	9° cot	9° sec	9° cosec	′
0	.13917	.99027	.14054	7.1154	1.0098	7.1853	.15643	.98769	.15838	6.3137	1.0215	6.3924	60
1	.13946	.99023	.14084	.1004	.0099	.1704	.15672	.98764	.15868	.3019	.0125	.3807	59
2	.13975	.99019	.14113	.0854	.0099	.1557	.15701	.98760	.15898	.2901	.0125	.3690	58
3	.14004	.99015	.14143	.0706	.0099	.1409	.15730	.98755	.15928	.2783	.0126	.3574	57
4	.14032	.99010	.14173	.0558	.0100	.1263	.15758	.98750	.15958	.2665	.0126	.3458	56
5	.14061	.99006	.14202	7.0410	.0100	7.1117	.15787	.98746	.15987	6.2548	.0127	6.3343	55
6	.14090	.99002	.14232	.0264	.0101	.0972	.15816	.98741	.16017	.2432	.0217	.3228	54
7	.14119	.98998	.14262	.0117	.0101	.0827	.15844	.98737	.16047	.2316	.0128	.3113	53
8	.14148	.98994	.14291	6.9972	.0102	.0683	.15873	.98732	.16077	.2200	.0128	.2999	52
9	.14176	.98990	.14321	.9827	.0102	.0539	.15902	.98727	.16107	.2085	.0129	.2885	51
10	.14205	.98986	.14351	6.9682	.0102	7.0396	.15931	.98723	.16137	6.1970	.0129	6.2772	50
11	.14234	.98982	.14380	.9538	.0103	.0254	.15959	.98718	.16167	.1856	.0130	.2659	49
12	.14263	.98978	.14410	.9395	.0103	.0112	.15988	.98714	.16196	.1742	.0130	.2546	48
13	.14292	.98973	.14440	.9252	.0104	6.9971	.16017	.98709	.16226	.1628	.0131	.2434	47
14	.14320	.98969	.14470	.9110	.0104	.9830	.16045	.98704	.16256	.1515	.0131	.2322	46
15	.14349	.98965	.14499	6.8969	.0104	6.9690	.16074	.98700	.16286	6.1402	.0132	6.2211	45
16	.14378	.98961	.14529	.8828	.0105	.9550	.16103	.98695	.16316	.1290	.0132	.2100	44
17	.14407	.98957	.14559	.8687	.0105	.9411	.16132	.98690	.16346	.1178	.0133	.1990	43
18	.14436	.98952	.14588	.8547	.0106	.9273	.16160	.98685	.16376	.1066	.0133	.1880	42
19	.14464	.98948	.14618	.8408	.0106	.9135	.16189	.98681	.16405	.0955	.0134	.1770	41
20	.14493	.98944	.14648	6.8269	.0107	6.8998	.16218	.98676	.16435	6.0844	.0134	6.1661	40
21	.14522	.98940	.14677	.8131	.0107	.8861	.16246	.98671	.16465	.0734	.0135	.1552	39
22	.14551	.98936	.14707	.7993	.0107	.8725	.16275	.98667	.16495	.0624	.0135	.1443	38
23	.14579	.98931	.14737	.7856	.0108	.8589	.16304	.98662	.16525	.0514	.0136	.1335	37
24	.14608	.98927	.14767	.7720	.0108	.8454	.16333	.98657	.16555	.0405	.0136	.1227	36
25	.14637	.98923	.14796	6.7584	.0109	6.8320	.16361	.98652	.16585	6.0296	.0136	6.1120	35
26	.14666	.98919	.14826	.7448	.0109	.8185	.16390	.98648	.16615	.0188	.0137	.1013	34
27	.14695	.98914	.14856	.7313	.0110	.8052	.16419	.98643	.16644	.0080	.0137	.0906	33
28	.14723	.98910	.14886	.7179	.0110	.7919	.16447	.98638	.16674	5.9972	.0138	.0800	32
29	.14752	.98906	.14915	.7045	.0111	.7787	.16476	.98633	.16704	.9865	.0138	.0694	31
30	.14781	.98901	.14945	6.6911	.0111	6.7655	.16505	.98628	.16734	5.9758	.0139	6.0588	30
31	.14810	.98897	.14975	.6779	.0111	.7523	.16533	.98624	.16764	.9651	.9139	.0483	29
32	.14838	.98893	.15004	.6646	.0112	.7392	.16562	.98619	.16794	.9545	.9140	.0379	28
33	.14867	.98889	.15034	.6514	.0112	.7262	.16591	.98614	.16824	.9439	.0140	.0274	27
34	.14896	.98884	.15064	.6383	.0113	.7132	.16619	.98609	.16854	.9333	.0141	.0170	26
35	.14925	.98880	.15094	6.6252	.0113	6.7003	.16648	.98604	.16884	5.9228	.0141	6.0066	25
36	.14953	.98876	.15123	.6122	.0114	.6874	.16677	.98600	.16914	.9123	.0142	5.9963	24
37	.14982	.98871	.15153	.5992	.0114	.6745	.16705	.98595	.16944	.9019	.0142	.9860	23
38	.15011	.98867	.15183	.5863	.0115	.6617	.16734	.98590	.16973	.8915	.0143	.9758	22
39	.15050	.98862	.15213	.5734	.0115	.6490	.16763	.98585	.17003	.8811	.0143	.9655	21
40	.15068	.98858	.15243	6.5605	.0115	6.6363	.16791	.98580	.17033	5.8708	.0144	5.9554	20
41	.15097	.98854	.15272	.5478	.0116	.6237	.16820	.98575	.17063	.8605	.0144	.9452	19
42	.15126	.98849	.15302	.5350	.0116	.6111	.16849	.98570	.17093	.8502	.0145	.9351	18
43	.15155	.98845	.15332	.5223	.0117	.5985	.16878	.98565	.17123	.8400	.0145	.9250	17
44	.15183	.98840	.15362	.5097	.0117	.5860	.16906	.98560	.17153	.8298	.0146	.9150	16
45	.15212	.98836	.15391	6.4971	.0118	6.5736	.16935	.98556	.17183	5.8196	.0146	5.9049	15
46	.15241	.98832	.15421	.4845	.0118	.5612	.16964	.98551	.17213	.8095	.0147	.8950	14
47	.15270	.98827	.15451	.4720	.0119	.5488	.16992	.98546	.17243	.7994	.0147	.8850	13
48	.15298	.98823	.15481	.4596	.0119	.5365	.17021	.98541	.17273	.7894	.0148	.8751	12
49	.15328	.98818	.15511	.4472	.0119	.5243	.17050	.98536	.17303	.7794	.0148	.8652	11
50	.15356	.98814	.15540	6.4348	.0120	6.5121	.17078	.98531	.17333	5.7694	.0149	5.8554	10
51	.15385	.98809	.15570	.4225	.0120	.4999	.17107	.98526	.17363	.7594	.0150	.8456	9
52	.15413	.98805	.15600	.4103	.0121	.4878	.17136	.98521	.17393	.7495	.0150	.8358	8
53	.15442	.98800	.15630	.3980	.0121	.4757	.17164	.98516	.17423	.7396	.0151	.8261	7
54	.15471	.98796	.15659	.3859	.0122	.4637	.17193	.98511	.17453	.7297	.0151	.8163	6
55	.15500	.98791	.15689	6.3737	.0122	6.4517	.17221	.98506	.17483	5.7199	.0152	5.8067	5
56	.15528	.98787	.15719	.3616	.0123	.4398	.17250	.98501	.17513	.7101	.0152	.7970	4
57	.15557	.98782	.15749	.3496	.0123	.4279	.17279	.98496	.17543	.7004	.0153	.7874	3
58	.15586	.98778	.15779	.3376	.0124	.4160	.17307	.98491	.17573	.6906	.0153	.7778	2
59	.15615	.98773	.15809	.3257	.0124	.4042	.17336	.98486	.17603	.6809	.0154	.7683	1
60	.15643	.98769	.15838	6.3137	.0125	6.3924	.17365	.98481	.17633	5.6713	.0154	5.7588	0
′	81° cos	81° sin	81° cot	81° tan	81° cosec	81° sec	80° cos	80° sin	80° cot	80° tan	80° cosec	80° sec	′

′	10° sin	10° cos	10° tan	10° cot	10° sec	10° cosec	11° sin	11° cos	11° tan	11° cot	11° sec	11° cosec	′
0	.17365	.98481	.17633	5.6713	1.0154	5.7588	.19081	.98163	.19438	5.1445	1.0187	5.2408	60
1	.17393	.98476	.17663	.6616	.0155	.7493	.19109	.98157	.19468	.1366	.0188	.2330	59
2	.17422	.98471	.17693	.6520	.0155	.7398	.19138	.98152	.19498	.1286	.0188	.2252	58
3	.17451	.98465	.17723	.6425	.0156	.7304	.19166	.98146	.19529	.1207	.0189	.2174	57
4	.17479	.98460	.17753	.6329	.0156	.7210	.19195	.98140	.19559	.1128	.0189	.2097	56
5	.17508	.98455	.17783	5.6234	.0157	5.7117	.19224	.98135	.19589	5.1049	.0190	5.2019	55
6	.17537	.98450	.17813	.6140	.0157	.7023	.19252	.98129	.19619	.0970	.0191	.1942	54
7	.17565	.98445	.17843	.6045	.0158	.6930	.19281	.98124	.19649	.0892	.0191	.1865	53
8	.17594	.98440	.17873	.5951	.0158	.6838	.19309	.98118	.19680	.0814	.0192	.1788	52
9	.17622	.98435	.17903	.5857	.0159	.6745	.19338	.98112	.19710	.0736	.0192	.1712	51
10	.17651	.98430	.17933	5.5764	.0159	5.6653	.19366	.98107	.19740	5.0658	.0193	5.1636	50
11	.17680	.98425	.17963	.5670	.0160	.6561	.19395	.98101	.19770	.0581	.0193	.1560	49
12	.17708	.98419	.17993	.5578	.0160	.6470	.19423	.98095	.19800	.0504	.0194	.1484	48
13	.17737	.98414	.18023	.5485	.0161	.6379	.19452	.98090	.19831	.0427	.0195	.1409	47
14	.17766	.98409	.18053	.5393	.0162	.6288	.19480	.98084	.19861	.0350	.0195	.1333	46
15	.17794	.98404	.18083	5.5301	.0162	5.6197	.19509	.98078	.19891	5.0273	.0196	5.1258	45
16	.17823	.98399	.18113	.5209	.0163	.6107	.19537	.98073	.19921	.0197	.0196	.1183	44
17	.17852	.98394	.18143	.5117	.0163	.6017	.19566	.98067	.19952	.0121	.0197	.1109	43
18	.17880	.98388	.18173	.5026	.0164	.5928	.19595	.98061	.19982	.0045	.0198	.1034	42
19	.17909	.98383	.18203	.4936	.0164	.5838	.19623	.98056	.20012	4.9969	.0198	.0960	41
20	.17937	.98378	.18233	5.4845	.0165	5.5749	.19652	.98050	.20042	4.9894	.0199	5.0886	40
21	.17966	.98373	.18263	.4755	.0165	.5660	.19680	.98044	.20073	.9819	.0199	.0812	39
22	.17995	.98368	.18293	.4665	.0166	.5572	.19709	.98039	.20103	.9744	.0200	.0739	38
23	.18023	.98362	.18323	.4575	.0166	.5484	.19737	.98033	.20133	.9669	.0201	.0666	37
24	.18052	.98357	.18353	.4486	.0167	.5396	.19766	.98027	.20163	.9594	.0201	.0593	36
25	.18080	.98352	.18383	5.4396	.0167	5.5308	.19794	.98021	.20194	4.9520	.0202	5.0520	35
26	.18109	.98347	.18413	.4308	.0168	.5221	.19823	.98016	.20224	.9446	.0202	.0447	34
27	.18138	.98341	.18444	.4219	.0169	.5134	.19851	.98010	.20254	.9372	.0203	.0375	33
28	.18166	.98336	.18474	.4131	.0169	.5047	.19880	.98004	.20285	.9298	.0204	.0302	32
29	.18195	.98331	.18504	.4043	.0170	.4960	.19908	.97998	.20315	.9225	.0204	.0230	31
30	.18223	.98325	.18534	5.3955	.0170	5.4874	.19937	.97992	.20345	4.9151	.0205	5.0158	30
31	.18252	.98320	.18564	.3868	.0171	.4788	.19965	.97987	.20375	.9078	.0205	.0087	29
32	.18281	.98315	.18594	.3780	.0171	.4702	.19994	.97981	.20406	.9006	.0206	.0015	28
33	.18309	.98309	.18624	.3694	.0172	.4617	.20022	.97975	.20436	.8933	.0207	4.9944	27
34	.18338	.98304	.18654	.3607	.0172	.4532	.20051	.97969	.20466	.8860	.0207	.9873	26
35	.18366	.98299	.18684	5.3521	.0173	5.4447	.20079	.97963	.20497	4.8788	0208	4.9802	25
36	.18395	.98293	.18714	.3434	.0174	.4362	.20108	.97957	.20527	.8716	.0208	.9732	24
37	.18424	.98288	.18745	.3349	.0174	.4278	.20136	.97952	.20557	.8644	.0209	.9661	23
38	.18452	.98283	.18775	.3263	.0175	.4194	.20165	.97946	.20588	.8573	.0210	.9591	22
39	.18481	.98277	.18805	.3178	.0175	.4110	.20193	.97940	.20618	.8501	.0210	.9521	21
40	.18509	.98272	.18835	5.3093	.0176	5.4026	.20222	.97934	.20648	4.8430	.0211	4.9452	20
41	.18538	.98267	.18865	.3008	.0176	.3943	.20250	.97928	.20679	.8359	.0211	.9382	19
42	.18567	.98261	.18895	.2923	.0177	.3860	.20279	.97922	.20709	.8288	.0212	.9313	18
43	.18595	.98256	.18925	.2839	.0177	.3777	.20307	.97916	.20739	.8217	.0213	.9243	17
44	.18624	.98250	.18955	.2755	.0178	.3695	.20336	.97910	.20770	.8147	.0213	.9175	16
45	.18652	.98245	.18985	5.2671	.0179	5.3612	.20364	.97904	.20800	4.8077	.0214	4.9106	15
46	.18681	.98240	.19016	.2588	.0179	.3530	.20393	.97899	.20830	.8007	.0215	.9037	14
47	.18709	.98234	.19046	.2505	.0180	.3449	.20421	.97893	.20861	.7937	.0215	.8969	13
48	.18738	.98229	.19076	.2422	.0180	.3367	.20450	.97887	.20891	.7867	.0216	.8901	12
49	.18767	.98223	.19106	.2339	.0181	.3286	.20478	.97881	.20921	.7798	.0216	.8833	11
50	.18795	.98218	.19136	5.2257	.0181	5.3205	.20506	.97875	.20952	4.7728	.0217	4.8765	10
51	.18824	.98212	.19166	.2174	.0182	.3124	.20535	.97869	.20982	.7659	.0218	.8967	9
52	.18852	.98207	.19197	.2092	.0182	.3044	.20563	.97863	.21012	.7591	.0218	.8630	8
53	.18881	.98201	.19227	.2011	.0183	.2963	.20592	.97857	.21043	.7522	.0219	.8563	7
54	.18909	.98196	.19257	.1929	.0184	.2883	.20620	.97851	.21073	.7453	.0220	.8496	6
55	.18938	.98190	.19287	5.1848	.0184	5.2803	.20649	.97845	.21104	4.7385	.0220	4.8429	5
56	.18967	.98185	.19317	.1767	.0185	.2724	.20677	.97839	.21134	.7317	.0221	.8362	4
57	.18995	.98179	.19347	.1686	.0185	.2645	.20706	.97833	.21164	.7249	.0221	.8296	3
58	.19024	.98174	.19378	.1606	.0186	.2566	.20734	.97827	.21195	.7181	.0222	.8229	2
59	.19052	.98168	.19408	.1525	.0186	.2487	.20763	.97821	.21225	.7114	.0223	.8163	1
60	.19081	.98163	.19438	5.1445	.0187	5.2408	.20791	.97815	.21256	4.7046	.0223	4.8097	0
′	79° cos	79° sin	79° cot	79° tan	79° cosec	79° sec	78° cos	78° sin	78° cot	78° tan	78° cosec	78° sec	′

NATURAL TRIGONOMETRIC FUNCTIONS

12° (complement 77°)

'	sin	cos	tan	cot	sec	cosec
0	.20791	.97815	.21256	4.7046	1.0223	4.8097
1	.20820	.97809	.21286	.6979	.0224	.8032
2	.20848	.97803	.21316	.6912	.0225	.7966
3	.20876	.97797	.21347	.6845	.0225	.7901
4	.20905	.97790	.21377	.6778	.0226	.7835
5	.20933	.97784	.21408	4.6712	.0226	4.7770
6	.20962	.97778	.21438	.6646	.0227	.7706
7	.20990	.97772	.21469	.6580	.0228	.7641
8	.21019	.97766	.21499	.6514	.0228	.7576
9	.21047	.97760	.21529	.6448	.0229	.7512
10	.21076	.97754	.21560	4.6382	.0230	4.7448
11	.21104	.97748	.21590	.6317	.0230	.7384
12	.21132	.97742	.21621	.6252	.0231	.7320
13	.21161	.97735	.21651	.6187	.0232	.7257
14	.21189	.97729	.21682	.6122	.0232	.7193
15	.21218	.97723	.21712	4.6057	.0233	4.7130
16	.21246	.97717	.21742	.5993	.0234	.7067
17	.21275	.97711	.21773	.5928	.0234	.7004
18	.21303	.97704	.21803	.5864	.0235	.6942
19	.21331	.97698	.21834	.5800	.0235	.6879
20	.21360	.97692	.21864	4.5736	.0236	4.6817
21	.21388	.97686	.21895	.5673	.0237	.6754
22	.21417	.97680	.21925	.5609	.0237	.6692
23	.21445	.97673	.21956	.5546	.0238	.6631
24	.21473	.97667	.21986	.5483	.0239	.6569
25	.21502	.97661	.22017	4.5420	.0239	4.6507
26	.21530	.97655	.22047	.5357	.0240	.6446
27	.21559	.97648	.22078	.5294	.0241	.6385
28	.21587	.97642	.22108	.5232	.0241	.6324
29	.21615	.97636	.22139	.5169	.0242	.6263
30	.21644	.97630	.22169	4.5107	.0243	4.6201
31	.21672	.97623	.22200	.5045	.0243	.6142
32	.21701	.97617	.22231	.4983	.0244	.6081
33	.21729	.97611	.22261	.4921	.0245	.6021
34	.21757	.97604	.22291	.4860	.0245	.5961
35	.21786	.97598	.22322	4.4799	.0246	4.5901
36	.21814	.97592	.22353	.4737	.0247	.5841
37	.21843	.97585	.22383	.4676	.0247	.5782
38	.21871	.97579	.22414	.4615	.0248	.5722
39	.21899	.97573	.22444	.4555	.0249	.5663
40	.21928	.97566	.22475	4.4494	.0249	4.5604
41	.21956	.97560	.22505	.4434	.0250	.5545
42	.21985	.97553	.22536	.4373	.0251	.5486
43	.22013	.97547	.22566	.4313	.0251	.5428
44	.22041	.97541	.22597	.4253	.0252	.5369
45	.22070	.97534	.22628	4.4194	.0253	4.5311
46	.22098	.97528	.22658	.4134	.0253	.5253
47	.22126	.97521	.22689	.4074	.0254	.5195
48	.22155	.97515	.22719	.4015	.0254	.5137
49	.22183	.97508	.22750	.3956	.0255	.5079
50	.22211	.97502	.22781	4.3897	.0256	4.5021
51	.22240	.97495	.22811	.3838	.0257	.4964
52	.22268	.97489	.22842	.3779	.0257	.4907
53	.22297	.97483	.22872	.3721	.0258	.4850
54	.22325	.97476	.22903	.3662	.0259	.4793
55	.22353	.97470	.22934	4.3604	.0260	4.4736
56	.22382	.97463	.22964	.3546	.0260	.4679
57	.22410	.97457	.22995	.3488	.0261	.4623
58	.22438	.97450	.23025	.3430	.0262	.4566
59	.22467	.97443	.23056	.3372	.0262	.4510
60	.22495	.97437	.23087	4.3315	.0263	4.4454

13° (complement 76°)

'	sin	cos	tan	cot	sec	cosec
0	.22495	.97437	.23087	4.3315	1.0263	4.4454
1	.22523	.97430	.23117	.3257	.0264	.4398
2	.22552	.97424	.23148	.3200	.0265	.4342
3	.22580	.97417	.23179	.3143	.0265	.4287
4	.22608	.97411	.23209	.3086	.0266	.4231
5	.22637	.97404	.23240	4.3029	.0266	4.4176
6	.22665	.97398	.23270	.2972	.0267	.4121
7	.22693	.97391	.23301	.2916	.0268	.4065
8	.22722	.97384	.23332	.2859	.0268	.4011
9	.22750	.97378	.23363	.2803	.0269	.3956
10	.22778	.97371	.23393	4.2747	.0270	4.3901
11	.22807	.97364	.23424	.2691	.0271	.3847
12	.22835	.97358	.23455	.2635	.0271	.3792
13	.22863	.97351	.23485	.2579	.0272	.3738
14	.22892	.97344	.23516	.2524	.0273	.3684
15	.22920	.97338	.23547	4.2468	.0273	4.3630
16	.22948	.97331	.23577	.2413	.0274	.3576
17	.22977	.97324	.23608	.2358	.0275	.3522
18	.23005	.97318	.23639	.2303	.0276	.3469
19	.23033	.97311	.23670	.2247	.0276	.3415
20	.23061	.97304	.23700	4.2193	.0277	4.3362
21	.23090	.97298	.23731	.2139	.0278	.3309
22	.23118	.97291	.23762	.2084	.0278	.3256
23	.23146	.97284	.23793	.2030	.0279	.3203
24	.23175	.97277	.23823	.1976	.0279	.3150
25	.23202	.97271	.23854	4.1921	.0280	4.3098
26	.23231	.97264	.23885	.1868	.0281	.3045
27	.23260	.97257	.23916	.1814	.0282	.2993
28	.23288	.97250	.23946	.1760	.0283	.2941
29	.23316	.97244	.23977	.1706	.0283	.2838
30	.23344	.97237	.24008	4.1653	.0284	4.2836
31	.23373	.97230	.24039	.1600	.0285	.2785
32	.23401	.97223	.24069	.1546	.0285	.2733
33	.23429	.97216	.24100	.1493	.0286	.2681
34	.23458	.97210	.24131	.1440	.0287	.2630
35	.23486	.97203	.24162	4.1388	.0288	4.2579
36	.23514	.97196	.24192	.1335	.0289	.2527
37	.23542	.97189	.24223	.1282	.0290	.2476
38	.23571	.97182	.24254	.1230	.0291	.2425
39	.23599	.97175	.24285	.1178	.0291	.2375
40	.23627	.97169	.24316	4.1126	.0292	4.2324
41	.23655	.97162	.24346	.1073	.0293	.2273
42	.23684	.97155	.24377	.1022	.0293	.2223
43	.23712	.97148	.24408	.0970	.0294	.2173
44	.23740	.97141	.24439	.0918	.0294	.2122
45	.23768	.97134	.24470	4.0867	.0295	4.2072
46	.23797	.97127	.24501	.0815	.0296	.2022
47	.23825	.97120	.24532	.0764	.0296	.1972
48	.23853	.97113	.24562	.0713	.0297	.1923
49	.23881	.97106	.24593	.0662	.0298	.1873
50	.23910	.97099	.24624	4.0611	.0299	4.1824
51	.23938	.97092	.24655	.0560	.0299	.1774
52	.23966	.97086	.24686	.0509	.0300	.1725
53	.23994	.97079	.24717	.0458	.0301	.1676
54	.24023	.97072	.24747	.0408	.0302	.1627
55	.24051	.97065	.24778	4.0358	.0302	4.1578
56	.24079	.97058	.24809	.0307	.0303	.1529
57	.24107	.97051	.24840	.0257	.0304	.1481
58	.24136	.97044	.24871	.0207	.0304	.1432
59	.24164	.97037	.24902	.0157	.0305	.1384
60	.24192	.97029	.24933	4.0108	.0306	4.1336

14° (complement 75°)

'	sin	cos	tan	cot	sec	cosec
0	.24192	.97029	.24933	4.0108	1.0306	4.1336
1	.24220	.97022	.24964	.0058	.0307	.1289
2	.24249	.97015	.24995	.0009	.0308	.1239
3	.24277	.97008	.25025	3.9959	.0308	.1191
4	.24305	.97001	.25056	.9910	.0309	.1144
5	.24333	.96994	.25087	3.9861	.0310	4.1096
6	.24361	.96987	.25118	.9812	.0311	.1048
7	.24390	.96980	.25149	.9763	.0311	.1001
8	.24418	.96973	.25180	.9714	.0312	.0953
9	.24446	.96966	.25211	.9665	.0313	.0906
10	.24474	.96959	.25242	3.9616	.0314	4.0859
11	.24502	.96952	.25273	.9568	.0315	.0812
12	.24531	.96944	.25304	.9520	.0316	.0765
13	.24559	.96937	.25335	.9471	.0316	.0718
14	.24587	.96930	.25366	.9423	.0317	.0672
15	.24615	.96923	.25397	3.9375	.0317	4.0625
16	.24643	.96916	.25428	.9327	.0318	.0579
17	.24672	.96909	.25459	.9279	.0319	.0532
18	.24700	.96901	.25490	.9231	.0320	.0486
19	.24728	.96894	.25521	.9184	.0320	.0440
20	.24756	.96887	.25552	3.9136	.0321	4.0394
21	.24784	.96880	.25583	.9089	.0322	.0348
22	.24813	.96873	.25614	.9042	.0323	.0302
23	.24841	.96866	.25645	.8994	.0323	.0256
24	.24869	.96858	.25676	.8947	.0324	.0211
25	.24897	.96851	.25707	3.8900	.0325	4.0165
26	.24925	.96844	.25738	.8853	.0326	.0120
27	.24953	.96837	.25769	.8807	.0327	.0074
28	.24982	.96829	.25800	.8760	.0327	.0029
29	.25010	.96822	.25831	.8713	.0328	3.9984
30	.25038	.96815	.25862	3.8667	.0329	3.9939
31	.25066	.96807	.25893	.8621	.0330	.9894
32	.25094	.96800	.25924	.8574	.0330	.9850
33	.25122	.96793	.25955	.8528	.0331	.9805
34	.25151	.96786	.25986	.8482	.0332	.9761
35	.25179	.96778	.26017	3.8436	.0333	3.9716
36	.25207	.96771	.26048	.8390	.0334	.9672
37	.25235	.96763	.26079	.8345	.0334	.9627
38	.25263	.96756	.26110	.8299	.0335	.9583
39	.25291	.96749	.26141	.8254	.0336	.9539
40	.25319	.96741	.26172	3.8208	.0337	3.9495
41	.25348	.96734	.26203	.8163	.0338	.9451
42	.25376	.96727	.26234	.8118	.0339	.9408
43	.25404	.96719	.26266	.8073	.0339	.9364
44	.25432	.96712	.26297	.8027	.0340	.9320
45	.25460	.96704	.26328	3.7983	.0341	3.9277
46	.25488	.96697	.26359	.7938	.0341	.9234
47	.25516	.96690	.26390	.7893	.0342	.9190
48	.25544	.96682	.26421	.7848	.0343	.9147
49	.25573	.96675	.26452	.7804	.0344	.9104
50	.25601	.96667	.26483	3.7759	.0345	3.9061
51	.25629	.96660	.26514	.7715	.0345	.9018
52	.25657	.96652	.26545	.7671	.0346	.8976
53	.25685	.96645	.26577	.7627	.0347	.8933
54	.25713	.96638	.26608	.7583	.0348	.8890
55	.25741	.96630	.26639	3.7539	.0349	3.8848
56	.25769	.96623	.26670	.7495	.0349	.8805
57	.25798	.96615	.26701	.7451	.0350	.8763
58	.25826	.96608	.26732	.7407	.0351	.8721
59	.25854	.96600	.26764	.7364	.0352	.8679
60	.25882	.96592	.26795	3.7320	.0353	3.8637

15° (complement 74°)

'	sin	cos	tan	cot	sec	cosec
0	.25882	.96592	.26795	3.7320	1.0353	3.8637
1	.25910	.96585	.26826	.7277	.0353	.8595
2	.25938	.96577	.26857	.7234	.0354	.8553
3	.25966	.96570	.26888	.7191	.0355	.8512
4	.25994	.96562	.26920	.7147	.0356	.8470
5	.26022	.96555	.26951	3.7104	.0357	3.8428
6	.26050	.96547	.26982	.7062	.0358	.8387
7	.26079	.96540	.27013	.7019	.0358	.8346
8	.26107	.96532	.27044	.6976	.0359	.8304
9	.26135	.96524	.27076	.6933	.0360	.8263
10	.26163	.96517	.27107	3.6891	.0361	3.8222
11	.26191	.96509	.27138	.6848	.0362	.8181
12	.26219	.96502	.27169	.6806	.0362	.8140
13	.26247	.96494	.27201	.6764	.0363	.8100
14	.26275	.96486	.27232	.6722	.0364	.8059
15	.26303	.96479	.27263	3.6679	.0365	3.8018
16	.26331	.96471	.27294	.6637	.0366	.7978
17	.26359	.96463	.27326	.6596	.0367	.7937
18	.26387	.96456	.27357	.6554	.0367	.7897
19	.26415	.96448	.27388	.6512	.0368	.7857
20	.26443	.96440	.27419	3.6470	.0369	3.7816
21	.26471	.96433	.27451	.6429	.0370	.7776
22	.26499	.96425	.27482	.6387	.0371	.7736
23	.26527	.96417	.27513	.6346	.0372	.7697
24	.26556	.96409	.27544	.6305	.0372	.7657
25	.26584	.96402	.27576	3.6263	.0373	3.7617
26	.26612	.96394	.27607	.6222	.0374	.7577
27	.26640	.96386	.27638	.6181	.0375	.7538
28	.26668	.96378	.27670	.6140	.0376	.7498
29	.26696	.96371	.27701	.6100	.0376	.7459
30	.26724	.96363	.27732	3.6059	.0377	3.7420
31	.26752	.96355	.27764	.6018	.0378	.7380
32	.26780	.96347	.27795	.5977	.0379	.7341
33	.26808	.96340	.27826	.5937	.0380	.7302
34	.26836	.96332	.27858	.5896	.0381	.7263
35	.26864	.96324	.27889	3.5856	.0382	3.7224
36	.26892	.96316	.27920	.5816	.0382	.7186
37	.26920	.96308	.27952	.5776	.0383	.7147
38	.26948	.96301	.27983	.5736	.0384	.7108
39	.26976	.96293	.28014	.5696	.0385	.7070
40	.27004	.96285	.28046	3.5656	.0386	3.7031
41	.27032	.96277	.28077	.5616	.0387	.6993
42	.27060	.96269	.28109	.5576	.0388	.6955
43	.27088	.96261	.28140	.5536	.0389	.6917
44	.27116	.96253	.28171	.5497	.0389	.6878
45	.27144	.96245	.28203	3.5457	.0390	3.6840
46	.27172	.96238	.28234	.5418	.0391	.6802
47	.27200	.96230	.28266	.5378	.0392	.6765
48	.27228	.96222	.28297	.5339	.0393	.6727
49	.27256	.96214	.28328	.5300	.0393	.6689
50	.27284	.96206	.28360	3.5261	.0394	3.6651
51	.27312	.96198	.28391	.5222	.0395	.6614
52	.27340	.96190	.28423	.5183	.0396	.6576
53	.27368	.96182	.28454	.5144	.0397	.6539
54	.27396	.96174	.28486	.5105	.0398	.6502
55	.27424	.96166	.28517	3.5066	.0399	3.6464
56	.27452	.96158	.28549	.5028	.0399	.6427
57	.27480	.96150	.28580	.4989	.0400	.6390
58	.27508	.96142	.28611	.4951	.0401	.6353
59	.27536	.96134	.28643	.4912	.0402	.6316
60	.27564	.96126	.28674	3.4874	.0403	3.6279

Lower headings (complements, read bottom-to-top): 77° for 12°, 76° for 13°, 75° for 14°, 74° for 15°, with columns cos, sin, cot, tan, cosec, sec.

NATURAL TRIGONOMETRIC FUNCTIONS

	16°						17°					
′	sin	cos	tan	cot	sec	cosec	sin	cos	tan	cot	sec	cosec
0	.27564	.96126	.28674	3.4874	1.0403	3.6279	.29237	.95630	.30573	3.2708	1.0457	3.4203
1	.27592	.96118	.28706	.4836	.0404	.6243	.29265	.95622	.30605	.2674	.0458	.4170
2	.27620	.96110	.28737	.4798	.0405	.6206	.29293	.95613	.30637	.2640	.0459	.4138
3	.27648	.96102	.28769	.4760	.0406	.6169	.29321	.95605	.30668	.2607	.0460	.4106
4	.27675	.96094	.28800	.4722	.0406	.6133	.29348	.95596	.30700	.2573	.0461	.4073
5	.27703	.96086	.28832	3.4684	.0407	3.6096	.29376	.95588	.30732	3.2539	.0461	3.4041
6	.27731	.96078	.28863	.4646	.0408	.6060	.29404	.95579	.30764	.2505	.0462	.4009
7	.27759	.96070	.28895	.4608	.0409	.6024	.29432	.95571	.30796	.2472	.0463	.3977
8	.27787	.96062	.28926	.4570	.0410	.5987	.29460	.95562	.30828	.2438	.0464	.3945
9	.27815	.96054	.28958	.4533	.0411	.5951	.29487	.95554	.30859	.2405	.0465	.3913
10	.27843	.96045	.28990	3.4495	.0412	3.5915	.29515	.95545	.30891	3.2371	.0466	3.3881
11	.27871	.96037	.29021	.4458	.0413	.5879	.29543	.95536	.30923	.2338	.0467	.3849
12	.27899	.96029	.29053	.4420	.0413	.5843	.29571	.95528	.30955	.2305	.0468	.3817
13	.27927	.96021	.29084	.4383	.0414	.5807	.29598	.95519	.30987	.2271	.0469	.3785
14	.27955	.96013	.29116	.4346	.0415	.5772	.29626	.95511	.31019	.2238	.0470	.3754
15	.27983	.96005	.29147	3.4308	.0416	3.5736	.29654	.95502	.31051	3.2205	.0471	3.3722
16	.28011	.95997	.29179	.4271	.0417	.5700	.29682	.95493	.31083	.2172	.0472	.3690
17	.28039	.95989	.29210	.4234	.0418	.5665	.29710	.95485	.31115	.2139	.0473	.3659
18	.28067	.95980	.29242	.4197	.0419	.5629	.29737	.95476	.31146	.2106	.0474	.3627
19	.28094	.95972	.29274	.4160	.0420	.5594	.29765	.95467	.31178	.2073	.0475	.3596
20	.28122	.95964	.29305	3.4124	.0420	3.5559	.29793	.95459	.31210	3.2041	.0476	3.3565
21	.28150	.95956	.29337	.4087	.0421	.5523	.29821	.95450	.31242	.2008	.0477	.3534
22	.28178	.95948	.29368	.4050	.0422	.5488	.29848	.95441	.31274	.1975	.0478	.3502
23	.28206	.95940	.29400	.4014	.0423	.5453	.29876	.95433	.31306	.1942	.0478	.3471
24	.28234	.95931	.29432	.3977	.0424	.5418	.29904	.95424	.31338	.1910	.0479	.3440
25	.28262	.95923	.29463	3.3941	.0425	3.5383	.29932	.95415	.31370	3.1877	.0480	3.3409
26	.28290	.95915	.29495	.3904	.0426	.5348	.29959	.95407	.31402	.1845	.0481	.3378
27	.28318	.95907	.29526	.3868	.0427	.5313	.29987	.95398	.31434	.1813	.0482	.3347
28	.28346	.95898	.29558	.3832	.0428	.5279	.30015	.95389	.31466	.1780	.0483	.3316
29	.28374	.95890	.29590	.3795	.0428	.5244	.30043	.95380	.31498	.1748	.0484	.3286
30	.28401	.95882	.29621	3.3759	.0429	3.5209	.30070	.95372	.31530	3.1716	.0485	3.3255
31	.28429	.95874	.29653	.3723	.0430	.5175	.30098	.95363	.31562	.1684	.0486	.3224
32	.28457	.95865	.29685	.3687	.0431	.5140	.30126	.95354	.31594	.1652	.0487	.3194
33	.28485	.95857	.29716	.3651	.0432	.5106	.30154	.95345	.31626	.1620	.0488	.3163
34	.28513	.95849	.29748	.3616	.0433	.5072	.30181	.95337	.31658	.1588	.0489	.3133
35	.28541	.95840	.29780	3.3580	.0434	3.5037	.30209	.95328	.31690	3.1556	.0490	3.3102
36	.28569	.95832	.29811	.3544	.0435	.5003	.30237	.95319	.31722	.1524	.0491	.3072
37	.28597	.95824	.29843	.3509	.0436	.4969	.30265	.95310	.31754	.1492	.0492	.3042
38	.28624	.95816	.29875	.3473	.0437	.4935	.30292	.95301	.31786	.1460	.0493	.3011
39	.28652	.95807	.29906	.3438	.0438	.4901	.30320	.95293	.31818	.1429	.0494	.2981
40	.28680	.95799	.29938	3.3402	.0438	3.4867	.30348	.95284	.31850	3.1397	.0495	3.2951
41	.28708	.95791	.29970	.3367	.0439	.4833	.30375	.95275	.31882	.1366	.0496	.2921
42	.28736	.95782	.30001	.3332	.0440	.4799	.30403	.95266	.31914	.1334	.0497	.2891
43	.28764	.95774	.30033	.3296	.0441	.4766	.30431	.95257	.31946	.1303	.0498	.2861
44	.28792	.95765	.30065	.3261	.0442	.4732	.30459	.95248	.31978	.1271	.0499	.2831
45	.28820	.95757	.30096	3.3226	.0443	3.4698	.30486	.95239	.32010	3.1240	.0500	3.2801
46	.28847	.95749	.30128	.3191	.0444	.4665	.30514	.95231	.32042	.1209	.0501	.2772
47	.28875	.95740	.30160	.3156	.0445	.4632	.30542	.95222	.32074	.1177	.0502	.2742
48	.28903	.95732	.30192	.3121	.0446	.4598	.30569	.95213	.32106	.1146	.0503	.2712
49	.28931	.95723	.30223	.3087	.0447	.4565	.30597	.95204	.32138	.1115	.0504	.2683
50	.28959	.95715	.30255	3.3052	.0448	3.4532	.30625	.95195	.32171	3.1084	.0505	3.2653
51	.28987	.95707	.30287	.3017	.0448	.4498	.30653	.95186	.32203	.1053	.0506	.2624
52	.29014	.95698	.30319	.2983	.0449	.4465	.30680	.95177	.32235	.1022	.0507	.2594
53	.29042	.95690	.30350	.2948	.0450	.4432	.30708	.95168	.32267	.0991	.0508	.2565
54	.29070	.95681	.30382	.2914	.0451	.4399	.30736	.95159	.32299	.0960	.0509	.2535
55	.29098	.95673	.30414	3.2879	.0452	3.4366	.30763	.95150	.32331	3.0930	.0510	3.2506
56	.29126	.95664	.30446	.2845	.0453	.4334	.30791	.95141	.32363	.0899	.0511	.2477
57	.29154	.95656	.30478	.2811	.0454	.4301	.30819	.95132	.32395	.0868	.0512	.2448
58	.29181	.95647	.30509	.2777	.0455	.4268	.30846	.95124	.32428	.0838	.0513	.2419
59	.29209	.95639	.30541	.2742	.0456	.4236	.30874	.95115	.32460	.0807	.0514	.2390
60	.29237	.95630	.30573	3.2708	.0457	3.4203	.30902	.95106	.32492	3.0777	.0515	3.2361
′	cos	sin	cot	tan	cosec	sec	cos	sin	cot	tan	cosec	sec
	73°						72°					

	18°						19°						
′	sin	cos	tan	cot	sec	cosec	sin	cos	tan	cot	sec	cosec	′
0	.30902	.95106	.32492	3.0777	1.0515	3.2361	.32557	.94552	.34433	2.9042	1.0576	3.0715	60
1	.30929	.95097	.32524	.0746	.0516	.2332	.32584	.94542	.34465	.9015	.0577	.0690	59
2	.30957	.95088	.32556	.0716	.0517	.2303	.32612	.94533	.34498	.8987	.0578	.0664	58
3	.30985	.95079	.32588	.0686	.0518	.2274	.32639	.94523	.34530	.8960	.0579	.0638	57
4	.31012	.95070	.32621	.0655	.0519	.2245	.32667	.94514	.34563	.8933	.0580	.0612	56
5	.31040	.95061	.32653	3.0625	.0520	3.2216	.32694	.94504	.34595	2.8905	.0581	3.0586	55
6	.31068	.95051	.32685	.0595	.0521	.2188	.32722	.94495	.34628	.8878	.0582	.0561	54
7	.31095	.95042	.32717	.0565	.0522	.2159	.32749	.94485	.34661	.8851	.0584	.0535	53
8	.31123	.95033	.32749	.0535	.0523	.2131	.32777	.94476	.34693	.8824	.0585	.0509	52
9	.31150	.95024	.32782	.0505	.0524	.2102	.32804	.94466	.34726	.8797	.0586	.0484	51
10	.31178	.95015	.32814	3.0475	.0525	3.2074	.32832	.94457	.34758	2.8770	.0587	3.0458	50
11	.31206	.95006	.32846	.0445	.0526	.2045	.32859	.94447	.34791	.8743	.0588	.0433	49
12	.31233	.94997	.32878	.0415	.0527	.2017	.32887	.94438	.34824	.8716	.0589	.0407	48
13	.31261	.94988	.32910	.0385	.0528	.1989	.32914	.94428	.34856	.8689	.0590	.0382	47
14	.31289	.94979	.32943	.0356	.0529	.1960	.32942	.94418	.34889	.8662	.0591	.0357	46
15	.31316	.94970	.32975	3.0326	.0530	3.1932	.32969	.94409	.34921	2.8636	.0592	3.0331	45
16	.31344	.94961	.33007	.0296	.0531	.1904	.32996	.94399	.34954	.8609	.0593	.0306	44
17	.31372	.94952	.33039	.0267	.0532	.1876	.33024	.94390	.34987	.8582	.0594	.0281	43
18	.31399	.94942	.33072	.0237	.0533	.1848	.33051	.94380	.35019	.8555	.0595	.0256	42
19	.31427	.94933	.33104	.0208	.0534	.1820	.33079	.94370	.35052	.8529	.0596	.0231	41
20	.31454	.94924	.33136	3.0178	.0535	3.1792	.33106	.94361	.35085	2.8502	.0598	3.0206	40
21	.31482	.94915	.33169	.0149	.0536	.1764	.33134	.94351	.35117	.8476	.0599	.0181	39
22	.31510	.94906	.33201	.0120	.0537	.1736	.33161	.94341	.35150	.8449	.0600	.0156	38
23	.31537	.94897	.33233	.0090	.0528	.1708	.33189	.94332	.35183	.8423	.0601	.0131	37
24	.31565	.94888	.33265	.0061	.0539	.1681	.33216	.94322	.35215	.8396	.0602	.0106	36
25	.31592	.94878	.33298	3.0032	.0540	3.1653	.33243	.94313	.35248	2.8370	.0603	3.0081	35
26	.31620	.94869	.33330	.0003	.0541	.1625	.33271	.94303	.35281	.8344	.0604	.0056	34
27	.31648	.94860	.33362	2.9974	.0542	.1598	.33298	.94293	.35314	.8318	.0605	.0031	33
28	.31675	.94851	.33395	.9945	.0543	.1570	.33326	.94283	.35346	.8291	.0606	.0007	32
29	.31703	.94841	.33427	.9916	.0544	.1543	.33353	.94274	.35379	.8265	.0607	2.9982	31
30	.31730	.94832	.33459	2.9887	.0545	3.1515	.33381	.94264	.35412	2.8239	.0608	2.9957	30
31	.31758	.94823	.33492	.9858	.0546	.1488	.33408	.94254	.35445	.8213	.0609	.9933	29
32	.31786	.94814	.33524	.9829	.0547	.1461	.33435	.94245	.35477	.8187	.0611	.9908	28
33	.31813	.94805	.33557	.9800	.0548	.1433	.33463	.94235	.35510	.8161	.0612	.9884	27
34	.31841	.94795	.33589	.9772	.0549	.1406	.33490	.94225	.35543	.8135	.0613	.9859	26
35	.31868	.94786	.33621	2.9743	.0550	3.1379	.33518	.94215	.35576	2.8109	.0614	2.9835	25
36	.31896	.94777	.33654	.9714	.0551	.1352	.33545	.94206	.35608	.8083	.0615	.9810	24
37	.31923	.94767	.33686	.9686	.0552	.1325	.33572	.94196	.35641	.8057	.0616	.9786	23
38	.31951	.94758	.33718	.9657	.0553	.1298	.33600	.94186	.35674	.8032	.0617	.9762	22
39	.31978	.94749	.33751	.9629	.0554	.1271	.33627	.94176	.35707	.8006	.0618	.9738	21
40	.32006	.94740	.33783	2.9600	.0555	3.1244	.33655	.94167	.35739	2.7980	.0619	2.9713	20
41	.32034	.94730	.33816	.9572	.0556	.1217	.33682	.94157	.35772	.7954	.0620	.9689	19
42	.32061	.94721	.33848	.9544	.0557	.1190	.33709	.94147	.35805	.7929	.0622	.9665	18
43	.32089	.94712	.33880	.9515	.0558	.1163	.33737	.94137	.35838	.7903	.0623	.9641	17
44	.32116	.94702	.33913	.9487	.0559	.1137	.33764	.94127	.35871	.7878	.0624	.9617	16
45	.32144	.94693	.33945	2.9459	.0560	3.1110	.33792	.94118	.35904	2.7852	.0625	2.9593	15
46	.32171	.94684	.33978	.9431	.0561	.1083	.33819	.94108	.35936	.7827	.0626	.9569	14
47	.32199	.94674	.34010	.9403	.0562	.1057	.33846	.94098	.35969	.7801	.0627	.9545	13
48	.32226	.94665	.34043	.9375	.0563	.1030	.33874	.94088	.36002	.7776	.0628	.9521	12
49	.32254	.94655	.34075	.9347	.0565	.1004	.33901	.94078	.36035	.7751	.0629	.9497	11
50	.32282	.94646	.34108	2.9319	.0566	3.0977	.33928	.94068	.36068	2.7725	.0630	2.9474	10
51	.32309	.94637	.34140	.9291	.0567	.0951	.33956	.94058	.36101	.7700	.0632	.9450	9
52	.32337	.94627	.34173	.9263	.0568	.0925	.33983	.94049	.36134	.7675	.0633	.9426	8
53	.32364	.94618	.34205	.9235	.0569	.0898	.34011	.94039	.36167	.7650	.0634	.9402	7
54	.32392	.94608	.34238	.9208	.0570	.0872	.34038	.94029	.36199	.7625	.0635	.9379	6
55	.32419	.94599	.34270	2.9180	.0571	3.0846	.34065	.94019	.36232	2.7600	.0636	2.9355	5
56	.32447	.94590	.34303	.9152	.0572	.0820	.34093	.94009	.36265	.7575	.0637	.9332	4
57	.32474	.94580	.34335	.9125	.0573	.0793	.34120	.93999	.36298	.7550	.0638	.9308	3
58	.32502	.94571	.34368	.9097	.0574	.0767	.34147	.93989	.36331	.7525	.0639	.9285	2
59	.32529	.94561	.34400	.9069	.0575	.0741	.34175	.93979	.36364	.7500	.0641	.9261	1
60	.32557	.94552	.34433	2.9042	.0576	3.0715	.34202	.93969	.36397	2.7475	.0642	2.9238	0
′	cos	sin	cot	tan	cosec	sec	cos	sin	cot	tan	cosec	sec	′
	71°						70°						

NATURAL TRIGONOMETRIC FUNCTIONS

′	20°						21°						22°						23°						′
′	sin	cos	tan	cot	sec	cosec	sin	cos	tan	cot	sec	cosec	sin	cos	tan	cot	sec	cosec	sin	cos	tan	cot	sec	cosec	′
0	.34202	.93969	.36397	2.7475	1.0642	2.9238	.35837	.93358	.38386	2.6051	1.0711	2.7904	.37461	.92718	.40403	2.4751	1.0785	2.6695	.39073	.92050	.42447	2.3558	1.0864	2.5593	60
1	.34229	.93959	.36430	.7450	.0643	.9215	.35864	.93348	.38420	.6028	.0713	.7883	.37488	.92707	.40436	.4730	.0787	.6675	.39100	.92039	.42482	.3539	.0865	.5575	59
2	.34257	.93949	.36463	.7425	.0644	.9191	.35891	.93337	.38453	.6006	.0714	.7862	.37514	.92696	.40470	.4709	.0788	.6656	.39126	.92028	.42516	.3520	.0866	.5558	58
3	.34284	.93939	.36496	.7400	.0645	.9168	.35918	.93327	.38486	.5983	.0715	.7841	.37541	.92686	.40504	.4689	.0789	.6637	.39153	.92016	.42550	.3501	.0868	.5540	57
4	.34311	.93929	.36529	.7376	.0646	.9145	.35945	.93316	.38520	.5960	.0716	.7820	.37568	.92675	.40538	.4668	.0790	.6618	.39180	.92005	.42585	.3482	.0869	.5523	56
5	.34339	.93919	.36562	2.7351	.0647	2.9122	.35972	.93306	.38553	2.5938	.0717	2.7799	.37595	.92664	.40572	2.4647	.0792	2.6599	.39207	.91993	.42619	2.3463	.0870	2.5506	55
6	.34366	.93909	.36595	.7326	.0648	.9098	.36000	.93295	.38587	.5916	.0719	.7778	.37622	.92653	.40606	.4627	.0793	.6580	.39234	.91982	.42654	.3445	.0872	.5488	54
7	.34393	.93899	.36628	.7302	.0650	.9075	.36027	.93285	.38620	.5893	.0720	.7757	.37649	.92642	.40640	.4606	.0794	.6561	.39260	.91971	.42688	.3426	.0873	.5471	53
8	.34421	.93889	.36661	.7277	.0651	.9052	.36054	.93274	.38654	.5871	.0721	.7736	.37676	.92631	.40673	.4586	.0795	.6542	.39287	.91959	.42722	.3407	.0874	.5453	52
9	.34448	.93879	.36694	.7252	.0652	.9029	.36081	.93264	.38687	.5848	.0722	.7715	.37703	.92620	.40707	.4565	.0797	.6523	.39314	.91948	.42757	.3388	.0876	.5436	51
10	.34475	.93869	.36727	2.7228	.0653	2.9006	.36108	.93253	.38720	2.5826	.0723	2.7694	.37730	.92609	.40741	2.4545	.0798	2.6504	.39341	.91936	.42791	2.3369	.0877	2.5419	50
11	.34502	.93859	.36760	.7204	.0654	.8983	.36135	.93243	.38754	.5804	.0725	.7674	.37757	.92598	.40775	.4525	.0799	.6485	.39367	.91925	.42826	.3350	.0878	.5402	49
12	.34530	.93849	.36793	.7179	.0655	.8960	.36162	.93232	.38787	.5781	.0726	.7653	.37784	.92587	.40809	.4504	.0801	.6466	.39394	.91913	.42860	.3332	.0880	.5384	48
13	.34557	.93839	.36826	.7155	.0656	.8937	.36189	.93222	.38821	.5759	.0727	.7632	.37811	.92576	.40843	.4484	.0802	.6447	.39421	.91902	.42894	.3313	.0881	.5367	47
14	.34584	.93829	.36859	.7130	.0658	.8915	.36217	.93211	.38854	.5737	.0728	.7611	.37838	.92565	.40877	.4463	.0803	.6428	.39448	.91891	.42929	.3294	.0882	.5350	46
15	.34612	.93819	.36892	2.7106	.0659	2.8892	.36244	.93201	.38888	2.5715	.0729	2.7591	.37865	.92554	.40911	2.4443	.0804	2.6410	.39474	.91879	.42963	2.3276	.0884	2.5333	45
16	.34639	.93809	.36925	.7082	.0660	.8869	.36271	.93190	.38921	.5693	.0731	.7570	.37892	.92543	.40945	.4423	.0806	.6391	.39501	.91868	.42998	.3257	.0885	.5316	44
17	.34666	.93799	.36958	.7058	.0661	.8846	.36298	.93180	.38955	.5671	.0732	.7550	.37919	.92532	.40979	.4403	.0807	.6372	.39528	.91856	.43032	.3238	.0886	.5299	43
18	.34693	.93789	.36991	.7033	.0662	.8824	.36325	.93169	.38988	.5649	.0733	.7529	.37946	.92521	.41013	.4382	.0808	.6353	.39554	.91845	.43067	.3220	.0888	.5281	42
19	.34721	.93779	.37024	.7009	.0663	.8801	.36352	.93158	.39022	.5627	.0734	.7509	.37972	.92510	.41047	.4362	.0810	.6335	.39581	.91833	.43101	.3201	.0889	.5264	41
20	.34748	.93769	.37057	2.6985	.0664	2.8778	.36379	.93148	.39055	2.5605	.0736	2.7488	.37999	.92499	.41081	2.4342	.0811	2.6316	.39608	.91822	.43136	2.3183	.0891	2.5247	40
21	.34775	.93758	.37090	.6961	.0666	.8756	.36406	.93137	.39089	.5583	.0737	.7468	.38026	.92488	.41115	.4322	.0812	.6297	.39635	.91810	.43170	.3164	.0892	.5230	39
22	.34803	.93748	.37123	.6937	.0667	.8733	.36433	.93127	.39122	.5561	.0738	.7447	.38053	.92477	.41149	.4302	.0813	.6279	.39661	.91798	.43205	.3145	.0893	.5213	38
23	.34830	.93738	.37156	.6913	.0668	.8711	.36460	.93116	.39156	.5539	.0739	.7427	.38080	.92466	.41183	.4282	.0815	.6260	.39688	.91787	.43239	.3127	.0895	.5196	37
24	.34857	.93728	.37190	.6889	.0669	.8688	.36488	.93105	.39189	.5517	.0740	.7406	.38107	.92455	.41217	.4262	.0816	.6242	.39715	.91775	.43274	.3109	.0896	.5179	36
25	.34884	.93718	.37223	2.6865	.0670	2.8666	.36515	.93095	.39223	2.5495	.0742	2.7386	.38134	.92443	.41251	2.4242	.0817	2.6223	.39741	.91764	.43308	2.3090	.0897	2.5163	35
26	.34912	.93708	.37256	.6841	.0671	.8644	.36542	.93084	.39257	.5473	.0743	.7366	.38161	.92432	.41285	.4222	.0819	.6205	.39768	.91752	.43343	.3072	.0899	.5146	34
27	.34939	.93698	.37289	.6817	.0673	.8621	.36569	.93074	.39290	.5451	.0744	.7346	.38188	.92421	.41319	.4202	.0820	.6186	.39795	.91741	.43377	.3053	.0900	.5129	33
28	.34966	.93687	.37322	.6794	.0674	.8599	.36596	.93063	.39324	.5430	.0745	.7325	.38214	.92410	.41353	.4182	.0821	.6168	.39821	.91729	.43412	.3035	.0902	.5112	32
29	.34993	.93677	.37355	.6770	.0675	.8577	.36623	.93052	.39357	.5408	.0747	.7305	.38241	.92399	.41387	.4162	.0823	.6150	.39848	.91718	.43447	.3017	.0903	.5095	31
30	.35021	.93667	.37388	2.6746	.0676	2.8554	.36650	.93042	.39391	2.5386	.0748	2.7285	.38268	.92388	.41421	2.4142	.0824	2.6131	.39875	.91706	.43481	2.2998	.0904	2.5078	30
31	.35048	.93657	.37422	.6722	.0677	.8532	.36677	.93031	.39425	.5365	.0749	.7265	.38295	.92377	.41455	.4122	.0825	.6113	.39901	.91694	.43516	.2980	.0906	.5062	29
32	.35075	.93647	.37455	.6699	.0678	.8510	.36704	.93020	.39458	.5343	.0750	.7245	.38322	.92366	.41489	.4102	.0826	.6095	.39928	.91683	.43550	.2962	.0907	.5045	28
33	.35102	.93637	.37488	.6675	.0679	.8488	.36731	.93010	.39492	.5322	.0751	.7225	.38349	.92354	.41524	.4083	.0828	.6076	.39955	.91671	.43585	.2944	.0908	.5028	27
34	.35130	.93626	.37521	.6652	.0681	.8466	.36758	.92999	.39525	.5300	.0753	.7205	.38376	.92343	.41558	.4063	.0829	.6058	.39981	.91659	.43620	.2925	.0910	.5011	26
35	.35157	.93616	.37554	2.6628	.0682	2.8444	.36785	.92988	.39559	2.5278	.0754	2.7185	.38403	.92332	.41592	2.4043	.0830	2.6040	.40008	.91648	.43654	2.2907	.0911	2.4995	25
36	.35184	.93606	.37587	.6604	.0683	.8422	.36812	.92978	.39593	.5257	.0755	.7165	.38429	.92321	.41626	.4023	.0832	.6022	.40035	.91636	.43689	.2889	.0913	.4978	24
37	.35211	.93596	.37621	.6581	.0684	.8400	.36839	.92967	.39626	.5236	.0756	.7145	.38456	.92310	.41660	.4004	.0833	.6003	.40061	.91625	.43723	.2871	.0914	.4961	23
38	.35239	.93585	.37654	.6558	.0685	.8378	.36866	.92956	.39660	.5214	.0758	.7125	.38483	.92299	.41694	.3984	.0834	.5985	.40088	.91613	.43758	.2853	.0915	.4945	22
39	.35266	.93575	.37687	.6534	.0686	.8356	.36893	.92945	.39694	.5193	.0759	.7105	.38510	.92287	.41728	.3964	.0836	.5967	.40115	.91601	.43793	.2835	.0917	.4928	21
40	.35293	.93565	.37720	2.6511	.0688	2.8334	.36921	.92935	.39727	2.5171	.0760	2.7085	.38537	.92276	.41762	2.3945	.0837	2.5949	.40141	.91590	.43827	2.2817	.0918	2.4912	20
41	.35320	.93555	.37754	.6487	.0689	.8312	.36948	.92924	.39761	.5150	.0761	.7065	.38564	.92265	.41797	.3925	.0838	.5931	.40168	.91578	.43862	.2799	.0920	.4895	19
42	.35347	.93544	.37787	.6464	.0690	.8290	.36975	.92913	.39795	.5129	.0763	.7045	.38591	.92254	.41831	.3906	.0840	.5913	.40195	.91566	.43897	.2781	.0921	.4879	18
43	.35375	.93534	.37820	.6441	.0691	.8269	.37002	.92902	.39828	.5108	.0764	.7026	.38617	.92242	.41865	.3886	.0841	.5895	.40221	.91554	.43932	.2763	.0922	.4862	17
44	.35402	.93524	.37853	.6418	.0692	.8247	.37029	.92892	.39862	.5086	.0765	.7006	.38644	.92231	.41899	.3867	.0842	.5877	.40248	.91543	.43966	.2745	.0924	.4846	16
45	.35429	.93513	.37887	2.6394	.0694	2.8225	.37056	.92881	.39896	2.5065	.0766	2.6986	.38671	.92220	.41933	2.3847	.0844	2.5958	.40205	.91531	.44001	2.2727	.0925	2.4829	15
46	.35456	.93503	.37920	.6371	.0695	.8204	.37083	.92870	.39930	.5044	.0768	.6967	.38698	.92209	.41968	.3828	.0845	.5841	.40301	.91519	.44036	.2709	.0927	.4813	14
47	.35483	.93493	.37953	.6348	.0696	.8182	.37110	.92859	.39963	.5023	.0769	.6947	.38725	.92197	.42002	.3808	.0846	.5823	.40328	.91508	.44070	.2691	.0928	.4797	13
48	.35511	.93482	.37986	.6325	.0697	.8160	.37137	.92848	.39997	.5002	.0770	.6927	.38751	.92186	.42036	.3789	.0847	.5805	.40354	.91496	.44105	.2673	.0929	.4780	12
49	.35538	.93472	.38020	.6302	.0698	.8139	.37164	.92838	.40031	.4981	.0771	.6908	.38778	.92105	.42070	.3770	.0849	.5787	.40381	.91484	.44140	.2655	.0931	.4764	11
50	.35565	.93462	.38053	2.6279	.0699	2.8117	.37191	.92827	.40065	2.4960	.0773	2.6888	.38805	.92164	.42105	2.3750	.0850	2.5770	.40408	.91472	.44175	2.2637	.0932	2.4748	10
51	.35592	.93451	.38086	.6256	.0701	.8096	.37218	.92816	.40098	.4939	.0774	.6869	.38832	.92152	.42139	.3731	.0851	.5752	.40434	.91461	.44209	.2619	.0934	.4731	9
52	.35619	.93441	.38120	.6233	.0702	.8074	.37245	.92805	.40132	.4918	.0775	.6849	.38859	.92141	.42173	.3712	.0853	.5734	.40461	.91449	.44244	.2602	.0935	.4715	8
53	.35647	.93431	.38153	.6210	.0703	.8053	.37272	.92794	.40166	.4897	.0776	.6830	.38886	.92130	.42207	.3692	.0854	.5716	.40487	.91437	.44279	.2584	.0936	.4699	7
54	.35674	.93420	.38186	.6187	.0704	.8032	.37299	.92784	.40200	.4876	.0778	.6810	.38912	.92118	.42242	.3673	.0855	.5699	.40514	.91425	.44314	.2566	.0938	.4683	6
55	.35701	.93410	.38220	2.6164	.0705	2.8010	.37326	.92773	.40233	2.4855	.0779	2.6791	.38939	.92107	.42276	2.3654	.0857	2.5681	.40541	.91414	.44349	2.2548	.0939	2.4666	5
56	.35728	.93400	.38253	.6142	.0707	.7989	.37353	.92762	.40267	.4834	.0780	.6772	.38966	.92096	.42310	.3635	.0858	.5663	.40567	.91402	.44383	.2531	.0941	.4650	4
57	.35755	.93389	.38286	.6119	.0708	.7968	.37380	.92751	.40301	.4813	.0781	.6752	.38993	.92084	.42344	.3616	.0859	.5646	.40594	.91390	.44418	.2513	.0942	.4634	3
58	.35782	.93379	.38320	.6096	.0709	.7947	.37407	.92740	.40335	.4792	.0783	.6733	.39019	.92073	.42379	.3597	.0861	.5628	.40620	.91378	.44453	.2495	.0943	.4618	2
59	.35810	.93368	.38353	.6073	.0710	.7925	.37434	.92729	.40369	.4772	.0784	.6714	.39046	.92062	.42413	.3577	.0862	.5610	.40647	.91366	.44488	.2478	.0945	.4602	1
60	.35837	.93358	.38386	2.6051	.0711	2.7904	.37461	.92718	.40403	2.4751	.0785	2.6695	.39073	.92050	.42447	2.3558	.0864	2.5593	.40674	.91354	.44523	2.2460	.0946	2.4586	0
′	cos	sin	cot	tan	cosec	sec	cos	sin	cot	tan	cosec	sec	cos	sin	cot	tan	cosec	sec	cos	sin	cot	tan	cosec	sec	′
	69°						68°						67°						66°						

NATURAL TRIGONOMETRIC FUNCTIONS

	24°						25°						26°						27°						
′	sin	cos	tan	cot	sec	cosec	sin	cos	tan	cot	sec	cosec	sin	cos	tan	cot	sec	cosec	sin	cos	tan	cot	sec	cosec	′
0	.40674	.91354	.44523	2.2460	1.0946	2.4586	.42262	.90631	.46631	2.1445	1.1034	2.3662	.43837	.89879	.48773	2.0503	1.1126	2.2812	.45399	.89101	.50952	1.9626	1.1223	2.2027	60
1	.40700	.91343	.44558	.2443	.0948	.4570	.42288	.90618	.46666	.1429	.1035	.3647	.43863	.89867	.48809	.0488	.1127	.2798	.45425	.89087	.50989	.9612	.1225	.2014	59
2	.40727	.91331	.44593	.2425	.0949	.4554	.42314	.90606	.46702	.1412	.1037	.3632	.43889	.89854	.48845	.0473	.1129	.2784	.45451	.89074	.51026	.9598	.1226	.2002	58
3	.40753	.91319	.44627	.2408	.0951	.4538	.42341	.90594	.46737	.1396	.1038	.3618	.43915	.89841	.48881	.0458	.1131	.2771	.45477	.89061	.51062	.9584	.1228	.1989	57
4	.40780	.91307	.44662	.2390	.0952	.4522	.42367	.90581	.46772	.1380	.1040	.3603	.43942	.89828	.48917	.0443	.1132	.2757	.45503	.89048	.51099	.9570	.1230	.1977	56
5	.40806	.91295	.44697	2.2373	.0953	2.4506	.42394	.90569	.46808	2.1364	.1041	2.3588	.43968	.89815	.48953	2.0427	.1134	2.2744	.45528	.89034	.51136	1.9556	.1231	2.1964	55
6	.40833	.91283	.44732	.2355	.0955	.4490	.42420	.90557	.46843	.1348	.1043	.3574	.43994	.89803	.48989	.0412	.1135	.2730	.45554	.89021	.51172	.9542	.1233	.1952	54
7	.40860	.91271	.44767	.2338	.0956	.4474	.42446	.90544	.46879	.1331	.1044	.3559	.44020	.89790	.49025	.0397	.1137	.2717	.45580	.89008	.51209	.9528	.1235	.1939	53
8	.40886	.91260	.44802	.2320	.0958	.4458	.42473	.90532	.46914	.1315	.1046	.3544	.44046	.89777	.49062	.0382	.1139	.2703	.45606	.88995	.51246	.9514	.1237	.1927	52
9	.40913	.91248	.44837	.2303	.0959	.4442	.42499	.90520	.46950	.1299	.1047	.3530	.44072	.89764	.49098	.0367	.1140	.2690	.45632	.88981	.51283	.9500	.1238	.1914	51
10	.40939	.91236	.44872	2.2286	.0961	2.4426	.42525	.90507	.46985	2.1283	.1049	2.3515	.44098	.89751	.49134	2.0352	.1142	2.2676	.45658	.88968	.51319	1.9486	.1240	2.1902	50
11	.40966	.91224	.44907	.2268	.0962	.4418	.42552	.90495	.47021	.1267	.1050	.3501	.44124	.89739	.49170	.0338	.1143	.2663	.45684	.88955	.51356	.9472	.1242	.1889	49
12	.40992	.91212	.44942	.2251	.0963	.4395	.42578	.90483	.47056	.1251	.1052	.3486	.44150	.89726	.49206	.0323	.1145	.2650	.45710	.88942	.51393	.9458	.1243	.1877	48
13	.41019	.91200	.44977	.2234	.0965	.4379	.42604	.90470	.47092	.1235	.1053	.3472	.44177	.89713	.49242	.0308	.1147	.2636	.45736	.88928	.51430	.9444	.1245	.1865	47
14	.41045	.91188	.45012	.2216	.0966	.4363	.42630	.90458	.47127	.1219	.1055	.3457	.44203	.89700	.49278	.0293	.1148	.2623	.45761	.88915	.51466	.9430	.1247	.1852	46
15	.41072	.91176	.45047	2.2199	.0968	2.4347	.42657	.90445	.47163	2.1203	.1056	2.3443	.44229	.89687	.49314	2.0278	.1150	2.2610	.45787	.88902	.51503	1.9416	.1248	2.1840	45
16	.41098	.91164	.45082	.2182	.0969	.4332	.42683	.90433	.47199	.1187	.1058	.3428	.44255	.89674	.49351	.0263	.1151	.2596	.45813	.88888	.51540	.9402	.1250	.1828	44
17	.41125	.91152	.45117	.2165	.0971	.4316	.42709	.90421	.47234	.1171	.1059	.3414	.44281	.89661	.49387	.0248	.1153	.2583	.45839	.88875	.51577	.9388	.1252	.1815	43
18	.41151	.91140	.45152	.2147	.0972	.4300	.42736	.90408	.47270	.1155	.1061	.3399	.44307	.89649	.49423	.0233	.1155	.2570	.45865	.88862	.51614	.9375	.1253	.1803	42
19	.41178	.91128	.45187	.2130	.0973	.4285	.42762	.90396	.47305	.1139	.1062	.3385	.44333	.89636	.49459	.0219	.1156	.2556	.45891	.88848	.51651	.9361	.1255	.1791	41
20	.41204	.91116	.45222	2.2113	.0975	2.4269	.42788	.90383	.47341	2.1123	.1064	2.3371	.44359	.89623	.49495	2.0204	.1158	2.2543	.45917	.88835	.51687	1.9347	.1257	2.1778	40
21	.41231	.91104	.45257	.2096	.0976	.4254	.42815	.90371	.47376	.1107	.1065	.3356	.44385	.89610	.49532	.0189	.1159	.2530	.45942	.88822	.51724	.9333	.1258	.1766	39
22	.41257	.91092	.45292	.2079	.0978	.4238	.42841	.90358	.47412	.1092	.1067	.3342	.44411	.89597	.49568	.0174	.1161	.2517	.45968	.88808	.51761	.9319	.1260	.1754	38
23	.41284	.91080	.45327	.2062	.0979	.4222	.42867	.90346	.47448	.1076	.1068	.3328	.44437	.89584	.49604	.0159	.1163	.2503	.45994	.88795	.51798	.9306	.1262	.1742	37
24	.41310	.91068	.45362	.2045	.0981	.4207	.42893	.90333	.47483	.1060	.1070	.3313	.44463	.89571	.49640	.0145	.1164	.2490	.46020	.88781	.51835	.9292	.1264	.1730	36
25	.41337	.91056	.45397	2.2028	.0982	2.4191	.42920	.90321	.47519	2.1044	.1072	2.3299	.44489	.89558	.49677	2.0130	.1166	2.2477	.46046	.88768	.51872	1.9278	.1265	2.1717	35
26	.41363	.91044	.45432	.2011	.0984	.4176	.42946	.90308	.47555	.1028	.1073	.3285	.44516	.89545	.49713	.0115	.1167	.2464	.46072	.88755	.51909	.9264	.1267	.1705	34
27	.41390	.91032	.45467	.1994	.0985	.4160	.42972	.90296	.47590	.1013	.1075	.3271	.44542	.89532	.49749	.0101	.1169	.2451	.46097	.88741	.51946	.9251	.1269	.1693	33
28	.41416	.91020	.45502	.1977	.0986	.4145	.42998	.90283	.47626	.0997	.1076	.3256	.44568	.89519	.49785	.0086	.1171	.2438	.46123	.88728	.51983	.9237	.1270	.1681	32
29	.41443	.91008	.45537	.1960	.0988	.4130	.43025	.90271	.47662	.0981	.1078	.3242	.44594	.89506	.49822	.0071	.1172	.2425	.46149	.88714	.52020	.9223	.1272	.1669	31
30	.41469	.90996	.45573	2.1943	.0989	2.4114	.43051	.90258	.47697	2.0965	.1079	2.3228	.44620	.89493	.49858	2.0057	.1174	2.2411	.46175	.88701	.52057	1.9210	.1274	2.1657	30
31	.41496	.90984	.45608	.1926	.0991	.4099	.43077	.90246	.47733	.0950	.1081	.3214	.44646	.89480	.49894	.0042	.1176	.2398	.46201	.88688	.52094	.9196	.1275	.1645	29
32	.41522	.90972	.45643	.1909	.0992	.4083	.43104	.90233	.47769	.0934	.1082	.3200	.44672	.89467	.49931	.0028	.1177	.2385	.46226	.88674	.52131	.9182	.1277	.1633	28
33	.41549	.90960	.45678	.1892	.0994	.4068	.43130	.90221	.47805	.0918	.1084	.3186	.44698	.89454	.49967	.0013	.1179	.2372	.46252	.88661	.52168	.9169	.1279	.1620	27
34	.41575	.90948	.45713	.1875	.0995	.4053	.43156	.90208	.47840	.0903	.1085	.3172	.44724	.89441	.50003	1.9998	.1180	.2359	.46278	.88647	.52205	.9155	.1281	.1608	26
35	.41602	.90936	.45748	2.1859	.0997	2.4037	.43182	.90196	.47876	2.0887	.1087	2.3158	.44750	.89428	.50040	1.9984	.1182	2.2346	.46304	.88634	.52242	1.9142	.1282	2.1596	25
36	.41628	.90924	.45783	.1842	.0998	.4022	.43208	.90183	.47912	.0872	.1088	.3143	.44776	.89415	.50076	.9969	.1184	.2333	.46330	.88620	.52279	.9128	.1284	.1584	24
37	.41654	.90911	.45819	.1825	.1000	.4007	.43235	.90171	.47948	.0856	.1090	.3129	.44802	.89402	.50113	.9955	.1185	.2320	.46355	.88607	.52316	.9115	.1286	.1572	23
38	.41681	.90899	.45854	.1808	.1001	.3992	.43261	.90158	.47983	.0840	.1092	.3115	.44828	.89389	.50149	.9940	.1187	.2307	.46381	.88593	.52353	.9101	.1287	.1560	22
39	.41707	.90887	.45889	.1792	.1003	.3976	.43287	.90145	.48019	.0825	.1093	.3101	.44854	.89376	.50185	.9926	.1189	.2294	.46407	.88580	.52390	.9088	.1289	.1548	21
40	.41734	.90875	.45924	2.1775	.1004	2.3961	.43313	.90133	.48055	2.0809	.1095	2.3087	.44880	.89363	.50222	1.9912	.1190	2.2282	.46433	.88566	.52427	1.9074	.1291	2.1536	20
41	.41760	.90863	.45960	.1758	.1005	.3946	.43340	.90120	.48091	.0794	.1096	.3073	.44906	.89350	.50258	.9897	.1192	.2269	.46458	.88553	.52464	.9061	.1293	.1525	19
42	.41787	.90851	.45995	.1741	.1007	.3931	.43366	.90108	.48127	.0778	.1098	.3059	.44932	.89337	.50295	.9883	.1193	.2256	.46484	.88539	.52501	.9047	.1294	.1513	18
43	.41813	.90839	.46030	.1725	.1008	.3916	.43392	.90095	.48162	.0763	.1099	.3046	.44958	.89324	.50331	.9868	.1195	.2243	.46510	.88526	.52538	.9034	.1296	.1501	17
44	.41839	.90826	.46065	.1708	.1010	.3901	.43418	.90082	.48198	.0747	.1101	.3032	.44984	.89311	.50368	.9854	.1197	.2230	.46536	.88512	.52575	.9020	.1298	.1489	16
45	.41866	.90814	.46101	2.1692	.1011	2.3886	.43444	.90070	.48234	2.0732	.1102	2.3018	.45010	.89298	.50404	1.9840	.1198	2.2217	.46561	.88499	.52612	1.9007	.1299	2.1477	15
46	.41892	.90812	.46136	.1675	.1013	.3871	.43471	.90057	.48270	.0717	.1104	.3004	.45036	.89285	.50441	.9825	.1200	.2204	.46587	.88485	.52650	.8993	.1301	.1465	14
47	.41919	.90790	.46171	.1658	.1014	.3856	.43497	.90044	.48306	.0701	.1106	.2990	.45062	.89272	.50477	.9811	.1202	.2192	.46613	.88472	.52687	.8980	.1303	.1453	13
48	.41945	.90778	.46206	.1642	.1016	.3841	.43523	.90032	.48342	.0686	.1107	.2976	.45088	.89258	.50514	.9797	.1203	.2179	.46639	.88458	.52724	.8967	.1305	.1441	12
49	.41972	.90765	.46242	.1625	.1017	.3826	.43549	.90019	.48378	.0671	.1109	.2962	.45114	.89245	.50550	.9782	.1205	.2166	.46664	.88444	.52761	.8953	.1306	.1430	11
50	.41998	.90753	.46277	2.1609	.1019	2.3811	.43575	.90006	.48414	2.0655	.1110	2.2949	.45140	.89232	.50587	1.9768	.1207	2.2153	.46690	.88431	.52798	1.8940	.1308	2.1418	10
51	.42024	.90741	.46312	.1592	.1020	.3796	.43602	.89994	.48449	.0640	.1112	.2935	.45166	.89219	.50623	.9754	.1208	.2141	.46716	.88417	.52836	.8927	.1310	.1406	9
52	.42051	.90729	.46348	.1576	.1022	.3781	.43628	.89981	.48485	.0625	.1113	.2921	.45191	.89206	.50660	.9739	.1210	.2128	.46741	.88404	.52873	.8913	.1312	.1394	8
53	.42077	.90717	.46383	.1559	.1023	.3766	.43654	.89968	.48521	.0609	.1115	.2907	.45217	.89193	.50696	.9725	.1212	.2115	.46767	.88390	.52910	.8900	.1313	.1382	7
54	.42103	.90704	.46418	.1543	.1025	.3751	.43680	.89956	.48557	.0594	.1116	.2894	.45243	.89180	.50733	.9711	.1213	.2103	.46793	.88376	.52947	.8887	.1315	.1371	6
55	.42130	.90692	.46454	2.1527	.1026	2.3736	.43706	.89943	.48593	2.0579	.1118	2.2880	.45269	.89166	.50769	1.9697	.1215	2.2090	.46819	.88363	.52984	1.8873	.1317	2.1359	5
56	.42156	.90680	.46489	.1510	.1028	.3721	.43732	.89930	.48629	.0564	.1120	.2866	.45295	.89153	.50806	.9683	.1217	.2077	.46844	.88349	.53022	.8860	.1319	.1347	4
57	.42183	.90668	.46524	.1494	.1029	.3706	.43759	.89918	.48665	.0548	.1121	.2853	.45321	.89140	.50843	.9668	.1218	.2065	.46870	.88336	.53059	.8847	.1320	.1335	3
58	.42209	.90655	.46560	.1478	.1031	.3691	.43785	.89905	.48701	.0533	.1123	.2839	.45347	.89127	.50879	.9654	.1220	.2052	.46896	.88322	.53096	.8834	.1322	.1324	2
59	.42235	.90643	.46595	.1461	.1032	.3677	.43811	.89892	.48737	.0518	.1124	.2825	.45373	.89114	.50916	.9640	.1222	.2039	.46921	.88308	.53134	.8820	.1324	.1312	1
60	.42262	.90631	.46631	2.1445	.1034	2.3662	.43837	.89879	.48773	2.0503	.1126	2.2812	.45399	.89101	.50952	1.9626	.1223	2.2027	.46947	.88295	.53171	1.8807	.1326	2.1300	0
′	cos	sin	cot	tan	cosec	sec	cos	sin	cot	tan	cosec	sec	cos	sin	cot	tan	cosec	sec	cos	sin	cot	tan	cosec	sec	′
	65°						64°						63°						62°						

NATURAL TRIGONOMETRIC FUNCTIONS

′	28° sin	28° cos	28° tan	28° cot	28° sec	28° cosec	29° sin	29° cos	29° tan	29° cot	29° sec	29° cosec
0	.46947	.88295	.53171	1.8807	1.1326	2.1300	.48481	.87462	.55431	1.8040	1.1433	2.0627
1	.46973	.88281	.53208	.8794	.1327	.1289	.48506	.87448	.55469	.8028	.1435	.0616
2	.46998	.88267	.53245	.8781	.1329	.1277	.48532	.87434	.55507	.8016	.1437	.0605
3	.47024	.88254	.53283	.8768	.1331	.1266	.48557	.87420	.55545	.8003	.1439	.0594
4	.47050	.88240	.53320	.8754	.1333	.1254	.48583	.87405	.55583	.7991	.1441	.0583
5	.47075	.88226	.53358	1.8741	.1334	2.1242	.48608	.87391	.55621	1.7979	.1443	2.0573
6	.47101	.88213	.53395	.8728	.1336	.1231	.48633	.87377	.55659	.7966	.1445	.0562
7	.47127	.88199	.53432	.8715	.1338	.1219	.48659	.87363	.55697	.7954	.1446	.0551
8	.47152	.88185	.53470	.8702	.1340	.1208	.48684	.87349	.55735	.7942	.1448	.0540
9	.47178	.88171	.53507	.8689	.1341	.1196	.48710	.87335	.55774	.7930	.1450	.0530
10	.47204	.88158	.53545	1.8676	.1343	2.1185	.48735	.87320	.55812	1.7917	.1452	2.0519
11	.47229	.88144	.53582	.8663	.1345	.1173	.48760	.87306	.55850	.7905	.1454	.0508
12	.47255	.88130	.53619	.8650	.1347	.1162	.48786	.87292	.55888	.7893	.1456	.0498
13	.47281	.88117	.53657	.8637	.1349	.1150	.48811	.87278	.55926	.7881	.1458	.0487
14	.47306	.88103	.53694	.8624	.1350	.1139	.48837	.87264	.55964	.7868	.1459	.0476
15	.47332	.88089	.53732	1.8611	.1352	2.1127	.48862	.87250	.56003	1.7856	.1461	2.0466
16	.47357	.88075	.53769	.8598	.1354	.1116	.48887	.87235	.56041	.7844	.1463	.0455
17	.47383	.88061	.53807	.8585	.1356	.1104	.48913	.87221	.56079	.7832	.1465	.0444
18	.47409	.88048	.53844	.8572	.1357	.1093	.48938	.87207	.56117	.7820	.1467	.0434
19	.47434	.88034	.53882	.8559	.1359	.1082	.48964	.87193	.56156	.7808	.1469	.0423
20	.47460	.88020	.53919	1.8546	.1361	2.1070	.48989	.87178	.56194	1.7795	.1471	2.0413
21	.47486	.88006	.53957	.8533	.1363	.1059	.49014	.87164	.56232	.7783	.1473	.0402
22	.47511	.87992	.53995	.8520	.1365	.1048	.49040	.87150	.56270	.7771	.1474	.0392
23	.47537	.87979	.54032	.8507	.1366	.1036	.49065	.87136	.56309	.7759	.1476	.0381
24	.47562	.87965	.54070	.8495	.1368	.1025	.49090	.87121	.56347	.7747	.1478	.0370
25	.47588	.87951	.54107	1.8482	.1370	2.1014	.49116	.87107	.56385	1.7735	.1480	2.0360
26	.47613	.87937	.54145	.8469	.1372	.1002	.49141	.87093	.56424	.7723	.1482	.0349
27	.47639	.87923	.54183	.8456	.1373	.0991	.49166	.87078	.56462	.7711	.1484	.0339
28	.47665	.87909	.54220	.8443	.1375	.0980	.49192	.87064	.56500	.7699	.1486	.0329
29	.47690	.87895	.54258	.8430	.1377	.0969	.49217	.87050	.56539	.7687	.1488	.0318
30	.47716	.87882	.54295	1.8418	.1379	2.0957	.49242	.87035	.56577	1.7675	.1489	2.0308
31	.47741	.87868	.54333	.8405	.1381	.0946	.49268	.87021	.56616	.7663	.1491	.0297
32	.47767	.87854	.54371	.8392	.1382	.0935	.49293	.87007	.56654	.7651	.1493	.0287
33	.47792	.87840	.54409	.8379	.1384	.0924	.49318	.86992	.56692	.7639	.1495	.0276
34	.47818	.87826	.54446	.8367	.1386	.0912	.49343	.86978	.56731	.7627	.1497	.0266
35	.47844	.87812	.54484	1.8354	.1388	2.0901	.49369	.86964	.56769	1.7615	.1499	2.0256
36	.47869	.87798	.54522	.8341	.1390	.0890	.49394	.86949	.56808	.7603	.1501	.0245
37	.47895	.87784	.54559	.8329	.1391	.0879	.49419	.86935	.56846	.7591	.1503	.0235
38	.47920	.87770	.54597	.8316	.1393	.0868	.49445	.86921	.56885	.7579	.1505	.0224
39	.47946	.87756	.54635	.8303	.1395	.0857	.49470	.86906	.56923	.7567	.1507	.0214
40	.47971	.87742	.54673	1.8291	.1397	2.0846	.49495	.86892	.56962	1.7555	.1508	2.0204
41	.47997	.87728	.54711	.8278	.1399	.0835	.49521	.86877	.57000	.7544	.1510	.0194
42	.48022	.87715	.54748	.8265	.1401	.0824	.49546	.86863	.57039	.7532	.1512	.0183
43	.48048	.87701	.54786	.8253	.1402	.0812	.49571	.86849	.57077	.7520	.1514	.0173
44	.48073	.87687	.54824	.8240	.1404	.0801	.49596	.86834	.57116	.7508	.1516	.0163
45	.48099	.87673	.54862	1.8227	.1406	2.0790	.49622	.86820	.57155	1.7496	.1518	2.0152
46	.48124	.87659	.54900	.8215	.1408	.0779	.49647	.86805	.57193	.7484	.1520	.0142
47	.48150	.87645	.54937	.8202	.1410	.0768	.49672	.86791	.57232	.7473	.1522	.0132
48	.48175	.87631	.54975	.8190	.1411	.0757	.49697	.86776	.57270	.7461	.1524	.0122
49	.48201	.87617	.55013	.8177	.1413	.0746	.49723	.86762	.57309	.7449	.1526	.0111
50	.48226	.87603	.55051	1.8165	.1415	2.0735	.49748	.86748	.57348	1.7437	.1528	2.0101
51	.48252	.87588	.55089	.8152	.1417	.0725	.49773	.86733	.57386	.7426	.1530	.0091
52	.48277	.87574	.55127	.8140	.1419	.0714	.49798	.86719	.57425	.7414	.1531	.0081
53	.48303	.87560	.55165	.8127	.1421	.0703	.49823	.86704	.57464	.7402	.1533	.0071
54	.48328	.87546	.55203	.8115	.1422	.0692	.49849	.86690	.57502	.7390	.1535	.0061
55	.48354	.87532	.55241	1.8102	.1424	2.0681	.49874	.86675	.57541	1.7379	.1537	2.0050
56	.48379	.87518	.55279	.8090	.1426	.0670	.49899	.86661	.57580	.7367	.1539	.0040
57	.48405	.87504	.55317	.8078	.1428	.0659	.49924	.86646	.57619	.7355	.1541	.0030
58	.48430	.87490	.55355	.8065	.1430	.0648	.49950	.86632	.57657	.7344	.1543	.0020
59	.48455	.87476	.55393	.8053	.1432	.0637	.49975	.86617	.57696	.7332	.1545	.0010
60	.48481	.87462	.55431	1.8040	.1433	2.0627	.50000	.86603	.57735	1.7320	.1547	2.0000
′	61° cos	61° sin	61° cot	61° tan	61° cosec	61° sec	60° cos	60° sin	60° cot	60° tan	60° cosec	60° sec

30° sin	30° cos	30° tan	30° cot	30° sec	30° cosec	31° sin	31° cos	31° tan	31° cot	31° sec	31° cosec	′
.50000	.86603	.57735	1.7320	1.1547	2.0000	.51504	.85717	.60086	1.6643	1.1666	1.9416	60
.50025	.86588	.57774	.7309	.1549	1.9990	.51529	.85702	.60126	.6632	.1668	.9407	59
.50050	.86573	.57813	.7297	.1551	.9980	.51554	.85687	.60165	.6621	.1670	.9397	58
.50075	.86559	.57851	.7286	.1553	.9970	.51578	.85672	.60205	.6610	.1672	.9388	57
.50101	.86544	.57890	.7274	.1555	.9960	.51603	.85657	.60244	.6599	.1674	.9378	56
.50126	.86530	.57929	1.7262	.1557	1.9950	.51628	.85642	.60284	1.6588	.1676	1.9369	55
.50151	.86515	.57968	.7251	.1559	.9940	.51653	.85627	.60324	.6577	.1678	.9360	54
.50176	.86500	.58007	.7239	.1561	.9930	.51678	.85612	.60363	.6566	.1681	.9350	53
.50201	.86486	.58046	.7228	.1562	.9920	.51703	.85597	.60403	.6555	.1683	.9341	52
.50226	.86471	.58085	.7216	.1564	.9910	.51728	.85582	.60443	.6544	.1685	.9332	51
.50252	.86457	.58123	1.7205	.1566	1.9900	.51753	.85566	.60483	1.6534	.1687	1.9322	50
.50277	.86442	.58162	.7193	.1568	.9890	.51778	.85551	.60522	.6523	.1689	.9313	49
.50302	.86427	.58201	.7182	.1570	.9880	.51803	.85536	.60562	.6512	.1691	.9304	48
.50327	.86413	.58240	.7170	.1572	.9870	.51827	.85521	.60602	.6501	.1693	.9295	47
.50352	.86398	.58279	.7159	.1574	.9860	.51852	.85506	.60642	.6490	.1695	.9285	46
.50377	.86383	.58318	1.7147	.1576	1.9850	.51877	.85491	.60681	1.6479	.1697	1.9276	45
.50402	.86369	.58357	.7136	.1578	.9840	.51902	.85476	.60721	.6469	.1699	.9267	44
.50428	.86354	.58396	.7124	.1580	.9830	.51927	.85461	.60761	.6458	.1701	.9258	43
.50453	.86339	.58435	.7113	.1582	.9820	.51952	.85446	.60801	.6447	.1703	.9248	42
.50478	.86325	.58474	.7101	.1584	.9811	.51977	.85431	.60841	.6436	.1705	.9239	41
.50503	.86310	.58513	1.7090	.1586	1.9801	.52002	.85416	.60881	1.6425	.1707	1.9230	40
.50528	.86295	.58552	.7079	.1588	.9791	.52026	.85400	.60920	.6415	.1709	.9221	39
.50553	.86281	.58591	.7067	.1590	.9781	.52051	.85385	.60960	.6404	.1712	.9212	38
.50578	.86266	.58630	.7056	.1592	.9771	.52076	.85370	.61000	.6393	.1714	.9203	37
.50603	.86251	.58670	.7044	.1594	.9761	.52101	.85355	.61040	.6383	.1716	.9193	36
.50628	.86237	.58709	1.7033	.1596	1.9752	.52126	.85340	.61080	1.6372	.1718	1.9184	35
.50653	.86222	.58748	.7022	.1598	.9742	.52151	.85325	.61120	.6361	.1720	.9175	34
.50679	.86207	.58787	.7010	.1600	.9732	.52175	.85309	.61160	.6350	.1722	.9166	33
.50704	.86192	.58826	.6999	.1602	.9722	.52200	.85294	.61200	.6340	.1724	.9157	32
.50729	.86178	.58865	.6988	.1604	.9713	.52225	.85279	.61240	.6329	.1726	.9148	31
.50754	.86163	.58904	1.6977	.1606	1.9703	.52250	.85264	.61280	1.6318	.1728	1.9139	30
.50779	.86148	.58944	.6965	.1608	.9693	.52275	.85249	.61320	.6308	.1730	.9130	29
.50804	.86133	.58983	.6954	.1610	.9683	.52299	.85234	.61360	.6297	.1732	.9121	28
.50829	.86118	.59022	.6943	.1612	.9674	.52324	.85218	.61400	.6286	.1734	.9112	27
.50854	.86104	.59061	.6931	.1614	.9664	.52349	.85203	.61440	.6276	.1737	.9102	26
.50879	.86089	.59100	1.6920	.1616	1.9654	.52374	.85188	.61480	1.6265	.1739	1.9093	25
.50904	.86074	.59140	.6909	.1618	.9645	.52398	.85173	.61520	.6255	.1741	.9084	24
.50929	.86059	.59179	.6898	.1620	.9635	.52423	.85157	.61560	.6244	.1743	.9075	23
.50954	.86044	.59218	.6887	.1622	.9625	.52448	.85142	.61601	.6233	.1745	.9066	22
.50979	.86030	.59258	.6875	.1624	.9616	.52473	.85127	.61641	.6223	.1747	.9057	21
.51004	.86015	.59297	1.6864	.1626	1.9606	.52498	.85112	.61681	1.6212	.1749	1.9048	20
.51029	.86000	.59336	.6853	.1628	.9596	.52522	.85096	.61721	.6202	.1751	.9039	19
.51054	.85985	.59376	.6842	.1630	.9587	.52547	.85081	.61761	.6191	.1753	.9030	18
.51079	.85970	.59415	.6831	.1632	.9577	.52572	.85066	.61801	.6181	.1756	.9021	17
.51104	.85955	.59454	.6820	.1634	.9568	.52597	.85050	.61842	.6170	.1758	.9013	16
.51129	.85941	.59494	1.6808	.1636	1.9558	.52621	.85735	.61882	1.6160	.1760	1.9004	15
.51154	.85926	.59533	.6797	.1638	.9549	.52646	.85020	.61922	.6149	.1762	.8995	14
.51179	.85911	.59572	.6786	.1640	.9539	.52671	.85004	.61962	.6139	.1764	.8986	13
.51204	.85896	.59612	.6775	.1642	.9530	.52695	.84989	.62003	.6128	.1766	.8977	12
.51229	.85881	.59651	.6764	.1644	.9520	.52720	.84974	.62043	.6118	.1768	.8968	11
.51254	.85866	.59691	1.6753	.1646	1.9510	.52745	.84959	.62083	1.6107	.1770	1.8959	10
.51279	.85851	.59730	.6742	.1648	.9501	.52770	.84943	.62123	.6097	.1772	.8950	9
.51304	.85836	.59770	.6731	.1650	.9491	.52794	.84928	.62164	.6086	.1775	.8941	8
.51329	.85821	.59809	.6720	.1652	.9482	.52819	.84912	.62204	.6076	.1777	.8932	7
.51354	.85806	.59849	.6709	.1654	.9473	.52844	.84897	.62244	.6066	.1779	.8924	6
.51379	.85791	.59888	1.6698	.1656	1.9463	.52868	.84882	.62285	1.6055	.1781	1.8915	5
.51404	.85777	.59928	.6687	.1658	.9454	.52893	.84866	.62325	.6045	.1783	.8906	4
.51429	.85762	.59967	.6676	.1660	.9444	.52918	.84851	.62366	.6034	.1785	.8897	3
.51454	.85747	.60007	.6665	.1662	.9435	.52942	.84836	.62406	.6024	.1787	.8888	2
.51479	.85732	.60046	.6654	.1664	.9425	.52967	.84820	.62446	.6014	.1790	.8879	1
.51504	.85717	.60086	1.6643	.1666	1.9416	.52992	.84805	.62487	1.6003	.1792	1.8871	0
59° cos	59° sin	59° cot	59° tan	59° cosec	59° sec	58° cos	58° sin	58° cot	58° tan	58° cosec	58° sec	′

NATURAL TRIGONOMETRIC FUNCTIONS

′	32°						33°						34°						35°						′
′	sin	cos	tan	cot	sec	cosec	sin	cos	tan	cot	sec	cosec	sin	cos	tan	cot	sec	cosec	sin	cos	tan	cot	sec	cosec	′
0	.52992	.84805	.62487	1.6003	1.1792	1.8871	.54464	.83867	.64941	1.5399	1.1924	1.8361	.55919	.82904	.67451	1.4826	1.2062	1.7883	.57358	.81915	.70021	1.4281	1.2208	1.7434	60
1	.53016	.84789	.62527	.5993	.1794	.8862	.54488	.83851	.64982	.5389	.1926	.8352	.55943	.82887	.67493	.4816	.2064	.7875	.57381	.81898	.70064	.4273	.2210	.7427	59
2	.53041	.84774	.62568	.5983	.1796	.8853	.54513	.83835	.65023	.5379	.1928	.8344	.55967	.82871	.67535	.4807	.2067	.7867	.57405	.81882	.70107	.4264	.2213	.7420	58
3	.53066	.84758	.62608	.5972	.1798	.8844	.54537	.83819	.65065	.5369	.1930	.8336	.55992	.82855	.67578	.4798	.2069	.7860	.57429	.81865	.70151	.4255	.2215	.7413	57
4	.53090	.84743	.62649	.5962	.1800	.8836	.54561	.83804	.65106	.5359	.1933	.8328	.56016	.82839	.67620	.4788	.2072	.7852	.57453	.81848	.70194	.4246	.2218	.7405	56
5	.53115	.84728	.62689	1.5952	.1802	1.8827	.54586	.83788	.65148	1.5350	.1935	1.8320	.56040	.82822	.67663	1.4779	.2074	1.7844	.57477	.81832	.70238	1.4237	.2220	1.7398	55
6	.53140	.84712	.62730	.5941	.1805	.8818	.54610	.83772	.65189	.5340	.1937	.8311	.56064	.82806	.67705	.4770	.2076	.7837	.57500	.81815	.70281	.4228	.2223	.7391	54
7	.53164	.84697	.62770	.5931	.1807	.8809	.54634	.83756	.65231	.5330	.1939	.8303	.56088	.82790	.67747	.4761	.2079	.7829	.57524	.81798	.70325	.4220	.2225	.7384	53
8	.53189	.84681	.62811	.5921	.1809	.8801	.54659	.83740	.65272	.5320	.1942	.8295	.56112	.82773	.67790	.4751	.2081	.7821	.57548	.81781	.70368	.4211	.2228	.7377	52
9	.53214	.84666	.62851	.5910	.1811	.8792	.54683	.83724	.65314	.5311	.1944	.8287	.56136	.82757	.67832	.4742	.2083	.7814	.57572	.81765	.70412	.4202	.2230	.7369	51
10	.53238	.84650	.62892	1.5900	.1813	1.8783	.54708	.83708	.65355	1.5301	.1946	1.8279	.56160	.82741	.67875	1.4733	.2086	1.7806	.57596	.81748	.70455	1.4193	.2233	1.7362	50
11	.53263	.84635	.62933	.5890	.1815	.8775	.54732	.83692	.65397	.5291	.1948	.8271	.56184	.82724	.67917	.4724	.2088	.7798	.57619	.81731	.70499	.4185	.2235	.7355	49
12	.53288	.84619	.62973	.5880	.1818	.8766	.54756	.83676	.65438	.5282	.1951	.8263	.56208	.82708	.67960	.4714	.2091	.7791	.57643	.81714	.70542	.4176	.2238	.7348	48
13	.53312	.84604	.63014	.5869	.1820	.8757	.54781	.83660	.65480	.5272	.1953	.8255	.56232	.82692	.68002	.4705	.2093	.7783	.57667	.81698	.70586	.4167	.2240	.7341	47
14	.53337	.84588	.63055	.5859	.1822	.8749	.54805	.83644	.65521	.5262	.1955	.8246	.56256	.82675	.68045	.4696	.2095	.7776	.57691	.81681	.70629	.4158	.2243	.7334	46
15	.53361	.84573	.63095	1.5849	.1824	1.8740	.54829	.83629	.65563	1.5252	.1958	1.8238	.56280	.82659	.68087	1.4687	.2098	1.7768	.57714	.81664	.70673	1.4150	.2245	1.7327	45
16	.53386	.84557	.63136	.5839	.1826	.8731	.54854	.83613	.65604	.5234	.1960	.8230	.56304	.82643	.68130	.4678	.2100	.7760	.57738	.81647	.70717	.4141	.2248	.7319	44
17	.53411	.84542	.63177	.5829	.1828	.8723	.54878	.83597	.65646	.5233	.1962	.8222	.56328	.82626	.68173	.4669	.2103	.7753	.57762	.81630	.70760	.4132	.2250	.7312	43
18	.53435	.84526	.63217	.5818	.1831	.8714	.54902	.83581	.65688	.5223	.1964	.8214	.56353	.82610	.68215	.4659	.2105	.7745	.57786	.81614	.70804	.4123	.2253	.7305	42
19	.53460	.84511	.63258	.5808	.1833	.8706	.54926	.83565	.65729	.5214	.1967	.8206	.56377	.82593	.68258	.4650	.2107	.7738	.57809	.81597	.70848	.4115	.2255	.7298	41
20	.53484	.84495	.63299	1.5798	.1835	1.8697	.54951	.83549	.65771	1.5204	.1969	1.8198	.56401	.82577	.68301	1.4641	.2110	1.7730	.57833	.81580	.70891	1.4106	.2258	1.7291	40
21	.53509	.84479	.63339	.5788	.1837	.8688	.54975	.83533	.65813	.5195	.1971	.8190	.56425	.82561	.68343	.4632	.2112	.7723	.57857	.81563	.70935	.4097	.2260	.7284	39
22	.53533	.84464	.63380	.5778	.1839	.8680	.54999	.83517	.65854	.5185	.1974	.8182	.56449	.82544	.68386	.4623	.2115	.7715	.57881	.81546	.70979	.4089	.2263	.7277	38
23	.53558	.84448	.63421	.5768	.1841	.8671	.55024	.83501	.65896	.5175	.1976	.8174	.56473	.82528	.68429	.4614	.2117	.7708	.57904	.81530	.71022	.4080	.2265	.7270	37
24	.53583	.84433	.63462	.5757	.1844	.8663	.55048	.83485	.65938	.5166	.1978	.8166	.56497	.82511	.68471	.4605	.2119	.7700	.57928	.81513	.71066	.4071	.2268	.7263	36
25	.53607	.84417	.63503	1.5747	.1846	1.8654	.55002	.83469	.65980	1.5156	.1980	1.8158	.56521	.82495	.68514	1.4595	.2122	1.7693	.57952	.81496	.71110	1.4063	.2270	1.7256	35
26	.53632	.84402	.63543	.5737	.1848	.8646	.55090	.83453	.66021	.5147	.1983	.8150	.56545	.82478	.68557	.4586	.2124	.7685	.57975	.81479	.71154	.4054	.2273	.7249	34
27	.53656	.84386	.63584	.5727	.1850	.8637	.55121	.83437	.66063	.5137	.1985	.8142	.56569	.82462	.68600	.4577	.2127	.7678	.57999	.81462	.71198	.4045	.2276	.7242	33
28	.53681	.84370	.63625	.5717	.1852	.8629	.55145	.83421	.66105	.5127	.1987	.8134	.56593	.82445	.68642	.4568	.2129	.7670	.58023	.81445	.71241	.4037	.2278	.7234	32
29	.53705	.84355	.63666	.5707	.1855	.8620	.55169	.83405	.66147	.5118	.1990	.8126	.56617	.82429	.68685	.4559	.2132	.7663	.58047	.81428	.71285	.4028	.2281	.7227	31
30	.53730	.84339	.63707	1.5697	.1857	1.8611	.55194	.83388	.66188	1.5108	.1992	1.8118	.56641	.82413	.68728	1.4550	.2134	1.7655	.58070	.81411	.71329	1.4019	.2283	1.7220	30
31	.53754	.84323	.63748	.5687	.1859	.8603	.55218	.83372	.66230	.5099	.1994	.8110	.56664	.82396	.68771	.4541	.2136	.7648	.58094	.81395	.71373	.4011	.2286	.7213	29
32	.53779	.84308	.63789	.5677	.1861	.8595	.55242	.83356	.66272	.5089	.1997	.8102	.56688	.82380	.68814	.4532	.2139	.7640	.58118	.81378	.71417	.4002	.2288	.7206	28
33	.53803	.84292	.63830	.5667	.1863	.8586	.55266	.83340	.66314	.5080	.1999	.8094	.56712	.82363	.68857	.4523	.2141	.7633	.58141	.81361	.71461	.3994	.2291	.7199	27
34	.53828	.84276	.63871	.5657	.1866	.8578	.55291	.83324	.66356	.5070	.2001	.8086	.56736	.82347	.68899	.4514	.2144	.7625	.58165	.81344	.71505	.3985	.2293	.7192	26
35	.53852	.84261	.63912	1.5646	.1868	1.8569	.55315	.83308	.66398	1.5061	.2004	1.8078	.56760	.82330	.68942	1.4505	.2146	1.7618	.58189	.81327	.71549	1.3976	.2296	1.7185	25
36	.53877	.84245	.63953	.5636	.1870	.8561	.55339	.83292	.66440	.5051	.2006	.8070	.56784	.82314	.68985	.4496	.2149	.7610	.58212	.81310	.71593	.3968	.2298	.7178	24
37	.53901	.84229	.63994	.5626	.1872	.8552	.55363	.83276	.66482	.5042	.2008	.8062	.56808	.82297	.69028	.4487	.2151	.7603	.58236	.81293	.71637	.3959	.2301	.7171	23
38	.53926	.84214	.64035	.5616	.1874	.8544	.55388	.83260	.66524	.5032	.2010	.8054	.56832	.82280	.69071	.4478	.2153	.7596	.58259	.81276	.71681	.3951	.2304	.7164	22
39	.53950	.84198	.64076	.5606	.1877	.8535	.55412	.83244	.66566	.5023	.2013	.8047	.56856	.82264	.69114	.4469	.2156	.7588	.58283	.81259	.71725	.3942	.2306	.7157	21
40	.53975	.84182	.64117	1.5596	.1879	1.8527	.55436	.83228	.66608	1.5013	.2015	1.8039	.56880	.82247	.69157	1.4460	.2158	1.7581	.58307	.81242	.71769	1.3933	.2309	1.7151	20
41	.53999	.84167	.64158	.5586	.1881	.8519	.55460	.83211	.66650	.5004	.2017	.8031	.56904	.82231	.69200	.4451	.2161	.7573	.58330	.81225	.71813	.3925	.2311	.7144	19
42	.54024	.84151	.64199	.5577	.1883	.8510	.55484	.83195	.66692	.4994	.2020	.8023	.56928	.82214	.69243	.4442	.2163	.7566	.58354	.81208	.71857	.3916	.2314	.7137	18
43	.54048	.84135	.64240	.5567	.1886	.8502	.55509	.83179	.66734	.4985	.2022	.8015	.56952	.82198	.69286	.4433	.2166	.7559	.58378	.81191	.71901	.3908	.2316	.7130	17
44	.54073	.84120	.64281	.5557	.1888	.8493	.55533	.83163	.66776	.4975	.2024	.8007	.56976	.82181	.69329	.4424	.2168	.7551	.58401	.81174	.71945	.3899	.2319	.7123	16
45	.54097	.84104	.64322	1.5547	.1890	1.8485	.55557	.83147	.66818	1.4966	.2027	1.7999	.57000	.82165	.69372	1.4415	.2171	1.7544	.58425	.81157	.71990	1.3891	.2322	1.7116	15
46	.54122	.84088	.64363	.5537	.1892	.8477	.55581	.83131	.66860	.4957	.2029	.7992	.57023	.82148	.69415	.4406	.2173	.7537	.58448	.81140	.72034	.3882	.2324	.7109	14
47	.54146	.84072	.64404	.5527	.1894	.8468	.55605	.83115	.66902	.4947	.2031	.7984	.57047	.82131	.69459	.4397	.2175	.7529	.58472	.81123	.72078	.3874	.2327	.7102	13
48	.54171	.84057	.64446	.5517	.1897	.8460	.55629	.83098	.66944	.4938	.2034	.7976	.57071	.82115	.69502	.4388	.2178	.7522	.58496	.81106	.72122	.3865	.2329	.7095	12
49	.54195	.84041	.64487	.5507	.1899	.8452	.55654	.83082	.66986	.4928	.2036	.7968	.57095	.82098	.69545	.4379	.2180	.7514	.58519	.81089	.72166	.3857	.2332	.7088	11
50	.54220	.84025	.64528	1.5497	.1901	1.8443	.55678	.83066	.67028	1.4919	.2039	1.7960	.57119	.82082	.69588	1.4370	.2183	1.7507	.58543	.81072	.72211	1.3848	.2335	1.7081	10
51	.54244	.84009	.64569	.5487	.1903	.8435	.55702	.83050	.67071	.4910	.2041	.7953	.57143	.82065	.69631	.4361	.2185	.7500	.58566	.81055	.72255	.3840	.2337	.7075	9
52	.54268	.83993	.64610	.5477	.1906	.8427	.55726	.83034	.67113	.4900	.2043	.7945	.57167	.82048	.69674	.4352	.2188	.7493	.58590	.81038	.72299	.3831	.2340	.7068	8
53	.54293	.83978	.64652	.5467	.1908	.8418	.55750	.83017	.67155	.4891	.2046	.7937	.57191	.82032	.69718	.4343	.2190	.7485	.58614	.81021	.72344	.3823	.2342	.7061	7
54	.54317	.83962	.64693	.5458	.1910	.8410	.55774	.83001	.67197	.4881	.2048	.7929	.57214	.82015	.69761	.4335	.2193	.7478	.58637	.81004	.72388	.3814	.2345	.7054	6
55	.54342	.83946	.64734	1.5448	.1912	1.8402	.55799	.82985	.67239	1.4872	.2050	1.7921	.57238	.81998	.69804	1.4326	.2195	1.7471	.58661	.80987	.72432	1.3806	.2348	1.7047	5
56	.54366	.83930	.64775	.5438	.1915	.8394	.55823	.82969	.67282	.4863	.2053	.7914	.57262	.81982	.69847	.4317	.2198	.7463	.58684	.80970	.72477	.3797	.2350	.7040	4
57	.54391	.83914	.64817	.5428	.1917	.8385	.55847	.82952	.67324	.4853	.2055	.7906	.57286	.81965	.69891	.4308	.2200	.7456	.58708	.80953	.72521	.3789	.2353	.7033	3
58	.54415	.83899	.64858	.5418	.1919	.8377	.55871	.82936	.67366	.4844	.2057	.7898	.57310	.81948	.69934	.4299	.2203	.7449	.58731	.80936	.72565	.3781	.2355	.7027	2
59	.54439	.83883	.64899	.5408	.1921	.8369	.55895	.82920	.67408	.4835	.2060	.7891	.57334	.81932	.69977	.4290	.2205	.7442	.58755	.80919	.72610	.3772	.2358	.7020	1
60	.54464	.83867	.64941	1.5399	.1922	1.8361	.55919	.82904	.67451	1.4826	.2062	1.7883	.57358	.81915	.70021	1.4281	.2208	1.7434	.58778	.80902	.72654	1.3764	.2361	1.7013	0
′	cos	sin	cot	tan	cosec	sec	cos	sin	cot	tan	cosec	sec	cos	sin	cot	tan	cosec	sec	cos	sin	cot	tan	cosec	sec	′
	57°						56°						55°						54°						

NATURAL TRIGONOMETRIC FUNCTIONS

′	36° sin	cos	tan	cot	sec	cosec	37° sin	cos	tan	cot	sec	cosec	38° sin	cos	tan	cot	sec	cosec	39° sin	cos	tan	cot	sec	cosec	′
0	.58778	.80902	.72654	1.3764	1.2361	1.7013	.60181	.79863	.75355	1.3270	1.2521	1.6616	.61566	.78801	.78128	1.2799	1.2690	1.6243	.62932	.77715	.80978	1.2349	1.2867	1.5890	60
1	.58802	.80885	.72699	.3755	.2363	.7006	.60205	.79846	.75401	.3262	.2524	.6610	.61589	.78783	.78175	.2792	.2693	.6237	.62955	.77696	.81026	.2342	.2871	.5884	59
2	.58825	.80867	.72743	.3747	.2366	.6999	.60228	.79828	.75447	.3254	.2527	.6603	.61612	.78765	.78222	.2784	.2696	.6231	.62977	.77678	.81075	.2334	.2874	.5879	58
3	.58849	.80850	.72788	.3738	.2368	.6993	.60251	.79811	.75492	.3246	.2530	.6597	.61635	.78747	.78269	.2776	.2699	.6224	.63000	.77660	.81123	.2327	.2877	.5873	57
4	.58873	.80833	.72832	.3730	.2371	.6986	.60274	.79793	.75538	.3238	.2532	.6591	.61658	.78729	.78316	.2769	.2702	.6218	.63022	.77641	.81171	.2320	.2880	.5867	56
5	.58896	.80816	.72877	1.3722	.2374	1.6979	.60298	.79776	.75584	1.3230	.2535	1.6584	.61681	.78711	.78363	1.2761	.2705	1.6212	.63045	.77623	.81219	1.2312	.2883	1.5862	55
6	.58920	.80799	.72921	.3713	.2376	.6972	.60320	.79758	.75629	.3222	.2538	.6578	.61703	.78693	.78410	.2753	.2707	.6206	.63067	.77605	.81268	.2305	.2886	.5856	54
7	.58943	.80782	.72966	.3705	.2379	.6965	.60344	.79741	.75675	.3214	.2541	.6572	.61726	.78675	.78457	.2746	.2710	.6200	.63090	.77586	.81316	.2297	.2889	.5850	53
8	.58967	.80765	.73010	.3697	.2382	.6959	.60367	.79723	.75721	.3206	.2543	.6565	.61749	.78657	.78504	.2738	.2713	.6194	.63113	.77568	.81364	.2290	.2892	.5854	52
9	.58990	.80747	.73055	.3688	.2384	.6952	.60390	.79706	.75767	.3198	.2546	.6559	.61772	.78640	.78551	.2730	.2716	.6188	.63135	.77549	.81413	.2283	.2895	.5839	51
10	.59014	.80730	.73100	1.3680	.2387	1.6945	.60413	.79688	.75812	1.3190	.2549	1.6552	.61795	.78622	.78598	1.2723	.2719	1.6182	.63158	.77531	.81461	1.2276	.2898	1.5833	50
11	.59037	.80713	.73144	.3672	.2389	.6938	.60437	.79670	.75858	.3182	.2552	.6546	.61818	.78604	.78645	.2715	.2722	.6176	.63180	.77513	.81509	.2268	.2901	.5828	49
12	.59060	.80696	.73189	.3663	.2392	.6932	.60460	.79653	.75904	.3174	.2554	.6540	.61841	.78586	.78692	.2708	.2725	.6170	.63203	.77494	.81558	.2261	.2904	.5822	48
13	.59084	.80679	.73234	.3655	.2395	.6925	.60483	.79635	.75950	.3166	.2557	.6533	.61864	.78568	.78739	.2700	.2728	.6164	.63225	.77476	.81606	.2254	.2907	.5816	47
14	.59107	.80662	.73278	.3647	.2397	.6918	.60506	.79618	.75996	.3159	.2560	.6527	.61886	.78550	.78786	.2692	.2731	.6159	.63248	.77458	.81655	.2247	.2910	.5811	46
15	.59131	.80644	.73323	1.3638	.2400	1.6912	.60529	.79600	.76042	1.3151	.2563	1.6521	.61909	.78532	.78834	1.2685	.2734	1.6153	.63270	.77439	.81703	1.2239	.2913	1.5805	45
16	.59154	.80627	.73368	.3630	.2403	.6905	.60552	.79582	.76088	.3143	.2565	.6514	.61932	.78514	.78881	.2677	.2737	.6147	.63293	.77421	.81752	.2232	.2916	.5799	44
17	.59178	.80610	.73412	.3622	.2405	.6898	.60576	.79565	.76134	.3135	.2568	.6508	.61955	.78496	.78928	.2670	.2739	.6141	.63315	.77402	.81800	.2225	.2919	.5794	43
18	.59201	.80593	.73457	.3613	.2408	.6891	.60599	.79547	.76179	.3127	.2571	.6502	.61978	.78478	.78975	.2662	.2742	.6135	.63338	.77384	.81849	.2218	.2922	.5788	42
19	.59225	.80576	.73502	.3605	.2411	.6885	.60622	.79530	.76225	.3119	.2574	.6496	.62001	.78460	.79022	.2655	.2745	.6129	.63360	.77365	.81898	.2210	.2926	.5783	41
20	.59248	.80558	.73547	1.3597	.2413	1.6878	.60645	.79512	.76271	1.3111	.2577	1.6489	.62023	.78441	.79070	1.2647	.2748	1.6123	.63383	.77347	.81946	1.2203	.2929	1.5777	40
21	.59272	.80541	.73592	.3588	.2416	.6871	.60668	.79494	.76317	.3103	.2579	.6483	.62046	.78423	.79117	.2639	.2751	.6117	.63405	.77329	.81995	.2196	.2932	.5771	39
22	.59295	.80524	.73637	.3580	.2419	.6865	.60691	.79477	.76364	.3095	.2582	.6477	.62069	.78405	.79164	.2632	.2754	.6111	.63428	.77310	.82043	.2189	.2935	.5766	38
23	.59318	.80507	.73681	.3572	.2421	.6858	.60714	.79459	.76410	.3087	.2585	.6470	.62092	.78387	.79212	.2624	.2757	.6105	.63450	.77292	.82092	.2181	.2938	.5760	37
24	.59342	.80489	.73726	.3564	.2424	.6851	.60737	.79441	.76456	.3079	.2588	.6464	.62115	.78369	.79259	.2617	.2760	.6099	.63473	.77273	.82141	.2174	.2941	.5755	36
25	.59365	.80472	.73771	1.3555	.2427	1.6845	.60761	.79424	.76502	1.3071	.2591	1.6458	.62137	.78351	.79306	1.2609	.2763	1.6093	.63495	.77255	.82190	1.2167	.2944	1.5749	35
26	.59389	.80455	.73816	.3547	.2429	.6838	.60784	.79406	.76548	.3064	.2593	.6452	.62160	.78333	.79354	.2602	.2766	.6087	.63518	.77236	.82238	.2160	.2947	.5743	34
27	.59412	.80437	.73861	.3539	.2432	.6831	.60807	.79388	.76594	.3056	.2596	.6445	.62183	.78315	.79401	.2594	.2769	.6081	.63540	.77218	.82287	.2152	.2950	.5738	33
28	.59435	.80420	.73906	.3531	.2435	.6825	.60830	.79371	.76640	.3048	.2599	.6439	.62206	.78297	.79449	.2587	.2772	.6077	.63563	.77199	.82336	.2145	.2953	.5732	32
29	.59459	.80403	.73951	.3522	.2437	.6818	.60853	.79353	.76686	.3040	.2602	.6433	.62229	.78279	.79496	.2579	.2775	.6070	.63585	.77181	.82385	.2138	.2956	.5727	31
30	.59482	.80386	.73996	1.3514	.2440	1.6812	.60876	.79335	.76733	1.3032	.2605	1.6427	.62251	.78261	.79543	1.2572	.2778	1.6064	.63608	.77162	.82434	1.2131	.2960	1.5721	30
31	.59506	.80368	.74041	.3506	.2443	.6805	.60899	.79318	.76779	.3024	.2607	.6420	.62274	.78243	.79591	.2564	.2781	.6058	.63630	.77144	.82482	.2124	.2963	.5716	29
32	.59529	.80351	.74086	.3498	.2445	.6798	.60922	.79300	.76825	.3016	.2610	.6414	.62297	.78224	.79639	.2557	.2784	.6052	.63653	.77125	.82531	.2117	.2966	.5710	28
33	.59552	.80334	.74131	.3489	.2448	.6792	.60945	.79282	.76871	.3009	.2613	.6408	.62320	.78206	.79686	.2549	.2787	.6046	.63675	.77107	.82580	.2109	.2969	.5705	27
34	.59576	.80316	.74176	.3481	.2451	.6785	.60968	.79264	.76918	.3001	.2616	.6402	.62342	.78188	.79734	.2542	.2790	.6040	.63697	.77088	.82629	.2102	.2972	.5699	26
35	.59599	.80299	.74221	1.3473	.2453	1.6779	.60991	.79247	.76964	1.2993	.2619	1.6396	.62365	.78170	.79781	1.2534	.2793	1.6034	.63720	.77070	.82678	1.2095	.2975	1.5694	25
36	.59622	.80282	.74266	.3465	.2456	.6772	.61014	.79229	.77010	.2985	.2622	.6389	.62388	.78152	.79829	.2527	.2795	.6029	.63742	.77051	.82727	.2088	.2978	.5688	24
37	.59646	.80264	.74312	.3457	.2459	.6766	.61037	.79211	.77057	.2977	.2624	.6383	.62411	.78134	.79876	.2519	.2798	.6023	.63765	.77033	.82776	.2081	.2981	.5683	23
38	.59669	.80247	.74357	.3449	.2461	.6759	.61061	.79193	.77103	.2970	.2627	.6377	.62433	.78116	.79924	.2512	.2801	.6017	.63787	.77014	.82825	.2074	.2985	.5677	22
39	.59692	.80230	.74402	.3440	.2464	.6752	.61084	.79176	.77149	.2962	.2630	.6371	.62456	.78097	.79972	.2504	.2804	.6011	.63810	.76996	.82874	.2066	.2988	.5672	21
40	.59716	.80212	.74447	1.3432	.2467	1.6746	.61107	.79158	.77196	1.2954	.2633	1.6365	.62479	.78079	.80020	1.2497	.2807	1.6005	.63832	.76977	.82923	1.2059	.2991	1.5666	20
41	.59739	.80195	.74492	.3424	.2470	.6739	.61130	.79140	.77242	.2946	.2636	.6359	.62501	.78061	.80067	.2489	.2810	.6000	.63854	.76958	.82972	.2052	.2994	.5661	19
42	.59762	.80177	.74538	.3416	.2472	.6733	.61153	.79122	.77289	.2938	.2639	.6352	.62524	.78043	.80115	.2482	.2813	.5994	.63877	.76940	.83022	.2045	.2997	.5655	18
43	.59786	.80160	.74583	.3408	.2475	.6726	.61176	.79104	.77335	.2931	.2641	.6346	.62547	.78025	.80163	.2475	.2816	.5988	.63899	.76921	.83071	.2038	.3000	.5650	17
44	.59809	.80143	.74628	.3400	.2478	.6720	.61199	.79087	.77382	.2923	.2644	.6340	.62570	.78007	.80211	.2467	.2819	.5982	.63921	.76903	.83120	.2031	.3003	.5644	16
45	.59832	.80125	.74673	1.3392	.2480	1.6713	.61222	.79069	.77428	1.2915	.2647	1.6334	.62592	.77988	.80258	1.2460	.2822	1.5976	.63944	.76884	.83169	1.2024	.3006	1.5639	15
46	.59856	.80108	.74019	.3383	.2483	.6707	.61245	.79051	.77475	.2907	.2650	.6328	.62615	.77970	.80306	.2452	.2825	.5971	.63966	.76865	.83218	.2016	.3010	.5633	14
47	.59879	.80090	.74064	.3375	.2486	.6700	.61268	.79033	.77521	.2900	.2653	.6322	.62638	.77952	.80354	.2445	.2828	.5965	.63989	.76847	.83267	.2009	.3013	.5628	13
48	.59902	.80073	.74809	.3367	.2488	.6694	.61290	.79015	.77568	.2892	.2656	.6316	.62660	.77934	.80402	.2437	.2831	.5959	.64011	.76828	.83317	.2002	.3016	.5622	12
49	.59926	.80056	.74855	.3359	.2491	.6687	.61314	.78998	.77614	.2884	.2659	.6309	.62683	.77915	.80450	.2430	.2834	.5953	.64033	.76810	.83366	.1995	.3019	.5617	11
50	.59949	.80038	.74900	1.3351	.2494	1.6681	.61337	.78980	.77661	1.2876	.2661	1.6303	.62706	.77897	.80498	1.2423	.2837	1.5947	.64056	.76791	.83415	1.1988	.3022	1.5611	10
51	.59972	.80021	.74946	.3343	.2497	.6674	.61360	.78962	.77708	.2869	.2664	.6297	.62728	.77879	.80546	.2415	.2840	.5942	.64078	.76772	.83465	.1981	.3025	.5606	9
52	.59995	.80003	.74991	.3335	.2499	.6668	.61383	.78944	.77754	.2861	.2667	.6291	.62751	.77861	.80594	.2408	.2843	.5936	.64100	.76754	.83514	.1974	.3029	.5600	8
53	.60019	.79986	.75037	.3327	.2502	.6661	.61405	.78926	.77801	.2853	.2670	.6285	.62774	.77842	.80642	.2400	.2846	.5930	.64123	.76735	.83563	.1967	.3032	.5595	7
54	.60042	.79968	.75082	.3319	.2505	.6655	.61428	.78908	.77848	.2845	.2673	.6279	.62796	.77824	.80690	.2393	.2849	.5924	.64145	.76716	.83613	.1960	.3035	.5590	6
55	.60065	.79951	.75128	1.3311	.2508	1.6648	.61451	.78890	.77895	1.2838	.2676	1.6273	.62819	.77806	.80738	1.2386	.2852	1.5919	.64160	.76698	.83662	1.1953	.3038	1.5584	5
56	.60088	.79933	.75173	.3303	.2510	.6642	.61474	.78873	.77941	.2830	.2679	.6267	.62841	.77788	.80786	.2378	.2855	.5913	.64189	.76679	.83712	.1946	.3041	.5579	4
57	.60112	.79916	.75219	.3294	.2513	.6636	.61497	.78855	.77988	.2822	.2681	.6261	.62864	.77769	.80834	.2371	.2858	.5907	.64212	.76660	.83761	.1939	.3044	.5573	3
58	.60135	.79898	.75264	.3286	.2516	.6629	.61520	.78837	.78035	.2815	.2684	.6255	.62887	.77751	.80882	.2364	.2861	.5901	.64234	.76642	.83811	.1932	.3048	.5568	2
59	.60158	.79881	.75310	.3278	.2519	.6623	.61543	.78819	.78082	.2807	.2687	.6249	.62909	.77733	.80930	.2356	.2864	.5896	.64256	.76623	.83860	.1924	.3051	.5563	1
60	.60181	.79863	.75355	1.3270	.2521	1.6616	.61566	.78801	.78128	1.2799	.2690	1.6243	62932	.77715	.80978	1.2349	.2867	1.5890	.64279	.76604	.83910	1.1917	.3054	1.5557	0
′	cos	sin	cot	tan	cosec	sec	cos	sin	cot	tan	cosec	sec	cos	sin	cot	tan	cosec	sec	cos	sin	cot	tan	cosec	sec	′
	53°						52°						51°						50°						

NATURAL TRIGONOMETRIC FUNCTIONS

43° (top) / 46° (bottom)

'	cosec	sec	cot	tan	cos	sin	'
0	1.4663	1.3673	1.0724	.93251	.73135	.68200	60
1	.4658	.3677	.0717	.93306	.73115	.68221	59
2	.4654	.3681	.0711	.93360	.73096	.68242	58
3	.4649	.3684	.0705	.93415	.73076	.68264	57
4	.4644	.3688	.0699	.93469	.73056	.68285	56
5	.4640	.3692	.0692	.93524	.73036	.68306	55
6	.4635	.3695	.0686	.93578	.73016	.68327	54
7	.4631	.3699	.0680	.93633	.72996	.68349	53
8	.4626	.3703	.0674	.93687	.72976	.68370	52
9	.4622	.3707	.0667	.93742	.72956	.68391	51
10	.4617	.3710	.0661	.93797	.72937	.68412	50
11	.4613	.3714	.0655	.93851	.72917	.68433	49
12	.4608	.3718	.0649	.93906	.72897	.68455	48
13	.4604	.3722	.0643	.93961	.72877	.68476	47
14	.4599	.3725	.0636	.94016	.72857	.68497	46
15	.4595	.3729	.0630	.94071	.72837	.68518	45
16	.4590	.3733	.0624	.94125	.72817	.68539	44
17	.4586	.3737	.0618	.94180	.72797	.68561	43
18	.4581	.3740	.0612	.94235	.72777	.68582	42
19	.4577	.3744	.0605	.94290	.72757	.68603	41
20	.4572	.3748	.0599	.94345	.72737	.68624	40
21	.4568	.3752	.0593	.94400	.72717	.68645	39
22	.4563	.3756	.0587	.94455	.72697	.68666	38
23	.4559	.3759	.0581	.94510	.72677	.68688	37
24	.4554	.3763	.0575	.94565	.72657	.68709	36
25	.4550	.3767	.0568	.94620	.72637	.68730	35
26	.4545	.3771	.0562	.94675	.72617	.68751	34
27	.4541	.3774	.0556	.94731	.72597	.68772	33
28	.4536	.3778	.0550	.94786	.72577	.68793	32
29	.4532	.3782	.0544	.94841	.72557	.68814	31
30	.4527	.3786	.0538	.94896	.72537	.68835	30
31	.4523	.3790	.0532	.94952	.72517	.68856	29
32	.4518	.3794	.0525	.95007	.72497	.68878	28
33	.4514	.3797	.0519	.95062	.72477	.68899	27
34	.4510	.3801	.0513	.95118	.72457	.68920	26
35	.4505	.3805	.0507	.95173	.72437	.68941	25
36	.4501	.3809	.0501	.95229	.72417	.68962	24
37	.4496	.3813	.0495	.95284	.72397	.68983	23
38	.4492	.3816	.0489	.95340	.72377	.69004	22
39	.4487	.3820	.0483	.95395	.72357	.69025	21
40	.4483	.3824	.0476	.95451	.72337	.69046	20
41	.4479	.3828	.0470	.95506	.72317	.69067	19
42	.4474	.3832	.0464	.95562	.72297	.69088	18
43	.4470	.3836	.0458	.95618	.72277	.69109	17
44	.4465	.3839	.0452	.95673	.72256	.69130	16
45	.4461	.3843	.0446	.95729	.72236	.69151	15
46	.4457	.3847	.0440	.95785	.72216	.69172	14
47	.4452	.3851	.0434	.95841	.72196	.69193	13
48	.4448	.3855	.0428	.95896	.72176	.69214	12
49	.4443	.3859	.0422	.95952	.72156	.69235	11
50	.4439	.3863	.0416	.96008	.72136	.69256	10
51	.4435	.3867	.0410	.96064	.72115	.69277	9
52	.4430	.3870	.0404	.96120	.72095	.69298	8
53	.4426	.3874	.0398	.96176	.72075	.69319	7
54	.4422	.3878	.0391	.96232	.72055	.69340	6
55	.4417	.3882	.0385	.96288	.72035	.69361	5
56	.4413	.3886	.0379	.96344	.72015	.69382	4
57	.4408	.3890	.0373	.96400	.71994	.69403	3
58	.4404	.3894	.0367	.96456	.71974	.69424	2
59	.4400	.3898	.0361	.96513	.71954	.69445	1
60	1.4395	1.3902	1.0355	.96569	.71934	.69466	0
'	sec	cosec	tan	cot	sin	cos	'

(bottom angle 46°)

42° (top) / 47° (bottom)

'	cosec	sec	cot	tan	cos	sin	'
0	1.4945	1.3456	1.1106	.90040	.74314	.66913	60
1	.4940	.3460	.1100	.90093	.74295	.66935	59
2	.4935	.3463	.1093	.90146	.74276	.66956	58
3	.4930	.3467	.1086	.90198	.74256	.66978	57
4	.4925	.3470	.1080	.90251	.74236	.66999	56
5	.4921	.3474	.1074	.90304	.74217	.67021	55
6	.4916	.3477	.1067	.90357	.74197	.67043	54
7	.4911	.3481	.1061	.90410	.74178	.67064	53
8	.4906	.3485	.1054	.90463	.74158	.67086	52
9	.4901	.3488	.1048	.90515	.74139	.67107	51
10	.4897	.3492	.1041	.90568	.74119	.67129	50
11	.4892	.3495	.1035	.90621	.74100	.67151	49
12	.4887	.3499	.1028	.90674	.74080	.67172	48
13	.4882	.3502	.1022	.90727	.74061	.67194	47
14	.4877	.3506	.1015	.90780	.74041	.67215	46
15	.4873	.3509	.1009	.90834	.74022	.67237	45
16	.4868	.3513	.1003	.90887	.74002	.67258	44
17	.4863	.3517	.0996	.90940	.73983	.67280	43
18	.4858	.3520	.0990	.90993	.73963	.67301	42
19	.4854	.3524	.0983	.91046	.73943	.67323	41
20	.4849	.3527	.0977	.91099	.73924	.67344	40
21	.4844	.3531	.0971	.91153	.73904	.67366	39
22	.4839	.3534	.0964	.91206	.73885	.67387	38
23	.4835	.3538	.0958	.91259	.73865	.67409	37
24	.4830	.3542	.0951	.91312	.73845	.67430	36
25	.4825	.3545	.0945	.91366	.73826	.67452	35
26	.4821	.3549	.0939	.91419	.73806	.67473	34
27	.4816	.3552	.0932	.91473	.73787	.67495	33
28	.4811	.3556	.0926	.91526	.73767	.67516	32
29	.4806	.3560	.0919	.91580	.73747	.67537	31
30	.4802	.3563	.0913	.91633	.73728	.67559	30
31	.4797	.3567	.0907	.91687	.73708	.67580	29
32	.4792	.3571	.0900	.91740	.73688	.67602	28
33	.4788	.3574	.0894	.91794	.73669	.67623	27
34	.4783	.3578	.0888	.91847	.73649	.67645	26
35	.4778	.3581	.0881	.91901	.73629	.67666	25
36	.4774	.3585	.0875	.91955	.73610	.67688	24
37	.4769	.3589	.0868	.92008	.73590	.67709	23
38	.4764	.3592	.0862	.92062	.73570	.67730	22
39	.4760	.3596	.0856	.92116	.73551	.67752	21
40	.4755	.3600	.0849	.92170	.73531	.67773	20
41	.4750	.3603	.0843	.92223	.73511	.67794	19
42	.4746	.3607	.0837	.92277	.73491	.67816	18
43	.4741	.3611	.0830	.92331	.73472	.67837	17
44	.4736	.3614	.0824	.92385	.73452	.67859	16
45	.4732	.3618	.0818	.92439	.73432	.67880	15
46	.4727	.3622	.0812	.92493	.73412	.67901	14
47	.4723	.3625	.0805	.92547	.73393	.67923	13
48	.4718	.3629	.0799	.92601	.73373	.67944	12
49	.4713	.3633	.0793	.92655	.73353	.67965	11
50	.4709	.3636	.0786	.92709	.73333	.67987	10
51	.4704	.3640	.0780	.92763	.73314	.68008	9
52	.4700	.3644	.0774	.92817	.73294	.68029	8
53	.4695	.3647	.0767	.92871	.73274	.68051	7
54	.4690	.3651	.0761	.92926	.73254	.68072	6
55	.4686	.3655	.0755	.92980	.73234	.68093	5
56	.4681	.3658	.0749	.93034	.73215	.68115	4
57	.4676	.3662	.0742	.93088	.73195	.68136	3
58	.4672	.3666	.0736	.93143	.73175	.68157	2
59	.4667	.3669	.0730	.93197	.73155	.68179	1
60	1.4663	1.3673	1.0724	.93251	.73135	.68200	0
'	sec	cosec	tan	cot	sin	cos	'

(bottom angle 47°)

41° (top) / 48° (bottom)

'	cosec	sec	cot	tan	cos	sin	'
0	1.5242	1.3250	1.1504	.86929	.75471	.65606	60
1	.5237	.3253	.1497	.86980	.75452	.65628	59
2	.5232	.3257	.1490	.87031	.75433	.65650	58
3	.5227	.3260	.1483	.87082	.75414	.65672	57
4	.5222	.3263	.1477	.87133	.75394	.65694	56
5	.5217	.3267	.1470	.87184	.75375	.65716	55
6	.5212	.3270	.1463	.87235	.75356	.65738	54
7	.5207	.3274	.1456	.87287	.75337	.65759	53
8	.5202	.3277	.1450	.87338	.75319	.65781	52
9	.5197	.3280	.1443	.87389	.75299	.65803	51
10	.5192	.3284	.1436	.87441	.75280	.65825	50
11	.5187	.3287	.1430	.87492	.75261	.65847	49
12	.5182	.3290	.1423	.87543	.75241	.65869	48
13	.5177	.3294	.1416	.87595	.75222	.65891	47
14	.5171	.3297	.1409	.87646	.75203	.65913	46
15	.5166	.3301	.1403	.87698	.75184	.65934	45
16	.5161	.3304	.1396	.87749	.75165	.65956	44
17	.5156	.3307	.1389	.87801	.75146	.65978	43
18	.5151	.3311	.1383	.87852	.75126	.66000	42
19	.5146	.3314	.1376	.87904	.75107	.66022	41
20	.5141	.3318	.1369	.87955	.75088	.66044	40
21	.5136	.3321	.1363	.88007	.75069	.66066	39
22	.5131	.3324	.1356	.88058	.75049	.66087	38
23	.5126	.3328	.1349	.88110	.75030	.66109	37
24	.5121	.3331	.1343	.88162	.75011	.66131	36
25	.5116	.3335	.1336	.88213	.74992	.66153	35
26	.5111	.3338	.1329	.88265	.74973	.66175	34
27	.5106	.3342	.1323	.88317	.74953	.66197	33
28	.5101	.3345	.1316	.88369	.74934	.66218	32
29	.5096	.3348	.1309	.88421	.74915	.66240	31
30	.5092	.3352	.1303	.88472	.74895	.66262	30
31	.5087	.3355	.1296	.88524	.74876	.66284	29
32	.5082	.3359	.1290	.88576	.74857	.66305	28
33	.5077	.3362	.1283	.88628	.74838	.66327	27
34	.5072	.3366	.1276	.88680	.74818	.66349	26
35	.5067	.3369	.1270	.88732	.74799	.66371	25
36	.5062	.3372	.1263	.88784	.74780	.66393	24
37	.5057	.3376	.1257	.88836	.74760	.66414	23
38	.5052	.3379	.1250	.88888	.74741	.66436	22
39	.5047	.3383	.1243	.88940	.74722	.66458	21
40	.5042	.3386	.1237	.88992	.74702	.66479	20
41	.5037	.3390	.1230	.89044	.74683	.66501	19
42	.5032	.3393	.1224	.89097	.74664	.66523	18
43	.5027	.3397	.1217	.89149	.74644	.66545	17
44	.5022	.3400	.1211	.89201	.74625	.66566	16
45	.5018	.3404	.1204	.89253	.74606	.66588	15
46	.5013	.3407	.1198	.89306	.74586	.66610	14
47	.5008	.3411	.1191	.89358	.74567	.66631	13
48	.5003	.3414	.1184	.89410	.74548	.66653	12
49	.4998	.3418	.1178	.89463	.74528	.66675	11
50	.4993	.3421	.1171	.89515	.74509	.66697	10
51	.4988	.3425	.1165	.89567	.74489	.66718	9
52	.4983	.3428	.1158	.89620	.74470	.66740	8
53	.4979	.3432	.1152	.89672	.74450	.66762	7
54	.4974	.3435	.1145	.89725	.74431	.66783	6
55	.4969	.3439	.1139	.89777	.74412	.66805	5
56	.4964	.3442	.1132	.89830	.74392	.66826	4
57	.4959	.3446	.1126	.89882	.74373	.66848	3
58	.4954	.3449	.1119	.89935	.74353	.66870	2
59	.4949	.3453	.1113	.89988	.74334	.66891	1
60	1.4945	1.3456	1.1106	.90040	.74314	.66913	0
'	sec	cosec	tan	cot	sin	cos	'

(bottom angle 48°)

40° (top) / 49° (bottom)

'	cosec	sec	cot	tan	cos	sin	'
0	1.5557	1.3054	1.1917	.83910	.76604	.64279	60
1	.5552	.3057	.1910	.83959	.76586	.64301	59
2	.5546	.3060	.1903	.84009	.76567	.64323	58
3	.5541	.3064	.1896	.84059	.76548	.64345	57
4	.5536	.3067	.1889	.84108	.76530	.64368	56
5	.5530	.3070	.1882	.84158	.76511	.64390	55
6	.5525	.3073	.1875	.84208	.76492	.64412	54
7	.5520	.3076	.1868	.84258	.76473	.64435	53
8	.5514	.3080	.1861	.84307	.76455	.64457	52
9	.5509	.3083	.1854	.84357	.76436	.64479	51
10	.5503	.3086	.1847	.84407	.76417	.64501	50
11	.5498	.3089	.1840	.84457	.76398	.64523	49
12	.5493	.3092	.1833	.84507	.76380	.64546	48
13	.5487	.3096	.1826	.84556	.76361	.64568	47
14	.5482	.3099	.1819	.84606	.76342	.64590	46
15	.5476	.3102	.1812	.84656	.76323	.64612	45
16	.5471	.3105	.1806	.84706	.76304	.64635	44
17	.5466	.3109	.1799	.84756	.76286	.64657	43
18	.5461	.3112	.1792	.84806	.76267	.64679	42
19	.5456	.3115	.1785	.84856	.76248	.64701	41
20	.5450	.3118	.1778	.84906	.76229	.64723	40
21	.5445	.3121	.1771	.84956	.76210	.64746	39
22	.5440	.3125	.1764	.85006	.76191	.64768	38
23	.5434	.3128	.1757	.85057	.76173	.64790	37
24	.5429	.3131	.1750	.85107	.76154	.64812	36
25	.5424	.3134	.1743	.85157	.76135	.64834	35
26	.5419	.3138	.1736	.85207	.76116	.64856	34
27	.5413	.3141	.1729	.85257	.76097	.64878	33
28	.5408	.3144	.1722	.85308	.76078	.64901	32
29	.5403	.3148	.1715	.85358	.76059	.64923	31
30	.5398	.3151	.1708	.85408	.76041	.64945	30
31	.5392	.3154	.1702	.85458	.76022	.64967	29
32	.5387	.3157	.1695	.85509	.76003	.64989	28
33	.5382	.3161	.1688	.85559	.75984	.65011	27
34	.5377	.3164	.1681	.85609	.75965	.65033	26
35	.5371	.3167	.1674	.85660	.75946	.65055	25
36	.5366	.3170	.1667	.85710	.75927	.65077	24
37	.5361	.3174	.1660	.85761	.75908	.65100	23
38	.5356	.3177	.1653	.85811	.75889	.65122	22
39	.5351	.3180	.1647	.85862	.75870	.65144	21
40	.5345	.3184	.1640	.85912	.75851	.65166	20
41	.5340	.3187	.1633	.85963	.75832	.65188	19
42	.5335	.3190	.1626	.86014	.75813	.65210	18
43	.5330	.3193	.1619	.86064	.75794	.65232	17
44	.5325	.3197	.1612	.86115	.75775	.65254	16
45	.5319	.3200	.1605	.86165	.75756	.65276	15
46	.5314	.3203	.1599	.86216	.75737	.65298	14
47	.5309	.3207	.1592	.86267	.75718	.65320	13
48	.5304	.3210	.1585	.86318	.75700	.65342	12
49	.5299	.3213	.1578	.86368	.75680	.65364	11
50	.5294	.3217	.1571	.86419	.75661	.65386	10
51	.5289	.3220	.1565	.86470	.75642	.65408	9
52	.5283	.3223	.1558	.86521	.75623	.65430	8
53	.5278	.3227	.1551	.86572	.75604	.65452	7
54	.5273	.3230	.1544	.86623	.75585	.65474	6
55	.5268	.3233	.1537	.86674	.75566	.65496	5
56	.5263	.3237	.1531	.86725	.75547	.65518	4
57	.5258	.3240	.1524	.86776	.75528	.65540	3
58	.5253	.3243	.1517	.86826	.75509	.65562	2
59	.5248	.3247	.1510	.86878	.75490	.65584	1
60	1.5242	1.3250	1.1504	.86929	.75471	.65606	0
'	sec	cosec	tan	cot	sin	cos	'

(bottom angle 49°)

NATURAL TRIGONOMETRIC FUNCTIONS

44°

′	sin	cos	tan	cot	sec	cosec	′
0	.69466	.71934	.96569	1.0355	1.3902	1.4395	60
1	.69487	.71914	.96625	.0349	.3905	.4391	59
2	.69508	.71893	.96681	.0343	.3909	.4387	58
3	.69528	.71873	.96738	.0337	.3913	.4382	57
4	.69549	.71853	.96794	.0331	.3917	.4378	56
5	.69570	.71833	.96850	1.0325	.3921	1.4374	55
6	.69591	.71813	.96907	.0319	.3925	.4370	54
7	.69612	.71792	.96963	.0313	.3929	.4365	53
8	.69633	.71772	.97020	.0307	.3933	.4361	52
9	.69654	.71752	.97076	.0301	.3937	.4357	51
10	.69675	.71732	.97133	1.0295	.3941	1.4352	50
11	.69696	.71711	.97189	.0289	.3945	.4348	49
12	.69716	.71691	.97246	.0283	.3949	.4344	48
13	.69737	.71671	.97302	.0277	.3953	.4339	47
14	.69758	.71650	.97359	.0271	.3957	.4335	46
15	.69779	.71630	.97416	1.0265	.3960	1.4331	45
16	.69800	.71610	.97472	.0259	.3964	.4327	44
17	.69821	.71589	.97529	.0253	.3968	.4322	43
18	.69841	.71569	.97586	.0247	.3972	.4318	42
19	.69862	.71549	.97643	.0241	.3976	.4314	41
20	.69883	.71529	.97700	1.0235	.3980	1.4310	40
21	.69904	.71508	.97756	.0229	.3984	.4305	39
22	.69925	.71488	.97813	.0223	.3988	.4301	38
23	.69945	.71468	.97870	.0218	.3992	.4297	37
24	.69966	.71447	.97927	.0212	.3996	.4292	36
25	.69987	.71427	.97984	1.0206	.4000	1.4288	35
26	.70008	.71406	.98041	.0200	.4004	.4284	34
27	.70029	.71386	.98098	.0194	.4008	.4280	33
28	.70049	.71366	.98155	.0188	.4012	.4276	32
29	.70070	.71345	.98212	.0182	.4016	.4271	31
30	.70091	.71325	.98270	1.0176	.4020	1.4267	30
31	.70112	.71305	.98327	.0170	.4024	.4263	29
32	.70132	.71284	.98384	.0164	.4028	.4259	28
33	.70153	.71264	.98441	.0158	.4032	.4254	27
34	.70174	.71243	.98499	.0152	.4036	.4250	26
35	.70194	.71223	.98556	1.0146	.4040	1.4246	25
36	.70215	.71203	.98613	.0141	.4044	.4242	24
37	.70236	.71182	.98671	.0135	.4048	.4238	23
38	.70257	.71162	.98728	.0129	.4052	.4233	22
39	.70277	.71141	.98786	.0123	.4056	.4229	21
40	.70298	.71121	.98843	1.0117	.4060	1.4225	20
41	.70319	.71100	.98901	.0111	.4065	.4221	19
42	.70339	.71080	.98958	.0105	.4069	.4217	18
43	.70360	.71059	.99016	.0099	.4073	.4212	17
44	.70381	.71039	.99073	.0093	.4077	.4208	16
45	.70401	.71018	.99131	1.0088	.4081	1.4204	15
46	.70422	.70998	.99189	.0082	.4085	.4200	14
47	.70443	.70977	.99246	.0076	.4089	.4196	13
48	.70463	.70957	.99304	.0070	.4093	.4192	12
49	.70484	.70936	.99362	.0064	.4097	.4188	11
50	.70505	.70916	.99420	1.0058	.4101	1.4183	10
51	.70525	.70895	.99478	.0052	.4105	.4179	9
52	.70546	.70875	.99536	.0047	.4109	.4175	8
53	.70566	.70854	.99593	.0041	.4113	.4171	7
54	.70587	.70834	.99651	.0035	.4117	.4167	6
55	.70608	.70813	.99709	1.0029	.4122	1.4163	5
56	.70628	.70793	.99767	.0023	.4126	.4159	4
57	.70649	.70772	.99826	.0017	.4130	.4154	3
58	.70669	.70752	.99884	.0012	.4134	.4150	2
59	.70690	.70731	.99942	.0006	.4138	.4146	1
60	.70711	.70711	1.00000	1.0000	.4142	1.4142	0

′	cos	sin	cot	tan	cosec	sec	′

45°

INDEX